Springer
Berlin
Heidelberg
New York
Barcelona
Budapest
Hong Kong
London
Milan
Paris
Santa Clara
Singapore
Tokyo

Birgit Pfitzmann

Digital Signature Schemes

General Framework and Fail-Stop Signatures

Springer

Author

Birgit Pfitzmann
Universität Hildesheim, Institut für Informatik
Gebäude Samelsonplatz 1, D-31141 Hildesheim, Germany
E-mail: pfitzb@informatik.uni-hildesheim.de

Cataloging-in-Publication data applied for

Die Deutsche Bibliothek - CIP-Einheitsaufnahme

Pfitzmann, Birgit:
Digital signature schemes : general framework and fail stop signatures / Birgit Pfitzmann. - Berlin ; Heidelberg ; New York ; Barcelona ; Budapest ; Hong Kong ; London ; Milan ; Paris ; Santa Clara ; Singapore ; Tokyo : Springer, 1996
(Lecture notes in computer science ; Vol. 1100)
ISBN 3-540-61517-2
NE: GT

CR Subject Classification (1991): C.2.0, C.2.4, D.2.1, D.4.6, E.3-4, F.3.1, J.1, K.6.5

1991 Mathematics Subject Classification: 94A60

ISSN 0302-9743
ISBN 3-540-61517-2 Springer-Verlag Berlin Heidelberg New York

Typesetting: Camera-ready by author
SPIN 10513291 06/3142 – 5 4 3 2 1 0 Printed on acid-free paper

Foreword

An increasing number of people, both inside and outside the science community, are fascinated by the current development and future prospects of what is known under the political or technical keywords, respectively, of "data superhighway" and "global information infrastructure", or "internet" and "world wide web". Fewer people, however, are aware that these facilities are a great challenge for our democratic societies to redefine the balance of power among their users and, accordingly, to invent new technical means to support users in maintaining their security goals of privacy (informational self-determination), confidentiality, integrity, availability, and non-repudiation.

Cryptology, a classical tool for confidentiality since ancient times, has offered completely new techniques for achieving security by the pioneering work of Diffie and Hellman in 1976 on asymmetric protocols that are based on pairs of secret and public keys. Since then, not only confidentiality, but also various kinds of integrity, non-repudiation and even anonymity are available. One basic component for these services is that of digital signatures, which offer network users the functionalities supplied by handwritten signatures in the paper-based world.

Engineering complex computing systems, such as global networks, requires a well-founded method to specify requirements, to design and implement components in a modular way, and to verify the final result. Building secure systems has to follow this procedure both for functional and for security-related aspects.

In this book, Birgit Pfitzmann makes essential contributions to the three dimensions discussed before: she presents an innovative class of digital signature schemes; these schemes enhance the autonomy and personal security of individual users; these schemes are thoroughly engineered.

More specifically, previous proposals for digital signatures suffer from the problem that a signer is basically unprotected if somebody succeeds in forging a signature. Of course, such an unhappy event should not occur, but, unfortunately, we cannot completely exclude the possibility. For the security (in terms of unforgeability) of all previous digital signature schemes is based on unproven assumptions in the theory of computational complexity, in particular on the famous conjecture $P \neq NP$. Now, in this text, a highly inventive and technically very intricate response is presented: the design of a digital signature scheme that provides a (claimed but not actual) signer, once a successful forgery has actually occurred, with the means to prove that forgery by demonstrating that the complexity assumption has been broken. Afterwards, in real life, the affected persons can agree to stop using the signature scheme. This feature motivates the name for the presented invention: fail-stop signature schemes.

Besides this core result, the book contains a rich world of other valuable contributions, which can be summarized as follows:

- For the first time, the book introduces a general and sophisticated framework in which previous and the innovative fail-stop digital signature schemes are systematically presented and evaluated.

- For the innovative fail-stop signature schemes, it precisely specifies the security requirements, develops a general method for constructing such schemes and for proving their security, presents modular concrete constructions, and evaluates them in terms of complexity theory.
- As a basic prerequisite, the mathematical theory of "collision-free families of functions" is elaborated and extended.

This book is essentially a dissertation (Ph. D. thesis) as submitted to the University of Hildesheim in 1993. It has been a great pleasure to observe how Birgit Pfitzmann insightfully combined many difficult techniques and results from various fields of computer science and mathematics, including logic-based specification, algorithmic complexity, probability theory, algebra, and cryptology. I greatly appreciate that the German *Gesellschaft für Informatik* (GI) honoured this excellent thesis in 1995 by an award for "foundations of informatics".

June 1996

Joachim Biskup
Institut für Informatik
Universität Hildesheim

Preface

Digital signature schemes are cryptologic schemes that provide a similar function for digital messages as handwritten signatures do for messages on paper: They guarantee the authenticity of a message to its recipient, and the recipient can prove this authenticity to third parties, such as courts, afterwards. Hence digital signatures are necessary wherever legal certainty is to be achieved for digital message exchange.

For practical applications, digital signatures are one of the two most important cryptologic primitives. In particular with the rise of electronic commerce on the Internet and the World Wide Web, they may become even more important than the better-known schemes for message secrecy.

The first part of this text presents a general framework of digital signature schemes, starting with the legal requirements, transforming them into a precise high-level specification, and deriving a classification of signature schemes according to their service, structural, and security properties.

The second part treats fail-stop signatures, a new class of digital signature schemes with particularly high security, in detail. In all previously known digital signature schemes, the security for signers was based on computational assumptions, i.e., an attacker with an unexpectedly good algorithm or unexpectedly large resources could forge signatures for which a signer would be held responsible exactly as for her real signatures. In a certain sense, this was proved to be inevitable. Fail-stop signature schemes improve upon it nevertheless: Forging a signature is as hard as in the most secure ordinary digital signature schemes, but if, for all that, someone succeeds in forging, the supposed signer can prove that this happened, or, more precisely, that the underlying assumption was broken. Thus one can relieve her from the responsibility for the signature. Additionally, one should stop the signature system or increase the security parameters.

Both parts are worked out in considerable detail. This may be seen as a negative consequence of this text being essentially my thesis. However, it may also be interesting in its own right, in particular for readers who have more experience with other parts of theoretical computer science than with cryptology, for two reasons:

The first part contains the first combination of cryptologic definitions of security with specification techniques from other parts of computer science. This introduces transparency into the modeling process of cryptology, i.e., a cryptologic security definition can be derived systematically and with some assurance that it expresses what was informally intended. I personally consider this the most important aspect of this work for the future, because it might help obtaining satisfactory definitions for "larger" cryptologic protocols, such as payment systems, which would be greatly needed both for the application of such schemes and for security evaluations of concrete proposals.

The second part contains mathematically rigorous security definitions and proofs. These are certainly not the first ones in cryptology, but surprisingly few have found their way into books. In particular, I am not aware of a book containing even a sketch of the formal definition of ordinary digital signature schemes. Instead, signature schemes and other larger cryptologic schemes, in contrast to small primitives like one-way functions, are often presented as "protocols" that only seem to allow heuristic treatment. Many theoretical computer scientists I met therefore did not regard such schemes as serious. I hope my rigorous treatment of details like probability spaces helps to alleviate such fears.

The text is self-contained with respect to the historical background and cryptologic primitives used. Prior acquaintance with basic notions of complexity theory, information theory, and temporal logic is useful in some chapters.

Chapters 1 to 3 can be seen as an extended introduction. In Chapter 1, the purposes of digital signature schemes and the resulting requirements on such schemes are discussed. A survey of the history of digital signature schemes is given in Chapter 2. Moreover, a lot of terminology is introduced in this way. In Chapter 3, the main new features of fail-stop signature schemes are briefly presented in an informal way.

The first main part centres around Chapter 5, which contains a sketch of a general formal definition and classification of digital signature schemes. Chapter 4 introduces some formal notation, and Chapter 6 leads back from the general classification to the types of schemes considered in the second part. This framework part is the newer part of this work. Calls for it arose because there was an increasing number of objects called digital signature schemes that did not fit previous definitions and either had no formal definition at all or each an entirely new one. It is semiformal, and large parts of it can be applied to many classes of cryptologic schemes, not only signature schemes. It should be completely formalized in such generality in the future.

The second main part contains the concrete fail-stop signature schemes. Chapter 6 belongs to this part as much as to the first part, because it presents an overview of new digital signature schemes and shows benefits they may offer in applications. Chapter 7 contains formal definitions of fail-stop signature schemes. The definitions are in the conventional style, but they are linked to the general definition from Chapter 5 in a semiformal way. Moreover, this chapter contains formal proofs of the relations between fail-stop signature schemes and ordinary ones and between different types of fail-stop signature schemes. Chapter 8 contains building blocks for actual constructions, and Chapter 9 and 10 contain those constructions. These constructions are sufficiently efficient to be used in practice. In Chapter 11, lower bounds on the efficiency achievable with fail-stop signature schemes and some newer schemes with an even higher degree of security are proved. The latter indicate that those schemes cannot be as efficient as fail-stop signature schemes. Altogether, fail-stop signature schemes seem to be the most viable way of offering signers in digital signature schemes security that does not rely on computational assumptions.

Large parts of Chapters 6 to 11 have been previously published, and mostly as joint work (except that this text is much more formal). The complete list of such publications is [WaPf89, Pfit89, WaPf90, PfWa90, Bleu90, BlPW91, PfWa91, PfWa91a, Pfit91, Pfit91a, HePP93], the manuscript [PePf95], and parts of [ChHP92]. They are referred to for larger results, but not for every detail. Another important article about fail-stop signature schemes is [HePe93]; parts of it are presented in Chapter 9. [Pfit93] is an extract of Chapter 5.

The thesis version of this text was submitted in September 1993; newer results are therefore presented in less detail.

Actually, I once thought that, given all these publications, it would be straightforward to work everything out formally and put Chapters 6 to 11 together in no time at all. This was a mistake. Whenever I wanted to use a "standard" cryptologic building block, it did not really fit. Nowadays I know I should not have been surprised when I first wanted to apply a certain multi-party computation protocol and the informal definition did not fit at all (see Section 7.5), because even the more formal definitions of such protocols are disputed. But I am still surprised, for instance, that I did not find a definition of zero-knowledge proof schemes that fits the application in Section 7.3, which seems very natural to me. This is one reason why I decided to present several constructions and proofs in even more detail than in most theoretical cryptology papers. I do not claim that each proof contains a brilliant idea, and the reader is free to skip them. (What else are the little landing places □ for?)

Acknowledgments

It is a real pleasure to try to invent charming sentences to thank all the people who helped me with this work by sharing ideas with me or contributing to a cosy working atmosphere or both.

With *Andreas Pfitzmann* and *Michael Waidner*, I have learned and worked on cryptology and security from the beginning, so that ideas of all three of us are often quite inseparable in any of our work. In particular, I owe to Michael the discovery that cryptology is a beautiful hobby and later the decision to make it my job, many serious and other discussions about formal models, and several joint publications that have been incorporated in this work. Andreas first noticed that there is useful work to be done in this field; then he was helpful from morning to nightfall, from the coffee supply to patiently listening to each day's success or failure, and producing lots of practical protocol ideas in between.

Naturally, I have also profited from the exchange of ideas with my other coauthors in parts of this work, *Gerrit Bleumer*, *David Chaum*, *Eugène van Heijst*, and *Torben Pedersen*. Even before, knowing David a little has been a great challenge, and his ideas were the starting point for much of our work — when someone insists long enough that I must have learnt cryptology *from* someone, then I say David. Gerrit was also the first to introduce a picturesque style into talks about fail-stop signatures and a very nice partner to share a room with (even though our ideas about room temperature differ by two degrees), and with Torben, I have had useful discussions about some topics we'd initially considered independently.

Joachim Biskup, my advisor, gave many valuable comments on and suggestions for my work, and it was stimulating to gain a broader view on security by looking over to the part of the group investigating information systems. I am also grateful that he gave me the chance to work with him at all — three of us, actually, knowing quite well what we wanted to do, constantly uttering opinions how everything should be run in the institute, and taking up just as much space as others who might work on his own ideas (of which there were plenty). Finally, he gave me back a reassuring belief that it is possible to reach some sort of power position and still act with reason and fairness.

Among our former students, *Manfred Böttger*, *Dirk Fox*, and *Andreas Ort* have given me helpful comments about fail-stop signatures, and together with *Ralf Aßmann* and Gerrit, we were very lucky to have a whole working group of reliable friends.

Our acclimatization in Hildesheim was supported by our colleagues *Jimmy Brüggemann* and *Christian Eckert*. Nowadays, the cosy working atmosphere is kept up by *Matthias Schunter*, too, who is also influencing the future directions of our work on general definitions, and *Ralf Menzel* and *Torsten Polle*. *Michaela Huhn* and *Peter Niebert* and a steady stream of colloquium talks in a department with a strong line in concurrency have helped my understanding of specifications in general.

I also thank *Eike Best* for agreeing to be the second referee of this work, for his encouragement to finish it and get it published, and for his comments on the text.

Anyway, I haven't found anything to complain about at the University of Hildesheim (well, this is not a place to mention photocopiers) — and this really means something, my friends say. Thus I find the decision of the current government of Lower Saxony to close our department and subsequently certainly the whole university deeply regrettable. I have enjoyed the personal atmosphere, the contacts among different research groups and different classes of staff, and the flexibility and openness for new ideas that only a fairly small department seems to be able to offer. Closing such places and cutting down research and education in general will be a loss for our society.

I am very grateful to *Johannes Buchmann*, too, who had agreed to be an advisor for this work if Andreas and I were unable to find two jobs somewhere else; it gave me a lot of security, and his questions first made me think about general definitions and classifications of signature schemes. Other people who contributed from afar by asking interesting questions first or sending unpublished literature are *Don Beaver*, *Gilles Brassard*, *Claude Crépeau*, *Ivan Damgård*, *Jacques Damon*, *Carl Meyer*, *Eiji Okamoto*, *Arend Rensink*, and *Moti Yung*. The Isaac Newton Institute in Cambridge (UK) hosted me while I applied the final finishing touches to this text.

Of course, this work would not exist without my parents and my grandmother either, although their interest in digital signatures has never quite equalled that in me as a person.

There seems to be a rule to mention how one produced one's text in this place; I typed much of mine on a latex mattress*, but in Word 5 on a portable Macintosh.

Hildesheim, June 1996 *Birgit Pfitzmann*

---

* dormabell Galaxie soft 100/200; Hildesheim 1992.

Contents

Tables

Figures

1 Requirements on Digital Signature Schemes

Digital signature schemes are to have the same functions for digital messages that handwritten signatures would have for documents on paper in the ideal case: They should provide message authentication that is provable to third parties in case of dispute [DiHe76], see Figure 1.1.

Like any digital information, digital signatures can be copied arbitrarily. This implies that the signatures of one and the same signer on different messages have to be completely different. It is therefore obvious that digital signatures cannot be any sort of digitalized version of handwritten signatures. Instead, digital signature schemes are specially developed classes of mathematical functions or interactive protocols.

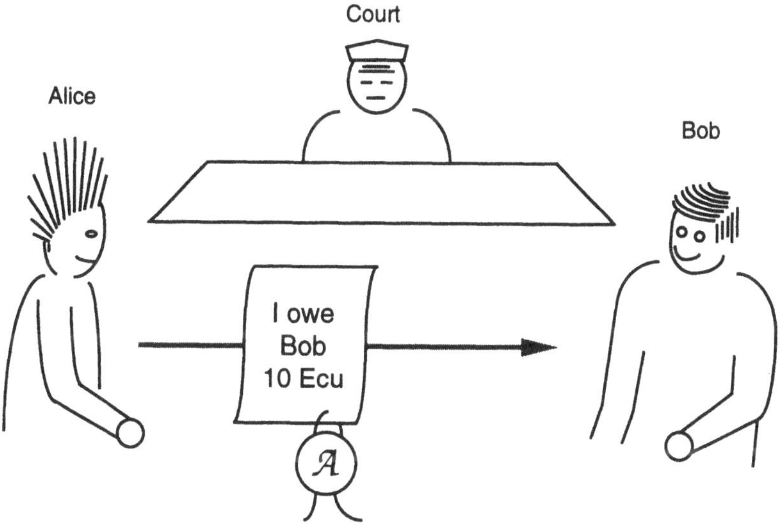

Figure 1.1. Example of the use of digital signatures.
Alice wants to send Bob a signed promissory note; the signature is represented by a seal. Bob should be convinced that this promissory note really comes from Alice, and if a dispute arises later, he should also be able to convince any court (shown in the background) of this fact. However, the exchange of the signature between Alice and Bob should be possible without calling in a third party.

1.1 Brief Survey of Applications

The use of digital signatures in practice has primarily been proposed in fields where handwritten signatures were used until now, but where one wants to transmit messages through digital communication networks. Examples of such fields are digital payment schemes, the use of network services that are not free of charge, buying information from commercial databases, and mail-order for normal goods using digital communication, or generally most of what is summarized under the buzzword electronic commerce.

Moreover, there are applications where documents are to be stored in digital form for other reasons. For instance, a digital signature is appropriate if a software company signs that a certain program is authentic, because the purchasers receive the program on a disk anyway. Another reason may simply be the efficiency of digital storage.

Last but not least, forging handwritten signatures has always been possible, and it is becoming easier with the development of photocopiers, and one must expect that machines can be constructed that can also copy the impression of the signature into the paper, in particular if signing on pads that can register the signing process becomes more common. Hence it can even be considered if handwritten signatures should be replaced, or at least complemented, by digital signatures for security reasons.

In addition to all these possible practical applications, digital signature schemes are important building blocks for many theoretical protocols in the field of distributed computing.

For all these reasons, digital signature schemes seem to be the part of modern cryptology that is most accepted in society and has the best chance of being promoted by governments and industry.

Thus, although the schemes presented in the sequel are mathematical objects and will be proved with respect to formal definitions, a short excursion into the legal and social significance of signatures seems worthwhile.

This holds all the more because fail-stop signature schemes are one of the main topics of this text, and their security feature that seemed impossible before could only be achieved by generalizing the previous definition of digital signature schemes (see Chapters 5 and 7). Such changes of definition, not uncommon in cryptology, may easily degenerate into arbitrariness, unless one thoroughly verifies that the generalized definitions still correspond to the informal ideas one has about digital signatures.

Another reason is that fail-stop signature schemes might improve the acceptability of digital signatures in law; this may even be their main advantage in practice (see Section 6.2). Of course, what cryptology can do in this field is only help by offering suitable schemes; decisions can only be made by jurisdiction or legislation.

1.2 Legal Significance of Signatures

As far as concrete law is concerned, this section only deals with the example of the Federal Republic of Germany. To my knowledge, the principles are very similar in other countries, at least in Western Europe and the Anglo-Saxon countries (see, e.g., [ABEP90]). In parts of the USA, digital signatures have recently been given some specific legal significance; [Schn96, p. 618, ABA95] may be points to start reading about the US situation.

In the Federal Republic of Germany, digital signatures do not have a specific, generally recognized legal significance at present. This does not mean that they cannot have any legal significance at all: They might, for instance, be used as one piece of evidence among others.

Nevertheless, the specification of digital signature schemes is influenced by the specific significance of handwritten signatures. This significance is slightly different in different fields of the law. (See [GoSc91], also for parts of the remainder of this section; but for the technical contents of that book, compare [Fox91a].) Considering the examples in Section 1.1, the two most important questions seem to be:

- Could digital signatures be used for those declarations of intention (German "Willenserklärungen" that have to be in writing ("Schriftform") according to BGB § 126 (the Civil Code) [BGB86]? (Remark: A declaration of intention is the basic step in German civil law; it comprises anything where a person expresses a wish that a certain legal effect should occur. In most cases, because of the autonomy of persons in civil law, the very declaration suffices for the legal effect to occur indeed. See, e.g., [Lare83].)
- Could digital signatures be treated like handwritten signatures in proofs by private documents ("Privaturkunden") according to ZPO §§ 416, 439, 440 (the code of civil procedure) [ZPO86]?

In these cases, the significance of handwritten signatures has two main components:

1. The signature is to make clear that the signer has indeed produced the signed document as a declaration of intention; it may later serve as a piece of evidence to this effect.
2. The warning function ("Warnfunktion"): The act of signing should call the signer's attention to the fact that he or she is about to carry out a legal transaction ("Rechtsgeschäft"). This protects persons from ill-considered acts.

Digital signatures cannot be produced by humans alone, because they require too complicated computations. (This will become clear in the following sections.) Thus they can only help fulfilling the first function. The second function must, instead, be guaranteed by a suitable user interface of the device that helps the person with the digital signatures. For example, each command to sign a message should be prompted by the question "Do you really want to sign the message ... ?". This would have to be complemented by a campaign telling all potential users what legal consequences giving digital signatures has.

The following considerations are therefore restricted to the first function. This function is sometimes subdivided into three parts:

a) The authenticity function ("Echtheitsfunktion"): The signature is to ensure that it is really the signer who has made the signed declaration of intention.
b) The identity function ("Identitätsfunktion"): The signature is to specify who has issued a document in the first place.

c) The closing function ("Abschlußfunktion"): The signature is to ensure that the document contains a complete declaration of intention, in contrast to sketches or beginnings of declarations.

This time, it is Function b) that cannot be fulfilled by the digital signatures themselves: With handwritten signatures, one requires that the identity can mainly be seen from the sequence of letters in the signature; such a sequence of letters does not exist with digital signatures. (In Section 2.3, it will become clear that the identity function is, instead, largely a matter of key distribution.) Of course, if courts maintain the requirement with the sequence of letters, digital signatures cannot be used at all. However, this seems to be a technical detail of legal interpretation, which could be changed without altering the function.

Function c), from a technical point of view, is a mixture of the warning function and the authenticity function: On the one hand, users are to be protected from signing sketches or beginnings of documents inadvertently; on the other hand, it has to be guaranteed that no part of a signed document can be deleted.

Thus, the technical discussion about digital signatures concentrates on the authenticity function: Anything that will be accepted as a certain user's digital signature on a certain declaration of intention must guarantee that exactly this user had indeed agreed to sign exactly this declaration of intention. Digital signatures must therefore be unforgeable in a sense as strong as possible, and it must be impossible to transfer a digital signature from one document to another. Hence digital signatures must be functions of both the message to be signed and the signer.

Note, however, that, contrary to widespread belief, a handwritten signature alone does not count as proof that a document has been issued by the supposed signer. According to § 416 ZPO, a signed private document does count as full proof that the declaration of intention it contains has been given by the signer; but before that, according to § 439, 440 ZPO, the authenticity of the signature has to be determined. The burden of proof ("Beweislast") is even with the recipient; theoretically, this means that in the case of dispute, the default value is that signatures have been forged. (In practice, however, courts might act differently.)

1.3 Consequences of the Legal Significance

Some more conclusions can be drawn from the legal considerations in the preceding section.

Assessment by Courts

If, for some technical restrictions, digital signatures are used that are not perfectly unforgeable, it is desirable that a court can judge how likely it is that a forgery took place. This implies, among other things, that the algorithms for digital signatures have to be publicly known.

Assessment by the Public

Not only courts, but the whole public should be able to test digital signatures and to judge their security: An important principle of states trying to guarantee the rights of their citizens is that cases are tried in open court. This principle is aimed at keeping courts under scrutiny and at the confidence into justice by the population. Both goals would be jeopardized if the public could not judge what was going on in the court.

No Trusted Third Parties

No so-called trusted third party should be needed in implementations of digital signature schemes, and in particular, no computerized third party.

Primarily, this is for the same fundamental reason as the previous point: Nobody is completely trusted a priori in constitutional and similar states, in contrast to absolutist ones. Only by mutual control does one hope to achieve that an honest majority prevails. For the same reason, on a larger scale, separation of powers is considered necessary. Moreover, one strives to let individuals act without interference by authorities as much as possible.

A computerized party is even worse, because at present, any complicated computer system can be misused by not only one, but many people, such as operators, maintenance personnel, and designers. In terms of fault tolerance: It is a series system with respect to trust, instead of a parallel system, as the judicial system should be.

Sometimes, it is put forward as an objection (often by banks) that many people will trust certain parties (such as banks). The statement may be true, but it is not a valid objection. First, with most people, this trust is founded on the very fact that these parties have been checked for a long time. (Most people do not have the opportunity to meet the directors, programmers etc. of their bank as fatherly family friends any more.) Secondly, even if most people do trust someone, this is no reason to require others to trust the same party, too.

Lest the preceding paragraphs should seem like an improper mixture of private and public law, some further distinctions have to be made: Of course, everybody can make private contracts about almost anything, e.g., about using anything called signatures in digital message exchange with anyone. These things would not have the significance of handwritten signatures. How much significance they would have as normal evidence is unclear: Courts might respect the contract; they might also regard it as invalid if it meant a serious disadvantage for one party, due to that party's inexperience with digital signatures, or if false promises were made. Especially with banks, one also has to consider that it may be unavoidable in practice to be a client of at least one of them. De facto, this puts banks in a similar position as states. Thus, it is appropriate to apply the same strict rules to them as to states.

A second reason for not having trusted third parties is practicality: At least a normal exchange of a signature should be possible just between the two parties concerned.

A third reason is that as long as the parties concerned are honest, their privacy should be protected, i.e., there should be no need for them to show all their declarations of intention to third parties, and not even the fact that they make any such declarations.

Equal Importance of Other System Parts

Most of what was just said for the digital signatures also has to hold for the surrounding protocol connecting the signatures to real identities (technically this will be key distribution), because the authenticity and identity function can only be provided if both the signature scheme and this protocol work correctly.

In practice, some third parties will usually take part in this protocol. However, the trust needed in them should be minimized by

- making them accountable for their actions, i.e., by providing ways for a court to distinguish between a fault of such a third party, including its personnel and equipment, on the one hand and a fault of a user on the other hand,
- measures for k-out-of-n trust, i.e., measures that guarantee security as long as at least k out of n such parties operate correctly, and
- diversity, i.e., allowing users some choice of what third parties they use.

Realizations are sketched in Section 2.3, "Key Distribution in Practice".

Blank Signatures

With digital signatures, people can pass their ability to sign on to others, because it consists of digital information alone. This has been regarded as a disadvantage over handwritten signatures. However, people can achieve almost the same effect by handing a large number of blank handwritten signatures to others. (The argument was used to substantiate that the information enabling people to sign should be kept hidden from them. However, that approach would be detrimental to the trust people can have in the security of their own signatures, and no really suitable hardware is to be expected in the near future anyway.)

1.4 Secure Hardware Support

Computing Signatures

As already mentioned in connection with the warning function, people will need devices to compute digital signatures for them. Thus one must assume that at least certain devices in the possession of people do not act against the will of their owners. For specifically designed end user devices, this can be a much more realistic assumption than that complicated central devices are uncorrupted, but it is still not trivial. One asset is the restricted access to the devices, another that the devices can be far less complicated, so that at least their design can be evaluated much better. People might also have the choice between devices from different producers (although, e.g., there are not that many producers of crypto chips). Of course, multi-user workstations are not of this type, and personal computers with largely open operating systems not really either.

On the other hand, one must take care that the complete computation is done on these devices. For instance, if the devices have no keyboard and display, like current smartcards, and all the inputs and outputs are transmitted through a device under someone else's control, like a point-of-sale terminal, the signer has no control over what message is actually signed. Consequently, this arrangement cannot provide the authenticity function, or at least no better than blank signatures can.

Storing Secret Data

Most people will need a device not only for computations, but even to store some secret data that they would otherwise have to remember; and most of the remaining people with a very good memory may not want to type so much data into the device for each signature. In this case, even a correct and helpful device becomes dangerous if it is lost or stolen or, e.g., with a normal size personal computer, if someone else simply gains access to it. One must therefore try to safeguard it against two kinds of attacks.

First, the finder or the thief of the device can try to use it exactly as the legitimate owner would. Thus the device must be given means to recognize its owner. Currently, passwords are used for this purpose. In this context, they are also called PIN, short for personal identification number. The security provided by passwords is rather weak, even if the device stops working after a few wrong attempts and the password is never transmitted through anyone else's device. (An improvement for the case where the thief has watched the owner type the password once is described in [MaIm91]; unfortunately, it seems to be too complicated for most people.) Additionally, one must ensure that owners recognize their devices so that they cannot be tricked into typing their password into a hostile device. Biometrics might be an alternative to passwords, but at present, most methods are neither reliable enough nor do they fit on the small devices considered (see, e.g., [DaPr89 Ch. 7, Fitz89]).

The second kind of attack is that thieves can try to extract the secrets from the device by other means. (Accidental finders are not likely to do so.) They are successful if they find either the password, with the device still intact, or the secret data for signing, without the device. Devices like smartcards are constructed with some measures for tamper-resistance, but their effectiveness is not clear, at least against attackers with access to a laboratory.

Outlook

For examples of what can go wrong if cryptologic systems are used in inappropriate environments, see [Pord93, PoRS93], where digital signatures in a scenario with PCs and smartcards were examined, and [Ande94]. More details about the design of trustworthy mobile user devices can be found in [PPSW95, PPSW96].

All the problems described in this section, 1.4, are important, and digital signatures should not be given too much legal significance before one has satisfactory solutions. Nevertheless, these problems are not problems of the digital signature schemes themselves. Therefore, in the remainder of this work, it is simply assumed that each person has found a reliable way of carrying out difficult computations and of storing secret data.

1.5 Relation to Other Types of Schemes

Three related types of cryptologic schemes are not always precisely distinguished from digital signature schemes:

1. mere authentication schemes (usually "symmetric"),
2. identification schemes, and
3. all kinds of secrecy schemes.

Mere (Symmetric) Authentication Schemes

Mere authentication schemes also serve to ensure the authenticity of messages: The recipient of a message with correct authentication can also be sure that the supposed sender has sent or agreed to send exactly this message. However, he cannot make anybody else believe this. In particular, the authentication does not help him in court. More precisely, from the point of view of a third party, the recipient could usually have produced the authenticated message just as well as the supposed sender. The purpose of these schemes is therefore to help people who trust each other to ensure that their messages have not been modified or forged by outsiders.

This symmetry between senders and recipients is usually reflected in the system structure; the schemes are then called symmetric authentication schemes (see Section 2.1). In contrast, digital signature schemes are sometimes called **asymmetric authentication schemes**. However, schemes exist that provide mere authentication and are not symmetric in this sense [OkOh91] (called non-transitive signature schemes there).

A cross between mere authentication schemes and signature schemes are authentication schemes with arbiters. These arbiters can settle disputes, but they must be trusted to a larger extent than courts with digital signature schemes, and there is no assessment by the public. See [Simm88, BrSt88] and, for an overview of newer articles, [JoSm95]. Some details, which differ in all these schemes, are mentioned in a footnote in Section 5.2.2.

Identification Schemes

Identification schemes only serve to authenticate a person or a device. In contrast to authentication schemes, this person or device does not want to transmit a particular message. Thus, identification schemes can mainly be used where certain people are to be granted physical access to buildings or areas: A small computer that they carry with them, e.g., on a smartcard, can carry out such an identification protocol. However, in situations where more digital communication follows after the original identification, all the following messages have to be authenticated, too.

From every authentication scheme (mere authentication or signatures), a corresponding identification scheme can be constructed; for instance, authenticated messages "I am now, ..., here, ...", with a time stamp, can be sent.[1] The reverse

---

1 Of course, this is no longer trivial if one makes requirements on the time and location of the person or device to be identified that one did not make in the authentication scheme. See [BeRo94] for a formal treatment of authentication with timeliness requirements, often called freshness, and [BrCh94] for some treatment of location.

implication does not hold, at least not with efficient constructions. This is sometimes overlooked: There are rather efficient identification schemes that are, in a certain model, provably secure. From those, digital signature schemes can be constructed, which are still rather efficient. However, these signature schemes are not provably secure any more. (See the Fiat-Shamir scheme [FiSh87, FeFS88] and several similarly constructed schemes, in the version where each participant chooses her own secret key.)

Secrecy Schemes

This third demarcation seems unnecessary from a purely scientific point of view, but for several practical reasons, it is not: Digital signature schemes, and authentication schemes generally, have nothing to do with keeping messages secret. For that purpose, one has secrecy schemes.

Apart from a historical idea that cryptology deals with secrecy, one reason why authentication and secrecy are sometimes mixed up is that some well-known authentication and secrecy schemes are constructed from the same basic functions, e.g., DES or RSA ([DES77, RiSA78], see Chapter 2). However, the basic functions are used differently in order to achieve the different purposes.

Another reason is that the following idea seems to suggest itself, and has indeed been proposed several times (e.g., with a small technical modification, in [DiHe76, RiSA78]): Assume one has a secrecy scheme, and one receives a ciphertext and deciphers it. If it yields a "sensible" message, it must have been a correct ciphertext produced by the supposed sender.

However, this idea has two major flaws: First, it can only be used for messages with inherent redundancy; otherwise, a predicate "sensible" does not even exist in an informal way. (If one adds redundancy to the message artificially, it is already a case of a different use for a different purpose.)

Secondly, secrecy schemes do not exclude that outsiders can transform one enciphered message into another sensible one. For example, consider the "one-time pad" or Vernam cipher, which is perfect as a secrecy scheme ([Vern26, Shan49], see also Section 2.2). Here, a message, represented as a bit string, is enciphered by XORing it with another bit string of the same length. The other bit string, the key, had been chosen randomly and agreed upon with the recipient. From the point of view of an outsider, for any given message, the ciphertext is perfectly random; hence the message is perfectly secret. Nevertheless, if the outsider inverts one or more bits of the ciphertext, exactly the same bits are inverted in the message after decryption, i.e., after the key has been XORed to the ciphertext. For instance, if the message is a digital money transfer order with a certain field for the amount, an outsider can tamper with the amount without any risk of being detected.

Hence, authentication schemes, and digital signature schemes in particular, cannot be treated as a variant of secrecy schemes, but need both definitions and constructions of their own.

1.6 A Variant: Invisible Signatures

Invisible signatures (usually, but not characteristically called "undeniable") are a kind of signatures providing more privacy than ordinary ones.

With ordinary digital signatures, a recipient can show a received signature to everybody else, even if there is no need to do so. For example, with the promissory note shown in Figure 1.1, the only real need for Bob to show the signature occurs if Alice is not willing to pay on the day for which the promise was made. However, Bob can also show the promissory note to all his friends in between. This can imply a breach of the privacy of Alice, who might want to keep private that she borrowed money, because the fact that the message is signed gives Bob more credibility than if he only told his friends that Alice borrowed money from him. Theoretically, one can say: If providing message authentication that is provable to third parties in case of dispute is regarded as the sole purpose of digital signature schemes, an ordinary digital signature scheme does too much.

This is why invisible signatures were introduced in [ChAn90]. (Conversely, if one says that the purpose of digital signature schemes is to imitate handwritten signatures as closely as possible, an invisible signature scheme does too little.)

An invisible signature cannot be shown to third parties without the help of the signer. If, however, the signer is forced to either deny or acknowledge a valid signature, e.g., in court, she cannot deny it.[2] In the same example as above, Bob's friends will not be able to test the validity of what Bob shows them as Alice's signature, because they cannot count on Alice's help. However, a court might force Alice to either deny or acknowledge the promissory note.

A related requirement of invisibility has explicitly been considered with mere authentication, but in a scenario with public keys, in [OkOh91].

2 This last feature gave rise to the original name "undeniable". However, it is a feature common to all signature schemes and therefore not characteristic. Moreover, the old terminology is very confusing with the noun "undeniability": It meant both that signatures cannot be denied and the characteristic feature that they cannot be shown round, which is called invisibility here.

2 History of Digital Signature Schemes

The schemes described in this section are the historical framework for the schemes and the classification proposed in the remainder of this work. Moreover, some of their components are reused in the new constructions. Therefore, this section does not only describe specifications, although those would be sufficient to delimit the new ideas, but contains sketches of some constructions, too.

Moreover, the history of digital signature schemes is so closely linked to the history of the related types of schemes mentioned in Section 1.5 that parts of the history of those also have to be outlined.

The organization of this section is only roughly chronological: The most essential ideas are in the right order, but related things are presented together. Chronological order with digital signature schemes, as with most other cryptologic subjects, means: Related to older work (Sections 2.1 and 2.2), someone has an informal idea (Section 2.3), and people happily start to construct schemes (Section 2.4). Later, problems are found even with those schemes that seemed to be the best ones so far (Section 2.5). Thus some people start to build provably secure schemes, and eventually, one even makes a definition (Section 2.6). I decided to keep this order, however questionable, in this informal section, because it gives the most realistic view of the state of the art — many publications still ignore that security definitions for digital signature schemes exist — and some of the previous work would not find a place in a more systematic approach.

2.1 Classical Cryptography

Working on the usual assumptions of classical cryptography, one would have thought that there is no such thing as a digital signature scheme: Classical cryptographic schemes assume that a sender and a recipient have a common secret, which is unknown to outsiders from whom the sender and the recipient want to protect themselves.

With privately used schemes, this secret may be the whole algorithm used. However, it was soon discovered that if a scheme is intended for widespread use, or to be carried out by machines, one cannot hope to keep the structure of the algorithm or the construction of the machines secret for a long time. Thus one divides the schemes into algorithms, which may be public, and certain parameters, called **keys**, which have to remain secret. (See, e.g., [DiHe76] for a brief sketch after [Kahn67].)

Nowadays, making algorithms public is not merely seen as unavoidable, but even as desirable: The security will be evaluated more thoroughly if the whole (scientific) public is invited to do so. Often, even a financial incentive is offered. Furthermore, if a scheme is not to be used solely by its inventor, some supervision is needed. For digital signature schemes, an additional reason was discussed in Section 1.3.

Hence, in classical cryptographic schemes, each pair or group of mutually trusting participants has a common secret key, and all the other information is public; the schemes are therefore automatically symmetric.

Primarily, secrecy schemes were considered, and no formal notion of security existed. Some even thought it impossible that such a notion could exist, the more so because several schemes had been broken for whose security mathematical arguments had been given. However, these arguments had only referred to some aspects of security, e.g., how many keys were possible (see, e.g., [DiHe76]).

2.2 Information-Theoretically Secure Symmetric Schemes

The first important step towards modern scientific cryptology[3] was Claude Shannon's work [Shan49]. There, for the first time, a precise (and, according to informal requirements, certainly sufficient) notion of security for any type of cryptologic scheme was defined: the information-theoretic security of secrecy schemes, sometimes called Shannon security. Roughly, the definition requires that a ciphertext provides an outsider with no additional information at all about the message. The information-theoretic notion means that the scheme is absolutely unbreakable, i.e., unbreakable even by attackers with unrestricted computing power and unrestricted memory.

However, in the same article it was proved that any secrecy scheme that is provably secure in this sense is equivalent to one-time pads (see Section 1.5) or even less efficient. Thus, for a while, there was no further research in this field. Besides, for most applications, one-time pads were regarded as too inefficient, because the length of the secret key, which has to be exchanged beforehand, must be at least equal to the overall length of the messages that might be sent later. Hence one continued to use other schemes in practice.

A similar work for authentication schemes was only published 15 years later: In [GiMS74], the information-theoretic, i.e., absolute security of symmetric authentication schemes was defined. Schemes complying with this definition are often called authentication codes. Like Claude Shannon's work, [GiMS74] already contains both concrete constructions of authentication codes and lower bounds on the achievable efficiency, and in particular, the key length. In contrast to secrecy schemes, however, the upper and lower bounds are not identical; furthermore, the constructions are less trivial. Therefore, there has been further research in this field.

3 The word "cryptology" is nowadays used for all schemes, or only all mathematical schemes, which enable parties who distrust each other or outsiders to cooperate in a useful way. For more types of cryptologic schemes than authentication and secrecy schemes, see, e.g., [Bras88, Schn96] or some subschemes in the later chapters of this text. "Cryptography" is sometimes regarded as a synonym and sometimes as more restricted, either to the construction of schemes (in contrast to cryptanalysis, for instance) or to secrecy schemes.

In particular, efficiently computable authentication codes where the key length only grows logarithmically with the length of the messages to be authenticated later were constructed in [WeCa81]. An improvement of this scheme and an overview of the literature in this field can be found in [BJKS94].

In practice, however, to this day, schemes with even greater efficiency are used for symmetric authentication, instead of information-theoretically secure ones; schemes about whose security no precise knowledge exists. Most common are certain modes of operation of the (former) Data Encryption Standard (DES). (See, e.g., [DES77] for the standard, [DaPr89] for modes of operation and possible applications, and [BiSh93] for new security examinations.)

2.3 Invention of Digital Signature Schemes

The idea that digital signature schemes might exist was first published in the directive article [DiHe76].

Structure

The fundamental idea in [DiHe76] was that there might be pairs of keys belonging together (see Figure 2.1): With one key, one can sign, whereas with the other key, one can only test signatures. Hence, the keys are called **signing key** and **test key**, respectively.

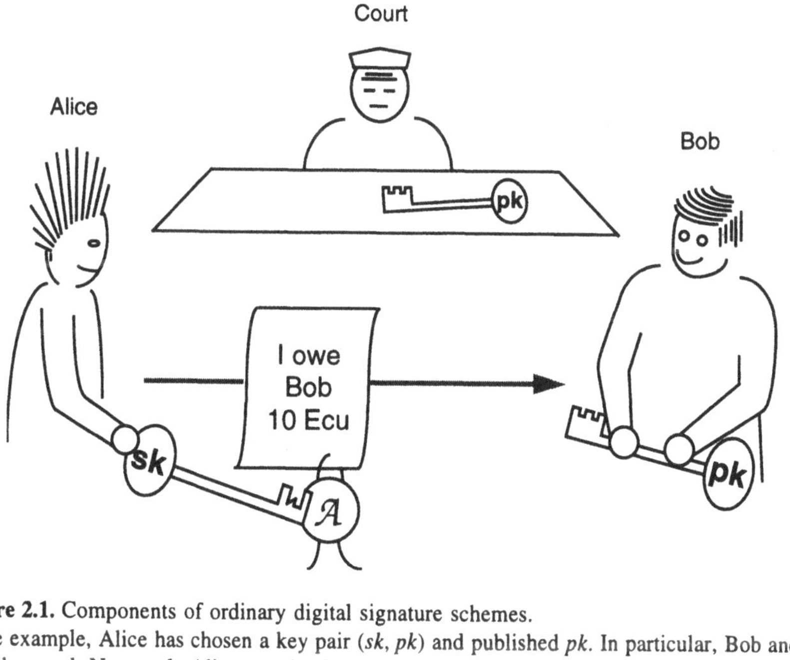

Figure 2.1. Components of ordinary digital signature schemes.
In the example, Alice has chosen a key pair (*sk*, *pk*) and published *pk*. In particular, Bob and the court know *pk*. Now, only Alice can sign her message with *sk*. Bob and the court accept a message as signed by Alice if and only if it passes the test with *pk*.

Such a scheme is intended to be used as follows: Everybody who may want to sign messages generates such a key pair. She keeps the signing key secret and publishes the test key. (For simplicity, signers will always be assumed to be female and recipients male, corresponding to the names used in the figures.) Alternatively, the two keys are therefore called **secret key** (or private key) and **public key**, respectively.

Everybody can now sign messages with their own signing keys, whereas all the other participants can test these signatures with the corresponding test key.

A bit more precisely, the components of an **ordinary digital signature scheme** and their interaction are usually depicted as in Figure 2.2.[4]

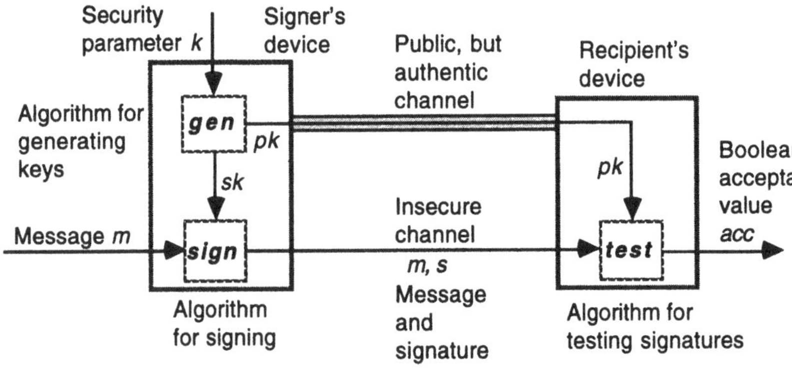

Figure 2.2. Components of ordinary digital signature schemes, more precisely.
Components in a strict sense are the algorithms ***gen***, ***sign***, and ***test***, which are written in bold face. Among them, ***gen*** and ***sign*** are probabilistic. The remaining values in italics are typical parameters and results of the algorithms. Devices and channels are not parts of the signature scheme and are only shown to illustrate the typical usage.

Security Limits

The main security requirement on such a digital signature scheme is, roughly speaking, that one cannot forge signatures although one knows the public key. A necessary (but not sufficient) condition for this is that one cannot compute the secret key from the public key.

One easily sees that such a scheme can never be information-theoretically, i.e., perfectly, secure. This was already mentioned in [DiHe76]: For practicality, there must be an upper bound on the length of signatures produced with signing keys and messages of a certain length. If forgers try all strings of up to this length, one by one, to see which ones pass the test with the public key for a given message, they are sure to find a valid signature on this message.

---

4 The word "ordinary" is used here because in later chapters, different schemes will be presented. Our previous publications used "conventional" instead, but some readers understood that as a synonym of "symmetric" or "without public keys".

The security of such digital signature schemes can therefore only be **computational**, i.e., hold in the sense of complexity theory: It relies on the fact that in reality, a forger has too little time to carry out the trivial forging algorithm, and that no much more efficient forging algorithm is available.

More unpleasantly, if all the algorithms that honest participants must carry out are polynomial-time, the same argument shows immediately that the complexity class of forging cannot be higher than NP (see [DiHe76, GaJo80]): A non-deterministic polynomial-time forging algorithm has just been shown. As $P \neq NP$ is a well-known unproven hypothesis in complexity theory, it cannot be expected that one can easily prove that forging is impossible in polynomial time in any such digital signature scheme. It is also quite unlikely that weaker, but still sufficient, lower bounds on the complexity of the forging problem can easily be proved.

Consequently, the security of such digital signature schemes can nowadays only rely on unproven assumptions. Of course, one tries to select assumptions that seem trustworthy for some reasons. A nice assumption would be $P \neq NP$. However, it was clear at once that the usual complexity-theoretic notion of infeasibility is not sufficient to say that forging is infeasible: This notion deals with the worst-case behaviour of algorithms, whereas forging must be infeasible on average, and even in most cases. More precise notions of security were only considered later, see Section 2.6. However, one can already say that until now, no digital signature scheme could be proved secure on the assumption $P \neq NP$. Hence one makes special computational assumptions about the infeasibility of some basic problem in the above-mentioned sense of "in most cases"; they are often called **cryptologic assumptions**.

The restriction to computational security is not necessarily a serious objection to the use of asymmetric authentication, because, as mentioned, most symmetric schemes used in practice are not information-theoretically secure either, nor has their security been proved in any stricter sense.

A consequence of computational security is that signature schemes usually depend on a so-called **security parameter**, which determines the length of the problem instances that are supposed to be infeasible. Thus, choosing a larger security parameter usually makes keys and signatures longer, and signing and testing more time-consuming, but one hopes that it makes forging signatures more difficult even more quickly, so that the gap between the complexities of the legal algorithms (*gen*, *sign*, and *test*) and of forging widens.

Near Relatives: Asymmetric Secrecy Schemes

The same idea with key pairs was first introduced for secrecy schemes in [DiHe76]: In this case, the first, more powerful, key is needed to decrypt messages, whereas with the second key, one can only encrypt. As before, the second key is published. Thus everybody can encrypt messages for the owner of a key pair and only the owner can decrypt them with the secret key. These schemes are called asymmetric secrecy schemes.[5]

5 The name public-key cryptosystems is also used. With some authors, it designates all asymmetric schemes, with others, asymmetric secrecy schemes only.

Key Distribution in Comparison with Symmetric Schemes

Digital signature schemes have one more advantage over symmetric authentication schemes, besides allowing disputes to be settled: Key distribution is simpler.

With all symmetric schemes, each pair of participants who want to communicate securely must have exchanged its own secret key. Thus they must have met privately before, at least if one takes a strict point of view. With asymmetric schemes, in contrast, only one public key per participant needs to be distributed.

For secrecy, one uses so-called hybrid schemes if efficiency is important and messages are long: The actual message is encrypted using an efficient symmetric scheme. The secret key used is authenticated and encrypted, using the less efficient asymmetric scheme, and sent as a prefix to the encrypted message. A special form of hybrid schemes can be constructed from mere asymmetric public key-distribution schemes: With the key-distribution scheme, no message can be exchanged, but a common secret key can be agreed upon [DiHe76].

Key Distribution in Practice

Notwithstanding the advantages mentioned above, distributing the test keys for a digital signature scheme is not trivial. By all means, the distribution has to be reliable. For instance, in Figure 2.1, it would be disastrous for Bob's security if Alice had told him one *pk*, and the court another. Similarly, it would be disastrous for Alice if the court worked with a wrong *pk* for which an attacker knew the corresponding secret key. Hence **reliable broadcast** is needed with its two characteristic properties consistency, i.e., all honest recipients receive the same value, and correctness, i.e., if the sender is honest, all honest recipients receive the value she intended to send.

In the theoretical treatment of digital signature schemes, one simply assumes that a reliable broadcast network can be used during a special key-distribution phase. Only the real messages, later on, are sent over arbitrary channels.

In most cases in practice, however, one cannot assume that any available communication network guarantees reliable broadcast in this sense. Restricted groups of participants can easily achieve reliable broadcast by meeting in one room. In larger groups, distribution using something like phone books, i.e., printed directories on paper, counts as fairly reliable: In this case, any falsification of the distribution is possible almost exclusively while the directories are being printed, it cannot easily be aimed at specific recipients, and it can usually be proved afterwards. Large-scale falsification can also be detected by comparing random samples.

For reasons of efficiency, one often prefers to distribute keys on the same digital communication network as normal messages, i.e., on the network where one will later protect messages using these very keys. Obviously, this cannot work from scratch, i.e., one has to assume that some keys have been distributed outside the network already. Then one can certify other keys. A **key certificate** is a signed message of the form "I, *C*, hereby certify that Person *A* has the key *pk*, where … ". The where-part contains technical details, such as the signature scheme to which *pk* belongs, the date of the signature, and the period of validity of the certificate, and should contain at least the following items:

- Restrictions desired by A, e.g., that pk can only be used in specific applications, or that pk is used on a multi-user workstation and A can therefore not take full responsibility for it.
- How sure C is of its statement, and thus how much liability it is willing to assume for it. E.g., C could state here how it has verified that pk really comes from A.

As desired in Section 1.3, the trust needed in the certifying parties can be minimized; in particular, these parties are accountable: If a recipient B shows a message signed with respect to a public key pk that he claims is A's and A denies this, the dispute can be settled as follows: First, the recipient has to show evidence why he believes the key is A's. This may be a handwritten signature by A herself, but usually it is a certificate by a party C. If C excluded liability in this certificate, it was at B's own risk that he trusted it. Otherwise, C has to show evidence why it believed that the key was A's. This may be a certificate by another party, but eventually some party will be reached that claims to have known it from A directly. This party must at least show a handwritten signature by A on pk and maybe demonstrate other measures it took against being fooled by a forged handwritten signature.

In this way, keys can be distributed both in a decentralized way as in the freely available program PGP [Zimm93, Garf95] and in the hierarchic manner suggested in the standard X.509 [ISO91, ISO95].

Some k-out-of-n trust and diversity can be achieved if more than one certificate with direct knowledge from A are required, and if anyone who certifies a key as being A's must first send the certificate to A via a specific notary public so that the real A hopefully has an opportunity to protest against a false certificate.

Key Generation

In this work, as in all publications in theory, it is assumed that participants generate their own secret keys, so that the keys deserve the attribute "secret". This procedure is also strongly recommended for practical applications.

Nevertheless, it has been proposed in practice that specific certification centres should also generate secret keys for the participants. Partly, this is explained by claiming that key generation were too inefficient for the devices of individual participants. However, keys for those digital signature schemes that might actually be used in practice can nowadays be generated on any personal computer and even on a smartcard in reasonable time. Thus this argument is at least obsolete. There is no political argument for any other party to know someone's signing key either (in contrast to secrecy schemes, where such arguments are put forward by security agencies, although I disagree with them and although such measures could not achieve the claimed goal of making messages of suspected criminals, but not of honest users, readable, because double-encryption and steganography are possible). Anyway, nobody has argued that the state should be able to forge signatures.

A more realistic problem is the generation of real random numbers for key generation. There are several methods, all of which have disadvantages. Fortunately, one does not need to make a choice, but should XOR several independently generated strings. At least one of them must be generated with user participation. See [PPSW96] for more details.

Relation Between Persons and Keys

The usual examples of the use of digital signatures assume that the relation between persons and public keys is bijective, at least at any given moment. This need not be the case in practice, and in theory not anyway.

On the one hand, although less frequently, keys may belong to more than one person, or to nobody at all. For instance, if a certain device signs all its outputs, and if several people can cause the device to make outputs, the key of this device can be seen as a common key of these people, whereas, if the device works automatically, its key cannot be seen as that of any person (or else, that of all its producers).

On the other hand, a person can own several keys.

First, this may happen without any specific goal. If digital signature schemes and their usage are not standardized, different organizations will use different signature schemes with their clients, and the keys will therefore be different, too. Even successive keys for the same purpose will have overlapping periods of validity.

Secondly, people may wish to restrict different keys to different purposes, e.g., one key used on an office workstation and a more secure key on a personal device.

Thirdly, one can use several keys to guarantee more privacy: Each public key can serve as a **pseudonym** of its owner. Under each of her pseudonyms, the person can perform transactions with organizations in a secure way; however, the organizations cannot join the information they collected about the person without her permission. For more details about the possibilities opened up by this approach, in particular in connection with credential schemes, and about the necessity of anchoring privacy so deeply in the technical systems, see, e.g., the surveys [Chau85, PfWP90, BüPf89, BüPf90], and for two newer papers, [Chau90, Chau92]. In particular, one can see that at least the same legal security can be achieved with these pseudonyms as with conventional approaches for many important legal transactions, most noticeably in digital payment schemes and the fair exchange of goods and payment. Thus the pseudonyms provide the functionality of the identity function of handwritten signatures.[6]

2.4 Intuitively Constructed Digital Signature Schemes

In [DiHe76], the idea of digital signatures was introduced, together with applications and discussions of possible approaches and security limits, but only a very inefficient concrete digital signature scheme could be presented.

---

6 In current law, signing with pseudonyms is permitted with handwritten signatures in Germany, although this rule seems to be aimed primarily at artist's names [Lare83]. In the USA, pseudonyms seem to be accepted in almost all cases.

One-Time Signatures

The first digital signature scheme, which was already described in [DiHe76], is Leslie Lamport's one-time signatures [Lamp79]. Although it was not very practical to begin with, the basic idea has been reused several times since (see Section 2.6) — and in some fail-stop signature schemes, too.

One starts with an arbitrary **one-way function** f. This means that f can be evaluated efficiently, but its inverse cannot. The latter must hold in a strong sense: For almost all images, it must be infeasible to compute any preimage. Some proposals for one-way functions, derived from classical cryptosystems, already existed at that time, because the use of such functions had been proposed for secure login procedures. According to [DiHe76], the first proposal was made by Roger Needham and the next ones in [EvKW74, Purd74].

As a secret key, for each bit that the signer may want to sign in future, she chooses two numbers $sk^{(i)}{}_0$ and $sk^{(i)}{}_1$ randomly from (a certain part of) the domain of f. She publishes all the images $pk^{(i)}{}_b := f(sk^{(i)}{}_b)$ as her public key. Later, if she wants to sign that the value of the i-th bit is b, she publishes $sk^{(i)}{}_b$. The recipient of a presumably signed message can easily test the correctness: For each bit b_i and its supposed signature s_i, he tests if $f(s_i) = pk^{(i)}{}_{b_i}$. The one-way property of f prevents forgeries.

This scheme is called a **one-time** signature scheme because each part of the secret key can be used only once, here for only one bit. (Later the term "one-time" will also be used for schemes where a complete message can be signed with each part of the secret key.) The most impractical feature of this scheme is the tremendous length of the public keys, because public keys have to be broadcast reliably at the beginning, whereas signatures need only be sent to one person and secret keys are simply stored.

Tree Authentication

One-time signature schemes became fairly practical with tree authentication [Merk90, Merk80, Merk82]. The former public keys are no longer published; instead, they are reduced to a short new public key. For this, they are used as the leaves of a binary tree (usually complete). The value of each inner node is computed by applying a **hash function** to its two children. The hash function, too, must have a one-way property in a strict cryptologic sense. The value pk of the root is the new public key. When one of the former "public" keys, $pk^{(i)}{}_b$, is used, it is authenticated with respect to pk. This can be achieved with overhead logarithmic in the size of the tree: Only the path from $pk^{(i)}{}_b$ to the root is shown, i.e., all the forefathers of $pk^{(i)}{}_b$ and their immediate children.

With similar hash functions, the messages can be reduced to constant length before they are signed bit by bit [DiHe76].

In more or less this form, and with one-way and hash functions of high efficiency, but unproven security, the scheme is nowadays still being considered for practical applications [Merk88, MeMa82 pp. 396-409, Meye91, Vaud92, BlMa94].

Trap-Door One-Way Permutations

An idea of how one might be able to construct efficient digital signature schemes was already described in [DiHe76]. Only with its realization in [RiSA78] did the idea of digital signatures, and of asymmetric cryptologic schemes in general, gain real popularity.

This idea is trap-door one-way permutations, i.e., permutations that are no longer one-way if one knows some secret "trap-door" information. More precisely, one should speak of trap-door one-way *families* of permutations. Such a family is defined as follows: There are three algorithms, called *gen*, *f*, and f^{-1}. A participant can use *gen* to generate a pair (*sk*, *pk*) of a secret and a public key for the family of permutations. Everyone who knows the public key can compute a certain permutation, $f(pk, \bullet)$, from the family, whereas only the secret key enables its owner to compute the inverse of this permutation.

In [DiHe76, RiSA78], a signature scheme is constructed from any trap-door one-way family of permutations in the following simple way: The secret and public key of the signature scheme are exactly those of the trap-door one-way permutations. The signer signs a message by applying the inverse permutation to it. Everybody else can test the signature by applying the permutation and checking that the result is the correct message.

For a comparison, note that with trap-door one-way permutations, the signer can compute a signature as a function of the message, whereas others, without the secret key, cannot do so. In contrast, if only a one-way function is given, as in the case with one-time signatures, the signer cannot compute anything that nobody else can. This is why, essentially, she had to choose all possible future signatures beforehand, which was most efficiently done bit by bit.

RSA

A trap-door one-way family of permutations was proposed in [RiSA78]. It was called RSA later.[7] The essential part of the secret key is two large primes

$$p, q,$$

and the essential part of the public key is the product

$$n := p \cdot q.$$

The main underlying cryptologic assumption is therefore that factoring large integers is infeasible. Concrete versions have later been called the **factoring assumption** (see Section 8.4). To this day, it has remained one of the two most important assumptions to base asymmetric cryptologic schemes on.

The factoring assumption implies that nobody except for the signer can compute $\phi(n) = (p-1)(q-1)$, Euler's totient function [RiSA78].

Additionally, the public key contains a number $e < n$ with $\gcd(e, \phi(n)) = 1$, where gcd denotes the greatest common divisor. The secret key contains the inverse

7 Usually, the secrecy and signature schemes constructed from this trap-door one-way family of permutations are also called RSA. However, there are several variants of those, as will be seen in Section 2.5. This can lead to confusion.

d of e modulo $\phi(n)$. The signer can compute d using the extended Euclidean algorithm. (A sketch of the necessary number theory and references are given in Chapter 8.) The permutation f corresponding to this public key (n, e) is defined by

$$f(m) := m^e \bmod n$$

for all $m \in \mathbb{Z}_n$, i.e., a discrete power function. One can see quite easily that the inverse of f can be computed as

$$f^{-1}(m) = m^d \bmod n.$$

Security discussions about RSA initially focused on two questions already raised in [RiSA78]: How hard is integer factoring? And are there other ways of inverting RSA than by factoring, or can one prove that these two problems are equally hard? None of these questions has found a final answer yet. For the first one, see Section 8.4.1, and for an overview of contributions to the second one, in particular the superencryption question, see, e.g., [DaPr89].

A third important question is if the signature scheme can be broken without breaking the trap-door one-way permutations. However, this question only came up later; see Section 2.5.

Further Intuitively Constructed Schemes

There were many attempts to construct alternatives to RSA. One goal was to improve upon the efficiency of RSA, the other, to base the schemes on cryptologic assumptions other than factoring. Within the latter, special interest was given to schemes where breaking seemed to have at least some relation to an NP-complete problem. In particular, according to a suggestion in [DiHe76], many signature schemes and asymmetric secrecy schemes were based on the knapsack problem, but always on knapsacks with special structures. However, so many knapsack schemes were broken that it is hard to trust any of them. Another well-known sequence of schemes with several broken variants is the Ong-Schnorr-Shamir schemes; they were based on the difficulty of solving polynomial equations modulo a composite number with unknown factors, and very efficient. For a good survey of these two types of schemes and several others, with an extensive bibliography, see [BrOd92], and for two newer results, [ScHö95, CoSV94].

The only serious rival to factoring as a cryptologic assumption to base asymmetric cryptologic schemes on that has emerged is the **discrete-logarithm assumption**. It was first suggested by John Gill for finite prime fields and used for a public key-distribution scheme in [DiHe76]. The idea is that discrete exponentiation, i.e., the operation

$$x \rightarrow g^x \bmod p,$$

for p prime and g a generator of the multiplicative group $\mathbb{Z}_p^*$, can be computed efficiently, whereas no efficient algorithm is known for the inverse, the so-called discrete logarithm. The first signature scheme based on this assumption is the ElGamal scheme [ElGa85]. Similarly to the situation with RSA, one can neither show that the ElGamal scheme is as hard to break as the discrete logarithm, nor does one have non-trivial lower bounds on the complexity of the discrete logarithm.

The practical complexity of the discrete logarithm has developed surprisingly similar to that of factoring (see Section 8.4.2), although no reduction between the two problems is known. As a consequence, the efficiency of the ElGamal scheme and RSA is rather similar, too.

Several variants of the ElGamal scheme have been suggested. On the one hand, the algorithms can be modified, e.g., see [Schn91, Rooi94, DSS92] for well-known ones and [Schn92, Pive93, NyRu95, HoMP95] for more variations. On the other hand, the same algorithms can be based on other families of cyclic groups: One only needs to know an efficient multiplication algorithm, generators, and the group order, and one must be willing to believe that computing discrete logarithms in the given family of groups is infeasible. Apart from multiplicative groups of other finite fields, the most well-known approach is to use **elliptic curves**, starting with [Mill86, Kobl87a]. For implementation issues and an overview of other literature, see [MeVa93]. The main reason for changing the group was that one believes that discrete logarithms might be harder to compute than in finite fields, so that one can use smaller security parameters and thus achieve higher efficiency. However, this was disproved for the elliptic curves that are easiest to handle [MeOV93], and thus it may be wise not to rely on it too much for any curve at present. For examples of other groups or related structures, see [Kobl89, BiBT94].

Anyway, one should be very careful with new cryptologic assumptions: Nowadays, the only criterion for their trustworthiness is how intensively they have been examined. Thus, roughly speaking, among those schemes that have not been broken, the oldest ones are most recommendable for practical use.

Another type of intuitively constructed schemes are the signature variants of provably secure identification schemes like [FiSh87, FeFS88, BDPW90], in the version where each participant chooses her own secret key, which were already mentioned in Section 1.5. They are based on normal cryptologic assumptions like factoring and so far unbroken. Similar schemes have also be constructed on assumptions that are not number-theoretic, from [Ster90] to [Poin95].

2.5 Problems, Countermeasures, and Emerging Security Notions

In Section 2.4, just as in the early literature, the notion of breaking had not been made precise. Implicitly, one assumed the following problem: Given the public key and a message, find a corresponding signature. However, one noticed that some schemes that seem infeasible to break in this sense are vulnerable if one allows stronger attacks and weaker forms of success.

First, the terminology that has later been developed for different types of attacks and success, e.g., in [GoMR88], is introduced.

Types of Attacks

The most important types of attacks, in the order of increasing strength, are:

- Key-only attack: The only information the attacker has to work on is the public key.
- Known-message attack (or general passive attack): The attacker is given the public key and some signed messages.
- Chosen-message or **active attack**: The attacker can choose some messages that the signer will sign for him before he must forge a signature on another message on his own.

  In the most general type of active attack, the attacker can choose those messages at any time. This is called an adaptive chosen-message attack. For technical reasons, weaker forms were considered where the attacker must choose all the messages before the signer publishes her public key or at least before the signer issues the first signature.

Types of Success

The most important types of success, in decreasing order, are:

- Total break: The attacker has found the secret key, or an equivalent way of constructing signatures on arbitrary messages efficiently.
- Selective forgery: The attacker has forged the signature on a message that he could select independently of the public key and before a possible active attack.
- **Existential forgery**: The attacker has forged the signature on a message that the signer has not signed, but the attacker could not choose what message.

In these terms, most of the breaks reported in Section 2.4 were total breaks after key-only attacks.

Problems

Early examples of weaker forms of breaking were the Rabin scheme and the Williams scheme: Both are similar to RSA, but constructed so that selective forgery with a passive attack was as hard as factoring. However, it was immediately noticed that the schemes could be totally broken with an active attack [Rabi79, Will80]. Another example was the signature-like scheme from [Rabi78]: It was noticed in [Yuva79] that an attacker could, with smaller overhead than one might have assumed, find two messages with the same signature, so that by asking the signer to sign one of them, he also obtains the signature on the other.

These attacks were not considered seriously until it was noticed, surprisingly late, that similar attacks are possible on RSA. The first attack simply uses that the secret RSA operation is a homomorphism [Davi82]; see also [DeMe82, Merr83]: By multiplying the signatures on two messages m_1 and m_2, one obtains the signature on the product $m_1 \cdot m_2$. Thus, if an attacker breaks his message into two factors and gets the signer to sign those, he can derive the signature on the chosen message. With a trick by Judy Moore, the attacker needs only one signature on a message of his choice [Denn84]. These are selective forgeries after chosen-message attacks, or, alternatively, existential forgeries after known-message attacks.

Existential forgery is even possible with a key-only attack in all signature schemes built from trap-door one-way permutations as described in Section 2.4: The attacker chooses a value and calls it a signature, computes the permutation with the public key, and calls the result a message.

By the way, the situation with the ElGamal scheme is similar to that with RSA, although that scheme is not directly constructed from trap-door one-way permutations: Existential forgery is possible with a key-only attack. However, no method for selective forgery with an active attack is known.

Assessment of Types of Attacks and Success

A known-message attack is perfectly realistic. A completely unrestricted adaptive chosen-message attack is not: If the signer signed arbitrary messages, there would be no need for forgery. However, restricted forms of active attacks certainly occur in practice: Almost every recipient of signatures will have some influence on what messages are signed, and in some situations, the recipient determines the message almost completely. For example, the signer might be a notary public who signs almost anything that clients ask her to; she only refuses to sign particularly ugly things, or always includes a correct time-stamp. The only way to make sure that one is on the safe side in all applications therefore seems to be to assume that the signer signs anything except one message for which a signature will be forged.

As to the types of success, a scheme where selective forgery is possible can obviously not be used in practice. Existential forgery may not always be harmful, because the message on which a signature was forged may be of no practical value to the attacker. However, one does not know what will be of practical value in all future applications of digital signature schemes, in particular, if data without inherent redundancy are signed. Hence, to be on the safe side, it seems necessary to assume that every signed message might be of value.

Ad-Hoc Countermeasures

There are two usual ad-hoc measures against the problems explained above (see, e.g., [DaPr80, Denn84]).

One is to add redundancy to messages before signing. In this case, only messages that fulfil a certain predicate are signed; this makes chosen-message attacks more complicated. Furthermore, a signature is only valid if the message fulfils the predicate; thus existential forgery in the original scheme seems unlikely to yield a valid message.

The other measure is to apply a one-way hash function to messages before signing. In this case, it seems unlikely that an attacker can find messages for a chosen-message attack where the hash values actually signed are useful to him. Furthermore, an existential forgery in the original scheme should yield a message whose preimage under the hash function is not known. Applying a hash function has the additional advantage that it makes the complete scheme more efficient, if the hash function is fast; actually, this is why this measure was originally proposed.

More Problems

The choice of good redundancy predicates or hash functions is not easy, in particular, if one wants the hash function to be fast. Weaknesses have been found in several proposed versions: For redundancy predicates, see [JoCh86], for hash functions, [DaPr85, Gira88, MiOl91].

More generally, the proposed schemes with redundancy or fast hash functions (often based on symmetric cryptologic schemes such as DES) have a rather chaotic overall structure, so that one cannot even hope that breaking them is equivalent to a well-examined problem such as factoring.

A recent technique is to show that at least the general principle of such a combined construction is sound by proving that the construction would be secure if the chaotic element were replaced by a random oracle [BeRo93]. Soundness in this sense was shown for the combination of trap-door one-way families of permutations and hash functions.

Nevertheless, where digital signature schemes are used in practice nowadays, or proposed for standardization, it is this kind of schemes. See, e.g., [GuQu91, Kali91, DSS91, Zimm93, Kent93, Bale93, ReSc95], and for more Internet pointers, <http://www.zurich.ibm.ch/Technology/Security/sirene/index.html>.

2.6 "Provably Secure" Digital Signature Schemes

First Attempts

The first attempts at proving the security of signature schemes were made in [Rabi78, Rabi79, Will80]. However, the proof sketch in [Rabi78] was on assumptions about the security of a symmetric cryptosystem that could not be seen as substantiated for any scheme. With the other two schemes, as mentioned in Section 2.5, the proof only dealt with an insufficient form of security. It was therefore proposed to use them with additional redundancy; this, however, destroys the proof even in its limited form.

Comprehensive Notion of Schemes and their Security

The first major step was to recognize that redundancy or hash functions are not some protocol around the "real" signature scheme. Instead, the signature scheme must comprise everything that happens with the message, and security must be proved for this complete scheme.

A second step was to formalize security not only as the infeasibility of computing the inverse of a function. Instead, the definition must comprise an active attack and exclude existential forgery.

Both has been done in [GoMR84, GoMR88], after an intermediate step in [GoMY83, GoMY83a]. The result is called the GMR definition here. Basically, a signature scheme is defined as a collection of algorithms *gen*, *sign*, and *test* (corresponding to Figure 2.2) such that, when the keys are correctly generated with *gen*, two properties hold:

- Signatures correctly generated with *sign* pass the corresponding test.
- If any polynomial-time attacker first communicates with a signer for a while, and then tries to compute a pair of a new message and a signature, the success probability is very small.

Actually, there are two further parameters in the definition, because the signature scheme described in the same article needs them: During key generation, the maximum number of messages to be signed must be fixed, and *sign* takes the number of the current message as an input.

Of course, proving the security of a scheme in this sense is not possible from scratch at present, see Section 2.3. Instead, one calls any cryptologic scheme "**cryptographically strong**"[8] or "provably secure" if it can be proved on what is regarded as a reasonable cryptologic assumption. Although this notion is not precise, there is general agreement about it: First, a reasonable cryptologic assumption should be concise, so that it is unlikely that easy ways to disprove it have been overlooked. This is the main difference to simply assuming that a whole cryptologic scheme is secure. Secondly, the assumption must have been examined thoroughly.

There are **concrete cryptologic assumptions**, such as the factoring assumption, and more general **abstract** ones, such as "a one-way function exists".

Cryptographically Strong Schemes

One reason why not much effort was spent on constructing provably secure digital signature schemes originally is that security in this sense was widely believed to be paradoxical, according to a remark in [Will80], misled by Rivest; see [GoMR88]. (The remark talks about "all constructive proofs"; however, it implicitly makes additional assumptions about the structure of such a proof.)

However, following a scheme provably secure against existential forgery after known-message attacks [GoMY83, GoMY83a], a scheme provably secure against existential forgery after adaptive chosen-message attacks was constructed in [GoMR84, GoMR88]. Actually, there is a general construction on the assumption that something called a trap-door claw-intractable family of permutation pairs exists, and a construction of such a family based on the factoring assumption.[9] The resulting scheme based on factoring is called **GMR** here. With some efficiency improvements it is practical, although, in most cases, slightly less efficient than pure RSA; see also [Gold87, FoPf91].

---

8 One might say "cryptologically strong" instead, if one adheres to the convention from Footnote 3. However, this term is established, and the convention is not always respected anyway.

9 Actually, they are simply called claw-free permutation pairs in [GoMR88]. The two name changes make the notation consistent with related collision-intractable or collision-free families of hash functions (see Section 8.5). The reasons are that the objects called claws do exist, it is only infeasible to find them, and that similar families without trap-doors are needed later.

Subsequently, one tried to find constructions on possibly weaker abstract assumptions. In [BeMi88, BeMi92], the assumption is the existence of a trap-door one-way family of permutations. This assumption was used for the efficient construction in [DiHe76] (see Section 2.4); however, a much more complicated construction was needed to avoid the problems mentioned in Section 2.5. It has a lot in common with one-time signatures and tree authentication. The constructions could be extended to arbitrary one-way permutations, i.e., not necessarily with trap-doors, in [NaYu89]. In a sense, this is not too surprising because no trap-doors were needed in the informal constructions of one-time signatures and tree authentication (see Section 2.4) either. Finally, the result was extended to any one-way function [Romp90]. The main problem in the last two cases was to construct appropriate hash functions.

With the current hierarchy of assumptions, one cannot hope for a more general result, because it was also shown quite easily in [Romp90] that a secure signature scheme yields a one-way function.

Alternative constructions are described in [BeGo90, Bras90, EvGM90, Bos92, BoCh93, DwNa94, CrDa95]. (The proof in [Bos92, BoCh93], however, is incomplete because it only treats known-message attacks; with obvious techniques it can only be completed for special cases, a small set of primes and constant message length.) Note that fail-stop signature schemes can also be used as ordinary digital signature schemes; see Section 7.4. In this sense, the construction from [HePe93] (see Section 9.3) with suitable measures from Chapter 10 was also the first reasonably efficient cryptographically strong ordinary digital signature scheme based on the discrete-logarithm assumption.

Some of the schemes listed above do not fit the GMR definition exactly, because they have more parameters or algorithms (see Section 5.3.2), but they will have a common definition in the general framework.

Some Remarks on Related Schemes

The search for convincing security notions and provably secure signature schemes was parallel with that for other types of cryptologic schemes.

The first big success were pseudo-random number generators, see, in particular, [BlMi84, Yao82a, ImLL89] and for an overview, [Gold95].

With asymmetric secrecy schemes, too, security is more than that it is hard to compute a plaintext, given the public key and a ciphertext. One problem, somewhat corresponding to existential forgery, is that an attacker may use a-priori knowledge about the plaintext, or be content with obtaining partial information about the plaintext; see, in particular, [GoMi84, Yao82a, MiRS88]. The other, harder problem is active (i.e., chosen-ciphertext) attacks [GoMT82]. There was a partial and interactive solution in [GaHY86, GaHY89]. [BlFM88] first sketched how the problem might be solved without interaction. [NaYu90] contains the first real proof; however, the active attack is restricted to the time before the ciphertext to be decrypted has been received. The general case is sketched in [RaSi92, DoDN91]. None of these constructions is practical so far, in contrast to the situation with signature schemes. Hence there were several attempts at schemes with partial security proofs; see [FrYu95]. In contrast to signature schemes, it seems unlikely that asymmetric secrecy schemes can be based on any one-way function, see [ImRu89].

For some overview of more general cryptologic tasks, see [Bras88, Schn96].

2.7 Special Variants

The picture of research about digital signature schemes is rounded off by a sketch of digital signature schemes with additional properties and modifications to the notion of signatures. Those that essentially fulfil the informal requirements from Chapter 1 will be called special signature schemes, the others signature-related schemes. Many of the properties can be combined.

2.7.1 Special Signature Schemes

Schemes with special security properties such as **fail-stop**, **dual**, and **information-theoretic security** will be treated in detail later (starting in Chapter 3 and with an overview in Chapter 6) and are therefore not treated here.

Invisible Signature Schemes

Invisible signatures (recall that this term is used instead of the uncharacteristic "undeniable") are signatures that the recipient cannot show around without the cooperation of the signer. The basic idea to achieve invisibility is that there is no test algorithm for signatures, which everybody can evaluate on their own, given the public key. Instead, a signature can only be verified by an interactive protocol between the signer and the current recipient [ChAn90]. In addition to this **verification protocol**, there is a special **disavowal protocol**, by which the signer can prove that some value is not a valid signature on a given message. This is necessary to distinguish, for instance in court, whether a supposed signer is not willing to verify a signature or whether the value is not a signature.

The security and efficiency of the original scheme from [ChAn90], and the improvement in [Chau91], is similar to that of RSA and the ElGamal scheme: It is based on a discrete-logarithm assumption, but not cryptographically strong. In particular, it is existentially forgeable with a key-only attack and selectively forgeable with chosen-message attacks, but one can try to counter these attacks with redundancy predicates or hash functions. This still holds for a newer practical scheme in [BCDP91], but this one is provably as secure as the somewhat more examined ElGamal scheme.

The article [BCDP91] also contains a theoretical construction from any one-way function.

Invisibility was not defined formally in the first publications about invisible signature schemes. Sketches of computational and information-theoretic invisibility are contained in [BCDP91, CBDP91] and [ChHP92], respectively. Neither is completely satisfactory yet.

A rather principal question about whether the current schemes, and any others, achieved satisfactory invisibility was raised in [DeYu91] and a sentence in [Chau91] (not present in the preproceedings version); however, it was answered quite satisfactorily in [Chau91a, CBDP91] (see also Section 5.2.12).

Schemes with **designated confirmer** [Chau95] are a variant of invisible signature schemes where a fourth party, called the confirmer, can also help to verify a signer's signature. The confirmer need not take part when a signature is issued, and signers need not trust it. In the current form (also in [Okam94]), the recipients have to trust the confirmer completely, i.e., if the confirmer refuses to verify a signature in court, the recipient cannot convince the court. Thus the schemes do not fulfil the informal requirements from Chapter 1. However, it seems no problem to equip these schemes in general and the scheme from [Chau95] in particular with a **confirmer disavowal** protocol, so that one can distinguish whether the confirmer refuses to cooperate or whether the signature is in fact wrong.

Properties to Improve Efficiency

Preprocessing and **on-line/off-line** computations [Schn91, EvGM90] are measures to perform part of the signing algorithm before the actual message is known. For the definition, this means that the signer has a local variable that is used and updated by the signing algorithm and also in between.

Batch signing or batch verification [Fiat90, NRVR95, YeLa95] are additional algorithms to produce or verify several signatures together faster than separately.

In **incremental** signature schemes [BeGG94, BeGG95], updates of a previously signed message can be signed faster than by an entirely new signature. Obviously, the signer needs local memory to store previous signatures. Two additional distinctions are whether this memory must be assumed to be uncorrupted, and whether it is allowed that a signature on an updated message gives information about the previous version of the message.

Server-aided signing or verification [MaKI90] are interactive protocols for a signer or verifier with very little computing power to delegate some of their computations to an untrusted device, called server, with higher computing power. This is primarily interesting for older smartcards without a special crypto chip. If the server is also the communication partner, one can see server-aided computation as a special case of interactive signing and verification. For the most recent schemes and more references, see [BéQu95, LiLe95].

2.7.2 Signature-Related Schemes

The following schemes are in many respects similar to signature schemes, but have particular properties so that they do not correspond to the informal requirements on replacements for handwritten signatures from Chapter 1. Of course, this is no criticism, because most of these schemes were deliberately invented for other applications. The original names containing "signature schemes" were retained. In the literature, the word "signature scheme" was also sometimes applied to symmetric authentication schemes; such schemes are not listed here.

Blind Signature Schemes

Blind signatures are signatures that the signer issues without being able to see the message she signs. However, she has the guarantee of signing only one message at a time. An important application is untraceable payment schemes: The bank signs so-called electronic coins using a blind signature scheme and sells them. Later, the owner of such a coin can pay with it, and the payee can deposit the coin at the bank again. The bank cannot trace the payment because it had not actually seen the coin the first time. The credentials mentioned in Section 2.3 also rely on certain forms of blind signatures; with some of them, more than one message is signed at a time. For more information, see, e.g., [Chau85, Chau89, Chau90, ChPe93].

Constructions of blind signatures require some action of the recipient, too, to transform what the signer really does into the form as a signed message. The efficient constructions rely on the multiplicative structure of RSA or similar basic signature schemes; in a sense, they employ selective forgery after a chosen-message attack in a positive way (see the references mentioned above and [ChEv87, EvHe92, CaPS95]). Cryptographically strong constructions are known, but impractical [Damg90, PfWa92a].

Restrictive blind signatures do not allow the recipient to get a completely arbitrary message signed; more precisely, the message itself is still arbitrary, but additional knowledge the recipient may have about it, such as a preimage of the message under a one-way function, is restricted. This is important in untraceable off-line payment schemes, see, e.g., [ChFN90, FrYu93, Bran94, Bran95].

Oblivious signatures [Chen94] are similar to blind signatures in that the signer does not know exactly what she signs, but they are even more restrictive than restrictive blind signatures: In one variant, the signer signs one out of n given messages without knowing which one the recipient has chosen, and in a second variant, she signs a specific message with one out of n given keys. Each time, the complexity is linear in n.

Group-Oriented Signature Schemes

Sometimes people sign in the name of a group or an organization. It may then be useful that the group as such has a public key so that recipients need not know which individuals belong to the group. If the group members trust each other, they can simply generate one secret key and give it to each group member. However, the task becomes more difficult if one of the following additional requirements is made:

- A certain quorum of group members is needed to produce a signature. This may be a simple threshold or a more complicated rule, e.g., two directors, or one director and two vice-directors, or ninety-nine employees; see, e.g., [Boyd86, Desm88, DeFr92, Lang95].
- Provisions are needed to deanonymize a particular signer later under certain circumstances (more precisely, if certain parties agree); see, e.g., [ChHe91, ChPe95, CrDS94].

Other differences are whether a group center is needed, to what extent it must be trusted, and how actively it has to take part; whether it is explicitly required that the specific signer within the group remains anonymous from the recipient, unless the specific deanonymization is made within the group; and whether members can dynamically enter or leave the group.

Other schemes do not have specific group keys, they only let a number of people who all have their own key pairs sign a message such that the result is shorter than the list of individual signatures would be, e.g., [Okam88, OhOk93].

Furthermore, signing is not the only operation that can be shared, see, e.g., [Pede91].

Terminology in this field is still somewhat untidy. Schemes where a quorum is needed are often called threshold signature schemes, because that is the most common case. Schemes where anonymity is guaranteed, but deanonymization is possible under certain circumstances, are briefly called group signature schemes. The term multisignatures usually means schemes without a group key.

Identity-Based Signature Schemes

In identity-based signature schemes, the public keys are simply the identities of their owners. The idea stems from [Sham85], and the most prominent example is [FiSh87]. However, these schemes do not fulfil the requirements from Section 1.3: A trusted third party generates all the secret keys. This is inevitable: Each secret key must fit an identity, and all participants except one are not to know it. As the participant with this identity has no computational advantage, she cannot compute her secret key either. (Most schemes like [FiSh87] have a variant with normal key generation; these were meant when such papers were referred to above.) For an intermediate form between ordinary and identity-based signature schemes, see [Gira91].

Moreover, from the application point of view, identity-based signature schemes are no different (except for the lower security) from ordinary digital signature schemes combined with key distribution via certificates by one center. In both cases, a signer has to contact the center once during key generation and distribution and obtain some information, either her secret key or the certificate. The center also has to broadcast a small amount of information, its own public key, to all recipients once. Later, the signer can sign and send the message and some authenticating information to the recipient in one single step; in the case with certificates this information consists of the signature and the certificate. The recipient can verify this information based solely on the signer's identity and the center's public key. The only advantage of the identity-based scheme may be that the length of the authenticating information is halved. (The situation is different with secrecy schemes, where the party with the certificate is not the one who sends the message.)

Arbitrated Signatures

Arbitrated signature schemes involve a kind of notary public in the process of signing [Akl82, MeMa82].

Signatures without Subliminal Channels

Signature schemes without **subliminal channels** have been developed for special applications where the message content is strictly controlled. In such cases, users must be prevented from encoding information in the signature instead. These schemes involve an additional party, usually called warden, in the process of signing. The warden is necessary to control the message content in the first place, but also plays an active role in the signing process; see, e.g., [Simm84, Desm88a, ChPe93].

3 Information-Theoretic Security for Signers: Introduction

Ever since the invention of digital signature schemes, it had been accepted that signers can only be secure in the computational sense and on cryptologic assumptions (see [DiHe76] and Section 2.3). One purpose of this work is to show that this need not be so, and to present several alternatives, in particular fail-stop signature schemes.

This short chapter elaborates on the preceding two sentences: It stresses the asymmetry between signers and recipients with ordinary digital signature schemes and briefly introduces the features of fail-stop signature schemes. In Section 3.1, it is shown why, with ordinary digital signature schemes, it is necessarily the signer whose security depends on the assumptions, although assigning responsibility and risks is a decision outside the digital signature scheme as a mathematical object, at least with the current definitions. In Section 3.2, one important idea is presented to show how signers can be made information-theoretically secure.

A complete overview of the signature schemes with new security properties is given in Chapter 6, after more terminology and classification criteria have been introduced in Chapters 4 and 5.

3.1 Problems with Ordinary Digital Signature Schemes

As described in Section 2.3, ordinary digital signature schemes, i.e., all schemes with the structure described there, can only be computationally secure and will rely on cryptologic assumptions. That is, even the most secure schemes (see Section 2.6) can be broken by an attacker with unexpected computing abilities, e.g., one who can factor unexpectedly large numbers (see Figure 3.1). This can either mean that the attacker has unexpectedly large computational resources or that he has found a fast algorithm disproving the assumption.

Consequences in the Case of Forgery

If an ordinary digital signature scheme is broken, the supposed signer of a message with a forged signature is defenseless: If the forger produces something that passes the test with the public key, any court will decide that the signature is valid, and the supposed signer will be held responsible.

The recipient of a signed message, in contrast, is absolutely secure: If he has checked that the signature passes the test with the public key, he knows that it will also do so in court, no matter if it is authentic or forged.

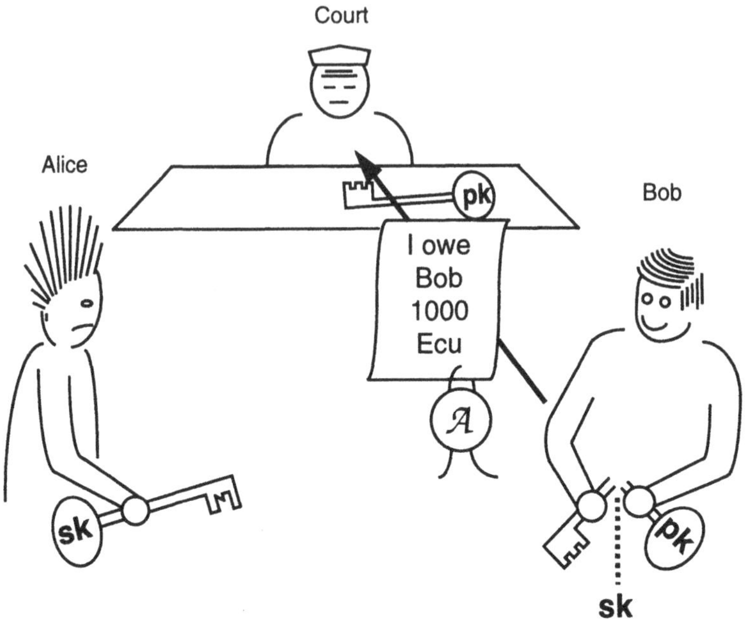

Figure 3.1. Situation with an ordinary digital signature scheme after a forgery

Why Forgeries Cannot be Handled Differently

That the signer is held responsible is, of course, only the (usual) technical view of what a court should do. A real court is not obliged to comply with it — recall that at least German courts are not obliged to acknowledge a handwritten signature either, see Section 1.2. It could believe the protestation by the supposed signer that a digital signature is a forgery, the more so because the signer can adduce that the signature scheme relies on an unproven assumption, no matter how long it has been examined.

However, if this were the case, recipients would not be secure at all any more: Even if the assumption is perfectly correct and no signature is ever forged, the real signers could deny their signatures in court, exactly like the supposed signer above. It is impossible for the court to distinguish the two cases. Hence, if recipients had to reckon with signatures being rejected in court, nobody would want to accept digital signatures from anybody whom they did not trust.

To sum up, if an ordinary digital signature scheme is used in the only sensible way, and if the underlying cryptologic assumption is broken, an attacker can forge signatures, and it is impossible to diagnose that this is happening (unless an honest person also finds out how the assumption can be broken). Furthermore, it is always the signer, not the recipient, who bears the risk.

3.2 One New Type: Fail-Stop Signature Schemes

In later chapters, several digital signature schemes will be presented or mentioned where at least the signer is information-theoretically secure, and sometimes even the recipient, too. The main point in overcoming the impossibility proof was to notice that digital signature schemes may have structures other than that described in [DiHe76] and made precise in the GMR definition (see Sections 2.3, 2.6).

The Fail-Stop Property

The first class of such new schemes, and the one treated in most detail here, are **fail-stop signature schemes** (see Figure 3.2). A fail-stop signature scheme contains all the components of an ordinary digital signature scheme, and, as long as the cryptologic assumption is not broken, works in the same way. However, if someone succeeds in forging a signature, in spite of the assumption, the supposed signer can *prove* that it is a forgery. More precisely: If the forged signature is shown to her, in order to make her responsible for it, she can prove that the underlying assumption has been broken.[10]

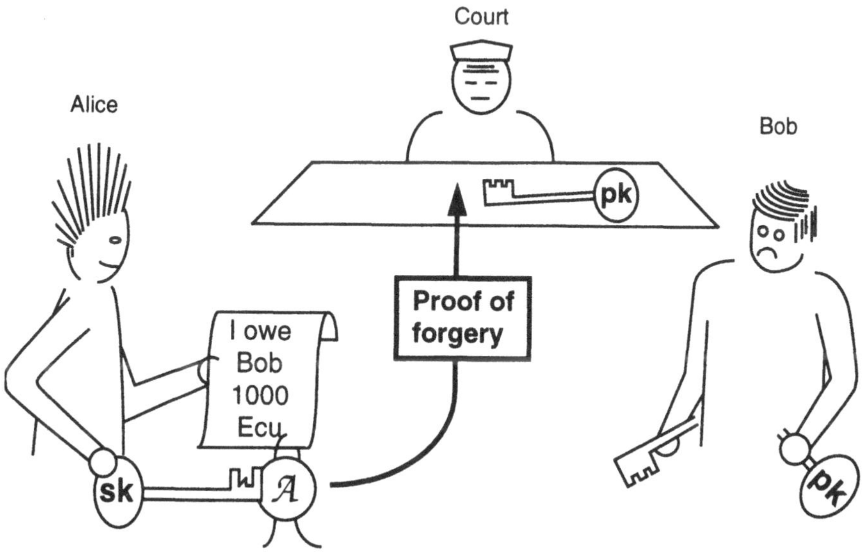

Figure 3.2. Situation with a fail-stop signature scheme after a forgery

10 Even more precisely (as will be seen in the formal definition in Section 7.1), the so-called proof of forgery that she produces is not a mathematical proof of such a statement, but a string with a certain property, and one part of the (mathematical) proof of the security of the scheme is that such strings are infeasible to construct, unless the assumption has been broken. For instance, if the security relies on the factoring assumption, a proof of forgery might be the factors of a number that should have been infeasible to factor. An alternative name might have been "evidence of forgery".

Thus one can relieve the signer from the responsibility for this signature. Additionally, one should stop the scheme or at least increase the security parameters. This gave rise to the name "fail-stop". (A related term is fail-stop processors, see [ScSc83]. A more intuitive illustration is old mechanical railway signals: The position the signal drops into if the wire breaks means stop for trains. Such systems are even called fail-safe, but being able to stop a broken digital signature scheme is not equally safe, even though safer than continuing to use it; see Section 6.2.)

Structure of Fail-Stop Signature Schemes

It is clear from the description of the fail-stop property that fail-stop signature schemes contain at least two new components, in addition to those from Figure 2.2:

- an algorithm to produce a **proof of forgery** from a forged signature and the secret key, and
- an algorithm that the remaining participants use to verify if something really is a proof of forgery.

For technical reasons, key generation is also modified, see Section 6.1.2.

Fail-stop signature schemes are therefore not comprised by the GMR definition (Section 2.6): They are a collection of more algorithms, the slightly different key generation will change even the formulation of those properties that the schemes have in common, and some additional requirements concerning the proofs of forgery are needed. Overcoming this problem is one of the purposes of Chapter 5. For particular definitions of secure fail-stop signature schemes, see Section 7.1.

4 Terminology

This chapter introduces formal notions used to formulate cryptologic security statements precisely and semiformal terminology for the following classification chapter.

Correct participants and attackers in cryptology carry out things like algorithms, protocols, or strategies. All these actions may be probabilistic. The actions prescribed for correct participants should be feasible, whereas actions of attackers may be infeasible or even non-computable. Sometimes, participants and/or attackers interact. Hence, the most basic formal notion is a probabilistic algorithm, and sometimes, one needs interactive algorithms and probabilistic and/or interactive functions, too.

With some variations, the formal notation used here is the standard notation of theoretical cryptology; I have primarily adapted mine from [GoMR88, GoMR89, Beav91].

4.1 General Notation

The length of a string, and also the size of a set, is denoted by $|\bullet|$. The length of a number is the length of the binary representation of that number; it is denoted by $|\bullet|_2$. The set of all non-empty bit strings is $\{0, 1\}^+$. Strings are included in quotes, ' ', except for the empty string ε.

4.2 Probabilities and Probabilistic Functions

Let S be a probability space. $P_S(e)$ denotes the probability of an element e and $P_S(E)$ that of an event E. Usually, S is omitted, because it is clear from the context. All well-known notations from probability theory are used. A probability space and its distribution are not always carefully distinguished.

If S is discrete, $[S]$ denotes the carrier set, i.e., the elements with non-zero probability.

If a value is chosen from S according to the given probability distribution and assigned to a variable x, this is denoted by $x \leftarrow S$. If the value of x is chosen from a given set X with uniform distribution, one also writes $x \in_R X$.

If $S_1, \ldots, S_n$ are n probability spaces ($n \in \mathbb{N}$) and p is an n-ary predicate, then

$$P(p(x_1, \ldots, x_n) \setminus x_1 \leftarrow S_1; \ldots; x_n \leftarrow S_n)$$

denotes the probability that the predicate $p(x_1, \ldots, x_n)$ is true if a value chosen from S_j has been assigned to x_j for $j := 1, 2, \ldots, n$, in this order.

The usual sign where I write "\" is "|". However, this notation describes the definition of a new probability space on n-tuples $(x_1, \ldots, x_n)$ from n given probability spaces rather than a conditional probability. Moreover, one can now formulate conditional probabilities in the newly defined probability space, such as

$$P(p(x_1, \ldots, x_n) | q(x_1, \ldots, x_n) \setminus x_1 \leftarrow S_1; \ldots; x_n \leftarrow S_n).$$

A **probabilistic function** f from a set X to a set Y is a function from X to the set of probability spaces on Y. The reason is that the relation of a probabilistic function to a probabilistic algorithm should be the same as that of a usual function to a deterministic algorithm. Hence for every input i, the term $f(i)$ denotes a probability space on Y.

Alternatively, one can represent a probabilistic function as a deterministic function with an additional random input. Then one writes $f(i, r)$, where r is chosen from a given probability space, and $f(i)$ is a random variable on the original space. Usually, r is uniformly distributed on a given set, such as the bit strings of a certain length, because it represents results of unbiased coin flips.[11]

The notation for probability spaces defined by successive assignments is particularly useful if the individual S_j's are defined by probabilistic functions or algorithms: One can write probabilities as

$$\mathrm{P}(p(x_1, \ldots, x_n) \setminus x_1 \leftarrow f_1(i_1); \ldots; x_n \leftarrow f_n(i_n)),$$

where the first input i_1 must be fixed, but later inputs i_j can contain former outputs x_l, $l < j$. This notation is sufficient to represent interaction of probabilistic actors with a small fixed number, n, of rounds. For more complicated interaction, interactive algorithms and functions are defined; see below.

4.3 Complexity

Feasible computations are usually expressed by probabilistic polynomial-time algorithms. For concreteness, Turing machines are used as the model of computation.[12]

In cryptology, **probabilistic algorithms** are usually represented as deterministic Turing machines with an additional input tape, the so-called random tape. The random tape contains a (potentially infinite) sequence of random bits. Each bit on this tape is read exactly once. The content (or each finite subsequence) is supposed to be uniformly distributed. If A is a probabilistic algorithm, $A(i)$ denotes the probability space on the outputs if A is run on input i (i.e., with i on the input tape — i does not include the content of the random tape). To cover non-terminating computations, the output space is augmented by an element $\uparrow$. The probabilistic function computed by A is not distinguished from A in the notation.

---

11 The advantage of the former notion seems to be that one need not bother about the length of the random string needed, whereas the latter notion yields more realistic notions of Turing reductions: In reality, one can use a probabilistic algorithm in a deterministic way by using special values r instead of random ones.

12 Alternatively, non-uniform complexity is used quite often, i.e., polynomial-size sequences of probabilistic circuits. (For details about non-uniform complexity, see [Schö85].) The argument for using non-uniform complexity is that allowing attackers to be non-uniform yields a stronger notion of security [GoMi84].

However, all existing security proofs are reduction proofs. To prove security against non-uniform attackers, one needs computational assumptions in the non-uniform model, too. Hence, all such theorems have a uniform and a non-uniform variant. As uniform reductions imply non-uniform reductions, but not vice versa, one has automatically proved both versions if one proves the uniform version [Pfit88, Gold91].

The running time of a "probabilistic polynomial-time algorithm" is deterministically polynomial, i.e., there is a polynomial Q such that the algorithm never needs more than $Q(k)$ steps on an input of binary length k. Of course, the random tape does not count as an input.[13]

Algorithms will sometimes only be defined on **restricted domains**. This means that neither the results nor the running time on inputs outside the domain are of interest. This corresponds to the promise problems from [EvYa80, EvSY84, GrSe88].

In asymptotic statements with an integer parameter k, the notion "for **sufficiently large** k" means "$\exists\, k_0\ \forall\, k \geq k_0$".

The notion of impossibility of a task for a polynomial-time attacker is neither worst-case complexity nor average-case complexity. Instead, as explained in Section 2.3, the success probability of an attacker has to be negligibly small, where the probability is taken over both the problem instances and the internal random choices of the attacker. A sequence $(P_k)_{k \in \mathbf{N}}$ of non-negative values is called **negligibly small** or superpolynomially small if for all $c > 0$ for sufficiently large k: $P_k < k^{-c}$. Some authors abbreviate this as "$P_k < 1/\text{poly}(k)$". Similarly, the sequence is called exponentially small if it is smaller than the inverse of some exponential function in k.

As mentioned in Section 2.3, the length of the instances of cryptologic problems is determined by so-called security parameters. Such parameters are represented in **unary** representation whenever they are input to an algorithm. For this, '1'^{k} denotes the unary representation of $k \in \mathbf{N}$.[14]

For a function f with integer inputs and integer outputs, an algorithm is said to compute f in unary iff it is a normal algorithm (i.e., not restricted to unary representation in its own computations) that expects each input in unary and computes the result in unary. For instance, if f has two inputs k and σ, such an algorithm computes '1'$^{f(k,\sigma)}$ from ('1'^{k}, '1'$^\sigma$). This notation is used for transformations of security parameters.

---

13 Although this is the usual type of algorithms in definitions and reduction proofs, e.g., in [GoMR88, GoMR89, Romp90, Gold93], expected polynomial-time algorithms are needed quite often. In particular, perfectly uniform random choice from a set whose size is not a power of two can only be done in expected polynomial time (see [FINN89]), and see Section 8.4.1 for prime number generation. I did not care about this more than others do, but I think the appropriate generalization would be to maintain deterministically polynomial time, because it is more realistic and a precondition for synchronism in multi-party scenarios, but to permit small error probabilities and small deviations from desired distributions in many places.

14 The reason for the unary representation is as follows: On the one hand, a security parameter is normally used as the input to a key-generation algorithm. On the other hand, it is supposed to denote the length of the keys generated, e.g., $k = 512$ for the generation of 512-bit keys. Thus, for the key-generation algorithm to be probabilistic polynomial-time in the usual sense, i.e., measured in the length of its input, the input cannot be k in binary representation.

4.4 Interaction

This section sketches definitions of interactive protocols or schemes and their properties. Selecting one detailed representation and rephrasing all old and new results in that terminology is beyond the scope of this text, but an overview of existing and conceivable variations is given and some additions are mentioned that would be needed for a general formal definition of signature schemes in the sense of Chapter 5. Before individual interactive functions and algorithms are defined, an overview of the environments they are used in is given.

4.4.1 Overview and Meta-Terminology

In general, one can identify the following **steps** in all definitions or informal descriptions of interactive protocols or protocol classes.

A. Static descriptions of the interactive systems. One complete description is called a **protocol** or **scheme**.[15]

   1. An important part is descriptions of the behaviour of individual actors. Here, the word **program** is used as a generalization of all types of algorithms and functions, and the two most important types of programs will be probabilistic interactive functions and interactive Turing machines.
   2. The rest of a static description is called the **structure description**. It contains parameters such as the possible numbers of actors, descriptions of connections, and initial states.

B. Concrete embodiments of a scheme or protocol, i.e., something that behaves according to the description. They are called **systems**.[16]

   The individual actors in a system are called **entities**, as in the OSI architectural model [Lini83]. Each entity behaves according to one of the given programs, but, depending on the structure description, there may be many entities with the same program. Entities may even be generated dynamically.[17,18]

C. The description of a class of possible **attackers**.

---

15 Both terms are allowed because "scheme" is the usual word with signature schemes, whereas "protocol" is usual with the 2-party and multi-party protocols mentioned below. If there is any distinction in the present context, then protocols are smaller than schemes, e.g., there is a verification protocol as a part of an invisible signature scheme.

16 This is not a general convention; in particular, some things called schemes in Chapter 2 for consistency are usually called systems.

17 The relation between programs and entities may be clarified by analogies in other terminologies: It is similar to the relation between a sequential program and a process, or, object-oriented, between an object type and an object.

18 Formal definitions are possible that never mention systems explicitly: One often defines the behaviour directly from the static description, see Step D. However, systems are at least the informal semantics of the protocols or schemes, i.e., the objects in the real world that are modeled.

D. The dynamic **behaviour** of the system with an attacker from the class and certain honest users.

If one wants to use protocols for some purpose, one needs two more steps:

E. **Requirements** or other types of **specification**.

F. A notion of **fulfilling** the requirements, or whatever the specification is, with certain degrees of security.

The steps are not always so nicely separated. In particular, Steps E and F are inseparable in conventional definitions of signature schemes. However, it is better if requirements are formalized for a whole class of schemes in terms of some interface behaviour, so that they are independent of the exact structure of the system and the assumptions about the attackers.

The following Sections 4.4.2 to 4.4.7 contain semiformal details about the 6 steps described above, as far as they are not specific to signature schemes.

Related Work in Cryptology

In cryptology, precise formulations of 2-party protocols and multi-party protocols for particular purposes exist, see, e.g., [GoMR89, Beav91, MiRo91] and their bibliography. The main purpose is zero-knowledge proof schemes (with 2 parties) and multi-party function evaluation, i.e., the joint evaluation of a function where each participant contributes a secret input at the beginning and obtains an output at the end. In contrast, signature schemes will be modeled as reactive systems, where users can make inputs and obtain outputs many times. The games in [GoMW87] are somewhat more general than joint function evaluation, but they have not been formalized yet. None of these formulations is sufficient for a general definition of signature schemes. (This is no criticism — they go much further in other directions.) Brief discussions of the differences can be found in the following sections. Particular versions of zero-knowledge proof schemes and multi-party function evaluation are used as subprotocols in the following; they are described more precisely where they are used (Sections 7.3 and 7.5.2).

4.4.2 Some Terminology about Specifications

Although specification corresponds to Step E, it is considered first, because it is unusual in cryptology and some of the terminology is needed in the following sections.

To specify requirements on a system independently of the system structure, one has to define an **interface**, as it is common practice with communication protocols (e.g., see [Lini83, Tane88]; personally, I learnt a lot from [Krum86]). The main object of the **specification** is the possible sequences of **events** at this interface, and an event is an input or output at one of the **access points**; see Figure 4.1.

The complete interface behaviour of a system is called the **service** that the system offers. The actors that interact with the system through the access points are called **users**.

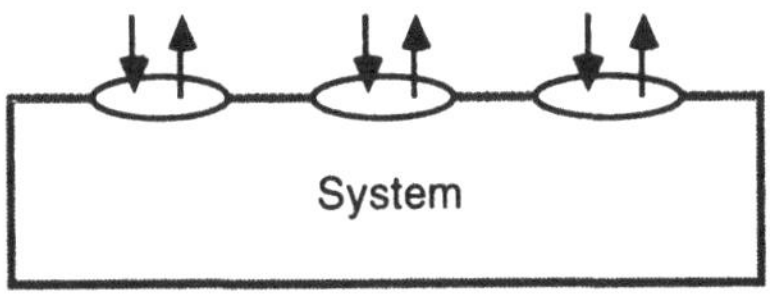

Figure 4.1. Parts of a specification

Some other words have been used less formally so far and maintain that meaning: **People** or **persons** mean people in the real world. A **device** is a hardware object in the real world, as in Section 1.4. "**Participant**" is used in an unspecific way for people together with their devices, i.e., something that is modeled by parts above and below the interface. A **role** refers to a user acting in a particular function; in this context it means using a particular access point.

4.4.3 Interactive Functions and Algorithms

Interactive Functions

A probabilistic interactive function is a probabilistic state-transition function, usually on a countable domain.[19] Hence it is characterized by three sets I, O, and S, the sets of possible inputs, outputs, and states, respectively, and a probabilistic function (see above) $f: I \times S \to O \times S$. (In contrast to the field of non-cryptologic protocol specification, the functions themselves, and not finite descriptions of them, are used here. Anyway, they are mainly used to model the unknown behaviour of computationally unrestricted attackers.)

Interactive Algorithms

Interactive Turing machines are the original model for interactive cryptologic protocols, i.e., they were used before interactive functions (see [GoMR85, GoMR89]). Hence they are not primarily defined as algorithms that compute interactive functions. In fact, one interactive Turing machine computes not one application of an interactive function, but a whole series of them from an initial to a final state, i.e., the complete life-time of an entity. It is a normal probabilistic Turing machine augmented by at least one special communication tape. Usually, one provides a way of signaling when a message written on such a tape has been completed, e.g., a special symbol in the tape alphabet; however, if synchronism is supervised locally, this is not necessary.

Most systems in cryptology are **synchronous**. For the programs, this means that they are defined in **rounds**: In each round, they receive some messages at the

19 As complexity is not considered here, the internal state of a component is not really interesting. Hence a notion that describes the pure input-output behaviour of a component might be more appropriate, e.g., as in [Gray92, Schu94]. However, the behaviour of connected components is much easier to describe with state-transition functions.

beginning and send some messages at the end. With interactive functions, this is clear; with interactive algorithms, it is only realistic in combination with a deterministic upper bound on the running time per round. With the complexity restrictions made on correct algorithms, this will always be the case. (However, synchronism would become a problem if expected polynomial-time algorithms were permitted, as discussed in a footnote to Section 4.3. Furthermore, I think synchronism is considered in an unrealistic way in the models of [Beav91, MiRo91] in the case of participants modeled by Turing machines without time bounds: There, a virtual global function is used that restarts participants for the next round when each of them has finished its previous round. The same model is used in [GoMR89], but in the 2-party scenario, it can be changed more easily.)

Details about Ports

With both interactive functions and interactive algorithms, some details can be formalized in various ways:

- How are different outputs (and inputs) distinguished in a program for an entity that interacts with several others?

  If the number of entities in a system and the connection structure is fixed in the protocol, each output of a state-transition function can be a tuple of values that represent the outputs on different channels. The individual output sets should be augmented by a special element *no_output*. With Turing machines, one can either use output tuples, too, or a separate tape for each simplex channel.

  If the program must allow the entity to interact with an arbitrary number of others, over an arbitrary number of channels, the entity has to know the actual numbers dynamically. In formalizations such as [Beav91, MiRo91] (although the really formal parts of both currently assume that n is fixed), the number, n, of entities would certainly be encoded in the initial state of the entity, as well as the identity of this individual entity, which is a number $i \in \{1, \ldots, n\}$.

  In any case, the different ways of outputting that are distinguished in a program will be called **ports**. (Informally, the word port will also be applied to entities and devices; it can be visualized as the place where these outputs come out, like an access point in an interface.)

  Similarly, input ports and input-output ports are defined.

- How are inputs and outputs handled that represent interface events, if one has the notion of an interface?
  - They are handled like other ports.
  - A usual alternative in cryptology is to represent them as the initial and final state of the entity. This is possible because in usual 2- and multi-party protocols, entities have only one input and one output that would be interpreted as interface events here.

In the general framework (Chapter 5), the first alternative is used, because signature schemes are modeled as reactive systems, which can interact with their users many times. In the definitions in the conventional style (Chapter 7), 2-party and multi-party subprotocols are handled in the conventional way.

Complexity

The complexity of an interactive Turing machine has only been defined for the case with one initial input (which would be called an interface input here). Complexity is then regarded as a function of the length of this initial input alone, and not the inputs from interaction with other entities.[20] This is reasonable: Otherwise an interactive Turing machine with the attribute polynomial-time could be forced into arbitrarily long computations by an unrestricted attacker who sends it arbitrarily long messages.

If one considers machines that react on many interface inputs, as they are needed in a general definition of signature schemes, one can choose to measure complexity as a function of the sum of the lengths of the interface inputs that occurred so far, or still of the initial state only. In particular situations, one might even make more special requirements, such as considering the time needed until the next output as a function of the most recent input only.[21]

Functions or Algorithms as Programs?

The programs (for the actions of honest participants) in definitions of cryptologic schemes are usually algorithms, but definitions in terms of functions exist, too. In the latter case, it is required that an algorithm that computes the function in polynomial time exists. The disadvantage in comparison with an algorithmic definition is that this would allow non-constructive proofs of the existence of the required algorithm, and such a scheme would be of no use in practice. However, algorithmic definitions can be seen as over-specifications: Participants who find more efficient algorithms that compute the same functions should be allowed to use them. A compromise is to use an algorithmic definition, but to define schemes as equivalent if the functions computed by corresponding algorithms are identical.

4.4.4 System Structure

In current cryptologic definitions, not much structure description is needed. Clearly, in 2-party protocols it is implicitly assumed that the 2 given programs are run by 2 entities with one channel between them. Multi-party protocols have been defined with a given number n of entities with different programs and an arbitrary set of channels, defined by probabilistic transport functions between ports [Beav91], or with one program, which may be executed by any number n of entities, and a fixed connection structure, such as point-to-point channels and broadcast channels between them all [MiRo91]. An important addition needed for a general definition of signature schemes is system structures that vary as a function of time.

---

20 For this reason, one must maintain the convention that an interactive Turing machine computes more than one application of an interactive function.

21 Related decisions are where one represents security parameters (see Section 5.2.4, "Initialization"), how active attacks on honest users are modeled (Section 5.4.2), and the formalization of availability of service (Section 5.2.7).

4.4.5 Attackers

Any attacker or any group of colluding attackers is represented by an **attacker strategy**, which is a probabilistic interactive function or Turing machine, like a correct entity.[22]

Considering particular attackers on particular systems can be subdivided in several ways: On the one hand, different aspects of the specification may be fulfilled in the presence of different types of attackers. On the other hand, each description of an attacker or a class of attackers must specify the following items:

1. How is the attacker connected to the rest of the system? In more intuitive words: To which parts of the system does the attacker have access, or, in distributed systems, how many participants may be dishonest? Is this constant throughout the lifetime of a system? Naturally, the answers depend on the type of systems considered.
2. What are the computational abilities of the attacker? Usually, as mentioned in Section 2.3, only one distinction is made: Attackers are either restricted to feasible computations, then they may use arbitrary polynomial-time interactive Turing machines; or computationally unrestricted, then they may use arbitrary probabilistic interactive functions. (For more distinctions, see, e.g., the footnote about non-uniform complexity in Section 4.3.)

Some informal terminology exists in connection with Item 1: An entity or a device that behaves as prescribed in the scheme is called **correct**; otherwise it is **corrupted**. Formally, a corrupted entity is no longer an individual part of a system; instead, one entity carrying out an attacker strategy usually takes the place (i.e., the connections) of several corrupted entities. More details are mentioned in Sections 5.4.1 and 5.4.2. A user or a participant is called **honest** or **dishonest**. With a user, this has no formal meaning so far, because no behaviour has been prescribed for users; however, honest and dishonest users will be treated differently in the notion of fulfilling a specification. With a participant, it means that both the user is honest or dishonest and the device is correct or corrupted.

4.4.6 System Behaviour

The behaviour of a system in interaction with certain attackers and users is defined by the possible sequences of its global states. This can be done in a natural way for the above-mentioned models of programs and connections. In particular, executing a protocol consisting of interactive functions means applying the actual functions many times. One such sequence of global states is called a **protocol execution** or

---

22 It may not be immediately clear why one can assume that attackers have a strategy — couldn't they make a new decision what to do next after every step of communication with the correct entities? However, this is equivalent: One can describe a global strategy as a complete, probabilistic decision tree, as in game theory, where for every history and every new reaction of the correct entities, the possible actions of the attackers in the next step, each with a probability, are listed.

a **run** (or trace) of the system. In the terminology of reactive systems, this is a linear-time model.

In a synchronous system, all messages sent at the end of one round are guaranteed to be received at the beginning of the next round. In practice, synchronism presupposes that messages are guaranteed to arrive within a certain period of time.

To be realistic, synchronism must be defined differently for attackers: They may send their own messages last in a round, so that they can already base their decision on the messages sent by others. This is called rushing attackers, see [Beav91, MiRo91].

Some parts of a behaviour are of particular interest: One is the restriction of the actions to those at the interface, i.e., the service. Another is the restriction to a given set of access points, because that may be what a set of honest users sees from the system. The **view** of an attacker is the restriction of a run to everything the attacker can see.

4.4.7 Degrees of Fulfilling

Formally, the degrees of security with which requirements or specifications can be fulfilled can only be defined when one has defined a class of requirements or specifications. Hence this subject is postponed to Section 5.4.3. Anyway, the most important criteria are whether small error probabilities are tolerated or not and whether security has really been proved. These criteria are closely related to the assumptions about the attackers (cf. Figure 5.16).

Note that the types of attacks mentioned in Section 2.5 now belong to the model of the behaviour of the honest users, and the types of success belong to the specification.

5 Properties of Digital Signature Schemes

This chapter contains a sketch of a general formal definition of signature schemes and a systematic classification of these schemes. The approach taken here can also be used for other types of cryptologic schemes.

The need for such a framework arose as follows in the context of a work whose original purpose was only to present fail-stop signature schemes and related schemes:

- First, there are quite a lot of such schemes with different properties, at least if all variations are counted, including those that are only sketched informally in Chapter 6. Hence at least an informal classification and terminology is needed to keep them in some order.
- Secondly, so far, any new type of signature scheme that had a formal definition at all needed a completely new one, as explained with fail-stop signature schemes at the end of Section 3.2. This is unsatisfactory: First, if they are all called signature schemes, they should have something in common, and secondly, new definitions in cryptology have turned out to be just as error-prone as new constructions.

  Hence the goal was one common definition that should at least cover the GMR definition, the schemes invented as ordinary digital signature schemes but not exactly fitting the GMR definition, and all the existing variants of fail-stop and invisible signature schemes, where "existing" means that a concrete construction has been proposed in the literature. Such a definition is sketched here.

  I even hope that this definition, if worked out with some additional refinements, will comprise everything that might be ever be called a signature scheme within the limit of the informal requirements of Chapter 1. Section 2.7 explained which of the known variants of signature schemes are signature schemes in this sense. Others could be defined and classified in a similar way.

This chapter is only semiformal. One reason is that the classification and the main ideas for the general definition should be of interest independently of any formalism; some formalism was only introduced into the classification to prevent misunderstanding. Moreover, a complete formalization at the level of generality where it would be most useful still seems a formidable task, at least if this includes formulating and proving a lot of theorems that one would intuitively expect to hold, so that one can check that the definition reflects intuition satisfactorily. Readers primarily interested in the formalization might look at Section 5.4.3, "Definition Sketches", and at the theorems sketched in Section 5.4.4 earlier.

Remark on Levels of Generality

If one formalizes this chapter, one should not do it for signature schemes only. Two more levels of generality seem appropriate:

- general cryptologic schemes, and

- schemes that might be called cryptologic transaction schemes, where small groups of users can have small subtasks (called transactions) carried out. For instance, this would include payment and credential schemes.

It is no use saying at this point which definitions would be made on which level (but see the subsection "Transactions" in Section 5.1.2), and it is not always mentioned in the following, but a formalist reader will be able to guess.

Overview of this Chapter

Section 5.1 contains the main ideas behind the definition and classification, some justification for these ideas, and general remarks about consequences and alternatives. Sections 5.2 to 5.4 contain the actual definitions and classification criteria (sorted according to service, structure, and degree of security, which is one of the main ideas of Section 5.1).

5.1 The Main Ideas

5.1.1 The Ideas and their Background

The basic ideas of the following classification are:

1. *The aspects*
   - *service,*
   - *structure, and*
   - *degree of security*

   of signature schemes are considered separately and almost independently.
2. *Signatures and keys are regarded as structural details, and not as the service.*

The main novelty about the first idea is that an interface for signature schemes has to be introduced. More precisely, it is an interface for the systems described by the schemes. In the terminology of Section 4.4.1, this means that Step E is separated from Step F.[23]

Of course, the placement of an interface is partly a matter of taste, in particular because several other definitions already exist: The systems are normally used in certain environments (for instance, systems described by the GMR definition must be used together with a counter keeping track of the number of messages authenticated), and one has some freedom as to where the system ends and where the environment begins.

Idea 2 now means that this interface is placed very "high", so that signatures and keys are only handled within the system, but do not appear in interface events.

23 An interesting similar approach was taken in [SyMe93] for key-distribution protocols usually treated with logics of authentication; see the remarks on those in Section 5.2.1.

Top-Down Justification

As a top-down motivation for specifying any service, one should consider what the users of the system expect.

With signature schemes, the most important application is that the users are people; then the specification should reflect the informal requirements of Sections 1.1 to 1.3. In this case, the natural thing to be represented by the formal interface is the real interface between people and their personal devices. Thus each access point corresponds to the keyboard and the display of such a device, and the events at the access point are the commands and responses exchanged between the person and the device. (Of course, commands and responses not referring to signing messages are not included, e.g., initial password checks or other applications implemented in the same device.)

Then the people do not really *need* to see their own signatures and keys, and parameters such as the number of messages authenticated so far. What they must see or even input themselves is primarily

- the *messages* to be authenticated or received,
- the *identities* of the signers, and
- the *decisions* whether a device accepted a message as authenticated or not.

Consequences for Entities and Programs

If the users of a system only bother about messages, identities, and decisions, the entities in the system have to take care of everything else.

In particular, if the signature schemes mentioned in the previous chapters are redefined in these terms, an entity below an access point of a signer generates the secret key for that signer, stores it, and performs all local administration, such as maintaining the above-mentioned counter for the messages authenticated so far (see Figure 5.1).

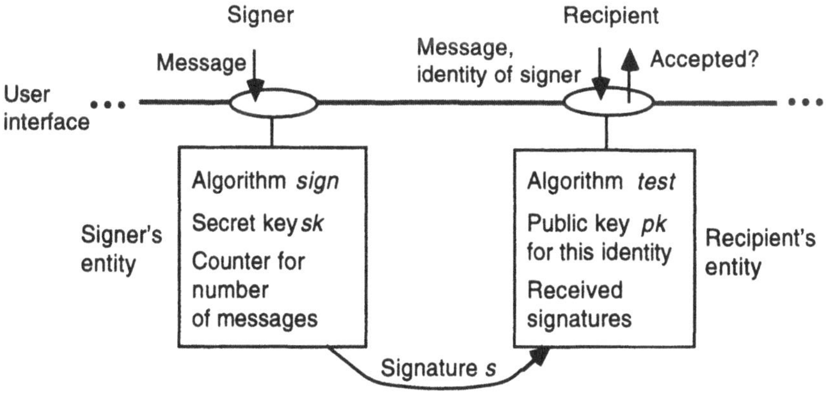

Figure 5.1. Example of interface events and entities if an ordinary digital signature scheme is modeled (incomplete).
Details about the interface events are discussed in Section 5.2.4.

Similarly, the entity below the access point of a recipient stores the public key and all the signatures received so far, picks them out if they have to be shown in court, and sends them to the court's entity. The entities also handle interactive subprotocols on their own. For instance, with an invisible signature scheme, once the signer and the recipient have given their entities the commands to sign and test a message and the entities are suitably connected, the entities do not only exchange the signature, but also carry out the interactive verification protocol and only tell their users the final results.

The programs in the signature scheme are descriptions of the behaviour of such entities.

Bottom-Up Justification

The bottom-up motivation for leaving well-known notions like signatures, keys, and the algorithm *sign* out of the service definition was that the service definition should be the same, or at least very similar, for everything currently called a signature scheme, and that these notions vary too much. To see this, consider the following examples[24]:

- Signing and testing may be more than algorithms; for instance, there is the interactive verification protocol of invisible signature schemes. Hence they must at least be defined as interactive programs.

  As a consequence, it is not clear whether all messages exchanged would be called the signature, or only the first one as it is currently done, or any other subset.
- There are schemes where a new signature depends on the number of previously authenticated messages; hence there is no reason to exclude that it depends on further local variables. Thus arbitrary local variables may have to be passed between different executions of the subprogram for signing within one entity.

  For efficiency, the complete secret key is even updated after each signature in some schemes. Hence one cannot easily maintain the notion of "the secret key". Instead, it should be treated like any other local variable used by the subprogram for signing.
- There are schemes without a public key in the usual sense; instead, every recipient has a different test key.
- A court need not test signatures in the same way as recipients. **Court**, in the technical sense, is short for any third party called on to settle a dispute. For instance, with fail-stop signature schemes and invisible signature schemes, the court also communicates with the signer in a dispute. In these cases, there must be an interactive program for settling disputes, which differs from that for testing, and signers and recipients need corresponding programs to interact with this one.

---

24 Throughout Chapter 5, the preferred examples are those signature schemes that have already been mentioned in Chapters 1 to 3. However, some cyclic dependencies cannot be avoided: The classification is to be *used* to present further schemes more systematically later, but part of the motivation was exactly those schemes.

All these generalizations can easily be realized in the entities described in the previous subsection.

The well-known notions like signatures, secret keys, and public keys, are redefined as structural properties of particularly simple types of signature schemes in Section 5.3.2.

5.1.2 Problems, Alternatives, and Simplifications

This section (5.1.2) is only relevant for a general formal definition, and not for the classification of signature schemes: It treats details that do not concern differences between signature schemes, but different possibilities to formalize all signature schemes.

Granularity of Entities

It must be decided how many different tasks are gathered in each entity, and correspondingly, how many different tasks are handled through each access point. In figures like Figure 5.1, this corresponds to the vertical separations between entities. Two decisions are quite canonical after Section 5.1.1:

- If one of the simpler signature schemes is modeled where secret and public keys exist, everything that happens with one secret key should happen within one entity, and everything that one recipient or court does with one public key should happen within one entity.
- Different people will usually use different access points to the system and different entities (or, in other words, one cannot gather *all* secret keys in one entity).

The remaining decisions are quite arbitrary; for the following, they are made as follows:

- There are three different types of access points: **signer access points, recipient access points**, and **court access points**. Thus if one person is both a signer and a recipient or a court, different entities handle these roles, and the corresponding commands are input at different access points. Correspondingly, a signature scheme contains three programs, one for each type of entity. They are called *signer_program*, *recipient_program*, and *court_program*, and the entities **signer's entity, recipient's entity** and **court's entity**.
- At an access point of a signer, only one identity is handled. With simple signature schemes, this means that only one secret key is handled within the entity.
- An access point of a recipient or a court handles all the identities of signers. With simple signature schemes, this means that an entity of a recipient or a court handles all the public keys. This has the advantage that the administration of the relation between identities of signers and public keys is hidden inside the system.

Connections: The Problems

The most serious problem with defining the service of a signature scheme (or any cryptologic transaction scheme) at a user interface is that a service can only be offered by a system consisting of both entities and connections. The intuitive idea of a signature scheme, however, is one of programs only, without descriptions of a connection structure. Otherwise, it would be a combined communication and signature scheme.

To see why the connections cannot be included in the scheme, consider the top-down motivation again: An entity of a signer corresponds to a personal device of that signer, e.g., a so-called super smartcard with keyboard and display. Usually, if asked to sign something, the device outputs the signature at a particular port. This is in conformance with the model described in Section 5.1.1 in so far as the signature is not (primarily) output at the user access point, i.e., the display. However, the signature does not arrive at the corresponding port of the recipient's device automatically — the device does not even need to know for which recipient it signs. The connection may be established in different ways:

- The ports of two devices may be plugged together, e.g., the user's super smartcard into the card reader of a point-of-sale terminal; then message transfer happens automatically.
- If the entities are processes in larger personal computers instead, an application program might include the signature into an e-mail message with the recipient's identity as an address,
- or into an e-mail message with a completely different address, because the recipient is traveling or uses several pseudonyms.

Hence what the collection of entities, as described in a signature scheme, does, is that they provide some service *if* they are properly connected, no matter how. To turn this into a formal definition, one must nevertheless formalize the condition "if properly connected".

Moreover, the connection structure meant by "if properly connected" is a function of time, in contrast to 2- or multi-party protocols customary in cryptology: The same output port of the entity of a signer may be connected to the input port of many different recipients, one after the other.

Even a connection between two given ports may be correct at some times and corrupted at others, e.g., because the devices are plugged together the first time and use e-mail the next time. This is not covered by usual models of attackers.

One therefore has to formulate requirements like "even if some previous signatures intended for a certain recipient got lost or were intercepted by an attacker, the recipient accepts a new signature if it reaches him." (Fulfilling this requirement is not trivial if both entities have memory.) The model used to express the current status of the connections in the requirements is now shown.

Connection Handling with Explicit Switching

The essential point about the model that will be used for connection handling is that exactly the one decision about connections that makes a difference for the service at the user interface is added to the interface. This decision is which entities are correctly connected at what time. This means (see Figure 5.2):

- The scheme consists mainly of programs, at least not of any channels.

- When a system is derived from the scheme, a special entity called switch is added that serves as a very abstract model of the network. It is connected to all the non-interface ports of the other entities and can establish connections between them.
- The control of the switch is seen as a part of the interface: There is one new connection-control access point, where one can input which connections are to be established.
- The inputs at this connection-control access point use the same identities as those used at the user interface, so that they are independent of the internal details of the system.

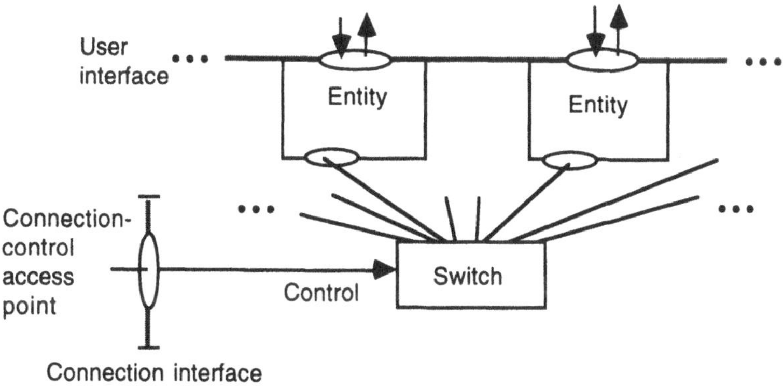

Figure 5.2. A connection structure where exactly the connection decision is a part of the interface.
The switch and the connection-control access point are essentially not parts of the signature *scheme*, but a model of an arbitrary network with just enough details to express what has to be known about the environment of the entities.

Remember that the switch is entirely virtual — in practice, connections are certainly established differently. In particular, the program of the switch is essentially not a component of a signature scheme, but fixed once and for all (see Section 5.3.1 for details). Its only purpose is to allow a definition of the following type: "A signature scheme consists of programs for standard entities (and a bit more) such that, if the entities *were* connected with such a switch, they would offer a certain service."

The benefit of the additional access point is that one can now use standard models of attackers: The virtual switch is assumed to be correct, and so are the connections between correct entities that it switches, but the dynamic behaviour of the attackers can be represented in the input events to the switch.

Alternatives for Connection Handling

As explicit switching may seem a strange model, some alternatives are sketched briefly:

- **Signature scheme as a layer.** One extreme is to consider the system consisting of the standard entities only. Then it is only a layer within a larger system, i.e., it has a network interface consisting of the non-interface ports of all the entities, in addition to the user interface. Of course, one would not specify the behaviour at the network interface completely, but only use formulas that describe that some messages are transported reliably as preconditions in the formulas that describe the behaviour at the user interface. This leads to more complicated service specifications than the model with explicit switching, but should result in exactly the same requirements on the programs from the signature scheme.
- **Automatic switching.** The other extreme is to keep connections out of the interface, i.e., to establish them automatically within the system. As long as no attackers are considered, this seems possible, although unrealistic.[25] Anyway, the dynamic behaviour of the attackers seems to be much harder to model in this way than with explicit switching.

Time

In a formal definition, a model of time is needed, both for the interface events and for message exchange within the system. For concreteness, the following simple, provisional model is assumed.

- There is global synchronism for everything within the system, i.e., a global notion of numbered rounds, see Section 4.4.6.

  This is not completely realistic, because personal devices are not always connected. In practice, entities only need a common idea of the length of rounds, and they must be able to synchronize when they are connected. The notion that all messages arrive in the next round, i.e., before any new messages are sent, is not very realistic either.
- If related inputs at several access points are necessary, for instance the signer's command to sign and the recipient's command to test in Figure 5.1, they are assumed to occur in the same round.

  This is not completely realistic either, at least if the users are people. However, it relieves the specification of the task of defining exact tolerances, and in fact, synchronization could be carried out by a surrounding system.

Note that it is realistic, but perhaps too much so for some types of specification, that the same model of time is used for interface events and for message exchange within the system, i.e., that one can see in the sequence of interface events how many rounds of internal operations occur between two interface events. Alternatively, one could abstract from such differences at the interface.[26]

---

[25] Recall that the signer usually does not input the identity of the intended recipient for signing. Hence the only way for the system to find out where to send the message is by checking which recipient currently inputs that he wants to test a message from this signer.

[26] In this case, one would have to consider carefully that activities in different parts of the system can overlap. This might be irrelevant in the correct systems, because with the decisions about transactions in the next subsection, overlapping transactions would be independent. However, attackers can introduce dependencies.

"Transactions"

The service of signature schemes and several other cryptologic schemes can be described conveniently by grouping interface events that are closely related (both logically and in time) together. Such groupings will be called transactions, although they do not have all the properties commonly associated with this word. For instance, the three interface events shown in Figure 5.1, i.e., the signer's command to sign, the recipient's command to test, and the output that the system produces, are grouped into a transaction called authentication. Examples from other schemes are a withdrawal of money or a transfer of money from one user to another in a payment scheme.

Transactions are not made explicit in the formalization: They are only used in didactic comments, whereas formal statements deal with interface events individually. However, if one defined more than only signature schemes, formalizing transactions might save some work.

All the following transactions have three properties in common. The first two can be seen as defining, the third one is a simplification.

- A service property: Within a transaction, a system has to react on certain previous inputs within a reasonable number of rounds, whereas at other times, it may be idle and wait for new inputs.
- A structural property: Within a transaction, the entities concerned expect to have fixed connections. (Hence the corresponding parts of the programs could be grouped together into subprotocols that are 2- or multi-party protocols in more or less the usual sense, e.g., a 2-party protocol for the authentication transaction.)
- The simplification: Only one transaction is permitted at one access point at one time. Inputs that try to start a new transaction before the previous transaction at the same access point has ended are simply ignored.

Transactions at disjoint sets of access points can be carried out in parallel. With global synchronism, where each message sent arrives in the next round, the simplification is not too unrealistic, because the entities participating in a transaction are kept quite busy and transactions terminate quickly. With more realistic models of time, one would have to permit overlapping transactions at a single access point. However, this would introduce many standard tasks of multi-processing into signature schemes, which is of no use in a classification.

5.2 Service

This section defines both the minimal service that is common to all signature schemes and special service properties that can be used to classify signature schemes. Section 5.2.1 discusses what kind of specification is used and why. Section 5.2.2 gives a brief informal overview of the actual service specification. Sections 5.2.3 to 5.2.7 contain details about the minimal service and about formalization in general. Additional service properties are considered in Sections 5.2.8 to 5.2.12.

5.2.1 What Kind of Specification?

The main characteristics of the following specification are:

- The specification is **descriptive**. It consists of several individual **requirements** describing properties that any sequence of interface events should have. In other words: Each requirement is a predicate on the set of sequences over the domain of the interface events, i.e., it characterizes some sequences as permitted and others as undesirable; see Figure 5.3.[27]
- Most of the requirements can conveniently be expressed in temporal logic, because certain events are required to happen sometime or never, respectively. Currently, however, the logic is only used to talk about sequences concisely and without writing too many indices. (See Section 5.4.4 for future possibilities.)
- The guideline for finding requirements is the interests of individual users or joint interests of small sets of users, see Figure 5.3. Such a set, a so-called **interest group**, must be mentioned explicitly with each requirement. Formally, it is a set of access points.
- Each requirement only deals with interface events at the access points of the interest group (and events at the connection-control access point).

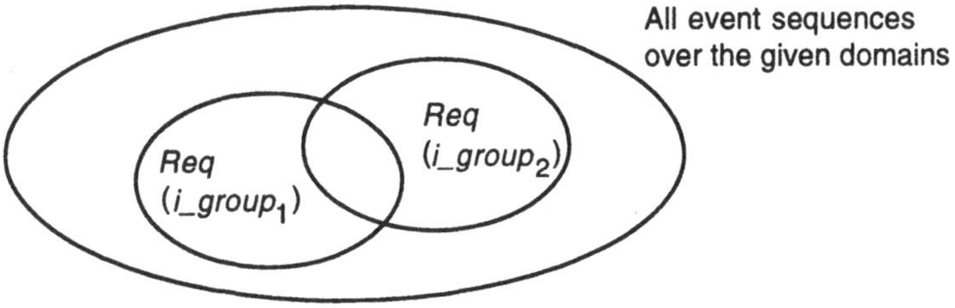

Figure 5.3. Example of the type of specification.
$Req(i\_group_j)$ denotes the set of sequences that fulfil the requirement made in the interest of a set of users, i_group_j. The two requirements are usually fulfilled with different degrees of security. Hence they cannot be replaced by one requirement that the sequence is in $Req(i\_group_1) \cap Req(i\_group_2)$.

Why a Descriptive Specification?

My primary reason to use a descriptive specification was that it seemed the natural way of expressing what I wanted to express, which should be as good a reason as any with a top-level specification. I expect that it will seem equally natural to readers used to logic specifications, and also to readers used to conventional definitions of

27 Not all requirements on cryptologic schemes can be expressed as predicates on event sequences, but fortunately, all minimal requirements on signature schemes can. Others require certain distributions, e.g., the service of a coin-flipping protocol, or privacy properties, i.e., they deal with the information or knowledge attackers can gain about the sequence of events at the interface to the honest users; see [PfWa94].

signature schemes, because those are descriptive, too, even though the requirements use details of the structure and the degree of security.

Nevertheless, readers used to general security models in cryptology [Yao82, Beav91, MiRo91] or more practical ones like [Dier91, Bisk93] might be surprised (if not, they can skip this subsection), because a usual notion in that field is that a secure system should fulfil the specification and do nothing else, or, more theoretically, have a minimum-knowledge property. This presupposes an unambiguous specification. At least in theory, this leads naturally to constructive specifications by reference implementations, usually simple centralized ones without attackers, which are to be simulated. They are often called ideal protocols or trusted-host specifications.

Such notions are very important for many purposes. However, I think they are not suitable for a general definition of signature schemes, nor for any classification: First, a general definition comprising several types of schemes must be ambiguous, hence the nothing-else aspect cannot be used with respect to it. Secondly, properties to be used in a classification need descriptive specifications: One does not want to write a completely new reference implementation each time, but make additional requirements with short descriptions. Thirdly, as most applications do not impose privacy requirements on signature schemes, a minimum-knowledge aspect is not even intended with most individual classes of signature schemes.

In the long run, I expect that descriptive specifications will often serve as top-level specifications, whereas constructive specifications will be used as refinements before the actual implementations. For instance, one could make trusted-host specifications of some individual types of signature schemes.

Why Interest Groups?

An informal reason for sorting requirements according to interest groups is that different users have different interests in real life, too. Such interests can easily be sketched in an informal way and are therefore a good starting point for a specification. Moreover, it is sensible to describe the interests of a certain group of users in terms of things that these users notice, i.e., the events at the access points where they have access.

A more formal reason for considering interest groups is that the subsequent security considerations for a requirement depend on the set of interested users, because users are regarded as mutually distrusting. To see this, consider structure and security for a moment (or wait for Section 5.4.1, where this paragraph is explained in more detail): Entities are usually supposed to belong to individual users, because they are in those users' devices. Entities belonging to users not interested in a requirement R are not guaranteed to be correct when R is proved. Moreover, this shows that making a requirement R on events at access points of users not interested in R would be of no use: In general, such a requirement could not be fulfilled in the desired sense, because these events are directly handled by entities that are not necessarily correct. For instance, a signature scheme cannot possibly prevent a dishonest court from rejecting correctly authenticated messages.

Combinations of the model of interest groups and of attackers inside the system can also be called a trust model, see [PfWa94, Schu95].

Remarks on Logics of Authentication

Logic specification of signature schemes may sound rather similar to the logics of authentication, often called BAN logic, from [BuAN90] and many subsequent articles. However, the purpose and consequently the approach are quite different. This is natural, because these logics were primarily designed to find errors in key-distribution protocols with symmetric schemes, which they do successfully.

- Logics of authentication are used to specify and prove protocols *using* cryptologic primitives, whereas here, the signature schemes themselves are to be specified.
- Logics of authentication assume very simple cryptologic primitives; hence they deal with individual algorithms and keys of those schemes. Thus a new type of logic would be needed for each new type of signature scheme, just as a new cryptologic definition was so far needed for each new type. Usually, e.g., in [LABW92], authentication is still assumed to be provided by a variant of a secrecy scheme, which, as explained in Section 1.5, is a structure that most signature schemes do not have. A more general abstraction would use the algorithms from the GMR definition, i.e., from Figure 2.2.
- If logics of authentication have a formal semantics, not the real cryptologic schemes are used, but algebraic abstractions [DoYa81, AbTu91]. Hence, if one finds an error with the logic, there was an error in the real protocol, but if one proves the algebraic abstraction to be secure, one is not sure that the real protocol is secure, too. Here, the real signature schemes are the semantics.

A more closely related approach was taken in [SyMe93], where requirements on the schemes usually treated with BAN logic were also formulated independently of the structure and in temporal logic. (The semantics is algebraic abstractions as above.) The general type of requirements is very similar, except that [SyMe93] has no explicit interface. Introducing one might be helpful there, too, because intuition seems to be needed to map, e.g., an accept statement from the requirements to something in the actual protocol, whereas here, it *is* the interface output of the protocol. Furthermore, an interface allows a separation of system entities and users, which is helpful because entities have prescribed programs and users do not.

For an overview of other related approaches, see [Mead95].

In future, the approaches might meet in logics for the design of complicated protocols, but using more general primitives and a real cryptologic semantics.

5.2.2 Overview of the Services of Signature Schemes

Any specification of the type explained above defines

- the types and possible numbers of *access points*,
- the *domains for the events* that can occur at such access points (one domain per type), grouped into transactions for didactic reasons,

- and the *requirements* of the different interest groups.

Moreover, this section 5.2 contains more than one such specification:

- a *minimal specification* for the general definition of signature schemes, and
- several *special service properties* for the classification of signature schemes.

A brief and incomplete overview of all these points is now given.

Types of Access Points

Three types of access points at the user interface are common to all signature schemes (see Section 5.1.2, "Granularity of Entities"): signer access points, recipient access points, and court access points.

Transactions and Events

Three types of transactions are common to all signature schemes.

- **Authentication** is a transaction between one signer and one recipient, where the signer wants to authenticate a message for the recipient, and the recipient wants to know if this authentication is correct. (Figure 5.1 showed a slightly simplified version of the interface events.)
- **Dispute** is a transaction between a recipient, a court, and possibly a signer, where the court has to decide whether a certain message had previously been authenticated by the signer.
- **Initialization** is a transaction to set up the possibility of carrying out authentications and disputes for one signer; it involves all participants. (It is the interface version of key generation and distribution.)

Minimal Requirements

"Minimal" are those requirements that all signature schemes have to fulfil; the following list starts with the ones that are most characteristic of signature schemes:

- The **requirement of the recipient on disputes**: Once a recipient has accepted a certain message as authenticated by a certain signer (in an authentication transaction), he should win disputes about that message in court. The only exception is with schemes like invisible signature schemes, where disputes only work if the signer cooperates.

  The interest group consists of the recipient and the court used in the dispute. (The requirement could not be fulfilled if the court were dishonest and manipulated its device.)
- The **requirement of the signer on disputes**: As long as a signer has not authenticated a certain message, i.e., not carried out authentication for it, nobody should be able to make a court believe that she did, at least if she disavows that message in court.

  The interest group consists of the signer and the court.
- **Unforgeability** is a joint requirement of a signer and a recipient: As long as the signer has not authenticated a certain message, nobody should be able to make the recipient believe that she did. (However, unforgeability seems to be a

consequence of the first two requirements in almost all cases, and one can justify not including unforgeability in the minimal requirements anyway; see Section 5.2.7.)

- **Effectiveness of authentication** is a joint requirement of a signer and a recipient, too: They should be able to perform authentication successfully if correct initialization took place.
- **Effectiveness of initialization.** Another joint requirement of a signer and at least one recipient or court is that they should be able to perform initialization successfully.
- **Correctness of initialization** is a joint requirement of an arbitrary set of participants: They want to obtain a consistent view about an initialization, even if the signer cheats and initialization is unsuccessful.
- **Availability of service** means that everybody can carry out transactions of their choice and transactions end within reasonable time.[28]

Additional Service Properties

In principle, one can define an arbitrary number of additional service properties. In the following, completeness is only aimed at with interesting properties of existing types of schemes. However, one can at least classify the properties somewhat further.

- **Stronger requirements**, i.e., concretizations where the minimal specification is ambiguous. The following classes are actually considered:
  - *Stronger requirements on disputes*, e.g., different versions of what happens if the signer does not cooperate in a dispute.
  - *User-friendliness*, i.e., the system behaviour in cases that can be regarded as user errors.

  One could also define *directedness of authentication* to mean that the authentication is only valid for particular recipients.
- **Multiple specifications**, i.e., different specifications intended for different degrees of security, which would be redundant otherwise. For instance, with fail-stop signature schemes one first requires that no forgeries occur, but secondly, if a forgery occurs nevertheless, it should be provable. This makes sense because the second requirement is to hold on weaker assumptions than the first one.
  - The *fail-stop* property is the only example of multiple specifications actually considered.

---

28 Now there is enough terminology to describe how the service of authentication schemes with arbiters (see Section 1.5) differs from that of digital signature schemes: In most of them, there is only one court, called an arbiter, and otherwise, the multiple arbiters do not decide independently, but cooperate to reach one common decision in a dispute. Effectiveness of authentication and effectiveness of initialization do not hold against the arbiter (or a sufficiently large subset of arbiters in [BrSt88]), and in some schemes, unforgeability does not hold against the arbiter either.

- **Special specification parameters** are also a type of concretization where the minimal specification is ambiguous. Specification parameters are explained in Section 5.2.5. The following examples are considered:
  - *Special message spaces.*
  - *Special message bounds*, i.e., restrictions on the number of messages that can be authenticated.
  - *Dependence of authentication on the recipients.*
- **Additional transactions** (i.e., extensions of the domains of interface events) and corresponding requirements. The following examples are considered:
  - Transactions to transfer authenticated messages from one recipient to another in the sense that the certainty that one can win disputes in court is transferred. Such transfers can work arbitrarily often (*arbitrary transferability*) or a fixed, finite number of times (*finite transferability*).
  - So-called *transfers of proofs of forgery* are considered in the subsection on the fail-stop property.
  - *Local* transactions.
  - Transactions for the *external verifiability* of the behaviour of participants.
  - More variants of *initialization* and *leaving*.
  - *Distributed* variants of transactions, such as authentication for more than one recipient simultaneously.[29]
- **Privacy requirements**. The only privacy requirement that has so far been considered is the *invisibility* of invisible signature schemes. (Recall that blind signature schemes and schemes without subliminal channels are not signature schemes in the sense of the minimal requirements.) One could also add normal confidentiality requirements with respect to outsiders.

Those properties that deal with parts that were regarded as outside the signature scheme in previous definitions can of course not easily be used to classify existing schemes. Examples are user-friendliness and variants of initialization and leaving.

How Much Detail Follows?

The following sections elaborate on this overview. The goal was to present enough details and formalism to guarantee that the type of specification cannot be misunderstood and that the classification is clear. Thus the interface events have been worked out completely and the two most important requirements, those on disputes,

---

29 One might wonder if it is a weakness of the separation of service and structure that so many properties have to be collected explicitly that did not have to be mentioned with previous approaches. However, this is not a consequence of the separation, but of permitting a more general structure than that of ordinary digital signature schemes. For instance, authentication with more than one recipient can easily be added to ordinary digital signature schemes, but not to invisible ones. Similarly, it is really not trivial that new recipients can enter later if key generation is interactive, as in [ChRo91]. The explicit description of the service should even be helpful, because it raises consciousness of properties that one may so far have tacitly assumed.

have been formalized. Three details in this formalization are tentative and should be finalized when more examples have been worked out: general conditions about correct connections, possible dependence of the authentication on recipients, and the termination of systems. The remaining minimal requirements and the special service properties are only discussed informally. It should not be too difficult to work them out in the same way (except, perhaps, for availability of service), but it was not worthwhile because the specification is not used in formal proofs in this text yet.

5.2.3 Remarks on the Generality of the Definition

This section briefly sketches in what way the definition surveyed in Section 5.2.2 is a general definition of all signature schemes, and where further generalization is possible. The main criterion was that a scheme should be included if and only if it can be used as a replacement for handwritten signatures in the sense of Sections 1.1 to 1.3. The main consequences were:

- The general definition should contain few transactions, because any transaction included here has to be offered by all schemes, i.e., they have to react on the corresponding input events in a way prescribed by the minimal requirements. Adding more transactions as special service properties is discussed in Section 5.2.11.
- The minimal requirements should be as weak as possible for legal security.

Deciding on the weakest possible minimal requirements is not trivial with respect to the **preconditions on the behaviour of the honest users**. For instance, the effectiveness of authentication clearly needs a precondition that the signer and the recipient input the same message, but it is not so clear how the users must use initialization for their requirements to be fulfilled. The conflicting factors are:

- Strong preconditions make the requirements weak and the definition general.
- Weak preconditions make the systems safer to use, i.e., small errors in the intended inputs do not lead to unspecified behaviour. This is particularly important if the systems are to be used directly by people.

In the following, strong preconditions are made, and stronger requirements with weaker preconditions are additional service properties (see Section 5.2.8, "User-Friendliness"). It should not be hard to devise general constructions that transform schemes fulfilling the minimal requirements into schemes fulfilling stronger, safer requirements.

Adding Types of Access Points

One point where the definition could be generalized further is that only signers, recipients, and courts determine the results of initialization and disputes.[30] This

[30] This is the only disputable decision of this type: Authentication is deliberately required to be a 2-party transaction (see Section 1.3); additional transactions can have arbitrary participants; and new participants can be added to initialization and disputes if they do not influence the results for the original participants (e.g., the observers in Section 5.2.11, "External Verifiability of the Behaviour of Participants").

excludes schemes comprising key distribution with key certificates from other parties (see Section 2.3). This was partly done on purpose, but also because a joint definition for both cases is rather complex. Moreover, if one allows such parties at all, one should allow any number of them and an arbitrary so-called access structure on them, i.e., a set consisting of those subsets that must collude in order to cheat.

Such a definition is now sketched. Apart from certification authorities, it covers confirmers in designated confirmer schemes (assuming that a confirmer disavowal protocol is added, see Section 2.7.1), and special risk bearers in fail-stop signature schemes (see Section 5.2.9). One obligatory requirement from Chapter 1 is that neither signers nor recipients should have to trust these parties in their requirements on disputes, i.e., the interest groups in those two requirements remain "the recipient and the court" and "the signer and the court". This excludes simple implementations where a trusted centre replaces the broadcast channel in initialization of a normal signature scheme — anyway, this could be treated by regarding the centre as a special implementation of a broadcast channel. Thus the following is a sketch of a minimal definition for the case where such parties can, to a certain extent, be held responsible for their actions.

A **signature-like scheme with accountable centres** (a special case of accountable third parties) has the usual three roles and an arbitrary number of others, which are collectively called centres. (For the same reasons as in Section 5.1.2, "Granularity of Entities", combinations like "centre and court" and "centre and recipient" are not considered separately.) The three common transactions are adapted as follows.

- Authentication remains unchanged.
- Disputes are between one recipient, one court, possibly one signer, and possibly all the centres. Thus all the access points of all new types may take part. The court's conclusion in a dispute may not only be that the message was or was not authenticated, but also that a certain subset of the centres is to blame.
- Initialization may be with all parties.

The minimal requirements are adapted as follows.

- The requirements of the signer and the recipient on disputes are unchanged.
- There is a new requirement of the centres on disputes that they are not blamed unduly.
- Unforgeability is often relaxed by adding the centres or the given subsets of them to the interest groups. Hence centres (or certain quorums of them) may be able to forge. One reason is that in the most important example, key certification, they *can*. (Designated confirmers cannot.) Moreover, it might not be too bad, because the requirements on disputes guarantee that if they ever forge indeed, this can be proved in court. It depends on the application if such an accountability after the fact is acceptable.
- Similarly, the effectiveness requirements are often relaxed by adding centres to the interest groups. However, it is still required that the participants have a consistent view and find someone to blame (not unduly) if something goes wrong.

Introducing accountable centres into signature schemes makes them more similar to authentication schemes with arbiters, but it is still required that any out of a large number of courts can decide and fulfil the original requirements on disputes.

5.2.4 Interface Events in Detail

This section gives a detailed description of the events that occur in the three common transactions. First the events at the user interface are treated, then those at the connection-control access point.

Formally, this section only defines domains. Informal statements like "the signer inputs a command x" mean that an input x belongs to the domain of events at a signer access point. More precisely, the domains are given as functions of basic domains for individual parameters, such as a message space M and sets of identities; Section 5.2.5 discusses where those basic domains come from. The meaning of the events is explained by showing how they occur together in transactions in correct runs of a system. The formal equivalent of these explanations is the requirements in Section 5.2.7.

Authentication

The most common transaction is authentication. The events at the signer access point and the recipient access point that form such a transaction are now described in detail. They are summarized in Figure 5.4, and some reasons for the decisions follow after the figure. (Remember that an example of what may happen under the interface was shown in Figure 5.1.)

- The signer inputs a command *'sign'* (i.e., the string *'sign'*) and the message m to be authenticated.[31]

  In a few classes of signature schemes, the signer must input the identity of the recipient, too. (None of the examples shown so far was of this type.) To cover all cases, a description $ids_{R,sign}$ of a set of identities of recipients is used. The value $Any := \epsilon$, i.e., the empty string, describes the set of all recipients, and the empty set $\emptyset$ is excluded. Note that authentication remains a transaction between only two parties — the meaning of a value $ids_{R,sign}$ with more than one element is that from the signer's point of view, any of the recipients $id_R \in ids_{R,sign}$ could be the one for whom the message is authenticated. Hence the standard case without restriction is $ids_{R,sign} = Any$.
- The recipient inputs a command *'test'*, the message m for which the test is to be carried out, and the identity id_S of the supposed signer.
- The recipient obtains an output acc, which denotes whether the message was accepted as authenticated. (No signature is output, as explained in Section 5.1.1.)

  In most schemes, acc is Boolean, where TRUE means accepted. In the general definition, any domain $Test\_results \supseteq \{\text{TRUE}, \text{FALSE}\}$ is permitted.

---

31 I hope that using the name *'sign'* for a command at the interface, while *sign* denotes an algorithm that may be carried out subsequently by an entity, is not confusing. In real life, one might replace string inputs by interactive graphical inputs anyway; however, modeling this would require a notion of refinement for the given type of specification.

Only TRUE and FALSE occur in the minimal requirements. Other results can be used in cases that remain unspecified in the minimal requirements, e.g., for error messages; see Section 5.2.8, "User-Friendliness".

- The signer obtains an output acc_S. The usual value is *'eot'* (end of transaction); it simply indicates that the access point has finished the transaction and is waiting for a new input. Other values may be error messages. The general case is covered by a domain $Sign\_results \neq \emptyset$.[32] In particular, a value *'key_used_up'* is needed for schemes where only a certain number of messages can be authenticated after any initialization, such as one-time signature schemes.

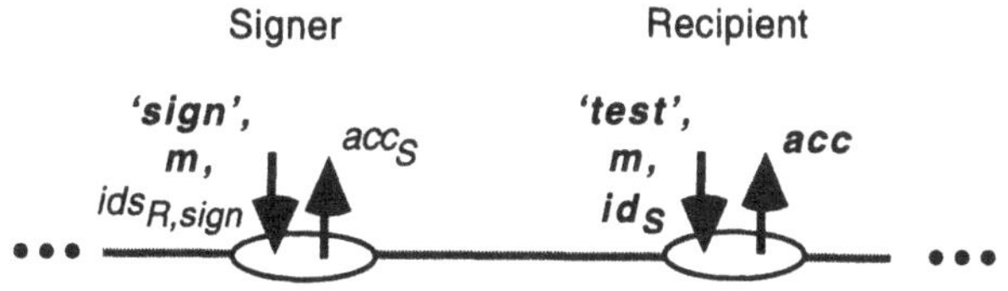

Figure 5.4. Interface events of authentication.
The boldface parameters are always necessary. Parameters in normal type have only been introduced to cover certain subtypes of the service.

In the rest of this subsection, some alternatives to the decisions made above are discussed.

Message as output for the recipient? As the signer inputs the message, and connections are assumed to be provided via the switch, one could have defined that the recipient obtains the message as an output, i.e., the signature scheme would include message transport. However, there might be applications where such a transport is not necessary. Moreover, the explicit input of the message gives the recipient more control over what his entity busies itself with. If one wants a scheme including message transport, one can easily build it using the scheme without transport, and one might add a prompt asking the recipient whether he really wants the message tested.

Identity of the signer. It may not be clear why the signer does not input her own identity in authentication, in particular because the secret key, which is a low-level identity, is an input in previous definitions (see Section 2.6).

First consider the top-down justification in Section 5.1.1: If the command *'sign'* is given to a personal device, there is no need to type one's name, i.e., one's high-level identity. The device always signs with the one secret key (or a generalization of such a key) stored in it anyway. The only time that identifying information is input to the device is during the password check or whatever the device does to recognize its legitimate user, but this is not a part of the signature scheme.

32 There is usually no need to tell the signer in acc_S whether the recipient accepted the message, because if both she and the recipient are honest, this should always be the case, and if one of them is dishonest, it does not really matter.

Secondly, from a purely theoretical point of view, consider what would happen if the identity was an input in such a service: If the specification would really permit all identities at all access points, everybody could enter the identity of somebody else. Hence there would be no security in the intuitive sense of the real world. (This cannot be avoided by declaring something as the identity that someone else *cannot* enter, such as a password or biometric information: The recipient and the court have to know an identity of the signer, and it is this very identity this paragraph deals with, because the requirements have to express facts like "if a signer with a certain identity did not authenticate a message, no court should believe that the signer with this identity did".)

A possibility that would work is that the signer enters the identity, but that only one identity works at this access point (i.e., the entity inside checks the identity), but that would be redundant.

For the case where a user can sign under several identities, one might have defined access points that handle a certain number of identities and where the currently used identity is an input (whereas in the definition above, such a user needs several access points — of course, they can be implemented on the same device). However, in practice, a signer would not want to input an identity, i.e., the string under which recipients and courts know her, but a local identifier such as "sign for bank" or "sign for credit card". This corresponds to the way access points are selected in software.

Additional parameters. Similar to the parameters $ids_{R,sign}$, one might allow other parameters that primarily give the system hints for possible optimizations. This would be the most elegant way of treating incremental signature schemes. Such parameters primarily affect the effectiveness of authentication, i.e., authentication will not work if they are wrong. For the general definition, one might try to add one parameter *others* with arbitrary relations that specify the correct use of *others*.

Dispute

A dispute involves events at two or three access points: a recipient access point, a court access point, and possibly the access point of the supposed signer. The supposed signer is defined as the one whose identity the court enters; the adjective "supposed" is sometimes omitted in the following.[33] The events described now are summarized in Figure 5.5, and some reasons for the decisions follow after the figure.

- The recipient inputs a command *'show'*, the message *m*, and the identity id_S of the signer.
- The court inputs a command *'decide'*, the message *m*, the identity id_S of the supposed signer, and possibly the identity of the recipient. As with the

33 Similarly, one may call the recipient a presumable or supposed recipient. However, in the following requirements, the signer is usually mentioned when her interests are considered, i.e., if she did not authenticate the message, whereas the recipient is usually mentioned when he did accept it as authenticated.

command *'sign'*, a parameter $ids_{R,dec}$ is provided to cover all cases, and the standard case is $ids_{R,dec} = Any$.

- If the supposed signer takes part, she inputs a command *'disavow'*, the message, and possibly the identity of the supposed recipient. The latter is represented in a parameter $ids_{R,dis}$.[34]
- The court obtains an output *acc*, which denotes whether the message was accepted as authenticated. Hence

  acc = TRUE means that the recipient has won the dispute, whereas

  acc = FALSE means that the supposed signer has won.

  In some schemes, not only these two results are possible. Hence any superset *Dispute_results* of {TRUE, FALSE} is permitted as the range of *acc*. Two cases occur in the following:

  First, in the service of fail-stop signature schemes, the fact that a proof of forgery has occurred in the system is represented at the interface by

  acc = *'broken'*.

  A beautiful, but unrealistic variant would be that the court finds out exactly who has produced a forgery. Realistically, with implementations of fail-stop signature schemes where different parts rely on different assumptions, there can be an output parameter *which_assumption* that distinguishes which assumption was broken.

  Secondly, if the signer is supposed to enter *'disavow'*, one must provide for the case that she refuses to take part. With some signature schemes, e.g., invisible ones, no real dispute takes place in this case. This is modeled as

  acc = *'not_cooperated'*.
- The recipient obtains an output acc_R. The usual value is *'eot'*, which indicates that the transaction has ended.[35] In general, any domain $Show\_results \neq \emptyset$ is permitted.
- If the signer has input a command, she also obtains an output acc_S from a domain $Disavow\_results \neq \emptyset$.

---

34 For the greatest possible generality, one might add parameters ids_C denoting possible courts in the commands of the signer and the recipient. In all schemes presented in the following, however, they would have the value *Any*.

Furthermore, there may be an alternative command *'agree'* for the case where the supposed signer takes part, but cannot or does not want to disavow the message. However, it is never really needed. It is mentioned again in Section 5.2.8.

35 As with the output to the signer in authentication, it is usually unnecessary that acc_R and the following acc_S indicate whether the message was accepted: The court can tell the signer and the recipient its decision outside the signature scheme. However, one might want such an output in case of imperfect security, so that the users can to some extent distinguish if the signature scheme failed or the court cheated and announced a wrong result; see also Section 5.2.11, "External Verifiability of the Behaviour of Participants".

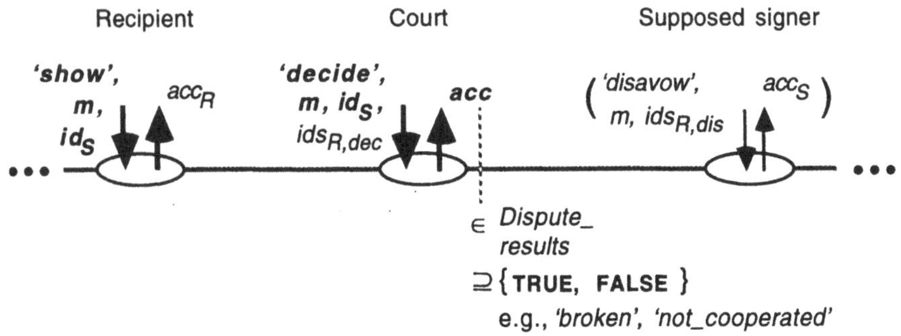

Figure 5.5. Interface events of a dispute.
Similar to Figure 5.4, the boldface events and parameters are always necessary, parameters in normal type have only been introduced to cover certain subtypes of the service, and events in parentheses actually do not occur in certain subtypes.

Initialization

Before the standard transactions can be performed, initialization must take place at the corresponding access points. Initialization at the interface represents key generation and key distribution within the system. Roughly, each user who takes part inputs a command *'init'*, and everybody obtains an output that denotes whether initialization was successful.[36] The main parameters of the interface events are identities, in particular, that of the future signer; however, several variants are conceivable as to which of the interface events have this parameter and whether more identities occur explicitly.

The most important distinction is that between initialization for a previously known identity and initialization for a newly created identity. Formally, this distinction defines which events have the identity of the signer as a parameter. For compactness, only the more common initialization for a previously known identity has been worked out in detail and is used in all subsequent sections.

Initialization for a previously known identity means that the identity that the signer will use in authentications and disputes has been defined outside the signature scheme. For instance, it may be a name and address, but also a previously known pseudonym. This type of identity has been assumed in the examples so far.

The following properties characterize initialization for a previously known identity:

- The signer's input does not contain her own identity,
- the inputs *'init'* at recipient and court access points have the identity id_S of the signer as a parameter,[37]

[36] One could have distinguished inputs *'init_as_signer'*, *'init_as_recipient'*, and *'init_as_court'*; however, the same information is implicit in the types of the access points.

[37] One could have defined that the recipients obtain the identity of the signer as an output instead. However, the choice made here seems slightly more flexible: The recipients can decide with whom they want to carry out initialization. This is particularly interesting in other, non-atomic variants of initialization.

- and none of the outputs has the identity of the signer as a parameter.

This type of initialization is shown in Figure 5.6.

The reasons why the signer does not input her own identity are similar to those with the command *'sign'*, although at a first glance, this may seem more strange now, because the secret information in the entities underneath, which will implicitly distinguish the access points during authentication, has not yet been generated.

However, in practice, the identity is present in the entity under an access point in the form of access to a broadcast channel under this previously known identity (for the time of initialization). For instance, with an ordinary digital signature scheme, the public key is broadcast on this channel inside the system during such an initialization. Similarly, if the system contained an authority that issues key certificates, the entity would need access to a secure channel to the authority under this identity, e.g., via the user who makes a handwritten signature. Note that the entities of all signers still use the same program; e.g., they use a particular port for broadcast outputs.

The purely theoretical reason is, as before, that if one could enter any identity at any access point, one could carry out initialization under the identities of others.

Initialization for a newly created identity is the generalized service representation of the following use of an ordinary digital signature scheme: Somebody generates a key pair, publishes the public key on an anonymous broadcast channel, and starts sending messages authenticated with the corresponding secret key. Thus the keys are not linked to any previously known identity, and in this simple case, one would usually regard the public key itself as the new identity.[38] Thus the identity for which this initialization took place is an output for all users who took part.

If each initialization is for a newly created identity, it is unrealistic to assume a particular access point for each future identity. For instance, a person will have only one device, which can be connected to an anonymous broadcast channel. Each time she wants an initialization for a newly created identity, she behaves in exactly the same way. Hence she should have a special access point just for initialization, and each initialization should yield a new access point, which handles the newly created identity. (The new access point should appear in the same environment where the access point used in the initialization is, so that the same user has access to it, for instance physically or with a password. However, this cannot be represented formally in the current model.) Hence the following events happen at the interface:

- The signer inputs her command *'init'* at the special access point,
- none of the inputs has an identity as a parameter[39],

---

38 More generally, with schemes where every entity of a recipient may obtain a different test key, the number of the round where the first broadcast within this initialization occurred is knowledge common to all the entities participating in this initialization and can therefore serve as the identity.

39 In contrast to previously known identities, one could now alternatively define that the signer inputs her own new identity. Her entity would generate a public key or whatever as before and additionally broadcast the identity. If someone chose an identity that any entity participating in this initialization knew to be already in use, all the entities would reject it.

- the special access point outputs an identity,
- a new access point with this identity appears,
- and the recipients and courts obtain the identity as an output, too.

The remaining decisions have to be made for both types of identities.

How many recipients take part? With most signature schemes, an initialization can be carried out with an arbitrary number of recipients. However, there are schemes where initialization is carried out with a fixed recipient. (For example, a signer may be a client of a bank and carry out initialization with the sole purpose of sending authenticated messages to the bank.) The set of possible numbers of recipients is called *Recipients_per_init*. The two above-mentioned cases are *Recipients_per_init* = $\mathbb{N}$ and *Recipients_per_init* = $\{1\}$.

Identities of recipients and courts. As with the other transactions, all cases are covered if the signer inputs a parameter $ids_{R,initS}$, which describes a set of recipients. The recipients and courts may need similar input parameters $ids_{R,initR}$ and $ids_{R,initC}$.

In contrast, I do not provide a parameter for the identities of the desired courts. This is related to the informal requirement "Assessment by the Public" in Section 1.3, i.e., every user should technically be able to assess the authenticity of anybody's messages. A signature scheme cannot guarantee this alone, because it seems necessary that all future courts take part in initialization (e.g., so that their entities can receive public keys), and only the application determines who takes part. However, there is at least no need to provide a parameter restricting the participating courts explicitly.

Outputs. Every user who took part in an initialization obtains an output denoting the success of this initialization. Sometimes this output is only Boolean. In other cases, it must denote which potential recipients took part successfully. To cover all cases, a value *acc* with a domain *Init_results* $\supseteq$ {TRUE, FALSE} and an additional parameter ids_{out} are provided. The meaning of *acc* = TRUE is basically that the signer behaved correctly and can now sign, and ids_{out} denotes those recipients and courts that can now test and decide.

Message bound. To cover cases where only a fixed number of messages can be authenticated after an initialization, there must be an input parameter to select this number, say N. It is called the message bound. Its domain is a subset *Message_bounds* of $\mathbb{N} \cup \{\infty\}$, where ∞ means that no upper bound exists. Recipients and courts input this number, too.[40] To be prepared for complexity considerations, N is always input in unary representation.

More parameters? I considered including the security parameters in the inputs to initialization. This would enable individual users to control their own security, and one could use different security parameters in different initializations in the same

---

40 The reason for this is technical: There are schemes where the complexity of initialization depends on N. The fact that all users input N into their own entities ensures that no attacker can trick entities of honest users into arbitrarily long computations.

system. (Now such a case is modeled as different systems derived from the same scheme.)

At present, however, the security parameters are regarded as internal details of the systems and represented in the initial states of each entity. The prevailing argument was: The goal is to define general notions like "a scheme *Scheme* fulfils a requirement *Req* computationally in the parameter *k* …", where both *Scheme* and *Req* are variables. This means that a sequence of systems Sys_k derived from *Scheme* fulfils a sequence of requirements Req_k. If *k* is a distinguished part of the entities, it is easy to define Sys_k formally. If *k* were an input parameter, it would formally be a parameter of the honest users and not of the system. This is not too bad, because a formal representation of honest users is needed anyway. However, one has to be able to talk about an honest user with parameter *k*, as far as a certain requirement is concerned. This seems difficult if *k* is one of many parameters and there can be different *k*'s in different initializations.

If the security parameters were included, they could collectively be called *par*, with a domain *Pars*, because they have no special meaning in a pure service specification. Anyway, it may be useful to include such a parameter *par* on whose value at least the minimal requirements do not depend, to provide for extensions of initialization necessitated by additional transactions. For the same reason as with the message bound *N*, all the users participating in initialization would have to input the same value *par*, and effectiveness of initialization would be guaranteed whenever they do this. This extension is omitted for brevity in the following.

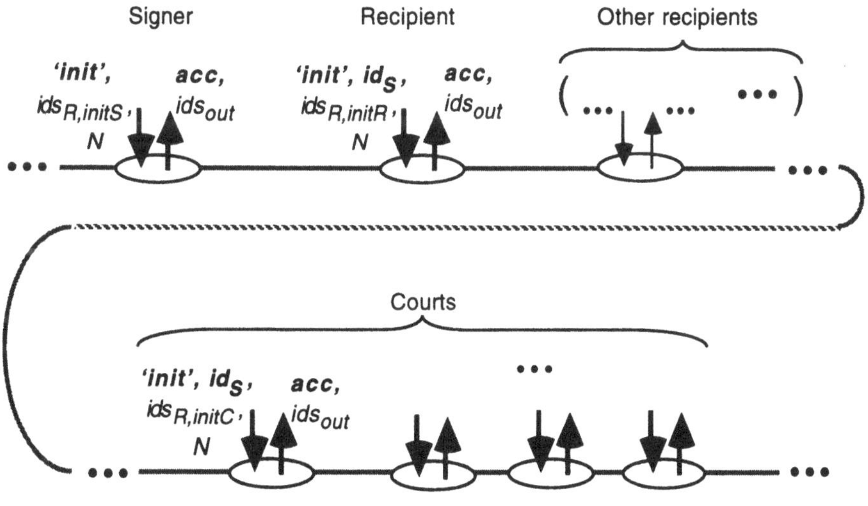

Figure 5.6. Interface events of initialization for a previously known identity.
As in Figures 5.4 and 5.5, the boldface events and parameters are always necessary, parameters in normal type have only been introduced to cover certain subtypes of the service, and events in parentheses actually do not occur in all subtypes.

Events at the Connection-Control Access Point

For connection handling with explicit switching (see Section 5.1.2), a domain for the inputs at the connection-control access point must be chosen. The following is a provisional sketch. For simplicity, the existence of connections is modeled, and not their establishment and release. In each round, the input at the connection-control access point designates the connections that exist between this round and the next one, i.e., it determines where messages sent in this round arrive in the next round. It is even sufficient if this input designates which access points are correctly connected for which type of transaction. The exact connections derived from these data (by the switch) are structural details. Hence a complete input event can be described in a variable *connections*, which contains a set of connection commands of the form

$$connection = (transaction\_type, access\_points),$$

where

- *transaction_type* $\in$ *Transaction_types*, and *Transaction_types* is a set of strings containing the elements *'authentication'*, *'dispute'*, and *'initialization'*[41], and
- *access_points* is a list of identities of access points taking part. The roles in which they do this, i.e., as signers, recipients, or courts, can be derived from the identities. A list was used instead of a set to provide numbering for multi-party subprotocols.

For each transaction type, a list type may be prescribed that defines how many access points of each type may be involved. For authentication and dispute, which are 2- and 3-party protocols, these types are clear. Very generally, one can define once and for all a set *List_types* and a function *type_of* that maps lists to their type. Then, for each transaction scheme, one can define a function *permitted_connections* that maps each transaction type to a set of permitted list types. However, general restrictions related to the number of user access points that take part have to be made.

5.2.5 Specification and System Parameters

The description of interface events in Section 5.2.4 contained several free variables, mostly denoting sets used as domains for parameters. This section discusses how these variables are bound. All the sets must be countable and non-empty, and for some of them, a restriction of the values they can assume is already known. Here is the complete list of them with some new restrictions.

a) The message space M, i.e., the domain for all parameters that were called m.
b) Sets Id_S, Id_R, and Id_C of identities. In particular, Id_S is the domain of all the parameters id_S, and Id_R is that of the elements of the sets described by the various parameters $ids_{R,x}$ with some identifier x. Their union is denoted by $Id := Id_S \cup Id_R \cup Id_C$. For simplicity, Id_S, Id_R, and Id_C are assumed to be

41 This set of strings is the first formal notion that deals with transactions.

disjoint. (This can be achieved by prefixing other identities, such as names and addresses, with letters 'S', 'R', and 'C'.)

c) The number and identities of access points. As only initialization for a previously known identity is considered further, the identities of the access points are exactly the sets Id_S, Id_R, and Id_C, and these sets can be assumed to be finite.

d) The exact domains of all the set parameters $ids_{R,x}$ are sorted out at the end of this section, because they are quite complicated and primarily needed to cover the more exotic types of signature schemes.

e) The set $Recipients\_per\_init \subseteq \mathbb{N}$.

f) The set $Dispute\_results \supseteq$ {TRUE, FALSE} and the related sets *Test_results*, *Sign_results*, *Show_results*, *Disavow_results*, and *Init_results*.

g) The set $Message\_bounds \subseteq \mathbb{N} \cup \{\infty\}$.[42]

h) The function *permitted_connections* (with some restrictions that have not been formalized).

Options

As long as a variable v such as those described above is free, it defines a family of specifications, $Spec_v$. Such a variable can be bound in two ways:[43]

1. **Specification parameters.** Each $Spec_v$ is regarded as a different specification, and any signature scheme *Scheme* must fulfil *one* of them.

   With each *Scheme*, it must be mentioned for which value $v \in V$ it fulfils the specification $Spec_v$. For instance, signature schemes for different message spaces $v = M$ will be permitted.

2. **System parameters.** The whole family $Spec := (Spec_v)_{v \in V}$ for some set V is regarded as one specification, and any signature scheme must fulfil *any* specification $Spec_v$ if it is embodied in a structure corresponding to parameter v. For instance, a signature scheme will be required to work with arbitrary sets Id_S of identities of signers, i.e., if $|Id_S|$ entities run the program for entities of signers and the switch can connect them under the given identities during initialization, the system should fulfil the service specification for the set Id_S (with a certain degree of security).

---

42 One might prescribe that *Message_bounds* is either infinite or contains ∞, so that an arbitrary number of messages can be authenticated somehow. However, schemes for authenticating one message only, i.e., with $Message\_bounds = \{1\}$, are interesting building blocks.

One could even define that *Message_bounds* is either $\{\infty\}$ or $\mathbb{N}$ itself, i.e., either no input N is needed or any number is possible. All known signature schemes have a variant that works for one of these cases. However, it is simpler if one can, for instance, restrict *Message_bounds* to powers of 2 in schemes with tree authentication.

43 Instead, one could also fix v once and for all, e.g., one could define that the message space of all signature schemes were the set of all bit strings. As the opposite extreme, one could make v an input parameter, e.g., in initialization or in a global transaction at the system start. But in both cases, that should have been done in Section 5.2.4 already.

Decisions

The numbers and identities of access points, i.e., Items b) and c), are regarded as system parameters. Hence every signature scheme must work for arbitrary finite sets of identities, say with $Id \subseteq \{0, 1\}^+$ for concreteness.

The only exception is that a restriction to one recipient is permitted. (However, there is still an arbitrary number of courts.) To represent this, a new variable *Recipients_total* $\subseteq \mathbb{N}$ is introduced, similar to *Recipients_per_init*. Its meaning is that Id_R only assumes values with $|Id_R| \in$ *Recipients_total*.

All the other parameters are specification parameters. This option gives the designer of individual signature schemes the greatest freedom, i.e., it yields the most general definition.

Sorting out Sets of Identities

The domains of the parameters $ids_{R,x}$ (Item d)) have not been given names yet, because a signature scheme may restrict some of these parameters in relation to others and to the actual participants in transactions. For concreteness, it is assumed that any subset other than *Any* is described by an enumeration of its elements, i.e., the domains *are* subsets of the power set $\mathcal{P}(Id_R)$. If the relations between the parameters were fixed once and for all, they could be formulated in the requirements and all the domains could be $\mathcal{P}(Id_R)$. However, it is more general to treat these relations as specification parameters, i.e., the designers of signature schemes can choose what relations their schemes support.

General remarks. The domains of these parameters must be chosen carefully:

1. The relations must be usable, both in practice and in the formal requirements. This means that each interest group must be able to check locally if its inputs fulfil the relations that occur in preconditions in their requirements.
2. The relations must be expressed as functions of Id_R, because the parameters must denote subsets of Id_R, which is a system parameter and therefore a variable in the specification.
3. Relations that are so stringent that the resulting signature schemes are uninteresting should be excluded. For instance, it should not happen that one can never authenticate a message because no suitable parameter $ids_{R,sign}$ exists.

The most general way to fulfil these requirements is not worked out here.

Notation for requirements. The concrete relations in all existing schemes are fairly simple; see Section 5.2.8, "Dependence of Authentication on the Recipient", and the requirements are at present formalized as simply as possible in this respect. The following restrictions are made:

- All participants in an initialization must input the same value as $ids_{R,initS}$, $ids_{R,initR}$, and $ids_{R,initC}$, respectively. It will be called $ids_{R,init}$.
- The output ids_{out} is exactly the set of recipients and courts who took part successfully, i.e., for whom guarantees will be given.

- If the signer takes part in disputes, the parameters of the court and the signer must be equal, i.e., $ids_{R,dec} = ids_{R,dis}$.

Thus only very little notation is needed in the requirements that have been formalized. There are

- a function $Ids_{R,init}$, where $Ids_{R,init}(Id_R)$ contains the permitted values of $ids_{R,init}$ if Id_R is the set of all identities of recipients, and
- a relation *suitable*, where $suitable(Id_R, ids_{out}, ids_{R,dec})$ means that $ids_{R,dec}$ is a permitted input in disputes if Id_R is the set of all identities of recipients and ids_{out} was the output in the corresponding initialization.

Note that not all instantiations of $Ids_{R,init}$ and *suitable* will fulfil Requirement 3 above.

Sketch of sensible additional restrictions. A sensible restriction on $Ids_{R,init}$ and *suitable* is to let them describe the permitted size of the parameters only. For instance, there may be a non-empty set $ids_{R,init\_sizes} \subseteq \mathbb{N} \cup \{\infty\}$, which means that $|ids_{R,init}| \in ids_{R,init\_sizes}$ is required. As the set must be non-empty and cannot contain 0, a signer and a recipient who want to carry out initialization together can always find a suitable parameter $ids_{R,init}$.

5.2.6 Towards Formalizations of Requirements

There are quite a lot of things to do before the requirements sketched in Section 5.2.2 can be written formally. This section starts with general notation; then notation to handle transactions follows, and finally, the correct use of initialization, which is a precondition in most requirements, is discussed and formalized.

Event Sequences

The requirements deal with sequences of sets of interface events; sets are used because several events may occur in the same round. An event at the user interface is represented as a triple

$$(identity, direction, value),$$

where

- *identity* denotes the access point where the event occurs; its domain is *Id*.
- $direction \in \{in, out\}$ denotes whether it is an input or an output event, and
- *value* is the value that is passed through the access point; the domains were described in Sections 5.2.4 and 5.2.5.

A variable *events* is defined whose value in each round is the current set of events at the user interface. Everything that is input in one round at one access point is regarded as one value. Hence *events* never contains more than one input per access point. Similarly, only values from the correct domains, as far as these domains are known statically, will appear in events. Hence such syntax checks are not modeled explicitly in the requirements.

The events at the connection-control access point in one round are completely described by the variable *connections*. All values of *connections* are assumed to be syntactically correct. Moreover, as overlapping transactions at the same access point are forbidden, it is assumed that elements *connection* whose lists *access_points* overlap have been deleted from *connections*.

Hence the event sequences are sequences of the values of the two variables *events* and *connections*. The sequences can be of arbitrary finite length.

Temporal Logic

A convenient formalism to talk about sequences without using many indices is temporal logic. A brief overview for readers unfamiliar with temporal logic follows. For precise definitions, see [MaPn91]. Corresponding to the sequences from the previous subsection, a linear-time logic with discrete, finite time is used.

A temporal formula is constructed from state formulas and logical and temporal operators.

A state formula is a formula from an underlying logic language, here normal predicate logic, that can be evaluated at an individual state of a sequence. In the present application, a state formula is therefore a formula about the variables *events* and *connections* in any given round and any number of auxiliary variables. The auxiliary variables are so-called rigid variables, i.e., they are assumed to have the same value in all rounds; see, for instance, the use of the message variable *m* below.

The following temporal operators are used (without the usual operator symbols to make the requirements readable for a casual user of temporal logic):

- "PREVIOUS *f*" means that the formula *f* is evaluated in the previous round, i.e., this formula holds in some round if *f* held in the previous round. In the very first round, PREVIOUS *f* never holds.
- "WEAK_PREVIOUS *f*" also means that *f* is evaluated in the previous round, but in the very first round, WEAK_PREVIOUS *f* always holds.
- "WEAK_NEXT *f*" means that *f* is evaluated in the next round. If no next round exists (because the sequence is finite), WEAK_NEXT *f* always holds (in contrast to an operator NEXT).
- "ALWAYS_IN_THE_PAST *f*" means that *f* holds now and has held in all earlier rounds.
- "HENCEFORTH *f*" means that *f* holds now and continues to hold in all following rounds.
- "*f* SINCE *g*" means that *g* held in some round (before now or now), and after that, *f* has held until (and including) now.
- "*f* BACK_TO *g*" is similar to SINCE, except that *g* is not guaranteed to have ever held; in that case, *f* must have held in all earlier rounds.
- "*f* UNTIL *g*" means that *g* will hold in some round (now or later), and before that, *f* always holds from now on.
- "*f* UNLESS *g*" is similar to UNTIL, except that *g* is not guaranteed to hold ever; in that case, *f* holds forever from now on.

A complete temporal formula is said to hold for a sequence if it holds in the first round.

Finally, ":=" is used to define a predicate on the left side as a syntactical equivalent of the formula on the right side; formal variables are permitted in the substitution. For instance, a modification of the operator SINCE is defined where f is no longer needed in the current round, but must already have started to hold in the round where g held:

$$f \text{ MODIFIED\_SINCE } g := g \vee \text{PREVIOUS}\,(f \text{ SINCE } (f \wedge g)).$$

General Predicates to Handle Transactions

This subsection defines abbreviations of frequently used formulas. Most of them correspond to the informal grouping of interface events into transactions. Two basic predicates denote that any input or output, respectively, occurs at a certain access point in the current round:

$$\begin{aligned} &input\_at(id) := \exists value\colon (id, in, value) \in events,\\ &output\_at(id) := \exists value\colon (id, out, value) \in events. \end{aligned}$$

The following predicate means that no output at all occurs at a set of access points, usually an interest group:

$$no\_output\_at(interest\_group) := \forall id \in interest\_group\colon \neg output\_at(id).$$

Now, valid inputs are defined. Inputs are invalid if they are ignored because they try to start a new transaction before the previous transaction at the same access point has ended (see Section 5.1.2). All transactions described so far, and all those that will be added for special classes of signature schemes, have exactly one input and one output at each access point concerned. Hence an input is valid if there has been no other input since the last output or since the start of the system. This is expressed as follows:

$$\begin{aligned} &valid\_input(id, value) :=\\ &\qquad (id, in, value) \in events\\ &\qquad \wedge \text{ WEAK\_PREVIOUS}\,((\neg input\_at(id)) \text{ BACK\_TO } output\_at(id)). \end{aligned}$$

Another predicate will be used to denote the value of the input at an access point *id* that a current output refers to. Starting from the round where the output occurs, this input is characterized as a previous valid input after which no other output occurred before now:

$$\begin{aligned} &previous\_valid\_input(id, value) :=\\ &\qquad \neg output\_at(id) \text{ MODIFIED\_SINCE } valid\_input(id, value). \end{aligned}$$

Finally, a correct connection during a certain transaction is defined. At present, the following complicated formalization is only used with initialization, whereas the 2- and 3-party transactions have simpler definitions. Requirements are considered from the point of view of an interest group and thus from a subset, *subset*, of the intended participants of the transaction. The set *subset* need not be the whole interest group, but those members of the interest group who intend to take part. Hence there should be an input (*transaction_type*, *access_points*) where *access_points* comprises this subset and is of the correct type. Moreover, the subset should be connected in the same way in each round of a transaction, i.e., the identities must appear in the same positions in the lists *access_points* throughout the transaction. Let *positions_in*(*subset*, *access_points*) denote those positions. (That is, *positions_in* is a fixed function, and each image *pos* is a mapping from *subset* to $\mathbb{N}$.) Then, for a variable *pos*, which denotes such positions, let

$$\begin{aligned}&\mathit{correct\_connection}(\mathit{transaction\_type}, \mathit{subset}, \mathit{pos}) := \exists \mathit{access\_points}:\\&\qquad (\mathit{transaction\_type}, \mathit{access\_points}) \in \mathit{connections}\\&\qquad \wedge\ \mathit{positions\_in}(\mathit{subset}, \mathit{access\_points}) = \mathit{pos}\\&\qquad \wedge\ \mathit{type\_of}(\mathit{access\_points}) \in \mathit{permitted\_connections}(\mathit{transaction\_type}).\end{aligned}$$

Intended Use of Initialization

The intended use of initialization is as follows: For each identity of a signer, id_S, there should be only one initialization. It should happen before any other transaction referring to id_S. (Transactions with other signers are possible before.) The signer, all courts, and all intended recipients should take part; they should input consistent parameters $ids_{R,init}$ and N; and the correct connection commands should be given.

A strong precondition in each minimal requirement (see Section 5.2.3) is that the members of the interest group behave in exactly this way.

Why is one initialization enough? One should check that the assumed user behaviour makes sense. In particular, one might think that several initialization attempts for the same identity id_S were useful in the following three types of situations.

1. The first attempt may be unsuccessful. However, effectiveness of initialization guarantees that the first initialization is successful if it is started correctly, correct connections are in place, and the signer is honest. Hence no repetition is needed in this case. Moreover, if an interest group not including the signer notices that initialization was unsuccessful (correctness of initialization guarantees that they agree on this), they know that the signer is dishonest, and hence repetition is of no use. Thus the only reason for a repetition might be that the connections were wrong the first time. However, one would then need additional requirements to ensure that the connections were at least good enough for the participants to agree that a repetition is needed.
2. If initialization is for a specific recipient only, the same signer might want additional initializations for other recipients. However, those have to be under different identities anyway in the model, because the identity of the signer is treated as the only identifier linking later transactions to the corresponding initialization. (For instance, if an ordinary digital signature scheme is represented, a court's entity must retrieve the public key of a signer according to id_S alone.) In such cases, a pair of pseudonyms of the signer and the recipient can serve as id_S.
3. Reinitialization may be needed because the message bound from the first initialization has been reached. However, as in the second situation, the reinitialization has to be under a new identity, so that each transaction can be linked to the correct initialization. In particular, it has been required that received

authenticated messages are valid in disputes indefinitely. Hence some information from the old initialization must be stored anyway. In practice, an identity id_S might contain the date when initialization was carried out.

Interesting states. Some formal predicates specifying correct initialization are now defined. An interest group can essentially be in one of three states with respect to an identity id_S:

- *No_init*: No initialization has taken place yet.
- *Correct_init_use*: One correct and successful initialization has taken place (where correct and successful refer to the interface view of the interest group).
- *Wrong_init*: An incorrect initialization or an attempt at a second initialization has taken place.

Furthermore, there is an intermediate state *During_init* during the first initialization. A state-transition diagram is shown in Figure 5.7.

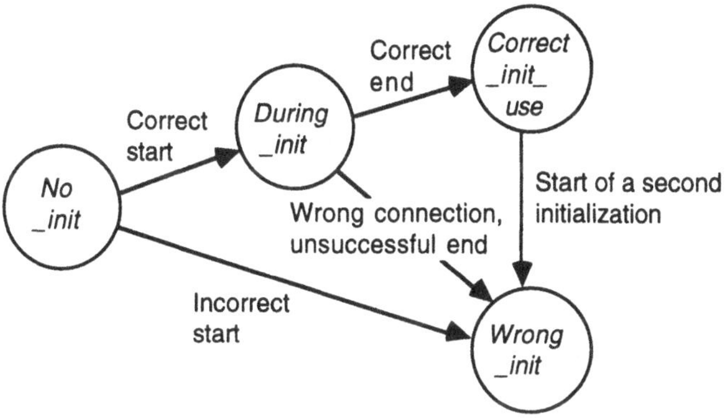

Figure 5.7. State-transition diagram for initializations.
Everything refers to one interest group and one identity of a signer.

Formal predicates. The first predicate models that the user with identity *id* tries to start initialization for the signer id_S in the current round. It reflects that initializations for id_S cannot be attempted at signer access points other than id_S. The parameters $ids_{R,init}$ and N are the set of possible recipients and the message bound that this user wants.

$$
\begin{aligned}
&init\_attempt(id, id_S, ids_{R,init}, N) := \\
&\qquad (\, id \in Id_S \rightarrow (id = id_S \wedge valid\_input(id, (\text{'}init\text{'}, ids_{R,init}, N)))) \\
&\qquad \wedge\, (id \in Id_R \cup Id_C \rightarrow valid\_input(id, (\text{'}init\text{'}, id_S, ids_{R,init}, N))).
\end{aligned}
$$

The next predicate represents that an interest group is in the state *No_init* at the beginning of the current round, i.e., no attempt at an initialization has been made prior to this round:

$no\_init(interest\_group, id_S) :=$
$\quad \forall id \in interest\_group\ \forall ids_{R,init} \in Ids_{R,init}(Id_R)\ \forall N \in Message\_bounds:$
$\quad\quad$ WEAK_PREVIOUS
$\quad\quad\quad$ ALWAYS_IN_THE_PAST $\neg\ init\_attempt(id, id_S, ids_{R,init}, N).$

In rounds where it is clear that one initialization for id_S has already taken place (and the following predicate will only be used in such contexts), the fact that a second initialization occurs among *interest_group* can simply be expressed by

$second\_init(interest\_group, id_S) :=$
$\quad \exists id \in interest\_group\ \exists ids_{R,init} \in Ids_{R,init}(Id_R)\ \exists N \in Message\_bounds:$
$\quad\quad init\_attempt(id, id_S, ids_{R,init}, N).$

The next predicate models that a set *interest_group* makes consistent inputs to start initialization for id_S, coming from the state *No_init*, and that all recipients in *interest_group* are among the intended recipients according to this initialization.

$correct\_init\_start(interest\_group, id_S, ids_{R,init}, N) :=$
$\quad (\forall id \in interest\_group: init\_attempt(id, id_S, ids_{R,init}, N))$
$\quad \wedge\ no\_init(interest\_group, id_S)$
$\quad \wedge\ interest\_group \cap Id_R \subseteq ids_{R,init}.$

Similarly, the next predicate models that an initialization comes to a successful end with the output parameter ids_{out} in the current round.[44]

$correct\_init\_end(interest\_group, ids_{out}) := \forall id \in interest\_group:$
$\quad (id, out, (\text{TRUE}, ids_{out})) \in events.$

A predicate for the entire transition from the state *No_init* to *Correct_init_use* is defined next. It is true in a round where an initialization ends successfully. Before that, there must have been a correct start of an initialization; and since this start, no other outputs may have occurred and correct connections must have been provided. The connections must already be in place in the round of the start and are no longer needed in the round with the end; the same holds for the absence of other outputs.[45]

$correct\_initialization(interest\_group, id_S, ids_{out}, N) :=$
$\quad correct\_init\_end(interest\_group, ids_{out})$
$\quad \wedge\ \exists pos\ \exists ids_{R,init} \in Ids_{R,init}(Id_R):$
$\quad\quad ((no\_output\_at(interest\_group)$
$\quad\quad\quad \wedge\ correct\_connection(\text{'}initialization\text{'}, interest\_group, pos))$
$\quad\quad$ MODIFIED_SINCE $correct\_init\_start(interest\_group, id_S, ids_{R,init}, N)).$

Finally, it is represented that an interest group is in the state *Correct_init_use* at the beginning of the current round (so that it can start another transaction in this round):

---

44 Here it is required that initialization ends at the same time for all participants. Otherwise the connections would be more complicated to handle. As initialization without centres usually works on broadcast channels, this is no serious restriction. However, it is not required here that all the recipients and courts of the interest group are in ids_{out}; this can be left to the correctness of initialization.

45 The predicate permits that an initialization ends in the very first round. This is unrealistic, but one should rather prove impossibility than exclude it in the definition.

$correct\_init\_use(interest\_group, id_S, ids_{out}, N) :=$
PREVIOUS
$(\neg second\_init(interest\_group, id_S)$
SINCE $correct\_initialization(interest\_group, id_S, ids_{out}, N))$.

The formal parameters in this predicate are exactly those values that make a difference for the future behaviour of the system, i.e., that have to be known in the requirements.

5.2.7 Minimal Requirements

In this section, the minimal requirements sketched in Section 5.2.2 are described in more detail. The two requirements on disputes are expressed in the formal notation introduced in Section 5.2.6. The others are discussed informally. As mentioned, the preconditions about connections, the relations between different parameters about identities of recipients, and the treatment of system termination are provisional.

Requirement of the Recipient on Disputes

The requirement of the recipient on disputes is, in fact, a requirement of an interest group consisting of a recipient, $id_R \in Id_R$, and a court, $id_C \in Id_C$.

The recipient wishes that any message he has accepted as authenticated should also be accepted by the court if a dispute about this message arises. However, in a minimal requirement fulfilled by invisible signature schemes, too, one has to allow the court to decide that the signer has not cooperated. Hence the result should be TRUE or *'not_cooperated'*.

An even weaker requirement of the recipient would be that the court does not obtain the output FALSE, but any other element of *Dispute_results* would be permitted. In particular, such a generalization would be needed if accountable centres were allowed, see Section 5.2.3. However, one must ensure that for each result, there is an interest group that wants to avoid it, at least under some circumstances such as disavowing. Otherwise one might end up with a scheme where courts always decide *'I_don't_know'*. Hence this generalization is not made here.

Furthermore, the precondition is made that the entities of the recipient and the court are in the state *Correct_init_use* (see Figure 5.7) during both the dispute and the execution of authentication where the recipient accepted the message, see Figure 5.8.

Now some predicates corresponding to the events in Figure 5.8 are defined. The first one is true exactly in a round where the recipient obtains the output that the message he had asked to test has been accepted.

$recipient\_accepts(id_R, m, id_S) :=$
$(id_R, out, \text{TRUE}) \in events$
$\wedge\, previous\_valid\_input(id_R, (\text{'}test\text{'}, m, id_S))$.

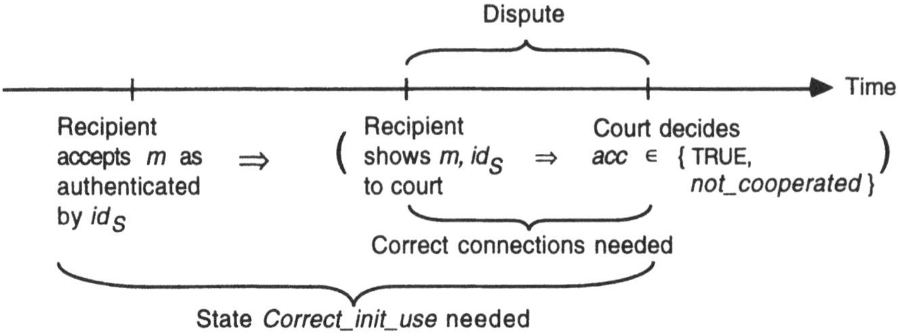

Figure 5.8. Sketch of the requirement of the recipient on disputes

The next predicate is true in a round where the recipient and the court start a dispute about this message consistently:

$$\begin{aligned} &\mathit{shows\_to}(id_R, id_C, m, id_S, ids_{R,dec}) := \\ &\qquad \mathit{valid\_input}(id_R, (\text{'}\mathit{show}\text{'}, m, id_S)) \\ &\qquad \wedge\ \mathit{valid\_input}(id_C, (\text{'}\mathit{decide}\text{'}, m, id_S, ids_{R,dec})). \end{aligned}$$

The permitted results of such a dispute are modeled next; the word "weakly" denotes that the output *'not_cooperated'* is possible.[46]

$$\begin{aligned} &\mathit{recipient\_weakly\_wins}(id_R, id_C) := \\ &\qquad ((id_C, \mathit{out}, \text{TRUE}) \in \mathit{events} \\ &\qquad\ \ \vee (id_C, \mathit{out}, \text{'}\mathit{not\_cooperated}\text{'}) \in \mathit{events}) \\ &\qquad \wedge\ \exists acc_R \in \mathit{Show\_results}\colon (id_R, \mathit{out}, acc_R) \in \mathit{events}. \end{aligned}$$

The proper connections are rather simple in this case: In each round, a connection between the recipient, the court, and possibly a signer must exist.

$$\begin{aligned} &\mathit{properly\_connected}(\text{'}\mathit{dispute}\text{'}, \{id_R, id_C\}) := \exists \mathit{access\_points}\colon \\ &\qquad (\text{'}\mathit{dispute}\text{'}, \mathit{access\_points}) \in \mathit{connections} \\ &\qquad \wedge\ (\mathit{access\_points} = (id_R, id_C) \\ &\qquad\quad \vee\ \exists id_S \in Id_S\colon \mathit{access\_points} = (id_R, id_C, id_S)). \end{aligned}$$

The previous three predicates, which were state formulas, are now combined into a temporal predicate that means that *if* a dispute is started correctly in the current round and correct connections are provided, it yields the correct result. The timing is as follows: There should be no other output until the correct result, except that it is no longer specified what the system does if the connections were wrong in the previous round. Of course, this exception only holds from the second round onwards. Hence the formula treats the first round separately, and then the remaining rounds after "WEAK_NEXT".

46 The requirement that the recipient obtains an output could have been deferred to the availability of service, but connections are easier to handle if the outputs are required to occur simultaneously. The value of this output is usually simply *'eot'*.

$recipient\_can\_weakly\_convince(id_R, id_C, m, id_S, ids_{R,dec}) :=$
$\quad shows\_to(id_R, id_C, m, id_S, ids_{R,dec})$
$\quad \to (recipient\_weakly\_wins(id_R, id_C)$
$\quad\quad \vee\ no\_output\_at(\{id_R, id_C\})$
$\quad\quad\quad \wedge$ WEAK_NEXT
$\quad\quad\quad\quad (no\_output\_at(\{id_R, id_C\})$
$\quad\quad\quad\quad$ UNLESS $(recipient\_weakly\_wins(id_R, id_C)$
$\quad\quad\quad\quad\quad \vee$ PREVIOUS $\neg properly\_connected(\text{'dispute'}, \{id_R, id_C\})))).$

The reason for using UNLESS, and not UNTIL, is that it is currently not guaranteed in the structure that sequences never end in the middle of transactions. Anyway, availability of service will be a general requirement that transactions do end.

Finally, the requirement can be assembled. The recipient and the court, i.e., the interest group, are formal parameters. The requirement says that whenever a recipient has accepted a message, he can from then on convince the court in the sense defined above, provided that both transactions occur in the state *Correct_init_use*. Recall that the predicate *suitable* defined what parameters $ids_{R,dec}$ can be used.

$Req_{rec}(id_R, id_C) :=$
$\quad \forall id_S \in Id_S\ \forall m \in M\ \forall ids_{out} \in \mathcal{P}(Id_R \cup Id_C)\ \forall N \in Message\_bounds:$
$\quad$ HENCEFORTH
$\quad\quad ((recipient\_accepts(id_R, m, id_S)$
$\quad\quad\quad \wedge\ correct\_init\_use(\{id_R, id_C\}, id_S, ids_{out}, N))$
$\quad\quad \to$ WEAK_NEXT $\forall ids_{R,dec}:$
$\quad\quad\quad ((suitable(Id_R, ids_{out}, ids_{R,dec}) \wedge id_R \in ids_{R,dec})$
$\quad\quad\quad \to (recipient\_can\_weakly\_convince(id_R, id_C, m, id_S, ids_{R,dec})$
$\quad\quad\quad\quad$ UNLESS $second\_init(\{id_R, id_C\}, id_S)))).$

Some explanations of the timing in this formula follow.

- The operator WEAK_NEXT is necessary because showing only works after accepting, i.e., from the next round on.
- Formally, *correct_init_use* is required in the round where the recipient accepts, whereas informally, it was required at the beginning of this execution of authentication. This makes no difference, because the definition of *recipient_accepts* says that the command to test was a previous valid input, i.e., initialization cannot have ended in between.
- Formally, attempts at a second initialization are excluded from the round after accepting until the round before the command to show the signature; informally, they should be excluded from the round where the recipient accepts until the end of the dispute. This makes no difference, because inputs in those other rounds would be invalid.

Requirement of the Signer on Disputes

The requirement of the signer on disputes is a requirement of an interest group consisting of a signer, $id_S \in Id_S$, and a court, $id_C \in Id_C$.

The signer wishes that the court should not accept a message as authenticated by her if she had not actually authenticated it. However, in a minimal requirement fulfilled by all signature schemes, this can only be required if the signer disavows. Furthermore, there is a precondition that the entities of the signer and the court are in the state *Correct_init_use* during the dispute (see Figure 5.9).

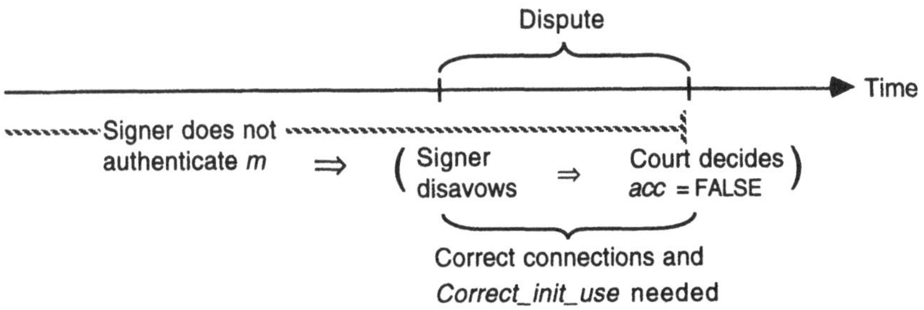

Figure 5.9. Sketch of the requirement of the signer on disputes.
The dotted line indicates the period of time where the signer must not have authenticated *m* for the result *acc* = FALSE to be guaranteed.

The events occurring in Figure 5.9 are formalized in the following predicates. The first predicate would hold in a round where the signer gave a command to sign the disputed message:

$$signer\_signs(id_S, m) := \exists ids_{R,sign} \subseteq Id_R\text{:}\quad valid\_input(id_S, (\text{'}sign\text{'}, m, ids_{R,sign})).$$

With this existential quantifier over $ids_{R,sign}$, the minimal requirement will allow the court to accept the message from a different recipient. This is important in practice: A parameter $ids_{R,sign} \neq Any$ is normally not used to restrict the recipients, but to enable optimization — even the efficiency of some ordinary digital signature schemes can greatly be improved if several messages have the same recipient and the signer inputs this fact to her entity [FoPf91].

Furthermore, the fact that validity of the signer's input was required means that the schemes *must* ignore commands to sign before other transactions have ended. One might weaken this.

The next predicate is true in the round where the signer and the court start a dispute consistently:

$$disavows(id_S, id_C, m, ids_{R,dec}) := valid\_input(id_S, (\text{'}disavow\text{'}, m, ids_{R,dec})) \wedge valid\_input(id_C, (\text{'}decide\text{'}, m, id_S, ids_{R,dec})).$$

The desired result of such a dispute is modeled next:

$$signer\_wins(id_S, id_C) := (id_C, out, \text{FALSE}) \in events \wedge \exists acc_S \in Disavow\_results\text{: } (id_S, out, acc_S) \in events.$$

The predicates for proper connections and a complete successful dispute are similar to those in the requirement of the recipient on disputes:

$$properly\_connected('dispute', \{id_S, id_C\}) := \exists access\_points: \\ ('dispute', access\_points) \in connections \\ \wedge (access\_points = (id_C, id_S) \\ \vee \exists id_R \in Id_R: access\_points = (id_R, id_C, id_S))$$

and

$$signer\_can\_convince(id_S, id_C, m, ids_{R,dec}) := \\ disavows(id_S, id_C, m, ids_{R,dec}) \\ \rightarrow (signer\_wins(id_S, id_C) \\ \vee no\_output\_at(\{id_S, id_C\}) \\ \wedge \text{WEAK\_NEXT} \\ (no\_output\_at(\{id_S, id_C\}) \\ \text{UNLESS } (signer\_wins(id_S, id_C) \\ \vee \text{PREVIOUS } \neg properly\_connected('dispute', \{id_S, id_C\})))).$$

Hence one obtains the following requirement:

$$Req_{sig}(id_S, id_C) := \\ \forall m \in M \ \forall ids_{out} \in \mathcal{P}(Id_R \cup Id_C) \ \forall N \in Message\_bounds: \\ \text{HENCEFORTH} \\ (correct\_initialization(\{id_S, id_C\}, id_S, ids_{out}, N) \\ \rightarrow \text{WEAK\_NEXT } \forall ids_{R,dec}: \\ (suitable(Id_R, ids_{out}, ids_{R,dec}) \\ \rightarrow (signer\_can\_convince(id_S, id_C, m, ids_{R,dec}) \\ \text{UNLESS } (signer\_signs(id_S, m) \\ \vee second\_init(\{id_S, id_C\}, id_S))))).$$

In Figure 5.9, it was required that the signer had not authenticated the message or attempted a second initialization until directly before the end of the dispute, whereas formally, it is only required until the beginning. However, the signer makes a valid input to disavow in this round and therefore cannot make any further valid inputs before the end of the dispute. In stronger requirements where the cooperation of the signer in the dispute is not a precondition, the formalization must follow the figure more closely.

Unforgeability

Unforgeability is a joint requirement of a signer, $id_S \in Id_S$, and a recipient, $id_R \in Id_R$: As long as the signer has not authenticated a particular message (defined as in the requirement of the signer on disputes), the recipient should not accept it (defined as in the requirement of the recipient on disputes). A precondition is that the recipient only inputs the command to test when he and the signer are in the state *Correct_init_use*. No correct connections are needed, except for those implicit in the correct use of initialization. The timing is shown in Figure 5.10.

Unforgeability is the main requirement on mere (usually symmetric) authentication schemes. However, it is a matter of taste if it should be among the minimal requirements on digital signature schemes. An intuitive argument for omitting unforgeability is that recipients do not always care who has authenticated a message. For

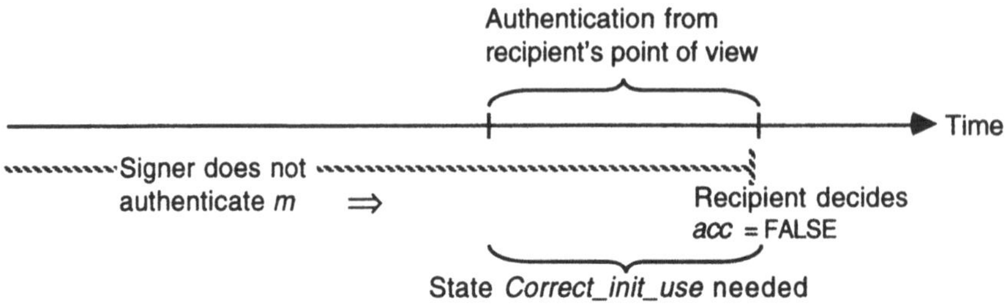

Figure 5.10. Sketch of unforgeability

instance, the recipient of an authenticated mail order only wants to be sure that he can claim his money in court. (Then, however, unforgeability might be required as a part of the availability of service: If forging were easy, there might be too many disputes.)

Formally, these considerations are of little importance, because unforgeability (or at least an intuitively sufficient, slightly weaker version of it) seems to be a consequence of the other requirements. In this case, it is unnecessary as a separate requirement. A proof sketch follows in Section 5.4.4.

However, if one considers signature-like schemes with accountable centres, one may forego unforgeability in favour of efficiency, see Section 5.2.3.

Effectiveness of Authentication

Effectiveness of authentication is a joint requirement of a signer, $id_S \in Id_S$, and a recipient, $id_R \in Id_R$. Basically, it means that if the signer inputs a command to sign a message and the recipient inputs the corresponding command to test the message from that signer, the recipient should obtain the output acc = TRUE. The signer should obtain some output, too, so that she knows that the transaction has ended.

A precondition is that the signer and the recipient are in the state *Correct_init_use* at the beginning of this transaction. Furthermore, the recipient must be among the possible recipients according to both the input $ids_{R,sign}$ and the corresponding initialization.

The only exception is that authentication need not work if the message bound N has been reached. Expressing this condition in temporal logic is probably not the most natural way, but it can be done with a flexible variable *counter* (i.e., *counter* may assume different values in different rounds — this is the opposite of a rigid variable), which is formally used to count executions of authentication.

Effectiveness of Initialization

Effectiveness of initialization is a requirement of an interest group consisting of a signer id_S and at least one recipient or court: If they input consistent commands to start an initialization for id_S (according to the predicate *correct_init_start*), the initialization should yield the result acc = TRUE for them all, provided they were in the state *No_init* and are correctly connected throughout the initialization.

When security is considered later, this requirement yields the statement that any subset of the participants that includes the signer can carry out initialization successfully even if all the other participants try to disturb them. This is why initialization sometimes needs identities as output parameters: If the structure of an implementation prescribes that more participants than the signer play an active part in initialization, they may always disrupt. Thus the best thing one can do is to detect disturbances and to finish initialization with fewer participants. In these cases, the users will want to know with whom initialization was finally successful.

Correctness of Initialization

While effectiveness of authentication can only be required if the signer is in the interest group, arbitrary interest groups require correctness of initialization: If they take part in an initialization correctly (defined as above), it is required that

- they all obtain identical results (acc, ids_{out}), i.e., they agree upon whether the initialization was successful or not and with whom,
- and none of them is excluded, i.e., all their identities are elements of ids_{out}.

The first of these properties is called consistency.

Availability of Service

So far, no requirement required that any output ever occurred. They only specified what the outputs should be *if* they occurred.

Availability of service is the general term for requirements that the system provides service with reasonable delay; in particular, deliberate denial of service should be impossible or at least hard. Such requirements are not present in most current definitions of types of signature schemes, because most of them fix a fairly simple structure, from which availability of service can easily be seen.

For cryptologic transaction schemes in general, one can distinguish the behaviour within and between transactions. Here, the assumptions from Section 5.1.2, "Time" and "Transactions", and the definition of valid inputs have simplified this considerably; it only remains to be required that every valid input at some access point is followed by an output at this access point within reasonable time. The interest group consists of this access point alone. This means that the access point returns to a state where the user can input commands for new transactions even if all the partners in the current transaction behave incorrectly.

Formally, one can use the operator EVENTUALLY from temporal logic, for instance, as ($\exists$*value*: *valid_input*(*id*, *value*)) $\rightarrow$ EVENTUALLY *output_at*(*id*). One must then take care in the definition of systems and their runs that all entities somehow finish their current transactions before a run ends, i.e., one cannot consider prefixes of runs. Moreover, such a specification does not reflect the reasonable time in which the output should occur.

One can also use formulas that prescribe an upper bound on the number of rounds after which an output occurs. This solves both problems mentioned above. However, in some schemes the number of rounds needed for a transaction depends on security parameters (which were modeled as system parameters, not specification parameters), e.g., the verification protocols of some invisible signature schemes.

Finally, one could use a special operator, such as SOON, which is to be interpreted in dependence on the security parameters; or one could use two different models of time inside the system and at the interface, so that the relation between these two notions is what depends on the parameters.

A problem that cannot be avoided by the signature scheme is that someone swamps other users outside the system, e.g., courts, with so much work that they can no longer perform the necessary work. However, as an explicit command from each transaction partner is needed in every transaction, no attack of this kind can happen inside the system.

5.2.8 Stronger Requirements

The first type of additional service properties is that some signature schemes fulfil stronger versions of the requirements on the results of the three common transactions, in particular disputes.

Strong Requirement of the Recipient on Disputes

As mentioned in Section 5.2.2, the recipient wishes that any message he has accepted as authenticated should also be accepted by a court in a subsequent dispute. A weaker minimal requirement was made because of invisible signature schemes (see Figure 5.8). Most signature schemes, however, fulfil the recipient's original wish.

One can easily obtain a formal version of this strong requirement of the recipient on disputes from the weak one by replacing the predicate *recipient_weakly_wins* by the predicate

$$\begin{aligned} &\mathit{recipient\_wins}(id_R, id_C) := \\ &\qquad (id_C, \mathit{out}, \text{TRUE}) \in \mathit{events} \\ &\qquad \wedge\, \exists acc_R \in \mathit{Show\_results}\colon (id_R, \mathit{out}, acc_R) \in \mathit{events}. \end{aligned}$$

For comparison with the following requirements of the signer, these two possibilities are represented in a small table (ignoring identity parameters to concentrate on the results of disputes):

Earlier	Start of dispute	Possible sets of permitted results
recipient_accepts	*shows_to*	{TRUE} {TRUE, *'not_cooperated'*}

Table 5.1. Overview of requirements of the recipient on disputes

Stronger Requirements of the Signer on Disputes

With the signer's requirements, there are more possibilities. The most important ones deal with the following question: What happens if the signer does not take part in a dispute about a message she has not authenticated?

- **Strong requirement of the signer on disputes.** Even if the signer does not cooperate, the court's output *acc* is FALSE. Hence an input *'disavow'* is unnecessary. This requirement is interesting in practice, because it means that one does not need provisions for finding the signer if one wants to carry out a fair dispute. It is sketched in Figure 5.11. No correct connections are needed.
- **Medium requirement of the signer on disputes.** If the signer does not cooperate, *acc* may be FALSE or *'not_cooperated'*, but not TRUE. The timing and the preconditions are identical to those in the strong requirement.

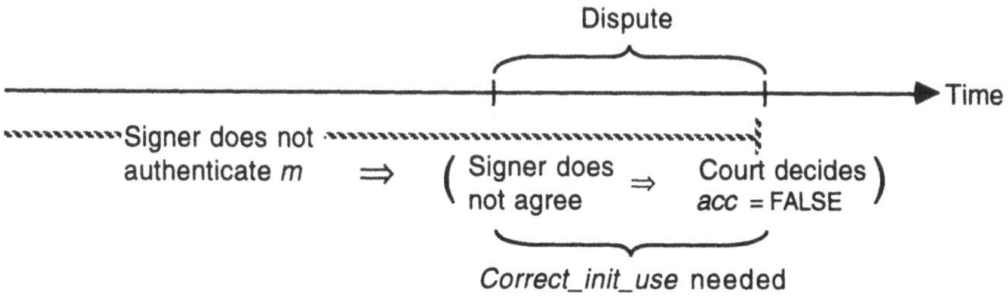

Figure 5.11. Strong requirement of the signer on disputes.
The dotted line indicates the period of time where the signer must not have authenticated *m* for the result *acc* = FALSE to be guaranteed.

The following Table 5.2 shows all variants that seem moderately sensible, including a command *'agree'* for a signer to agree to having authenticated the message.[47]

Earlier	Start of dispute	Possible sets of permitted results
¬*signer_signs*	*'disavow'*	• {FALSE}
	No command	• **{FALSE}** • **{FALSE, *'not_cooperated'*}** • **No restriction**
	'agree'	• No restriction • {TRUE} • Same set as with "No command"
signer_signs	*'disavow'*	• No restriction
	No command	• No restriction • {FALSE, *'not_cooperated'*}
	'agree'	• No restriction • {TRUE}

Table 5.2. Overview of conceivable requirements of the signer on disputes.
The most important distinction is in bold type. "No restriction" formally means the set Dispute_results.

47 One scheme from the literature, [FuOO91], is not covered by this table, because the signer can both agree and disavow in one dispute. However, I cannot imagine an application.

Now some explanations of less important requirements from Table 5.2 follow.

- If the signer inputs a correct command *'agree'* in the dispute, one need not make any restriction on the outcome. (That is, the command *'agree'* is superfluous.)
  One conceivable alternative, as shown in the table, is to require that the outcome is TRUE in that case. However, this subsection deals with requirements in the interest of the signer and the court, and if they are honest and the signer agrees to having authenticated the message, a formal dispute need not be carried out anyway.
  Another conceivable alternative is to make the same requirement as if the signer did not input anything. However, in this case the input is useless.
- The only requirement ever made in the interest of the signer if she has in fact authenticated the message, i.e., in the lower half of Table 5.2, is the one from invisible signature schemes: There, the recipient should not be able to convince a third party, i.e., a court, that the message had been authenticated, unless the signer cooperates. However, the requirement one could make here is only a special case of invisibility, which also deals with dishonest third parties.

Important Combinations

The following combinations of requirements of the recipient and the signer on disputes are important, because they occur in practice:

- **2-party disputes.** The strong requirements of both the recipient and the signer are made. Thus, if the recipient has accepted the message as authenticated, the court's output is TRUE, and if the signer has not authenticated the message, the court's output is FALSE, even if the signer does not disavow. Hence one can carry out all disputes with 2 parties.
  Ordinary digital signature schemes and the information-theoretically secure digital signature schemes of [ChRo91, PfWa92] are of this type.
- **3-party disputes at the signer's discretion.** The weak requirement of the recipient and the medium requirement of the signer are combined. Thus the recipient tolerates that the result is sometimes *'not_cooperated'* although he had accepted the message as authenticated, and the signer tolerates that if she has not authenticated a message, but fails to take part in a dispute about it, the result may be *'not_cooperated'*, too.
  Essentially, this means that it is at the signer's discretion whether the 3-party dispute can be carried out. Of course, one needs rules outside the system to decide under which circumstances the refusal of the signer to cooperate can be taken as a sign of guilt. For instance, if a real, legal court acts in the role of court, this might be the case, whereas no signer could reasonably be expected to cooperate if friends of the recipient play court.
  This combination is offered by invisible signature schemes.
- **3-party disputes at the recipient's discretion.** The strong requirement of the recipient and the weak requirement of the signer are combined. Thus it is necessary to find the signer before one can carry out a fair dispute, because if

she does not disavow, the recipient may win the dispute although the signer never authenticated the message.

Essentially, this means that although disputes are 3-party protocols, they can take place whenever the recipient wants, and it is only in the signer's own interest to take part.

This combination occurs in some versions of fail-stop and dual signature schemes, see below.

User-Friendliness

As mentioned in Section 5.2.3, one can make stronger versions of most requirements, to make the systems safer to use. For example, one might add an output *'you cannot test anything yet, initialize first'* to the domain *Test_results* and require that it occurs whenever a recipient inputs *'test'* before *'init'* for some identity id_S. Similarly, one can require the system to recognize and reject attempts at a second initialization for the same identity. Then one can relax the preconditions about the correct use of initialization.

Directedness of Authentication

As there is a parameter $ids_{R,sign}$ describing intended recipients, one might also want to use it to restrict the validity of an authentication to these recipients. This means that nobody else should be able to win disputes about the authenticated message in court, i.e., the requirement of the signer on disputes would be strengthened. The interest group would contain the signer and the court (in contrast to invisibility, which may otherwise seem related).

A general measure to construct a scheme with directedness of authentication from an arbitrary given signature scheme is that the signer's entity prefixes $ids_{R,sign}$ to the message before authenticating it with the given scheme. The formalization of who has won the dispute is given by $ids_{R,dec}$, which usually describes just one recipient.

Several variants are conceivable; in particular, the intended recipients may or may not belong to the interest group. If they do, one can alternatively define that someone else has won the dispute by the fact that none of the intended recipients has input the corresponding command *'show'*. In this case, one will combine a given signature scheme with a secrecy scheme for messages between entities. This should work with most signature schemes, but not always, because it is conceivable that later authentications with the attacker as the intended recipient divulge former authentications.

5.2.9 Multiple Specifications for Different Degrees of Security

As several degrees of security exist with which specifications can be fulfilled, one can make multiple specifications for the same scheme, one for each degree of security. Typically, one degree of security, *high*, is higher than another one, *low*, in the sense that any requirement fulfilled with the degree *high* is also fulfilled with the degree *low*. One can make more or stronger requirements for the lower degree of security, or, equivalently, on stronger assumptions about the type of attacks that may occur. In fault tolerance, this is known as graceful degradation [AnLe81]. The fail-stop property is the only example of multiple specifications in the following.[48]

Fail-Stop Property

Generally. Generally and informally, a fail-stop property can be expressed as follows: On a strong assumption (i.e., with a degree *low*), one has the service one really wants; but if the assumption turns out to be wrong, the system at least notifies its users of this case, instead of producing wrong outputs that look correct. In fault tolerance, this corresponds to raising an *exception* [AnLe81]. Hence one or more special values, such as *'broken'*, are needed in the output domains. In the specification for the degree *low*, these outputs are required never to occur, and all the requirements that one really wants (e.g., those from Section 5.2.7) are made. In the so-called fall-back specification for the degree *high*, some of the original requirements are relaxed so that the results can be either *'broken'* or what they should have been originally.

In signature schemes. The fail-stop property of signature schemes specifically deals with the two requirements on disputes. In principle, it can be combined with any versions of those (see Section 5.2.8). In the following, only signature schemes without outputs *'not_cooperated'* are considered, i.e., not invisible signature schemes. Hence the strong requirement of the recipient on disputes is used. In contrast, a fall-back version of the minimal requirement of the signer on disputes is used in all current schemes, i.e., the participation of the signer is needed to obtain the output *'broken'* in disputes. (Recall that it was the signer who computed the proof of forgery in Figure 3.2.)

Hence the following fall-back requirements are made (with the usual preconditions about the correct use of initialization and correct connections in the dispute, and the same interest groups as before):

- **Strong fall-back requirement of the recipient on disputes.** Once a recipient has accepted a certain message as authenticated by a certain signer, a court should obtain a result $acc \in$ {TRUE, *'broken'*} in a dispute about this message.
- **Weak fall-back requirement of the signer on disputes.** As long as a signer has not authenticated a certain message, a court should obtain a result $acc \in$ {FALSE, *'broken'*} in a dispute about this message, at least if the signer disavows.

These were the two requirements for the degree *high*. In addition, there is the requirement that the output *'broken'* only occurs when it is correct, i.e., when the assumption has been broken. In other words, for the degree *low* it is required that this output does not occur at all.

48 Moreover, the fail-stop property will only be used with two specific degrees of security: *low* is "on a cryptologic assumption" and *high* "information-theoretically". In principle, other combinations are also possible, for instance that *low* needs an upper bound on the number of attackers and *high* means that more attackers are tolerated.

- **Correctness of *'broken'*.** The output *acc* = *'broken'* should never occur in disputes. The interest group consists of the court in this dispute.

These new requirements and the original ones are illustrated in Figure 5.12.

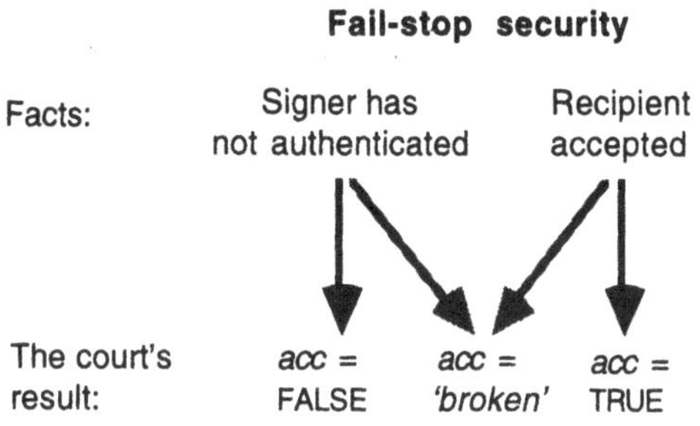

Figure 5.12. Requirements on the court's output in schemes with a fail-stop property. Black arrows show the strong requirements for the low degree of security, i.e., for normal situations. (It is assumed that honest users behave sensibly in the details that are not shown in the figure, e.g., the signer disavows if she has not authenticated.) Grey arrows show transitions that are additionally possible in extreme situations. Transitions without any arrow are excluded with both degrees of security.

For a comparison, other types of security are already shown in Figure 5.13.

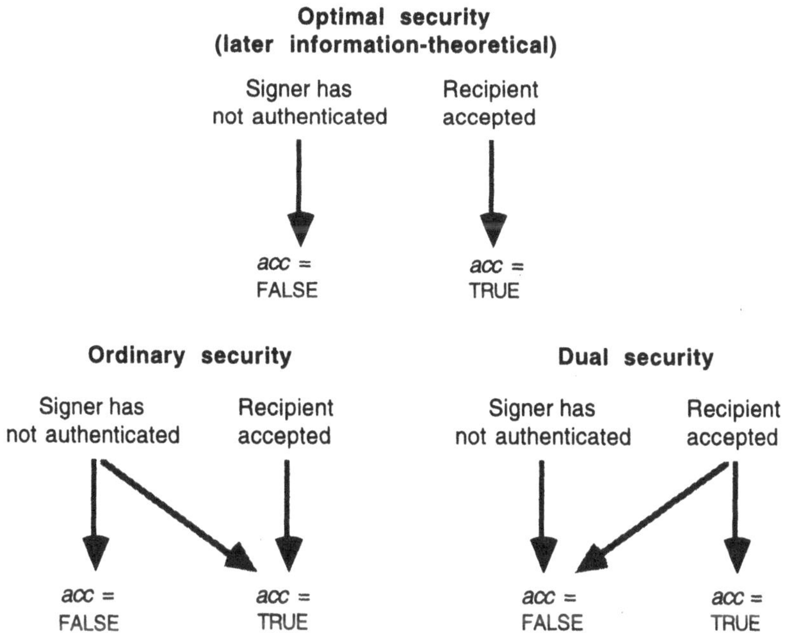

Figure 5.13. Requirements on the court's output in other types of security.

These security types are mainly treated in Section 5.4.3. With the "ordinary" type of security, known from ordinary digital signature schemes, the requirement of the recipient on disputes is guaranteed with the high degree of security, whereas the court may wrongly decide for the recipient in extreme situations. To its right, a type of security dual to ordinary security is shown.

The fail-stop property is stronger than both these types: One can simulate ordinary security by identifying *'broken'* with TRUE and dual security by identifying *'broken'* with FALSE.

At the top, the optimal situation is shown, where the court always decides correctly. Fail-stop security would therefore be placed in the middle of this diagram.

Combinations

The strong requirement of the recipient and the weak requirement of the signer on disputes (for the degree *low*) are consequences of the three new requirements on disputes, if they are in fact used in situations where the degree *high* is higher than the degree *low*. Hence they need not be proved separately for concrete fail-stop signature schemes.

However, one can add the strong requirement of the signer for the degree *low*. Then the signer can only be wrongly made responsible for a message if both the assumption for the degree *low* has been broken and she fails to take part in the dispute. This seems to be a suitable combination in practice, because signers might lose their devices or die. See Section 7.1.4 for realizations.

The remaining requirements, i.e., those on authentication and initialization, are usually made for the degree *high*, except for unforgeability, which is in the specification for the degree *low* only.

Special Risk Bearers

In this subsection, a weaker version of the fail-stop property is explained. In the notation of Section 5.2.3, it yields a signature-like scheme with accountable centres. Such schemes are called **fail-stop signature schemes with special risk bearers**. Where a distinction is necessary, the real signature schemes with a fail-stop property as described above are called **full fail-stop signature schemes**, and their property a full fail-stop property.

The idea is that there may be special users who are held responsible if the output *'broken'* occurs. Such people are called risk bearers. For instance, an insurance may have to pay up in this case, or the party that has introduced the signature scheme, or always the recipient and not the signer. In this case, the correctness of *'broken'* is only required in the interest of the court in that dispute plus at least one risk bearer, and the original requirements of the signer and the recipient are relaxed so as to allow the output *'broken'* even for the degree *low*.

Thus the full fail-stop property is one where everybody is regarded as a risk bearer (except that they do not have special access points for their role as risk bearers then). The full fail-stop property is useful, for instance, if one wants unforgeability in the original sense, or if the system is completely stopped once the output *'broken'* occurs and everybody considers this a nuisance.

The modifications in the specification brought about by special risk bearers are now summarized with a few more details than in Section 5.2.3.[49]

- There are special access points for risk bearers.
- All risk bearers may take part in each initialization, and the identities of the risk bearers that took part successfully are denoted by an additional output parameter $ids_{Risk,out}$.
- Risk bearers do not take part in any other transactions.

The requirements are altered as follows:

- The requirements of the recipient and the signer on disputes (with the original interest groups) are weakened: Neither the signer nor the recipient minds if the court's output is *'broken'*. (Compare the third paragraph in the subsection "Requirement of the Recipient on Disputes" in Section 5.2.7.) Thus these requirements become identical to the fall-back requirements, which belong to the degree *high*, and can be omitted if *high* is higher than *low*.
- The correctness of *'broken'* is required in the interest of the court in the given dispute and any risk bearer. Hence any single risk bearer can guarantee that the output *'broken'* does not occur (with the degree *low*).
- Unforgeability is weakened by requiring it in the interest of groups consisting of the signer, the recipient, and any risk bearer. Thus all risk bearers together may be able to forge.
- Effectiveness of authentication is unchanged.
- Effectiveness of initialization is weakened by requiring it in the interest of groups consisting of the signer, at least one recipient or court, and any risk bearer.
- Correctness of initialization is extended by a requirement in the interest of the signer and at least one recipient or court: If initialization is not successful, then $ids_{Risk,out} = \emptyset$, i.e., it is clear that the failure was due to cheating by all risk bearers. (More intuitively, as initialization is no longer guaranteed to be effective even if the signer is honest, one should be able to distinguish whose fault it was if something goes wrong.) Naturally, consistency is also required for $ids_{Risk,out}$, and each risk bearer requires not to be excluded, i.e., that its identity is in $ids_{Risk,out}$.
- Availability of service remains unchanged.

Effectiveness of initialization can be omitted in this case, because it follows from the remaining requirements, see Section 5.4.4.

49 The following requirements are stronger than the minimal ones for signature-like schemes with accountable centres. In particular, effectiveness of authentication is required even if all risk bearers are dishonest; this is needed when schemes with one risk bearer are used as building blocks for full fail-stop signature schemes.

Transferability of Proofs of Forgery

If one wants to stop the whole system after an output *'broken'* and convince many people that this was necessary, it should be possible to transfer the knowledge that the scheme has been broken. (Otherwise, the signer and the recipient would have to repeat the dispute in front of everybody.) This property is called transferability of proofs of forgery. There is an additional transaction called **transfer of a proof of forgery** between two courts.[50] The court that wants to transfer the knowledge enters *'transfer_proof'*, and the other court enters *'test_proof'* and obtains an output $acc \in \{$*'broken'*, *'not_broken'*$\}$.[51] There are two additional requirements:

- **Effectiveness of transfers of proofs of forgery.** If a court has once obtained an output *'broken'*, either in a dispute or after entering *'test_proof'*, and now carries out a transfer of a proof of forgery with another court, that court obtains the output acc = *'broken'*, too. The interest group consists of the two courts in the transfer.
- **Correctness of *'broken'*, Part 2.** The value acc = *'broken'* never occurs in transfers of proofs of forgery. The interest group consists of the receiving court in that transfer, or, if special risk bearers are considered, that court together with any risk bearer.

The first requirement is made for the degree *high*, the second one for the degree *low*.

5.2.10 Special Specification Parameters

Special Message Spaces

Normally, one requires that arbitrary messages can be authenticated, i.e., the message space M is the set of all strings over an alphabet, say $\{0, 1\}^+$. This is the case in the GMR definition. (In this sense, something like RSA is a signature scheme only in combination with the description of how arbitrarily long messages are mapped into blocks.)

However, in some applications, e.g., in payment schemes, one knows that all messages to be authenticated are very short, and some signature schemes have more efficient versions for this case. This is why signature schemes for arbitrary message spaces were allowed in Section 5.2.5. It is only assumed that the message space is non-empty.[52]

---

50 One might extend this to all types of participants, but as every user is assumed to be technically able to act as a court, this simpler version is sufficient to convince all users.

51 If one wanted more specific notions of what has been broken, the interface events could have parameters, such as the parameter *which_assumption* or the identity of the signer from the original dispute.

52 Note that the message space is independent of internal details of the system. This is important for applications, and in this framework it is clear because the message space belongs to the service. Nevertheless, in conventional descriptions of signature schemes, the message space is sometimes allowed to depend on a key or at least a security parameter, because such a dependence naturally arises in constructions. Here this will be called schemes for signing message blocks; they are only regarded as subprotocols.

Special Message Bounds

It was already explained in a footnote to Section 5.2.5 that it is useful to have signature schemes with restricted message bounds. In particular, pure one-time signature schemes, where only one message can be authenticated, are interesting building blocks for more general schemes.

Dependence of Authentication on the Recipients

Dependence of authentication on the recipients deals with the input parameters $ids_{R,x}$ and their precise domains in certain situations. As mentioned before, the cases that actually occur in the literature are all rather simple.

- **No dependence on the recipient.** All parameters are always *Any*. Hence one can as well omit them. This is the usual case with ordinary digital signature schemes.
- **Fixed recipient.** There is only one recipient in the system, i.e., $|Id_R| = 1$. Formally, this is expressed by $Recipients\_total = \{1\}$. All the remaining parameters can then be *Any*, i.e., they can be omitted.

  Particularly efficient implementations of fail-stop and dual signature schemes (see Figure 5.12) and of the ordinary digital signature scheme GMR (see [FoPf91]) exist in this case.
- **One recipient per initialization.** The total number of recipients is arbitrary, but only one recipient takes part in each initialization. This case is very similar to the previous one. Formally, it is expressed by $Recipients\_per\_init = \{1\}$, and each domain $Ids_{R,init}(Id_R)$ consists of all the one-element subsets of Id_R. The remaining parameters can be *Any* again, i.e., they can be omitted.

The following cases can also be useful:

- **Few recipients.** If there are few recipients in the system overall or per initialization, it can be more efficient to use several copies of an efficient scheme for a fixed recipient than a general scheme.
- **Recipient known in authentication.** This means that the parameters $ids_{R,sign}$ are 1-element subsets of ids_{out} of the corresponding initialization. Such inputs can be useful if signers have some recipients to whom they send many authenticated messages, because some of the efficiency improvements for fixed recipients can be applied dynamically [FoPf91]. In these cases, the disputes do not depend on the recipient, i.e., $ids_{R,dec} = ids_{R,dis} = Any$.

5.2.11 Additional Transactions

As mentioned in Section 5.2.2, several signature schemes offer more than the three common transactions. The interface events and corresponding requirements of important ones occurring in practice are now presented.

Transferability in General

Transferability means that a recipient who has accepted a message as authenticated by a certain signer can transfer it to a second recipient in such a way that the second recipient is also sure that he can win disputes about the message. In the minimal service specification, no possibility for such transfers is provided. (Showing the message to the second recipient as in a dispute does not always help, because disputes may be 3-party transactions, whereas these transfers should be 2-party transactions.) In fact, not all signature schemes offer transferability, and it is even the purpose of invisible signature schemes that they do not.

In the service specification, transferability is realized by a transaction **transfer** between two recipients.

Arbitrary Transferability

Arbitrary transferability is the special case where the second recipient is in exactly the same position with respect to the authenticated message as the first recipient, and therefore, an arbitrary number of transfers can take place.

In this case, the transaction transfer is a combination of previously known interface events: The first recipient enters $show(m, id_S)$, and the second recipient enters $test(m, id_S)$ and obtains an output *acc*. The first recipient also obtains an output, usually *'eot'*. More generally, new interface events $transfer(m, id_S)$ and $obtain(m, id_S)$ could be introduced, but they are not needed in the existing schemes.

There is one new requirement, the **effectiveness of transfers**: If someone once accepted a message as authenticated and now a transfer is started consistently, the new recipient obtains the output *acc* = TRUE (under the precondition of the state *Correct_init_use* and correct connections in the new transfer).

This definition and the requirement of the recipient on disputes imply what the second recipient in a transfer would require from disputes, because there is no formal difference between accepting a message as authenticated in authentication and in a transfer.[53]

Finite Transferability

Finite transferability is a weaker form where the recipient in a transfer is not in the same position as the original recipient: The certainty about the fact that one can win disputes about this message may decrease with each transfer, so that only a finite number λ of successive transfers is guaranteed. (This happens in the extension to [ChRo91] described in [PfWa92], whereas [ChRo91] has no transferability; see Section 6.3.4.[54]) This restriction only refers to transfers in series, whereas the number of transfers by the same recipient is not restricted. The parameter λ can be a specification parameter or an input parameter in initialization (as a component of the general parameter *par* omitted for brevity, see the end of "Initialization" in Section 5.2.4).

---

53 One might think that in signature schemes with arbitrary transferability, disputes in court could be replaced by transfers, i.e., the recipient of an authenticated message and the court would carry out a transfer transaction for that message. However, this is not possible in general, because different requirements may be fulfilled with different degrees of security. For instance, a successfully forged fail-stop signature can be transferred successfully, but it will be recognized as a forgery during a dispute in court.

54 In [PfWa92, Waid91], signature schemes with finite transferability were called pseudosignature schemes, to distinguish them from ordinary ones with arbitrary transferability.

In the case of finite transferability, the transaction transfer has a new parameter i, called the **acceptance level**. It is defined so that one can guarantee that in the i-th transfer, the message is still accepted with acceptance level i. Thus higher acceptance levels mean lower degrees of certainty, i.e., fewer future transfers.

Thus a transfer is defined by the following interface events: The first recipient inputs $show(m, id_S, i)$, and the second recipient inputs $test(m, id_S, i)$ and obtains a Boolean output *acc*. The first recipient also obtains an output, usually *'eot'*.

The command $test(m, id_S)$ from authentication could be called $test(m, id_S, 0)$ now, and $show(m, id_S)$ from a dispute could be called $show(m, id_S, \lambda + 1)$.[55]

Effectiveness of transfers is now defined as follows: A recipient can transfer a message further with any higher acceptance level, until the level λ is reached. That is, if the message was accepted in a transfer where he had input $test(m, id_S, i)$ with $i < \lambda$ (or in authentication), and now he enters $show(m, id_S, j)$ for some $j > i$ and someone else enters $test(m, id_S, j)$, that user's output will be TRUE, too (under the precondition of the state *Correct_init_use* and correct connections in the new transfer).

The **requirement of the recipient on disputes** is extended to recipients in transfers (with $i \leq \lambda$). If one has required **unforgeability**, it is extended so that nobody accepts a message as authenticated with any acceptance level as long as a signer has not authenticated it.

With these requirements, one recipient can indeed transfer an authenticated message to arbitrarily many other recipients: If he accepted it with acceptance level i, he can transfer it to them all with acceptance level $i + 1$. Hence, if one draws transfers as a tree in the natural way, effectiveness of transfers is guaranteed in any tree of depth λ.

Local Transactions

Local transactions, i.e., transactions involving only one access point, can be added quite easily to most schemes. For instance, a transaction where the signer asks how many messages can still be authenticated at a certain access point is useful. Recipients might also be interested to know with which signers they have already carried out initialization and what authenticated messages they have received.

Another transaction might exist for the duplication of an access point in some schemes. This is useful if a person wants to use several devices. (As mentioned in Section 1.3, some people regard this property as undesirable. But, e.g., consider a bank where many messages have to be authenticated.) One may also want to keep back-ups in case the main device breaks down or gets lost. With simple versions of ordinary digital signature schemes, this can be implemented by copying the same key into several entities. In general, if there are message bounds to be considered and local memory exists, more complicated implementations with more complicated specifications would be needed.

---

55 In many cases, the implementation of *show* does not depend on the parameter i — the entity simply passes a received signature on. However, implementations of *test* do depend on i.

External Verifiability of the Behaviour of Participants

External verifiability of the behaviour of participants in a transaction essentially means that there is a variant of this transaction where additional parties can observe the original participants and decide whether they behave correctly. Such a property has not been required explicitly in any previous definition of signature schemes, but it can easily be fulfilled with some types of schemes and may be needed in some applications. The same property will be needed for other types of schemes in Sections 7.3 and 7.5.2 (zero-knowledge proofs and multi-party function evaluation), and the need for it may become clearer there.

Generally. External verifiability of an output *o* of a transaction type *trans* is defined as follows: One or more additional users, called **observers**, take part in the extended transaction.

- The inputs and outputs of the original users are unchanged.
- Each observer inputs a command *'observe_trans'* with all the parameters that the original users claim to input.
- Each observer obtains an output *o_observed*. Its domain is the union of the domain of *o* and the value *'cheating'*. The value *'cheating'* means that the participant *id* where the output *o* should occur has been caught cheating, so that it cannot be determined what *o* should be.

The following requirements are made:

- In the interest of any observer and the participant *id* where *o* occurs, this observer's output *o_observed* should be equal to *o*.
- For any other interest group *interest_group* that has a requirement on *o*, and any observer *obs*, the same requirement is made on the output *o_observed* of this observer in the interest of $(\mathit{interest\_group} \setminus \{id\}) \cup \{obs\}$, except that *o_observed* may have the value *'cheating'* instead.

Usually, consistency of observations is also required, i.e., all honest observers should obtain identical results. However, this will be a consequence of a general structural requirement, see Section 5.3.2, "Structure for External Verifiability".

Authentication. For the output *acc* in authentication, external verifiability means that each observer inputs a command *'observe_authentication'* with the parameters m, ids, and $ids_{R,sign}$. Each observer receives an output *acc_observed* according to the following requirements (where the latter is derived from the effectiveness of authentication):

- In the interest of this observer and the recipient, *acc_observed* = *acc*.
- In the interest of this observer and the signer, *acc_observed* ∈ {TRUE, *'cheating'*}.

External verifiability of authentication is useful if the signer authenticates a message in exchange for something; e.g., the promissory note in Figure 1.1 may be exchanged for money. Immediately during this exchange, there may be a disagreement: The recipient claims that he could not accept the promissory note as authenticated and will not pay, whereas the signer claims that she has authenticated it correctly and wants her money now, because the recipient can force her to pay it back later. This disagreement can be settled by an observer.[56]

Note that the goal is not to convince the observer of the authentication, i.e., he need not obtain enough information to win disputes, but to convince him that the *recipient* has obtained enough information to win disputes. Furthermore, the signer cannot simply execute authentication with the observer, and the observer hand the results to the recipient, because the observer need not be generally trusted; e.g., there may be many independent observers.

External verifiability of authentication is easy to realize with the structure of ordinary digital signature schemes or fail-stop signature schemes, where everybody applies the same function *test* to signatures. However, it is certainly non-trivial in schemes where different recipients and courts use different tests, and it is not even trivial with invisible signature schemes, although all recipients use the same test program: As the verification protocol is interactive, the decision of the recipient may depend on internal values randomly chosen during the protocol execution — although in the existing invisible signature schemes, it does not, so that they are in fact externally verifiable.

Dispute. External verifiability of the output *acc* of the court in a dispute corresponds to the informal requirement made in Section 1.3, "Assessment by the Public". It means: If the court is honest, the observing public obtains the same result as the court. Otherwise, each of them either catches the court cheating within the dispute transaction or knows that the output *acc* of the court's correct entity (which they cannot see, and which a dishonest court may have manipulated) must be equal to her own observed value. Thus, if the court announces a different decision, the observers also know that the court is cheating.

With the structure of ordinary digital signature schemes and fail-stop signature schemes, disputes are always externally verifiable, because the function *test* and the verification of proofs of forgery are non-interactive and equal for everybody. With current invisible signature schemes, disputes are not externally verifiable if the court carries out the disavowal protocol with the signer, because if the signer and the court collude, the signer can disavow a valid signature in a way that cannot be noticed. (Technically this works by the court only posing challenges that it knows the signer can answer in a challenge-response protocol.) However, if the recipient carries out the disavowal protocol with the signer instead, and the court observes, the dispute is externally verifiable.

Other Transactions for Initialization and Leaving

Some schemes may offer a special kind of initialization for new recipients who enter the system later and missed the normal initialization of some signers. This is easy to realize if initialization within the system is non-interactive. In signature-like schemes with accountable centres, non-atomic initialization may even be the standard case,

---

[56] This problem can also be handled outside the signature scheme; e.g., the same court who might later have to decide whether the signer must pay the money back is now informed of the disagreement and settles the potential dispute in advance. However, the solution with external verifiability is more flexible.

e.g., if inside the system, the entities of recipients only request public keys from a directory of certified keys when they need them. One might also think about a transaction for a user to leave the system. Transactions to convert the system, or parts of it, into a different one are also known, e.g., invisible signatures can be converted into normal ones, see [BCDP91]. Of course, adding transactions implies adding requirements on their outputs.

Distributed and Combined Variants

An extension of external verifiability is distributed variants of transactions, e.g., a variant of authentication where several recipients take part and either all of them accept the message as authenticated or none does. In contrast to observers, all these recipients should be able to win disputes about the message.

Transactions can also be combined. For instance, batch signing combines several authentications. If this should be visible at the interface, inputs *'sign'* with several messages as parameters are needed. (Instead, it could be regarded as an internal optimization, but not with the simple model of time chosen here.)

Remarks on Formalization

In what sense are the minimal requirements still fulfilled in schemes with additional transactions? Entirely new transactions, such as transfers and local transactions, are no problem. Variants of the three minimal transactions that do not modify the interface events at the three standard access points are no problem either, e.g., external verifiability. Other variants can be a problem. In particular, a specific input for batch signing cannot be represented as (*'sign'*, m, $ids_{R,sign}$), not even with the additional parameter *others*. Nevertheless, it has to be considered in the predicate *signer_signs* in Section 5.2.7. In such cases, the minimal requirements are only guaranteed if the interest group restricts itself to the minimal transactions. Otherwise the general definition must be made even more abstract by basing predicates such as *signer_signs* on abstract properties of inputs, instead of the inputs themselves; these properties have to be specified for each new type of input.

5.2.12 Privacy Requirements

Privacy requirements are not considered in detail in this text. They are quite different from all the others, which could be called **integrity requirements** (apart from availability of service, which would be called an availability requirement), and which said what outputs should occur at each access point. Moreover, integrity requirements are only guaranteed if the user of the access point belongs to the interest group and the corresponding entity is therefore assumed to be correct (see Section 5.2.1). In contrast, **privacy requirements** deal explicitly with the knowledge attackers can obtain. The following sketches are conventional mixtures of service and structure.

Invisibility

Invisibility has already been introduced in Sections 1.6 and 2.7. It means that the recipient has no way of convincing a third party that he has carried out authentication with the signer, unless the signer takes part in a dispute. Thus neither the recipient nor the third party are in the interest group, and their entities may be corrupted.

The formal requirement has some similarity to a zero-knowledge property. It says that whatever the recipient and his entity can do after an execution of authentication with an honest signer, he could, on average, have done equally well without the authentication. Hence, whatever he does, it does not convince a third party that authentication must have taken place for him to be able to act like this.[57] The principal question mentioned in Section 2.7 was that such formalizations, like those of zero-knowledge, only deal with the situation where the recipient has first received an authenticated message and then wants to show it round. One may also want to exclude that several people gather right away and try to carry out authentication in a way that they are all convinced of the authenticity of the message.[58]

Normal Confidentiality Requirements

One could also consider normal confidentiality requirements in the interest of all participants in a transaction, e.g., that attackers do not learn anything about the messages that honest users authenticate for each other. In general, one would use combinations of normal signature schemes and secrecy schemes inside the system, but, as mentioned under "Directedness of Authentication" in Section 5.2.8, this will not always be trivial.

5.3 Structure

As the service of digital signature schemes has been defined at an interface, one can consider implementations with arbitrary structure, e.g., even centralized ones. However, only decentralized ones as sketched in Section 5.1 are defined to *be* signature schemes: Two people meeting in the desert (where they would never go without their mobile personal devices) should be able to exchange authenticated messages. More precisely:

- There must be one entity per access point, as in Figure 5.1; this entity is said to belong to the identity of this access point.
- Only the entities under the access points concerned take part in a transaction.

These minimal structural requirements, called **locality**, are described in a little more detail in Section 5.3.1. Similar requirements would be made on general cryptologic transaction schemes, such as secrecy, payment, and credential schemes. Section 5.3.2 describes additional structural properties that characterize special classes of

---

57 Authentication is not completely zero-knowledge, however, because it enables the recipient to win disputes. Formally, the core of the difference is that the recipient has gained knowledge with respect to the signer, but not with respect to others.

58 One might also try to regard invisibility as a special case of a general minimum-knowledge property, instead of as a new service requirement; see Section 5.2.1, "Why a Descriptive Specification?".

signature schemes. Primarily, they are complexity restrictions, but they also affect the attainable security; see Section 5.4.

5.3.1 Minimal Structural Requirements

A signature **scheme** mainly consists of feasible programs for local entities, i.e., a triple of probabilistic polynomial-time interactive algorithms,

$$Programs = (signer\_program, recipient\_program, court\_program),$$

and the tuple of specification parameters from Section 5.2.5, say

$$MainScheme = (spec\_pars, Programs).$$

If a scheme with more types of access points is implemented, there are additional programs.

The only other component is a rudimentary program for the switch, i.e., the virtual network component, which is described below.

Ports. The only fact related to locality that can be seen statically in the programs is what ports they use. Each program has at least the following input-output ports (where everything except for the names is so far only an informal explanation):

- An interface port, which is used for the interface events. In figures, it is drawn on top of the entities. Each interface port yields an access point.
- A 2-party port, which is mainly used in 2-party transactions, such as authentication.
- A 3-party port, which is used in addition to the 2-party port in 3-party transactions.
- A broadcast port, which is mainly used for broadcast under the previously known identities in initialization, see Section 5.2.4.

Switch program. The larger part of the switch program can be defined once and for all, i.e., it need not be a component of every signature scheme. The switch has one so-called interface port (corresponding to the connection-control access point) and other ports that can be connected with the ports of the other entities. It is memory-less; in each round, it evaluates the current input *connections* and transports messages between its other ports accordingly between this round and the next one. Hence its program is a mapping from pairs *connection* = (*transaction_type*, *access_points*) to concrete connections.

Parts of this mapping are also defined once and for all. In particular, for each correct pair (*'authentication'*, (id_S, id_R)), the switch connects the 2-party ports of those two entities with a point-to-point channel, and similarly, it has a fixed scheme for connecting 2- and 3-party ports of entities in disputes.

For initialization, the switch usually connects the broadcast ports of the participants with broadcast channels. However, the number and types of channels used in initialization are not restricted, i.e., this part of the mapping must be defined in the scheme. Moreover, each new type of transaction must be represented in the switch program.

Remark on enforcing the correct use of ports. It is not prescribed that the programs only use the dedicated ports in authentication and disputes, so as to guarantee locality. However, the fixed part of the definition of the switch program ensures that only these ports are connected, and it does not really matter if the programs try to use other ports, too. Moreover, such a property might sometimes be hard to see statically from the programs.

Deriving Systems from Schemes

A **system** is an instantiation of a scheme with certain system parameters. These are the sets of identities, Id_S, Id_R, Id_C, as mentioned in Section 5.2.5, and additional security parameters. Given a scheme and the system parameters, the instantiation is defined as follows:

- For each identity, there is one entity; it executes the program corresponding to its type.
- Each entity has the system parameters and its own identity as its initial state.
- One additional entity executes the switch program. Its ports are connected to each port of the other entities, except for the interface ports; see Figure 5.2.

With any precise notion of interactive algorithms, it is clear how the system behaviour, i.e., global runs of such a system (in interaction with users) are defined. The interface, and thus the restriction to interface behaviour, is defined by the interface ports of all the entities.

5.3.2 Additional Structural Properties

This section contains criteria that characterize signature schemes whose structure is less complex than the general case. Moreover, all the familiar notions of signatures, signing and test algorithms, secret keys, test keys, and public keys, are redefined for special classes of signature schemes. All the properties are described in terms of the systems derived from the schemes.

Generally, the following criteria can be used to classify the structure of distributed systems:

- The type of connections, e.g., if broadcast channels or only point-to-point channels are available.
- The communication complexity, i.e., how much use is made of the various channels. This is an important criterion for practicality, because communication is often slow or expensive.
- The internal complexity of the entities, i.e., time and memory requirements.
- Other internal properties of the entities, which simplify conventional definitions rather than the system itself, e.g., whether an entity updates its memory after each transaction.

Several of these criteria can be applied to each transaction individually. In particular, initialization is often allowed to be more complex than authentication and disputes.

Non-Interactive Authentication

Non-interactive authentication means that during an execution of authentication, the signer's entity just sends something to the recipient's entity; there is no feedback from the recipient's entity. For instance, ordinary digital signature schemes and fail-stop signature schemes are of this type. Invisible signature schemes are not, because of the interactive verification protocol, nor are schemes with server-aided signing or verification if the server is the transaction partner. Note that such server-aided schemes offer exactly the same service as ordinary digital signature schemes and are only distinguished by this structural difference.

The main advantage of non-interactive authentication is that the signer can simply send an authenticated message off, e.g., by electronic mail, whereas an interactive protocol requires an on-line connection.

In signature schemes with non-interactive authentication, the message that the signer's entity sends during authentication can be called the **signature**.

Furthermore, the actions of the entities of the signer and the recipient during non-interactive authentication correspond to the old algorithms ***sign*** and ***test*** (as in Figure 2.2 and Section 2.6). However, they have other parameters in general than in ordinary digital signature schemes: Each input consists of the parameters from the respective user input and a local variable that describes the complete current memory content of the entity — there is no notion of keys in general. Similarly, the output consists of the interface output and the new memory content. Both *sign* and *test* may be probabilistic.

Other Aspects of the Communication Complexity of Authentication

As authentication will be used far more often than the other two transactions, it is important to restrict its communication complexity. (Disputes can be expected to be rare if a secure signature scheme is used, because nobody can gain anything from them, at least in a formal sense.) It was already prescribed in the minimal structural requirements that only a point-to-point channel can be used.

In the case of interactive authentication, as with all interactive protocols, an important criterion is the **round complexity**, i.e., the number of rounds needed. Message complexity, the number of separate messages sent during a protocol execution, essentially equals round complexity in 2-party protocols, but **bit complexity**, the number of bits sent, is as important as usual. The bit complexity of non-interactive authentication is the length of the signature.

Communication Complexity of Other Transactions

The complexity of other transactions can be classified like that of authentication. Only the current minima are sketched in the following.

If a scheme has 2-party **disputes**, they are often non-interactive. However, no non-interactive 3-party dispute is known, i.e., none where the entities of the signer and the recipient each send a message to the court's entity in the first round and the court's entity immediately decides. Instead, as with fail-stop signature schemes, the court's entity at least forwards information from the recipient's entity to the signer's entity.

As to **initialization**, it had been assumed in Section 5.2 that no signature scheme could exist without it and that a broadcast channel would be needed. One might ask if this is true.

Informally, initialization is needed because authentication is completely digital and carried out over an insecure channel. Hence the signer's entity must possess digital information that enables it to act differently from any potential forger, at least on average. This information must be related to some information the recipient has in connection with the identity of this signer. Hence a secure channel under this identity must have existed at some time.

The question whether a **broadcast channel** is needed is important because reliable broadcast is very hard to realize in practice. Informally, broadcast seems to be necessary because the information that the entities of the signer, the recipient, and all courts have must be somehow consistent. One can probably prove the necessity of broadcast (or of introducing centres with at least the restrictions sketched in Section 5.2.3) formally at least for the more powerful types of signature schemes by the following approach: With signature schemes with finite transferability (and even more easily with arbitrary transferability), efficient reliable broadcast protocols can be constructed [DoSt83, PfWa92]. Hence, if such a signature scheme could be established without initial reliable broadcast, one would obtain reliable broadcast from scratch. In some senses of security, this is known to be impossible [PeSL80, GrYa89]. A brief sketch of a more general proof is contained in [DoDw91], which also mentions the application to the necessity of broadcast channels in signature schemes.

In all known signature schemes with a fail-stop property, transfers of proofs of forgery are non-interactive. The one message sent is called a **proof of forgery**. These schemes follow the structure described in Section 3.2 even more closely: In a dispute, the signer's entity computes this same proof of forgery from the forged signature and sends it to the court, and the court verifies it exactly as in a transfer.

Transfers in all existing signature schemes with arbitrary or finite transferability are non-interactive. Most of them are with non-interactive authentication, too, and in the transfer, the original signature is simply passed on. Only the test carried out by the recipient's entity depends on the acceptance level i in signature schemes with finite transferability.

"Memory-less" Signing

The term "memory-less" signing (from [Gold87]) does not mean that the entity of a signer does not need any memory: Even between transactions, some secret information has to be stored. Instead, it means that this memory is read-only after initialization; in particular, no information about authentication transactions needs to be stored. In this case, the constant secret information is called the **secret key**.

Although "memory-less" signing has been given some importance, e.g., in [Gold87, GoMR88], the only qualitative advantage I see is that it implies that the signer's access point can easily be duplicated (see Section 5.2.11, "Local

Transactions"). However, all present schemes that are not "memory-less" also permit some duplication, although less flexibly: In these schemes, later authentications do not depend on the content of messages authenticated before, but only on the number of such messages and some random information. With each of these schemes, there is a method to share out consistent random information so that, e.g., two devices sign as if one of them were signing the first $N/2$ messages and the other the second $N/2$ messages, where N is the message bound. Of course, if information has to be stored for future disputes, one may need both devices in a dispute.

Important schemes *without* memory-less signing are

- the original variants of cryptographically strong schemes such as GMR,
- schemes with preprocessing and on-line/off-line computations, which offer the same service as ordinary digital signature schemes and are only distinguished by the addition of memory to their structure, and
- incremental signature schemes.

"Memory-less" Receiving and Deciding

Entities of recipients cannot be "memory-less" in the same sense as entities of signers, because they must store some information about each authenticated message they have received in case of disputes. Hence, "memory-less" receiving is used to denote that the actions of the recipient's entity in authentication do not depend on previous authentications and disputes.

The constant information that the entity uses in each test is called a **test key**. (It is not necessarily a public key, though, because different recipients and courts may have different constant test keys.)

Schemes with more than one recipient per initialization (see Section 5.2.10, "Dependence of Authentication on the Recipients") are almost always "memory-less"; at least, testing a new message must work no matter whether the earlier messages from the same signer had the same recipient or not. Similarly, courts are almost always "memory-less". In contrast, the efficiency of schemes with fixed recipient or one recipient per initialization can often be improved by giving up "memory-less" receiving (see [FoPf91] or Section 10.6).

Public Keys

So far, the only case where a clear notion of public keys exists is the least complex form of initialization: If the signer's entity just broadcasts one message to all other entities, this message is called a public key. More generally, a public key can be defined if

1. the outputs acc and ids_{out} (and $ids_{Risk,out}$ in fail-stop signature schemes with special risk bearers) of all the entities participating in an initialization are a (common) deterministic function of the messages sent on broadcast channels,
2. and, if acc = TRUE, the memory content of the entities of all participating recipients and courts at the end of initialization is also a (common) deterministic function of the messages sent on broadcast channels.

This memory content will be called the **public key**.[59]

The first property implies the consistency part of the correctness of initialization.

I see no real benefit in the existence of a public key in a general setting, because in contrast to properties like non-interactive authentication, it does not reduce any complexity parameter. Nevertheless, public keys occur naturally in many constructions.

Standard Structure for External Verifiability

If external verifiability of the behaviour of participants is required (see Section 5.2.11), a structural requirement is usually made, too: The entities of the observers should only observe the messages between the original entities, and not send any messages themselves. For this purpose, the channels used in the normal implementation of the transaction are extended to broadcast channels including the observers' entities as receivers. Moreover, it is required that the decisions of the observers are deterministic. This ensures the consistency of observations.

In contrast, if a distributed variant of a transaction is required, an arbitrary protocol between all the entities concerned is allowed.

5.4 Security

This section describes degrees of security. A short overview was already given in Sections 4.4.5 to 4.4.7. A degree of security is primarily defined for one scheme and one requirement, not for a complete specification. It is characterized by the attackers that are tolerated and the notion of "fulfilling" the requirement. Most of this section can be used for all cryptologic transaction schemes.

Section 5.4.1 describes how the attackers are connected to the rest of a system derived from the scheme, and Section 5.4.2 models the behaviour of the honest users. Thus, after these two sections, the actual systems are known whose runs have to be considered. Section 5.4.3 shows the usual combinations of the assumptions about the computational abilities of the attackers and the notions of fulfilling. Section 5.4.4 contains theorems and proof sketches one could hope to work out if Sections 5.3 and 5.4 were completely formal. Some are general, others specific to signature schemes.

In contrast to Sections 5.2 and 5.3, there are no special subsections for minimal and stronger security properties. The criteria introduced in Sections 5.4.1 and 5.4.2 are almost identical for all signature schemes (and many other cryptologic transaction schemes), and Section 5.4.3 is a classification all over.

---

59 One might try to generalize this notion further by omitting the explicit requirement that the acceptance value and the public key are functions of broadcast messages. However, it might then depend on the attackers if everybody has the same public key, and thus the simplicity of the notion is lost.

5.4.1 Access of Attackers to System Parts

Locality as a Security Property

The model of the access of attackers to system parts reflects locality, like the minimal structural requirements:

> *Whenever a requirement of a certain interest group is considered, only the entities belonging to this interest group are assumed to be correct.*

This was already anticipated in Section 5.2.1, "Why Interest Groups". Recall that an interest group is formally a set of identities, and that the entities belonging to it are those that are directly connected to the access points with these identities. This may be called the standard attacker model of cryptology. Combined with suitably small interest groups, it may also be called the standard trust model.

The intuitive justification for this model is that people are regarded as (potentially) mutually distrusting, i.e., the designer of a signature scheme should not *force* them to trust others with respect to their authenticated messages, and that no mutually trusted hardware is assumed (see Section 1.3, "No Trusted Third Parties").[60]

In addition to the entities belonging to the interest groups, the switch is assumed to be correct, as explained in Section 5.1.2, "Connection Handling with Explicit Switching".

Cooperation of Attackers

With all the integrity requirements on signature schemes, it is tolerated that all corrupted entities collude, as almost always in cryptology. Hence, when a certain requirement is considered, all entities not belonging to the interest group are replaced by one big entity.[61] This entity may be completely malicious, i.e., it does its best to cheat the honest users.[62] An example is shown in Figure 5.14.

Access to Channels

The access of attackers to channels is usually restricted as follows: Connections that are explicitly required at the interface (as inputs to the connection-control access point) are assumed to guarantee integrity and availability, i.e., they transport

---

60 With some cryptologic schemes, the access of attackers to system parts is restricted in other ways, e.g., to less than 1/3 of the entities. However, for all schemes with legal relevance, locality as a security property is important.

61 Invisibility, however, can only be defined with at least two different attacker entities, and the same holds for the absence of subliminal channels.

62 This is a usual worst-case assumption in cryptology, because intentional attacks, and not physical failures, are studied. Nevertheless, two intermediate cases are sometimes considered: First, someone might be curious, but not malicious enough to let an entity deviate from its program, i.e., they would only carry out additional computations with the information received. This case mainly has applications to privacy requirements. Secondly, someone might be malicious, but not risking to be caught. Hence they might let entities deviate from their programs as long as this cannot be detected, e.g., by choosing numbers with a particular algorithm instead of randomly. This is sometimes assumed with "trusted" centers.

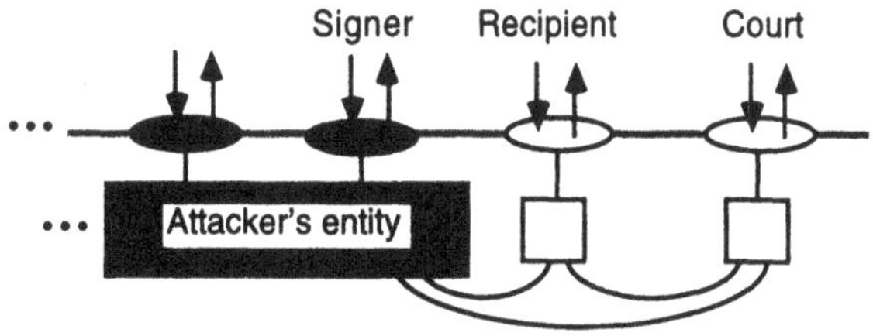

Figure 5.14. Example of a system with attackers.
The figure shows the system when the requirement of the recipient on disputes is considered for a specific recipient and a specific court. The dark part denotes the attacker and is arbitrary.

messages exactly as specified. This is modeled by assuming that the switch and all the connections it switches are correct. (Connections between the same entities at other times may be corrupted.) Confidentiality on these channels is not guaranteed, i.e., the attackers also obtain the data.

In particular, broadcast channels are assumed to be reliable even if some of the entities connected to them are corrupted. Thus, if a correct entity sends a message, all receivers receive exactly this message and know that it comes from this entity, and even if the sender is corrupted, it cannot trick the recipients into receiving different messages. One often speaks of the "broadcast assumption" if a broadcast channel is present in the structure of a system.

Some Special Properties

Small additions or subtractions to the usual assumptions about the access of attackers to system parts exist in some signature schemes.

Private channels. Some signature schemes need point-to-point channels in initialization that keep messages confidential (in addition to integrity and availability), i.e., only the intended receiver obtains any information. This must be mentioned explicitly in the degree of security, and can only be applied to schemes where the switch program contains two types of point-to-point channels.

Authentic channels.[63] Sometimes, point-to-point channels are needed in initialization where integrity and availability are not sufficient — the receiver must also be able to recognize the identity of the sender. This means that the identity of the sender is appended to the message on the channel, as with a broadcast channel.

Private and authentic storage. So far, it was assumed that data stored in correct entities is completely private, i.e., an attacker can neither read nor modify it. However, it is sometimes useful to distinguish how much of the data really has to be secret, because private storage is hard to implement in practice — one needs

63 Terminology with channels varies: First, one could speak of a "channel guaranteeing authenticity", because the messages are authentic, not the channel. Secondly, "secure channel" is more common, but it is sometimes used as "private channel" was used above. Similarly, "private" can be used for confidentiality alone, and so can "secret".

Moreover, special assumptions about channels can also be seen as structural properties, because they concern the switch program.

tamper-resistant devices, or one must be very sure that nobody ever gains access to a device. For large amounts of data, it is easier to implement storage that is only authentic, i.e., where an attacker may learn the data, although he cannot modify them. For example, one can copy the data on several diskettes and keep them in different places. To ensure integrity, the data can either be kept in places like safes where a breach of security would at least be noticed, or they can be authenticated with a symmetric authentication scheme, so that only the key and short authenticators must be stored in the tamper-resistant device. Then the loss of all copies but one can be tolerated.[64]

An example of this distinction in fail-stop signature schemes is given in Section 10.4. The related distinction between authentic and untrusted storage was made for incremental signature schemes [BeGG95]. One can also regard server-aided computation as related if the server is a larger untrusted device of the same user.

5.4.2 Influence of Attackers on Honest Users

The formal reason for modeling the honest users is that one cannot define runs of the system without them: One needs some source for the user inputs. A more intuitive reason for modeling the honest users is that this is where the active attacks described in Section 2.5 come in: One must decide to what extent the behaviour of honest users might be influenced by the attackers.

In the following, two formal models of essentially the same idea are presented. Some discussions of their relative merits follow. The section concludes with discussions of how conventional definitions of active attacks fit into these models. Actually, the general model with interfaces seems to simplify the treatment of active attacks in definitions considerably.

Two Models

Essentially, one obtains the best degree of security if one universally quantifies over the behaviour of the honest users: No matter what the honest users do, the requirements are fulfilled. Such a model automatically covers all conceivable active attacks, because behaviours resulting from an influence by an attacker are just behaviours, too. It is rather a natural model, too — for instance, how could one know anything about how an honest user selects the messages she authenticates? (This is in contrast to the behaviour of correct entities, which act according to programs.)

Of course, the notion "universally quantifies" was not precise, because it was not clear where such a quantifier would be placed in what formula. Hence two precise models are now presented. The first one is simpler and sufficient for all integrity requirements (and thus all the minimal requirements on signature schemes), whereas the second one is more intuitive and can also be used with privacy requirements.

---

64 Secret sharing schemes, introduced in [Blak79, Sham79], can be used to approach this situation for private storage, too. However, in this case, several shares must remain intact for the secret to be recovered and must be recollected each time the secret is used.

In the first model, the honest users are integrated into the attacker strategy, as shown in Figure 5.15. (However, the correct entities are still correct.) This is called the model with **direct access**, because the attackers have direct access to the access points under consideration.

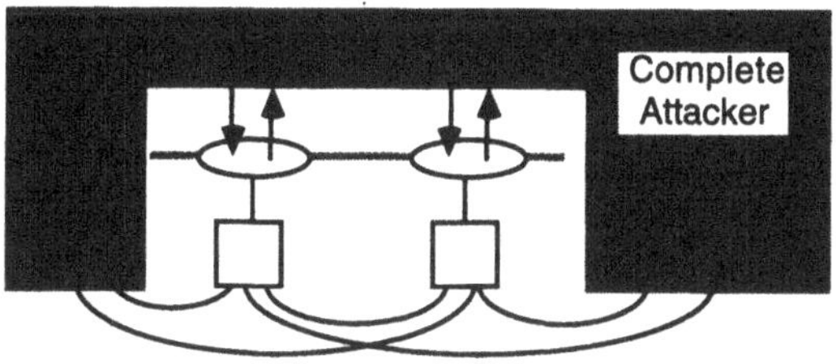

Figure 5.15. Model of an active attack on two honest users, version with direct access.
Correct entities and access points about which requirements are made are white, the attacker is dark. "Direct access" means that the honest users are integrated into the attacker strategy.

In the second model, there are explicit entities representing honest users. As shown in Figure 5.16, they have special ports where they communicate with the attacker, i.e., where the attacker can influence them. This is called the model with **indirect access**.

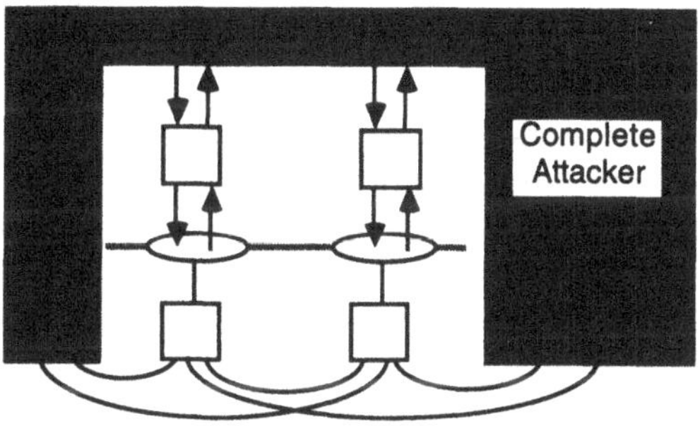

Figure 5.16. Model of an active attack, version with indirect access.
Correct entities and access points about which requirements are made are white, the attacker is dark; the white entities above the interface represent the honest users.

In the second model, the computational abilities of the entities representing the honest users have to be restricted in the same way as those of the attackers. Apart from this restriction, there will be normal universal quantifiers over their programs in the same place in the formulas in Section 5.4.3 as the quantifier over the attacker strategy.

Discussions Common to Both Models

Relation to the preconditions on user behaviour in the requirements. Neither model mentions any preconditions on user behaviour, because the requirements fully deal with those already: The models in this section mean that no matter how the honest users behave, the requirements are fulfilled (in some sense to be defined in Section 5.4.3), and the requirements say that if the users take certain elementary precautions such as using initialization correctly, the system guarantees them some other properties.

Computational restrictions on honest users. In both models, the honest users are assumed to be computationally restricted whenever the attacker is (implicitly in the model with direct access and explicitly in that with indirect access). This is not quite the announced universal quantifier over all behaviours. On the one hand, however, it is rather a reasonable restriction — why should attackers be less powerful than honest users. On the other hand, the restriction is necessary, because an unbounded honest user might inadvertently help an attacker to break a system. For example, assume an unrestricted honest user were in the habit of factoring numbers that she received in authenticated messages, and to sign the factors before answering. Then, if the implementation of the signature scheme relied on factoring, an active attacker could easily induce this user to factor public keys. (This can be seen as a generalization of the argument in [MiRS88] why the so-called message finder is needed in [GoMi84].)

Separation of users and entities. The separation between users and their entities in this framework is useful here, because it automatically excludes some particularly stupid user behaviour. For instance, one would otherwise have to explicitly exclude honest users that tell the attacker their secret keys, because no signature scheme could possibly protect them. Now, the formal users simply have no access to the secret information in the entities. This is a reasonable restriction; e.g., we have no idea what letters a user writes, but her letters might be expected to be independent of the implementation of the signature scheme.

Linking behaviour above and below the interface. After the previous paragraph, it may seem strange that the behaviour of the honest users in the model with direct access has been linked to activities below the interface. However, the attacker can base its influence on details of the corrupted entities, and then the behaviour of the honest users may depend on those, too. Still, the behaviour remains independent of internal details of the correct entities.

Equivalence for integrity requirements. For requirements in the sense of Section 5.2.1, where sequences of interface events are classified into permitted ones and undesirable ones, one can easily see that the two models are equivalent (both with and without computational restrictions on honest users and attackers):

First consider a situation in the first model. It is described by an attacker strategy $\tilde{A}_1$. Then an attacker can achieve exactly the same sequences of interface events in the second model by using the strategy $\tilde{A}_2 := \tilde{A}_1$, if the honest users only pass messages on between the attacker and the interface; and these particular honest users have to be considered, because there is a universal quantifier over the strategies of the honest users.

Secondly, consider a situation in the second model. It consists of an attacker strategy $\tilde{A}_2$ and one strategy H_i for each honest user. The combination of these strategies is a strategy $\tilde{A}_1$, which achieves exactly the same sequences of interface events in the first model. (Recall from Section 4.4.5 that strategies are nothing but programs; and it is presupposed that with all sensible formalizations of interactive programs, several interacting entities can be described by one program again.)

Differences Between the Models

Intuitiveness. A disadvantage of the first model is that it may be intuitively unconvincing: Why does one make requirements at all if the honest users give the attackers direct access to their access points? For instance, if an attacker wants to forge a signature, why doesn't he use the signer's access point to authenticate the message in the normal way? Formally, of course, one can either argue with the equivalence to the second model, or say that nobody has yet come up with another model that is certainly on the safe side, i.e., that certainly covers all the possible behaviours of all honest users.

Privacy requirements. For privacy requirements, which deal with the knowledge of attackers, the model with indirect access must be used.

Formally, one can see that the equivalence proof cannot be used with privacy requirements: If one combines an attacker strategy $\tilde{A}_2$ and the strategies H_i of the honest users from the model with indirect access into an attacker strategy $\tilde{A}_1$ in the model with direct access, the attacker gains knowledge that only the honest users had in the model with indirect access.

Restricted attacks. In the model with indirect access, one *can* model restricted attacks if one needs them. For instance, passive attacks are modeled by honest users that do not react on anything from the outside world, but choose their inputs, e.g., the messages they authenticate, according to some predefined probability distribution. This is unrealistic in most situations. A better example might be that honest users choose some initialization parameters carefully and without influence from outside, but may be influenced later.

Relation to Conventional Notions of Active Attacks

Attacks above and below the interface. One formal definition of an active attack might be that it is any attack where the attacker lets his entities deviate from their prescribed programs. The behaviour of the honest users and the influence of the attackers on them has nothing to do with active attacks in this sense, because no programs for users exist. Instead, this type of active attack was considered in Section 5.4.1, where the access of attackers to parts below the interface was considered.

Notion from the GMR definition. The notion of an active attack in the GMR definition corresponds to the one in this section (although no notion of interface exists, of course): In an adaptive chosen-message attack, the attacker can, for a while, choose messages that the signer's entity will sign, i.e., he completely takes over the role of the honest user for a while, but without gaining access to the entity itself, e.g., he does not get the secret key.

Generalization. Both models presented above consider active attacks on all types of access points, i.e., not only on signers, but also on recipients and courts.

This does not mean that the GMR definition is too weak: Active attacks only make a difference if they are directed against users whose entities act depending on internal secrets. (Otherwise, a passive attacker can simulate on his own how the correct entity would have reacted if he had used an active attack.) With the structure of ordinary digital signature schemes and fail-stop signature schemes, the entities of recipients and courts do not have such secrets. In contrast, with schemes where different recipients have different test keys, an attacker might try to find out somebody's test key by asking him to test lots of supposedly authenticated messages and observing the results. Such active attacks on recipients are dangerous for information-theoretically secure signature schemes, and they were originally overlooked [ChRo91].

Finally, note that an active attacker may not only influence the inputs of the honest users, but also see the outputs. For example, the poor recipient who was made to test lots of junk signatures might tell everybody around him: "Have you also had such troubles with e-mail this morning? I received 105 authenticated messages and only 2 were correct." The attacker might even answer: "No, I haven't; let me see if I can help", to find out which were the two that passed the test.

Application to Connections

In the current application, the connection-control access point is treated like an access point of an honest user, because it is mentioned in the requirements and the entity that belongs to it, i.e., the switch, is assumed to be correct. Hence the attacker has direct or indirect access to it, precisely as to the access points of the honest users.

5.4.3 Computational Assumptions and Notions of Fulfilling

This section treats combinations of

- restrictions on the computational abilities of the attackers and
- notions of fulfilling, in particular,
  - error probabilities and
  - the assumptions needed in the proof of security (from "no assumption needed" to "no proof provided").

All individual criteria have been mentioned before, except that it remains to be formalized in what probability spaces the error probabilities are defined and how large they may be.

Combinations for One Requirement

Originally, the criteria treated in this section are rather different, but specific combinations of them are usual. For an arbitrary single requirement, such typical combinations are summarized in Figure 5.17.

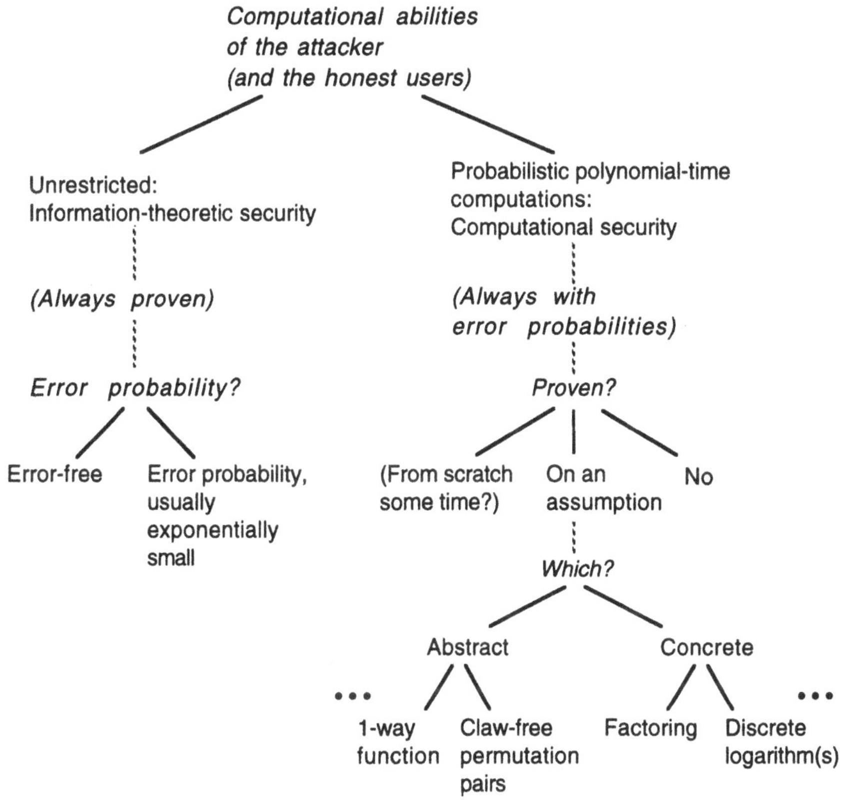

Figure 5.17. Typical computational restrictions and degrees of fulfilling (for a single requirement).

Questions are in italics and reached from the parent node by dotted lines; answers are in normal type and reached by normal lines. As to the items in parentheses, it is just experience that nobody claims information-theoretic security without some proof, but it should be provable in some models that a restriction to computational security only makes sense in combination with error probabilities (see Section 5.4.4, "General Theorems").

Definition Sketches

Assuming the formal details in all the previous sections were filled in, all ingredients would now be ready for the definition of a security semantics for the type of specification introduced in Sections 5.2.1 and 5.2.6. In particular, the probability spaces where the error probabilities are defined would be clear, and approximately how the quantifiers are placed in the security definitions. To show that this is indeed so, some notation is now assigned to concepts that were sketched in the previous sections.

The model of honest users with direct access is used.

The security semantics must define under which conditions a scheme *Scheme* fulfils a requirement *Req* with a given degree of security, *degree*. This could boldly be written as

$$Scheme \models_{degree} Req.$$

At least classes of signature schemes and requirements that can be made on them have been sketched. The notion should be easily extendible to arbitrary cryptologic transaction schemes. The requirements are not restricted to temporal logic, but can be any functions that assign a set of permitted sequences of interface events to each interest group of a certain type, as in Figure 5.3. (Recall that the interest group was a free variable in each requirement.) Hence let *I_groups*(*Req*) be the domain of interest groups for this requirement, and for each *i_group* ∈ *I_groups*(*Req*), let *Req*(*i_group*) denote the set of permitted sequences if this particular interest group is considered.

It has also been sketched how systems are derived from a scheme and certain system parameters, say *sys_pars*, from a domain *Sys_pars*(*Scheme*).[65] Thus one could speak of a system *Sys*(*Scheme*, *sys_pars*).

Moreover, the access of attackers to system parts was defined once and for all. (More generally, different versions could be distinguished in *degree*.) Hence, for each interest group *i_group* of the correct type, let

$$Sys(Scheme,\ sys\_pars,\ i\_group)$$

denote the system obtained from *Sys*(*Scheme*, *sys_pars*) by retaining only those entities that belong to the interest group *i_group* and the virtual network entity, the switch.

Furthermore, the port structure of an attacker that can communicate with such a system is known from the access of attackers to system parts and the model of honest users. Thus one has a class

$$Attacker\_class(Scheme,\ Req)$$

of permitted attackers.[66] Each individual attacker strategy $\tilde{A}$ from this class has *sys_pars* and *i_group* as parameters in its initial state. Thus, in contrast to *Scheme* and *Req*, these parameters are not encoded into the attacker strategy, but an attacker strategy must work for them all. (This will make a difference when computationally restricted attackers are considered, and it is clear if one regards a security parameter in *sys_pars*.)

It should be clear how such an attacker and a system interact. The combined system could be written as

---

65 The domain usually does not depend on the individual scheme much, but, e.g., the domain of the system parameter Id_R was dependent on the specification parameter *Recipients_total*, which is part of the scheme.

66 The parameter *Req* is necessary because it determines the type of the interest groups, which determines the ports that the attacker needs.

$$Combine[Sys(Scheme, sys\_pars, i\_group), \tilde{A}(sys\_pars, i\_group)]$$

with a general operator *Combine*. This is a closed system and the initial states of all the entities are given, hence it is an object for which runs would have been defined. The runs have probabilities, which are given by the random choices within both the attacker and the correct part of the system. This might be written as

$$run \leftarrow Combine[Sys(Scheme, sys\_pars, i\_group), \tilde{A}(sys\_pars, i\_group)],$$

i.e., the system is identified with the probability space it defines on runs. For the requirements, only the restrictions of the runs to the events at the access points in the interest group are considered. This could be written as the runs with an additional restriction operator, e.g.,

$$i\_events \leftarrow Combine[Sys(Scheme, sys\_pars, i\_group), \tilde{A}(sys\_pars, i\_group)]|_{i\_group}.$$

If *Scheme* and *Req* are regarded as fixed, one can abbreviate this as

$$i\_events \leftarrow I\_events(sys\_pars, i\_group, \tilde{A}).$$

Each sequence *i_events* either is an element of the set *Req(i_group)*, i.e., fulfils the requirement, or not. One can therefore define the probability

$$\mathrm{P}_{\tilde{A}}(sys\_pars, i\_group) := \mathrm{P}(i\_events \in Req(i\_group) \setminus i\_events \leftarrow I\_events(sys\_pars, i\_group, \tilde{A})).$$

This is the probability that the degrees of security deal with.[67]

Information-theoretic security without error probability. For the simplest case, the definition can now be completed: The scheme *Scheme* fulfils the given requirement *Req* information-theoretically without error probability if for all attackers $\tilde{A} \in Attacker\_class(Scheme, Req)$, all system parameters $sys\_pars \in Sys\_pars(Scheme)$, and all interest groups $i\_group \in I\_groups(Req)$, all sequences of interface events at the interest group fulfil *Req*, i.e.,

$$\mathrm{P}_{\tilde{A}}(sys\_pars, i\_group) = 1.$$

Error probabilities. Generally, a class of functions regarded as "very small" can be given, and one requires that the function $1 - \mathrm{P}_{\tilde{A}}(sys\_pars, i\_group)$ is "very small" for all attackers $\tilde{A} \in Attacker\_class(Scheme, Req)$.

Suitable classes of very small functions are those where the probability decreases superpolynomially or exponentially in one of the security parameters, say *k*. However, one must take care with the remaining system parameters. In the order of increasing security, one can leave them constant while *k* tends to infinity, or let them grow at most polynomially with *k*, or universally quantify over them after the quantifier over *k*. Moreover, some requirements may only be fulfilled if more than one security parameter tends to infinity. Examples can be seen in later chapters.

67 It is important that a linear-time model is used in the probabilities: One obtains security statements of the form "the probability is small that an attacker manages to carry out a successful initialization and to forge later". The alternative would be conditional statements, such as "the conditional probability is small that an attacker can forge, given that initialization was successful", which are not true in most existing schemes.

Before presenting general definitions of all sensible possibilities, one should try them out in some theorems about combinations of requirements and systems.

Computational security. For computational security, the quantifier over the attacker strategies is restricted to $\tilde{A} \in PPA \cap Attacker\_class(Scheme, Req)$, where *PPA* denotes the class of probabilistic polynomial-time interactive algorithms. In this case, one can at most allow other system parameters to grow polynomially with the security parameters under consideration, and one usually requires superpolynomially small error probabilities only.

Combinations of Degrees of Security in Signature Schemes

So far, degrees of security have been defined for individual requirements. As there are several minimal requirements on signature schemes (and more for special types of service), many different combinations are possible. This subsection considers some important combinations.

Primarily, the two requirements on disputes are considered (and related additional requirements, such as fail-stop properties), and only information-theoretic and computational security are distinguished. Unforgeability, as mentioned, is a consequence of these two requirements. The other requirements are usually fulfilled information-theoretically.

The following terms will be used for complete **security types** (as anticipated in Figure 5.12):

- **Ordinary security** is the type of security that ordinary digital signature schemes offer: The requirement of the signer on disputes is fulfilled computationally only, that of the recipient information-theoretically, and there is no fail-stop property. If transferability is required, the effectiveness of transfers also holds information-theoretically.
- **Dual security** is dual to ordinary security: The requirement of the signer on disputes is fulfilled information-theoretically, that of the recipient computationally only, and there is no fail-stop property. If transferability is required, the effectiveness of transfers need only hold computationally.
- **Fail-stop security** has been described in Section 5.2.9; the degree *low* is now computationally and *high* is information-theoretically. Thus the fall-back requirements of both the signer and the recipient on disputes are fulfilled information-theoretically and the correctness of *'broken'* computationally.
- **Information-theoretic security** means that the requirements of both the signer and the recipient on disputes hold information-theoretically.

The fifth possible combination, where the requirements of both the signer and the recipient on disputes hold computationally only, has not occurred in practice so far.

As sketched after Figure 5.13, schemes with fail-stop security can be used as schemes with either ordinary or dual security, if one identifies the output *'broken'* with TRUE or FALSE, respectively, i.e., if one assigns the responsibility for authenticated messages either always to the signer or always to the recipient even if the scheme has been broken.

5.4.4 Sketches of Expected Theorems and Proofs

In the following, some theorems are sketched that should be provable if the formalization is adequate.

General Theorems

This subsection sketches theorems that are not specific to signature schemes.

First, if the requirements are restricted to temporal logic, general temporal validity (i.e., the fact that a formula holds for all sequences over the given domain) should trivially imply security validity with every degree of security.

As to proof rules, modus ponens is not trivial. It can be seen as a test for robust classes of "very small" functions: Let requirements R_1, R_2, and $R := (R_1 \rightarrow R_2)$ be given. Modus ponens means that the validity of R_1 and R for a scheme with a certain degree of security implies the validity of R_2. For given parameters $\tilde{A}$, *sys_pars*, and *i_group*, let P_1, P_2, and P denote the probabilities $P_{\tilde{A}}(sys\_pars, i\_group)$ for the respective requirements. Obviously, $(1 - P_2) \leq (1 - P_1) + (1 - P)$. Hence modus ponens can be used if the sum of two "very small" functions is still "very small".

Whenever a requirement holds for a scheme in the interest of a certain interest group, it also holds in the interest of any larger interest group with the same degree of security. This should be clear because more entities are correct if the interest group is larger, and correct entities are a special case of an attacker strategy.

I also expect that computational restrictions only make sense in combination with allowing error probabilities, at least in models where the complexity of an interactive entity is regarded as a function of its initial state alone or where honest users are modeled as computationally restricted. Then the correct part of the system is polynomial-time in its initial state and therefore only reacts on parts of polynomial length of the input from an unrestricted attacker. Hence with mere guessing, a computationally restricted attacker has a very small chance of doing exactly what a certain unrestricted attacker would do, as far as it is seen by the correct entities. Hence if a requirement is not fulfilled information-theoretically without error probability, such a restricted attacker has a small probability of success, too.

Unforgeability as a Consequence of Other Requirements

It was already mentioned in Sections 5.2.2 and 5.2.7 that unforgeability seems to be a consequence of the other requirements, with restrictions of minor importance. A proof of this statement is now sketched. The restrictions are:

- The existence of at least one honest court is assumed, i.e., unforgeability is proved with an interest group consisting of one signer, id_S, one recipient, id_R, and one court. This restriction is of minor importance in practice because every user who can serve as a recipient or a signer should technically be able to serve as a court. Thus there will be a correct court entity.
- Availability of service is assumed in addition to the two requirements on disputes, and disputes must be available a little longer than authentication if system termination is considered.

It is assumed that the given requirements hold with a common degree of security (which may be the minimum of the degrees with which they were originally shown to hold).

Assume an attacker strategy $\tilde{A}$ breaks unforgeability with significant probability, i.e., it produces sequences of interface events where *recipient_accepts*(id_R, m, id_S) for some $m \in M$ occurs before *signer_signs*(id_S, m), although initialization is used correctly at the access points of the interest group.

Now another attacker strategy A^* is constructed that breaks the conjunction of the two requirements on disputes with the same probabilities. The idea is that this strategy must start a dispute when the other strategy has succeeded in forging. Hence it first simulates $\tilde{A}$ and keeps track of all commands to sign or test, so that it notices when $\tilde{A}$ has succeeded in forging. This can be done using $\tilde{A}$ as a black box, i.e., as a kind of Turing reduction on reactive systems; see Figure 5.18.

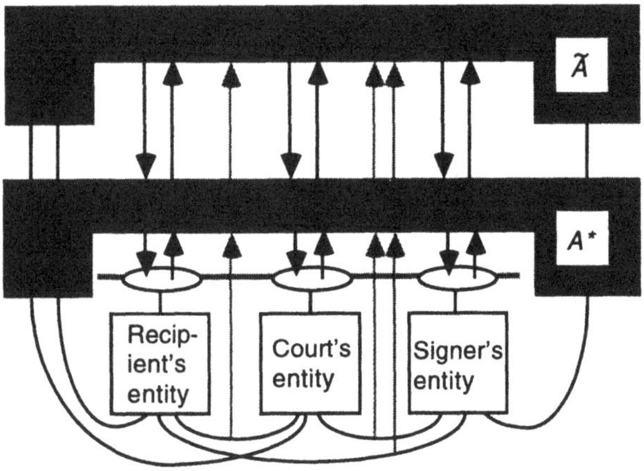

Figure 5.18. Simulation in the proof of unforgeability.
The attacker strategy A^* attacks three correct entities; the attack is based on a black-box simulation of the attacker strategy $\tilde{A}$. A^* succeeds if the resulting sequences of events at the shown interface do not fulfil the requirements (with significant probability). Grey arrows are taps on connections.

After a forgery, A^* stops simulating $\tilde{A}$ and starts a dispute about the forgery, i.e., it inputs all the correct commands at the access points of the interest group and provides the correct connections at the connection-control access point. (And it makes no further inputs.) Before that, it may have to wait until previous transactions at those access points end; availability of service guarantees that this happens.

Availability of service also guarantees that the dispute ends. If the court's output is neither TRUE nor '*not_cooperated*', the requirement of the recipient is not fulfilled, because *recipient_accepts*(id_R, m, id_S) had occurred. If it is TRUE or '*not_cooperated*', the requirement of the signer is not fulfilled, because *signer_signs*(id_S, m) had not occurred until the forgery and A^* made no further inputs since.

Together with modus ponens, this contradicts the original requirements.

Initialization in Fail-Stop Signature Schemes with Special Risk Bearers

In Section 5.2.9, it was mentioned that effectiveness of initialization need not be required explicitly for fail-stop signature schemes with special risk bearers. It is now sketched that correctness of initialization indeed implies effectiveness of initialization in these schemes.

It has to be shown that an initialization yields acc = TRUE if the signer, a recipient or court, and a risk bearer id_{Risk} are honest. First, correctness of initialization in the interest of the signer and the recipient or court means that either acc = TRUE or $ids_{Risk,out} = \emptyset$. Secondly, $ids_{Risk,out} \neq \emptyset$ follows from the correctness of initialization in the interest of the risk bearer, which means that $id_{Risk} \in ids_{Risk,out}$.

Necessity of Error Probabilities

One could try to achieve all information-theoretic security without an error probability. This subsection shows that this is impossible by giving proof sketches of the following statements:

1. The requirements of the recipient and the signer on disputes cannot both be fulfilled without error probability.
2. If the requirement of the signer on disputes (or the fall-back requirement) is fulfilled without error probability, the requirement of the recipient on disputes (or the correctness of *'broken'*) is not fulfilled at all.
3. If the requirement of the signer on disputes is fulfilled information-theoretically, the requirement of the recipient on disputes cannot be fulfilled without error probability.

Although Statement 1 follows from Statement 2, we start with an easy proof of it. The proof shows that even the weaker symmetric authentication is impossible without error probability. (For symmetric authentication schemes with the standard structure, this result is implicit in [GiMS74].) Consider unforgeability: During authentication, correct connections are not a precondition. Hence, when a recipient's entity carries out its program after a command (*'test'*, m, id_S), any other entity could be connected to its 2-party port. As the whole scheme is assumed to be digital, the only difference between the signer's entity and a potential forger is information stored in the signer's entity. A forger can make a guess at this information and carry out the correct program that the signer's entity would carry out for m, based on the guessed information. If the guess is correct, the forgery is accepted because of the effectiveness of authentication, at least with high probability.[68]

Consequently, the requirements of the signer and the recipient on disputes cannot both be fulfilled information-theoretically without an error probability: If a

---

68 Here the structural property that authentication is a 2-party transaction is used, i.e., that effectiveness of authentication holds if the entities of the signer and the recipient are connected at their 2-party ports and no other connection is made. If all entities took part, the argument would not be valid, because some messages of the real signer would be guaranteed to reach the recipient, because channels were assumed to be secure against denial of service.

successful forgery has occurred, they are contradictory. (This is a special case of the argument that unforgeability follows from the other minimal requirements.)

For Statement 2, assume once more that a forger guesses the complete secret information of the signer's entity and then carries out authentication with the recipient's entity for a certain message. If he guesses correctly, the recipient accepts with very high probability. Furthermore, if the requirement of the signer is fulfilled without error probability, a court rejects with probability 1 in a subsequent dispute. If, instead of the forger, the signer simply authenticates the same message with her correct secret information, the recipient and the court are in exactly the same situation as they were with the successful forger, and the court will also reject with probability 1. This behaviour is feasible for the signer, and therefore the recipient cannot even be computationally secure.

The same argument applies to the fall-back requirement of the signer, if there is a fail-stop property: If that were error-free, the court's output in the dispute would be FALSE or *'broken'* with probability 1. The former contradicts the requirement of the recipient, the latter the correctness of *'broken'*.

For Statement 3, assume that the requirement of the recipient on disputes is error-free. Thus, whenever an execution of authentication with the recipient's entity leads to acc = TRUE, the recipient will win a subsequent dispute in court. A computationally unrestricted attacker comprising the recipient's entity can search for a sequence of messages that would lead to acc = TRUE if the correct recipient's entity received them in authentication. Then this attacker can win disputes deterministically. Hence the requirement of the signer can only be fulfilled against computationally restricted attackers in this case.

A consequence of these statements is that subdividing the security types from Section 5.4.3, "Combinations of Degrees of Security in Signature Schemes", according to the error probabilities in their information-theoretic parts does not yield many new types.

- With ordinary security, the recipient may or may not be secure without an error probability. (In ordinary digital signature schemes, he is.)
- With dual security, the signer can only be secure with an error probability.
- With fail-stop security, there is an error probability in the fall-back requirement of the signer on disputes. The fall-back requirement of the recipient on disputes may or may not be fulfilled without an error probability.
- With information-theoretic security, there is an error probability for both parties.

For all these types, realizations exist (see Chapter 6). Here and in the following, terms like "computational security for the signer" are used as abbreviations for statements like "the requirement of the signer on disputes is fulfilled against computationally restricted attackers".

6 Overview of Existing Schemes with Other than Ordinary Security

This chapter presents an overview of existing schemes with other than ordinary security. Recall that "existing" means that a concrete construction has been proposed in the literature. Section 6.1 contains an overview of these schemes within the classification from Chapter 5, i.e., their service, structural, and security properties, and the complete bibliography of these schemes. Section 6.2 discusses possible benefits of the new schemes in applications. Section 6.3 presents ideas for actual constructions in an informal way and contains references to the remaining chapters.

6.1 Properties

The security types considered are fail-stop, dual, and information-theoretic security. In other words, the schemes considered here offer information-theoretic security for signers, i.e., either the requirement or the fall-back requirement of the signer on disputes is fulfilled information-theoretically.

6.1.1 Top-Level Classification

It is not useful to consider all possible combinations of service, structure, and degree of security one by one, because there are far more possible combinations than existing schemes. (However, one could try to do so in future, i.e., either invent a scheme, or prove impossibility, or explain why the combination only has disadvantages even if one takes efficiency into account.) Instead, classes are defined according to a few important criteria, and within each class, the existing schemes with their remaining properties are listed.

When looking for suitable classes, it is useful to know that the original goals of all the work in this field were the new security types and reasonable efficiency, and as a starting point, only the service and the structure of ordinary digital signature schemes were known. Hence one tried to achieve the goals somehow, making changes to the service and structure when necessary. Discovering what a variety of services and structures one could allow under the name "signature scheme" was a side effect. Consequently, the top-level classes are the security types.

The next two levels of the classification will be the presence or absence of

- invisibility and
- interactive authentication.

The reason is that these two properties, like the security types, have always been seen as so clear deviations from ordinary digital signature schemes that, if present in a signature scheme, they are mentioned in the name. In fact, invisibility makes quite a difference to the legal environment needed for signatures (see Section 5.2.8,

"3-party disputes at the signer's discretion"), and interactive authentication has considerable practical disadvantages.

Using these three levels of classification and omitting classes for which no schemes have yet been proposed, one obtains the classes shown in Figure 6.1. In particular, invisibility implies interactive authentication, at least in current schemes. Moreover, 3-party disputes at the signer's discretion have only occurred together with invisibility. Hence the term "normal", as opposed to "invisible", only denotes schemes with 2-party disputes or 3-party disputes at the recipient's discretion. The individual classes are considered in the following subsections.

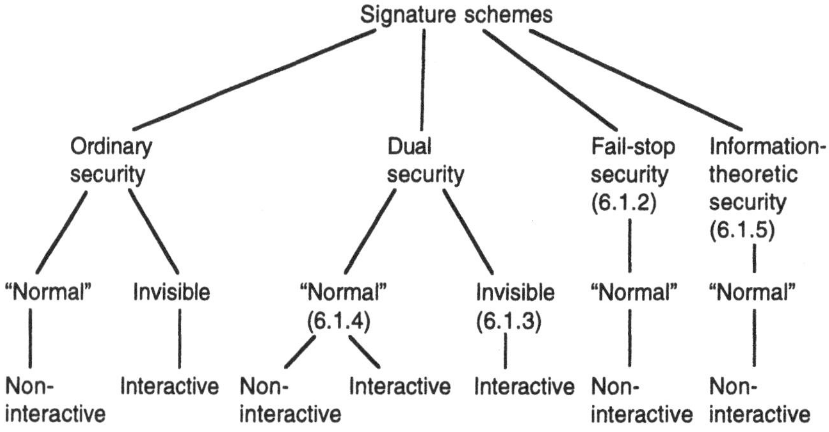

Figure 6.1. Classes of existing signature schemes and the sections where they are treated. The term "normal", as opposed to "invisible", is short for 2-party disputes or 3-party disputes at the recipient's discretion; "interactive" and "non-interactive" refer to authentication.

6.1.2 Fail-Stop Signature Schemes

Signature schemes with fail-stop security have so far been considered in [WaPf89, WaPf90, Pfit89, PfWa90, Bleu90, BlPW91, PfWa91, PfWa91a, Pfit91, Pfit91a, Heij92, HePe93, HePP93, DaPP94, Pfit94, Wilh94], where [DaPP94] contains some joint work with Moti Yung. A preliminary implementation exists in [Wilh93].

As shown in Figure 6.1, all these schemes are with non-interactive authentication, i.e., the notion of a signature exists, and without invisibility. Additional service properties they have in common are:

- 3-party disputes at the recipient's discretion. (However, many schemes additionally fulfil the strong requirement of the signer on disputes on the computational assumption.)
- Arbitrary transferability among those users who are possible recipients according to initialization.
- Transferability of proofs of forgery.

- External verifiability of both authentication and disputes can be added without modifying the original programs.

Additional common structural properties are:

- Public keys exist (see Section 5.3.2).
- Transfers of proofs of forgery are non-interactive, i.e., explicit proofs of forgery exist.

In the following, these properties are taken for granted; hence the name "**fail-stop signature scheme**" is restricted to schemes with these properties.[69]

The main variations are in the number of risk bearers and how the risk bearers participate in initialization, and in the number of recipients and the consequences on testing signatures. Furthermore, the existing schemes vary in the message space, the cryptologic assumption that the correctness of *'broken'* relies on, and in efficiency.

Number of Risk Bearers and Complexity of Initialization

Fail-stop security without further attributes means that the correctness of *'broken'* is required in the interest of each court individually. However, schemes with fewer special risk bearers (see Section 5.2.9) are important, because they can be much more efficient. For an overview, see Figure 6.2.

The reason for the importance of risk bearers is that all their entities play an active role in initialization. This is necessary because the correctness of *'broken'* is in the interest of any pair of a risk bearer and a court, i.e., they want computing a proof of forgery to be infeasible for attackers. With current definitions and computational assumptions, infeasibility is only defined for problem instances chosen according to a given distribution. Hence a correct entity must take part in the choice. (For instance, in a scheme based on factoring, the factors of one or more numbers might count as a proof of forgery, and the correct entity ensures that the other participants do not construct all the numbers by multiplying factors.) Thus either all courts or all risk bearers have to take part. As it is intended that every user can act as a court, there are at least as many courts as risk bearers; hence it is more efficient if the risk bearers take part.

Initialization is therefore greatly simplified if there is only one risk bearer: Its entity can locally generate such a problem instance and broadcast it; this message is called a **prekey**. In the most efficient case, the signer's entity can simply select a secret and a public key based on this prekey and broadcast the public key; this is called 2-message initialization. The same prekey can even be used by all signers. (Such a joint initialization for several signers would belong to "Other Transactions for Initialization and Leaving" in Section 5.2.11.)

A slightly more complex case occurs if the prekey must fulfil certain conditions for the signer to be secure, e.g., that it is a number with exactly 2 prime factors. If

[69] It would be more systematic to use this name for all signature schemes with fail-stop security. But it would be awkward to list all additional properties in the name of each type of scheme, and this use of the term is nearer to previous formal definitions of fail-stop signature schemes.

the signer's entity cannot verify these conditions on its own, the risk bearer's entity may have to give the signer's entity an interactive proof of the correctness (see Section 7.3).

If there are many risk bearers, initialization can be much more complex. However, all existing fail-stop signature schemes are based on a construction with only one risk bearer, and the additional measures to accommodate several risk bearers are very similar for all these constructions, see Section 7.5. (Sketches were contained in [Pfit89, PfWa90].)

In particular, a construction exists that transforms any fail-stop signature scheme for a fixed risk bearer with 2-message initialization into one for many risk bearers where initialization only needs two rounds: In the first round, the entity of each risk bearer broadcasts a separate prekey; in the second round, the signer's entity broadcasts a public key. More generally, one can use parallel replications of the initialization of any fail-stop signature scheme for a fixed risk bearer, see Section 7.5.1. This sounds quite efficient; however, it has so far implied that the complexity of the other transactions grows linearly with the number of risk bearers. In contrast, versions with more complex initialization exist where the complexity of the other transactions is not larger than in the case with one risk bearer, see Section 7.5.2.

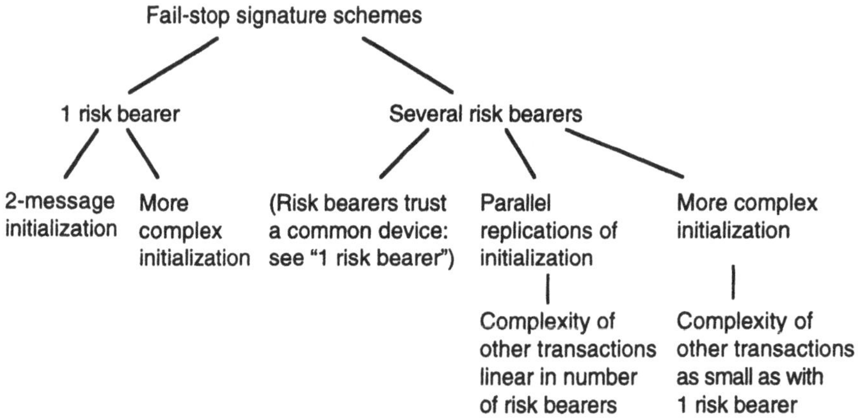

Figure 6.2. Existing fail-stop signature schemes, classified according to risk bearers

Note that according to the description above, the entities of courts and recipients do not send any messages in the initialization of existing fail-stop signature schemes with special risk bearers; they only receive messages that are broadcast by the entities of the signer and the risk bearers.

Number of Recipients and Complexity of Tests

The second service property in which existing fail-stop signature schemes differ is the dependence of authentication on the recipients (see Section 5.2.10). This classification is independent of that according to risk bearers. However, the cases with a fixed risk bearer and a fixed recipient often occur together: If the signature scheme is used by clients of an organization, such as a bank, to send messages to this organization, the organization is the only recipient and can also be the only risk bearer.

Similar to the convention with risk bearers, a fail-stop signature scheme without further attributes is assumed to provide the most general service, i.e., no dependence on the recipient, but more restricted schemes can be more efficient, in particular in their test algorithms. The two most common cases are (see Figure 6.3):

- **No dependence on the recipient.** As mentioned in Section 5.3.2, such schemes are usually with "memory-less" receiving, but not always. A related structural property, however, is common to all existing schemes in this class: The court's entity in a dispute acts as follows.

  1. A signature is received from the recipient's entity and tested with the same algorithm *test* that entities of recipients use in authentication.[70]
  2. If the signature does not pass this test, the court's entity outputs *acc* = FALSE and stops. Otherwise, it forwards the signature to the signer's entity.
  3. If it receives an answer from the signer's entity, it uses an algorithm *verify* to verify that the answer is a valid proof of forgery. If yes, the output is *acc* = *'broken'*, otherwise *acc* = TRUE.

  The same algorithm *verify* is used to verify transferred proofs of forgery.

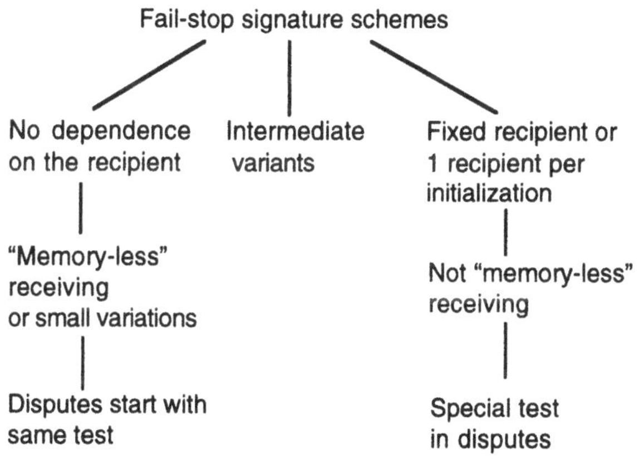

Figure 6.3. Existing fail-stop signature schemes, classified according to the dependence on the recipient

70 The conventions made so far ensure that this is possible:
- An algorithm *test* exists because of non-interactive authentication.
- After initialization, the entities of courts and recipients have the same public key.
- As there is no dependence on the recipient, the entity of a recipient can test any signature even if the signer has given many signatures to other recipients before. Hence its actions in authentication have at least a special case where no information has been changed since initialization, i.e., where the parameters of *test* are only the message and the public key. This is the case the court's entity can use.

If receiving *is* "memory-less", in addition to all the conventions made so far, the special structure sketched in Section 3.2 has been reached.

- **Fixed recipient or one recipient per initialization.** With all existing fail-stop signature schemes, what one gains by this restriction is efficiency in authentication, in particular, in the algorithm *test*, because the recipient's entity can store information from previous signatures. On the other hand, this implies that a court's entity cannot use the same test for a signature as the recipient's entity, i.e., disputes are not constructed as above.

Message Space

A fail-stop signature scheme without an attribute "for the message space M" is assumed to be for a general message space, for concreteness the set of all non-empty bit strings. All existing types of fail-stop signatures schemes (according to the other criteria) have such a variant, except for one theoretical construction from [DaPP94]. With some types, more efficient variants for very short messages exist. However, the difference is much larger with early, rather inefficient schemes than with new ones that are efficient anyway.

Each existing scheme is based on a construction for signing one message block. However, the block size usually depends on a security parameter; hence these subprotocols are not signature schemes for a certain given message space in the sense of Chapter 5 (cf. Section 9.1).

Cryptologic Assumptions and Efficiency

All types of fail-stop signature schemes, as far as service is concerned, could be built very early on the abstract assumption that a claw-intractable family of permutation pairs exists, i.e., the assumption from [GoMR88], except that trap-doors are not even needed; see [Pfit89, PfWa90].

This implies that all types of schemes also exist both on the factoring assumption and on a discrete-logarithm assumption (with [Damg88]).

Nowadays, more efficient constructions based directly on either of these two concrete assumptions exist [HePe93, HePP93] (see also [PePf95], and Section 9.4 contains a new variant with 2-message initialization based on the factoring assumption).

For the case with a fixed recipient and a fixed risk bearer, the difference in efficiency to ordinary digital signature schemes is very small. The schemes with no dependence on the recipient are practical, too, although probably not efficient enough for some applications at present. If the risk bearer trusts a fast, but not cryptographically strong hash function, efficiency can be improved further. (Table 11.1 shows details, and [Wilh94] contains concrete optimizations.) If several risk bearers trust a physical assumption and let one trusted device act for them all in initialization, there is no change — this might be the case with large organizations. Otherwise, with a large number of risk bearers, only the schemes based on the discrete-logarithm assumption seem feasible, but it would still be useful if the risk bearers trusted a non-cryptologic source of random bits, such as old tables of random numbers (see Remark 9.16).

The abstract assumptions on which fail-stop signature schemes can be built have recently been weakened. On the basis of [NOVY93], there is a construction from arbitrary one-way families of permutations (personal communication with Moti Yung and [DaPP94]). An intermediate step is a construction from so-called statistically hiding bit commitment schemes with non-interactive opening and public verification, which was contained more or less implicitly in [PfWa90]. These constructions only allow to sign messages of previously known size, and they only allow inefficient ways of signing many messages.

Moreover, [DaPP94] contains a construction from an arbitrary so-called collision-intractable family of hash functions, which is fairly efficient at least if one trusts a fast, but not cryptographically strong hash function, and may therefore be a reasonable alternative if number-theoretic assumptions should be disproved.

There is still no construction from an arbitrary one-way function and no equivalence proof, i.e., none of the above-mentioned primitives can so far be constructed from arbitrary fail-stop signature schemes (but one-way functions can). However, [DaPP94] contains a construction of bit commitment schemes with the properties mentioned above from rather a large subclass of fail-stop signature schemes.

6.1.3 Invisible Signature Schemes with Dual Security

Only a few schemes exist in this class so far [ChHP92, HePe93]. Anyway, invisible signature schemes are automatically with 3-party disputes at the signer's discretion, without any transferability, and currently with interactive authentication. In addition, the existing schemes share the following structural properties, similar to the existing fail-stop signature schemes:

- Public keys exist.
- In initialization, the entities of courts never send any messages.

In the following, these properties are taken for granted; hence the name "**dual invisible signature scheme**" is restricted to schemes with these properties.

Number of Recipients and Complexity of Initialization

The main variation is in the dependence on the recipients. Their role is similar to that of the risk bearers in fail-stop signature schemes: To guarantee computational security for each recipient, even if many other participants are attacking, the entities of all recipients must take part in initialization. Hence initialization is much simpler if it is for a fixed recipient.

Structure of Authentication and Disputes

The structure of authentication and disputes in existing dual invisible signature schemes resembles that of existing invisible signature schemes with ordinary security, not that of fail-stop signature schemes. The protocol carried out during authentication is of the following restricted form:

1. In the first round, the entity of the signer sends a value to the entity of the recipient. This value is called the **invisible signature**, and it is the only value that the recipient's entity stores.

2. The entities carry out a so-called zero-knowledge proof that the invisible signature is correct. Roughly, this is an interactive protocol that convinces the recipient's entity that the invisible signature is a correct function of the message and a secret key that corresponds to the given public key, without telling it anything else about the secret key. This part is called the **verification protocol**.

Disputes work as follows:

1. The recipient's entity sends the invisible signature to the court's entity, who passes it on to the signer's entity.
2. If the signer disavows, her entity gives the court's entity a zero-knowledge proof (see above) that the invisible signature is *not* correct. This is called the **disavowal protocol**.

Message Space, Cryptologic Assumptions, and Efficiency

The situation with messages spaces, cryptologic assumptions, and efficiency is similar to that with fail-stop signature schemes.

Schemes without further attributes allow all bit strings to be authenticated. There is not so much efficiency to be gained by restricting the message space as in old fail-stop signature schemes anyway. But again, all existing schemes are based on constructions for short message blocks.

Dual invisible signature schemes can be constructed from any claw-intractable family of permutation pairs, and more efficient constructions based directly on the factoring assumption or the discrete-logarithm assumption exist [ChHP92]. However, they are still a lot less efficient than the most efficient fail-stop signature schemes, although the invisible signatures themselves are not longer than fail-stop signatures and not more complex to compute. However, the verification protocol needs σ rounds of communication to achieve an error probability of about $2^{-\sigma}$, and the complexity of each round is about that of computing a signature. (It seems possible to parallelize this protocol, although this has not been proved in detail [ChHP92], but anyway, the bit complexity remains.)

The scheme in [HePe93] is distinguished by the fact that the signatures are convertible, i.e., the signer can turn them into "normal", transferable signatures when invisibility is no longer needed and if she wants to economize on the interactive verification and disavowal protocols.

6.1.4 "Normal" Signature Schemes with Dual Security

"Normal", i.e., not invisible signature schemes with dual security exist primarily as special variants of fail-stop signature schemes: As mentioned under Figure 5.12 and at the end of Section 5.4.3, one can turn a fail-stop signature scheme into one with dual security by replacing the output *acc* = *'broken'* by FALSE. The only condition is that the recipient is also regarded as a risk bearer, if it is a scheme with special risk bearers. Hence one obtains dual signature schemes with fixed recipient from fail-stop signature schemes with one risk bearer, and general dual signature schemes from full fail-stop signature schemes.

Only one direct construction (with small variations) of a "normal" signature scheme with dual security exists [PfWa91a, Pfit91a]. It was introduced for efficiency when no really efficient fail-stop signature schemes existed yet. It can be based on any fail-stop signature scheme and on the weak theoretical assumptions, it is still much more efficient for long messages than the fail-stop signature schemes. On the concrete assumptions, factoring and discrete logarithm, however, it is currently obsolete. Because of its interactive authentication, the scheme was not even called a signature scheme originally, but "3-phase protocol". Furthermore, it is restricted to a fixed recipient.

One can adapt the construction to a small number of recipients, but the efficiency decreases rapidly. This variant is so far the only example of a signature scheme where the parameter $ids_{R,sign}$ is really needed.

6.1.5 Schemes with Information-Theoretic Security

Signature schemes with information-theoretic security are easy to classify: Only one scheme exists so far ([ChRo91] with improvements and extensions in [PfWa92, Waid91]). With the conventions from Chapter 5, it is not even quite a signature scheme: In contrast to all other schemes, it does not withstand arbitrary active attacks (see Section 5.4.2). It offers the following service:

- No transferability [ChRo91] or finite transferability [PfWa92, Waid91].
- Authentication does not depend on the recipient.
- 2-party disputes.
- The message space can be arbitrary (in [PfWa92, Waid91] only).

The structural properties are:

- Non-interactive authentication.
- Disputes are non-interactive, too. If the scheme is finitely transferable, a dispute is a special case of the non-interactive transfer of a signature.
- Initialization is very complex: All entities of recipients and courts play an active role in a protocol in several rounds over a broadcast channel. Each entity has its own specific test key at the end.

The special problem with the degree of security is due to the fact that the entities of recipients and courts have secret information and divulge some of it in authentication and disputes, in contrast to all other existing signature schemes. Hence not only the signer, but also recipients and courts are vulnerable to active attacks, as described at the end of Section 5.4.2. This seems to be a more difficult problem than active attacks on signers, because each signature is issued only once, whereas it may be tested very often.[71]

---

[71] One could try to introduce a parameter for the maximum number of tests a recipient or court carries out with respect to a given initialization, similar to the message bound for the number of authentications. However, this would entail further changes to the requirements — at present, it is required that any recipient can have any received authenticated message disputed at any time.

Although no signature scheme with information-theoretic security against general active attacks is known, it has been shown in [PfWa92, Waid91] that the extension of the scheme from [ChRo91] can be used within any deterministically polynomial-time protocol (with some additional requirements that the protocol uses the signature scheme in a "reasonable" way — with the new type of definition, they simply mean that the signature scheme is only used through its interface). A protocol defines when and from whom a recipient is willing to accept messages and to test their authenticity; hence one can determine upper bounds on the information an attacker can gain and set the security parameters of the signature scheme accordingly. This degree of security can be described if the model with indirect access is used (see Figure 5.15), and the entities representing the honest users are exactly the entities from the given protocol.

Anyway, the existing scheme is so inefficient that it can only be used in theory, i.e., to implement larger distributed protocols without computational assumptions. For this purpose, the security is sufficient. To a certain extent, it can even be proved that information-theoretically secure signature schemes are necessarily very inefficient: The length of each signature grows linearly in the number of participants who can test it, that is, in the number of both recipients and courts [HePP93, PePf95]; see Section 11.6. (With the new general definitions from Chapter 5, one would have to extend those proofs somewhat.)

There exists a distributed variant of authentication for this scheme (see Section 5.2.11), i.e., a protocol where either all the recipients accept a signature or none does [PfWa92b]. This is not trivial, even if reliable broadcast channels are given, because the entities of the recipients have different test keys.

6.2 Possible Applications and Legal Significance

This section discusses possible benefits of the new types of signature schemes in applications. It resumes Section 3.1, where some problems with ordinary digital signature schemes were sketched, which can now be described as problems with ordinary security. Hence it is now discussed what advantages other security types may have with respect to the legal and social requirements from Chapter 1.

It is not hard to imagine that a scheme with information-theoretic security would greatly increase the legal security of digital signatures. However, as mentioned in Section 6.1.5, such schemes are currently impractical and it seems that they will never be very efficient. Hence their social implications are not very relevant. In contrast, practical schemes with fail-stop or dual security exist. Hence the only two topics of this section are

1. benefits of dual security and
2. benefits of fail-stop security.

To rule out misunderstanding: The claim in the first topic is

- not "dual security is better than ordinary security",

- but "having dual security and ordinary security to choose from is better than having only one of them".

6.2.1 Possible Benefits of Dual Security

Use in Message Exchange

The first advantage of having schemes with ordinary security and others with dual security is that one can make one party information-theoretically secure in a message exchange: If *A* and *B* exchange messages signed with an ordinary digital signature scheme, both are only computationally secure — if the cryptologic assumption is broken, signatures of both of them can be forged and their requirements as signers on disputes are not fulfilled. If both use a signature scheme with dual security, nothing is gained. However, if *A* uses a scheme with dual security for messages she authenticates, and *B* signs with an ordinary digital signature scheme, *A* is information-theoretically secure: Her requirement as the signer in disputes about her own messages is fulfilled information-theoretically, and so is her requirement as the recipient in disputes about *B*'s messages.

Asymmetry Between Parties

Being able to offer information-theoretic security to one out of two parties is most interesting in applications with an a-priori asymmetry between the parties. Asymmetry primarily means that there is a stronger and a weaker partner; Figure 6.4 illustrates this. It is useful to make the weaker partner information-theoretically secure.

Asymmetry is most marked if one party has the functions of a system operator of the signature scheme, such as a bank that introduces the signature scheme in a digital payment scheme. For concreteness, the following details are presented for this important case. More precisely, they apply whenever a large organization introduces a digital signature scheme for digital message exchange with its clients, and most clients are individuals. (However, if the clients also exchange messages with each other, fail-stop security is needed for similar benefits.)

Some reasons for making clients information-theoretically secure in a payment scheme are:

- The bank is the stronger partner in several ways. It can select the signature schemes and security parameters and thus provide for its own security. Moreover, it can inform itself about how trustworthy the cryptologic assumption is, both initially and while the scheme is in use, whereas many clients will already be deterred by the name of a factoring or discrete-logarithm assumption.

  Note that this argument is more about liberty and psychology than about computer science: One might say that the security for the bank is so important that any cryptologic assumption that a bank can trust ought to be trustworthy enough for anybody else, too. First, however, there is the undefined word "can": Why should someone else be convinced that an assumption can be trusted just because a bank does trust it? And why should they even be forced to trust

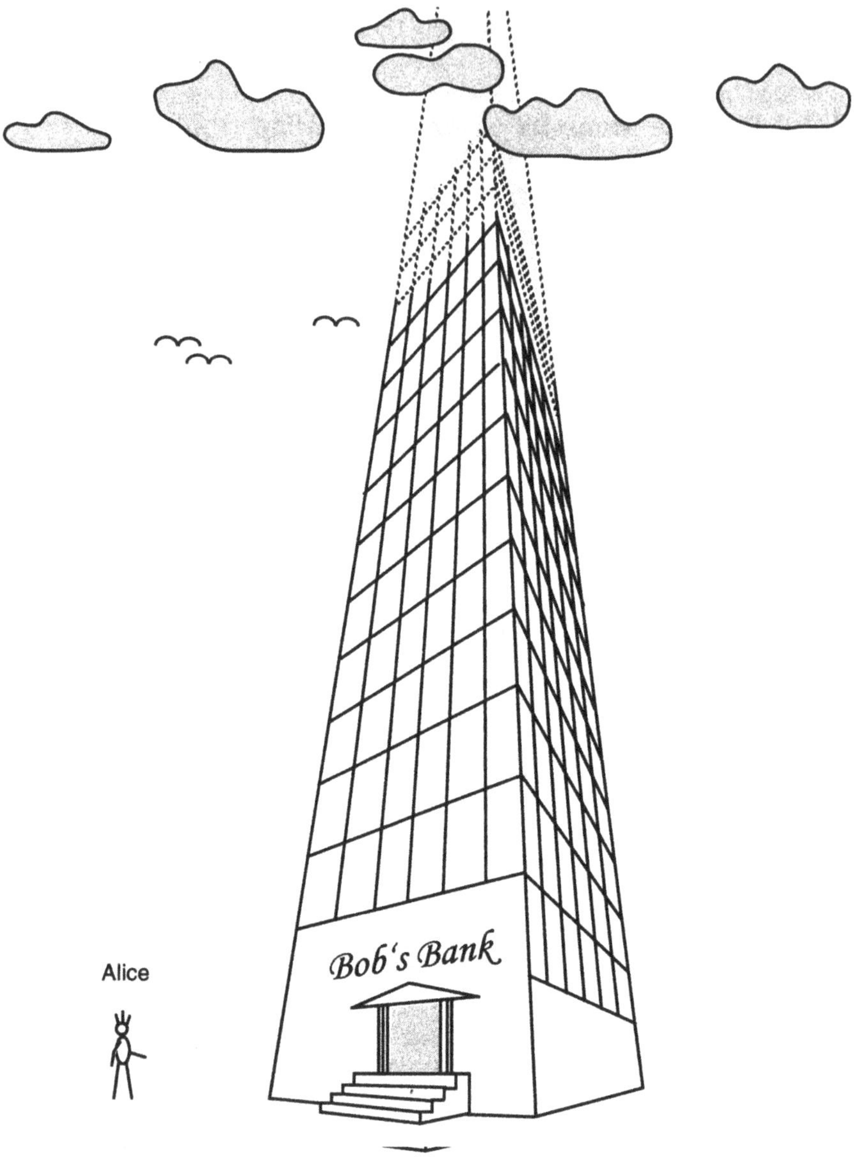

Figure 6.4. Illustration of an asymmetry between two parties

such an assumption? (And people cannot very well avoid using whatever payment schemes the banks offer.) Secondly, trust has a value in itself: It is not only important that a scheme is not broken; people should also feel good about it while they have to use it.

- The bank is the party that can stop the system. Hence there is a kind of external fail-stop property if the bank is the only party whose security is based on a cryptologic assumption: If anyone breaks the assumption, the only party that can be cheated is the bank; the bank naturally notices this and can stop the system. In contrast, if clients could be cheated, and a forger would carefully cheat a limited number of clients only, the bank would not be likely to believe them that this was happening.

- If a majority of clients were security-conscious, the first banks introducing such a scheme would have market advantages.
- The fact that clients are information-theoretically secure might increase the legal acceptance of the scheme, i.e., in the more likely case where the cryptologic assumption is *not* broken, the bank might be more secure that the clients' signatures are indeed recognized in court than if the clients were using a scheme with ordinary security.

  To see this, recall that a real court is not obliged to comply with the technical view of how it has to decide; it could believe a supposed signer that an ordinary digital signature is a forgery (see Section 3.1). A court should be far less likely to do so if it is proven that clients are information-theoretically secure.[72]

The arguments dealing with the fact that a payment system might be broken, and how this situation could be handled, should not make one think that such a situation could ever be harmless, even if the system could be stopped almost immediately. Hence an external or system-internal fail-stop property should not seduce one into choosing risky security parameters. Furthermore, one may regard the arguments dealing with the knowledge that the system has not been broken, in particular the last one, as more important than those dealing with the consequences if it has been broken.

Efficiency in Asymmetric Situations

The case described above, i.e., where one large organization exchanges messages with its clients and only the clients use a signature scheme with dual security to authenticate their messages, is exactly the case where existing signature schemes with dual security are almost as efficient as existing ordinary digital signature schemes. In particular, if a fail-stop signature scheme is used as a dual signature scheme, as described in Section 6.1.4, the organization is both the only risk bearer and the only recipient, which leads to the most efficient versions in the classifications shown in Figures 6.2 and 6.3. In particular, if there is 2-message initialization, the organization can easily publish its prekey for the clients' signatures together with its own public key.

72 Remember, however, that this is only half of the problem a court faces in practice: Apart from the unproven cryptologic assumptions, there were unproven assumptions about physical security; see Section 1.4. Of course, dual or fail-stop security does not help if the signer's secret information is physically stolen — no digital authentication scheme can: Once a forger has the signer's complete secret information, it is impossible to distinguish him from the signer by digital means. Hence if a signer claims that her device was stolen and the PIN found out, it is not clear how a court should decide.

6.2.2 Possible Benefits of Fail-Stop Security

The possible benefits of a fail-stop signature scheme used as a dual signature scheme have already been discussed in Section 6.2.1. Hence this section concentrates on the advantages of fail-stop security that cannot be achieved by a combination of schemes with ordinary and dual security.

Roughly, the advantages are the same as in Section 6.2.1, but they are no longer restricted to scenarios where small individuals exchange messages with a large organization that sets up the signature system.

- With a fail-stop property, one can make clients of organizations, or individuals in general, information-theoretically secure even if they exchange authenticated messages with each other. Of course, this means that one must find other risk bearers. This might be the organization that introduces the system, e.g., a bank that introduces a digital payment scheme where clients exchange authenticated messages, such as cheques, with each other (in contrast to a system based on remittances as assumed above). In a more general application, one would need an insurance. The arguments, in particular the psychologic and social ones, for making the organization bear the risk are the same as above.

  Of course, selecting risk bearers arbitrarily only works for financial risks (and even there, only to a certain extent). In a large-scale application in the real world, the fail-stop property would make individuals safe from a strong risk, but still leave them with a smaller risk, such as higher insurance premiums or having to use handwritten signatures again.

  On the other hand, one should not neglect that one non-financial risk is completely averted in a system with fail-stop security: Nobody can wrongly be branded as a cheater or as quarrelsome. If a cryptologic assumption is broken, it may be much better that the losses are distributed equally and everybody knows that this is due to a common disaster, than that some signers (or recipients) are made responsible while everybody else believes that they were the ones who tried to cheat.

- Next, of course, there is the fail-stop property as such, i.e., the fact that the scheme can be stopped in consensus if the cryptologic assumption has been broken. How much damage may have occurred up to this time depends on the application: Forgeries are proved in disputes. If a person who has broken the cryptologic assumption only cheats by proving her own signatures to be forgeries in court, the system will be stopped as soon as any recipient sues her for one of her signatures. If the cheater also forges signatures of other users, the system may be stopped earlier, because a proof of forgery will also be constructed when a recipient of a forged signature tells the supposed signer about this signature privately.

  Theoretical applications exist where no damage at all can occur in such a period, e.g., Byzantine agreement and untraceable communication [WaPf89, WaPf90]. For applications in practice, however, it must be repeated that a fail-stop property cannot serve as an excuse for taking the selection of a trustworthy cryptologic assumption and sufficiently large security parameters lightly.

- The fact that any forgery can be recognized unambiguously might increase the legal acceptance of the scheme. In particular, everybody might be more secure that courts comply with the technical view of how they have to settle disputes if the correctness of this view does not rely on unproven assumptions. For the same reason, a fail-stop property might be interesting if one wants to give digital signatures the same legal significance as handwritten signatures, because any fail-stop signature that has not been proved to be a forgery guarantees the authenticity function information-theoretically (as far as the mathematical part of the system is concerned).

As in the previous section, one can regard the last point and the psychologic aspects of the first one as the most important arguments, because they concern the more likely case that the system is not broken — if one really expected the system to be broken, one had better refrain from using it in the first place (unless in parallel with other schemes).

6.3 Important Construction Ideas

This section gives a short overview of important ideas used in the construction of signature schemes with other than ordinary security. Only abstract ideas are presented; the number-theoretic ideas follow in Chapter 8.

One principle is common to all these constructions: Even in the information-theoretic sense, the secret information in a signer's entity cannot be uniquely determined from public information.

In schemes where secret keys and public keys exist, this implies that many possible secret keys correspond to the same public key, see Figure 6.5. That a secret key *sk* and a public key *pk* correspond to each other means that the pair (*sk*, *pk*) is a possible outcome of key generation.

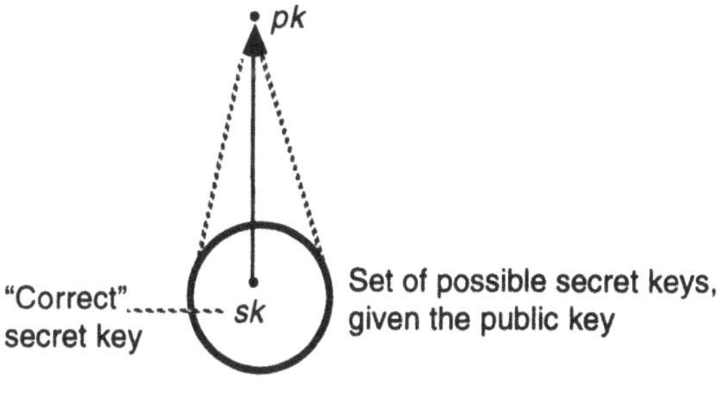

Figure 6.5. Many-one relation between secret and public keys.
The "correct" secret key is defined as the one that the signer's entity actually has.

Usually, at least 2^σ equally probable secret keys correspond to each public key if one aims at information-theoretic security with an error probability of at most $2^{-\sigma}$:

Then the **correct secret key**, i.e., the one that the signer's entity actually has, can only be guessed with a probability of $2^{-\sigma}$.[73]

Similar relations hold in schemes with a more complex structure. Furthermore, the term "public information" can be extended to "all the information that an attacker may know". In particular, this includes all the signatures that the signer's entity has already produced.

6.3.1 Construction of Fail-Stop Signature Schemes

Basic Construction Idea

The basic idea for existing signature schemes with fail-stop security is presented for schemes with the simple structure shown in Figure 3.2, i.e., with secret and public keys and "memory-less" signing and receiving. Even for schemes with this structure, however, the following construction is not compulsory; some deviations are explained below. Any value that passes the test with the public key (for a given message) is called an **acceptable signature**.

The basic idea is that every message m has many different acceptable signatures, of which the signer can construct only one (unless she breaks the cryptologic assumption); see Figure 6.6. This one is called the **correct signature**. Of course, the set of the acceptable signatures on m must still be small in comparison with the complete signature space, so that it is infeasible for a computationally restricted forger to find any acceptable signature.

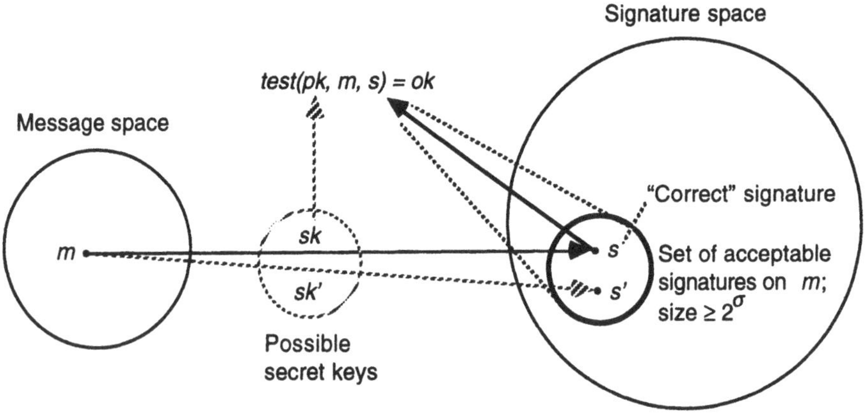

Figure 6.6. Acceptable and correct signatures

73 Of course, a many-one relation between secret and public information is not sufficient for security; but once one has a formal definition, one can formally prove that it is necessary. However, this is not completely trivial: The security for the signer need not be violated in every single case where the secret information in her entity can be guessed. A formal treatment for a standard case of fail-stop signature schemes can be seen in Section 11.3.

In the information-theoretic sense, an attacker can always compute the set of the acceptable signatures on a message *m* (for the same reason as forging ordinary digital signatures cannot be harder than NP, see Section 2.3). The new feature is: Even a computationally unrestricted attacker does not have sufficient information to determine which of the many acceptable signatures is the correct one.

Of course, when proving this for a concrete construction, one must carefully consider all the information that the attacker has. In particular, he knows that the correct signature is constructed by signing the message with a secret key *sk* that corresponds to the public key *pk*. Fortunately, as known from Figure 6.5, many secret keys are possible, and each of them would yield an acceptable signature. One alternative key, *sk'*, and the corresponding alternative signature, *s'*, are shown in Figure 6.6. It is now assumed that there are still many acceptable signatures that could be the correct one from the point of view of the attacker.

Consequently, a forged signature will be different from the correct signature with very high probability, such as *s'* in Figure 6.7. If this forged signature is shown to the signer (as in Figure 3.2), or rather her entity, the signer's entity knows two acceptable signatures on the same message, because it can compute the correct signature on the same message, too.

This will be sufficient for a proof of forgery. The pair of two signatures on the same message can either immediately count as a proof of forgery, as illustrated in Figure 6.8, or there can be a procedure that constructs a simpler proof from such a pair. For instance, such a proof could be a factor of a number that the signer should not have been able to factor (see Section 6.1.2, "Number of Risk Bearers ...").

Regarding two different acceptable signatures on the same message (and for the same public key) as a proof that the scheme has been broken is sound because it was assumed that the signer herself can compute only one acceptable signature, unless she breaks the cryptologic assumption.

The signer will also know only one of the secret keys corresponding to her public key; this is compulsory if different secret keys lead to different signatures.

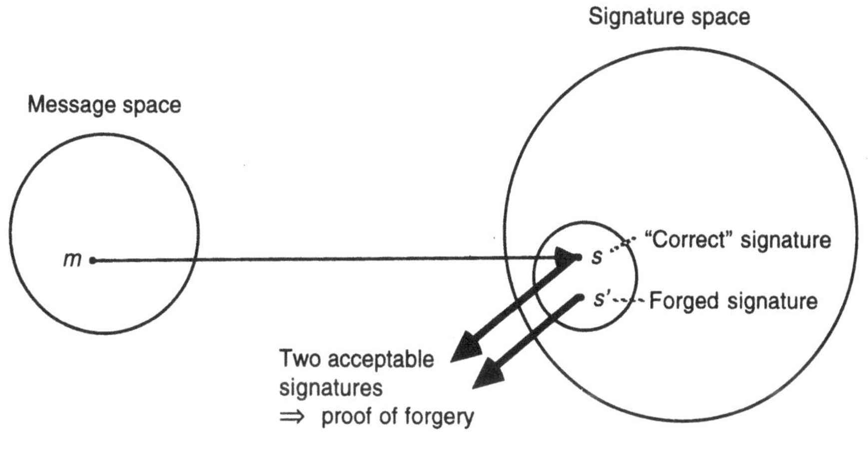

Figure 6.7. Construction of a proof of forgery

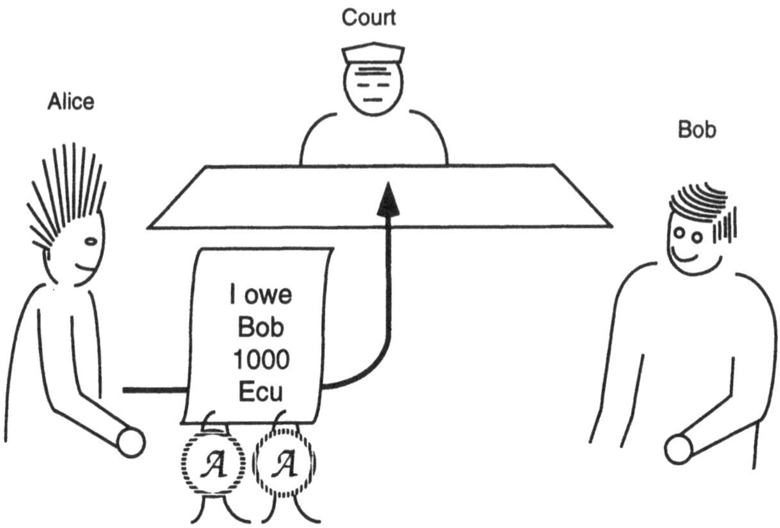

Figure 6.8. Usual type of proof of forgery

Deviations from the Basic Construction Idea

The construction sketched above is only the simplest case; in particular, the signer may know more than one secret key and more than one acceptable signature. Two examples show this. As a starting point, assume that a secure fail-stop signature scheme according to the construction above is given.

First, each secret key is augmented by a random bit at the end. Everything else remains unchanged. The security of the scheme is obviously unaffected, and the signer knows two possible secret keys for each public key.

Secondly, each signature is augmented by a random bit at the end, and two acceptable signatures on the same message only count as a proof of forgery if they differ in more than the last bit. The security of the scheme is unaffected again, and the signer knows two acceptable signatures on each message.

A third example follows in the subsection on signing long messages.

Important Building Blocks: Bundling Functions

From the description above, one can guess that a certain class of functions will play an important role in constructions, in particular as functions mapping secret keys on public keys. These functions have two properties:

- Every image (e.g., *pk*) has many preimages (e.g., many possible *sk*'s).
- It must be computationally infeasible to find a **collision**, i.e., a pair of values with the same image (e.g., two secret keys corresponding to the same public key); see Figure 6.9. Such functions are called **collision-intractable**.[74]

[74] "Collision-free" is the most established equivalent term, but it sometimes gives the wrong impression that collisions do not exist at all. "Collision-resistant" has also been used, and "computationally collision-free" would seem appropriate, too.

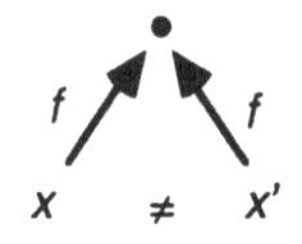

Figure 6.9. A collision: The pair (x, x') is an f-collision.

A rather general class of such functions will be called **bundling functions**. There are subclasses with additional properties, too. For precise definitions and constructions, see Chapter 8.

A First Step: Signing One Message Block

All existing fail-stop signature schemes are constructed in two steps[75]: First, a scheme for signing only one message block of a certain length is constructed, where the block length may depend on the security parameters. Then the scheme is extended so that many messages of arbitrary or at least predefined length can be signed.

The first step of the constructions will follow the basic construction idea explained above exactly (see Chapter 9). The second step has two parts: There are extensions to predefined message spaces and extensions to large message bounds (see Chapter 10).

Signing Long Messages (Message Hashing)

The extensions to arbitrary message spaces do not vary much. If the desired message space M is the set of all bit strings, messages will be hashed before signing. At first sight this might seem impossible with fail-stop signature schemes: Given a signature on a message m, a computationally unrestricted attacker can usually find another message m' that is mapped to the same short string by the hash function. Hence, this attacker knows the correct signature on m', too, in contrast to Figure 6.6. Fortunately, this is not a problem, because such a forgery gives the signer's entity a collision of the hash function. If the hash function is from a collision-intractable family, i.e., if it is computationally infeasible to find collisions, the signer cannot construct a collision by herself. Hence such a collision can count as a proof of forgery. See Section 10.1 for more details.

If the desired message space M consists of short messages only, one has to define embeddings of M into the sequence of message-block spaces given by the first step of the construction.

75 This is not proven to be the only possible construction. The only known related theorem is the lower bound in Section 11.3, which says that the number of secret random bits a signer needs grows linearly with the number of messages she can sign. It is therefore quite natural to use schemes where each signature depends on "its own" random bits, so that it can be computed quickly, and one can see this as an operation from a one-time signature scheme. However, a rather impractical scheme exists which is not of this type, see Remark 10.24.

Signing Many Messages (Tree Authentication)

The easiest way more messages can be signed if one has a scheme for signing one message is to prepare as many keys as one intends to sign messages. However, this is not very practical. In particular, the communication complexity of initialization would be very high, because all the public keys would have to be distributed on a reliable broadcast channel, such as a phone book. Hence, the most important goal of the constructions is to guarantee short public keys.

One basic idea for these constructions is tree authentication. If one starts with the type sketched in Section 2.4, the same addition is needed as with message hashing: The hash functions used must be collision-intractable, and their collisions count as proofs of forgery.

Two types of tree authentication exist. The one mentioned so far will be called **bottom-up tree authentication**, the other one **top-down tree authentication** [Merk88, GoMR88]. The former leads to shorter signatures, the latter is more flexible. Its basic idea is that new public keys are authenticated using old keys. Fail-stop versions of both are presented in Sections 10.2 and 10.3, respectively. Section 10.4 contains a variant of top-down tree authentication that only needs a small amount of private storage. This may be important in practice, see the end of Section 5.4.1.

A scheme that does not need tree authentication is presented in [Pfit94]. This leads to very short signatures, but it has computational disadvantages. Furthermore, it relies on stronger cryptologic assumptions than the other schemes.

Many variations and combinations of the basic types of tree authentication are conceivable. Some are presented and compared in [Wilh94]. Furthermore, efficiency improvements exist that exploit special properties of the underlying scheme for signing one message block, see Section 10.5.

Resulting Efficiency

The complexity of the most efficient schemes for signing one message block is almost as low as that of efficient ordinary digital signature schemes. The same holds if message hashing is added. (Note that this subsection assumes a fixed risk bearer or any other version that has the same effect on the efficiency of authentication, cf. Figure 6.2.)

In schemes with arbitrary message bounds, one must send a whole branch of an authentication tree as a signature, and the whole branch must be tested. This means that the complexity of each authentication grows logarithmically with the overall number of messages to be authenticated. (However, it has not been proved that this is necessary.) To compare this with the efficiency of ordinary digital signature schemes, one must distinguish two cases:

- If one considers cryptographically strong schemes only, the same holds for all existing ordinary digital signature schemes. Recently, however, a scheme that achieves fairly short signatures in practice by specific flat trees was presented [DwNa94].[76]

---

[76] The scheme from [BoCh93] has not been considered here because of the insufficient proof, see Section 2.6.

- If one considers all schemes that look moderately secure, such as RSA with the additional measures described in Section 2.5, ordinary digital signature schemes exist where the complexity of one authentication is independent of the overall number of messages to be authenticated. In this case, one usually decides to trust fast hash functions, too, so that long messages can be signed fast.

  If one uses such a fast hash function in bottom-up tree authentication for a fail-stop signature scheme, the overhead for the tree part (for trees of reasonable size, such as depth 20) is small in comparison with the actual signature, at least in time complexity. (This is why one-time signature schemes with tree authentication are still considered in practice, see Section 2.4.)

A table with a more precise complexity comparison can be found in Section 11.6.

Simplifications with Fixed Recipient

As mentioned in Section 6.1.2, more efficient constructions exist for the case of a fixed recipient, which is rather important in practice (see Section 6.2). They can be seen as special variants of tree authentication that exploit the fact that the recipient's entity can store information about the current tree. Hence only one new leaf, instead of one complete branch, has to be sent and tested during each authentication, see Section 10.6. The complexity of fail-stop signature schemes with fixed recipient is therefore comparable to that of ordinary digital signature schemes.

6.3.2 Construction of Invisible Signature Schemes with Dual Security

Existing dual invisible signature schemes share half of the basic construction idea with fail-stop signature schemes (see Section 6.1.3 and Figures 6.5 and 6.6): Given the public key, there are many possible secret keys and many possible invisible signatures, of which the signer knows only one. This one is called the **correct** invisible signature. Even a computationally unrestricted attacker will not have enough information to determine the correct invisible signature. Hence a forged invisible signature will be different from the correct one with high probability.

However, the incorrectness of a forged invisible signature cannot be exploited in the same way as with fail-stop signatures: There is no such notion as acceptable invisible signatures that are infeasible to construct for computationally restricted forgers — without the verification protocol with the signer's entity, invisible signatures look like something everybody could easily have produced. In fact, in existing constructions, the set of possible invisible signatures, given the message and the public key, is still the whole signature space, as illustrated in Figure 6.10.

Hence the idea of using two acceptable signatures on the same message as a proof of forgery cannot be applied. Instead, the signer's entity proves to the court's entity (using a zero-knowledge proof scheme) that its correct signature, say s, is different from the forged signature, say s', that has been shown to the court's entity. The exact statement it proves is:

"I know a secret key sk that corresponds to pk and leads to an invisible signature $s \neq s'$."

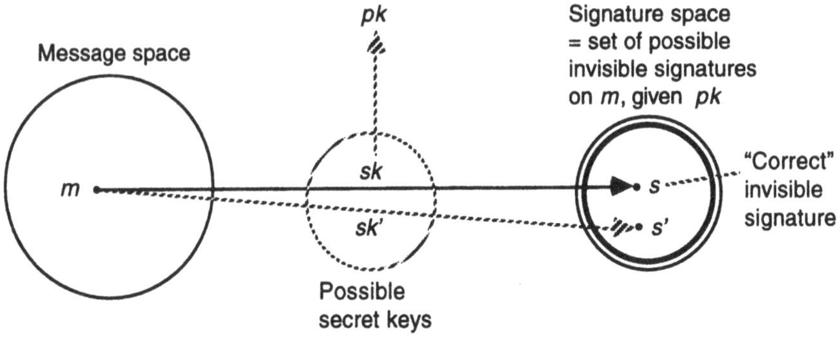

Figure 6.10. Possible and correct invisible signatures in existing schemes

For precise notions of proofs of knowledge, see [BeGo93] and its bibliography.[77] Assuming that proofs of knowledge do what one intuitively thinks, this construction guarantees the signer information-theoretic security: Whenever the attacker has guessed the invisible signature wrong, the signer's entity can prove this statement. On the other hand, as a signer only knows one secret key, unless she breaks the cryptologic assumption, she cannot disavow her correct signature in this way.[78]

Similar to the situation with fail-stop signature schemes, this construction is not compulsory, important building blocks are bundling functions, and all existing schemes are based on constructions for signing only one message block. For more details, see [ChHP92].

6.3.3 Construction of "Normal" Signature Schemes with Dual Security

As mentioned in Section 6.1.4, the usual method to obtain a non-invisible signature scheme with dual security is to use a fail-stop signature scheme and to identify *'broken'* with FALSE. The properties of the only other existing scheme of this type were sketched there, too.

The basic construction idea for this scheme is to combine a fail-stop signature scheme that is only efficient for very short messages with an ordinary digital signature scheme so that only very short messages have to be signed with the fail-stop signature scheme. The main steps of authentication for a message m and a signer id_S are:

---

77 One really needs a proof of knowledge, and not a better-known proof of language membership, because what the correct signature is cannot be defined relative to the public key and the message: It depends on which of the possible secret keys a signer (or her entity) knows.

78 Note that only dual security has been achieved, and not a fail-stop property: The court's entity cannot distinguish the situation where an attacker shows a random number s', claiming it were an invisible signature, and the signer disavows s', from the situation where the cryptologic assumption has been broken. Hence the court's result is acc = FALSE in both cases, never acc = *'broken'*.

- **Transaction description.** The recipient's entity signs the following message with the ordinary digital signature scheme and sends it to the signer's entity: "The i-th message of signer id_S is m."
- **Ok.** If the transaction description is correct, the signer's entity signs one single bit, which can be interpreted as "ok", with its i-th fail-stop signature, and sends this signature to the recipient's entity.

Recall that the recipient is fixed; hence his entity can store the counter i. Furthermore, the notion of the "i-th fail-stop signature" is clearly defined in the fail-stop signature schemes that would be used here (and any fail-stop signature scheme could be modified in this way): Either a scheme with tree authentication would be used or the theoretical construction from [DaPP94], where as many keys have to be prepared as one intends to sign messages.

In a dispute about this message, the court's entity decides as follows:

- First, the recipient's entity has to present a number i and the signer's ok that she authenticated the i-th message.
- If the signer's entity can compute a proof of forgery for this fail-stop signature, the result is acc = FALSE. Otherwise, it must present the transaction description for the i-th message with the signature of the recipient's entity. If this transaction description contains a different message m', the result is acc = FALSE, otherwise acc = TRUE.

To prevent mischief, one can add a preliminary step where the signer's entity sends an ordinary digital signature on the transaction description to the recipient's entity. The mischief would be that an attacker starts authentication in the name of a signer. The attacker cannot really gain anything by this, but it reduces the availability of service, because the recipient can only use each value i once.

The scheme is efficient even with a fail-stop signature scheme where messages are signed bit by bit. As promised, the requirement of the signer on disputes is fulfilled information-theoretically: It only relies on the fail-stop signatures and that the correct transaction descriptions are stored. The requirement of the recipient on disputes is fulfilled computationally: In order to cheat him, someone must either present a proof of forgery or forge the recipient's signature on a wrong transaction description.

More details can be found in [PfWa91a, Pfit91a].

6.3.4 Construction of Schemes with Information-Theoretic Security

This section sketches the information-theoretically secure signature schemes from [ChRo91, PfWa92, Waid91]. These schemes are with non-interactive authentication and 2-party disputes; hence one can speak of signatures and of testing them.

The first basic idea is that the entities of all recipients and courts must have different test keys, i.e., there is no public key. Thus an unrestricted attacker does not know how a recipient's entity tests a signature, and therefore the attack by exhaustive search mentioned under "Security Limits" in Section 2.3 is no longer applicable.

If the signer's entity used an independently chosen key of an information-theoretically secure symmetric authentication scheme with each recipient's or court's entity, forgery would obviously only be possible with exponentially small error probability. However, such a scheme would not fulfil the requirement of the recipient on disputes. A first extension is that a signature s consists of many parts s_i, one for each potential recipient or court, so that each entity can test the signature by testing the corresponding part. Hence a signature no longer depends on the recipient. However, this only works for honest signers: A dishonest signer can issue a signature where the part for the intended recipient is correct, but the parts for all courts are wrong.

The second idea in [ChRo91] was therefore that the signer should not know which of the parts of the signature are for whom, and that there are many parts for each recipient and court. Assume for a moment that this can be done. Then no matter how many wrong and correct parts a cheating signer puts in a signature, it is very improbable that all the parts for the intended recipient are correct, whereas all the parts for a certain court are wrong. Hence the entities of recipients and courts need only use different tests:

- A recipient's entity accepts a signature if *all* its parts are correct, whereas
- a court's entity accepts a signature if at least *one* of its parts is correct.

This guarantees that the requirement of the recipient on disputes is fulfilled. The requirement of the signer on disputes is also still fulfilled because the individual parts are information-theoretically unforgeable.

However, such signatures do not offer transferability: If the entity of the second recipient used the same test as the court's entity, the requirement of this second recipient on disputes could be broken with non-negligible probability (if he is given a "signature" where very few parts are correct). If it used the same test as the entity of the first recipient, transferability could be broken with non-negligible probability (if a first recipient is given a "signature" where most, but not all the parts are correct). Finite transferability can be achieved by providing more versions of the test: The entity of the next recipient in a transfer always requires fewer of its parts to be correct than the previous one. For details, see [PfWa92, Waid91].

Now an initialization protocol remains to be constructed where the signer's entity exchanges many keys of a symmetric authentication scheme with the entities of recipients and courts, but the signer cannot find out which of them were exchanged with whom. The basic idea is that (instead of the signer's entity) the entities of recipients and courts generate the keys that are for them, and send them to the signer's entity anonymously. The basic method for information-theoretically secure anonymous sending on an untrusted network is the DC-net from [Chau88]. It is combined with several tricks to ensure that all the entities of recipients and courts succeed in sending a sufficient number of keys (even in the presence of disrupters who try to use the anonymous channel all the time), and that only the signer's entity learns these keys (if the signer is honest) and nobody is excluded as a disrupter who did not disrupt. Thus in this scheme, effectiveness and correctness of initialization are non-trivial. For details, see the original literature.

7 Conventional Definitions of Fail-Stop Signature Schemes and General Reductions

In this chapter, conventional definitions of fail-stop signature schemes are given and several general properties are proved.

The actual definition of so-called standard fail-stop signature schemes is contained in Section 7.1. In Section 7.2, relations to alternative or additional security properties are shown. Section 7.3 presents fail-stop signature schemes with prekey, an important subclass, and proves simplified security criteria for them. Section 7.4 shows the relation between standard fail-stop signature schemes and ordinary digital signature schemes. Section 7.5 contains constructions of schemes with many risk bearers from schemes with one risk bearer.

7.1 Definition

Previous formal definitions of fail-stop signature schemes [Pfit89, PfWa90, PePf95] were derived bottom-up from the GMR definition of ordinary digital signature schemes with only those extensions that occurred in the constructions, as in Section 3.2. Thus, compared with the general definition, they have all the restrictions listed in Section 6.1.2 and a few more, which seemed too technical to be mentioned there.

Here the same type of definition is presented with small generalizations only (except that only the case with one risk bearer had been formalized before), so that no significant changes were needed in the proofs made according to the previous definition, in particular the lower bounds in Chapter 11. If one wants a fully general formal definition, it is better to formalize Chapter 5. The five remaining restrictions are denoted by $restr_1$ to $restr_5$. Such schemes are called **standard fail-stop signature schemes**.

However, the definition is now derived semiformally top-down from the general definition. This should clarify

- what is implicitly assumed about the complete entities when only certain algorithms are defined (such as the use of old proofs of forgery in disputes, see Section 7.1.1),
- that there are in fact some restrictions in such a definition,
- and why certain types of active attacks are considered and others not.

Section 7.1.1 explains why one can concentrate on schemes with special risk bearers. The components of the schemes are derived in Section 7.1.2 and summarized formally in Definitions 7.1 to 7.3. The requirements, which are now mixed with considerations of structure and degree of security, are studied in Sections 7.1.3 to 7.1.5.

7.1.1 Concentrating on Schemes with Special Risk Bearers

The following sections concentrate on standard fail-stop signature schemes with special risk bearers. In particular, the formal versions of the definitions and constructions are only presented for such schemes.

One reason is that the formal definitions of full fail-stop signature schemes can be derived from the informal discussions just like those with special risk bearers.

The other reason is that, as mentioned in Section 5.2.9, a full fail-stop signature scheme is closely related to a scheme with special risk bearers where each user who acts as a signer, recipient, or court, also has a risk bearer's access point available.[79] In fact, if a scheme is given where an arbitrary number of risk bearers can take part, one can construct a full fail-stop signature scheme as follows: Each entity of the new scheme consists of two parts; one part acts like a risk bearer's entity and the other like an entity of a signer, recipient, or court, respectively, from the underlying scheme. As risk bearers' entities only take part in initialization, this only concerns the program parts for initialization (if those can be identified statically). The outer parts of all entities must handle the fact that the two parts share their ports.

If an algorithm from the following definitions is carried out in entities of both risk bearers and another role (e.g., the algorithm *res* below), one can of course construct the combined entity more efficiently. To formalize such details, one needs the omitted definition of full fail-stop signature schemes.

The case with one risk bearer is given special attention. First, it is particularly simple. Secondly, as mentioned in Section 6.1.2, all existing fail-stop signature schemes are based on constructions with only one risk bearer; hence a special definition simplifies the proofs of these constructions. Thirdly, only this case was treated in previous definitions, and it should become clear how those definitions are related to the ones given here.

7.1.2 Top-Down Derivation of the Components

The components of a fail-stop signature scheme in the general definition are programs for the different types of entities. The components in a conventional definition are parts of these programs corresponding to particular transactions, or even to one round within such a transaction. Thus the transactions are now considered one by one and decomposed into algorithms. Two notations are used:

- **Algorithmic.** Where efficient constructions are presented, algorithmic notation that keeps track of the current memory contents of entities is needed.
- **Functional.** If one is only interested in the functions computed, notation is simplified if one works with static parameters, such as the complete sequence of random bits an entity uses, although in practice those bits are generated

[79] Actually, the difference could not be seen at all in previous definitions and constructions, because there was no notion of entities and access points, only of algorithms and people. However, this often led to the notions of recipients and risk bearers being mixed up.

dynamically. (This is related to considering the pure input-output behaviour of an interactive function.)

The more detailed algorithmic notation is used for the original definitions, and the functional notation is derived from it.

Initialization

General restrictions and their consequences for outputs. The following restrictions on initialization were made in Section 6.1.2:

- Public keys exist. This means that the acceptance values *acc* of all participants are a deterministic function of the messages that were broadcast, and so are the values ids_{out} (and $ids_{Risk,out}$) that denote who took part successfully and the memory contents *pk* of the entities of courts and recipients (and risk bearers) at the end of a successful initialization.
- If there are special risk bearers, the entities of courts and recipients do not send any messages; they only receive messages that are broadcast by the entities of the signer and the risk bearers.

For notational convenience, a public key is also defined if initialization is unsuccessful; let $pk := \varepsilon$ if acc = FALSE.

If there are special risk bearers, the parameter ids_{out} is omitted, because the entities of recipients and courts do not play an active role.

The algorithm for computing all these public results is called the result algorithm,

$$res.$$

Thus, *res* computes a tuple $pub := (acc, ids_{Risk,out}, pk)$ or (acc, ids_{out}, pk) from the messages that were broadcast. It is an interactive algorithm with input ports only. Alternatively, it could have been described as a normal algorithm that gets one input consisting of all messages that were broadcast and their round numbers and senders. However, for availability of service, the entity may have to stop listening after a while if the signer and the risk bearers cheat and go on and on, and thus the whole input may never be collected. (And in reality, the algorithm would be carried out interactively anyway.)

As an additional result of initialization, the signer's entity obtains a secret value. It is called *sk_temp*, a temporary secret key, because it may change later. (That is, it is not necessarily a secret key in the sense of Section 5.3.2.) If initialization is not successful, $sk\_temp := \varepsilon$ is assumed for simplicity.

Security parameters. As some requirements on a fail-stop signature scheme have to be fulfilled information-theoretically and others only computationally, it is natural to consider two security parameters. They are called σ and k, where σ measures the information-theoretic security and k the computational security. The primary role of σ is that the error probability in the fall-back requirement of the signer on disputes decreases exponentially with σ. In other words, σ determines the probability that the signer is cheated with unprovable forgeries. The primary role of k is to ensure the correctness of *'broken'*, i.e., the larger k is, the harder it should be to compute valid proofs of forgeries (and thus forgeries in the first place).

As usual, the security parameters are represented in unary when they are inputs to algorithms.

Message bound. The message bound N is also an input to each algorithm in key generation, and it is also represented in unary.

However, one must take care with sets *Message_bounds* that contain the element ∞. For this, the convention

$$\text{'1'}^{\infty} := \text{'0'}$$

is made. Hence, if $N = \infty$, i.e., if an arbitrary number of messages can be signed after key generation, the complexity of key generation is only determined by the remaining parameters, whereas, if a finite message bound N has to be known, the complexity of key generation may grow polynomially with N. In other expressions, the case $N = \infty$ is treated as usual, e.g., $i \le \infty$ for all $i \in \mathbb{N}$ is considered to be true.[80]

Case with one risk bearer. In the special case with one risk bearer, the resulting structure of initialization is as follows (see Figure 7.1):

There is a two-party protocol for entities of one signer and one risk bearer with additional reliable broadcast channels where any number of entities of courts and recipients may listen, too. The interactive algorithm for the signer's entity is called A (for Alice, as usual) and that for the entity of the risk bearer B (because he is often the recipient, Bob). Both A and B may be — and will be — probabilistic. The random bit strings used by A and B are called r_A and r_B, respectively.

The triple (A, B, *res*) is called *Gen*, the key-generation protocol.

As a two-party protocol does not need identities internally, the only input parameters of A and B are the security parameters and the message bound. When the parameters k, σ, and N are clear from the context, they are abbreviated as

$$par := (\text{'1'}^k, \text{'1'}^\sigma, \text{'1'}^N).$$

The interactive algorithms and their parameters are summarized in Figure 7.1.[81]

80 One would not lose much by disallowing $N = \infty$: Schemes that can be used with $N = \infty$ can also be used with a very large finite N. One would then have to assume that key generation in practice did not read the complete representation of N in unary; otherwise it would take an unjustified amount of time. Hence the chosen representation is more realistic with respect to complexity. A disadvantage is that it leads to sums of probabilities with an infinite number of non-zero terms, e.g., in the proof of Lemma 7.20. I did not treat the order of summation carefully, but summing according to increasing length should always work.

81 None of the previous definitions is structured like this. The original ones in [Pfit89, PfWa90] only consider a special case (called schemes with prekey in Section 7.3), and do not formalize the role of the risk bearer's entity in it. The generalization in [PePf95] does not contain the algorithm *res*. Instead, the entities of the signer and the risk bearer just output *acc* and the public key in some joint way. The advantage of having *res* and its output $ids_{Risk,out}$, apart from greater generality, is that it enables courts and recipients to distinguish whether the reason for an unsuccessful initialization lies with the signer or the risk bearer. This is necessary to fulfil the requirements on initialization. Furthermore, *res* is needed if a scheme with one risk bearer is used as a building block in a scheme with many risk bearers according to Construction 7.36, where cheaters must be excluded to ensure overall effectiveness.

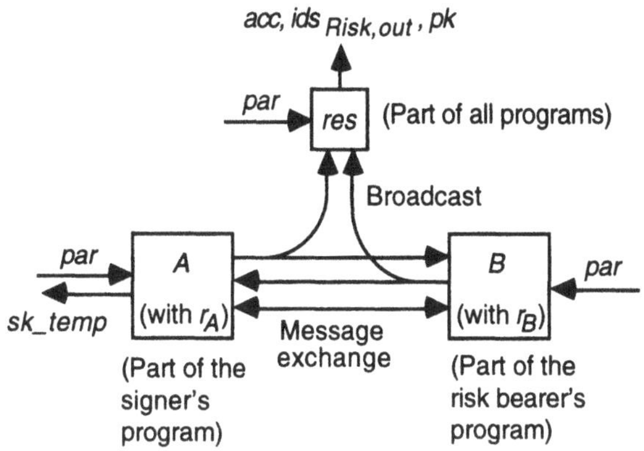

Figure 7.1. Components and parameters of a correct initialization in a conventional definition of standard fail-stop signature schemes with one risk bearer

Implicitly assumed actions. Some actions of the entities in the sense of the general definition are not part of the algorithms mentioned above. However, for initialization they are quite trivial: First, a two-party protocol in the usual sense assumes a dedicated channel for the message exchange between the two parties. Thus an entity carrying out an algorithm *A* or *B* has to select the correct port for each outgoing message and to check that incoming messages have arrived at the correct port. Secondly, the entities must distinguish which of the inputs and outputs of the interactive algorithms are interface events and which are exchanged with local memory. Thirdly, the entities have already evaluated the parameter *'init'* when the interactive algorithms are called.

Many risk bearers. In the case with any number of special risk bearers, the 2-party protocol (*A*, *B*) in *Gen* is replaced by a multi-party protocol between one entity of a signer and an arbitrary number of entities of risk bearers. The signer's algorithm is called *A* again, the (common) algorithm for each risk bearer *B*, and any number of entities of recipients and courts can listen on broadcast channels and use the algorithm *res* to compute the results. The interactive algorithms of the multi-party protocol can use the numbers $\{1, \ldots, R\}$ as identities as usual, if there are *R* risk bearers. It is implicitly assumed that the entities realize the mapping between these numbers and the external identities.

Functional notation. The secret value *sk_temp* is exactly the secret information that the signer's entity stores at the end of initialization. However, more secret random bits may be generated later. (Formally, they are read from a random tape.) It is sometimes useful to have a notation for all the secret information that a signer's entity ever uses. Hence let r_A be a sufficiently long string of random bits[82], and let

82 It may be infinite, like the content of the random tape. In most existing schemes, an upper bound is known (as a function of *par*). The existence of such a bound is guaranteed if entities are polynomial-time in their initial states (see Section 4.4.3, "Complexity"). In the following, however, the other model is used: The complexity of *sign* is allowed to depend on the message length, too.

$$sk := (sk\_temp, r_A).$$

Furthermore, let $Gen^{(f)}$ be the functional version of *Gen*, augmented by the random choice of r_A. Thus the complete outcome of $Gen^{(f)}$ can be described by a tuple $(acc, ids_{Risk,out}, pk, sk)$, or, abbreviated[83], (pub, sk).

Authentication

According to Section 6.1.2, standard fail-stop signature schemes are with non-interactive authentication. Hence, as described in Section 5.3.2, one can identify two non-interactive algorithms *sign* and *test*. Moreover, there is no dependence on the recipient.

Signing as an algorithm. Signing is allowed to be probabilistic and with memory.[84] Thus the algorithm *sign* has two inputs, the current memory content sk_temp_{old} and the message m, and two outputs, the signature s and the new memory content, sk_temp_{new}:[85]

$$(s, sk\_temp_{new}) \leftarrow sign(sk\_temp_{old}, m).$$

If the message bound is reached, *sign* need not output further signatures, and in all existing constructions, it does not. This property will even be required as the restriction $restr_1$; it simplifies the treatment of the information an attacker can obtain from a signer's entity and is without loss of generality. From that point onward, the memory content *sk_temp* remains unchanged — it may still be needed in disputes.

Signing as a function. The functional notation avoids the temporary variables: Each signature is regarded as a deterministic function of the complete secret information, *sk*, and the sequence of messages up to the one to be signed. (Thus, the functional version of signing as an interactive algorithm extending over all executions of authentication is considered.) To make this work, one has to anticipate that disputes are not allowed to change the value of *sk_temp*. A message sequence of length $i \in \mathbb{N}_0$ is written as

$$\underline{m} = (m_1, \ldots, m_i).$$

The functional version of signing m_i, if the previous messages were $m_1, \ldots, m_{i-1}$, and if $i \le N$, is therefore written as

$$s := sign^{(f)}(sk, i, \underline{m}).$$

---

83 With a slight abuse of notation, $(acc, ids_{Risk,out}, pk, sk)$ and (pub, sk) are identified, although they have different parentheses. Similar identifications will tacitly be made with similar abbreviations below.

84 In all existing constructions, signatures only depend on the *number* of previously signed messages, not on the contents of those messages. This was prescribed in the definitions in [Pfit89, PfWa90], as in the GMR definition, but no longer in [PePf95].

85 Neither the public key nor the security parameters are inputs to *sign*, although they are known to the entity. This is without loss of generality: If these values are needed for signing, they can be included in *sk_temp*. Similarly, the security parameters will not be inputs wherever *pk* is, because they can be included in *pk*. However, they will be inputs to all attacker algorithms, because otherwise, they would *have* to be included in *pk*.

The parameter i was introduced so that signatures on earlier messages in a sequence $\underline{m}$ can be denoted, too.

The value s is called the **correct** signature on m_i (given the complete sequence $\underline{m}$). However, this notion is only defined relative to an execution of key generation with the correct algorithm A and to given random bits r_A. Intuitively, it only says which signature the entity of an honest signer will use, and not how many other signatures a dishonest signer may know.

Test. The conventional definition is only formalized for the case where *test* is deterministic and receiving is "memory-less" (restriction $restr_2$).

Hence *test* is a polynomial-time algorithm that, on input the public key pk, a message $m \in M$, and a supposed signature s on m, outputs either acc = TRUE or acc = FALSE, i.e.,

$$acc := test(pk, m, s).$$

Any value s that passes this test is called an **acceptable** signature on m (see Figure 6.6). This notion can be used more generally than that of a correct signature, because it only depends on the public value pk.

Note that *test* has only been defined for messages from the message space, M. Hence the result of applying *test* to a message outside M is not specified. In particular, arbitrary values s might be acceptable signatures on such wrong messages. Thus a certain precondition on the behaviour of honest users is made here, as in Section 5.2.3 — one could provide more user-friendly schemes that reject wrong messages. However, whether wrong messages *can* be recognized is not so much a problem of the signature scheme as of the person selecting the message space. In particular, only the present definition implies that a signature scheme for a general message space, such as $\{0, 1\}^+$, is also a signature scheme for any subset, which is a theorem that would intuitively be expected.

Disputes and Transfers of Proofs of Forgery

The structure of disputes in standard fail-stop signature schemes was almost completely described in Section 6.1.2 (Subsection "Number of Recipients and Complexity of Tests") by the actions of the court's entity: In Step 1, the court's entity tests the signature with the algorithm *test* defined above. (Now *test* is memory-less anyway, i.e., no special case is needed.) In Step 2, this signature is sent to the signer's entity, which can answer with a string called a proof of forgery. In Step 3, the court's entity verifies this proof.

The corresponding action of the recipient's entity is simple: It sends a stored signature to the court's entity. The signer's entity acts as follows:

1. It looks if it has already stored a proof of forgery; if yes, it sends it to the court's entity.[86]

---

[86] To see why this is necessary, consider the basic construction idea from Section 6.1.2, and in particular, Figures 6.7 and 6.8: A proof of forgery shows the attacker the correct signature on a message. He could use it in a future dispute. The signer would lose that dispute if her entity had not stored the forged signature from the first dispute. Formally, this condition is used in the proof sketch of Lemma 7.5.

2. Otherwise it tries to compute a new proof of forgery. If the computation succeeds, it sends the resulting proof and stores it for future disputes.

The only parts of these protocols one sees in the conventional definition are two non-interactive algorithms, *prove* for the computation of proofs of forgery and *verify* for their verification. In particular, storing and retrieving a proof of forgery are only implicitly assumed, because the proof of forgery is not a part of *sk_temp*.

Transfers of proofs of forgery were required to be non-interactive, and their structure is very simple: One entity sends the proof of forgery, and the other verifies it with *verify*.

Computing proofs of forgery. If *prove* is regarded as an algorithm, its inputs are the current secret information, *sk_temp*, a message $m \in M$, and a value s that is supposed to be a signature[87] on m. As mentioned above, a restriction, $restr_3$, is made that computing proofs of forgery does not change the value of *sk_temp*. Hence the only output is a bit string $proof \in \{0, 1\}^*$. A special value *not_a_forgery*, say the empty string ε for concreteness, is provided for cases where the algorithm "notices" that it cannot find a valid proof of forgery. In any case, one can write

$$proof \leftarrow prove(sk\_temp, m, s).$$

In fact, a restriction, $restr_4$, is made that the algorithm *always* outputs *not_a_forgery* or a valid proof of forgery. This is without much loss of generality: Given any scheme without this restriction, one can adapt the signer's entity so that it stores the public key and tests the result *proof* of the old algorithm *prove* with *verify* before it outputs it, so that it can output *not_a_forgery* instead of invalid proofs.[88]

If one is only interested in functional aspects, one can regard proving forgeries as a deterministic function of *sk* and the complete sequence of messages signed so far, instead of *sk_temp*. For convenience, the previous signatures are also regarded as an input, although they can be derived from the other inputs. A pair of a message sequence and the corresponding signature sequence is called a history, $hist = ((m_1, \ldots, m_i), (s_1, \ldots, s_i))$. Hence one writes

$$proof := prove^{(f)}(sk, m, s, hist).$$

Verifying proofs of forgery. Proofs of forgery are usually verified by entities of courts, i.e., based on public information. The same restrictions as with *test* are made, i.e., verification is deterministic and memory-less ($restr_5$). Hence *verify* is a polynomial-time algorithm that, on input the public key and a string *proof*, outputs TRUE or FALSE. If the output is TRUE, the string *proof* is called a **valid** proof of forgery. One can write this with a Boolean variable *valid* as

$$valid := verify(pk, proof).$$

---

87 The algorithm *prove* is primarily intended to be used on acceptable signatures. However, the general definition yields more convenient notation. If s is not an acceptable signature, the output is usually *not_a_forgery*.

88 This restriction is needed to prove that certain complicated active attacks need not be considered with the fall-back requirement of the signer on disputes; see Section 7.1.3.

One could generalize *verify* by using the message and the disputed signature as additional inputs, i.e., *valid* := *verify*(*pk*, *m*, *s*, *proof*), as in [PePf95]. However, this would induce several complications:

- In the transfer of a proof of forgery, the message and the signature have to be transferred, too, because the proof cannot be verified without them. Hence, not the output *proof* of the algorithm *prove*, but the triple *proof** := (*m*, *s*, *proof*) would be the proof of forgery in the sense of Section 5.3.2.
- One has to be careful with future disputes after the one where the first proof of forgery was computed. There are two possibilities:
  - One could allow the signer's entity to use the old proof of forgery and the old message and signature to show that the scheme has already been broken. Thus it transfers *proof** = (*m*, *s*, *proof*) to the court's entity, and *proof** can be verified given only the public key. Hence this possibility is equivalent to the chosen one.
  - One could make proofs of forgery really specific to one message and one signature. However, one must then take care that seeing the earlier proof of forgery does not make it easier for an attacker to make unprovable forgeries on new messages. Such a statement is not made in any of the current conventional definitions of fail-stop signatures. I did not consider it worth while to work such distinctions out, because one should stop the whole system after a valid proof of forgery anyway.[89]

Definitions

Before the components of standard fail-stop signature schemes (in a conventional definition) are summarized in Definition 7.1, the specification parameters from Section 5.2.5 must be considered. Several of them have already been fixed for all standard fail-stop signature schemes, e.g., the set *Dispute_results* and everything to do with sets of identities of recipients, because no dependence on the recipient is prescribed. Others cannot be seen in a conventional definition, such as *Sign_results*. Two parameters remain, the message space and the set of message bounds.

Definition 7.1. The **components of a standard fail-stop signature scheme with one risk bearer** for a non-empty message space $M \subseteq \{0,1\}^+$ and a non-empty set $Message\_bounds \subseteq \mathbb{N} \cup \{\infty\}$ are a 5-tuple (*Gen*, *sign*, *test*, *prove*, *verify*) where

- *Gen*, the key-generation protocol, is a triple (*A*, *B*, *res*).

  A and *B* are probabilistic polynomial-time interactive algorithms with two input and output ports each; one pair is called 2-party ports and the other

[89] Nevertheless, independent of whether proofs of forgery are specific to one message and one signature or not, one cannot assume in the security definition that the system *is* stopped, because according to Chapter 5, it is up to the users whether they carry out transfers of proofs of forgeries or not. In the model, this cannot be changed because the system cannot guarantee distribution of proofs of forgery, because reliable channels are not assumed to be available all the time. In practice, too, proofs of forgery might not always be distributed fast enough to prevent further disputes.

broadcast ports.[90] The result algorithm, *res*, is a deterministic polynomial-time interactive algorithm with two input ports only. *A*, *B*, and *res* only have to be defined for initial inputs of the form $par := (\text{'1'}^k, \text{'1'}^\sigma, \text{'1'}^N)$ with $k, \sigma \in \mathbb{N}$ and $N \in Message\_bounds$. For $N = \infty$, the convention $\text{'1'}^\infty := \text{'0'}$ is used. *B* has no output, *A* has one output, *sk_temp*, and *res* outputs a triple $pub := (acc, ids_{Risk,out}, pk)$, where *acc* is Boolean and $ids_{Risk,out}$ is a subset of $\{1\}$.

The execution of the complete protocol *Gen* is defined by an execution of *A*, *B*, and *res*, combined as in Figure 7.1: The 2-party ports of *A* and *B* are connected with a point-to-point channel and the broadcast ports with broadcast channels, which also lead to the input ports of *res*. Hence *Gen* defines probabilistic assignments of the form

$$(acc, ids_{Risk,out}, pk, sk\_temp) \leftarrow Gen(\text{'1'}^k, \text{'1'}^\sigma, \text{'1'}^N)$$

or, equivalently,

$$(pub, sk\_temp) \leftarrow Gen(par).$$

Note that all outputs have been defined with only one instance of *res*, although in reality, an arbitrary number of entities of recipients and courts execute *res*: As *res* is deterministic and only works on broadcast messages, all the entities obtain the same result.

- *sign* is a probabilistic polynomial-time algorithm that, on input a value sk_temp_{old} and a message $m \in M$, outputs a pair (s, sk_temp_{new}) or the value *'key_used_up'*. The output *s* is called a signature.[91]

  The definition of *sign* can be restricted to values sk_temp_{old} that can actually occur. This is expressed as $sk\_temp_{old} \in SK\_Temp$ for a set *SK_Temp*.
- *test* is a deterministic polynomial-time algorithm that, on input a triple (pk, m, s) with $m \in M$, outputs an acceptance value $acc \in \{\text{TRUE}, \text{FALSE}\}$. If the output is TRUE, *s* is called an **acceptable** signature on *m* (for this public key, *pk*).

  The definition of *test* can be restricted to values *pk* that can actually occur, i.e., where (TRUE, $\{1\}$, *pk*) is a possible output of *res*.
- *prove* is a probabilistic polynomial-time algorithm that, on input a value *sk_temp*, a message $m \in M$, and a value *s* that is supposed to be a signature on *m*, outputs a bit string $proof \in \{0, 1\}^+ \cup \{not\_a\_forgery\}$. An output other than *not_a_forgery* is called a proof of forgery.

  The definition of *prove* can be restricted to values $sk\_temp \in SK\_Temp$.
- *verify* is a deterministic polynomial-time algorithm that, on input a pair $(pk, proof)$, outputs a value $valid \in \{\text{TRUE}, \text{FALSE}\}$. If the output is TRUE, *proof* is called a **valid** proof of forgery for *pk*.

  The definition of *verify* can be restricted to values *pk* that can actually occur, i.e., where (TRUE, $\{1\}$, *pk*) is a possible output of *res*.

These components must have the following properties:

---

90 Recall from Section 4.4.3 that interface inputs and outputs are not represented by ports in the conventional definitions.

91 One cannot speak of a correct signature here in the algorithmic definition, because no connection to an original sk_temp_0 is given.

a) The domain *SK_Temp* comprises the original temporary secret keys and is closed against up to *N* applications of *sign* with arbitrary messages $m \in M$.

b) An output *proof* of *prove* is either *not_a_forgery* or a valid proof of forgery.

c) The output *'key_used_up'* occurs as the result of *sign* if and only if the message bound has been reached.

More precisely, these properties mean:

a) If an execution of *Gen* with the correct algorithm of the signer, *A*, and the correct algorithm *res*, but an arbitrary, computationally unrestricted attacker strategy $\tilde{B}$ in the place of *B*, leads to an outcome (TRUE, {1}, *pk*, *sk_temp*), then $sk\_temp \in SK\_Temp$. Furthermore, if sk_temp_{old} can be reached from such an *sk_temp* by applying *sign* to messages from *M* up to *N* times, then $sk\_temp_{old} \in SK\_Temp$.

b) For all $sk\_temp_{old} \in SK\_Temp$ reached from an outcome (TRUE, {1}, *pk*, *sk_temp*) of key generation, as in Part a), all possible outputs *proof* of $prove(sk\_temp_{old}, m, s)$ with $m \in M$ and an arbitrary *s* are either *not_a_forgery* or fulfil *verify*(*pk*, *proof*) = TRUE.

c) If sk_temp_{old} can be reached from an original *sk_temp*, defined as in Part a), by applying *sign* up to *N*–1 times, no output of $sign(sk\_temp_{old}, m)$ with $m \in M$ is *'key_used_up'*. In contrast, if sk_temp_{old} can be reached by applying *sign* exactly *N* times, *'key_used_up'* is the only possible output of $sign(sk\_temp_{old}, m)$.

d) The components are said to be polynomial-time in the interface inputs alone if *test* works in time polynomial in *pk* and *m* alone, *prove* in *sk_temp* and *m*, and *verify* in *pk*.[92] ♦

Note that the restrictions $restr_2$, $restr_3$, and $restr_5$ are implicit in the definition, and $restr_1$ and $restr_4$ have been required explicitly as Properties c) and b).

The following definition generalizes Definition 7.1 to an arbitrary number of risk bearers. It is not quite as rigorous as the previous one, because no formalization of multi-party protocols and, in particular, their execution with attackers has been fixed.

Definition 7.2. The **components of a standard fail-stop signature scheme with an arbitrary number of risk bearers** for a non-empty message space $M \subseteq \{0, 1\}^+$ and a non-empty set $Message\_bounds \subseteq \mathbb{N} \cup \{\infty\}$ are defined as in Definition 7.1, except for the key-generation protocol *Gen*. It is still defined as a triple (*A*, *B*, *res*), where *res* is called the result algorithm. The differences are:

- Inputs: *A* and *res* need an initial input of the form $par = (\text{'1'}^k, \text{'1'}^\sigma, \text{'1'}^N, \text{'1'}^R)$, where $R \in \mathbb{N}$ stands for the number of risk bearers' entities taking part.[93] *B*

92 This property, which will guarantee availability of service in the chosen model, is only defined here, but not always required, because that would exclude the general abstract construction with message hashing, unless the notion of hash functions were modified significantly. However, the constructions with concrete collision-intractable families of hash functions can be modified to have this property (see Section 10.1).

93 The use of the same notation *par* for the different parameters in Definitions 7.1 and 7.2 is on purpose, just as with *A*, *B*, and *res*: Some of the later definitions can now be formalized for both cases together.

needs an input (*par*, *i*), where *i* stands for the internal identity of this particular entity of a risk bearer.

- Execution: In an execution of *Gen*, one entity executing *A* and *R* entities executing *B* are connected with both point-to-point channels (not necessarily private) and broadcast channels (and the algorithms *A* and *B* must have the appropriate ports). *res* is still a deterministic polynomial-time interactive algorithm with input ports only, and those input ports are connected to the broadcast channels. Note that one can still define all outputs with only one instance of *res*.
- Outputs: The outputs are unchanged, except that $ids_{Risk,out}$ is now a subset of $\{1, \ldots, R\}$. ♦

Definition 7.3 (Functional notation). The names of the algorithms in Definitions 7.1 and 7.2 can also be used for the (probabilistic or deterministic) functions realized by these algorithms. However, this notation is only used with *test* and *verify*. For the three other components, the following probabilistic functions are defined:

a) In *Gen*, the algorithm *A* is replaced by a probabilistic interactive function $A^{(f)}$ that first calls the probabilistic interactive function defined by *A* and then chooses an additional random string r_A with uniform distribution, where r_A is long enough to make *N* future applications of *sign* and an arbitrary number of applications of *prove* possible. It may be infinite if no a-priori bound is known. The output of $A^{(f)}$ is denoted by $sk := (sk\_temp, r_A)$. With a slight abuse of the notation of Section 5.3.2, it is called a secret key, because it is constant.

   The resulting protocol and the probabilistic function it defines are called $Gen^{(f)}$. Thus $Gen^{(f)}$ defines probabilistic assignments of the form

$$(acc, ids_{Risk,out}, pk, sk) \leftarrow Gen^{(f)}(par).$$

b) A deterministic function $sign^{(f)}$ is defined as follows: On input $sk = (sk\_temp, r_A)$ with $sk\_temp \in SK\_Temp$ and a message sequence $\underline{m} = (m_1, \ldots, m_i) \in M^i$ with $i \in \mathbb{N}_0$ and $i \leq N$, the algorithm *sign* is used repeatedly to sign the messages in the given order, with corresponding updates of *sk_temp* and using the random bits from r_A. Thus the output of $sign^{(f)}$ is a sequence $\underline{s} = (s_1, \ldots, s_i)$ of signatures; one can write

$$\underline{s} := sign^{(f)}(sk, \underline{m}).$$

   The projection to the *j*-th signature (with $1 \leq j \leq i$), i.e., the *j*-th component of the result $\underline{s}$, is denoted by an additional parameter *j*. This is written as

$$s_j := sign^{(f)}(sk, j, \underline{m}).$$

   The latter notation is also defined for sequences of more than *N* messages, as long as $j \leq N$.

c) A deterministic function $prove^{(f)}$ is defined as follows: On input (*sk*, *m*, *s*, *hist*), where $sk = (sk\_temp, r_A)$ with $sk\_temp \in SK\_Temp$ and $hist = (\underline{m}, \underline{s})$, where $\underline{m} = (m_1, \ldots, m_i) \in M^i$ with $i \in \mathbb{N}_0$ and $i \leq N$, the algorithm *sign* is used repeatedly to sign the messages in $\underline{m}$, with corresponding updates of *sk_temp* and using the random bits from r_A. This yields a value sk_temp_i.[94] Now $prove(sk\_temp_i, m, s)$ is used to compute the result *proof*. ♦

Note that the functional notation does not treat the case $i > N$. The following formal security definitions implicitly take Property c) from Definition 7.1 for granted, i.e., they do not treat what a signer's entity might do in authentications after the message bound has been reached, because it does not do anything.

7.1.3 Breaking Down the Minimal Requirements

Security of a fail-stop signature scheme, in the context of a conventional definition, means that the minimal requirements from Sections 5.2.7 and 5.2.9 are restated in terms of the algorithms from Definitions 7.1 and 7.2 or the functions from Definition 7.3, each with the appropriate degree of security. Access of attackers to entities is modeled by replacing algorithms that would be in these entities by an arbitrary other algorithm or function. This algorithm must also comprise the influence of attackers on honest users, i.e., the active attacks. Moreover, it obtains all messages as parameters that the attacker can observe on channels that are not private.

The requirements are now considered one by one. The two original requirements on disputes from Section 5.2.7 can be omitted: According to Section 5.2.9, "Combinations", they follow from the fall-back requirements on disputes and the correctness of *'broken'* in full fail-stop signature schemes, and in the case with special risk bearers as accountable centres, they were omitted on purpose.

Fall-Back Requirement of the Recipient on Disputes

The fall-back requirement of the recipient on disputes is that once the recipient has accepted a message m as authenticated by a signer, a court in a dispute about this message should obtain a result $acc \in \{\text{TRUE}, \textit{'broken'}\}$.

Lemma 7.4. The fall-back requirement of the recipient on disputes is fulfilled information-theoretically without error probability purely by the structure assumed for standard fail-stop signature schemes. ♦

Note that the proof cannot be formalized with the components defined in Section 7.1.2, because it only deals with their assumed use in the entities in the sense of Chapter 5.

Proof sketch of Lemma 7.4. The recipient's entity only accepts m as authenticated by a signer id_S if $test(pk, m, s) = \text{TRUE}$, where pk is a public key from a successful initialization under the identity id_S. The only step of a dispute where the court's entity can output a result other than TRUE or *'broken'* is Step 2, and then only if $test(pk^*, m, s^*) = \text{FALSE}$, where pk^* and s^* are what the court's entity regards as the public key belonging to id_S and the signature. This cannot happen if $pk^* = pk$ and $s^* = s$, because *test* is deterministic. As s^* has been received directly from the recipient's entity on a reliable channel, $s^* = s$ is clear. Furthermore, there is a precondition that exactly one initialization under the identity id_S has been carried

[94] In concrete constructions, sk_temp_i can often be expressed as a much simpler function of *hist*; this is why $\underline{s}$ was included in the parameters.

out, both the recipient and the court took part, and a reliable broadcast channel was used. Hence both entities obtained their local versions of the public key by applying the deterministic algorithm *res* to the same messages. Hence $pk^* = pk$, too. □

Hence this requirement is never mentioned again.

Fall-Back Requirement of the Signer on Disputes

The fall-back requirement of the signer on disputes is that, as long as she has not authenticated a certain message and is willing to disavow, a court should obtain a result $acc \in$ {FALSE, *'broken'*} in a dispute about this message. This requirement has to be fulfilled information-theoretically with an exponentially small error probability, and only the entities of the signer and the court are assumed to be correct.

The success of an attacker strategy is represented in the conventional definition in terms of the outcomes of the algorithms used internally in the dispute: The attacker strategy must find values m and s where

- m is a message not previously signed by the signer,
- s is a valid signature on m (so that the dispute does not end with acc = FALSE in Step 2), and
- if the algorithm *prove* is used to prove the forgery, the result is not a valid proof of forgery.

Moreover, active attacks have to be considered, i.e., the attacker may induce the signer and the court to perform an arbitrary number of authentications and disputes. However, only a restricted active attack has been considered formally in previous conventional definitions: The attacker only initiates authentications before the one dispute where he tries to achieve the result acc = TRUE. It is now shown that this restriction is in fact without loss of generality for standard fail-stop signature schemes. However, the restriction $restr_4$ is used, which was not made explicitly in previous definitions.

Lemma 7.5. If a standard fail-stop signature scheme guarantees the fall-back requirement of the signer on disputes against attackers that only initiate authentications and then one dispute, it also guarantees this requirement against general active attacks. ♦

Proof sketch. Let an attacker strategy $\tilde{B}$ of the non-restricted type be given. Another attacker strategy B^* of the restricted type is constructed that has at least the same probability of success, using $\tilde{B}$ as a black box (similar to Figure 5.18). First, B^* simulates $\tilde{B}$ and keeps track of the history. Whenever $\tilde{B}$ would start authentication with the correct entity of the signer, B^* does so, too. However, when $\tilde{B}$ wants to start a dispute, B^* makes a more complicated decision. First, it simulates $\tilde{B}$ one step further to see if it would send an acceptable signature on the disputed message m to the correct court's entity. B^* can do this without involving the correct entities, because they would not send anything in this step.

a) If no acceptable signature would be sent, the court's entity would decide acc = FALSE without even calling on the signer's entity. Hence B^* can give these results to $\tilde{B}$ without involving the correct entities.

b) If an acceptable signature s would be sent and the message m has not yet been signed by the correct entity of the signer (i.e., s is a successful forgery), B^* decides that this is the one dispute where it tries its luck. Hence it starts the dispute with the two correct entities and sends s to the court's entity in Step 1. Independent of the result of this dispute, B^* stops afterwards.

c) If an acceptable signature s would be sent, but m has already been signed by the correct entity of the signer, B^* does not carry out the dispute with the correct entities. Instead, it tells $\tilde{B}$ that the signer's entity sent *not_a_forgery* and the court's entity obtained the result TRUE (although this is not necessarily what the correct entities would have done, see below).

The new strategy B^* is obviously of the required restricted type. It remains to be shown that B^* succeeds with at least the same probability as $\tilde{B}$.

- In authentications and in disputes of Type a), B^* and $\tilde{B}$ act identically.
- For disputes of Type b), it has to be shown that B^* does not lose anything by stopping afterwards. There are only two cases: If the court's entity outputs TRUE, both B^* and $\tilde{B}$ have succeeded, and there is no need to continue. If the court's entity outputs *'broken'*, the signer's entity must have computed a valid proof of forgery and will reuse it in all future disputes. Hence $\tilde{B}$ can never succeed later, and B^* can just as well stop.
- Disputes of Type c) are the critical case, because it is not clear that B^* simulates the correct entities correctly.[95] This is why the restriction $restr_4$ had to be made, i.e., that any output of *prove* other than *not_a_forgery* is a valid proof of forgery. Now it is at least clear that if B^*'s simulation is wrong, the signer's entity would have computed a valid proof of forgery and thus $\tilde{B}$ could never have succeeded afterwards. Hence B^* cannot do worse in this case, and in the other case, it continues exactly like $\tilde{B}$. □

Thus the conventional definition of the security for the signer, Definitions 7.12 to 7.14, will only consider the restricted active attacks.

Correctness of *'broken'*

Correctness of *'broken'* means that a correct entity of a court should not produce the output *'broken'* in a dispute or a transfer of a proof of forgery. With the structure assumed for standard fail-stop signature schemes, this output depends on an application of *verify*, hence the requirement means that no valid proofs of forgery should occur. This requirement is fulfilled computationally only, and if there are special risk bearers, one of their entities is assumed to be correct.

---

95 Of course, it is to be expected in conjunction with other requirements that the signer can usually not disavow messages she has really signed. However, this has certainly not been required for the case where the value s that $\tilde{B}$ sends is different from the signature, say s', that the signer's entity had made on the same message. I considered making a restriction that correct entities never attempt to compute proofs of forgery for messages they have signed. This could be done without loss of generality from a functional point of view by letting entities store all signed messages and search through them. However, it would be a considerable loss in efficiency compared with algorithms *prove* in existing schemes.

In previous definitions, this requirement has been considered almost without active attacks, i.e., the attacker only takes part in one initialization (where he may try to cheat, of course) and then immediately tries to compute a valid proof of forgery. It is now shown that this is without loss of generality in standard fail-stop signature schemes.

Lemma 7.6. If a standard fail-stop signature scheme guarantees the correctness of *'broken'* against attackers that only take part in one initialization and one dispute, it also guarantees this requirement against general active attacks. ♦

Proof sketch. The correct entities are those of the court that applies *verify* and, if special risk bearers are considered, one risk bearer. By the assumed structure of standard fail-stop signature schemes, the court's entity only applies the deterministic algorithms *res*, *test*, and *verify* to information that is known to the attacker. Hence an attacker can simulate all the actions of the court's entity on his own and does not need active attacks on it. (More formally, this could be written as a reduction, as in the previous proof sketch.) The risk bearer's entity only carries out initializations. By the precondition about correct use of initialization, cheating does not count if it involves more than one initialization for the same signer's identity id_S. Initializations for other identities are completely independent, hence an attacker can simulate them on his own. □

This restricted requirement will be formalized in Definition 7.11.

Unforgeability

It was sketched in Section 5.4.4 that unforgeability is a consequence of the other requirements. This will be proved formally for standard fail-stop signature schemes below. Unforgeability is therefore not a part of the definition of a secure standard fail-stop signature scheme, but it will be formalized in Definition 7.22.

Unforgeability means that as long as a signer has not signed a certain message, nobody should be able to make a recipient accept it as signed by her. It is only required computationally. In a full fail-stop signature scheme, the entities of the signer and the recipient in question are assumed to be correct. In the case with special risk bearers, one risk bearer is added to the interest group, as mentioned in Section 5.2.9.

In previous definitions, the only active attacks were that the attacker makes the signer's entity sign messages.

Lemma 7.7. If a standard fail-stop signature scheme guarantees both unforgeability against attackers that only initiate authentications and correctness of *'broken'*, it also guarantees unforgeability against general active attacks. ♦

Proof sketch. Active attacks on the recipient can be omitted, because the attacker can simulate the actions of the recipient's entity on his own: It applies the algorithms *res* and *test* to values known to the attacker, and in disputes, it sends a previously received signature. The risk bearer's entity can be treated as in the proof sketch of Lemma 7.6.

It is a bit harder to see why it is useless for the attacker to carry out disputes with the signer's entity.[96] By restriction $restr_4$, the signer's entity in such a dispute either outputs *not_a_forgery* or a valid proof of forgery. If the latter could happen with significant probability, the signer and the attacker together could break the correctness of *'broken'*, similar to the sketch of the proof that unforgeability is a consequence of the other requirements in Section 5.4.4.[97] Thus the attacker can always use *not_a_forgery* to simulate such disputes. □

Effectiveness of Authentication

Effectiveness of authentication in standard fail-stop signature schemes means that any signature s computed with the correct signing algorithm should pass the corresponding test, if exactly one correct initialization was made, unless the message bound has been reached. Only the signer's and the recipient's entity are assumed to be correct. Hence, if special risk bearers are considered, the signer's algorithm A has been carried out correctly in initialization, but no entity needs to have carried out the risk bearers' algorithm B correctly. The result algorithm *res* has been applied correctly, because the results of the two correct entities are considered.

Active attacks on the recipient are useless, as before, and active attacks on the signer do not make much difference here either: An attacker can only influence the value *sk_temp* that the signer's entity will use by choosing the messages to be signed, but *sk_temp* will be universally quantified anyway. Hence no active attack will be seen in the conventional definition, Definition 7.10.

Effectiveness of Initialization

This requirement need not be formalized, because in the case with risk bearers it follows from the correctness of initialization, as sketched in Section 5.4.4, and according to Section 7.1.1, only this case is formalized.

Correctness of Initialization

Consistency of initialization is achieved automatically in standard fail-stop signature schemes because the result is a deterministic function of broadcast messages.

The requirement that no honest participant is excluded must be made explicitly. For schemes with special risk bearers, this means:

- If the signer is regarded, the entities of the signer and at least one recipient or court are assumed to be correct. Hence A and *res* are carried out correctly, but B not necessarily. It must be guaranteed that either acc = TRUE or $ids_{Risk,out} = \emptyset$.

---

[96] Again, it would be simpler if the restriction $restr_4$ had been replaced by the restriction that the signer's entity only tries to compute a proof of forgery if it receives a successful forgery, i.e., a valid signature s on a message m that it has not signed before. Then the attacker could just as well carry out authentication for m with the correct recipient's entity and send it this s and thus break unforgeability immediately.

[97] At the level of entities, this argument seems to need an honest court, which is not assumed here. However, the conventional definition of the correctness of *'broken'*, as sketched in the previous subsection and formalized in Definition 7.11, only says that it should be infeasible to compute a valid proof of forgery, as long as any risk bearer is honest.

- If a risk bearer is regarded, the entities of this risk bearer and at least one recipient or court are assumed to be correct. Hence this instance of *B* and *res* are carried out correctly, but *A* and possible further instances of *B* not necessarily. It must be guaranteed that the identity *i* of this risk bearer is an element of $ids_{Risk,out}$ (where $i = 1$ in the case with only one risk bearer).

This will be formalized in Definition 7.9.

Availability of Service

It is shown that availability of service is provided in every standard fail-stop signature scheme whose components are polynomial-time in the interface inputs alone. The assumed entities do not do anything between transactions, and in each transaction, they carry out a constant number of algorithms from Definition 7.1 or 7.2, respectively, and some storage operations. Each algorithm from *Gen* is polynomial-time in the parameters *par*, i.e., in the initial state of the entity, even if it interacts with more powerful attackers, due to the conventions made in Section 4.4.3. Hence the length of *pk* and the original *sk_temp* are polynomial in those parameters, too. Each application of *sign*, *test*, *prove*, or *verify* is polynomial-time in the message, which is an interface input at each entity, and a key. Hence one obtains inductively that the length of all further values *sk_temp* and all running times are polynomial in the initial state and the sum of the length of messages input to the entity so far.

Hence this requirement is not mentioned again.

7.1.4 Breaking Down Additional Service Properties

Before the requirements that remain from Section 7.1.3 are formalized, the additional service properties that standard fail-stop signature schemes should have according to Section 6.1.2 are considered. It turns out that most of these requirements are automatically fulfilled according to the assumed structure of the entities around the algorithms from Definition 7.1 or 7.2, respectively. The only remaining one, the strong requirement of the signer on disputes in the case with special risk bearers, can be fulfilled by similar structural measures.

Stronger Requirements on Disputes

As mentioned in Section 5.2.9, "Combinations", it is useful in practice to add the strong requirement of the signer on disputes for the degree *low* to the minimal requirements. This means that on a computational assumption, the following is required even if the signer does not take part in a dispute:

- In a full fail-stop signature scheme, the court's output has to be FALSE.
- If special risk bearers are considered, this requirement can be weakened in the same way as the minimal requirement of the signer on disputes: The output may be FALSE or *'broken'*. (However, with the construction below, this weakening is not necessary.)

Lemma 7.8. A secure full standard fail-stop signature scheme, i.e., one that fulfils all the minimal requirements, also fulfils the strong requirement of the signer on disputes computationally. ♦

Proof sketch. This proof sketch uses some of the expected general theorems from Section 5.4.4. It has to be shown that the court's output in a dispute is neither *'broken'* nor TRUE. These outputs can only occur if an acceptable signature on the disputed message is shown in Step 1 of the dispute. If an attacker strategy $\tilde{B}$ could do this with significant probability, an attacker strategy B^* could act like $\tilde{B}$ until such a situation occurs and then let the signer disavow. Then the court's output would be TRUE or *'broken'* again. As the signer has now disavowed, this contradicts the conjunction of the weak requirement of the signer on disputes and the correctness of *'broken'*. □

If special risk bearers are considered, the strong requirement of the signer on disputes is no longer fulfilled automatically: All the risk bearers together may be able to forge a signature. Instead of showing it to a recipient to break unforgeability, they can use it in Step 1 of a dispute. Unless the signer shows a proof of forgery, they win this dispute.

However, this requirement can be fulfilled by organizational measures, i.e., measures that do not concern the algorithms from Definition 7.1 or 7.2, respectively. The idea is to add the signer to the risk bearers, so that the result of a dispute is guaranteed not to be *'broken'* in the interest of the signer and the court. Then the proof sketch above can be applied again. Adding the signer to the risk bearers can be done in two ways:

- Outside the signature scheme: The person who uses the signer's access point is given a risk bearer's access point (and entity), too.
- Inside the signature scheme: The signer's entity consists of two parts. One part acts like the original signer's entity, the other like a risk bearer's entity, and there is a little administration so that both parts can share the same ports.

Hence the strong requirement of the signer on disputes is not mentioned again.

Arbitrary Transferability

Arbitrary transferability is easy to achieve as a consequence of the existence of public keys and non-interactive authentication: The entity of the former recipient of a signed message can simply pass the signature on, and the entity of the new recipient tests it with the normal algorithm *test*. (Signatures had to be stored anyway in case of disputes.) The effectiveness of transfers, i.e., the requirement that the new recipient should accept the signature, is guaranteed information-theoretically without error probability because both entities have the same public key.

Transferability of Proofs of Forgery

Transfers of proofs of forgery have already been described in Section 7.1.2. Effectiveness of transfers of proofs of forgery is clear, because the entities of both courts use the same deterministic algorithm *verify* and the same public key.

Similarly, the correctness of *'broken'* for such transfers is the same as the normal correctness of *'broken'* for disputes.

External Verifiability of the Behaviour of Transaction Partners

External verifiability of authentication is easy to achieve because authentication is non-interactive, public keys exist, and *test* is deterministic and memory-less ($restr_2$): If the message exchange during authentication, i.e., sending the signature, takes place on a reliable broadcast channel (as it is standard when external verifiability is considered), all entities that took part in initialization can test the signature with the same public key.

Disputes, too, are easy to verify externally: The observers can test both the signature sent in Step 1 of the dispute and verify the proof of forgery if the signer's entity sends one. Hence they can check the behaviour of the court.

One can also easily achieve that authentication can be repeated (and then with external verification) if someone doubts afterwards that it took place, and in particular, if the recipient claims that he did not receive the signature. One can either sign the same message again, which usually leads to a different signature, because *sk_temp* has changed, or the signer's entity can store the signature or enough information to reconstruct exactly the same signature on the message. The latter may be useful in situations where the message bound is small for some reason, so that one does not want to "lose" signatures with repetitions. In neither case does the recipient gain more possibilities to win disputes, or an attacker to cheat, than without the repetition.

7.1.5 Formal Security Definitions

In this section, those security definitions are formalized that were semiformally shown to be sufficient in the two previous sections. They are made in the order of increasing complexity (determined by the number of transactions to be considered), which is inverse to the order in which they were considered so far. Hence, after some notation, there are definitions of

- correctness of initialization,
- effectiveness of authentication,
- security for risk bearers, which is the conventional name for the security definition derived from the requirement "correctness of *'broken'*" (similar to the conventions at the end of Chapter 5), and
- security for the signer.

Notation with One Risk Bearer

First, some notation about the execution of the key-generation protocol *Gen* with attackers is defined. Most of it is the usual notation for 2-party protocols with attackers.

Attacker strategies replacing A or B are called $\tilde{A}$ and $\tilde{B}$, respectively. The resulting protocols if the other algorithm and *res* are still correct are denoted by

$Gen_{\tilde{A},B}$ and $Gen_{A,\tilde{B}}$. These protocols are executed like correct 2-party protocols by alternation of A and $\tilde{B}$, or $\tilde{A}$ and B, respectively.

- Inputs. The inputs to the attacker strategies are the parameters, *par*, just as with the correct algorithms. The random strings used are called $r_{\tilde{A}}$ and $r_{\tilde{B}}$, respectively.
- Output of $\tilde{B}$. If the risk bearer is cheating, he may store his view of the protocol execution and try to exploit it later. This view of a protocol execution is defined as a list containing the random string $r_{\tilde{B}}$ as far as $\tilde{B}$ used it and all the messages sent by A and $\tilde{B}$. (Recall that the risk bearer can see all the messages sent by A.) In a conventional definition, this storing is modeled as an extra output $aux_{\tilde{B}}$ of $\tilde{B}$. If the special case $\tilde{B} = B$ is considered, $aux_{\tilde{B}} := \varepsilon$ is used (the empty string).[98]

  Hence, an outcome of $Gen_{A,\tilde{B}}$ is denoted as $(acc, ids_{Risk,out}, pk, sk\_temp, aux_{\tilde{B}})$ or $(pub, sk\_temp, aux_{\tilde{B}})$.
- Output of $\tilde{A}$. Similarly, $\tilde{A}$ obtains an additional private output $aux_{\tilde{A}}$, which it may try to exploit later. In the case $\tilde{A} = A$, $aux_{\tilde{A}} := \varepsilon$ is used.

  Hence, an outcome of $Gen_{\tilde{A},B}$ is denoted as $(acc, ids_{Risk,out}, pk, sk\_temp, aux_{\tilde{A}})$ or $(pub, sk\_temp, aux_{\tilde{A}})$.[99]

The probability spaces defined by protocol executions with given parameters are written $Gen_{\tilde{A},B}(par)$ and $Gen_{A,\tilde{B}}(par)$, respectively. The functional notation is adapted accordingly.

Notation with Many Risk Bearers

In the case with many risk bearers, three situations have to be considered:

- If only *res* and A are executed correctly, the attacker strategy replacing all instances of B is called $\tilde{B}$, and the resulting protocol is written $Gen_{A,\tilde{B}}$. The inputs to $\tilde{B}$ are the parameters, *par*. As above, an output $aux_{\tilde{B}}$ of $\tilde{B}$, usually its view, is an additional outcome.
- If only *res* and one instance of B are executed correctly, the attacker strategy replacing A and the other instances of B is written $\tilde{A}$ (i.e., a cheating signer with the help of some risk bearers), and the resulting protocol is written $Gen_{\tilde{A},B}$. The inputs to $\tilde{A}$ are *par* and the internal identity i of the correct risk bearer's entity, i.e., the same number i that B obtains as an input. $\tilde{A}$ computes an additional private output $aux_{\tilde{A}}$.
- If *res*, A, and one instance of B are executed correctly, the attacker strategy replacing the other instances of B is written $\tilde{O}$ (an outsider with the help of some risk bearers), and the resulting protocol is written $Gen_{A,B,\tilde{O}}$. The inputs to $\tilde{O}$ are *par* and the internal identity i of the correct risk bearer's entity, i.e., the same number i that B obtains as an input. $\tilde{O}$ has a private output $aux_{\tilde{O}}$.

---

98 If this notation were only used for "real" attackers, one could assume without loss of generality that $aux_{\tilde{B}}$ is always the complete view.

99 It is without loss of generality to assume that $\tilde{A}$ outputs two values, *sk_temp* and $aux_{\tilde{A}}$. This leads to more convenient notation in the case $\tilde{A} = A$, e.g., in the proof of Theorem 7.24.

The probability spaces defined by protocol executions with given parameters are written $Gen_{A,\tilde{B}}(par)$, $Gen_{\tilde{A},B}(par, i)$, and $Gen_{A,B,\tilde{O}}(par, i)$, respectively, and the functional notation is adapted accordingly.

Correctness of Initialization

Correctness of initialization can easily be translated into the results of the protocol *Gen*.

Definition 7.9. A standard fail-stop signature scheme provides correctness of initialization if it has the following properties. For all probabilistic interactive functions $\tilde{A}$ and $\tilde{B}$ and all parameters *par* according to Definition 7.1 or 7.2, respectively:

a) For the signer: In every execution of $Gen_{A,\tilde{B}}(par)$, i.e., for all tuples $(acc, ids_{Risk,out}, pk, sk\_temp, aux_{\tilde{B}}) \in [Gen_{A,\tilde{B}}(par)]$, either acc = TRUE or $ids_{Risk,out} = \emptyset$.

b) • For the risk bearer, if there is only one: In every execution of $Gen_{\tilde{A},B}(par)$, the output $ids_{Risk,out}$ is $\{1\}$.

  • For the *i*-th of several risk bearers: In every execution of $Gen_{\tilde{A},B}(par, i)$ with $i \le R$ (where *R* is the last parameter of *par*, in unary as always), the output $ids_{Risk,out}$ contains the element *i*. ♦

Effectiveness of Authentication

The definition of effectiveness of authentication deals with arbitrary signatures in the sequence of signatures; hence the functional notation is used.

Definition 7.10. Let a standard fail-stop signature scheme be given.

a) $Bad_{eff}(N)$ is defined as the set of **bad outcomes** of key generation, as far as effectiveness of authentication with message bound *N* is concerned. This means that key generation seemed correct, but nevertheless it can happen that a correctly signed message does not pass the test. More formally, $Bad_{eff}(N)$ is the set of tuples $(acc, ids_{Risk,out}, pk, sk)$ with

  • acc = TRUE,

  • but there exists a message sequence $\underline{m} = (m_1, \ldots, m_j) \in M^j$ with $j \in \mathbf{N}$ and $j \le N$ and $test(pk, m_j, s_j)$ = FALSE for $s_j := sign^{(f)}(sk, j, \underline{m})$.

b) The scheme provides **error-free** effectiveness of authentication iff for all probabilistic interactive functions $\tilde{B}$, all parameters *par* as in Definition 7.1 or 7.2, respectively, with '1'^{N} as their second component, no possible outcome of key generation is bad, i.e.,

$$((acc, ids_{Risk,out}, pk, sk, aux_{\tilde{B}}) \in [Gen^{(f)}{}_{A,\tilde{B}}(par)] \\ \Rightarrow (acc, ids_{Risk,out}, pk, sk) \notin Bad_{eff}(N)).$$

c) It provides effectiveness of authentication with an **exponentially small error probability** iff for all $\tilde{B}$ and *par* as in Part b), the probability that the first four components of the outcome of $Gen^{(f)}{}_{A,\tilde{B}}(par)$ are in $Bad_{eff}(N)$ is at most $2^{-\sigma}$ (where σ is the second parameter from *par*).[100] ♦

Note that the error probability in Part c) is only taken over key generation (in the functional version), and not over the messages. Hence, as anticipated in Section 7.1.3, arbitrary active attacks have been hidden in the quantifier over the message sequence: If the keys are not in $Bad_{eff}(N)$, there is no message sequence for which authentication is not effective, hence it does not matter whether the attacker or an honest user chooses the messages, and whether adaptively or not.

Security for Risk Bearers

Security for risk bearers means that the requirement "correctness of *'broken'* " is fulfilled in the computational sense. According to Section 7.1.3, it is sufficient to consider an attacker who takes part in key generation and then immediately tries to compute a valid proof of forgery. These two parts of the attacker strategy are called $\tilde{A}_1$ and $\tilde{A}_2$.

The statement of the definition is that the probability that the attacker finds a valid proof of forgery is negligibly small in the parameter k.

It has to be decided how the other two parameters, σ and N, are treated. The simplest way is to fix them first and then let k tend to infinity; but then k depends on σ and N. The definition becomes more general if all parameters are allowed to grow simultaneously. However, σ and N must remain polynomial in k, so that the attacker strategy, which gets them as inputs, only has time polynomial in k. The following definition is the strongest one with this property: For a given k, it considers all σ's and N's smaller than an arbitrary polynomial in k. Alternatively, one could use arbitrary, but fixed dependencies, i.e., $\sigma = fsig(k)$ and $N = fn(k)$ for arbitrary functions *fsig* and *fn* that are polynomial-time computable in unary. All reductions in this text work in both models, but the reductions in the chosen model are usually less efficient than in the other one.[101]

As computationally restricted attackers are considered, algorithmic notation is used.

---

100 This notion of "exponentially small" is defined by an explicit upper bound, as in previous conventional definitions. A benefit is that one can decide what error probability one is willing to tolerate and set σ accordingly. A disadvantage is that the sum of two exponentially small functions need not be exponentially small in this sense, i.e., this formalization does not yield modus ponens automatically (see Section 5.4.4, "General Theorems"). Hence different properties have to be defined with different error probabilities, and some explicit computations with σ are needed.

101 I am not aware of any discussion in the literature about the best method to handle such situations, not even of any formal treatment of more than one security parameter. As to message bounds, I have at least compared the articles about provably secure ordinary digital signature schemes: The definition in [GoMR88] skips this point, but the forger seems to ask for a number i of signatures that is fixed before k. [BeMi92] does not need a message bound. [NaYu89, Romp90] do not define the message bound as a separate parameter in the correct scheme, but as a fixed polynomial in k. The rest do not make their own definitions.

Consequently, the different types of parameter transformations occurring in the following reductions, which look "standard", do not seem to be standard yet, and in general, I preferred writing a proof of 10 lines to explaining in 5 lines why it was trivial.

Definition 7.11. A standard fail-stop signature scheme is **secure for risk bearers** iff for all probabilistic polynomial-time interactive algorithms $\tilde{A}_1$ and non-interactive $\tilde{A}_2$ (the two parts of the attacker strategy) and all polynomials *Qsig*, *Qn* (determining the growth of σ and N as functions of k):

a) In the case with one risk bearer:

$\forall c > 0\ \exists k_0\ \forall k \geq k_0\ \forall \sigma \leq Qsig(k)\ \forall N \in Message\_bounds$ with $N \leq Qn(k)$ or $N = \infty$, and for $par := (\text{'1'}^k, \text{'1'}^\sigma, \text{'1'}^N)$:

$$P(acc = \text{TRUE} \wedge verify(pk, proof) = \text{TRUE} \setminus (acc, ids_{Risk,out}, pk, sk\_temp, aux_{\tilde{A}}) \leftarrow Gen_{\tilde{A}_1,B}(par); proof \leftarrow \tilde{A}_2(par, acc, ids_{Risk,out}, pk, sk\_temp, aux_{\tilde{A}})) < k^{-c}.$$

b) In the case with an arbitrary number of risk bearers, the additional parameters R for the total number of risk bearers and i for the internal identity of the correct risk bearer have to be considered. For simplicity, R is fixed before k, so that i can be fixed, too. Hence

$\forall R\ \forall i \leq R\ \forall c > 0\ \exists k_0\ \forall k \geq k_0\ \forall \sigma \leq Qsig(k)\ \forall N \in Message\_bounds$ with $N \leq Qn(k)$ or $N = \infty$, and for $par := (\text{'1'}^k, \text{'1'}^\sigma, \text{'1'}^N, \text{'1'}^R, i)$:

$$P(acc = \text{TRUE} \wedge verify(pk, proof) = \text{TRUE} \setminus (acc, ids_{Risk,out}, pk, sk\_temp, aux_{\tilde{A}}) \leftarrow Gen_{\tilde{A}_1,B}(par); proof \leftarrow \tilde{A}_2(par, acc, ids_{Risk,out}, pk, sk\_temp, aux_{\tilde{A}})) < k^{-c}.$$

◆

Security for the Signer

Security for the signer will be defined in two ways. The reason is that previous definitions avoided the concept of probabilistic interactive functions in favour of better-known notions. (This could originally be done because only simple versions of key generation were considered.) Now it is simpler to make a "forward" definition that deals explicitly with an interactive attacker strategy that carries out authentications and one dispute. This section contains such a forward definition. The "backward" definition from previous publications and a proof that it is slightly (and unnecessarily) stronger than the forward definition are presented in Section 7.2.1. Nevertheless, some of the later sections are based on the backward definition.

As this definition deals with unrestricted attackers, functional notation is used. First, some notation about forgeries is introduced.

Definition 7.12. Let a standard fail-stop signature scheme for a message space M and a set *Message_bounds* be given.

a) The set of possible **histories**, given a secret key sk and a message bound N, is

$$Hist(sk, N) := \{(\underline{m}, \underline{s}) \mid \exists j \in \mathbf{N}: j \leq N \wedge \underline{m} \in M^j \wedge \underline{s} = sign^{(f)}(sk, \underline{m})\}.$$

Intuitively, a history is the view of an attacker of what happened after key generation: An attacker of the restricted type described in Section 7.1.3 only lets the signer sign messages and observes the resulting signatures.

b) The set of **previously signed messages**, given a history $hist = (\underline{m}, \underline{s})$ with $\underline{m} = (m_1, \ldots, m_j)$, is

$$M(hist) := \{m_1, \ldots, m_j\}.$$

This set is relevant because an attacker can only cheat successfully by producing an acceptable signature on a message not in this set.

c) The set of **successful forgeries**, given an acceptance value *acc* (representing the result of key generation), a public key *pk*, and a history *hist*, is defined by

$$Forg(\text{TRUE}, pk, hist) := \{f = (m, s) \mid test(pk, m, s) = \text{TRUE} \wedge m \in M \setminus M(hist)\},$$

$$Forg(\text{FALSE}, pk, hist) := \emptyset.$$

Thus a successful forgery is a pair of a message and an acceptable signature on it, where the message was not previously signed.[102] If key generation was not successful, forging cannot be successful either, because no honest court would carry out a dispute; more formally, successful initialization is a precondition in the requirement of the signer on disputes.

d) A **provable forgery**, given a secret key *sk*, a public key *pk*, and a history *hist*, is a value *f* that the honest signer can prove to be a forgery, i.e., the signer obtains a valid proof of forgery by applying the algorithm *prove* to *f*.[103] This is expressed by the following predicate *provable*:

$$provable(sk, pk, hist, f) :\Leftrightarrow verify(pk, prove^{(f)}(sk, m, s, hist)) = \text{TRUE}. \quad \blacklozenge$$

The next definition introduces notation for the attacker strategy and its interaction with the signer's entity. According to Section 7.1.3, restricted attacker strategies of the following type are considered:

1. First, the attacker carries out key generation with the real signer's entity and the correct algorithm *res*. This part of the attacker strategy is called $\tilde{B}$.
2. Then the attacker interacts with the real signer's entity, choosing messages to be signed. This part of the attacker strategy is called *F* (the forger). *F* starts with the information $aux_{\tilde{B}}$ that $\tilde{B}$ obtained in key generation; this expresses the fact that $\tilde{B}$ and *F* are parts of one coordinated strategy. At some point, *F* outputs a value $f = (m, s)$ as a forgery and stops.

Definition 7.13. Let a standard fail-stop signature scheme and an attacker strategy $(\tilde{B}, F)$, consisting of two probabilistic interactive functions of the appropriate type, be given.

a) The probability distribution defined by the interaction of *F* with the real signer's entity, where
   - the signer's entity starts with a secret key *sk* as its input,
   - *F* has inputs *par*, *pub*, and $aux_{\tilde{B}}$,
   - and the results are the history *hist* and the output *f* of *F*,

---

[102] It does not matter that this set contains correct signatures, too, because it is only used to characterize the values an attacker can choose from when starting a dispute where he wants to have any chance of cheating the signer.

[103] *f* need not be a successful forgery, i.e., anything is called a provable forgery that looks like one to the algorithms *prove* and *verify*. In the following, however, this notion is usually applied to the successful forgeries an attacker has to use when trying to cheat the signer.

is denoted by

$$(hist, f) \leftarrow Auths^{(f)}{}_{S,F}(par, pub, aux_{\tilde{B}}, sk).$$

More formally, $Auths^{(f)}{}_{S,F}$ is defined as the execution of a 2-party protocol between F and the interactive function S defined by repeated application of *sign* to the messages received from F. The output *hist* is defined as $(\underline{m}, \underline{s})$, where $\underline{m}$ is the sequence of messages that F sent to S or, if F sent more than N messages, the first N of them, and $\underline{s}$ is the sequence of signatures that S sent back.

b) The probability of any event E in the probability space that results if both parts of the attacker strategy interact with the real signer's entity is abbreviated by $P_{\tilde{B},F,par}(E)$, i.e., for all parameters *par* as in Definition 7.1 or 7.2, respectively,

$$P_{\tilde{B},F,par}(E) := P(E \setminus (pub, sk, aux_{\tilde{B}}) \leftarrow Gen^{(f)}{}_{A,\tilde{B}}(par); \\ (hist, f) \leftarrow Auths^{(f)}{}_{S,F}(par, pub, aux_{\tilde{B}}, sk)).$$

This probability space is defined on tuples $(pub, sk, aux_{\tilde{B}}, hist, f)$ where *pub* is of the form $pub = (acc, ids_{Risk,out}, pk)$, and the components of such tuples will always be used with these names.

c) Two events are defined in the probability space from Part b):
   - *Forge* is the event that F has produced a successful forgery, i.e., it is defined by the predicate $f \in Forg(acc, pk, hist)$.
   - *Provable* is the event that the result of F is a provable forgery, i.e., it is defined by the predicate $provable(sk, pk, hist, f)$. ♦

The security for the signer against attacker strategies as described above means that the probability that the attacker succeeds in computing a successful forgery that the signer cannot prove to be a forgery is very small. This criterion can be formulated quite simply with the notation introduced in the previous definition.

Definition 7.14. A standard fail-stop signature scheme is **secure for the signer "forwards"** iff for all probabilistic interactive functions $\tilde{B}$ and F (representing a cheating risk bearer colluding with a forger) and all parameters *par* as in Definition 7.1 or 7.2, respectively,

$$P_{\tilde{B},F,par}(Forge \wedge \neg Provable) \leq 2^{-\sigma},$$

where σ is the second parameter from *par*. ♦

Recall that the event *Forge* can only occur if key generation was successful. Hence Definition 7.14 correctly represents that successful initialization is a precondition in the requirement of the signer on disputes.

Note that it is not possible to replace the probability in Definition 7.14 by $P_{\tilde{B},F,par}(\neg Provable \mid Forge)$: A forger might decide to forge only if $\tilde{B}$ was lucky and produced bad keys. This only happens with very small probability, but if it does, the conditional probability may be large.[104]

[104] This is easier to see in schemes with prekey (see Definition 7.31): There, $\tilde{B}$ might generate a prekey that is not good, and with an exponentially small probability, the prekey passes the zero-knowledge proof nevertheless. In this very unlikely case, nothing is guaranteed.

Summary

Definition 7.15. A standard fail-stop signature scheme is called **secure** iff it fulfils Definitions 7.9, 7.10, 7.11, and 7.14. ♦

7.2 Relations Between Security Properties

This section contains additional definition of security properties and proofs of their relations to the defining properties of standard fail-stop signature schemes:

- The backward definition of the security for the signer and the proof that it is slightly stronger than the forward definition.
- The definition of unforgeability and the proof that it follows from the security for the signer and the risk bearers (with a stronger version if the backward definition of the security for the signer is used).

7.2.1 Security for the Signer "Backwards"

The backward definition of the security for the signer considers the a-posteriori probabilities of successful forgeries being provable. The scheme is considered secure if these probabilities are very small, even for the best choice of a forgery from the point of view of an attacker. For the first definitions of security against unrestricted attackers by considering a-posteriori probabilities of secret information, see [Shan49, GiMS74].

The first definition deals with the information an attacker strategy has when it selects a forgery. Whether the forgery is provable or not depends only on the secret key *sk* of the signer's entity, apart from the information known to the attacker. Hence it is interesting which secret keys the signer's entity could possibly have from the point of view of the attacker. These possible secret keys correspond to the dotted circle in the middle of Figure 6.6, except that the history and the auxiliary output $aux_{\tilde{B}}$ from key generation were omitted in the figure for simplicity.

Definition 7.16. The set of **possible secret keys**, given the strategy $\tilde{B}$ that the attacker used in key generation and values *par*, *pub*, $aux_{\tilde{B}}$, and *hist*, is defined as follows:

$$SK_{\tilde{B}}(par, pub, aux_{\tilde{B}}, hist) :=$$
$$\{sk \mid (pub, sk, aux_{\tilde{B}}) \in [Gen^{(f)}{}_{A,\tilde{B}}(par)] \ \wedge \ hist \in Hist(sk, N)\},$$

where N is the message bound from *par*. ♦

The definition of security works backwards, too:

- First, a particular instance of the information an attacker has is defined as "good" (from our point of view, or that of the honest signer) if it leaves so much uncertainty about *sk* that any successful forgery is provable with high a-posteriori probability.
- Next, an outcome of key generation is called good if no matter what messages will later be signed, the information that an attacker obtains will always be good.

- Finally, it is required that the outputs of key generation are good with very high probability.

Definition 7.17. Let a standard fail-stop signature scheme, an attacker strategy $\tilde{B}$, and parameters *par* as in Definition 7.1 or 7.2, respectively, be given.

a) The probability of any event E in the probability space defined by the key generation alone is abbreviated as $P_{\tilde{B},par}$, i.e., for all parameters *par*,
$$P_{\tilde{B},par}(E) := P(E \setminus (pub, sk, aux_{\tilde{B}}) \leftarrow Gen^{(f)}{}_{A,\tilde{B}}(par)).$$
This probability space is defined on tuples $(pub, sk, aux_{\tilde{B}})$ where pub is of the form $pub = (acc, ids_{Risk,out}, pk)$, and the components of such tuples will always be used with these names.

b) The set $GoodInf_{\tilde{B}}(par)$ of **good information** known to the attacker is defined as follows: If $pub = (acc, ids_{Risk,out}, pk)$ and $hist = (\underline{m}, \underline{s})$, then
$$(pub, aux_{\tilde{B}}, hist) \in GoodInf_{\tilde{B}}(par) :\Leftrightarrow \forall f \in Forg(acc, pk, hist):$$
$$P_{\tilde{B},par}(provable(sk, pk, hist, f) \mid pub, aux_{\tilde{B}}, sign^{(f)}(sk, \underline{m}) = \underline{s})$$
$$\geq 1 - 2^{-\sigma-1},$$
where σ is the second parameter from *par*. The first two terms in the condition of the probability are, as usual, abbreviations for the events that the corresponding components of the tuples in the probability space have exactly the given values pub and $aux_{\tilde{B}}$. Hence the probability is in fact an a-posteriori probability given all the information known to the attacker, or, in other words, given that $sk \in SK_{\tilde{B}}(par, pub, aux_{\tilde{B}}, hist)$. Thus $GoodInf_{\tilde{B}}(par)$ contains those results of key generation and histories where, no matter how the attacker selects a successful forgery f, the likelihood that it is unprovable is very small.

c) The set $GoodKeys_{\tilde{B}}(par)$ of **good keys**, or, more precisely, good outcomes of key generation, is defined as follows:
$$(pub, sk, aux_{\tilde{B}}) \in GoodKeys_{\tilde{B}}(par) :\Leftrightarrow \forall hist \in Hist(sk, N):$$
$$(pub, aux_{\tilde{B}}, hist) \in GoodInf_{\tilde{B}}(par).$$
Thus an outcome is called good if it guarantees that no matter what messages will be signed, the information known to the attacker will be good, and thus any successful forgery will be provable with high likelihood.

d) When the attacker strategy and the parameters are clear from the context, the events that the information or the keys are good are abbreviated by *GoodInf* and *GoodKeys*, respectively. This notation is used in both the probability space with the distribution $P_{\tilde{B},par}$ and that with $P_{\tilde{B},F,par}$. Hence
   - *GoodInf* means $(pub, aux_{\tilde{B}}, hist) \in GoodInf_{\tilde{B}}(par)$, and
   - *GoodKeys* means $(pub, sk, aux_{\tilde{B}}) \in GoodKeys_{\tilde{B}}(par)$.

e) A standard fail-stop signature scheme is called **secure for the signer "backwards"** iff for all probabilistic interactive functions $\tilde{B}$ and all parameters *par*:
$$P_{\tilde{B},par}(\neg GoodKeys) \leq 2^{-\sigma-1},$$
where σ is the second security parameter from *par*.

f) The following additional requirement is often made with security for the signer backwards: If the entities of the signer and all risk bearers act correctly in key generation, the resulting keys are always good. In the case with one risk bearer, this can simply be written as

$$P_{B,par}(\neg GoodKeys) = 0. \qquad \blacklozenge$$

Remark 7.18. Note how unsuccessful key generation has been treated: If acc = FALSE, then $Forg(acc, pk, hist) = \emptyset$ by definition. Hence the conditions for membership in $GoodInf_{\tilde{B}}(par)$ and $GoodKeys_{\tilde{B}}(par)$ are always fulfilled. Thus the security definition means that any attacker in key generation with very high probability either gets caught as a cheater or ends up with good keys. ♦

Theorem 7.19 (Security backwards and forwards). In standard fail-stop signature schemes, security for the signer backwards implies security for the signer forwards. ♦

The main part of this theorem is contained in the following lemma, which is later (in Section 7.2.2) also used to obtain stronger versions of Theorem 7.19 for restricted attackers.

Lemma 7.20. If a standard fail-stop signature scheme is secure for the signer backwards, then for all attacker strategies $(\tilde{B}, F)$ as in Definition 7.13 and all parameters par as in Definition 7.1 or 7.2, respectively:

$$P_{\tilde{B},F,par}(Forge \wedge \neg Provable) \le P_{\tilde{B},par}(\neg GoodKeys) + 2^{-\sigma-1} P_{\tilde{B},F,par}(Forge),$$

where σ is the second parameter from par. ♦

Before the fairly long proof, note that this lemma is easy to believe: The first summand is the probability that the cheating risk bearer(s) can produce a bad key pair. The second summand deals with good keys. In this case, every successful forgery can be proved with probability at least $1 - 2^{-\sigma-1}$ (by Definition 7.17b); hence one should expect the probability of unprovable successful forgeries to be at most $2^{-\sigma-1}$ times the probability that any successful forgery is produced. The formal proof has to deal with the fact that all these probabilities are in different probability spaces.

Proof of Theorem 7.19 from Lemma 7.20. The first summand is bounded by $2^{-\sigma-1}$ according to Definition 7.17e, and the probability in the second summand is at most 1. This immediately yields the desired result. □

Proof of Lemma 7.20. Let $\tilde{B}$, F, and par be fixed throughout the proof.

A. The probability to be computed is first partitioned according to good and bad keys:

$$\begin{aligned} &P_{\tilde{B},F,par}(Forge \wedge \neg Provable) \\ &\quad \le P_{\tilde{B},F,par}(\neg GoodKeys) + P_{\tilde{B},F,par}(Forge \wedge \neg Provable \wedge GoodKeys) \\ &\quad \le P_{\tilde{B},par}(\neg GoodKeys) + P_{\tilde{B},F,par}(Forge \wedge \neg Provable \wedge GoodInf). \end{aligned}$$

For the first summand, it was used that the event $GoodKeys$ only depends on key generation, and not on the actions of F, i.e., it only depends on the first of the two probabilistic assignments that define the probabilities $P_{\tilde{B},F,par}$.

For the second summand, it was used that *GoodKeys* implies *GoodInf* in the given probability space. This is true because *hist* is a result of an interaction of F and the real signer's entity, and thus $hist \in Hist(sk, N)$.

Thus it only remains to be shown that

$$P_{\tilde{B},F,par}(Forge \wedge \neg Provable \wedge GoodInf) \leq 2^{-\sigma-1}\, P_{\tilde{B},F,par}(Forge). \qquad (1)$$

B. The proof of Inequality (1) is based on the inequalities from Definition 7.17b. They are a-posteriori probabilities given the information known to the attacker, which will be abbreviated as

$$inf := (pub, aux_{\tilde{B}}, hist).$$

Hence the probability is partitioned according to these values:

$$P_{\tilde{B},F,par}(Forge \wedge \neg Provable \wedge GoodInf) = \sum_{\substack{inf \in GoodInf_{\tilde{B}}(par) \\ f \in Forg(acc,pk,hist)}} (P_{\tilde{B},F,par}(inf, f) \cdot P_{\tilde{B},F,par}(\neg Provable \mid inf, f)). \qquad (2)$$

The second factor in each summand already looks similar to the probabilities in Definition 7.17b, but the probability is still over both key generation and the subsequent interaction. It will be shown that this does not matter, i.e., it will be proved below that for all $inf \in GoodInf_{\tilde{B}}(par)$ and $f \in Forg(acc, pk, hist)$:

$$P_{\tilde{B},F,par}(\neg Provable \mid inf, f) < 2^{-\sigma-1}. \qquad (3)$$

Substituting (3) into (2) then yields

$$\begin{aligned} P_{\tilde{B},F,par}&(Forge \wedge \neg Provable \wedge GoodInf) \\ &< 2^{-\sigma-1} \sum_{\substack{inf \in GoodInf_{\tilde{B}}(par) \\ f \in Forg(acc,pk,hist)}} P_{\tilde{B},F,par}(inf, f) \\ &= 2^{-\sigma-1}\, P_{\tilde{B},F,par}(GoodInf \wedge Forge) \\ &\leq 2^{-\sigma-1}\, P_{\tilde{B},F,par}(Forge). \end{aligned}$$

This is the desired Inequality (1). Hence only (3) remains to be shown.

C. For the proof of (3), let $inf = (pub, aux_{\tilde{B}}, hist) \in GoodInf_{\tilde{B}}(par)$ and $f \in Forg(acc, pk, hist)$ be fixed, where $hist = (\underline{m}, \underline{s})$. Definition 7.17b implies

$$P_{\tilde{B},par}(\neg provable(sk, pk, hist, f) \mid pub, aux_{\tilde{B}}, sign^{(f)}(sk, \underline{m}) = \underline{s}) < 2^{-\sigma-1}. \quad (4)$$

Thus it suffices to show that the probabilities in (3) and (4) are equal. Both are conditional probabilities where only *sk* is still free. The following more general statement is shown: The conditional distributions of *sk* are identical in the two cases, i.e., for any *sk*,

$$P_{\tilde{B},F,par}(sk \mid pub, aux_{\tilde{B}}, hist, f) = P_{\tilde{B},par}(sk \mid pub, aux_{\tilde{B}}, sign^{(f)}(sk, \underline{m}) = \underline{s}). \quad (5)$$

Informally, this means that the attacker has no additional information about the secret key from taking part in the choice of the history adaptively (and, obviously, from choosing his own forgery f). When (5) has been shown, the probabilities that the predicate $\neg provable(sk, pk, hist, f)$ holds are also identical in the two cases, which finishes the proof.

D. Now, (5) remains to be proved for any given sk. First, the left side of (5) is separated into the two steps with $\tilde{B}$ and F, respectively. For this, an abbreviation for the probabilities in the second step is introduced: For any event E, let

$$P_{F,par,pub,aux_{\tilde{B}},sk}(E) := P(E \mid (hist, f) \leftarrow Auths^{(f)}{}_{S,F}(par, pub, aux_{\tilde{B}}, sk)).$$

Then for any given sk,

$$\begin{aligned} &P_{\tilde{B},F,par}(sk \mid pub, aux_{\tilde{B}}, hist, f) \\ &= \frac{P_{\tilde{B},F,par}(sk, pub, aux_{\tilde{B}}, hist, f)}{P_{\tilde{B},F,par}(pub, aux_{\tilde{B}}, hist, f)} \\ &= \frac{P_{\tilde{B},par}(sk, pub, aux_{\tilde{B}})\, P_{F,par,pub,aux_{\tilde{B}},sk}(hist, f)}{\sum_{sk^*} P_{\tilde{B},par}(sk^*, pub, aux_{\tilde{B}})\, P_{F,par,pub,aux_{\tilde{B}},sk^*}(hist, f)}. \end{aligned}$$

The range of sk^* can be restricted to values $sk^* \in SK_{\tilde{B}}(par, pub, aux_{\tilde{B}}, hist)$, because for the others, one of the factors is 0. Moreover, only $sk \in SK_{\tilde{B}}(par, pub, aux_{\tilde{B}}, hist)$ needs to be considered, because otherwise both sides of (5) are zero. It is now shown that in this case, the second factors of all the terms are equal, so that they can be canceled out. Hence it is shown that for the given values pub, $aux_{\tilde{B}}$, $hist$, and f, a constant C exists such that for all $sk^* \in SK_{\tilde{B}}(par, pub, aux_{\tilde{B}}, hist)$,

$$P_{F,par,pub,aux_{\tilde{B}},sk^*}(hist, f) = C. \tag{6}$$

Given (6), the proof of (5), and thus the proof of the lemma, finishes as follows:

$$\begin{aligned} &P_{\tilde{B},F,par}(sk \mid pub, aux_{\tilde{B}}, hist, f) \\ &= \frac{P_{\tilde{B},par}(sk, pub, aux_{\tilde{B}})}{\sum_{sk^* \in SK_{\tilde{B}}(par,pub,aux_{\tilde{B}},hist)} P_{\tilde{B},par}(sk^*, pub, aux_{\tilde{B}})} \\ &= \frac{P_{\tilde{B},par}(sk, pub, aux_{\tilde{B}})}{\sum_{sk^*: sign^{(f)}(sk^*, \underline{m}) = \underline{s}} P_{\tilde{B},par}(sk^*, pub, aux_{\tilde{B}})} \\ &= \frac{P_{\tilde{B},par}(sk, pub, aux_{\tilde{B}})}{P_{\tilde{B},par}(pub, aux_{\tilde{B}}, sign^{(f)}(sk, \underline{m}) = \underline{s})} \\ &= P_{\tilde{B},par}(sk \mid pub, aux_{\tilde{B}}, sign^{(f)}(sk, \underline{m}) = \underline{s}). \end{aligned}$$

In the third line, it was used that for all the values sk^* where $sign^{(f)}(sk^*, \underline{m}) = \underline{s}$ holds, but $sk^* \in SK_{\tilde{B}}(par, pub, aux_{\tilde{B}}, hist)$ does not, the probability $P_{\tilde{B},par}(sk^*, pub, aux_{\tilde{B}})$ is zero.

E. Formula (6) remains to be shown. Informally, this means: If the forger has obtained a certain history, and then looks at the possible secret keys, obtaining exactly this history was equally probable for all of them. The only really intuitive meaning of this fact is that it implies (5), i.e., it implies that the a-posteriori probabilities of the possible secret keys are not biased by the fact that the history was chosen adaptively.

Formula (6) can be shown as follows (with the definition of the execution of a 2-party protocol): The probability in (6) is defined by an alternation of the signer's interactive algorithm, S, and the forger, F. Hence it is the product of the probabilities that the next message or signature sent still belongs to *hist* if all previous ones do so. In the functional notation used here, S is deterministic, and $sk^* \in SK_{\tilde{B}}(par, pub, aux_{\tilde{B}}, hist)$ implies $sign^{(f)}(sk^*, \underline{m}) = \underline{s}$. Hence all the probabilities on the signer's side are 1. Consequently, the forger's view in each step is identical for all these secret keys, and hence the probability distribution of the next message chosen by the forger must be identical, too.

This finishes the proof of (6), and thus the proof of the lemma. □

Remark 7.21. The converse of Theorem 7.19 is not true. For instance, consider the following stupid variant of a secure fail-stop signature scheme: If a message equals the secret key, the signer's entity adds the string *'Hey, this was my secret key'* to the signature. The probability that this ever happens is small for any attacker strategy (because the attacker would have to guess the secret key first), hence the security for the signer forwards is still fulfilled. However, for each successful outcome of key generation, there exist histories containing this message-signature pair, and then the forger can produce unprovable successful forgeries, because he knows the secret key. (For details about the (im-)probability of guessing the secret key and proving correct signatures to be forgeries, see the constructions and Section 11.3.) ♦

7.2.2 Unforgeability

This section contains the proof that secure standard fail-stop signature schemes also provide unforgeability. According to Section 7.1.3, restricted attacker strategies of the following type are considered:

1. • In a scheme with only one risk bearer, key generation is carried out entirely without the attacker. In order to be able to apply Lemma 7.20, the correct B is regarded as a special case of an attacker strategy, i.e., the protocol is written $Gen^{(f)}{}_{A,B}$, and the results are (pub, sk, aux_B) with $aux_B = \varepsilon$.
   • In a scheme with several risk bearers, all but one risk bearer may be attacking. Hence a protocol $Gen^{(f)}{}_{A,B,\tilde{O}}$ is executed, where $\tilde{O}$ is a probabilistic polynomial-time interactive algorithm. The outcome is $(pub, sk, aux_{\tilde{O}})$.

   To unify the notation, the indices of *aux* may be omitted.
2. Then the attacker interacts with the real signer's entity, choosing messages to be signed. This part of the attacker strategy is called F, the forger. It is a probabilistic polynomial-time algorithm and starts with the information *par*, *pub*, and *aux*. At some point, F outputs a value $f = (m, s)$ as a forgery and stops.

The forger F is successful if m is none of the previously signed messages and s is an acceptable signature on m.

Note that these forgers are special cases of those considered with the security for the signer. In the case with several risk bearers, let $\tilde{B}$ denote the combination of B and $\tilde{O}$. Hence the definition of unforgeability deals with the same probabilities $P_{\tilde{B},F,par}$ as the forward definition of the security for the signer.

As unforgeability will be a consequence of the security for both the signer and the risk bearers, both security parameters, k and σ, may have to tend to infinity. The definition of the precise relation between them corresponds to the following theorem; it can be generalized.

Definition 7.22.

a) A standard fail-stop signature scheme with one risk bearer provides **unforgeability** in both security parameters iff for all probabilistic polynomial-time interactive algorithms F and all polynomials $Qsig$, Qn (determining the growth of σ and N as functions of k):

$\forall c > 0\ \exists k_0\ \forall k \geq k_0\ \forall \sigma \leq Qsig(k)\ \forall N \in Message\_bounds$ with $N \leq Qn(k)$ or $N = \infty$: If $par := (\text{'}1\text{'}^k, \text{'}1\text{'}^\sigma, \text{'}1\text{'}^N)$, then (with the notation from Definition 7.13)

$$P_{B,F,par}(Forge) \leq k^{-c} + 2^{-\sigma}.$$

b) The scheme provides unforgeability in k alone iff, with the same notation and quantifiers,

$$P_{B,F,par}(Forge) \leq k^{-c}.$$

c) In a scheme with several risk bearers, it is required that for all probabilistic polynomial-time interactive algorithms $\tilde{O}$ and F and all polynomials $Qsig$ and Qn, and if $\tilde{B}$ denotes the combination of one correct risk bearer's algorithm B and $\tilde{O}$:

$\forall R\ \forall i \leq R\ \forall c > 0\ \exists k_0\ \forall k \geq k_0\ \forall \sigma \leq Qsig(k)\ \forall N \in Message\_bounds$ with $N \leq Qn(k)$ or $N = \infty$: If $par := (\text{'}1\text{'}^k, \text{'}1\text{'}^\sigma, \text{'}1\text{'}^N, \text{'}1\text{'}^R, i)$, then

$$P_{\tilde{B},F,par}(Forge) \leq k^{-c} + 2^{-\sigma},$$

or

$$P_{\tilde{B},F,par}(Forge) \leq k^{-c},$$

respectively. ♦

Remark 7.23. In the case where unforgeability depends on both security parameters, one can derive a normal-looking formula for unforgeability in one security parameter l by computing both k and σ as functions of l. For instance, if $k := \sigma := l$, one can use $Qsig := k$ and obtains: For all $c > 0$, there exist l_0 such that $P_{\tilde{B},F,par}(Forge) \leq l^{-(c+1)} + 2^{-l}$ for all $l \geq l_0$. There exists l^* such that $2^{-l} \leq l^{-(c+1)}$ for all $l \geq l^*$. Hence for all $l \geq \max\{l_0, l^*\}$:

$$P_{\tilde{B},F,par}(Forge) \leq l^{-c}.$$ ♦

Theorem 7.24 (Unforgeability).

a) Any secure standard fail-stop signature scheme provides unforgeability in both security parameters.

b) If there is only one risk bearer, and if Definition 7.17f is fulfilled, i.e., correct key generation only yields good keys, unforgeability in k alone is guaranteed. ♦

Proof. Let F, and in the case of several risk bearers $\tilde{O}$, be given, and let $\tilde{B}$ and *par* be defined accordingly. As F and $\tilde{O}$ are probabilistic polynomial-time, a signer who tries to break the security for risk bearers can use these algorithms as subroutines in the following way:

1. The signer executes *Gen* with the correct risk bearer's entity, using the correct algorithm A, or A and $\tilde{O}$, respectively.
2. The signer locally executes F alternately with her real signing algorithm to obtain a "forgery" $f = (m, s)$.
3. Finally, she uses *prove* to compute a proof of forgery for f.

Informally, the proof proceeds as follows: Assume that F computes successful forgeries with non-negligible probability. On the one hand, the security for the signer against an attacker using F then implies that Step 3 yields a valid proof of forgery with non-negligible probability. (Note that it makes no formal difference whether the signer or an attacker carries out F.) On the other hand, this means that when a cheating signer acts as described above, it contradicts the security for risk bearers. Hence the assumption must have been wrong; this proves unforgeability.

This proof is now formalized (but not as an indirect proof). Primarily, it has to be shown that the informal argument is in the correct probability spaces.

A. First, corresponding to the notation of Definition 7.11, Step 1 is formalized as an algorithm $\tilde{A}_1$ and Steps 2 and 3 as $\tilde{A}_2$.

- In the case with one risk bearer, $\tilde{A}_1$ is the correct A. Hence Step 1 is an execution of $Gen_{\tilde{A}_1,B}(par) = Gen_{A,B}(par)$, and its outcome is a tuple $(pub, sk\_temp, aux_{\tilde{A}})$, where $pub = (acc, ids_{Risk,out}, pk)$ and $aux_{\tilde{A}} = aux_A = \varepsilon$.
- In the case with several risk bearers, $\tilde{A}_1$ is the combination of A and $\tilde{O}$. Hence Step 1 is an execution of $Gen_{\tilde{A}_1,B}(par) = Gen_{A,B,\tilde{O}}(par)$. Its outcome is a tuple $(pub, sk\_temp, aux_{\tilde{A}})$, where $aux_{\tilde{A}} = aux_{\tilde{O}}$.
- $\tilde{A}_2$, on input $(par, pub, sk\_temp, aux_{\tilde{A}})$, first executes F in interaction with *sign* (as in Definition 7.13a, but in algorithmic notation): The inputs to F are $(par, pub, aux_{\tilde{A}})$, and *sk_temp* is updated with each application of *sign*. The results of Step 2 are a new temporary secret key from the last application of *sign* and the output f of F. Hence this step is denoted by

  $$(sk\_temp_{new}, f) \leftarrow Auths_{S,F}(par, pub, aux_{\tilde{A}}, sk\_temp).$$

  If f is a pair (m, s), the output of $\tilde{A}_2$ is $proof \leftarrow prove(sk\_temp_{new}, m, s)$. This corresponds to Step 3.

The probability that a signer using $\tilde{A}_1$ and $\tilde{A}_2$ successfully cheats the risk bearer is abbreviated by

$$\begin{aligned} P_{broken}(par) \;:=\; & \mathrm{P}(acc = \mathrm{TRUE} \wedge verify(pk, proof) = \mathrm{TRUE} \setminus \\ & (acc, ids_{Risk,out}, pk, sk\_temp, aux_{\tilde{A}}) \leftarrow Gen_{\tilde{A}_1,B}(par); \\ & proof \leftarrow \tilde{A}_2(par, acc, ids_{Risk,out}, pk, sk\_temp, aux_{\tilde{A}})). \end{aligned}$$

B. Now it is shown formally that $P_{broken}(par)$ is at least equal to the probability that an attacker using F produces a provable forgery. First, the case with one risk bearer is treated. In the first equation, the definitions of $\tilde{A}_1$ and $\tilde{A}_2$ for one risk bearer are used, and then algorithmic notation is replaced with equivalent functional notation.

$$\begin{aligned}
P_{broken}(par) &= \mathrm{P}(acc = \mathrm{TRUE} \wedge verify(pk, proof) = \mathrm{TRUE} \setminus \\
&\qquad (acc, ids_{Risk,out}, pk, sk_temp, \varepsilon) \leftarrow Gen_{A,B}(par); \\
&\qquad (sk_temp_{new}, (m, s)) \leftarrow Auths_{S,F}(par, pub, \varepsilon, sk_temp); \\
&\qquad proof \leftarrow prove(sk_temp_{new}, m, s)) \\
&= \mathrm{P}(acc = \mathrm{TRUE} \wedge verify(pk, proof) = \mathrm{TRUE} \setminus \\
&\qquad (acc, ids_{Risk,out}, pk, sk, \varepsilon) \leftarrow Gen^{(f)}{}_{A,B}(par); \\
&\qquad (hist, (m, s)) \leftarrow Auths^{(f)}{}_{S,F}(par, pub, \varepsilon, sk); \\
&\qquad proof := prove^{(f)}(sk, m, s, hist)) \\
&= \mathrm{P}(acc = \mathrm{TRUE} \wedge verify(pk, prove^{(f)}(sk, m, s, hist)) = \mathrm{TRUE} \setminus \\
&\qquad (acc, ids_{Risk,out}, pk, sk, \varepsilon) \leftarrow Gen^{(f)}{}_{A,B}(par); \\
&\qquad (hist, (m, s)) \leftarrow Auths^{(f)}{}_{S,F}(par, pub, \varepsilon, sk)).
\end{aligned}$$

The two probabilistic assignments are precisely those that define the probabilities $\mathrm{P}_{B,F,par}$, because the correct risk bearer's algorithm B outputs $aux_B = \varepsilon$. Hence

$$\begin{aligned}
P_{broken}(par) &= \mathrm{P}_{B,F,par}(acc = \mathrm{TRUE} \wedge provable(sk, pk, hist, f)) \\
&\geq \mathrm{P}_{B,F,par}(Forge \wedge Provable).
\end{aligned}$$

The last inequality holds because the event $Forge$ implies $acc = \mathrm{TRUE}$.

C. The analogue of Part B with several risk bearers first yields:

$$\begin{aligned}
P_{broken}(par) &= \mathrm{P}(acc = \mathrm{TRUE} \wedge verify(pk, prove^{(f)}(sk, m, s, hist)) = \mathrm{TRUE} \setminus \\
&\qquad (acc, ids_{Risk,out}, pk, sk, aux_{\tilde{O}}) \leftarrow Gen^{(f)}{}_{A,B,\tilde{O}}(par); \\
&\qquad (hist, (m, s)) \leftarrow Auths^{(f)}{}_{S,F}(par, pub, aux_{\tilde{O}}, sk)).
\end{aligned}$$

As above, the two probabilistic assignments are precisely those that define the probabilities $\mathrm{P}_{\tilde{B},F,par}$, because $\tilde{B}$ was defined as the combination of B and $\tilde{O}$, and its auxiliary output is $aux_{\tilde{O}}$, too. Hence, as above,

$$P_{broken}(par) \geq \mathrm{P}_{\tilde{B},F,par}(Forge \wedge Provable).$$

D. In the case with one risk bearer, B is now also called $\tilde{B}$, so that the results of Parts B and C are written identically.

The proof of Part a) of the theorem can be finished quite easily. First the security for the signer from Definition 7.14 is used:

$$\begin{aligned}
\mathrm{P}_{\tilde{B},F,par}(Forge) &= \mathrm{P}_{\tilde{B},F,par}(Forge \wedge Provable) + \mathrm{P}_{\tilde{B},F,par}(Forge \wedge \neg Provable) \\
&\leq P_{broken}(par) + 2^{-\sigma}.
\end{aligned}$$

The first summand was defined as the probability from the security for risk bearers (Definition 7.11). Using this definition immediately yields the desired result.

E. Part b) of the theorem is proved with Lemma 7.20. For the case $\tilde{B} = B$, it says

$$\mathrm{P}_{B,F,par}(Forge \wedge \neg Provable) \leq \mathrm{P}_{B,par}(\neg GoodKeys) + 2^{-\sigma-1}\,\mathrm{P}_{B,F,par}(Forge).$$

The first summand is zero according to Definition 7.17f. Therefore (with the general equation $\mathrm{P}(E \wedge E^*) = \mathrm{P}(E) - \mathrm{P}(E \wedge \neg E^*)$):

$$\mathrm{P}_{B,F,par}(Forge \wedge Provable) \geq (1 - 2^{-\sigma-1})\,\mathrm{P}_{B,F,par}(Forge),$$

or, conversely,

$$\begin{aligned} P_{B,F,par}(Forge) &\leq (1-2^{-\sigma-1})^{-1} P_{B,F,par}(Forge \wedge Provable) \\ &\leq 2\, P_{broken}(par). \end{aligned}$$

As above, application of Definition 7.11 immediately yields the desired result. (If c is given, there exists k_0 so that $P_{broken}(par) < k^{-(c+1)}$ for all $k \geq k_0$. Then $P_{B,F,par}(Forge) < 2k^{-(c+1)} \leq k^{-c}$ for $k \geq \max(k_0, 2)$.) □

7.3 Fail-Stop Signature Schemes with Prekey

This section presents a special class of standard fail-stop signature schemes with one risk bearer, where the structure of the key-generation protocol is a rather special case of that allowed in Definition 7.1. Almost all existing constructions belong to this class. (The theoretical construction based on bit commitments or one-way families of permutations from [DaPP94] does not.)

The primary benefit is not particularly low complexity, although that sometimes results, too, but that parts of the public key can be reused in several executions of key generation, and that security proofs become more modular. The former is an important precondition for the constructions of schemes for signing many messages from schemes for signing one message (see Section 6.3.1 and Chapter 10). Informally, this simpler key generation works as follows:

- First, the risk bearer's entity generates and publishes a value *prek*, called a prekey.
- Next, the risk bearer's entity may have to convince the signer's entity that *prek* has been chosen correctly, or at least that *prek* is good enough for the signer to be secure, but without disclosing too much information about *prek*. The notion of "good enough" will be modeled by a set *Good* of so-called good prekeys.

  If the signer's entity does not need the help of the risk bearer's entity in this step, i.e., if it can test *prek* locally, one obtains the simplest form of key generation, the 2-message initialization from Section 6.1.2.
- If the signer's entity is convinced, it generates a secret key and a corresponding public value *mk*, called the main public key, based on *prek*. The complete public key consists of *prek* and *mk*.[105]

For example, the prekey may be a number $n = p \cdot q$, and the risk bearer's entity may have to convince the signer's entity that n really has exactly two prime factors, but without showing it these factors, before the signer's entity generates the secret key and the main public key as certain numbers modulo n.

Additionally, as zero-knowledge proof schemes have error probabilities, but some properties of standard fail-stop signature schemes were required without an error probability, one sometimes has to consider all prekeys that a signer's entity may possibly accept. They are represented by a set *All*.

---

[105] In previous publications, *mk* was called *pk*, but this may lead to confusion with the pair $pk = (prek, mk)$.

7.3.1 Appropriate Zero-Knowledge Proof Schemes

The standard tools for convincing someone of something without giving too much information away are zero-knowledge proof schemes, originally defined in [GoMR89]. There are several such definitions, which differ in certain details. Unfortunately, I could not find any that has the properties needed here, in particular, with respect to the treatment of polynomial-time provers, although usual schemes seem to have them. Hence a definition of what I regard as the minimal properties needed in the present application is given, but no new schemes are presented. Remarks about the origin of the various parts of the definition and further possible generalizations follow below.

The definition assumes that one party has to generate a value K (usually some sort of key — in the present application the prekey) with a certain probability distribution *Corr* (for "correct") and needs a generation algorithm *gen* for this task, and another party wants to be convinced that K is an element of a set *Good*. The first party is called the prover, the second party the verifier. More precisely, both the distribution and the set are parametrized with security parameters, and there is a precondition that all values generated with the correct distribution are elements of *Good*.

Moreover, external verifiability of the proof scheme as defined in Section 5.2.11 is needed (for the algorithm *res* of the signature schemes): Someone who observes the prover and the verifier during a proof should be able to tell if K should have been accepted as good. Note that the goal is not to convince the observer that K is good (in fact, if the prover and the verifier collude, they can make the observer think that a proof was accepted although K is not good). The goal is that any observer can settle disputes between the prover and the verifier. This is necessary if the proof is used in a surrounding protocol. If the verifier complains that the prover has not given an acceptable proof, but the prover says that the verifier is lying, one may not be able to continue with the outer protocol. Now, if everybody else has been observing, they have a consistent view of which of the prover and the verifier is lying and may exclude the liar from the protocol or take similar measures.[106]

Definition 7.25 (Zero-knowledge proof scheme with generation algorithm, goodness predicate, and external verifiability). Let a pair (*CorrFam*, *GoodFam*) be given where

- $CorrFam := (Corr_{k,\sigma})_{k,\sigma \in \mathbb{N}}$ is a family of probability distributions, called the correct distributions, and
- $GoodFam := (Good_{k,\sigma})_{k,\sigma \in \mathbb{N}}$ is a family of sets,
- such that for all $k, \sigma \in \mathbb{N}$,

$$[Corr_{k,\sigma}] \subseteq Good_{k,\sigma}.$$

106 It would not help if the prover executed a proof with each observer, because a cheating prover could give some of them acceptable proofs and others not. Then, as nobody is globally trusted, one cannot take consistent measures, because either the prover can be lying or those observers who say they did not obtain an acceptable proof.

(That is, the carrier set of the correct distribution consists of good values only, but they need not be the only good values.)

The components of a zero-knowledge proof scheme with generation algorithm and external verifiability for the pair (*CorrFam*, *GoodFam*) are an algorithm *gen* and a triple *ZKP* := (*P*, *V*, *Obs*) with the following structure (see Figure 7.2 at the end of this definition):

- *gen*, the generation algorithm, is a probabilistic polynomial-time algorithm that, on input $par^* := ('1'^k, '1'^\sigma)$ with $k, \sigma \in \mathbb{N}$, outputs a pair of values (*K*, *aux*).
  Informally, *K* is the value that had to be generated originally, and *aux* is an auxiliary value that will help the prover to convince the verifier.
- *P*, the prover's algorithm, is a probabilistic polynomial-time interactive algorithm with one input-output port. Its initial input is a triple (par^*, *K*, *aux*) with par^* as above and (*K*, *aux*) ∈ [$gen(par^*)$]; and it does not produce a final output.
  Informally, this is the algorithm for the person who generated a value *K* with *gen* and now wants to convince someone that *K* is good.
- *V*, the verifier's algorithm, is a probabilistic interactive algorithm with one input-output port. Its initial input is a pair (par^*, *K*) with par^* as above, and it outputs a Boolean value *acc*. It has to work in time polynomial in the input par^* alone. (Hence it is polynomial-time when regarded as an interactive algorithm where only par^* is the initial input and *K* may be sent by the attacker.)
  Informally, this algorithm is used to verify that *K* is good in interaction with the prover; *acc* = TRUE means that the verifier is convinced.
- *Obs*, the observer's algorithm, is a deterministic interactive algorithm with two input ports only. Its initial input is a pair (par^*, *K*) with par^* as above, and it outputs a value *acc_observed* with the range {TRUE, FALSE, *'cheating'*}. It has to work in time polynomial in the input par^* alone.
  Informally, corresponding to Section 5.2.11, an observer listens to the prover and the verifier and observes whether the verifier should be convinced.

Execution of the protocol is denoted as follows (similar to the notation with *Gen* and shorter than the usual notation from the literature would be if one added *Obs* there):

- A correct execution of all the three algorithms, where *P* and *V* are connected with reliable broadcast channels that also lead to the input ports of *Obs*, and where the inputs par^* and *K* are the same for all three (see Figure 7.2), is denoted by a probabilistic assignment

  $$(acc, acc\_observed) \leftarrow ZKP(par^*, K, aux).$$

  The outputs have been defined with only one instance of *Obs*, although there may be several observers in reality, because *Obs* is deterministic and only works on broadcast messages, i.e., all observers obtain the same result.
- A cheating prover is represented by a probabilistic interactive function $\tilde{P}$, which has the same inputs as *P*. The execution of $\tilde{P}$, *V*, and *Obs* is denoted by

  $$(acc, acc\_observed) \leftarrow ZKP_{\tilde{P},V}(par^*, K, aux).$$

- A cheating verifier is represented by a probabilistic interactive algorithm $\tilde{V}$. In addition to the inputs and outputs that V has, it may have both an additional input $aux_{\tilde{V},in}$ and an additional output $aux_{\tilde{V},out}$.[107] The execution of P, $\tilde{V}$, and Obs is denoted by

$$(acc, acc\_observed, aux_{\tilde{V},out}) \leftarrow ZKP_{P,\tilde{V}}(par^*, K, aux, aux_{\tilde{V},in}).$$

Note that P and V (and $\tilde{P}$ and $\tilde{V}$) obtain the same results if they are carried out without observers and with only a point-to-point channel between them.

These components must have the following security properties:

a) **Correct generation.** For all $k, \sigma \in \mathbb{N}$, the first component, K, of $gen(\text{'1'}^k, \text{'1'}^\sigma)$, is distributed according to $Corr_{k,\sigma}$.

b) **Completeness (Effectiveness of proofs).**[108] If K has been generated correctly, a correct prover can always convince a correct verifier. More precisely: For all $par^* = (\text{'1'}^k, \text{'1'}^\sigma)$ with $k, \sigma \in \mathbb{N}$ and $(K, aux) \in [gen(par^*)]$, the output acc is TRUE in every execution of $ZKP(par^*, K, aux)$.

c) **Soundness (Requirement of the verifier on proofs).** If K is not even good, no cheating prover can convince a correct verifier with more than an exponentially small probability. More precisely: For all probabilistic interactive functions $\tilde{P}$, all parameters $par^* = (\text{'1'}^k, \text{'1'}^\sigma)$ with $k, \sigma \in \mathbb{N}$, and all values $K \notin Good_{k,\sigma}$ and aux:

$$P(acc = \text{TRUE} \setminus (acc, acc\_observed) \leftarrow ZKP_{\tilde{P},V}(par^*, K, aux)) \le 2^{-\sigma-1}.$$

d) **Zero-knowledge.** A cheating verifier cannot obtain additional knowledge from a correct prover by an execution of the proof scheme in the following sense: Any information she can obtain by an execution of the protocol with the real prover, she could have computed on her own with almost the same probability distribution. "Almost the same" means that no probabilistic polynomial-time algorithm can distinguish the two probability distributions. The information that she has obtained is represented in $aux_{\tilde{V},out}$. Moreover, one has to consider the a-priori information $aux_{\tilde{V},in}$. More precisely:

  - For all probabilistic polynomial-time interactive algorithms $\tilde{V}$ (the cheating verifier),
  - there exists a (non-interactive) probabilistic polynomial-time algorithm Sim, called the **simulator** (this is the algorithm that the verifier could use to compute on her own what $\tilde{V}$ computes after the interaction), such that
  - for every probabilistic polynomial-time algorithm Inf (representing a-priori information derived from K and aux in a feasible way),

---

107 The most important case where $aux_{\tilde{V},in}$ actually occurs is if several zero-knowledge proofs for the same value K are executed: Then $aux_{\tilde{V},in}$ is the information that cheating verifiers may have gathered in previous executions, i.e., it consists of old values $aux_{\tilde{V},out}$.

108 "Completeness" is the usual name for such properties in the literature, but "effectiveness of proofs" fits better with the terminology in Chapter 5. The same holds for the two names of the following property.

- the ensembles of probability distributions induced by $ZKP_{P,\tilde{V}}$ and *Sim*, where *Sim* gets the same inputs that $\tilde{V}$ would have, and $aux_{\tilde{V},in}$ is generated as *Inf*(*K*, *aux*), are computationally indistinguishable.

  This means that no probabilistic polynomial-time algorithm *Dist* should be able to distinguish them in the following sense: The distinguisher gets an input drawn according to either of the distributions, and informally, it outputs 0 if it thinks it has seen a result of $ZKP_{P,\tilde{V}}$ and 1 if it thinks it has seen a result from the simulator. Indistinguishability means that this does not work well, i.e., the output 0 occurs with almost the same probability for both types of inputs. Hence one requires the following for all polynomials *Qsig*:

  $\forall c > 0\ \exists k_0\ \forall k \geq k_0\ \forall \sigma \leq Qsig(k)$, and for $par^* := (\text{`1'}^k, \text{`1'}^\sigma)$: If one abbreviates the inputs to the zero-knowledge proof by

  $$in := (par^*, K, aux, aux_{\tilde{V},in}),$$

  the difference[109]

  $$\Delta_{in} := |\mathrm{P}(Dist(ZKP_{P,\tilde{V}}(in)) = 0) - \mathrm{P}(Dist(Sim(par^*, K, aux_{\tilde{V},in})) = 0)|$$

  is small on average. (Here, the first probability is taken over the random choices of P, $\tilde{V}$, and *Dist*, and the second one over those of *Sim* and *Dist*.) This means that

  $$E(\Delta_{in}) \leq k^{-c}$$

  for the expected value in the probability space on *in* defined by the assignments

  $$(K, aux) \leftarrow gen(par^*);\ aux_{\tilde{V},in} \leftarrow Inf(K, aux).$$

e) **External verifiability.**

- External verifiability requirement of the prover. For all probabilistic interactive functions $\tilde{V}$, all parameters $par^* = (\text{`1'}^k, \text{`1'}^\sigma)$, and all values $(K, aux) \in [gen(par^*)]$ and $aux_{\tilde{V},in}$: The observer's output *acc_observed* in all executions of $ZKP_{P,\tilde{V}}(par^*, K, aux, aux_{\tilde{V},in})$ is either TRUE or *'cheating'*, i.e., the observer either thinks that the verifier should be convinced or catches the verifier cheating.
- External verifiability requirement of the verifier. For all probabilistic interactive functions $\tilde{P}$, all parameters $par^* = (\text{`1'}^k, \text{`1'}^\sigma)$, and all values *K* and *aux*: The observer's result *acc_observed* in all executions of $ZKP_{\tilde{P},V}(par^*, K, aux)$ is equal to *acc*, i.e., the observer thinks that the verifier should be convinced if and only if the verifier is convinced. ♦

The components are summarized in Figure 7.2.

[109] Recall that *Sim* works on inputs of the form $(par^*, K, aux_{\tilde{V},in})$, like $\tilde{V}$. For simplicity, *Sim* is required to output triples $(acc, acc\_observed, aux_{\tilde{V},out})$ like $ZKP_{P,\tilde{V}}$, although this means that *Sim* simulates both $\tilde{V}$ and *Obs*, instead of $\tilde{V}$ only. This does not make the definition stricter, because any combination of $\tilde{V}$ and *Obs* is another admissible cheating verifier $\tilde{V}^*$.

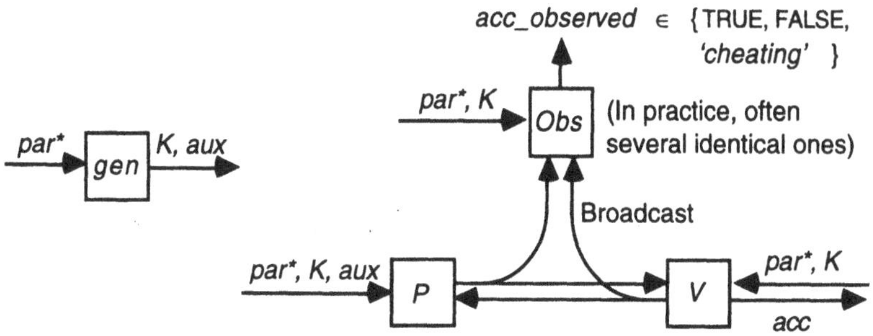

Figure 7.2. Components of a zero-knowledge proof scheme with generation algorithm and external verifiability, and their parameters in a correct execution

Remark 7.26 (Different definitions of zero-knowledge proof schemes). Definitions of zero-knowledge proof schemes vary in several respects. Here is a list of the decisions made above and the corresponding references.

- **Degrees of security.** Soundness, i.e., the requirement of the verifier on proofs, is guaranteed information-theoretically, and the zero-knowledge property computationally only. The dual type of zero-knowledge proof schemes exists, too; they are often called perfect zero-knowledge arguments, see [BrCr90]. Here, however, the verifier is the signer's entity, and hence a scheme had to be selected where the properties in the interest of the verifier are guaranteed information-theoretically. (Proof schemes where both properties are information-theoretical exist, too, but only for special languages.)

  Sometimes, a small error probability in the effectiveness of proofs is permitted, e.g., in [GoMR89], but concrete proof schemes never seem to have one. If one were introduced here, it should be exponentially small in σ.

- **Interest groups.** Nothing has been specified for values K that are good, but cannot be generated with *gen*. This corresponds to a specification in terms of interest groups: If the prover belongs to an interest group, there will be a precondition that his entity has correctly generated K with *gen*; this concerns effectiveness of proofs and the zero-knowledge property. Soundness is in the interest of the verifier, and the verifier only wants to know that K is good.

  Such a gap is unusual in definitions of zero-knowledge proof schemes, but it also exists in [BeYu93] for special proof schemes (non-interactive ones, which have a different definition).

- **Polynomial-time provers.** The prover's part in the protocol has been represented by a polynomial-time algorithm, P. In most definitions, the prover is computationally unrestricted. (See [GoMR89, ToWo87, GoOr94] and even [BoFL91], which claims to deal with practical cases. [Kili91] treats polynomial-time reductions between different provers, but does not contain a definition with polynomial-time provers either.) This corresponds to the idea that languages with interactive proofs are a complexity-theoretic generalization of NP, where a polynomial-time verifier does not only obtain one witness from a more powerful party, but can ask the powerful party many questions.

Of course, a prover of the same complexity as the verifier can only help the verifier if he has an auxiliary input related to K. This is mentioned in [GoMW91, Footnote 3], but the first definition that really treats this case seems to be in [Gold91, Gold93]. However, effectiveness of proofs is there defined as follows: For each K, there *exists* a value *aux* such that the proof works. Thus it is not clear if an actual generation algorithm *gen* produces such a value *aux* where the proof works, and not even if any feasible generation algorithm exists that produces K together with such a value. This is why I made the generation algorithm explicit, instead of defining a proof scheme for a language.

Consequently, I saw no need to require the proof scheme to be zero-knowledge for all distributions on triples (K, *aux*, $aux_{\tilde{V},in}$) that can be generated in polynomial time, which is the definition in [Gold93]. Instead, I concentrated on the actual distribution of (K, *aux*) and only assumed that arbitrary other information based on (K, *aux*) may be available.[110]

- **Auxiliary input.** The auxiliary a-priori information $aux_{\tilde{V},in}$ was first introduced in [ToWo87, Oren87]. It is necessary if one wants to prove that the composition of several zero-knowledge proofs is still zero-knowledge.
- **Uniform complexity.** Most definitions are non-uniform, i.e., they use circuit complexity. A uniform definition was given in [Gold93], and this (mainly Remark 18) was adapted here.
- **Two security parameters** have been used here. Usually, there is only one (or even none — then the security is measured as a function of the length of the input K exclusively), and strictly exponential decrease of the error probability in the soundness is not required. In the present application, however, it is needed. Anyway, most existing zero-knowledge proof schemes are repetitions of one basic round, and the error probability decreases exponentially with the number of rounds. Hence the number of such rounds would be a linear function of σ.

  One could generalize this aspect further by using new security parameters for the zero-knowledge proof scheme, instead of the indices to the family of distributions. However, one must then be careful with the relation between these parameters when they all tend to infinity.

  Moreover, it does not seem to be required anywhere else that the verifier and the observer need time polynomial in the security parameters only, because it is unusual to regard K as a value that may be internal to a larger system, as it is needed here.
- **External verifiability** is usually not required. ♦

110 One could make the definition stricter (so that individual schemes become more widely applicable) by assuming that a relation between values K and *aux* is given and requiring effectiveness for all pairs from this relation, and the zero-knowledge property for any generation algorithm that generates values K together with related values *aux*.

Another conceivable variation in the treatment of the generation algorithm is to assume that the given distribution is not only on values K, but on pairs (s, K), where s is some secret information related to K. Then *gen* must produce triples (s, K, *aux*) such that the first two components have the correct distribution.

The easiest case of a proof scheme as defined above is that the verifier can verify if K is good on her own. This is formalized in the following definition, and the subsequent lemma simply says that such a local verification is indeed a special case of a zero-knowledge proof scheme in the sense of Definition 7.25, so that this special case does not need special treatment.

Definition 7.27 (Local verifiability). Let a pair (*CorrFam*, *GoodFam*) as in Definition 7.25 be given. It is called locally verifiable if there is

- a probabilistic polynomial-time generation algorithm *gen* that, on input ('1'^{k}, '1'$^\sigma$), outputs a value K with the distribution $Corr_{k,\sigma}$, and
- a non-interactive and deterministic algorithm V that decides membership in *GoodFam* in time polynomial in the inputs '1'^{k} and '1'$^\sigma$ alone. It is called the local verification algorithm. Thus $V($'1'^{k}, '1'$^\sigma$, $K)$ = TRUE $\Leftrightarrow K \in Good_{k,\sigma}$. ♦

No auxiliary output *aux* is generated this time, because the prover only needed *aux* to convince the verifier in the zero-knowledge proof.

Lemma 7.28. Let a pair (*CorrFam*, *GoodFam*) as in Definition 7.25 be given. If it is locally verifiable with algorithms *gen* and V as in Definition 7.27, a zero-knowledge proof scheme with generation algorithm and external verifiability for (*CorrFam*, *GoodFam*) is given by

- the algorithm *gen** that generates a value K just like *gen*, but outputs (K, ε), and
- $ZKP := (P, V, Obs)$ where P does nothing at all and $Obs := V$, i.e., the observer locally verifies K, too. ♦

Proof. Correct generation follows from the precondition on *gen*. Effectiveness of proofs follows immediately from the precondition $[Corr_{k,\sigma}] \subseteq Good_{k,\sigma}$. Soundness is just the definition of V. Zero-knowledge is clear because P does not send anything, hence it cannot divulge anything; formally, one can use $Sim := \tilde{V}$. The external verifiability requirement of the prover is shown like the effectiveness of proofs, and the external verifiability requirement of the verifier is fulfilled because $Obs = V$ and both are deterministic. □

Remark 7.29 (Varying *GoodFam*). Let a zero-knowledge proof scheme (*gen*, *ZKP*) in the sense of Definition 7.25 for a pair (*CorrFam*, *GoodFam*) be given. If $GoodFam' := (Good'_{k,\sigma})_{k,\sigma \in \mathbb{N}}$ is a second family of sets and $Good'_{k,\sigma} \supseteq Good_{k,\sigma}$ for all $k, \sigma \in \mathbb{N}$, then (*gen*, *ZKP*) is a zero-knowledge proof scheme in the sense of Definition 7.25 for (*CorrFam*, *GoodFam'*), too. This is obvious because the only security property where the sets of good keys are mentioned is soundness, and there, $K \notin Good'_{k,\sigma}$ implies $K \notin Good_{k,\sigma}$, and hence the original soundness property can be applied. ♦

Remark 7.30 (Existence of zero-knowledge proof schemes). Zero-knowledge proof schemes exist for all languages in NP under certain computational assumptions, but of course, those schemes have not been constructed and proved with respect to the definition made here. [GoMW91] works with arbitrarily powerful provers and in the non-uniform model, but makes a remark that the proof should also work for provers with arbitrary auxiliary inputs. [Gold93] is for polynomial-time provers and uniform, but, as mentioned, only proves the *existence* of a value *aux* for which the proof works. The proofs of these schemes (in particular of the construction of schemes for all NP-languages from one concrete scheme for one concrete language) are a bit sketchy, but I guess that they work if an arbitrary witness *aux* is given and that they offer external verifiability.

If this is so, there exists at least one inefficient zero-knowledge proof scheme for every possible generation problem of values *K* in a two-party scenario, as they will occur in the following: Let

- a probabilistic polynomial-time algorithm *gen* that defines the correct generation of such values *K* from parameters $par^* := ('1'^k, '1'^\sigma)$, and
- a corresponding family *GoodFam*

be given. Define

- *CorrFam* as the family of distributions defined by *gen*, and
- gen^* as the algorithm that behaves like *gen*, but additionally outputs the random string used in this process as *aux*.

The graph of *gen*, i.e., the set of pairs (par^*, K) with $K \in [gen(par^*)]$, is a language in NP, and gen^* generates elements in it together with a witness *aux*. Let *ZKP* be a zero-knowledge proof scheme for that language that works with arbitrary witnesses and offers external verifiability. Then (gen^*, ZKP) is a zero-knowledge proof scheme in the sense of Definition 7.25 for (*CorrFam*, *CorrFam*). According to Remark 7.29, it also works for (*CorrFam*, *GoodFam*). ♦

For the problems occurring in the following concrete constructions, more efficient zero-knowledge proof schemes are known.

7.3.2 Definition of Schemes with Prekey

Definition 7.31. The components of a standard fail-stop signature scheme with prekey are defined like those of a general standard fail-stop signature scheme with one risk bearer, except that the key-generation protocol and the verification of proofs of forgery are constructed from simpler components (*CorrFam*, *GoodFam*, (*AllFam*, *all_test*), (gen_B, ZKP), gen_A, *mk_test*) and *verify_simple*, where:

- $CorrFam := (Corr_{k,\sigma})_{k,\sigma \in \mathbf{N}}$ is a family of probability distributions, called the **correct prekey distributions**.
- $GoodFam := (Good_{k,\sigma})_{k,\sigma \in \mathbf{N}}$ is a family of sets, called the **family of good prekeys**. Intuitively, it represents prekeys good enough for the signer to be secure. Let $Good := \bigcup_{k,\sigma} Good_{k,\sigma}$.
- $AllFam := (All_{k,\sigma})_{k,\sigma \in \mathbf{N}}$ is a family of sets, called the **family of all acceptable prekeys**, and *all_test* decides membership in this family in time polynomial in the security parameters alone.[111] Hence *all_test* is an algorithm

[111] Instead of being a separate component of the signature schemes, (*AllFam*, *all_test*) could be a component of the zero-knowledge proof schemes, in particular because parts of *V* and *Obs* may be equal to *all_test*. However, I did not want to change the definition of zero-knowledge proof schemes more than necessary.

that, on input ('1'^{k}, '1'$^\sigma$, *prek*), outputs TRUE if $prek \in All_{k,\sigma}$ and FALSE otherwise, in time polynomial in the inputs '1'^{k} and '1'$^\sigma$ alone. Let $All := \bigcup_{k,\sigma} All_{k,\sigma}$.

- (gen_B, *ZKP*) is a **zero-knowledge proof scheme** with generation algorithm and external verifiability for (*CorrFam*, *GoodFam*). (See Definition 7.25, and note that the following Property a) contains the precondition for that definition.) The components of *ZKP* are called *P*, *V*, and *Obs*.

  The outputs of gen_B are written (*prek*, *aux*). The first output, *prek*, is called a **prekey**; the second output, *aux*, is only needed to convince the signer's entity of the correctness of *prek* in the zero-knowledge proof. Note that the inputs to gen_B are only the two security parameters par^* = ('1'^{k}, '1'$^\sigma$), and not the message bound *N*.
- gen_A, the **main key-generation algorithm**, is a probabilistic polynomial-time algorithm. On input the parameters *par* = ('1'^{k}, '1'$^\sigma$, '1'^{N}) with $k, \sigma \in \mathbb{N}$ and $N \in$ *Message_bounds* and a prekey $prek \in All_{k,\sigma}$, it generates a pair (*sk_temp*, *mk*), where *sk_temp* is called the temporary secret key and *mk* the **main public key**.

  A functional version, $gen_A^{(f)}$, is defined as usual: It outputs (*sk*, *mk*), where *sk* consists of *sk_temp* and a random string r_A.
- *mk_test*, the **main public key test**, is a deterministic algorithm that, on input (*par*, *prek*, *mk*), where *par* = ('1'^{k}, '1'$^\sigma$, '1'^{N}) with $k, \sigma \in \mathbb{N}$ and $N \in$ *Message_bounds* and $prek \in All_{k,\sigma}$, and in time polynomial in the inputs *par* and *prek* alone, outputs TRUE or FALSE. A main public key that passes this test is called acceptable.
- *verify_simple*, the **simplified verification algorithm**, is a probabilistic polynomial-time algorithm that, on input a pair (*prek*, *proof*) with $prek \in All$, outputs a value $valid \in$ {TRUE, FALSE}. (Hence the difference is that the proof of forgery is verified given only the prekey, not the complete public key.)

These components must have the following additional properties:

a) Good and acceptable prekeys. All correctly generated prekeys are good and acceptable; more precisely, for all $k, \sigma \in \mathbb{N}$,

$$[Corr_{k,\sigma}] \subseteq Good_{k,\sigma} \subseteq All_{k,\sigma},$$

and the length of the elements of $All_{k,\sigma}$ is polynomial in *k* and σ, i.e., there is a polynomial *Q* such that $|prek| \le Q(k, \sigma)$ for all $k, \sigma \in \mathbb{N}$ and all $prek \in All_{k,\sigma}$.[112]

[112] This length restriction and subsequent ones are needed to ensure availability of service, here in the sense that the running time is polynomial in the interface inputs alone, because values like prekeys and main public keys may be sent to some participants by attackers. (Note that even if membership in a family of sets can be tested in polynomial time, the length of the set elements is not automatically polynomially restricted, because the test may depend on substrings only.) The restrictions are without much loss of generality, because the correct values can be generated in polynomial time, i.e., an upper bound on their length exists.

b) Acceptable main public keys. All correctly generated main public keys are acceptable, i.e., for all $par = (\text{‘1’}^k, \text{‘1’}^\sigma, \text{‘1’}^N)$ with $k, \sigma \in \mathbb{N}$ and $N \in$ *Message_bounds* and all prekeys $prek \in All_{k,\sigma}$,

$$((sk\_temp, mk) \in [gen_A(par, prek)] \Rightarrow mk\_test(par, prek, mk) = \text{TRUE}),$$

and the length of acceptable main public keys is polynomial in the length of *par* and *prek*.

c) If it is desired that *verify* is polynomial-time in the interface inputs alone, *verify_simple* must be polynomial-time in *prek* alone.

The corresponding components *A*, *B*, *res*, and *verify* required in Definition 7.1 are defined in terms of these simpler components as follows. The input to *A*, *B*, and *res* is of the form $par = (\text{‘1’}^k, \text{‘1’}^\sigma, \text{‘1’}^N)$ with $k, \sigma \in \mathbb{N}$ and $N \in$ *Message_bounds*, and the abbreviation $par^* := (\text{‘1’}^k, \text{‘1’}^\sigma)$ is used.

- *A* first expects to receive a value *prek* from the risk bearer's entity on the broadcast channel and tests it with *all_test*(*par**, *prek*). If the result is FALSE, it stops. Otherwise, it carries out the verifier's part, *V*, of the zero-knowledge proof scheme on input (*par**, *prek*), using the broadcast channel for all messages. This gives a result acc_A. If acc_A = FALSE, it stops. Otherwise, it executes $gen_A(par, prek)$ to obtain values *sk_temp* and *mk*. It broadcasts *mk*, the main public key, and outputs *sk_temp*.
- *B* first carries out $gen_B(par^*)$ to obtain values *prek* and *aux*. Then it carries out the prover's part, *P*, of the zero-knowledge proof scheme on input (*par**, *prek*, *aux*), using the broadcast channel for all messages.
- *res* first expects to receive a value *prek* from the risk bearer's entity on the broadcast channel and tests it with *all_test*(*par**, *prek*). If the result is FALSE, it outputs (FALSE, $\emptyset$, ε) and stops. Otherwise, it performs the observer's part, *Obs*, of the zero-knowledge proof scheme on input (*par**, *prek*). The result is a value *acc_observed*.
  - If *acc_observed* = *‘cheating’*, i.e., the signer (who is the verifier) has been caught cheating in the proof, the output is (FALSE, $\{1\}$, ε).
  - If *acc_observed* = FALSE, i.e., the observer thinks that the risk bearer was not convincing as a prover, the output is (FALSE, $\emptyset$, ε).
  - If *acc_observed* = TRUE, i.e., the observer thinks that the proof was ok, it expects a value *mk* from the signer's entity on the broadcast channel. If none arrives, or if *mk_test*(*par*, *prek*, *mk*) = FALSE, the output is (FALSE, $\{1\}$, ε) again. Otherwise, the output is

$$(\text{TRUE}, \{1\}, (prek, mk)).$$

- *verify*, on input (*pk*, *proof*) with *pk* = (*prek*, *mk*), simply calls *verify_simple*(*prek*, *proof*).

  The domain of the first parameter consists of values *pk* = (*prek*, *mk*) where parameters $par = (\text{‘1’}^k, \text{‘1’}^\sigma, \text{‘1’}^N)$ exist such that $prek \in All_{k,\sigma}$ and *mk_test*(*par*, *prek*, *mk*) = TRUE. This domain is denoted by

$$PK\_All.$$

It has to be shown that these components are admissible in Definition 7.1:

First, A, B, and *res* are polynomial-time in their initial inputs *par*. With A, this holds because *all_test* and V are polynomial-time in *par** alone, and any value *prek* used as an input to gen_A has been accepted by *all_test*, so that its length is polynomial in *par** by Property a). With B, it is obvious. The algorithm *res* starts with *all_test* and *Obs*, which are polynomial-time in *par** alone. If it carries out *mk_test*, which is polynomial-time in *par* and *prek*, the value *prek* has been accepted by *all_test*, and hence its length is polynomial in that of *par**. Finally, if *res* has to output *mk*, this value has been accepted by *mk_test*, and hence its length is polynomial in *par* and *prek* by Property b), where the length of *prek* has already been shown to be polynomial in that of *par*.

Secondly, one can easily see from the definition of *res* that *verify* has been defined for all values *pk* that can actually occur.

Furthermore, it suffices to define *test* for the same values $pk \in PK\_All$ as *verify*. Similarly, a value *sk_temp* can only be an original temporary secret key (as in the requirement on *SK_Temp* in Definition 7.1) if there exist parameters par = ('1'^{k}, '1'$^\sigma$, '1'^{N}) as above, a prekey $prek \in All_{k,\sigma}$, and a value *mk* such that $(sk\_temp, mk) \in [gen_A(par, prek)]$. Define

$$SK\_Temp_{orig}$$

and

$$SK\_Temp_{orig}(prek)$$

as the set of all these values and those for a fixed value *prek*, respectively. ♦

Remark 7.32. The use of the broadcast channel in the correct case (which should be the most common case) and the involvement of recipients and courts can be reduced as follows: After *prek* has been published, and if it passes *all_test*, the entities of the signer and the risk bearer first try to execute their algorithms P and V on the point-to-point channel. The signer's entity broadcasts its result *acc*. If it is TRUE, i.e., there is no disagreement between the signer and the risk bearer, it immediately publishes *mk*, too. Otherwise, the proof must be repeated on the broadcast channel as in Definition 7.31. ♦

Remark 7.33. The restriction that the validity of proofs of forgery depends on *prek* alone, and not on *mk*, is sensible, because *prek* is the part of the key that protects the risk bearer, whose entity generates it. The restriction is also without much loss of generality: Given a general scheme, one can define an equivalent restricted scheme (whose components are distinguished from the given ones by asterisks): Use $prek^* := (par, prek)$ and $proof^* := (mk, proof)$ and define $verify\_simple^*(prek^*, proof^*) := mk\_test(par, prek, mk) \wedge verify((prek, mk), proof)$. The equivalence holds, although verification is now executed on a value *mk* sent by the signer in the proof of forgery, because the choice of *mk* and *proof* in Definition 7.11 are two consecutive actions of the signer. One only has to take care with the growth of N in relation to k in that case, if one wants *verify_simple* to be polynomial-time in *prek* alone. ♦

7.3.3 Security of Schemes with Prekey

As the zero-knowledge proof scheme in a standard fail-stop signature scheme with prekey is required to be secure in itself, and *all_test* decides membership in *All* correctly, it is natural to reduce the security of such a scheme to criteria that only deal with the remaining components. This is done in the following theorem. The criteria are considerably simpler than the original definitions, because interaction in key generation no longer has to be considered. The constructions in Chapters 9 and 10 only have to be proved with respect to these criteria.

Theorem 7.34 (Simplified security criteria). If a standard fail-stop signature scheme with prekey fulfils the following three criteria, then

a) it is secure,

b) effectiveness of authentication is error-free, and

c) the slightly stronger security for the signer backwards, including Definition 7.17f, holds.

The criteria are:

1. **Effectiveness of authentication.** For all acceptable prekeys and all key pairs based on it, all correct signatures are acceptable.[113]

   More precisely: For all parameters $par = ('1'^k, '1'^\sigma, '1'^N)$ with $k, \sigma \in \mathbb{N}$ and $N \in Message\_bounds$, all prekeys $prek \in All_{k,\sigma}$, all pairs $(sk, mk) \in [gen_A^{(f)}(par, prek)]$, all message sequences $\underline{m} = (m_1, \ldots, m_j) \in M^j$ with $j \in \mathbb{N}$ and $j \le N$, the correct signature $s_j := sign^{(f)}(sk, j, \underline{m})$ passes the test with $pk := (prek, mk)$, i.e., $test(pk, m_j, s_j) = \text{TRUE}$.

2. **Security for the risk bearer.** If the risk bearer's entity generates the prekey correctly, it is infeasible to find a valid proof of forgery for it.

   More precisely: For all probabilistic polynomial-time algorithms $\tilde{A}^*$ and all polynomials $Qsig$ (determining the growth of σ as a function of k):

   $\forall c > 0\ \exists k_0\ \forall k \ge k_0\ \forall \sigma \le Qsig(k)$ and for $par^* := ('1'^k, '1'^\sigma)$:

   $$P(verify\_simple(prek, proof) = \text{TRUE} \setminus prek \leftarrow Corr_{k,\sigma};\ proof \leftarrow \tilde{A}^*(par^*, prek)) < k^{-c}.$$

3. **Security for the signer.** If a prekey is good and the signer's entity bases its main key generation on it, the resulting keys are good in a sense very similar to Definition 7.17. More precisely:

   - For any parameters $par = ('1'^k, '1'^\sigma, '1'^N)$ with $k, \sigma \in \mathbb{N}$ and $N \in Message\_bounds$ and any prekey $prek \in All_{k,\sigma}$, the probability of an event E in the probability space resulting from the signer's main key generation is denoted by

   $$P_{par,prek}(E) := P(E \setminus (sk, mk) \leftarrow gen_A^{(f)}(par, prek)).$$

113 If this criterion were only made for good prekeys, the scheme would still be secure, but effectiveness of authentication would only be error-free if the risk bearer's entity acted correctly.

- The set *GoodInf(par, prek)* of **good information** known to the attacker is defined as follows: If $pk = (prek, mk)$ and $hist = (\underline{m}, \underline{s})$, then

$$(mk, hist) \in GoodInf(par, prek) :\Leftrightarrow \forall f \in Forg(\text{TRUE}, pk, hist): \\ P_{par,prek}(provable(sk, pk, hist, f) \mid mk, sign^{(f)}(sk, \underline{m}) = \underline{s}) \\ \geq 1 - 2^{-\sigma-1},$$

where σ is the second parameter from *par*.

- The following requirement is made: For all parameters $par = (\text{'1'}^k, \text{'1'}^\sigma, \text{'1'}^N)$ with $k, \sigma \in \mathbb{N}$ and $N \in Message\_bounds$, all prekeys $prek \in Good_{k,\sigma}$, all key pairs $(sk, mk) \in [gen_A{}^{(f)}(par, prek)]$, and all possible histories $hist \in Hist(sk, N)$,

$$(mk, hist) \in GoodInf(par, prek). \qquad \blacklozenge$$

The criteria in Theorem 7.34 could be regarded as the security definition of the signature scheme where the zero-knowledge proof is replaced by a trusted oracle that simply tells the entities of the signer and the observing recipients and courts whether the prekey is good. The criteria say that if the risk bearer's entity generates the prekey correctly and the signer has to select *proof* without obtaining additional information, the requirement of the risk bearer is fulfilled, and that the requirements of the signer are fulfilled if the prekey is good. Hence the proof of Theorem 7.34 mainly elaborates that the zero-knowledge proof scheme is as good as such a trusted oracle for practical purposes.

Moreover, note that Theorem 7.34 says that correctness of initialization no longer has to be required explicitly.

Proof sketch of Theorem 7.34. For Part a) of the theorem, the four parts of the security definition (Definition 7.15) are treated in Parts A to D of the following proof. However, effectiveness of authentication in Part B of the proof is immediately proved in the error-free sense, which also yields Part b) of the theorem. Similarly, in Part D of the proof, security for the signer backwards (Definition 7.17e) is proved immediately; this implies security for the signer forwards according to Theorem 7.19 and is required in Part c) of the theorem. The requirement from Definition 7.17f is proved in Part E.

A. Correctness of initialization (Definition 7.9).

- For the signer: By the definition of *res*, the output acc = FALSE and $ids_{Risk,out} = \{1\}$ can only occur if either *acc_observed* = *'cheating'* or the signer's entity fails to send an acceptable *mk*. The former is excluded by the external verifiability requirement of the verifier on the proof scheme. The latter could only happen to an honest signer if acc_A = FALSE, because all correctly generated main public keys are acceptable. However, the external verifiability requirement of the verifier on the proof scheme guarantees that this can only happen if *acc_observed* is FALSE, too, and then *res* does not expect *mk* anyway.
- For the risk bearer: By the definition of *res*, an output $ids_{Risk,out} \neq \{1\}$ can only occur if *res* does not receive an acceptable prekey or if *acc_observed* = FALSE. The former cannot happen to an honest risk bearer, because all correctly

generated prekeys are acceptable, and the latter is excluded by the external verifiability requirement of the prover on the proof scheme.

B. Effectiveness of authentication (Definition 7.10). Let $\tilde{B}$ be given and let (TRUE, $ids_{Risk,out}$, pk, sk) be an outcome of key generation, i.e., of $Gen^{(f)}{}_{A,\tilde{B}}(par)$ for some parameters par = ('1'^{k}, '1'$^\sigma$, '1'^{N}) as above. By construction of *res*, the value *pk* must be of the form (*prek*, *mk*), where *prek* is an acceptable prekey and *mk* has been received from *A*. By construction of *A*, *mk* has been generated with $gen_A(par, prek)$. Hence one can apply Criterion 1 of Theorem 7.34, and it yields that this outcome is not in $Bad_{eff}(N)$. This means error-free effectiveness of authentication.

C. Security for the risk bearer (Definition 7.11). The precondition of Criterion 2 of Theorem 7.34 means that valid proofs of forgery are infeasible to find if the risk bearer's entity only generates a prekey. It has to be shown that they are still infeasible to find if the risk bearer's entity carries out the additional zero-knowledge proof. Hence, essentially, it has to be shown that the formalization of "zero-knowledge" means what it should. The formalization of the following proof sketch should be similar to the proofs about the composition of zero-knowledge proofs in [GoOr94, ToWo87, Gold93]. An overview of this part of the proof is given in Figure 7.3. Finally, it has to be considered that the attacker in the criterion does not have '1'^{N} as a parameter, whereas the attacker in Definition 7.11 has.

Hence, assume that the signature scheme is not secure for the risk bearer, i.e., contrary to Definition 7.11a, two algorithms $\tilde{A}_1$ and $\tilde{A}_2$ (the two parts of the attacker strategy) find valid proofs of forgery after the complete key generation with significant probability. $\tilde{A}_1$ first carries out the zero-knowledge proof with *B* in the role of a verifier $\tilde{V}$ and then has to publish *mk*. With small modifications, it can be separated into an algorithm $\tilde{V}$ followed by an algorithm $\tilde{A}_1^*$ that generates *mk*, given all the results of $\tilde{V}$. Therefore, the composition $\tilde{A}_2^*$ of $\tilde{A}_1^*$ and $\tilde{A}_2$ generates both *mk* and *proof*, given the prekey and the additional output of $\tilde{V}$, and *proof* is a valid proof of forgery with significant probability.

Now let $\tilde{A}_2^*$ use a result of the simulator *Sim* of $ZKP_{P,\tilde{V}}$, instead of a result of the real zero-knowledge proof. If this would make a significant difference in $\tilde{A}_2^*$'s ability to produce a valid proof of forgery, the composition of $\tilde{A}_2^*$ and *verify* could serve as a distinguisher, in contradiction to the zero-knowledge property. Hence the composition $\tilde{A}$ of *Sim* and $\tilde{A}_2^*$ is an algorithm that finds a main public *mk* and a valid proof of forgery *proof* for it with significant probability, given just *par* and *prek*.

Hence the proof of the following statement has been sketched (where *verify* has been substituted by its definition): There exist polynomials *Qsig* and *Qn* and a constant $c > 0$ such that

$$\forall k_0\ \exists k \geq k_0\ \exists \sigma \leq Qsig(k)\ \exists N \in Message\_bounds \text{ with } N \leq Qn(k) \text{ or } N = \infty:$$

$$\begin{aligned} &P(verify\_simple(prek, proof) = \text{TRUE} \setminus \\ &\qquad prek \leftarrow Corr_{k,\sigma};\ (mk, proof) \leftarrow \tilde{A}(\text{'1'}^k, \text{'1'}^\sigma, \text{'1'}^N, prek)) \\ &> k^{-c}. \end{aligned}$$

Finally, a similar algorithm $\tilde{A}*$ is defined that does not have '1'^{N} as an input: $\tilde{A}*$ tries the values $N := \infty, 1, 2, \ldots, Qn(k)$ one by one, i.e., it calls $\tilde{A}*$('1'^{k}, '1'$^\sigma$, '1'^{N}, *prek*). If an output (*mk*, *proof*) fulfils *verify_simple*(*prek*, *proof*) = TRUE, $\tilde{A}*$ outputs *proof* and stops. Obviously, $\tilde{A}$ runs in polynomial time. Moreover, its success probability is at least the maximum of the success probabilities of the individual iterations, because no unsuccessful stop is possible in an earlier iteration. This is the desired contradiction to Criterion 2 of Theorem 7.34.

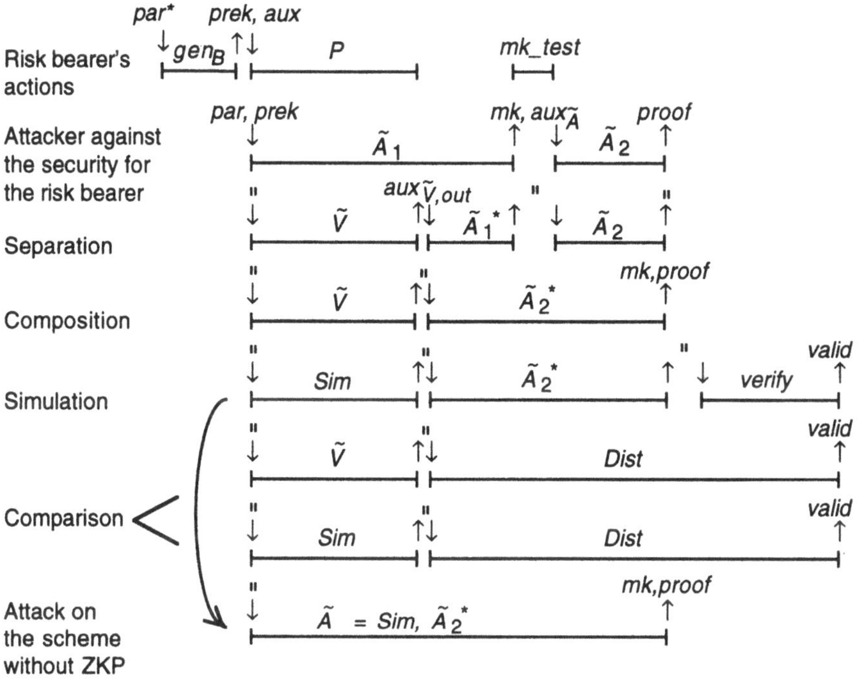

Figure 7.3. Security for the risk bearer when giving a zero-knowledge proof concerning the prekey.
Each row corresponds to a step of the proof in the text. Only the most important input and output parameters of the algorithms are shown. The order from left to right is chronologic; algorithms aligned with each other either interact, or are identical, or simulate each other.

D. Security for the signer backwards (Definition 7.17e). It is first shown that all information containing a good prekey is good in the sense of Definition 7.17b and c. More precisely, let an attacker strategy $\tilde{B}$ and parameters *par* = ('1'^{k}, '1'$^\sigma$, '1'^{N}) be given. It is shown that for all (*pub*, *sk*, $aux_{\tilde{B}}$) ∈ $[Gen^{(f)}{}_{A,\tilde{B}}(par)]$ with *pub* = (TRUE, $ids_{Risk,out}$, *pk*) and *pk* = (*prek*, *mk*),

$$prek \in Good_{k,\sigma} \Rightarrow (pub, sk, aux_{\tilde{B}}) \in GoodKeys_{\tilde{B}}(par). \qquad (*)$$

For this, it has to be shown that (*pub*, $aux_{\tilde{B}}$, *hist*) ∈ $GoodInf_{\tilde{B}}(par)$ for all *hist* ∈ *Hist*(*sk*, *N*). Let such a history *hist* = ($\underline{m}$, $\underline{s}$) be given. Criterion 3 of Theorem 7.34 can be applied, because it is clear from the construction of *A* in Definition 7.31 that

$(sk, mk) \in [gen_A{}^{(f)}(par, prek)]$. This yields $(mk, hist) \in GoodInf(par, prek)$. Hence it remains to be shown for (*) that

$$((mk, hist) \in GoodInf(par, prek) \Rightarrow (pub, aux_{\tilde{B}}, hist) \in GoodInf_{\tilde{B}}(par)).$$

Let any successful forgery $f \in Forg(acc, pk, hist)$ be given, and remember acc = TRUE. Hence

$$P_{\tilde{B},par}(provable(sk, pk, hist, f) \mid pub, aux_{\tilde{B}}, sign^{(f)}(sk, \underline{m}) = \underline{s}) \geq 1 - 2^{-\sigma-1}$$

has to be derived from

$$P_{par,prek}(provable(sk, pk, hist, f) \mid mk, sign^{(f)}(sk, \underline{m}) = \underline{s}) \geq 1 - 2^{-\sigma-1}.$$

The former probability extends over the choice of the prekey by $\tilde{B}$, the execution of the zero-knowledge proof, and the choice of sk and mk by the signer's entity, whereas the latter only extends over the choice of sk and mk when $prek$ is given and no zero-knowledge proof takes place. It is shown that the resulting probabilities are nevertheless equal.

First, there is a condition that the prekey is $prek$ in the first probability, hence probabilities from the choice of the prekey do not matter.

The main reason for equality is that in both cases, the choice of sk and mk is formally carried out as $(sk, mk) \leftarrow gen_A{}^{(f)}(par, prek)$ (by definition of A and $P_{par,prek}$), i.e., it is not based on any information from the zero-knowledge proof in the former case. In other words, the behaviour of the signer's entity in the zero-knowledge proof is completely independent of its choice of sk and mk, once the prekey is given, and hence it cannot give additional information about that choice. Hence the zero-knowledge proof and $aux_{\tilde{B}}$ can be omitted in the former probability, too.

This finishes the proof sketch of (*). A detailed proof would look similar to that of Lemma 7.20.

Furthermore, recall that acc = FALSE implies $(pub, sk, aux_{\tilde{B}}) \in GoodKeys_{\tilde{B}}(par)$, too (Remark 7.18). Hence the probability

$$P_{\tilde{B},par}(\neg GoodKeys)$$

is bounded by the probability that acc = TRUE although $prek \notin Good_{k,\sigma}$.

It is now shown that the probability of this event is at most $2^{-\sigma-1}$: By the definition of res, this implies $acc\_observed$ = TRUE; and with the external verifiability requirement of the verifier on the proof scheme, acc_A = TRUE, too. The soundness of the proof scheme means that for any bad prekey and any auxiliary value aux that $\tilde{B}$ might choose, the probability that acc_A = TRUE after the zero-knowledge proof is at most $2^{-\sigma-1}$. Hence the overall probability that $\tilde{B}$ chooses a bad prekey and that this prekey is accepted in the zero-knowledge proof is at most $2^{-\sigma-1}$, too, as required.

E. Finally, Definition 7.17f remains to be shown, i.e., if the entities of the signer and the risk bearer act correctly in key generation, the resulting keys are always good. This is clear because $prek \in Good_{k,\sigma}$ always holds in this case, and (*) means that keys resulting from a good prekey are always good. □

Remark 7.35. If the good prekeys are locally verifiable, and thus there is no error probability in the soundness of the zero-knowledge proof scheme, there is no real use for the family *AllFam* any more, and *all_test* can be omitted. ♦

One advantage of schemes with prekey is that after one zero-knowledge proof (or one local verification), a signer's entity can base many successive secret keys and main public keys on the same prekey without further interaction with the risk bearer's entity. This is important in the constructions for signing many messages from a scheme for signing one message mentioned in Section 6.3.1 (see Chapter 10 for more details). Informally, one can already see that this does not weaken security: The security for the risk bearer is unchanged because the risk bearer's entity does not do anything new. The probability that an attacker can cheat the signer with an unprovable successful forgery for one out of N key pairs (chosen independently) is at most N times the probability that he can do so for one key pair and therefore still exponentially small (as long as N grows at most polynomially in the security parameters).

Remark 7.36. As mentioned in Section 6.1.2, "Number of Risk Bearers and Complexity of Initialization", the same prekey can even be used for all signers. Hence the risk bearer's entity can publish one prekey without knowing what signers will take part. For instance, this is useful if the risk bearer is a bank and the signers are varying clients. Every signer's entity carries out a zero-knowledge proof with the risk bearer's entity once and can then base many successive secret keys and main public keys on this prekey. The only change this makes for security is that the risk bearer's entity now carries out more than one zero-knowledge proof and hence one really needs a definition of zero-knowledge that permits the composition of such proofs.

If the prekey is locally verifiable, key distribution is identical to ordinary digital signature schemes after the initial publication of the prekey: Every new signer simply publishes her main public key (except that, if the local verification of the prekey yielded FALSE, the signer would have to call on recipients and courts to punish the risk bearer). ♦

7.4 Relation to Ordinary Digital Signature Schemes

It was sketched under Figure 5.12 and at the end of Section 5.4.3 that fail-stop security is stronger than ordinary security. This is now shown formally for the conventional definition of standard fail-stop signature schemes. Actually, two statements are shown:

1. Full standard fail-stop signature schemes themselves provide ordinary security if the output *'broken'* in disputes is replaced with TRUE. The same holds for schemes with special risk bearers if the signer plays the role of a risk bearer, too.

2. Any standard fail-stop signature scheme (full or with special risk bearers) can be used to construct **standard** ordinary digital signature schemes, if standard ordinary digital signature schemes are defined as those with the structure allowed in the GMR definition or insignificant generalizations thereof.

One can easily see that the first statement, when broken down as in Sections 7.1.3 and 7.1.4, is nothing else than unforgeability: Replacing *'broken'* in disputes with TRUE means that the result of a dispute only depends on Step 1 — the result is TRUE if and only if the recipient's entity can show an acceptable signature. (The interest group now consists of the signer and the court, and of the signer and a recipient in unforgeability. However, this does not make a formal difference, because the court's entity carries out *res* and *test* just like the entity of a recipient in standard fail-stop signature schemes.) Hence the first statement has been proved in Section 7.2.2.

Nevertheless, standard fail-stop signature schemes used in this way are not standard ordinary digital signature schemes, mainly because the latter have non-interactive key generation. However, if the output *'broken'* in disputes is replaced with TRUE, no risk remains for anybody except for the signer. Hence one can permit the signer's entity to carry out the complete key generation on its own.

Moreover, standard ordinary digital signature schemes have only one security parameter. This can be realized by choosing $k = \sigma$. Finally, the algorithms *prove* and *verify* are not needed; they are simply omitted in the construction.

A precise definition of standard ordinary digital signature schemes in the notation used here is omitted for brevity; it can easily be adapted from [GoMR88] and seen in the proof below.

Theorem 7.37. From every secure standard fail-stop signature scheme, a secure standard ordinary digital signature scheme can be constructed as follows. Without loss of generality, a scheme with one risk bearer can be used — if a scheme with several risk bearers is given, let $R := 1$ constantly.

- Key generation: On input $par^* := (\text{'1'}^l, \text{'1'}^N)$, where l is the new security parameter and N is the message bound, the signer's entity sets $par := (\text{'1'}^l, \text{'1'}^l, \text{'1'}^N)$ and carries out the entire protocol *Gen*(*par*) on its own. This yields an outcome $(acc, ids_{Risk,out}, pk, sk\_temp)$. If acc = TRUE, it broadcasts *pk* as its public key.

  If the fail-stop signature scheme is with prekey, the zero-knowledge proof and *all_test* can be omitted.
- Signing and testing work as in the given standard fail-stop signature scheme.

  (This presupposes a small generalization of the GMR definition: Signing may use arbitrary memory, not only a counter of the previously signed messages.) ♦

Proof. First, key generation is always successful according to Definition 7.9a and b. (Note that there is no formal difference between the execution of *Gen* by one party and by two parties.) This is not an explicit requirement with standard ordinary digital signature schemes, but it is implicitly required that every execution of key generation yields a key pair. Moreover, the zero-knowledge proof and *all_test* in a scheme with prekey can be omitted, because correct prekeys are always accepted.

Effectiveness of authentication follows immediately from Definition 7.10. Usually, error-free effectiveness of authentication is required with standard ordinary digital signature schemes. This is guaranteed if effectiveness of authentication is error-free in the underlying standard fail-stop signature scheme, or at least in the case of correct execution of *Gen*, i.e., with $\tilde{B} = B$. In particular, this is the case if a standard fail-stop signature scheme with prekey is used (Theorem 7.34b).

The only other formal security requirement on standard ordinary digital signature schemes is unforgeability. It follows immediately from Theorem 7.24 and Remark 7.23. □

7.5 Constructions with Many Risk Bearers

This section sketches how standard fail-stop signature schemes with many risk bearers can be constructed from standard fail-stop signature schemes with only one risk bearer. Recall that this also yields constructions of full standard fail-stop signature schemes (see Section 7.1.1).

The properties of the following two constructions were already mentioned in Section 6.1.2, "Number of Risk Bearers and Complexity of Initialization" and "Cryptologic Assumptions and Efficiency". Both constructions are general, i.e., they can be applied to arbitrary schemes. More efficient constructions are possible in special cases; see Section 7.5.2, "Special Versions", and Remark 9.16. (It is not even necessary that schemes with many risk bearers are constructed from schemes with one risk bearer at all, although all existing constructions are.)

7.5.1 Replication of Initialization

The idea of the first construction is that each risk bearer's entity executes the original protocol *Gen* with the signer's entity once, and all the resulting keys are used in parallel. This construction is conceptually simple and leads to a feasible initialization protocol. Its disadvantage is that the resulting keys are long, and the complexity of authentication and disputes grows linearly with the number of risk bearers.

Construction 7.38. Let the components of a secure standard fail-stop signature scheme with one risk bearer be given. The components of a scheme with an arbitrary number of risk bearers (for the same message space and the same message bounds) are constructed as follows. They are written with an asterisk to distinguish them from the components of the underlying scheme.

- Key generation: If the parameters are $par^* = (\text{'1'}^k, \text{'1'}^{\sigma^*}, \text{'1'}^N, \text{'1'}^R)$, the key-generation protocol Gen^* consists of R phases. These phases can be executed in parallel if one wants to minimize the round complexity, but they are now represented sequentially.

  In the i-th phase, the entities of the signer and the i-th risk bearer execute $Gen(par)$, where $par := (\text{'1'}^k, \text{'1'}^{\sigma}, \text{'1'}^N)$ with $\sigma := \sigma^* + \lceil \log_2(R) \rceil$. (Recall that each risk bearer's entity has its internal identity, $i \in \{1, ..., R\}$, as an input parameter and therefore knows in which phase it is active.) This means that the signer's entity executes A, the entity of the i-th risk bearer executes B, and all entities apply the result algorithm *res*. The signer's entity uses new random bits for each execution of A. Let the outcome of the i-th phase be $(acc_i, ids_{Risk,out,i}, pk_i, sk\_temp_i)$. Recall that $ids_{Risk,out,i}$ is either $\{1\}$ or $\emptyset$.

The global results are defined as follows:

$$ids_{Risk,out} := \{i \mid ids_{Risk,out,i} = \{1\}\},$$

i.e., each risk bearer has taken part successfully iff his entity took part successfully in the phase where it played an active role.

The whole initialization is successful iff the signer has never been caught cheating and at least one of the risk bearers has taken part successfully. For this, define Boolean values $ids_{Sign,out,i}$ to be TRUE iff the signer was not caught cheating in the i-th phase, i.e.,

$$ids_{Sign,out,i} :\Leftrightarrow acc_i \vee (ids_{Risk,out,i} = \emptyset),$$

and let

$$acc := ids_{Sign,out,1} \wedge \ldots \wedge ids_{Sign,out,R} \wedge (ids_{Risk,out} \neq \emptyset).$$

The keys consist of all the partial keys from the successful phases: If acc = FALSE, then $pk := sk\_temp := \varepsilon$, and otherwise

$$pk := (pk_i)_{i \in ids_{Risk,out}},$$

and $$sk\_temp := (sk\_temp_i)_{i \in ids_{Risk,out}}.$$

The individual algorithms A^*, B^*, and res^* can easily be derived from this global description.

- Signing: The input to $sign^*$ consists of a value $sk\_temp_{old} = (sk\_temp_{old,i})_{i \in ids_{Risk,out}}$ and a message m. The signature consists of one part per (successful) risk bearer; a part is computed as

$$(s_i, sk\_temp_{new,i}) \leftarrow sign(sk\_temp_{old,i}, m).$$

  The complete output of $sign^*$ is the pair (s, sk_temp_{new}) with $s := (s_i)_{i \in ids_{Risk,out}}$ and $sk\_temp := (sk\_temp_{new,i})_{i \in ids_{Risk,out}}$, unless any of the parts is '*key_used_up*': then the complete output is '*key_used_up*', too.

- Test: The input to the algorithm $test^*$ is a triple (pk, m, s) with $pk = (pk_i)_{i \in ids_{Risk,out}}$ and $s = (s_i)_{i \in ids_{Risk,out}}$. Each part of the signature is tested with the corresponding part of the public key, and all parts must be correct. Hence the result acc is TRUE iff

$$\forall i \in ids_{Risk,out}\colon test(pk_i, m, s_i) = \text{TRUE}.$$

- Proving forgeries: The input to $prove^*$ is a triple (sk_temp_{old}, m, s) with sk_temp_{old} and s as above. A proof of forgery consists of one part per (successful) risk bearer; a part is computed as

$$proof_i \leftarrow prove(sk\_temp_{old,i}, m, s_i).$$

  If any of the parts is *not_a_forgery*, the output *proof* is *not_a_forgery*, too. Otherwise, $proof := (proof_i)_{i \in ids_{Risk,out}}$.

- Verifying proofs of forgery: The input to *verify** is a pair (*pk*, *proof*) as above. The proof of forgery is considered valid if all its parts are valid. Hence the result *valid* is TRUE iff

$$\forall i \in ids_{Risk,out}: verify(pk_i, proof_i) = \text{TRUE}. \qquad \blacklozenge$$

Theorem 7.39. Construction 7.38 is a secure standard fail-stop signature scheme if the underlying scheme with one risk bearer is secure. Moreover, effectiveness of authentication is error-free if it is error-free in the underlying scheme. ♦

Proof sketch. All the algorithms are obviously polynomial-time in the correct parameters. Next, the properties required in Definition 7.2, which refers to Definition 7.1, are shown, and then the four security properties.

a) The definition of *sign** has been made for the set $SK\_Temp^* := \bigcup_{R \in \mathbb{N}} SK_{Temp}{}^R$, and it obviously has the required closure properties.
b) The property that all outputs of *prove** are *not_a_forgery* or valid proofs of forgery follows immediately from the corresponding property of the underlying scheme and the definition that *proof* is set to *not_a_forgery* if any component $proof_i$ would be *not_a_forgery*.
c) The property that the output *'key_used_up'* occurs if and only if the message bound has been reached follows immediately from the same property of the underlying scheme.
d) **Correctness of initialization.**
   - For the signer: The correctness of initialization in the underlying scheme implies for each phase that either acc_i = TRUE or $ids_{Risk,out,i} = \emptyset$. (As the signer's entity carries out each phase independently, the information gained in previous phases cannot help the attacker: He could simulate those phases on his own by playing both roles in them.) Hence $ids_{Sign,out,i}$ =TRUE for all i. The definition of *acc* therefore implies either *acc* = TRUE or $ids_{Risk,out} = \emptyset$, which was to be shown.
   - For the i-th risk bearer: The correctness of initialization in the underlying scheme implies that in the i-th phase, the output $ids_{Risk,out,i}$ is $\{1\}$. This implies $i \in ids_{Risk,out}$, which was to be shown.
e) **Effectiveness of authentication.** First, it is shown that if an outcome of key generation in the new scheme is bad, at least one of the outcomes of the individual phases is also bad: Let $(acc, ids_{Risk,out}, pk, sk) \in Bad_{eff}{}^*(N)$, and let $s = sign^{(f)}(sk, j, \underline{m})$ be a signature in the new scheme that does not pass the test with *pk*. Thus one of its parts, say s_i, does not pass the test with pk_i, where $i \in ids_{Risk,out}$. Hence $key_i' := (\text{TRUE}, ids_{Risk,out,i}, pk_i, sk_i)$ is in $Bad_{eff}(N)$, where sk_i consists of sk_temp_i and that part $r_{A,i}$ of the random string r_A from *sk* that has been used when working with sk_temp_i.[114] To see that key_i' is in fact the outcome of an individual phase, acc_i = TRUE remains to be shown. In fact,

114 More precisely, all continuations of this random string must be considered. Similarly, the probabilities below are not trivial, because $r_{A,i}$ need not be situated at fixed positions of r_A.

acc = TRUE implies $ids_{Sign,out,i}$ = TRUE, and with $i \in ids_{Risk,out}$, this yields acc_i = TRUE.

The probability that an outcome of key generation in the new scheme is in $Bad_{eff}{}^*(N)$ is therefore at most R times the probability that an outcome of key generation in the underlying scheme is in $Bad_{eff}(N)$. (This holds because the signer's entity performs the algorithm A from the underlying key generation R times independently. The attacker need not act independently, but whatever he does in one of the phases is a permissible attacker strategy for the underlying scheme, because he could have simulated the other phases on his own.)

Hence, if this probability is zero in the underlying scheme, it is zero in the new scheme, too, and otherwise it is bounded by $R\,2^{-\sigma} \le 2^{-\sigma^*}$.

f) **Security for risk bearers.** Assume that an attacker strategy (consisting of $\tilde{A}_1^*$ and $\tilde{A}_2^*$) can cheat the i-th of R risk bearers in the new scheme with significant probability, i.e., the formula in Definition 7.11b is not fulfilled for these values R and i.

The output acc of the complete key generation can only be TRUE if $ids_{Sign,out,i}$ = TRUE, i.e., if the attacker strategy is not caught cheating in Phase i. Correctness of initialization of the underlying scheme implies that the honest risk bearer is not caught cheating either, i.e., $ids_{Risk,out,i} = \{1\}$. Hence this phase is successful, i.e., acc_i = TRUE.

Furthermore, $verify^*(pk, proof)$ = TRUE implies $verify(pk_i, proof_i)$ = TRUE.

Hence this attacker strategy carries out key generation from the underlying scheme with the one correct risk bearer's entity and then computes a valid proof of forgery for the resulting public key, pk_i, with significant probability. This contradicts Definition 7.11a (with a slightly larger polynomial $Qsig$ than $Qsig^*$).

g) **Security for the signer.** Assume the contrary of Definition 7.14. Then an attacker strategy $(\tilde{B}, F)$ and parameters par^* exist such that, with probability greater than $2^{-\sigma^*}$, the result of $Gen_{A,\tilde{B}}(par)$ is acc = TRUE, and then F finds an unprovable successful forgery $f = (m, s)$.

For this, the parts s_i of s must be acceptable signatures for the partial public keys pk_i that are actually used, and at least one value $f_i := (m, s_i)$ must be unprovable. As in Part e), acc = TRUE and $i \in ids_{Risk,out}$ imply acc_i = TRUE.

According to the pigeon-hole principle, there must be at least one i for which this happens with probability greater than $2^{-\sigma^*} / R$. Hence an attacker strategy $(\tilde{B}_i, F_i)$ on the underlying scheme is now considered that acts as if it were attacking in the i-th phase of the new scheme: $\tilde{B}_i$ simulates $\tilde{B}$ in key generation, but only carries out Phase i with the real signer's entity and plays the signer's role itself in the remaining phases of $\tilde{B}$. (This is possible because the actions of the signer's entity in the different phases are independent.) Next, F_i simulates F. Whenever F asks for a message to be signed, F_i asks the real signer's entity to sign it, which gives a part s_i, and produces the remaining parts itself. Finally, F_i proposes the part f_i of F's forgery as a forgery in the underlying scheme.

This strategy cheats successfully in the underlying scheme with probability greater than $2^{-\sigma^*} / R$, and thus greater than $2^{-\sigma}$. This contradicts the security of the underlying scheme. □

7.5.2 Multi-Party Function Evaluation in Initialization

The idea behind the second construction of standard fail-stop signature schemes with many risk bearers is that the risk bearers' entities should somehow agree on one common public key from the underlying scheme with only one risk bearer [PfWa90]. Similarly, the signer's entity should have only one temporary secret key. The remaining algorithms, *sign*, *test*, *prove*, and *verify*, can then be the same as in the underlying scheme.

The obvious advantage of this construction is that the complexity of authentication and disputes is independent of the number of risk bearers. The disadvantage is that a general suitable key-generation protocol is very inefficient; however, see the last subsection for more efficient special cases. (Moreover, due to problems with definitions of multi-party function evaluation protocols, I did not even dare to call the security considerations below a proof sketch.)

For the transformation of an arbitrary key-generation protocol *Gen* with one risk bearer into a protocol *Gen** that generates keys with the same distribution, but in a way that many risk bearers can trust them, a multi-party function evaluation protocol is used.

Multi-party Function Evaluation Protocols

As mentioned in Section 4.4.1, "Related Work in Cryptology", multi-party protocols have almost exclusively been considered for the evaluation of (probabilistic) functions. The informal definition of a multi-party protocol that securely evaluates a function f on n inputs, $x_1, \ldots, x_n$, which are assumed to be contributed by n different users, is that the protocol has exactly the same effect for all users, honest and dishonest, as an evaluation by a trusted host would have. Such a trusted host would receive each input x_i secretly from the i-th user, apply f, and output $y := f(x_1, \ldots, x_n)$ to everybody (or, if f is probabilistic, a value y distributed according to $f(x_1, \ldots, x_n)$) [Yao82]. In particular, the multi-party function evaluation protocol should guarantee:

- Correctness: All honest users obtain the same result y. The result is distributed according to $f(x_1, \ldots, x_n)$, where x_i is the intended input if the i-th user is honest, and otherwise a value chosen independently of the x_j's of the honest users.
- Privacy: The attacker should not learn anything about the inputs of honest users from the protocol execution that he could not have inferred from the result y and his own inputs alone.

For discussions of the many pitfalls lying between this intuitive idea and a formal definition, see [Beav91, MiRo91]. (Furthermore, [MiRo91] only considers deterministic functions.)

Variants exist where each user obtains a different output y_i secretly from the trusted host. If probabilistic functions are considered, the results may be correlated, i.e., there is a global probabilistic function F that maps n-tuples $(x_1, \ldots, x_n)$ to n-tuples $(y_1, \ldots, y_n)$, and the i-th user obtains y_i as a result.

Most concrete proposals of multi-party function evaluation protocols are not only protocols for one particular function, but general transformation techniques that can be used to derive a suitable protocol for any given function.

Idea for the Application

To apply a multi-party function evaluation protocol to key generation, which is an interactive protocol, it is useful to regard *Gen* as one probabilistic function. This has implicitly been done all the time: *Gen* maps values *par* to tuples (acc, $ids_{Risk,out}$, pk, sk_temp). Hence a trusted host performing the entire key generation, i.e., *A*, *B*, and *res*, will be simulated.[115] The correctness of initialization implies that *acc* and $ids_{Risk,out}$ are always TRUE and {1}, respectively, in this case. Hence one can omit them. The trusted host would tell the signer's entity both *sk* and *pk*, and the other entities obtain *pk* only.

This global function is now evaluated with a multi-party function evaluation protocol by the entities of the signer and the risk bearers. Recall that the entities of recipients and courts do not send any messages during initialization of a standard fail-stop signature scheme with special risk bearers; they are treated in a special subsection below.

So far, there are no private inputs x_i. However, the protocol that will actually be used, from [ChDG88, Damg88a], realizes probabilistic functions with an extra input *r*, in addition to the private inputs, and *r* is assumed to come from a globally trusted source of random bits. Such a source is not assumed here. Instead, it can be simulated with the same degree of security as the rest of the protocol if *r* is computed as the XOR of secret random strings $r_1, \ldots, r_n$, where r_i is contributed by the *i*-th user of the protocol (which, in the present application, is an outer part of the entity of the signer or a risk bearer, not a user of the signature scheme). This initial XOR is treated as a normal part of the function to be evaluated. Thus these secret random strings are now the only private inputs.

Problems with Disrupters

Unfortunately, the degree of security needed here is different from those usually considered with multi-party function evaluation: Almost all proposals consider the case where less than half of the entities participating are corrupted (see [Beav91, MiRo91] for the newest definitions and more references, [GoMW87, BeGW88, ChCD88, RaBe89] for influential constructions, and [FrGY92] for an overview). In fact, it can be proved that multi-party function evaluation protocols fulfilling the strict definition above can only exist in this case [Clev86, BeGW88], even if the attackers are computationally restricted. The basic problem is that one must deal with disrupters, i.e., attackers stopping in the middle of the protocol execution. Then the remaining entities must be able to simulate the rest of the computation.

---

115 Even when multi-party protocols that simulate interactive functions or reactive systems are defined, this should be more efficient than simulating the interactive algorithm *B* of the risk bearer or all the individual protocol steps.

Furthermore, only *Gen*, and not $Gen^{(f)}$, needs to be simulated, because the signer's entity can generate its future random bits alone.

However, there are some protocols without this last property, i.e., they simply stop if an attacker disrupts. Moreover, there are situations where an entity is caught cheating and the protocol stops, too. This is not quite what a trusted host would have done, but in exchange, an arbitrary number of attackers can be tolerated. The first such protocol is [ChDG88]. (However, that article does not contain a correct definition of what the protocol guarantees if attackers may try to disrupt, and the proof does not really treat this case either.) For the newest protocols and more references, see [Beav90, GoLe91, CrGT95].[116]

In their pure form, none of these protocols would guarantee effectiveness of initialization, which has been required in the interest of each pair of the signer and one risk bearer. Hence each time the entity of a risk bearer disrupts or is caught cheating, the protocol has to be restarted without it. With R risk bearers, at most $R - 1$ repetitions are necessary. Repetition may bias the randomness of the result: An attacker can disrupt in one of the last steps of the protocol, when he already knows what the final result will be, and thus exclude results he does not like. (Hence this type of protocol would not make much sense if it were, e.g., used to generated one trusted random bit.) However, if cryptologic keys are chosen, the only important property is that nobody can cheat with respect to those keys with significant probability. The probability that the attacker manages to obtain a key for which he can cheat in $R - 1$ repetitions of the protocol should be at most $(R - 1)$ times the probability that he can do this in the original scheme. (Of course, this statement has not been proved for lack of definitions.) As all the probabilities of cheating are negligibly small, a constant factor of $R - 1$ can be tolerated.

Role of Recipients and Courts

An algorithm res^* is needed that the entities of recipients and courts can execute, too. They do not take part in the multi-party function evaluation actively, but they observe the complete protocol execution, which is performed on broadcast channels anyway. (The following means that the protocol from [ChDG88] can easily be equipped with external verifiability as defined in Section 5.2.11.)

- Whenever one of the active entities is to be excluded, the algorithm res^* checks if this decision is correct. One can easily see from the protocol description in [ChDG88] that this decision only depends on broadcast messages, and not on any internal secrets of the active entities. The global result acc^* is TRUE if the entities of the signer and at least one risk bearer remain and execute the multi-party function evaluation protocol without disruption, and $ids_{Risk,out}{}^*$ consists of the identities of the remaining risk bearers.

116 The main addition in the newer references is a property called fairness. Roughly, it means that if the protocol is stopped, the attackers and the honest participants have approximately the same amount of information about what the result would have been. This property is not needed in the present application. Furthermore, the newer references do not have the property called "special protection for the signer" below. Hence [ChDG88] is used in the following. It may, however, be possible to add that property to newer protocols and thus to obtain protocols relying on weaker cryptologic assumptions.

- If $acc^* = \text{TRUE}$, i.e., there was a non-disrupted protocol execution, the algorithm res^* computes the result pk of this execution, too. One can easily see from the protocol description in [ChDG88] that this can be done given the broadcast messages only.

Special Protection for the Signer

The protocol from [ChDG88] has one more special property needed here: One participant (P_n in the notation used there) can be protected information-theoretically. Here, this role is offered to the signer. Hence, even if all risk bearers cooperate, they can neither break the correctness of the result, except by disrupting, nor obtain any information about the secret input and output of the signer's entity.

Details About the Degree of Security

The protocol from [ChDG88] can be implemented with different types of so-called bit commitment schemes. (A commitment is similar to putting a secret in a locked box and giving the box to someone else or putting it in a public place, so that one can no longer change the secret, but nobody else can see it yet. Later, one can unlock the box and show everybody what the secret was. See [BrCC88] for details.) In the present application, an information-theoretically unforgeable one must be used by all the entities of risk bearers, because this guarantees that the probability of undetected cheating by a risk bearer is exponentially small [ChDG88, p. 106]. The signer's entity, however, must use an information-theoretically hiding one.

The security for the users of the multi-party function evaluation protocol, except for the one who is protected information-theoretically, relies on the so-called quadratic-residuosity assumption. Hence the security for risk bearers in a fail-stop signature scheme based on this protocol also relies on this assumption.

Security Considerations

One can briefly check that all the required security properties have at least been thought of. Beforehand, note that a protocol where a trusted host executes *Gen* using the XOR of random strings contributed by its users is as good as one where a trusted host randomly chooses its own random string, as long as at least one user is honest, i.e., one string is chosen randomly. (Recall that the strings of the attackers are independent of this one, because it is given to the trusted host secretly.) Hence one can concentrate on this protocol.

a) Correctness of initialization. One can easily see from the protocol description in [ChDG88] that no correct entity can ever be excluded as cheating. (The entities only have to publish secret information that they used in deterministic computations, and the others redo these computations and compare the result.) This implies immediately that all honest risk bearers remain in $ids_{Risk,out}{}^*$, and that, as long as the signer is honest, $acc = \text{FALSE}$ can only happen if all risk bearers have been excluded.

b) Effectiveness of authentication. An attacker strategy can achieve that the outcome of key generation is in $Bad_{eff}(N)$ in two ways: Either it succeeds in cheating without being caught in the multi-party function evaluation. This can only happen with exponentially small probability, because the signer's entity is correct. Or the result lies in $Bad_{eff}(N)$ by chance. This is impossible if effectiveness of authentication in the underlying scheme is error-free (at least after correct execution of *Gen*). Otherwise, it can only happen with exponentially small probability in one execution of the protocol, and by disruptions, an attacker can increase this probability by a factor of less than R. Hence the overall probability is still exponentially small.

c) Security for risk bearers: The security for risk bearers in the underlying fail-stop signature scheme guarantees, in particular, that it is infeasible to compute valid proofs of forgery for public keys chosen by a correct execution of *Gen* with significant probability. As discussed above, the multi-party function evaluation protocol with repetitions should guarantee that, as long as one risk bearer's entity executes the protocol correctly, a computationally restricted attacker cannot bias the result so much or obtain so much additional information that valid proofs of forgery become significantly easier to compute.

d) Security for the signer: Because of the special protection for the signer, even a computationally unrestricted attacker does not obtain more information from the multi-party function evaluation than from a completely correct execution of *Gen* (with XOR), and cannot bias the resulting keys more than by the disruptions. Hence the probability that an attacker strategy outputs an unprovable successful forgery for these keys should be at most R times larger than in the underlying scheme with one risk bearer.

Special Versions

If the protocol *Gen* is particularly simple, the construction with a multi-party function evaluation protocol can be simplified, too.

1. If the underlying fail-stop signature scheme with one risk bearer is with prekey (Definition 7.31), the zero-knowledge proof and *all_test* can be omitted in the representation of the function *Gen*: If A, B, and *res* are executed correctly, the result of these steps is always $acc_A = acc\_observed =$ TRUE.

   Moreover, only the security for the signer relies on the correct execution of the main key-generation algorithm gen_A. Hence gen_A can be executed by the signer's entity alone. All other entities can test *mk* locally.

   Thus only the prekey-generation algorithm gen_B remains to be simulated by the multi-party function evaluation protocol. Note that the signer's entity still has to take part in this protocol to ensure that the resulting prekey is good.

2. A particularly simple case occurs if the prekey-generation algorithm gen_B can be decomposed into

   - the uniformly random choice of a string r of a certain length, where r need not be kept secret, and
   - a deterministic algorithm that computes *prek* from r.

   Then each entity can evaluate the deterministic algorithm on its own, and multi-party function evaluation is only needed for the choice of r. Hence a so-called coin-flipping protocol is sufficient. However, one has to take care that the coin-flipping protocol is secure in the sense of multi-party function evaluation, whereas the normal definition only requires that the result is unbiased, i.e., it does not exclude that an attacker might obtain useful auxiliary information about the result, such as its factorization. Nevertheless, coin-flipping is considerably more efficient than the general case.

In this case, it is also quite realistic to rely on non-cryptographic generation of r, e.g., using old random number tables.

3. If the prekey is locally verifiable, one can consider letting the entities of the risk bearers carry out the prekey generation without the signer's entity, because the signer's entity can verify the correctness of the prekey afterwards. This may be worth while if one wants to use the same prekey for all signers, as in Remark 7.36. However, one must take some care to fulfil effectiveness and correctness of initialization.

   For this, in each repetition of the multi-party function evaluation, one of the risk bearers is protected information-theoretically, as the signer was so far. Moreover, if such a repetition ends without a disruption, all remaining risk bearers' entities perform the local verification. If the prekey is not good, the risk bearer who was protected information-theoretically is excluded and the protocol is repeated. All this can be externally verified by the observing entities of recipients and courts. Moreover, when some remaining risk bearers' entities have finally agreed on a prekey, the observers verify that prekey, and if it is not good, they set acc := FALSE and $ids_{Risk,out} := \emptyset$.

   Now, however, there is an exponentially small error probability in the information-theoretic correctness of initialization in the interest of risk bearers. This was not permitted in Definition 7.9, but it could be permitted according to the general definition in Chapter 5.

All these simplifications can be applied to the construction of efficient fail-stop signature schemes based on the discrete-logarithm assumption, see Remark 9.16.

Remark 7.40. Although coin-flipping is more efficient than general multi-party function evaluation, it is not trivial. In particular, the coin-flipping protocol given in [Damg88a] (and which seems to have been well-known in cryptologic folklore for some time) as a subprotocol for the general multi-party function evaluation protocol from [ChDG88] is incorrect: There, the entities first make commitments on random bits and then open these commitments in the same order as they made them. With some commitment schemes, this allows attackers to make their commitments as blinded versions of previous commitments and to open their commitments when they have seen how the previous commitments were opened. Hence attackers can completely determine the result of the coin-flipping protocol. This can be repaired by opening the commitments in inverse order. (This is simpler than adding zero-knowledge proofs or even using non-malleable commitments [DoDN91].) However, a correctness proof would be complicated because of the same problems with definitions and disrupters as with general multi-party function evaluation protocols; it is therefore beyond the scope of this text. ♦

8 Building Blocks

This chapter contains building blocks for existing constructions of fail-stop signature schemes in bottom-up order. Sections 8.1 and 8.2 are purely mathematical, whereas Sections 8.3 to 8.5 consider computational aspects.

8.1 Some Group and Number Theory

This section collects some facts from group and number theory that will be used in the following.

The general facts in Sections 8.1.1 and 8.1.2, which are stated without proof, can be found in almost any introduction to algebra or elementary number theory, respectively; most readers will know them anyway. For others, [Lips81] might be a suitable choice, together with the introduction of [Kran86] or [Kobl87] or a "real" number theory book such as [IrRo90, Hass64]. The facts in Sections 8.1.3 to 8.1.5 are more special to cryptology; they are given with sufficient explanation.

8.1.1 Basic Facts from Group Theory

Group Order

For any group G, the number of its elements, $|G|$, is called the order of G.

If H is a subgroup of G, then $|H|$ divides $|G|$ (Lagrange's theorem).

Thus if the order of G is prime, G only has the trivial subgroups G and $\{1\}$ (where G is written multiplicatively).

Element Order and Cyclic Groups

If G is written multiplicatively and $g \in G$, the order of g, written ord(g), is the smallest $i \in \mathbb{N} \cup \{\infty\}$ with $g^i = 1$. For all $j, l \in \mathbb{Z}$:

$$g^j = g^l \Leftrightarrow j \equiv l \bmod \mathrm{ord}(g).$$

The powers of g form a subgroup of G, denoted by $<g>$, with $|<g>| = \mathrm{ord}(g)$. The element g is called a generator of G if $<g> = G$. A group that has a generator is called cyclic.

Easy consequences are:

The order of any element g divides the group order. In particular, $g^{|G|} = 1$ for all $g \in |G|$; this is Fermat's little theorem.

Any cyclic group G is isomorphic to the additive group of integers modulo $|G|$. For any generator g, the exponentiation function $exp_g(x) := g^x$ is an isomorphism into G. The inverse is the discrete-logarithm function log_g. In particular, G is Abelian, i.e., commutative.

In a group of prime order p, any element other than 1 is a generator: The order of $<g>$ can only be 1 or p.

If the order n of a cyclic group $G = \langle g \rangle$ is not prime, there is a unique subgroup of order t for each divisor t of n. This subgroup is cyclic, too, and generated by $g^{n/t}$. It consists of exactly those elements g^* of G whose order divides t, i.e., with $g^{*t} = 1$.

Homomorphism Theorem

Let ψ be a homomorphism from a group G to a group H. Consequences of the so-called homomorphism theorem are:

For all $h \in \psi(G)$, the size of the preimage set $\psi^{-1}(h)$ is the same. It equals $|ker(\psi)|$, where $ker(\psi)$ denotes the kernel, i.e., the elements mapped to 1. One has $|ker(\psi)| \cdot |\psi(G)| = |G|$.

Actually, all the groups used in the following are Abelian. Thus for each subgroup H of G, a factor group G/H is defined. The function that maps each element of G to its class in G/H is called the canonical mapping.

8.1.2 Basic Facts about Rings of Integers Modulo *n*

Most of the following facts are only needed in the constructions based on the factoring assumption. There, the basic structure used is the ring of integers modulo n, where n is a chosen number that is hopefully hard to factor. Particular attention is paid to quadratic residues and square roots, because the squaring function plays an important part in the following schemes.

The Rings

For any positive integer n, the ring of integers modulo n is denoted by $\mathbb{Z}_n$ and its multiplicative group by $\mathbb{Z}_n^*$. Elements of $\mathbb{Z}$ and their residue classes are not distinguished in the notation.

A number y is in $\mathbb{Z}_n^*$ if and only if $\gcd(y, n) = 1$. The order of $\mathbb{Z}_n^*$ is $\phi(n)$, where ϕ denotes Euler's totient function.

For any prime p, the ring $\mathbb{Z}_p$ is a field, because $\mathbb{Z}_p^* = \mathbb{Z}_p \backslash \{0\}$.

Chinese Remainder Theorem

If $n = q_1 \cdot \ldots \cdot q_i$, where the q_j's are pairwise relatively prime, i.e., their greatest common divisors are 1, the Chinese remainder theorem says that $\mathbb{Z}_n$ is isomorphic to the direct product of the rings $\mathbb{Z}_{q_j}$. The isomorphism from $\mathbb{Z}_n$ to the direct product is given by the canonical reductions modulo q_j. An efficient method to compute the inverse, i.e., to compute $y \bmod n$ from the values $y \bmod q_j$, is the so-called Chinese remainder algorithm. Usually, the q_j's are taken to be the different prime powers from the factorization of n.

Generators Modulo Prime Powers

The Chinese remainder theorem reduces the problem of determining the structure of rings $\mathbb{Z}_n$ to rings $\mathbb{Z}_{p^r}$ for prime powers p^r. The most important theorem about the latter is that for $p \neq 2$, each multiplicative group $\mathbb{Z}_{p^r}^*$ is cyclic.

A generator is also called a primitive root modulo p^r. The total number of generators is $\phi(\phi(p^r))$; this is easy to see from the above-mentioned isomorphism to the additive group modulo $\phi(p^r)$, like many other properties.

Quadratic Residues and Square Roots

A quadratic residue modulo n is an element of $\mathbb{Z}_n^*$ that has a square root. The set of quadratic residues, denoted by QR_n, is a subgroup. Thus $y \in QR_n :\Leftrightarrow \exists w: w^2 \equiv y \bmod n$. The remaining elements are called quadratic nonresidues (although they are residues and not quadratic).

For an odd prime p, exactly half of the elements of $\mathbb{Z}_p^*$ are quadratic residues, and each one has two square roots $\pm w$. The quadratic residues are characterized by the Legendre symbol $(\frac{y}{p})$, which is defined as +1 if y is a quadratic residue and −1 otherwise (and 0 for $y \equiv 0 \bmod p$). The Legendre symbol can be computed efficiently with Euler's criterion: $(\frac{y}{p}) = y^{(p-1)/2}$.

Modulo a prime power, p^r, where $p \neq 2$, a number y is a quadratic residue if and only if it is one modulo p. Furthermore, each quadratic residue has two square roots again. This can be seen by considering the isomorphism with the additive group modulo $\phi(p^r) = (p-1)p^{r-1}$: If g is a generator, exactly the elements g^e with an even exponent e are the quadratic residues, and $g^{e/2}$ and $g^{(e+\phi(p^r))/2}$ are the roots.

The situation modulo a general odd n can be derived with the Chinese remainder theorem: A number y is a quadratic residue modulo n if and only if it is one modulo each prime factor of n. If n has i distinct prime factors, the number of square roots of each quadratic residue is 2^i, and $|QR_n| = |\mathbb{Z}_n^*| / 2^i$.

One can define a homomorphism χ_n that maps each y to the complete information about how quadratic it is: If $p_1, \ldots, p_i$ are the distinct prime factors of n, e.g., in decreasing order, let $\chi_n(y) := ((\frac{y}{p_1}), \ldots, (\frac{y}{p_i}))$. The kernel of χ_n is QR_n.

Jacobi Symbol

The Jacobi symbol is another generalization of the Legendre symbol: its multiplicative extension to arbitrary odd numbers as the lower parameter. Thus the Jacobi symbol of y modulo n is denoted by $(\frac{y}{n})$; it only depends on $y \bmod n$ and takes the values 1 and −1 on $\mathbb{Z}_n^*$ and 0 outside; and it is multiplicative in both its parameters, i.e., $(\frac{y}{n})(\frac{y'}{n}) = (\frac{yy'}{n})$ and $(\frac{y}{n})(\frac{y}{n'}) = (\frac{y}{nn'})$ always hold.

The subgroup of residues with Jacobi symbol +1 is denoted by $\mathbb{Z}_n^*(+1)$.

Obviously, the Jacobi symbol can be derived from χ_n. It is +1 for all quadratic residues, i.e., $QR_n \subseteq \mathbb{Z}_n^*(+1)$, and in general, $\mathbb{Z}_n^*(+1)$ is much larger than QR_n: It always contains half or all of the elements of $\mathbb{Z}_n^*$.

The Jacobi symbol is interesting because it can be computed efficiently for any pair of numbers, by use of the so-called law of quadratic reciprocity. Actually, one would often be more interested in deciding quadratic residuosity, but no probabilistic polynomial-time algorithm for that is known, unless the prime factors of n are additional inputs. (A cryptologic assumption that deciding quadratic residuosity is infeasible has been used several times in the literature, e.g., in the multi-party function evaluation protocol used in Section 7.5.2, but it is not needed in the following.) Thus $\mathbb{Z}_n^*(+1)$ serves as a recognizable extension of QR_n.

8.1.3 Generalized Blum Integers

Most cryptologic schemes based on the factoring assumption use (positive) integers with additional properties, in particular integers with exactly two different prime factors. The most general class used in the following is that of generalized Blum integers: Let

$$GeneralBlum := \{n = p^s q^t \mid p, q \text{ prime} \wedge s, t \text{ odd} \wedge p \equiv q \equiv 3 \bmod 4\}.$$

A subclass is that of (normal) Blum integers,

$$Blum := \{n = p\,q \mid p, q \text{ prime} \wedge p \equiv q \equiv 3 \bmod 4\},$$

named after [Blum82]. (However, this name has been used for several similar classes of numbers by various authors.) Now the special properties that make generalized Blum integers interesting for cryptology are listed.

Jacobi Symbols of Square Roots

Let n be any generalized Blum integer and $n = p^s q^t$ its factorization. The Jacobi symbol of any y modulo n is $(\frac{y}{n}) = (\frac{y}{p})^s (\frac{y}{q})^t = (\frac{y}{p}) (\frac{y}{q})$.
Euler's criterion implies $(\frac{-1}{p}) = (\frac{-1}{q}) = -1$, because $p \equiv q \equiv 3 \bmod 4$. This yields two further important facts:

First, $(\frac{-1}{n}) = +1$, but -1 is not a quadratic residue, i.e., $-1 \in \mathbb{Z}_n^*(+1) \setminus QR_n$.

Secondly, the two roots $\pm w_p$ of a quadratic residue mod p have different Legendre symbols, and similarly for q. Hence the four roots of a quadratic residue mod n are mapped to all the four different values (1, 1), (1, –1), (–1, 1), and (–1, –1) by χ_n. In particular, two of them have the Jacobi symbol +1; they form a pair $\pm w$; and exactly one of them is a quadratic residue.

In particular, this implies that squaring is a permutation on QR_n if n is a generalized Blum integer.

Recognizing Generalized Blum Integers

Some of the importance of generalized Blum integers stems from the fact that there is a fairly efficient zero-knowledge proof scheme for them [GrPe88], whereas none is known for Blum integers (nor a local verification algorithm for generalized Blum integers).

In the following, Blum integers will primarily serve as correct prekeys of standard fail-stop signature schemes (or components of such prekeys), and generalized Blum integers count as good in one of these schemes. Thus, with the notation of Section 7.3.1, a prover has to generate a Blum integer n with some given distribution $Corr_{k,\sigma}$, and a verifier must be convinced that n is at least a generalized Blum integer.

Naturally, the sketch of the zero-knowledge proof in [GrPe88] is not with respect to Definition 7.25. Moreover, it assumes a random source trusted by both the prover and the verifier, simply saying that such a source could be implemented by various cryptologic techniques. Working out this proof is outside the scope of this text, but it should be possible if one takes care about the following points:

- The auxiliary value *aux* the generation algorithm *gen* has to produce is the factorization of n.
- The coin-flipping protocol, i.e., the protocol used to simulate the trusted random source, must offer one party information-theoretic security. This role is offered to the verifier in the zero-knowledge proof scheme (and thus the signer in the fail-stop signature scheme).
- As mentioned in Section 7.5.2, "Special Versions", the normal definition of a coin-flipping protocol is not that it simulates a trusted random source, but only that it produces an unbiased result. Thus it is not trivial that a zero-knowledge proof scheme that is secure with a trusted random source is still secure with an arbitrary coin-flipping protocol. Hence one has to make a new proof of the whole zero-knowledge proof scheme. Alternatively, one can hope that a theorem will eventually be proved that replacing a probabilistic function within a larger protocol with a multi-party function evaluation protocol does not decrease the security of the larger protocol significantly; then one can use a coin-flipping protocol that is secure in the sense of a multi-party function evaluation protocol.
- If the coin-flipping protocol works bit by bit, the efficiency of the scheme in [GrPe88] is considerably reduced.
- One can easily see that the scheme in [GrPe88] offers external verifiability. However, one must take care that the coin-flipping protocol used offers external verifiability, too.

8.1.4 Williams Integers

A special class of Blum integers is that of the following Williams integers, named after [Will80]:

$$Will := \{n = pq \mid p, q \text{ prime} \wedge p \equiv 3 \bmod 8 \wedge q \equiv 7 \bmod 8\}.$$

Their special property used in the following (as in [Will80, GoMR88]) is that 2 has the Jacobi symbol -1 modulo any of them. This follows from the second supplement to the law of quadratic reciprocity:

$$\left(\tfrac{2}{n}\right) = (-1)^{(n^2-1)/8}.$$

If n is a generalized Williams integer, then

$$n \equiv pq \equiv 3 \cdot 7 \equiv 5 \bmod 8 \Rightarrow n^2 \equiv 25 \bmod 16 \Rightarrow (n^2-1)/8 \text{ is odd.}$$

8.1.5 The Density of Primes

Most cryptologic schemes need large prime numbers. Hence it is important to know how many prime numbers of a certain size there are.

The basic theorem in this field is the well-known prime-number theorem,

$$\pi(n) \sim \frac{n}{\ln(n)},$$

where $\pi(n)$ is the number of primes in the set $\{1, ..., n\}$, ln denotes the natural logarithm, and $\sim$ means that the quotient of the two sides tends to 1 for $n \to \infty$. (See [HaWr79, Chapter 1].)

Sometimes, primes in certain congruence classes are needed, e.g., $p \equiv 3 \bmod 4$ for Blum integers. For such cases, Dirichlet's prime-number theorem states that in a certain sense, primes are equally distributed over the possible congruence classes: Given any modulus ν, there are roughly equally many primes congruent $\xi \bmod \nu$ for all $\xi \in \mathbb{Z}_\nu^*$. If $\pi_{\nu,\xi}(n)$ denotes the number of primes in the set $\{1, ..., n\}$ that are congruent to $\xi \bmod \nu$, the theorem says

$$\pi_{\nu,\xi}(n) \sim \frac{1}{\phi(\nu)} \frac{n}{\ln(n)}.$$

(See [Kran86] for more information.) With $\nu = 1$ and $\xi = 0$, the normal prime-number theorem is a special case.

The prime-number theorems considered all the primes up to a certain limit. If one is only interested in large primes, e.g., primes with a given binary length k, the following statement is more interesting: For all $n \in \mathbb{N}$:

$$\pi_{\nu,\xi}(2n) - \pi_{\nu,\xi}(n) \sim \frac{1}{\phi(\nu)} \frac{n}{\ln(n)}.$$

The proof is a rather straightforward application of Dirichlet's prime-number theorem and some o-calculus.

As prime-number generation is a part of the correct operation of the schemes presented in the following, one may be interested in concrete statements for given k, such as $k = 512$, although the asymptotic statements made above are sufficient for the following proofs. Here is one from [RoSc62]; I do not know if an analogue for primes in congruence classes is known: For all $n \geq 21$,

$$\pi(2n) - \pi(n) \geq \frac{3}{5} \frac{n}{\ln(n)}.$$

8.2 Functions with Large Preimage Sets

This section presents basic functions where every image has a large number of preimages (see Section 6.3.1 for some motivation). This property is called a **bundling property** (see Figure 8.1). The function is said to be of **bundling degree** d if every image has at least d preimages. Functions with a bundling property only serve a cryptologic purpose if they are collision-intractable. In this section, however, only their mathematical properties are collected.

Section 8.2.1 treats the discrete-logarithm case and Section 8.2.3 the factoring case. Both sections are slightly more comprehensive than needed in this text, because these function classes may have more applications in future. In between, Section 8.2.2 contains an abstract construction from pairs of permutations on a common domain, because some aspects of the factoring case are a special case of this construction.

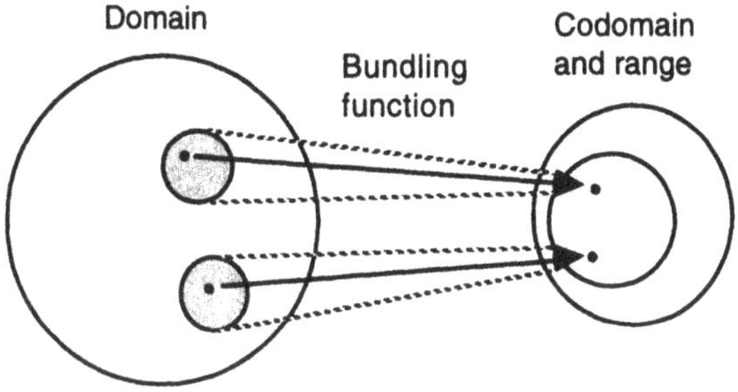

Figure 8.1. A bundling function.
The small grey circles are individual preimage sets; the bundling property guarantees that they are of a certain minimum size d, the bundling degree. The range need not be the whole codomain.

8.2.1 Discrete-Logarithm Case: Tuple Exponentiation

The basic functions with a bundling property in the discrete-logarithm case are simply products of several exponentiations. This is called tuple exponentiation or, if the number of components is known to be μ, μ-tuple exponentiation.[117] Pair exponentiation seems to have been first used like this in [BoCP88], larger tuples in [ChHP92].

In General Groups

The following notation is used.

Definition 8.1. Let H be an Abelian group of order q (not yet necessarily prime) and $\mu \in \mathbb{N}$.

a) For any tuples $\underline{g} = (g_1, \ldots, g_\mu) \in H^\mu$ and $\underline{x} = (x_1, \ldots, x_\mu) \in \mathbb{Z}^\mu$, let
$$\underline{g}^{\underline{x}} := g_1^{x_1} \bullet \ldots \bullet g_\mu^{x_\mu}.$$
The exponents only need to be defined modulo q because of Fermat's little theorem; hence the same notation can be used for tuples $\underline{x} = (x_1, \ldots, x_\mu) \in \mathbb{Z}_q^{\ \mu}$.

b) For any given μ and $\underline{g}$, the μ-tuple exponentiation function with basis $\underline{g}$ from $\mathbb{Z}_q^{\ \mu}$ to H is denoted by $exp_{\underline{g}}$, i.e.,
$$exp_{\underline{g}}(\underline{x}) := \underline{g}^{\underline{x}}.$$

c) For $\underline{x} = (x_1, \ldots, x_\mu)$, $\underline{y} = (y_1, \ldots, y_\mu) \in \mathbb{Z}_q^{\ \mu}$, denote the inner product by
$$\underline{x}\,\underline{y} := x_1 y_1 + \ldots + x_\mu y_\mu.$$

d) Zero tuples or vectors are written as $\underline{0}$. The number of components will always be clear from the context. ♦

117 A more usual name is vector exponentiation; however, there is not always a vector space, and it is useful to have μ in the name.

Some simple mathematical properties of tuple exponentiation follow.

Lemma 8.2.

a) For any $\mu \in \mathbb{N}$ and any μ-tuple $\underline{g} \in H^\mu$, the function $exp_{\underline{g}}$ is a homomorphism:
$$exp_{\underline{g}}(\underline{x} + \underline{y}) = \underline{g}^{(\underline{x} + \underline{y})} = \underline{g}^{\underline{x}}\, \underline{g}^{\underline{y}} = exp_{\underline{g}}(\underline{x})\, exp_{\underline{g}}(\underline{y}).$$

b) If H is cyclic, tuple exponentiation is an inner product followed by a normal exponentiation: If $\underline{g} = (g_1, \ldots, g_\mu)$ and g is a generator of H, each g_i can be written in the form $g_i = g^{e_i}$, and
$$exp_{\underline{g}}(\underline{x}) = \underline{g}^{\underline{x}} = g^{e_1 x_1} \bullet \ldots \bullet g^{e_\mu x_\mu} = g^{\underline{e}\,\underline{x}}.$$
One can say that it *is* an inner product on $\mathbb{Z}_q{}^\mu$, where one copy of $\mathbb{Z}_q{}^\mu$ has been replaced with an isomorphic image H^μ. ♦□

In Groups of Prime Order

The most important case is that where the group order, q, is prime. Then $\mathbb{Z}_q$ is a field, and as its multiplicative group is cyclic, a tuple-exponentiation equation corresponds to a linear equation in the exponents (by Lemma 8.2b). Hence one can determine the number of solutions to such equations.[118]

In this section, only 2-tuple or pair exponentiation is treated; other statements follow where they are needed.

Lemma 8.3. Let H be a group of prime order q, and $\underline{g} = (g_1, g_2)$ a pair of generators of H. Then for each $x_1 \in \mathbb{Z}_q$, the function $exp_{\underline{g}}(x_1, \bullet)$: $\mathbb{Z}_q \to H$ is bijective. In other words, for any $z \in H$ and any x_1, there is exactly one x_2 with $exp_{\underline{g}}(x_1, x_2) = z$. ♦

Proof. The easiest proof is that the function $x_2 \to g_2{}^{x_2}$ is bijective, and so is multiplication by a constant $g_1{}^{x_1}$.

More systematically, one can use Lemma 8.2b, using g_1 as the generator g: For any $z \in H$, g_2 and z can be represented as $g_2 = g_1{}^{e_2}$ and $z = g_1{}^{e^*}$. Then
$$\underline{g}^{\underline{x}} = z \Leftrightarrow g_1{}^{x_1 + e_2 x_2} = g_1{}^{e^*} \Leftrightarrow x_1 + e_2\, x_2 \equiv e^* \bmod q.$$
As g_2 is a generator, $e_2 \neq 0$. Hence this linear equation has exactly one solution x_2.[119] □

Corollary 8.4 (Bundling degree). If H is a group of prime order q and $\underline{g}$ a pair of generators of H, every image z of the pair exponentiation function $exp_{\underline{g}}$ has exactly q preimages. Thus $exp_{\underline{g}}$ is of bundling degree q. ♦

Another consequence of Lemma 8.3 is that the result z gives no (Shannon) information about the first parameter, x_1, of $exp_{\underline{g}}(x_1, x_2)$, if x_2 is chosen uniformly at random. This is called a **hiding property**, because the result z hides x_1 perfectly.

---

118 Of course, computing the linear equation corresponding to a given tuple exponentiation equation is related to computing discrete logarithms, and computationally restricted participants will not be able to exploit it (see Section 8.5.3).

119 Note that it has been used that q is prime: The well-known theorems about the number of solutions to linear equations only hold over fields.

8.2.2 A Construction from Pairs of Permutations

Assume that a pair (f_0, f_1) of permutations on a common domain D is given. From this pair, functions B and B_σ (for $\sigma \in \mathbb{N}$) with bundling properties will be constructed. ("B" stands for bundling.) The construction is due to [GoMR88], but it was only used for collision-intractability there, i.e., no bundling property was shown.

The idea of the construction is as follows: f_0 and f_1 are two functions such that each element z of D has one preimage under each of them, i.e., two preimages altogether. One can reinterpret them as one function where each z has two preimages by declaring the index 0 or 1 an additional parameter. To obtain many preimages for each z, instead of only 2, the application of this function is iterated. The resulting function is called B, and its restriction to exactly σ iterations B_σ.

Definition 8.5 (Iterated function or permutation). If f_0 and f_1 are functions on a common domain D, and if it is clear from the context which functions are meant[120], let B denote the function

$$B: \{0, 1\}^* \times D \to D,$$
$$B(b_1 b_2 \ldots b_l, y) := f_{b_1}(f_{b_2}(\ldots f_{b_l}(y) \ldots)),$$

where $b_1, b_2, \ldots, b_l$ are the individual bits of the bit string that is the first parameter (see Figure 8.2). The restriction of B to strings of length σ as the first parameter is called B_σ, i.e.,

$$B_\sigma: \{0, 1\}^\sigma \times D \to D$$

with $B_\sigma(b, y) := B(b, y)$. Similarly, if the given functions have an index K (usually some sort of key), i.e., if they are called $f_{0,K}$ and $f_{1,K}$, the resulting functions are called

$$B_K \text{ and } B_{\sigma,K}. \qquad \blacklozenge$$

For instance, $B(\text{'1011'}, y) = f_1(f_0(f_1(f_1(y))))$. In Figure 8.2, an application of f_0 is drawn as an arrow to the upper right, and an application of f_1 as an arrow to the upper left. Thus an application of B is a sequence of arrows starting from y, and the bits b_i are used to select in which direction to go.

Lemma 8.6. If f_0 and f_1 are permutations on their domain D, the iterated functions B and B_σ have the following properties:

a) The restriction $B(b, \bullet)$ is a permutation on D for each $b \in \{0, 1\}^*$. In other words, for any $z \in D$ and any bit string b, exactly one y exists with $B(b, y) = z$.

b) For all $\sigma \in \mathbb{N}$, the function B_σ is of bundling degree 2^σ. More precisely, each $z \in D$ has exactly 2^σ preimages. ♦

Proof. a) The function $B(b, \bullet)$ is a composition of permutations and thus a permutation, too.

---

120 More formally, one would have to define B as an operator mapping function pairs to new functions, but the additional notation would not be justified in the following.

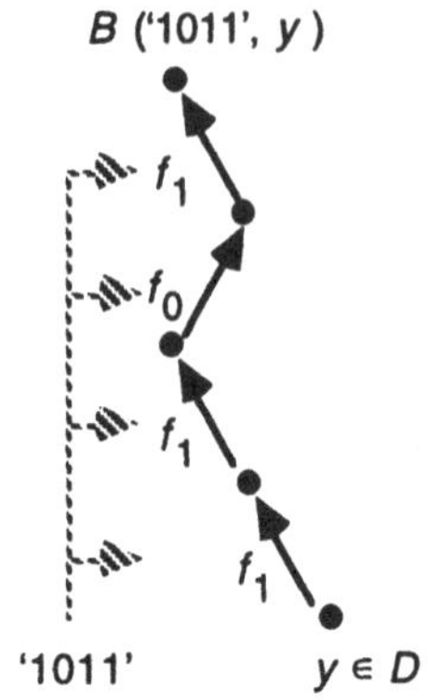

Figure 8.2. Example of the function B

b) According to Part a), for each string b of length σ, there is exactly one value y_b with $B_\sigma(b, y_b) = z$. There are 2^σ strings of length σ. Thus the 2^σ pairs (b, y_b) are the preimages of z under B_σ. (Note that the values y_b need not be different.) □

Figure 8.3 shows a preimage set with the same graphical conventions as in Figure 8.2.

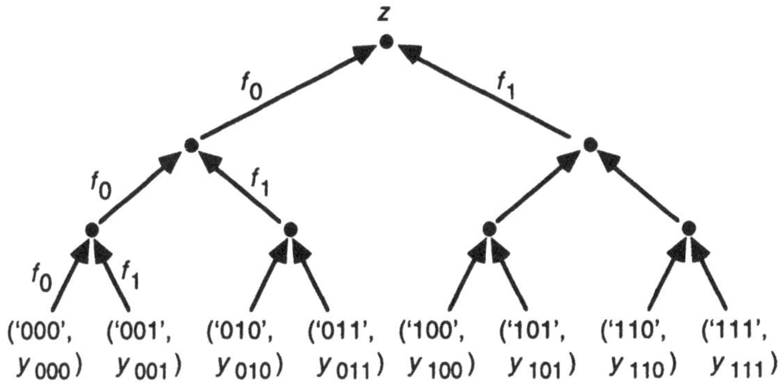

Figure 8.3. The bundling property of B_σ.
The figure shows the 2^σ preimages (b, y_b) of a value z under B_σ for the case $\sigma = 3$.

Part a) of this lemma corresponds to Lemma 8.3 for the discrete-logarithm case and has the same consequence: The result z gives no (Shannon) information about the first parameter, b, if the second parameter, y, is chosen uniformly at random from D. This is a **hiding property** again.

Remark 8.7. One can generalize the constructions from this section and their computational aspects treated in Section 8.5.4 to larger tuples of permutations than pairs, similar to the construction of hash functions in [Damg88]. (Some performance analysis of the hash functions can be found in [Fox91].) However, most of the special constructions in the factoring case cannot be extended easily; hence the notational overhead of the generalization did not seem worth while. ♦

8.2.3 Factoring Case: Iterated Squaring and Doubling (Or: A Useful Homomorphism on an Ugly Group)

All the functions presented in this section are based on the squaring function modulo n, which is a permutation on QR_n if n is a generalized Blum integer (see Section 8.1.3). Before these functions are defined, two generalizations are made:

- Permutations will later be needed on sets where membership can be decided efficiently. Hence QR_n is replaced by a related set called RQR_n. (The computational aspects, however, are treated later.)
- Some properties also hold if n is not a generalized Blum integer. Thus one can sometimes omit a zero-knowledge proof (see the end of Section 8.1.3) and use a more efficient local verification algorithm. Hence most definitions are presented for more general integers n.

Overview of this Section

1. First, the domains and pairs of functions, $f_{0,n}$ and $f_{1,n}$, on them are defined.
2. For the special case where n is a generalized Blum integer, it is shown that $f_{0,n}$ and $f_{1,n}$ are permutations, and Lemma 8.6 is exploited.

The remaining steps are taken for any $n \in 4\mathbb{N} + 1$. Thus $n \equiv 1 \bmod 4$, $n > 1$, and by the so-called first supplement to the law of quadratic reciprocity, $(\frac{-1}{n}) = +1$.[121]

3. A closed form of the iterated function B_n (see Definition 8.5) is presented.
4. It is shown that the restrictions $B_{\sigma,n}$ of B_n are homomorphisms. For this purpose, an ugly-looking group structure is defined on the domains. (Actually, a slightly modified version $B^*_{\sigma,n}$ of the general $B_{\sigma,n}$ is considered, where the first parameter is interpreted as a number, instead of a string.)
5. The fact that $B^*_{\sigma,n}$ is a homomorphism will later be of interest in its own right. Now, however, a result about the size of preimage sets is derived from it, i.e., a weaker form of the result of Step 2, but for more general n.

Domains and Function Pairs

First, some simple number-theoretic statements needed in Definition 8.9 are collected.

Lemma 8.8.

a) For any $n \in 4\mathbb{N} + 1$, the sets $\{\pm 1\}$ and $\pm QR_n$ are subgroups of $\mathbb{Z}_n{}^*$. (The abbreviations mean $\{\pm 1\} := \{1, -1\}$ and $\pm QR_n := QR_n \cup -QR_n$.)

---

[121] One can generalize everything to all odd numbers, but the restriction that the Jacobi symbol of -1 modulo n is $+1$ simplifies the representation and makes the resulting constructions a little more efficient, and it is so easy to verify locally that the generalization does not seem worth while.

b) If n is a generalized Blum integer, then $\pm QR_n = \mathbb{Z}_n{}^*(+1)$. ♦

Proof. Part a) is clear. For Part b), recall that $-1 \in \mathbb{Z}_n{}^*(+1) \setminus QR_n$ (Section 8.1.3). This proves the inclusion $\mathbb{Z}_n{}^*(+1) \supseteq \pm QR_n$ and $|\pm QR_n| = 2|QR_n|$. The considerations around χ_n in Section 8.1.2 imply $|QR_n| = 1/4\ |\mathbb{Z}_n{}^*|$ and $|\mathbb{Z}_n{}^*(+1)| = 1/2\ |\mathbb{Z}_n{}^*|$ for generalized Blum integers. Thus $|\mathbb{Z}_n{}^*(+1)| = |\pm QR_n|$. Together with the inclusion, this implies that the sets are equal. □

Definition 8.9 (Replaced quadratic residues).

a) For any generalized Blum integer n, let the replaced quadratic residues modulo n be the factor group

$$RQR_n := \mathbb{Z}_n{}^*(+1) / \{\pm 1\} = \pm QR_n / \{\pm 1\}.$$

b) For arbitrary integers $n \in 4\mathbb{N} + 1$, one can distinguish a small and a large generalization of RQR_n:

$$RQR_n^{<} := \pm QR_n / \{\pm 1\},$$

and

$$RQR_n^{>} := \mathbb{Z}_n{}^*(+1) / \{\pm 1\}.$$

c) For future computational purposes, each element of these factor groups, i.e., a set $\{\pm y\} = \{y, n - y\}$ with $1 \le y < n$, is represented by its smaller member, which can be characterized by the condition $y < n/2$. This yields the following identifications:

$$RQR_n^{<} = \{y \in \mathbb{Z} \mid 1 \le y < n/2 \wedge (y \in QR_n \vee n - y \in QR_n)\}$$

and

$$RQR_n^{>} = \{y \in \mathbb{Z} \mid 1 \le y < n/2 \wedge (\tfrac{y}{n}) = 1\}.$$

d) The canonical mappings from $\pm QR_n$ to $RQR_n^{<}$ and from $\mathbb{Z}_n{}^*(+1)$ to $RQR_n^{>}$ in this representation are denoted by $|\bullet|$, because they would be the usual absolute value on $\mathbb{Z}$ if $\mathbb{Z}_n$ were represented symmetrically (i.e., by the numbers with the smallest absolute values).[122]

e) To keep track of which group is used, multiplication in the factor groups $RQR_n^{<}$ and $RQR_n^{>}$ is denoted by $\circ$. Thus, with all the identifications, one can write $y \circ y' = |yy'|$. ♦

Note that, as the notation suggests,

$$RQR_n^{<} \subseteq RQR_n^{>},$$

and if n is a generalized Blum integer, then $RQR_n^{<} = RQR_n^{>} = RQR_n$.

As promised, for generalized Blum integers (where squaring was a permutation on QR_n), squaring will be shown to be a permutation on RQR_n, too.[123] Thus it is now

---

122 Although in theory the representation from Part c) will always be assumed, in practice a series of multiplications in $RQR_n^{<}$ or $RQR_n^{>}$ can be carried out in the set $\{1, \ldots, n\}$, with only one application of $|\bullet|$ at the end.

123 Squaring is not a permutation on any of QR_n, $RQR_n^{<}$, or $RQR_n^{>}$ for arbitrary n, not even in $4\mathbb{N} + 1$. For instance, if $n = pq$ with p, q prime and $p \equiv q \equiv 1 \bmod 4$, then $\chi_n(-1) = (1, 1)$. Hence either all the four roots of a quadratic residue are quadratic residues again, or none is. Thus squaring is 4-to-1 on QR_n. The four roots form two different classes in $\pm QR_n/\{\pm 1\}$; thus squaring is not 1-to-1 on $RQR_n^{<}$ either. Even more obviously, squaring is not a permutation on $RQR_n^{>}$ in general, because its range is at most the subset $RQR_n^{<}$.

introduced as one function of a pair, so that the results of Section 8.2.2 can be applied.

Definition 8.10 (Function pair). (Adapted from [GoMR88].) For any $n \in 4\mathbb{N} + 1$, two functions

$$f_{0,n}, f_{1,n}: RQR_n^{\gtrless} \rightarrow RQR_n^{\lessgtr}$$

are defined by

$$f_{0,n}(x) := x^2,$$
$$f_{1,n}(x) := 4 \circ x^2.$$

The index n may be omitted if it is clear from the context. Note that the range is indeed at most $RQR_n^{\lessgtr}$, because squaring maps into $RQR_n^{\lessgtr}$ and $4 = 2^2 \in RQR_n^{\lessgtr}$. ♦

According to the conventions in Definition 8.5, the following functions have now been defined, too:

$$B_n: \{0, 1\}^* \times RQR_n^{\gtrless} \rightarrow RQR_n^{\lessgtr}$$

with

$$B_n(b_1 b_2 \ldots b_l, y) = f_{b_1}(f_{b_2}(\ldots f_{b_l}(y) \ldots)),$$

and their restrictions $B_{\sigma,n}$ to strings of length σ. The restriction of B_n to $\{0, 1\}^* \times RQR_n^{\lessgtr}$ can be denoted by $B_n^{\lessgtr}$, if the distinction is important.

Strong Properties of B_n for Generalized Blum Integers

Lemma 8.11 (Permutations). (Adapted from [GoMR88].)

a) If n is a generalized Blum integer, $f_{0,n}$ and $f_{1,n}$ are permutations on RQR_n.

b) If n is a generalized Blum integer, the restriction $B_n(b, \bullet)$ is a permutation on RQR_n for each $b \in \{0, 1\}^*$. In other words, for any image $z \in RQR_n$ and any bit string b, there is exactly one $y \in RQR_n$ with $B_n(b, y) = z$. ♦

Proof. a) The canonical mapping induces an isomorphism from QR_n to RQR_n. (In other words, QR_n is a set of representatives and multiplication in RQR_n is represented by multiplication in QR_n.) Thus all the properties of the squaring function in QR_n are carried over to RQR_n. In particular, $f_{0,n}$ is a permutation.

Now $f_{1,n}$ is the composition of a permutation, $f_{0,n}$, and multiplication by 4. Multiplication is a permutation, too, because $4 \in RQR_n$.

b) Given Part a), this is just Lemma 8.6a. □

Part b) of this lemma corresponds to Lemma 8.3 for the discrete-logarithm case, and it has the same two consequences:

1. The restrictions $B_{\sigma,n}$ have a bundling property (see Lemma 8.6b and Figure 8.3).
2. The result z gives no (Shannon) information about the first parameter, b, if the second parameter, y, is chosen uniformly at random from RQR_n. This is a **hiding property** again.

The first consequence was not made a part of the lemma because the same result for more general n is Lemma 8.17. In contrast, the second consequence is special to generalized Blum integers.

Closed Representation of B_n

The idea of the following closed representation of B_n, which can be found in [Gold87] with a close look, is quite easy: In each iteration, the original parameter y is squared, and sometimes a 4 is multiplied to it. All the previous 4's are also squared. Thus, if the length of b is l, the result must be $4^\beta \circ y^{2^l}$ for some β.

Lemma 8.12. For each string $b = b_1 b_2 \ldots b_l$, let $num(b) := b_1 + 2b_2 + \ldots + 2^{l-1} b_l$, i.e., interpret b as a binary number written backwards. Then

$$B_n(b, y) = 4^{num(b)} \circ y^{2^l}$$

for all $n \in 4\mathbb{N} + 1$ and $y \in RQR_n^>$. ♦

Proof. The proof is by induction over l.

For $l = 1$, $B_n(b, y) = f_{b_1}(y)$, where $f_0(y) = y^2 = 4^0 \circ y^{2^1}$ and $f_1(y) = 4^1 \circ y^{2^1}$, as required.

If the lemma has already been shown for $l - 1$, it can be shown for l as follows: Let $b' := b_1 b_2 \ldots b_{l-1}$, and note that $num(b) = num(b') + 2^{l-1} b_l$. Hence

$$\begin{aligned} B_n(b, y) &= f_{b_1}(f_{b_2}(\ldots f_{b_{l-1}}(f_{b_l}(y) \ldots)) = B_n(b', f_{b_l}(y)) = B_n(b', 4^{b_l} \circ y^2) \\ &= 4^{num(b')} \circ (4^{b_l} \circ y^2)^{2^{l-1}} = 4^{num(b') + 2^{l-1} b_l} \circ y^{2 \cdot 2^{l-1}} = 4^{num(b)} \circ y^{2^l}. \end{aligned}$$ □

If one considers the restrictions $B_{\sigma,n}$ to strings b of length σ, the numbers $num(b)$ are between 0 and $2^\sigma - 1$. It is useful to define a variant of $B_{\sigma,n}$ directly on numbers.

Definition 8.13. For all $n \in 4\mathbb{N} + 1$ and $\sigma \in \mathbb{N}$, let

$$B^*_{\sigma,n}: \{0, \ldots, 2^\sigma - 1\} \times RQR_n^> \rightarrow RQR_n^<$$

be defined by $$B^*_{s,n}(a, y) := 4^a \circ y^{2^s}.$$

The restriction of $B^*_{\sigma,n}$ to $\{0, \ldots, 2^\sigma - 1\} \times RQR_n^<$ can be denoted by $B^{*<}_{\sigma,n}$, if the distinction is important. ♦

Lemma 8.12 can now be written as $B_n(b, y) = B^*_{\sigma,n}(num(b), y)$ if the length of b is σ.

The Functions $B^*_{\sigma,n}$ as Homomorphisms

If one already knows that one wants $B^*_{\sigma,n}$ to be a homomorphism for some reason, one can more or less derive what the corresponding group operation on its domain must be, if such an operation exists. This was done in [Bleu90, BlPW91]. The result, however, turned out to be a special case of [Bena87, Section 2.6].

Definition 8.14 (Group operation). For all $n \in 4\mathbb{N} + 1$ and $\sigma \in \mathbb{N}$, the domain of $B^*_{\sigma,n}$ is abbreviated as

$$G_{\sigma,n} := \{0, \ldots, 2^\sigma - 1\} \times RQR_n^>,$$

and an operation $*$ on $G_{\sigma,n}$ is defined by

$$(a, y) * (a', y') := ((a + a') \bmod 2^\sigma, y \circ y' \circ 4^{(a+a') \operatorname{div} 2^\sigma}).$$ ♦

Remark 8.15. The same construction can be applied to any other Abelian group G instead of $RQR_n^>$, any element g of G instead of 4, and any $r \in \mathbb{N}$ instead of 2^σ, and one can always prove an analogue of Theorem 8.16. This was also shown in [Bena87] already. In particular, one can define a subgroup of $G_{\sigma,n}$ as

$$G_{\sigma,n}^< := \{0, \ldots, 2^\sigma-1\} \times RQR_n^<. \qquad \blacklozenge$$

Theorem 8.16 (Groups and homomorphisms). Let $n \in 4\mathbb{N}+1$ and $\sigma \in \mathbb{N}$.

a) The set $G_{\sigma,n}$ with the operation $*$ is an Abelian group; its neutral element is $(0, 1)$.

b) The function $B_{\sigma,n}^*$ is a homomorphism from $G_{\sigma,n}$ to $RQR_n^<$. ♦

Proof. Both parts of the theorem can be proved by direct and rather tedious computation. Now a more systematic proof is shown where the group is derived from the direct product

$$Prod := \mathbb{Z} \times RQR_n^>$$

by identifying 2^σ from $\mathbb{Z}$ with 4 from $RQR_n^>$. This means that a subgroup

$$Sub := \langle (2^\sigma, 4^{-1}) \rangle = \{(a' 2^\sigma, 4^{-a'}) \mid a' \in \mathbb{Z}\}$$

of *Prod* is defined, and that $(G_{\sigma,n}, *)$ is proved to be isomorphic to the factor group

$$G'_{\sigma,n} := Prod \,/\, Sub.$$

a) It is first shown that $G_{\sigma,n}$, viewed as a subset of *Prod*, is a set of representatives of $G'_{\sigma,n}$:

- Let $(a, y) \in Prod$ be given, and let $a = a' 2^\sigma + a''$ with $0 \le a'' < 2^\sigma$. Then $(a'', y \circ 4^{a'})$ is a representative of (a, y) in $G_{\sigma,n}$, because their quotient is $(a' 2^\sigma, 4^{-a'}) \in Sub$.
- If (a, y) and (a', y') are two elements of $G_{\sigma,n}$, their quotient in *Prod* is $(a - a', y \circ y'^{-1})$. As $|a - a'| < 2^\sigma$, this quotient can only be an element of *Sub* if it is $(0, 1)$. Hence two different elements of $G_{\sigma,n}$ are in different classes in $G'_{\sigma,n}$.

Hence $G_{\sigma,n}$ with the operation induced by that on $G'_{\sigma,n}$ is an Abelian group with the neutral element $(0, 1)$. It is now shown that this operation is $*$: The product of $(a, y), (a', y') \in G_{\sigma,n}$ in *Prod* is $(a + a', y \circ y')$, and its representative in $G_{\sigma,n}$ is $((a + a') \bmod 2^\sigma, y \circ y' \circ 4^{(a+a') \operatorname{div} 2^\sigma})$, as required.

b) If the definition of $B_{\sigma,n}^*$ is extended to *Prod* (with the same defining equation), one can easily see that it is a homomorphism on that group. Furthermore, $B_{\sigma,n}^*(2^\sigma, 4^{-1}) = 4^{(2^\sigma)} \circ (4^{-1})^{2^\sigma} = 1$, and hence the whole subgroup *Sub* lies in the kernel of $B_{\sigma,n}^*$. Thus $B_{\sigma,n}^*$ can be defined on the factor group $G'_{\sigma,n}$ in the canonical way and is a homomorphism there, and thus, with the proof of Part a), also on $G_{\sigma,n}$. □

Size of the Preimage Sets of $B_{\sigma,n}^*$ for General n

As $B_{\sigma,n}^*$ is a homomorphism, the facts stated in Section 8.1.1 easily yield a lower bound on the number of preimages of each element that has any preimage at all. The idea is that the domain of $B_{\sigma,n}^*$ is much larger than the codomain; hence the preimage sets must be large on average. As all the preimage sets of a homomorphism are of equal size, every single one of them must be large.

Lemma 8.17.

a) For all $n \in 4\mathbb{N} + 1$ and $\sigma \in \mathbb{N}$, each element z in the range of $B^*_{\sigma,n}$ has at least 2^σ preimages, i.e.,

$$z \in B^*_{\sigma,n}(G_{\sigma,n}) \Rightarrow |B^{*\,-1}_{\sigma,n}(z)| \geq 2^\sigma.$$

Thus $B^*_{\sigma,n}$ is of bundling degree 2^σ.

b) The same holds for the restrictions $B^{*<}_{\sigma,n}$. ♦

Proof. With the homomorphism theorem,

$$|B^{*\,-1}_{\sigma,n}(z)| = |ker(B^*_{\sigma,n})| = |G_{\sigma,n}| \,/\, |B^*_{\sigma,n}(G_{\sigma,n})| \geq 2^\sigma\, |RQR^{>}_n| \,/\, |RQR^{<}_n| \geq 2^\sigma.$$

Similarly,

$$|B^{*<-1}_{\sigma,n}(z)| = |ker(B^{*<}_{\sigma,n})| = |G^{<}_{\sigma,n}| \,/\, |B^{*<}_{\sigma,n}(G^{<}_{\sigma,n})| \geq 2^\sigma\, |RQR^{<}_n| \,/\, |RQR^{<}_n| = 2^\sigma. \square$$

8.3 Some Efficient Algorithms

In order to see that the algorithms in the following schemes and some reductions used in proofs are efficient, one needs to know some simple facts from computational number theory.

The standard book in this field is still [Knut81], but quite a lot of literature exists, in particular on special tricks for cryptologic schemes. Only sequential algorithms are mentioned here, and a complete bibliography would exceed the scope of this section. Some precise descriptions and comparisons of algorithms suited for a practical high-speed software implementation, and more references, can be found in [Fox91].

Modular Multiplication

The basic operation in most of the following schemes is modular multiplication. (Elliptic curve arithmetic, on which some of the schemes could be based instead, is not described here; see, e.g., Kobl87].) It is assumed that $\mathbb{Z}_n$ is represented by the numbers $\{0, \ldots, n-1\}$. A modular multiplication can be computed with one multiplication and one division. A multiplication of l-bit numbers on a machine with word length w can easily be performed with $\lceil l/w \rceil^2$ word multiplications. Division takes a small number of word multiplications more.

There are asymptotically faster ways of multiplying. However, it is a general belief that the fastest algorithm, from [ScSt71], only becomes worth while for numbers larger than those typically used in cryptology (see, e.g., [Guin91]). The intermediate Karatsuba algorithm has its cross-over point somewhere near the typical size, depending on the concrete implementation, see, e.g., [Aßma89]. Thus saying that multiplication is $O(l^2)$ is a conservative estimate in theory and realistic in practice.

Similarly, one does not deviate much from $O(l^2)$ with division in practice, although one can be faster asymptotically: The only usual alternative to standard division is the Montgomery method, where the representation of residue classes by numbers is changed in such a way that modular multiplication can be done without division [Mont85]. Instead, there is a so-called reduction operation. It has two implementation variants, which are not always carefully distinguished. The first one uses two calls to a multiplication subroutine. With numbers of the typical size, this is no use if one has a good implementation of division; it should, however, be faster with larger numbers, where Karatsuba multiplication would be used. The efficiency of the second reduction variant, which uses word multiplications directly, is between that of standard multiplication and division.

Inversion, Chinese Remainder Algorithm, and Jacobi Symbol

Modular inverses can be computed efficiently with the extended Euclidean algorithm. However, this is somewhat slower than modular multiplication and asymptotically $O(l^3)$.

The Chinese remainder algorithm is very efficient after a little precomputation that can be done once and for all in cryptologic situations; for two congruences modulo numbers of length $l/2$ it needs one modular and one non-modular multiplication of numbers of length $l/2$.

Consequently, if one has to carry out computations modulo a composite modulus n whose factors are known, it is often advantageous to compute modulo each of the factors separately and to combine the results with the Chinese remainder algorithm at the end [QuCo82].

As mentioned, Jacobi symbols can be evaluated using the law of quadratic reciprocity, which yields an algorithm similar to the Euclidean algorithm and of asymptotic complexity $O(l^3)$.

Exponentiation

Exponentiation can be computed efficiently in any family of groups where an efficient multiplication algorithm is given, due to the well-known square-and-multiply algorithm. It needs l^* squarings and, on average, $l^*/2$ multiplications for an l^*-bit exponent.

If the group order $|G|$ is known, long exponents should be reduced modulo $|G|$ first.

The number of multiplications can be reduced. Techniques for the case where the basis is a variable can be found in [Knut81, BoCo90, SaDi93]; however, none of them achieves less than l^* squarings and multiplications altogether. (For more details, see the next subsection, "μ-Tuple Exponentiation".) If the basis g is fixed and only the exponent varies, precomputation of some powers of g can help to a reduction to about $l^*/\log_2(l^*)$ multiplications [BGMW93].[124]

Specially for modular exponentiation with an l-bit basis and an l^*-bit exponent, all this means an asymptotic complexity of $O(l^2 l^*)$. It is useful to have a squaring

---

124 Note that everything also holds for groups written additively: The product $x \cdot g$ of a group element g with an element x of $\mathbb{Z}$, which is defined by repeated addition, can be computed with $log_2(x)$ doublings and some additions.

routine that is faster than general multiplication; almost a factor of 2 can be gained. With a composite modulus whose factorization is known, one should apply the Chinese remainder theorem so that one can use faster multiplication of smaller numbers and reduce the exponent.

μ-Tuple Exponentiation

The product of several exponentiations, i.e., a μ-tuple exponentiation $\mathbf{g}^{\mathbf{x}}$ as in Definition 8.1, can be computed more efficiently than by computing all the products $g_i^{x_i}$ separately and multiplying them. In the following, small tuples are often used, e.g., with $\mu = 3$. In such cases, the simplest technique (attributed to Shamir in [ElGa85]) is an extension of the square-and-multiply algorithm that evaluates exponents from left to right: After each squaring, the intermediate result is multiplied with a product $\prod g_i^{b_i}$, where b_i is the appropriate bit of x_i. A table with the 2^{μ} possible products $\prod g_i^{b_i}$ is precomputed. For $\mu = 3$, this yields l^* squarings and, on average, $7/8 l^*$ multiplications if all three exponents are of length l^*.

One can even reduce the number of multiplications similar to methods for normal exponentiation at the cost of more precomputation, e.g., by multiplying with higher powers only after a certain number of squarings. More elaborate techniques can be found in [BoCo90].

8.4 Concrete Cryptologic Assumptions

As mentioned in Section 6.1.2, efficient fail-stop signature schemes can be constructed on the two most common concrete cryptologic assumptions, factoring and discrete logarithm, and theoretical constructions on possibly weaker abstract assumptions exist. However, although one usually talks of *the* factoring assumption etc., there are several possible variants. Therefore, brief discussions of both assumptions and the corresponding generation of problem instances, such as numbers that seem hard to factor, follow.

8.4.1 Integer Factoring

"The" Factoring Assumption

The first assumption is that factoring large integers is infeasible. Only Williams integers will be needed, i.e., those with exactly two prime factors p and q; where $p \equiv 3 \bmod 8$ and $q \equiv 7 \bmod 8$.[125] More precisely, the following assumption from [GoMR88] is used.

---

[125] As far as number-theoretic properties are concerned, one could permit generalized Williams integers, similar to generalized Blum integers, of the form $p^s q^t$. However, in a factoring assumption, large exponents s and t would mean small prime factors if n is always of approximately the same length, and numbers with small prime factors are easier to factor.

Definition 8.18.

a) For all $k \in \mathbb{N}$, let

$$Will_k := \{n = p\,q \in Will \mid |p|_2 = |q|_2 = k\}.$$

b) The factoring assumption is that for all probabilistic polynomial-time algorithms $\tilde{F}$ (that try to factor), all constants $c > 0$ and k sufficiently large:

$$P(f \text{ is a nontrivial divisor of } n \setminus n \in_R Will_k; f \leftarrow \tilde{F}(n)) < k^{-c}. \qquad \blacklozenge$$

State of the Art

The state of the art of factoring a few years ago is summarized in [LeLe90]. Since then, one significant new algorithm, the number field sieve, was invented; see the bibliography in [LeLe93, pp.1-3]. To state the time complexity of the best known algorithms, the following abbreviation is usual:

$$L_n[\tfrac{1}{i}; c] := (e^{\ln(n)^{1/i}\ln(\ln(n))^{(i-1)/i}})^{c + o(1)}.$$

The best general-purpose algorithms used in practice until recently have expected running times of $L_n[\frac{1}{2}; c]$ with small constants c (between 1 and $\sqrt{4/3}$, depending on whether one only considers algorithms whose running time has been proved). As time complexity is usually measured in terms of the length of the input, not of the input n itself, this is superpolynomial, but not strictly exponential because of the square root in the exponent. The number field sieve only has a third root in the exponent, i.e., $L_n[\frac{1}{3}; c]$ with c around 2.

In practice, general numbers, i.e., numbers without known special number-theoretic properties, have been factored up to about 130 decimal digits, i.e., 430 bits [AGLL95]. The number field sieve has reached almost 120 digits [DoLe95] and is expected to surpass the other algorithms soon.

A future challenge arises from quantum computing, because [Shor94] showed that factoring is possible in random polynomial time on this machine model. For introductions, see [Brow94, BeVa93]. I cannot say anything about how soon this may be realistic (unless by copying from the references). Moreover, this is not the only new model of highly parallel computation; see, e.g., [Beav95].

Generation of Uniformly Distributed Williams Integers

An actual cryptologic scheme needs a concrete algorithm gen_{Will} to generate Williams integers, and usually, in contrast to the assumption above, the resulting distribution is not exactly uniform. The assumption that would really be needed is that factoring is infeasible if the numbers are generated by gen_{Will}. Moreover, most algorithms used in practice are only expected polynomial-time.

First, note that one can achieve an exactly uniform distribution by repeatedly choosing numbers p and q of length k and in the appropriate congruence classes, randomly and testing them for primality, until two primes have been found. According to the prime-number theorems, the search ends after an expected polynomial number of trials. However, the fastest known deterministic primality test is slightly superpolynomial [AdPR83, CoLe87], and the only completely proved algorithm that recognizes primes without error in expected polynomial time (i.e., a ZPP algorithm in the notation of [BaDG88]), which is [AdHu87] together with [Rabi80], is regarded as even less practical. On a certain assumption about the density of primes in medium-sized intervals, one can use the algorithm from [GoKi86] instead. (The assumption is weaker than the so-called Cramer's conjecture, which says $\pi(n + \lceil \ln(n)^2 \rceil) > \pi(n)$ for sufficiently large n. Even without this assumption, a factoring assumption for the resulting distribution should be a consequence of that made above.)

If one wants a deterministically polynomial-time algorithm that only outputs prime numbers, and where the corresponding factoring assumption follows from that made above, one has to rely on Cramer's conjecture (see above) and search for each prime from some random number upwards in steps of two, and test each number with the pure Miller primality test [Mill76], which relies on the extended Riemann hypothesis.

In practice, one normally uses a small number of iterations of the Rabin-Miller test [Rabi80], where one might end up with a composite number with a very small probability (i.e., it is a co-R algorithm). Fortunately, the factoring assumption for the resulting distribution is a consequence of the one above: For k sufficiently large, the a-posteriori error probability, even after only one iteration of the test, decreases faster than the inverse of any polynomial in k (see [DaLP93]), and it decreases exponentially in the number of additional iterations. Thus, even if there were an algorithm that factored all numbers with more than two prime factors quickly, it would not have a significant impact on the overall probability of factoring the chosen numbers. Hence, the algorithm using the Rabin-Miller test is a reasonable choice for a probabilistic polynomial-time algorithm gen_{Will} such that the factoring assumption implies for all probabilistic polynomial-time algorithms $\tilde{F}$, all $c > 0$, and sufficiently large k:

$$P(f \text{ is a nontrivial divisor of } n \mid n \leftarrow gen_{Will}(\text{'}1\text{'}^k); f \leftarrow \tilde{F}(n)) < k^{-c}.$$

This algorithm gen_{Will} is assumed in the following, but any other algorithm for which the previous sentence is true could be used instead (provided it can be adapted to output the factors of n, too, as an auxiliary input for a zero-knowledge proof), and if anyone wanted to use an algorithm where this property cannot be proved, the last inequality should be taken directly as the corresponding factoring assumption.

An alternative to the use of the Rabin-Miller test are algorithms as in [Maur95] that generate numbers that are always prime, but with an unproven distribution.

Weak Numbers

If one considers numbers of fixed and rather small size (e.g., 512 bits at present), known polynomial-time algorithms that succeed in factoring with a superpolynomially, but subexponentially, small probability asymptotically may still succeed with a reasonable probability in practice. In particular, this holds for Pollard's $p - 1$ method [Poll74], which works well if all the prime factors of $p - 1$ are fairly small, and a corresponding $p + 1$ method [Will82]. (For a brief survey and a guide to more literature, see [LeLe90].) What has to be regarded as dangerous in practice is discussed in [BrDL93].

Hence it is usually suggested that the numbers $p - 1$ and $q - 1$ (and perhaps also $p + 1$ and $q + 1$) should have large prime factors p' and q', respectively. (An additional well-known requirement that $p' - 1$ and $q' - 1$ should have large prime factors, too, only deals with special attacks on RSA and need not be considered in schemes provably as hard as factoring.) Methods to generate such numbers with more or less modified distribution can be found in [Gord85, Bach88, Maur95].

However, the elliptic curve factoring algorithm (see [LeLe90] for a short description) restricted to a few curves succeeds with the same probability as the algorithms mentioned above, and the overhead is larger by a small integer factor only. Hence one could also exclude numbers that would be factored by such an algorithm; this, however, is impossible, because there is a large choice of curves. (This has now also been observed in [Miha94].) Therefore I think one had better increase the size of the numbers.

Variations with the Type of the Numbers

Other possible variations in the factoring assumption concern the number of prime factors of n and the congruence classes and length of these factors.

The condition about two large prime factors is common to almost all cryptologic schemes based on a factoring assumption. At present, numbers of this type are among the hardest instances of all known factoring algorithms. Anyway, they are a non-negligible fraction of the numbers of any fixed size (this can easily be seen by applying the prime-number theorem to the possible factors), and therefore a factoring assumption for numbers with two prime factors is a consequence of any similar assumption for numbers of a more general structure.

Blum integers and Williams integers are often used, too. Because of Dirichlet's prime-number theorem, asymptotically about half of all prime numbers are congruent to 3 mod 4, and among these, about half are congruent to 3 mod 8. Hence the factoring assumption made above is a consequence of one for arbitrary numbers with two prime factors.

The condition that the length of the factors is exactly equal is rather strict. In practice, one might fix the length in words only or even start with the required length l of n (i.e., $l = 2k$ here) and a bound α and require only $|p|_2, |q|_2 \geq \alpha l$; see [Maur95]. This would require a more general factoring assumption for each α.

8.4.2 Discrete Logarithm

The second assumption used in the following is that groups H of prime order q exist where computing discrete logarithms is infeasible, i.e., an assumption slightly different from that mentioned in Section 2.4. (Some benefits of groups of prime order were already shown in Section 8.2.1.)

Abstract Assumption

The following abstract assumption is unusual in the sense that it considers different interest groups. One party selects the group where computing discrete logarithms is assumed to be hard. The other party needs to be sure that what has been generated is a group at all, and of prime order, and with some more properties defined below. (This is similar to the notions of correctly generated and good or acceptable prekeys, and indeed, the description of a selected group will be a part of the prekey in the schemes in Section 9.3.) As local verifiability is required here, the notion is represented by a family of sets All_k, representing all acceptable groups.

Definition 8.19.

a) A **family of groups of prime order** has the following components:

- Key generation.
  - A probabilistic polynomial-time algorithm *gen*, the group-generation algorithm, that, on input '1'^{k} with $k \in \mathbb{N}$ (the security parameter), outputs a prime q and a value *desc* (representing the description of a group $H_{q,desc}$ of order q).
  - A family of sets $(All_k)_{k \in \mathbb{N}}$ of pairs $(q, desc)$ (representing all descriptions of groups acceptable to the party that has not chosen the group). Let $All := \bigcup_k All_k$.
  - An algorithm *group_verification* that, on input a triple ('1'^{k}, q, *desc*), decides if $(q, desc) \in All_k$ in time polynomial in the first input alone.[126]
- A family of groups, $(H_{q,desc})_{(q,desc) \in All}$. The group elements must be (represented as) tuples of bit strings.[127]
- Algorithms that, with a first input $(q, desc) \in All$ and in time polynomial in this input alone,
  - choose random elements in $H_{q,desc}$ with uniform distribution,
  - test membership in $H_{q,desc}$, and
  - compute the group operations in $H_{q,desc}$.[128]

  Note that these were 5 algorithms, one for each operation, but each one for all pairs $(q, desc)$. They have not been given explicit names; instead, they are written "$\in_R$", "$\in$", and with the usual notation for group operations. The first algorithm is probabilistic.

These components must have the following additional properties:

α) All correctly generated group descriptions are acceptable, i.e., $[gen(\text{'1'}^k)] \subseteq All_k$ for all $k \in \mathbb{N}$, and the length of the elements of All_k is polynomial in k.

---

126 The condition that tests should be polynomial-time in a subset of their inputs only and the upper bounds on the size of all acceptable keys (here and in the following) have the same purpose as with prekeys and their verification: The algorithms will be used by entities that may get some of their inputs from an attacker, whereas the entities must be polynomial-time in their own initial values and interface inputs.

127 This is because computations in these groups will be considered, and the model of computation is on tuples of bit strings.

128 This means multiplication, inversion, and finding the neutral element. An algorithm computing the neutral element can also be constructed from the others: One can choose a random element and multiply it with its inverse. However, one can usually find the neutral element more efficiently.

β) Properties of all acceptable groups: For all $k \in \mathbb{N}$ and all $(q, desc) \in All_k$, the value q is a prime number with $q > 2^k$, and the order of the group $H_{q,desc}$ is q.

b) One says that **the discrete logarithm is hard** in such a family of groups iff for every probabilistic polynomial-time algorithm $\tilde{A}$, the probability is negligibly small that $\tilde{A}$, on input a correctly generated group description and two random elements of the group (one of them a generator), finds the discrete logarithm of these two elements.

More precisely: $\forall c > 0\ \exists k_0\ \forall k \geq k_0$:

$$P(e = log_g(g^*) \setminus (q, desc) \leftarrow gen(\text{`1'}^k);\ g \in_R H_{q,desc} \setminus \{1\};\ g^* \in_R H_{q,desc};\ e \leftarrow \tilde{A}(\text{`1'}^k, q, desc, g, g^*)) < k^{-c}.$$

c) The **abstract discrete-logarithm assumption** is that a family of groups of prime order where the discrete logarithm is hard exists. ♦

Remark 8.20. Definition 8.19a implies that the length of the elements of all acceptable groups is polynomial in that of $(q, desc)$, because uniformly distributed random elements can be chosen in polynomial-time. Hence the length is also polynomial in k. ♦

Remarks about Possible Variations

Three further conceivable generalizations of Definition 8.19a have been omitted, because no example follows where they are needed, and hence the additional notation did not seem justified:

- The condition $q > 2^k$, which is unusual in cryptology, is needed because the size of the group also determines the information-theoretic part of the security of the following schemes. Instead, one might introduce a second security parameter σ for that purpose, where σ might, in theory, be smaller than k. However, algorithms *gen* used in practice first generate a prime q of approximately k bits anyway if they are given the input '1'^{k}. Moreover, this condition is exploited in the current construction of hash functions (Construction 8.50).
- A zero-knowledge proof scheme could be permitted instead of local verifiability, or, as with prekeys, two families of good and all acceptable groups.
- The requirement that the group elements are immediately, and thus uniquely, represented by strings could be omitted. For instance, an element of a factor group could then be represented by any of its representatives in the original group, whereas with the current definition, one set of representatives must be fixed. Additionally, an algorithm that tests equality of elements of $H_{q,desc}$ would be needed. However, this would yield two notions of equality, that of group elements and that of the strings representing them, and with all occurrences of random choices, one would have to decide whether the group element or the string or both have to be distributed uniformly. Moreover, there would be problems in the construction of hash functions (Construction 8.50), where group elements are mapped into strings.

Other more or less formal abstract discrete-logarithm assumptions, such as in [BoKK90, McCu90, OkSS93] differ in the following points (apart from the absence of sets All_k): Does one need

- to compute inverses,
- to test group membership,
- to know the group order, and
- to test that the group has been chosen correctly, and if yes, is a probabilistic test or an interactive proof sufficient?

Usually, the condition that random elements can be generated is missing; instead, *gen* generates the group together with one generator. For groups of known prime order q, this is equivalent, because a random element $\neq 1$ can serve as a generator, and conversely, random elements can be generated from one generator by exponentiation with random numbers modulo q.

Moreover, if the groups are not cyclic, one can partition the discrete-logarithm problem into a decision problem whether a discrete logarithm exists and the computation.

Note that the assumption, as formalized above, only means that computing discrete logarithms is infeasible for people who did not take part in the choice of the group, because $\tilde{A}$ only gets the results q and *desc* as inputs. The same held for the factoring assumption, where it is obvious that someone who generates n might know the factors. Here, however, it is generally believed that even the person who chooses the group cannot compute discrete logarithms, except for certain multiplicative groups modulo primes, which can, however, be excluded from the family [Gord93, Euro93].

Concrete Discrete-Logarithm Assumption: Subgroups of Prime Fields

The most well-known and well-investigated discrete-logarithm assumption is that for multiplicative groups of finite prime fields, i.e., the cyclic groups $\mathbb{Z}_p^*$ of order $p - 1$.[129] It is called the standard discrete-logarithm assumption in the following. Of course, $p - 1$ is even and therefore not a prime, hence these groups cannot be used directly here.

If $p - 1$ has a large prime factor q, then $\mathbb{Z}_p^*$ has a unique cyclic subgroup of prime order q. This group is called $H_{q,p}$. According to Section 8.1.1, it can be specified as

$$H_{q,p} := \{g^* \in \mathbb{Z}_p^* \mid g^{*q} = 1\}.$$

These groups are used in the following. In the notation of Definition 8.19, $desc := p$ is used as the description of the group (together with q). Group elements are represented as numbers modulo p as usual. Thus the following type of assumptions is made, where the group-generation algorithm is still a free parameter:

---

129 Similar to the situation with factoring, one often excludes primes p where $p - 1$ has no large prime factors, because computing discrete logarithms is much easier in that case [PoHe78].

Definition 8.21.

a) A **generation scheme for subgroups of prime fields** is a triple of
   - a probabilistic polynomial-time algorithm *gen* (the group-generation algorithm),
   - a function *len_p*,
   - and a polynomial-time algorithm *len_p** that computes *len_p* in unary,

   where *gen*, on input '1'^{k} with $k \in \mathbb{N}$, outputs a pair (q, p) of primes with
   $$q > 2^k \wedge q \mid (p-1) \wedge |p|_2 \le len\_p(k).$$

b) One says that **the discrete logarithm is hard** for such a generation scheme, or that the **concrete discrete-logarithm assumption** holds for it, iff for every probabilistic polynomial-time algorithm $\tilde{A}$, for all $c > 0$ and for k sufficiently large,
   $$P(e = log_g(g^*) \setminus (q, p) \leftarrow gen(\text{'}1\text{'}^k);\ g \in_R H_{q,p}\setminus\{1\};\ g^* \in_R H_{q,p};\ e \leftarrow \tilde{A}(\text{'}1\text{'}^k, q, p, g, g^*))$$
   $$< k^{-c}.$$ ♦

Construction 8.22. Let a generation scheme for subgroups of prime fields be given (see Definition 8.21a). The corresponding family of groups of prime order is defined by the following components:

- Key generation:
  - The same algorithm *gen* as in the generation scheme is used.
  - The sets All_k are defined as
    $All_k := \{(q, p) \in \mathbb{N} \times \mathbb{N} \mid q, p \text{ prime} \wedge q > 2^k \wedge q \mid (p-1) \wedge |p|_2 \le len\_p(k)\}$.
  - The algorithm *group_verification*, on input ('1'$^k, q, p$), first tests if $|q|_2 \le |p|_2 \le len\_p(k)$; this can be done in time polynomial in k. If yes, it continues and tests if $q > 2^k$ and $q \mid (p-1)$, and if p and q are prime. As discussed with the factoring assumption, the Rabin-Miller test is used in practice, although it introduces an exponentially small error probability into some properties (but not into availability of service). These tests take time polynomial in the length of q and p, which were already verified to be polynomial in k.
- The groups $H_{q,p}$ are the unique subgroups of order q of $\mathbb{Z}_p^*$, as defined above.
- The additional algorithms work as follows:
  - Uniformly random elements of $H_{q,p}$ can be chosen as $(p-1)/q$-th powers of random elements of $\mathbb{Z}_p^*$.
  - Membership of g^* in $H_{q,p}$ can be tested by first testing membership in $\mathbb{Z}_p^*$ and then testing if $g^{*q} = 1$.
  - The group operations are simply those of $\mathbb{Z}_p^*$. ♦

Lemma 8.23. If the discrete logarithm is hard for the given generation scheme for subgroups of prime fields, Construction 8.22 is a family of groups of prime order where the discrete logarithm is hard. ♦

Proof. All the algorithms are obviously polynomial-time in the correct parameters. What remains to be shown is Properties α) and β) from Definition 8.19a and that the discrete logarithm is hard according to Definition 8.19b.

α) All correctly generated group descriptions are acceptable by the construction of *gen* and *All*, and the length of an element (q, p) of All_k is bounded by $2len\_p(k)$.

β) Clear by the definitions.

b) That the discrete logarithm is hard is the same formula as in Definition 8.21b. □

State of the Art

For multiplicative groups of prime fields, i.e., corresponding to the standard discrete-logarithm assumption, the situation is very similar to factoring: The state of the art a few years ago is summarized in [LeLe90, McCu90, LaOd91]. Since then, a number field sieve algorithm has been invented [Gord93a], and its running time is of the order $L_n[\frac{1}{3}; c]$, whereas the time complexity of the best algorithms used in practice so far is of the order $L_n[\frac{1}{2}; c]$, both with small constants c.

In practice, discrete logarithms have been computed for primes p of about 200 bits. However, not so much work has gone into computing discrete logarithms as into factoring.

On quantum computers, computing discrete logarithms is possible in random polynomial time [Shor94].

Generation Algorithms

Different proposals for the group-generation algorithm *gen* have the following in common: First, q is chosen as a random prime of a certain length, and then the values $p := d\,q + 1$ with factors d from a certain range are tested for primality. The proposals vary in the range of d. In some cases, e.g., if only $d = 2$ is used, the choice of q must also be repeated if none of the possible p's is prime.[130]

It seems to be generally believed, at present, that any of these algorithms *gen* leads to a sensible discrete-logarithm assumption. E.g., in the proposed standard DSS [DSS91], following [Schn91], p is chosen according to the standard discrete-logarithm assumption (i.e., between 512 and 1024 bits long) and q is much smaller (160 bits), corresponding to an assumption that no special subexponential discrete-logarithm algorithm for subgroups exists.

If one wants a relation with the standard discrete-logarithm assumption, one must ensure that the quotient $d = (p-1)/q$, i.e., the index of the subgroup, is only polynomial in k.

In this case, any method to compute discrete logarithms in the subgroup $H_{q,p}$ leads to a method to compute discrete logarithms in $\mathbb{Z}_p{}^*$ with overhead polynomial in k (following ideas from [PoHe78]): Given $g, g^* \in \mathbb{Z}_p{}^*$, first compute the

130 Note that the sets All_k in Construction 8.22 are useful, although with most of these algorithms *gen*, testing membership in $[gen('1'^k)]$ is not infeasible. For instance, consider the algorithm *gen* that searches for the smallest d such that $p := d\,q + 1$ is prime. Then the membership test for All_k only needs two primality tests, whereas a membership test for $[gen('1'^k)]$ would have to verify that no value $d'q + 1$ with $d' < d$ is prime.

discrete logarithm e^* of g^{*d} with respect to g^d in $H_{q,p}$. Thus $g^{de^*} = g^{*d}$. Hence $de^* \equiv log_g(g^*)\, d \bmod p-1$, and $e := log_g(g^*)$ can be searched for among the d solutions to this congruence.

Heuristically, one assumes that a non-negligible percentage of primes p has a large prime factor q in this sense (see, e.g., [Maur92]). Then the standard discrete-logarithm assumption implies a similar assumption for primes with this property, because one can find d (and thus q) by trial division if only p is given. Moreover, if *gen* generates primes with this property uniformly, or with small deviations only, the same assumption holds for the primes generated by *gen*.

Anyway, primes p with one very large prime factor q are usually regarded as the hardest cases for discrete-logarithm algorithms.

If *gen* generates primes where p is much larger than q, the concrete discrete-logarithm assumption in Definition 8.21b is no longer related to the standard discrete-logarithm assumption, but to the certified discrete-logarithm assumption [BoKK90, ChDG88]. Its difference to the standard discrete-logarithm assumption is that the algorithm that tries to compute discrete logarithms is given the prime factorization of $p - 1$ as an additional input. Hence it is the stronger of the two assumptions. In the given case, the prime factor q is a partial factorization. Moreover, it is not clear if an efficient discrete-logarithm algorithm with respect to generators of the subgroups would yield an efficient discrete-logarithm algorithm with respect to generators of the complete groups.

Other Concrete Discrete-Logarithm Assumptions

Three other concrete discrete-logarithm assumptions that could be used are mentioned.

If $p = 2q + 1$, one can use the **factor group** $H'_{q,p} := \mathbb{Z}_p^*/\{\pm 1\}$, instead of a subgroup [ChAn90]. It can be represented by the numbers $1, \ldots, q$. An advantage of this group is that there is an efficiently computable bijection ι from $H'_{q,p}$ to $\mathbb{Z}_q$: Map q to 0 and the remaining numbers to themselves. (Of course, any discrete-logarithm function is a bijection, too, but hopefully not efficiently computable.) This means that exponentiation and similar functions from $\mathbb{Z}_q$ to $H'_{q,p}$ can be iterated in a simple way.

Multiplicative groups or subgroups of **other finite fields** can also be used. In particular, fields $GF(2^k)$ have been proposed as an alternative to prime fields, because they give rise to particularly efficient hardware implementations. However, in software they are usually not practical, because the hardware multiplication operation cannot be exploited. Additionally, the number 2^k used must be larger than p in the other case. For overviews of discrete-logarithm algorithms for this case, see [LeLe90, Section 3.17, McCu90]; [GoMc93] contains practical results up to $k = 500$; and the best algorithm used in practice is of the order $L_n[\frac{1}{3}; c]$. Moreover, only very few such fields exist; hence one has to trust the stronger assumption that computing discrete logarithms is infeasible in particular groups (instead of randomly chosen groups) for each security parameter.

As mentioned in Section 2.4, **elliptic curves** are a fashionable candidate for the implementation of cryptologic schemes based on a discrete-logarithm assumption. One problem with them is that it is not easy to determine the order and the group structure of a randomly chosen curve — in contrast to all previously mentioned groups they are not necessarily cyclic. This was an important reason to consider special curves such as supersingular ones. In answer to such doubts, [Kobl91] describes an algorithm that generates elliptic curves of prime order, together with a generator g, in expected polynomial time.

Remark 8.24. In the algorithm in [Kobl91], page 210, the two instructions "go back to step (2)" must be replaced by "go back to step (1)" to be consistent with the proof of the theorem and Remark 1 on page 212. ♦

It is easy to see that the remaining requirements made in the abstract discrete-logarithm assumption hold for this algorithm. Furthermore, once the order q of the group is known, it can be verified much quicker: If the curve is defined over a field $\mathbb{Z}_p$, its order is known to be in the interval $p + 1 \pm 2\sqrt{p}$. Hence, if q is from this interval, $g^q = 1$, and $g \neq 1$, then the group order must be q, because any multiple would be too large.

The running time of the algorithm is a polynomial of a rather high degree; however, with recent advances in implementations of Schoof's algorithm for determining the order of a curve, it is becoming feasible for numbers of the desired size (see the last sections of [LeMo95]).

Although discrete logarithms on elliptic curves may be harder to compute than others in the normal sense, they do not help against quantum computation: Shor's result that computing discrete logarithms is possible in random quantum polynomial time was extended to arbitrary families of groups in [BoLi95].

8.5 Collision-Intractable Function Families

8.5.1 Overview

The property that makes all the functions with bundling properties, and also some other functions such as hash functions, interesting for cryptology is that it is infeasible to find collisions, i.e., two values with the same image; see Figure 8.4 (and Figure 6.9). For precision, this notion and two related ones are given formal definitions.

Definition 8.25 (Collisions and related notions).

a) For any function f, an f-collision is defined as a pair of values, (x, x'), from the domain of f with $x \neq x'$ and $f(x) = f(x')$.

b) For a pair (f_0, f_1) of functions with the same codomain, a claw is defined as a pair of values, (x, x'), from the respective domains with $f_0(x) = f_1(x')$.

   More generally, for a tuple $(f_0, \ldots, f_\mu)$ of functions with the same codomain, a claw can be defined as a pair of values together with indices of functions, i.e., $((i, x), (i', x'))$, with $i \neq i'$ and $f_i(x) = f_{i'}(x')$.

c) If a function f and a relation $\approx$ on the domain of f are given, an f-collision with respect to $\approx$ is defined as a pair of values, (x, x'), from the domain of f with $x \not\approx x'$ and $f(x) = f(x')$. This notion will only be used for relations $\approx$ that are reflexive and symmetric. ♦

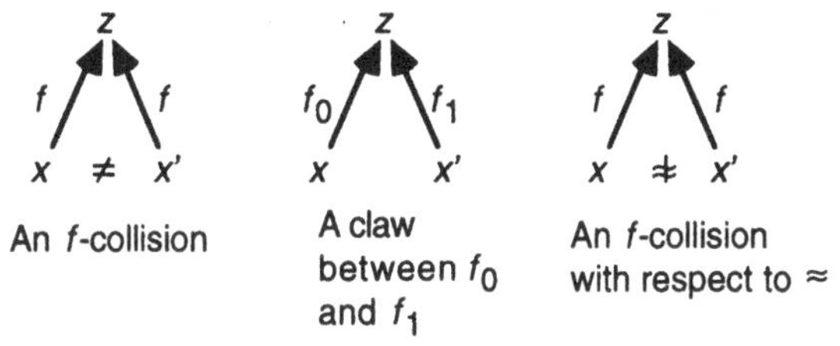

Figure 8.4. Collisions and related notions

If the function f is specified by an algorithm, one must take care what its intended domain is, because an algorithm may produce results even outside this domain.[131] Values should only be regarded as a collision if they are in the domain. (For instance, they must have the correct Jacobi symbol in the factoring case — this is why the sets RQR_n, where membership can be decided efficiently, were introduced.)

Collision-intractability is the computational property that it is infeasible to find collisions. It is only defined for families of functions: For any single function that has a collision in the mathematical sense, there is an algorithm with constant running time that, independent of any input, always outputs this collision.[132]

Classes of Collision-Intractable Function Families

Several classes of collision-intractable functions can be defined. Important ones are collision-intractable families of

- bundling functions, i.e., functions with a bundling property,
- bundling homomorphisms, i.e., bundling functions that are also homomorphisms of Abelian groups,
- hash functions, i.e., functions that map arbitrarily long bit strings to short ones, and
- fixed-size hash functions, i.e., functions that map bit strings of a certain length to shorter strings.

---

131 One could exclude this by requiring algorithms to stop with an error message outside their intended domains. However, it is often more efficient to separate the membership test for the domain from the algorithm that computes the function. For instance, the squaring function on RQR_n would become very inefficient if each application included the computation of the Jacobi symbol of the input; and in many situations, the input is the result of a previous squaring and therefore in the correct domain anyway.

132 This implies that collision-intractable hash functions as used in practice (e.g., [SHS92]) are formally undefinable.

Important classes with other properties related to collision-intractability are families of

- hiding functions; the simplest case are functions with two parameters where the result gives no Shannon information about the first parameter and that are collision-intractable with respect to equality of the first parameter — they yield efficient commitments to long strings,
- hiding homomorphisms, i.e., hiding functions that are also homomorphisms of Abelian groups, and
- permutation pairs where it is infeasible to find claws; their existence is used as an abstract cryptologic assumption.

Detailed definitions are presented in Section 8.5.2. Figure 8.5 gives an overview of these classes and their use in later chapters and in the dual invisible signature schemes from [ChHP92]. The folding functions mentioned in the figure are a special type of hash functions defined and used for greater efficiency in [PfWa90]: They are intended for the case where several values from the range of the hash function have to be hashed again, instead of arbitrary strings (e.g., in tree authentication). However, they are not absolutely necessary in the following.

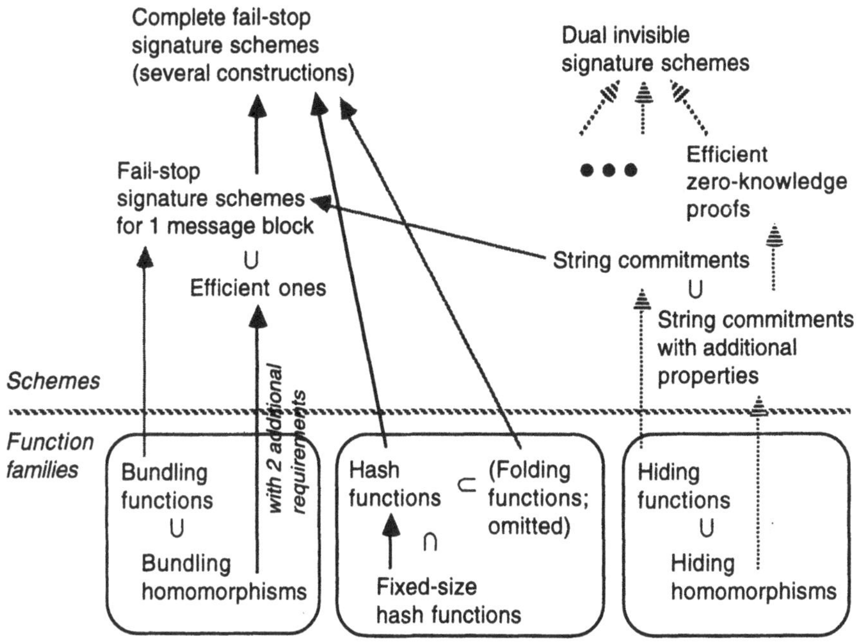

Figure 8.5. Function families: Overview and some applications.
Signs "⊂" denote inclusion of classes, black arrows denote constructions presented in detail in the following chapters, dashed arrows denote constructions in [ChHP92], and grey arrows other possible constructions.

Apart from defining more such classes, one can also define details within each definition in different ways, e.g., requirements on the domains and membership tests (similar to the discrete-logarithm assumptions). In particular, all the following definitions contain sets *Good* and *All* of good keys or all acceptable keys, i.e., they make provisions for different interest groups; the use of these sets is considered in Remark 8.38. Furthermore, not all the simple relations between the definitions that one could prove are mentioned below.

Constructions of Collision-Intractable Function Families

All the classes of function families shown in Figure 8.5 can be constructed both on the abstract discrete-logarithm assumption (see Section 8.5.3) and on the factoring assumption (see Section 8.5.5), and those without homomorphism properties also on the abstract assumption that a claw-intractable family of permutation pairs exists (see Section 8.5.4). An overview of these constructions is given in Figures 8.6 and 8.7. The top layer of both figures is identical to the bottom layer of Figure 8.5.

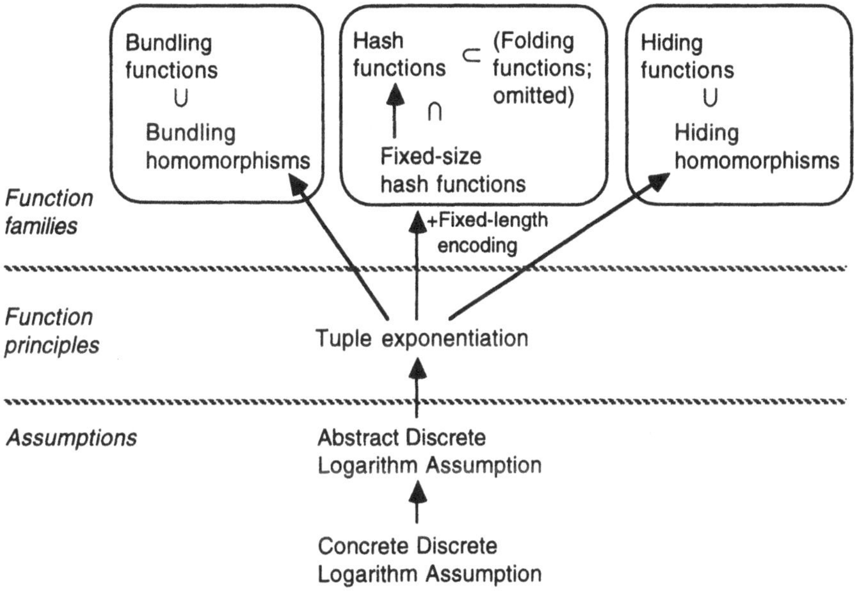

Figure 8.6. Function families: Discrete-logarithm case.
Signs "⊂" denote inclusion; arrows denote constructions.

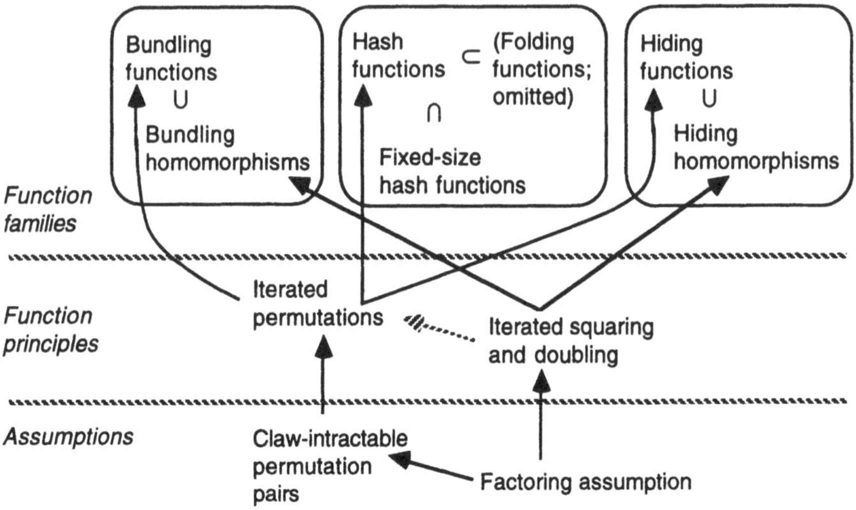

Figure 8.7. Function families: Cases of factoring and claw-intractable permutation pairs. Signs "⊂" denote inclusion; arrows denote constructions. The diagram at the bottom commutes, i.e., iterated squaring and doubling is the special case of iterated permutations where the construction of claw-intractable permutation pairs on the factoring assumption is used.

8.5.2 Definitions

This section contains the definitions of the classes of function families listed in the overview, see Figure 8.5. At the end of this section, Table 8.1 summarizes how the definitions differ in details.[133]

Claw-Intractable Permutation Pairs

Claw-intractable permutation pairs were introduced in [GoMR88]. This subsection contains a strong and a weak version of the definition, now without trap-doors. It may be helpful to know that the weak version will be used in the factoring case if one does not want to use a zero-knowledge proof, and thus the modulus n is not necessarily a generalized Blum integer.

Definition 8.26. **A strong claw-intractable family of permutation pairs** has the following components:

- A probabilistic polynomial-time algorithm *gen*, the key-generation algorithm, that, on input '1'^{k} with $k \in \mathbb{N}$, outputs a value K, called a key (representing the description of a permutation pair).

[133] As mentioned before, the definitions could be relaxed by allowing more algorithms to be probabilistic and allowing more small error probabilities. In particular, one could restrict more properties to good keys (which are assumed to be verified with zero-knowledge proofs and thus with error probabilities), instead of all acceptable keys (which are assumed to be locally verifiable).

- Families $GoodFam := (Good_k)_{k\in\mathbb{N}}$ and $AllFam := (All_k)_{k\in\mathbb{N}}$ of sets (called the sets of good keys and all acceptable keys, respectively). Let $Good := \bigcup_k Good_k$ and $All := \bigcup_k All_k$.
- A family of sets $(D_K)_{K\in All}$, and a family of pairs of functions on them, $((f_{0,K}, f_{1,K}))_{K\in All}$, i.e., for $i := 0, 1$:

$$f_{i,K}: D_K \to D_K.$$

- Two polynomial-time algorithms f_0 and f_1. Each f_i computes a whole family of functions, i.e., on input $K \in All$ and $x \in D_K$, it outputs $f_{i,K}(x)$.
- Additional algorithms (where the first one is probabilistic) that, with a first input $K \in All$ and in time polynomial in this input alone
  - choose random elements in D_K, where the distribution must be uniform if $K \in Good$, and
  - test membership in D_K.

  They have not been given explicit names, because they will be written "$\in_R$" and "$\in$".

These components must have the following additional properties:

a) Good and acceptable keys: All correctly generated keys are good and acceptable; more precisely, $[gen(\text{'}1\text{'}^k)] \subseteq Good_k \subseteq All_k$ for all $k \in \mathbb{N}$, and the length of the elements of All_k is polynomial in k.

b) Length restrictions: The length of the elements of D_K for $K \in All$ is polynomial in that of K.

c) Permutations: For $K \in Good$, the functions $f_{0,K}$ and $f_{1,K}$ are permutations.

d) Claw-intractability: For every probabilistic polynomial-time algorithm $\tilde{A}$, the probability that $\tilde{A}$, on input a correctly generated key K, outputs a claw between $f_{0,K}$ and $f_{1,K}$ is negligibly small. More precisely: $\forall c > 0\ \exists k_0\ \forall k \geq k_0$:

$$P(f_{0,K}(x) = f_{1,K}(x') \wedge x, x' \in D_K \setminus K \leftarrow gen(\text{'}1\text{'}^k);\ (x, x') \leftarrow \tilde{A}(\text{'}1\text{'}^k, K)) < k^{-c}.$$

♦

Definition 8.27. A **weak claw-intractable family of permutation pairs** is defined like a strong one, except that $f_{0,K}$ and $f_{1,K}$ are only required to be permutations if K has been generated correctly, i.e., if $K \in [gen(\text{'}1\text{'}^k)]$ for some k. ♦

Remark 8.28. With both these definitions, one can test in polynomial time if a claw has been found for a given acceptable key, i.e., on input (K, x, x') with $K \in All$. ♦

Bundling Functions and Homomorphisms

The basic building blocks for the following efficient fail-stop signature schemes are collision-intractable families of bundling homomorphisms. Their mathematical part was prepared in Section 8.2: For both the factoring and the discrete-logarithm case, homomorphisms with a bundling property were presented, i.e., each image has many preimages.

As in the definition of standard fail-stop signature schemes, two security parameters are used to measure the security of the two different properties, which are often in the interest of different parties: k determines the computational security against collision-finding, and τ determines the bundling degree, which will be 2^{τ}. (When bundling homomorphisms are used in fail-stop signature schemes, τ will be related to σ, which determines the information-theoretic security for the signer; one can already regard τ as a parameter that measures how unlikely it is that someone, given an image z, guesses correctly which preimage someone else has chosen.)

This leads to the following definition:

Definition 8.29. A **collision-intractable family of bundling functions** has the following components:

- A probabilistic polynomial-time algorithm *gen*, the key-generation algorithm, that, on input ('1'^{k}, '1'$^{\tau}$) with $k, \tau \in \mathbb{N}$, outputs a value K, called a key (representing the description of a function).
- Families $GoodFam := (Good_{k,\tau})_{k,\tau \in \mathbb{N}}$ and $AllFam := (All_{k,\tau})_{k,\tau \in \mathbb{N}}$ of sets (called the sets of good keys and all acceptable keys, respectively). Let $Good := \bigcup_{k,\tau} Good_{k,\tau}$ and $All := \bigcup_{k,\tau} All_{k,\tau}$.
- Two families of sets, $(G_K)_{K \in All}$ and $(H_K)_{K \in All}$, and a family of functions between them, $(h_K)_{K \in All}$, i.e.,
$$h_K: G_K \to H_K.$$
- A polynomial-time algorithm h that computes the whole family of functions, i.e., on input $K \in All$ and $x \in G_K$, it outputs $h_K(x)$.
- Additional algorithms (where the first one is probabilistic) that, with a first input $K \in All$ and in time polynomial in this input alone,
  - choose random elements in G_K, where the distribution must be uniform if $K \in Good$, and
  - test membership in G_K and H_K.

  They have not been given explicit names, because they will be written "$\in_R$" and "$\in$".

These components must have the following additional properties:

a) Good and acceptable keys: All correctly generated keys are good and acceptable; more precisely, $[gen(\text{'1'}^k, \text{'1'}^{\tau})] \subseteq Good_{k,\tau} \subseteq All_{k,\tau}$ for all $k, \tau \in \mathbb{N}$, and the length of the elements of $All_{k,\tau}$ is polynomial in k and τ.

b) Length restrictions: The length of the elements of G_K and H_K for $K \in All$ is polynomial in that of K.

c) Bundling property: For all $k, \tau \in \mathbb{N}$ and all $K \in Good_{k,\tau}$: Each $z \in h_K(G_K)$ has at least 2^{τ} preimages under h_K.

d) Collision-intractability: For every probabilistic polynomial-time algorithm $\tilde{A}$, the probability that $\tilde{A}$, on input a correctly generated key K, outputs an h_K-collision is negligibly small.

   More precisely: For all polynomials *Qtau* (determining the growth of τ as a function of k): $\forall c > 0\ \exists k_0\ \forall k \geq k_0\ \forall \tau \leq Qtau(k)$:

$$P(h_K(x) = h_K(x') \wedge x \neq x' \wedge x, x' \in G_K \setminus K \leftarrow gen('1'^k, '1'^\tau); \quad (x, x') \leftarrow \tilde{A}('1'^k, '1'^\tau, K)) < k^{-c}.$$ ♦

Note that one can test in polynomial time if a collision has been found for a given key $K \in All$.

The bundling homomorphisms, which are defined next, are basically bundling functions that are homomorphisms.

Definition 8.30. A **collision-intractable family of bundling homomorphisms** is a collision-intractable family of bundling functions with the following additional properties and components:

a) For each $K \in All$, the sets G_K and H_K are Abelian groups and h_K is a homomorphism between them.
b) Polynomial-time algorithms are given that, with a first input $K \in All$, compute the group operations in G_K and H_K. (They do not need explicit names in the following.) ♦

In abstract constructions, the domains G_K are written additively and the codomains H_K multiplicatively. This notation corresponds to the discrete-logarithm case, where h_K is tuple exponentiation. Note that homomorphisms automatically have a bundling property if the domain is sufficiently larger than the codomain, as in Lemma 8.17.

Hiding Functions and Homomorphisms

Hiding functions are functions where an argument is hidden information-theoretically in the result, i.e., they have the hiding property mentioned in Section 8.2. They are not needed in the following, but they are important applications of both tuple exponentiation and iterated squaring and doubling, and they are building blocks for dual invisible signature schemes, see [ChHP92].

Specialists will see at once that the relevance of hiding functions is that they yield information-theoretically hiding commitment schemes on large domains, also called **string commitments**, in contrast to the usual bit commitments. (The string commitments in [Naor91] are of the dual type, i.e., computationally hiding and information-theoretically unforgeable.) One only has to supplement the zero-knowledge proof scheme and the local verification algorithm for the families of sets of good keys and all acceptable keys.[134] Hiding functions were first informally mentioned in [ChFN90], but without a construction.

The definition is quite similar to that of bundling functions, except that one must decide what can be hidden by the hiding function. The following definition is very general in this respect: There is an arbitrary family of domains S_K, i.e., what can be hidden may depend on the key.

---

134 Moreover, the homomorphism property can be exploited for efficient zero-knowledge proofs of knowledge showing that the secrets hidden in two commitments are equal [ChHP92, Pede92] and, given some additional conditions that are fulfilled in the following constructions, that the secrets are unequal [ChHP92].

Furthermore, note that not all information-theoretically hiding string commitments have to be constructed from hiding functions; in particular, there may be more interaction.

Another way in which the following definition is rather general is *where* an element ξ of S_K is hidden. So far, it was always the first parameter of a function h in two parameters, i.e., one chooses a second parameter y, computes $z := h(\xi, y)$, and says that ξ is hidden in z. The general idea is maintained: ξ is first extended to something larger, say x (which was $x = (\xi, y)$ so far) and $z := h(x)$ is computed. Now, however, one needs an explicit algorithm to extract ξ from x again. It is called π, because it is the projection to the first component if $x = (\xi, y)$. Conversely, one needs an algorithm *choose* that extends ξ to x, see Figure 8.8.[135]

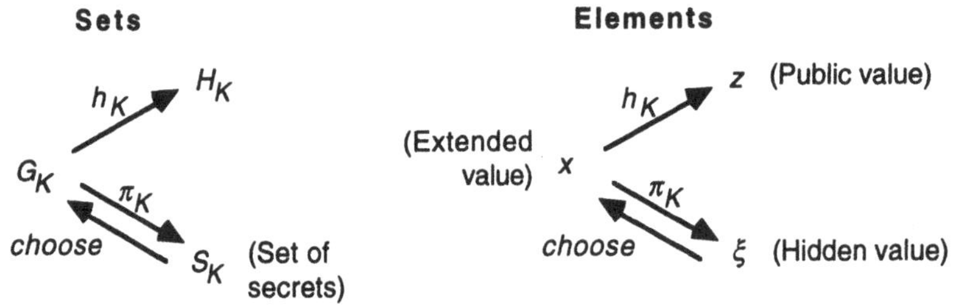

Figure 8.8. Notation with families of hiding functions

Definition 8.31. A **collision-intractable family of hiding functions** has the following components:

- A probabilistic polynomial-time algorithm *gen*, the key-generation algorithm, that, on input '1'^{k} with $k \in \mathbb{N}$, outputs a value K, called a key (representing the description of a function).
- Families $GoodFam := (Good_k)_{k \in \mathbb{N}}$ and $AllFam := (All_k)_{k \in \mathbb{N}}$ of sets (called the sets of good keys and all acceptable keys, respectively). Let $Good := \bigcup_k Good_k$ and $All := \bigcup_k All_k$.
- Three families of sets:
  - $(S_K)_{K \in All}$ are called the sets of secrets (their elements are the objects that are hidden by the hiding function),
  - $(G_K)_{K \in All}$ are the domains of the actual hiding functions (their elements are the extended values constructed from secrets), and
  - $(H_K)_{K \in All}$ are the codomains of the actual hiding functions (their elements are the values that can be made public without compromising the secrets),

  and two families of functions between them, $(h_K)_{K \in All}$ and $(\pi_K)_{K \in All}$, with

  $$h_K: G_K \to H_K,$$

  and

  $$\pi_K: G_K \to S_K,$$

[135] One may think that this generalization is an unnecessary complication, because in all the following examples, ξ is in fact a pair (x, y). However, when group structures on these sets are introduced, the group structure on the Cartesian product in the factoring case is not a direct product.

where h_K is the actual hiding function and π_K maps an extended value to the secret that it represents (see Figure 8.8).

- Polynomial-time algorithms h and π that compute the whole families of functions, i.e., on input $K \in All$ and $x \in G_K$, they output $h_K(x)$ and $\pi_K(x)$, respectively.
- A probabilistic polynomial-time algorithm *choose* that chooses a random extended value for a given secret, i.e., on input (K, ξ), where $K \in All$ and $\xi \in S_K$, it outputs an element of $\pi_K^{-1}(\xi)$, where the distribution must be uniform if $K \in Good$.
- Additional algorithms (the former of them probabilistic) that, with a first input $K \in All$ and in time polynomial in this input alone
  - choose random elements in S_K with uniform distribution, and
  - test membership in S_K, G_K and H_K, respectively.

  They have not been given names, because they will be written "$\in_R$" and "$\in$".

These components must have the following additional properties:

a) Good and acceptable keys: All correctly generated keys are good and acceptable; more precisely, $[gen(\text{'}1\text{'}^k)] \subseteq Good_k \subseteq All_k$ for all $k \in \mathbb{N}$, and the length of the elements of All_k is polynomial in k.

b) Length restrictions: The length of the elements of G_K and H_K for $K \in All$ is polynomial in that of K.

c) Hiding property: For each $K \in Good$:
   - All $\xi \in S_K$ have equally many extensions in G_K, i.e., the size of the set $\pi_K^{-1}(\xi)$ is independent of ξ.
   - If a value $z \in h_K(G_K)$ is known, the size of the set $h_K^{-1}(z) \cap \pi_K^{-1}(\xi)$ is independent of $\xi \in S_K$.

d) Collision-intractability with respect to equal π-images (i.e., one cannot find two different secrets and extensions of them that are mapped to the same public value)[136]: For every probabilistic polynomial-time algorithm $\tilde{A}$: $\forall c > 0\ \exists k_0\ \forall k \geq k_0$:

$$P(h_K(x) = h_K(x') \wedge \pi_K(x) \neq \pi_K(x') \wedge x, x' \in G_K \setminus K \leftarrow gen(\text{'}1\text{'}^k); (x, x') \leftarrow \tilde{A}(\text{'}1\text{'}^k, K)) < k^{-c}.$$

◆

Remark 8.32. The hiding property guarantees that if values ξ with an arbitrary a-priori probability distribution are hidden by extending them with *choose*, applying h_K, and making the outcome z public, the a-posteriori probability of each ξ is equal to its a-priori probability. The definition could be generalized by allowing *choose* to produce a non-uniform distribution even if $K \in Good$ and formalizing the hiding property directly as in this remark. ◆

---

136 This is the terminology of Definition 8.25c with the relation $\approx$ defined on G_K by $\xi \approx \xi' :\Leftrightarrow \pi(\xi) = \pi(\xi')$.

Similar to bundling homomorphisms, hiding homomorphisms are basically hiding functions that are homomorphisms.

Definition 8.33. A **collision-intractable family of hiding homomorphisms** is a collision-intractable family of hiding functions with the following additional properties and components:

a) For each $K \in All$, the sets S_K, G_K, and H_K are Abelian groups and both π_K and h_K are homomorphisms.

b) Polynomial-time algorithms are given that, with a first input $K \in All$, compute the group operations in S_K, G_K, and H_K. (They do not need explicit names in the following.) ♦

Lemma 8.34. For families of hiding homomorphisms, the hiding property from Definition 8.31c can be replaced by the following shorter statement:

- For each $K \in Good$, the product homomorphism $\psi_K := (h_K, \pi_K)$: $G_K \to h_K(G_K) \times S_K$ is surjective. ♦

Proof. For each $K \in Good$, the two parts of the hiding property must be shown.

a) According to the homomorphism theorem, all non-empty sets $\pi_K^{-1}(\xi)$ are of the same size. Moreover, as ψ_K is surjective, π_K is surjective, too, i.e., all these sets are non-empty.

b) First, one easily sees that ψ_K is really a homomorphism. (Generally, this is a part of the universal mapping property of direct products.) Secondly, each set $h_K^{-1}(z) \cap \pi_K^{-1}(\xi)$ is a preimage $\psi_K^{-1}(z, \xi)$. Hence the homomorphism theorem and surjectivity imply that all these sets are of the same size. □

Hash Functions

As with most other classes of function families, there is not only one definition of collision-intractable families of hash functions.

In particular, one has to decide what the results of the hash function are allowed to be. In the original definition in [Damg88], an entirely different finite codomain H_K is allowed for each key K, and there is no bound on the length of the elements of these codomains, i.e., of the hash values. This makes certain restrictions necessary when the functions are used to hash messages before they are signed, unless the signature scheme has the message space $\{0, 1\}^+$. Hence more restricted codomains like in [Damg90a, Pfit89] are used here.

Moreover, the following definition differs from the original one in the use of sets of all acceptable keys.

Note that a weaker notion of families of hash functions exists, too, so-called families of universal one-way hash functions [NaYu89]. However, in the applications to fail-stop signature schemes, collision-intractability is needed.

Definition 8.35. A **collision-intractable family of hash functions** has the following components:

- A probabilistic polynomial-time algorithm *gen* that, on input '1'^{k} with $k \in \mathbb{N}$, outputs a value K, called a key (representing the description of a function).

- A family $AllFam := (All_k)_{k \in \mathbb{N}}$ of sets (called the sets of all acceptable keys). Let $All := \bigcup_k All_k$.
- A function len: $\mathbb{N} \to \mathbb{N}$, called the length function (denoting the length of the hash values in terms of the security parameter), and a polynomial-time algorithm that computes len in unary.[137]
- A family of functions, $(hash_K)_{K \in All}$, with
$$hash_K: \{0, 1\}^+ \to \{0, 1\}^{len(k)}$$
for all $k \in \mathbb{N}$ and $K \in All_k$. The results are called hash values.
- A polynomial-time algorithm *hash* that computes the whole family of functions, i.e., on input $K \in All$ and a bit string m, it outputs the hash value $hash_K(m)$.

These components must have the following additional properties:[138]

a) Acceptable keys: All correctly generated keys are acceptable, i.e., $[gen(`1'^k)] \subseteq All_k$ for all $k \in \mathbb{N}$, and the length of the elements of All_k is polynomial in k.
b) Collision-intractability: For every probabilistic polynomial-time algorithm $\tilde{A}$, for all $c > 0$ and for k sufficiently large:
$$P(hash_K(m) = hash_K(m') \wedge m \neq m' \wedge m, m' \in \{0, 1\}^+ \setminus K \leftarrow gen(`1'^k); (m, m') \leftarrow \tilde{A}(`1'^k, K)) < k^{-c}.$$ ♦

Definition 8.36. A collision-intractable family of fixed-size hash functions has the following components:

- A probabilistic polynomial-time algorithm *gen*, the key-generation algorithm, that, on input $`1'^k$ with $k \in \mathbb{N}$, outputs a value K, called a key (representing the description of a function).
- A family $AllFam := (All_k)_{k \in \mathbb{N}}$ of sets (called the sets of all acceptable keys). Let $All := \bigcup_k All_k$.
- A function len: $\mathbb{N} \to \mathbb{N}$, called the length function (denoting the length of the hash values in terms of the security parameter), a polynomial-time algorithm that computes len in unary, and a value $k_{len} \in \mathbb{N}$ (denoting from where on the hash functions are length-reducing).
- A family of functions, $(hash_K)_{K \in All}$, with
$$hash_K: \{0, 1\}^k \to \{0, 1\}^{len(k)}$$
for all $k \in \mathbb{N}$ and $K \in All_k$. The results are called hash values.
- A polynomial-time algorithm *hash* that computes the whole family of functions, i.e., on input $K \in All_k$ and a bit string m of length k, it outputs the hash value $hash_K(m)$.

---

137 Such an algorithm can also be constructed from the others: On input $`1'^k$, call $gen(`1'^k)$ to generate a key K, compute $h_K(`0')$, and replace it by a string of ones of equal length. However, one can usually compute the length more efficiently.

138 One might wonder what the sets of all acceptable keys are for, because none of the following properties is based on them. However, it has already been required that the algorithm h computes a function with a certain codomain in polynomial time for these keys.

These components must have the following additional properties:

a) Acceptable keys: All correctly generated keys are acceptable, i.e., $[gen('1'^k)] \subseteq All_k$ for all $k \in \mathbb{N}$, and the length of the elements of All_k is polynomial in k.
b) Length-reducing: For all $k \in \mathbb{N}$ with $k \geq k_{len}$, the hash values are shorter than the inputs, i.e., $len(k) < k$.[139]
c) Collision-intractability: For every probabilistic polynomial-time algorithm $\tilde{A}$, for all $c > 0$ and for k sufficiently large:

$$P(hash_K(m) = hash_K(m') \wedge m \neq m' \wedge m, m' \in \{0, 1\}^k \setminus K \leftarrow gen('1'^k);\ (m, m') \leftarrow \tilde{A}('1'^k, K)) < k^{-c}.$$ ♦

Remark 8.37 (Short collision proofs). It was mentioned in a footnote to Definition 7.1 that only a modification to the definition of hash functions would guarantee availability of service if a standard fail-stop signature scheme is combined with message hashing using an arbitrary collision-intractable family of hash functions. The reason is that collisions can be arbitrarily long compared with the key in Definition 8.35. The modification would be to add a polynomial-time algorithm *prove_collision* that transforms any collision into a (short) string *collision_proof* and an algorithm *verify_collision* that verifies such strings in time polynomial in the key alone. The requirements are that every collision yields a valid collision proof (for all acceptable keys) and that it is infeasible to find collision proofs (for correctly generated keys). ♦

Remarks on Good Keys

Remark 8.38 (Good keys).

a) One can easily see that all the definitions in this section, 8.5.2, are invariant against making the sets of good keys or the sets of all acceptable keys smaller, provided all correctly generated keys are still considered good, and all good keys are still considered acceptable. For instance, if a collision-intractable family of bundling functions is given, and one replaces the sets $Good_{k,\tau}$ with sets $Good'_{k,\tau}$ where $[gen('1'^k, '1'^\tau)] \subseteq Good'_{k,\tau} \subseteq Good_{k,\tau}$ for all $k, \tau \in \mathbb{N}$, one has a collision-intractable family of bundling functions again. Hence it is useful to construct concrete families with the largest possible sets of good and acceptable keys.
b) The definitions of correctly generated keys and good keys were made so that zero-knowledge proof schemes in the sense of Definition 7.25 can be applied: The party that needs collision-intractability generates the key and gives the other party a zero-knowledge proof that the key is good. The family *CorrFam* of

139 In [Damg90a], length-reduction is required for all $k \in \mathbb{N}$. Of course, $k = 1$ should be excluded anyway, but constructions are simpler if larger bounds are permitted. For instance, if a family of groups where the discrete logarithm is hard does not contain any group whose elements are shorter than 10 bits, a construction of fixed-size hash functions from it will not yield any function that hashes to less than 10 bits. One could use different, trivial constructions for small k's, but it does not seem worth while.

correct distributions is, of course, that induced by the key-generation algorithm. A generation algorithm, and not only distributions, was required in the individual families so that Remark 7.30 can be applied: It should guarantee that at least an inefficient zero-knowledge proof scheme exists for each such function family.

c) One could generalize the key generation of all the classes of function families by permitting arbitrary 2-party key-generation protocols with external verifiability. Key generation would then be similar to that of arbitrary standard fail-stop signature schemes with one risk bearer (Definition 7.1), not just that of standard fail-stop signature schemes with prekey.

d) With all the following constructions of one class of function families from another one, it could be shown how a zero-knowledge proof scheme for good keys (and a local verification algorithm for all acceptable keys) of the given family yields one for the newly constructed family. Instead, however, it would probably be better to prove some general theorems about parameter transformations in zero-knowledge proof schemes. ♦

Table

The following table summarizes some properties required from some of the classes of function families defined above. However, it is not shown whether each property is required for all acceptable keys, or all good keys, or only all correctly generated keys.

	Bundling	Hiding	Hash
Security parameters	k, τ	k	k
Sets and functions	$h_K: G_K \to H_K$	$h_K: G_K \to H_K$, $\pi_K: G_K \to S_K$	$hash_K: \{0, 1\}^+ \to \{0, 1\}^{len(k)}$
Additional algorithms	"$\in_R$" in G_K, "$\in$" in G_K, H_K	$choose: S_K \to G_K$, ("inverts" π_K) "$\in_R$" in S_K, "$\in$" in all three	len
Information-theoretic requirements	$\geq 2^\tau$ preimages	$z := h_K(x)$ gives no information about $\xi := \pi_K(x)$	—
Computational requirements	Collision-intractable	Collision-intractable with respect to equal π-images	Collision-intractable

Table 8.1. Overview of the definitions of function families

8.5.3 Constructions in the Discrete-Logarithm Case

This section contains the constructions of function families, as defined in Section 8.5.2, on the abstract discrete-logarithm assumption. For an overview, see Figure 8.6; some details are summarized in Table 8.2. The earliest of the following constructions seems to have been the use of pair exponentiation as string commitments, i.e., hiding functions, in [BoCP88] (extending bit commitment schemes from [BoKK90, ChDG88]). As all these constructions are based on μ-tuple exponentiation, a general theorem about the collision-intractability of tuple exponentiation is proved first.

Collision-Intractability of General Tuple Exponentiation

This subsection considers the collision-intractability of tuple exponentiation. It is shown that it is infeasible to find $exp_{\underline{g}}$-collisions for tuples of generators of groups of prime order where the discrete logarithm is hard. First, a related simpler notion, that of multiplicative relations between given generators, is defined.

Definition 8.39. Let H be an Abelian group of order q and $\underline{g}$ a μ-tuple of elements of H. (Later, q will usually be prime and $\underline{g}$ a tuple of generators.) A **$\underline{g}$-relation** is a multiplicative dependency between the components of $\underline{g}$, i.e., a tuple $\underline{v}$ that fulfils the following predicate:

$$rel(\underline{g}, \underline{v}) \;:\Leftrightarrow\; \underline{v} \in \mathbb{Z}_q^{\;\mu} \wedge \underline{v} \neq \underline{0} \wedge \underline{g}^{\underline{v}} = 1. \qquad \blacklozenge$$

If q is prime and the isomorphism between H and $\mathbb{Z}_q$ is used, a $\underline{g}$-relation corresponds to a linear dependency between the exponents (cf. Lemma 8.2b). This is good to have in mind in the mathematical parts, but it cannot be exploited computationally.

The following lemma collects a few simple dependencies between $\underline{g}$-relations, collisions, and discrete logarithms that should not get lost in the long computational parts. (Some of them are not needed in the following.)

Lemma 8.40 (Mathematical parts). Let H be an Abelian group of order q and $\underline{g}$ a μ-tuple of elements of H.

a) $\underline{g}$-relations are exactly the non-zero elements of the kernel of $exp_{\underline{g}}$.

b) Relations and collisions are closely related:
   - If $\underline{v}$ is a $\underline{g}$-relation, then $(\underline{v}, \underline{0})$ is an $exp_{\underline{g}}$-collision.
   - If $(\underline{x}, \underline{x}')$ is an $exp_{\underline{g}}$-collision, then $\underline{x} - \underline{x}'$ is a $\underline{g}$-relation.

c) Discrete logarithms are special cases of relations: If $\underline{g} = (g, g^*)$, where g is a generator of H, and if $e = log_g(g^*)$, then $\underline{v} := (e, -1) = (e, q-1)$ is a $\underline{g}$-relation.

d) Conversely, if q is prime and $\underline{g} = (g, g^*)$, where g is a generator of H, each $\underline{g}$-relation yields the discrete logarithm: If $\underline{g}^{\underline{v}} = 1$ with $\underline{v} = (v_1, v_2) \neq (0, 0)$, then

$$v_2 \neq 0 \wedge log_g(g^*) = -v_1 v_2^{-1} \;\; (\text{in } \mathbb{Z}_q). \qquad \blacklozenge$$

Proof. a) and b) follow immediately from the definitions. (Note that $\underline{g}^{\underline{0}} = 1$ and that $exp_{\underline{g}}$ is a homomorphism by Lemma 8.2a.) For c), note that $g^* = g^e$ immediately implies $g^e g^{*-1} = 1$.

As to d), the precondition immediately implies $g^{*\,v_2} = g^{-v_1}$. First, assume that $v_2 = 0$: Then $g^{-v_1} = g^{*0} = 1$. As g is a generator, i.e., $\mathrm{ord}(g) = q$, this implies $-v_1 \equiv 0 \bmod q$. Thus $(v_1, v_2) = (0, 0)$, which contradicts the precondition. Hence in fact $v_2 \neq 0$. Now the fact that q is prime implies that $-v_1 v_2^{-1}$ exists and $g^* = g^{-v_1 v_2^{-1}}$. □

Before stating the main theorem of this section, one must decide how large the tuples $\underline{g}$ of generators are for which someone tries to find $exp_{\underline{g}}$-collisions. For $\mu = 2$, the proof is simple (see Case 1 below) and was known in [BoCP88].

The first generalization is to assume that μ, the size of the tuples, is arbitrary, but fixed before the security parameter k. This was done in [ChHP92]. Tuple exponentiation for $\mu \geq 2$ was also considered in [ChEG88] already, but the theorem stated there (without proof) neither easily implies nor is easily implied by the theorems needed in the other articles.

Now, similar to the treatment of the parameters σ and N in the security for risk bearers in standard fail-stop signature schemes, a more general version is proved where μ is only bounded by a polynomial $Qmu(k)$. One can easily see in the proof that one obtains a more efficient reduction by restricting the theorem to arbitrary, but fixed dependencies $\mu = fmu(k)$, where *fmu* is polynomial-time computable in unary. Proof sketches for that case are also given in [Bran93, BeGG94]. As I already had the following proof at that time, and its reduction even seems to be slightly tighter, I simply kept it here. Tuples of non-constant length will be needed in Construction 8.50.

Theorem 8.41 (Collision-intractability of poly(k)-tuple exponentiation in groups of prime order). Let a family of groups of prime order be given where the discrete logarithm is hard. For every probabilistic polynomial-time algorithm $\tilde{A}$ (that tries to compute collisions) and every polynomial Qmu (determining the growth of μ as a function of k):

$\forall c > 0\ \exists k_0\ \forall k \geq k_0\ \forall \mu \leq Qmu(k)$:

$$P((\underline{x}, \underline{x}') \text{ is an } exp_{\underline{g}}\text{-collision} \setminus (q, desc) \leftarrow gen(\text{`}1\text{'}^k);\ \underline{g} \in_R (H_{q,desc} \setminus \{1\})^{\mu}; \\ (\underline{x}, \underline{x}') \leftarrow \tilde{A}(\text{`}1\text{'}^k, \text{`}1\text{'}^{\mu}, q, desc, \underline{g})) \\ < k^{-c}.$$

♦

The input parameter '1'$^{\mu}$ is redundant, because it can be derived from $\underline{g}$, but it corresponds to the conventions about system parameters used in the rest of this text and yields simpler notation in the proof.

In view of Lemma 8.40b, one can easily see that it suffices to prove that it is infeasible to find relations in the same family of groups and for tuples of the same sizes μ. (Actually, the infeasibility of both tasks is equivalent, but only this implication is needed in the following.)

Lemma 8.42 (Relation-intractability in groups of prime order). Let a family of groups of prime order be given where the discrete logarithm is hard. For every probabilistic polynomial-time algorithm $\tilde{A}$ and every polynomial Qmu:

$\forall c > 0\ \exists k_0\ \forall k \geq k_0\ \forall \mu \leq Qmu(k)$:

$$P(rel(\underline{g}, \underline{v}) \setminus (q, desc) \leftarrow gen(\text{`}1\text{'}^k);\ \underline{g} \in_R (H_{q,desc} \setminus \{1\})^{\mu}; \\ \underline{v} \leftarrow \tilde{A}(\text{`}1\text{'}^k, \text{`}1\text{'}^{\mu}, q, desc, \underline{g})) \\ < k^{-c}.$$

♦

Proof of Theorem 8.41 from Lemma 8.42. Assume that an algorithm $\tilde{A}$ contradicts Theorem 8.41. Then the algorithm $\tilde{A}'$ that first calls $\tilde{A}$ and then sets $\underline{v} := \underline{x} - \underline{x}'$ if the output of $\tilde{A}$ is $(\underline{x}, \underline{x}')$, finds relations with the same probabilities. □

Proof of Lemma 8.42. Assume that an algorithm $\tilde{A}$ contradicts Lemma 8.42 for a polynomial *Qmu* and a constant $c > 0$. Throughout the proof, $\mu \geq 2$ can be assumed, because relations for $\mu = 1$ do not exist.

Case 1: *Qmu* = 2. If *Qmu* is the constant 2, i.e., all the tuples are pairs, Lemma 8.40d implies that the algorithm $\tilde{A}'$ that first calls $\tilde{A}$ and then outputs $x := -v_1 v_2^{-1}$ whenever $v_2 \neq 0$ contradicts the discrete-logarithm assumption. (It only makes a negligible difference in the probabilities that both components of $\underline{g}$ are generators in the lemma, but not in the discrete-logarithm assumption.) Hence the assumed algorithm $\tilde{A}$ cannot exist.

Case 2: General *Qmu*. In this case, the assumed algorithm $\tilde{A}$ is used to construct an algorithm $\tilde{A}^*$ that contradicts Case 1, i.e., $\tilde{A}^*$ finds relations between pairs of generators.

$\tilde{A}^*$: On input ('1'^{k}, '1'^{2}, q, *desc*, $\underline{g}^*$) with $\underline{g}^* = (g_1^*, g_2^*)$:

For $\mu := 2$ to $Qmu(k)$, carry out the following 4 steps:

1. Choose $\underline{R} := (r_{i,j}) \in \mathbb{Z}_q^{\mu \times 2}$ randomly with $\underline{r}_i \neq \underline{0}$, i.e., $(r_{i,1}, r_{i,2}) \neq (0, 0)$, for all i.
2. Compute the μ-tuple
$$\underline{g} := ext(\underline{g}^*, \underline{R}),$$
where $$g_i := \underline{g}^{*\,\underline{r}_i},$$
i.e., $g_i = g_1^{*r_{i,1}} g_2^{*r_{i,2}}$. (The name "*ext*" stands for an extension from 2 to μ generators.) If a component g_i is not a generator, i.e., $g_i = 1$, output $\underline{v}^* := \underline{r}_i$ and stop.
3. Run $\tilde{A}$ on input ('1'^{k}, '1'$^\mu$, q, *desc*, $\underline{g}$) and call the result $\underline{v}$.
4. Compute the matrix product
$$\underline{v}^* := red(\underline{v}, \underline{R}) := \underline{v}\,\underline{R}.$$
(The name "*red*" stands for a reduction of the relation from μ to the original 2 generators.) If $\underline{v}^*$ is a $\underline{g}^*$-relation, output it and stop.

Outline of the rest of the proof. $\tilde{A}^*$ obviously runs in time polynomial in the length of its inputs. It remains to be shown that it finds $\underline{g}^*$-relations with significant probability. The outline of this proof is as follows:

- If $\tilde{A}^*$ stops in Step 2 for any μ, it always outputs a $\underline{g}^*$-relation.
- Otherwise, the tuple $\underline{g}$ that is input to $\tilde{A}$ in Step 3 is a random tuple (even for fixed $\underline{g}^*$); thus $\tilde{A}$ finds a $\underline{g}$-relation inside $\tilde{A}^*$ with the same probability as if it were used on its own.
- One can easily see that whenever $\tilde{A}$ was successful, the reduction in Step 4 leads to a value $\underline{v}^*$ with $\underline{g}^{*\underline{v}^*} = 1$. Thus $\underline{v}^*$ is a $\underline{g}^*$-relation whenever it is non-zero.
- It is not excluded that $\underline{v}^* = \underline{0}$, i.e., that $\tilde{A}^*$ is not successful although $\tilde{A}$ was. However, it is shown that this happens with negligible probability. The idea for this (main) part of the proof is that $\tilde{A}$ must base its decision about $\underline{v}$ on its inputs alone, i.e., on the description of the group and $\underline{g}$, not on the other information known in $\tilde{A}^*$. In particular, there are many possible $\underline{R}$'s and $\underline{g}^*$'s that could

have led to $\underline{g}$. For each fixed $\underline{g}$ and $\underline{v}$, it will be shown that for a vast majority of the possible $\underline{R}$'s and $\underline{g}^*$'s, the reduction in Step 4 leads to a value $\underline{v}^* \neq \underline{0}$.

Now this is shown more formally.[140]

Notation and top level of the proof. The connection between the success probabilities of $\tilde{A}$ and $\tilde{A}^*$ is shown for any given group, i.e., for fixed ('1'^{k}, q, *desc*), and even for each pair $\underline{g}^*$, i.e., when the probability is only over the random choices of $\tilde{A}^*$. If k, q, and *desc* are clear from the context, $H_{q,desc}$ is abbreviated as H and the success probabilities as

$$P_{succ}(\mu, \underline{g}) := P(rel(\underline{g}, \underline{v}) \setminus \underline{v} \leftarrow \tilde{A}(\text{`1'}^k, \text{`1'}^\mu, q, desc, \underline{g})),$$
$$P^*_{succ}(\underline{g}^*) := P(rel(\underline{g}^*, \underline{v}^*) \setminus \underline{v}^* \leftarrow \tilde{A}^*(\text{`1'}^k, \text{`1'}^2, q, desc, \underline{g}^*)),$$

for any μ-tuple $\underline{g}$ and any pair $\underline{g}^*$ of generators of H. The averages over all the tuples are

$$P_{succ,av}(\mu) := P(rel(\underline{g}, \underline{v}) \setminus \underline{g} \in_R (H\setminus\{1\})^\mu; \underline{v} \leftarrow \tilde{A}(\text{`1'}^k, \text{`1'}^\mu, q, desc, \underline{g})),$$
$$P^*_{succ,av} := P(rel(\underline{g}^*, \underline{v}^*) \setminus \underline{g}^* \in_R (H\setminus\{1\})^2; \underline{v}^* \leftarrow \tilde{A}^*(\text{`1'}^k, \text{`1'}^2, q, desc, \underline{g}^*)).$$

It is proved below that for any pair of generators, $\underline{g}^*$, and any μ with $2 \le \mu \le Qmu(k)$,

$$P^*_{succ}(\underline{g}^*) \ge (1 - q^{-1})\, P_{succ,av}(\mu). \qquad (0)$$

Given (0), the proof of the lemma is finished as follows: First, taking the average over $\underline{g}^*$ yields

$$P^*_{succ,av} \ge (1 - q^{-1})\, P_{succ,av}(\mu) \ge (1 - 2^{-k})\, P_{succ,av}(\mu).$$

Secondly, the average over the group generation is taken on both sides. (To write this step formally, one would have to give $P^*_{succ,av}$ and $P_{succ,av}(\mu)$ additional indices q and *desc*.) By the assumption about $\tilde{A}$, there is an infinite set $\mathcal{K}$ of values k with the following property: There exists $\mu \le Qmu(k)$ such that $\tilde{A}$, given a μ-tuple of generators, outputs a relation with a probability of at least k^{-c}. For all $k \in \mathcal{K}$, one obtains

$$\begin{aligned}
&P(rel(\underline{g}^*, \underline{v}^*) \setminus (q, desc) \leftarrow gen(\text{`1'}^k); \underline{g}^* \in_R (H_{q,desc}\setminus\{1\})^2;\\
&\qquad \underline{v}^* \leftarrow \tilde{A}^*(\text{`1'}^k, \text{`1'}^2, q, desc, \underline{g}^*))\\
&\ge (1 - 2^{-k})\, P(rel(\underline{g}, \underline{v}) \setminus (q, desc) \leftarrow gen(\text{`1'}^k); \underline{g} \in_R (H_{q,desc}\setminus\{1\})^\mu;\\
&\qquad \underline{v} \leftarrow \tilde{A}(\text{`1'}^k, \text{`1'}^\mu, q, desc, \underline{g}))\\
&\ge (1 - 2^{-k})\, k^{-c}.
\end{aligned}$$

In particular, this is larger than $k^{-(c+1)}$ for $k \ge 2$, and thus the desired contradiction to the statement proved in Case 1. Hence the assumed algorithm $\tilde{A}$ cannot exist, which proves the lemma.

---

140 This is a strong statement for practical security: $\tilde{A}^*$ translates instances for the security parameter k into instances for $\tilde{A}$ for the same k and only induces a negligible increase in the error probability. Moreover, if one knows how μ depends on k, i.e., a fixed dependency $\mu = fmu(k)$ is given, $\tilde{A}$ only has to be called once, i.e., the reduction is very efficient.

For specialists: The fact that the success probability of $\tilde{A}^*$ on any *given* pair of generators is almost as high as the success probability of $\tilde{A}$ overall is not surprising: Like the discrete-logarithm problem, the problems are random self-reducible; see [ToWo87] for a definition.

Thus Inequality (0) remains to be proved. Recall that k, q, and *desc* are regarded as fixed in this inequality. Furthermore, let a value μ with $2 \le \mu \le Qmu(k)$ and a pair of generators, $\underline{g}^*$, of H be fixed.

Outline formally. The proof outlined above deals with the intermediate results $\underline{g}$ and $\underline{v}$ in the iteration of $\tilde{A}^*$ with the value μ. Hence an algorithm $\tilde{A}^*_\mu$ is defined that only performs this iteration of $\tilde{A}^*$ and outputs $\underline{g}$ and $\underline{v}$, too. (For completeness, define $\underline{v} := \tilde{A}(\text{'1'}^k, \text{'1'}^\mu, q, desc, \underline{g}) := \underline{0}$ if $\underline{g}$ is not a tuple of generators, i.e., if $\tilde{A}^*$ stops in Step 2.) Moreover, the constant input '1'^{2} is omitted with $\tilde{A}^*_\mu$.

Let S_μ be the probability space defined by

$$(\underline{g}, \underline{v}, \underline{v}^*) \leftarrow \tilde{A}^*_\mu(\text{'1'}^k, q, desc, \underline{g}^*),$$

and let $P^*_{succ}(\mu, \underline{g}^*)$ be the success probability of $\tilde{A}^*_\mu$, i.e.,

$$P^*_{succ}(\mu, \underline{g}^*) := \mathrm{P}_{S_\mu}(rel(\underline{g}^*, \underline{v}^*)).$$

The first point of the outline formally means that for all tuples $(\underline{g}, \underline{v}, \underline{v}^*) \in [S_\mu]$,

$$(\underline{g} \notin (H\backslash\{1\})^\mu \Rightarrow rel(\underline{g}^*, \underline{v}^*)). \tag{1}$$

If (1) has been shown, one can concentrate on the other case, where $\underline{g}$ is a tuple of generators. Formally, this concentration is expressed by applying the following formula, which holds for any events B, C with $\neg C \Rightarrow B$ in any probability space:

$$\begin{aligned}\mathrm{P}(B) &= \mathrm{P}(C \wedge B) + \mathrm{P}(\neg C \wedge B) = \mathrm{P}(C)\,\mathrm{P}(B \mid C) + \mathrm{P}(\neg C)\\ &\ge (\mathrm{P}(C) + \mathrm{P}(\neg C))\,\mathrm{P}(B \mid C) = \mathrm{P}(B \mid C) = \mathrm{P}(C)^{-1}\,\mathrm{P}(B \wedge C).\end{aligned}$$

Here this implies

$$P^*_{succ}(\mu, \underline{g}^*) \ge \mathrm{P}_{S_\mu}(\underline{g} \in (H\backslash\{1\})^\mu)^{-1}\ \mathrm{P}_{S_\mu}(rel(\underline{g}^*, \underline{v}^*) \wedge \underline{g} \in (H\backslash\{1\})^\mu). \tag{1*}$$

The second point of the outline says that all tuples $\underline{g}$ of generators have the same probability. If this is true, it must be the total probability that a tuple of generators is chosen divided by the number of such tuples. Thus one can hope to show for any tuple $\underline{g}' \in (H\backslash\{1\})^\mu$:

$$\mathrm{P}_{S_\mu}(\underline{g}') = \frac{\mathrm{P}_{S_\mu}(\underline{g} \in (H\backslash\{1\})^\mu)}{(q-1)^\mu}. \tag{2}$$

If (2) has been proved, it can be exploited in (1*) as follows (where $\underline{g}'$ is now called $\underline{g}$ again):

$$\begin{aligned}P^*_{succ}(\mu, \underline{g}^*) &\ge \mathrm{P}_{S_\mu}(\underline{g} \in (H\backslash\{1\})^\mu)^{-1} \sum_{\underline{g} \in (H\backslash\{1\})^\mu} \mathrm{P}_{S_\mu}(\underline{g})\,\mathrm{P}_{S_\mu}(rel(\underline{g}^*, \underline{v}^*) \mid \underline{g})\\ &= (q-1)^{-\mu} \sum_{\underline{g} \in (H\backslash\{1\})^\mu} \mathrm{P}_{S_\mu}(rel(\underline{g}^*, \underline{v}^*) \mid \underline{g})\\ &= (q-1)^{-\mu} \sum_{\underline{g} \in (H\backslash\{1\})^\mu} \sum_{\underline{v}} \mathrm{P}_{S_\mu}(\underline{v} \mid \underline{g})\,\mathrm{P}_{S_\mu}(rel(\underline{g}^*, \underline{v}^*) \mid \underline{g}, \underline{v})\\ &\ge (q-1)^{-\mu} \sum_{\underline{g} \in (H\backslash\{1\})^\mu} \sum_{\underline{v}:rel(\underline{g},\underline{v})} \mathrm{P}_{S_\mu}(\underline{v} \mid \underline{g})\,\mathrm{P}_{S_\mu}(rel(\underline{g}^*, \underline{v}^*) \mid \underline{g}, \underline{v}).\end{aligned} \tag{2*}$$

Intuitively, the last inequality means a restriction to those values $\underline{v}$ where $\tilde{A}$ was successful. Now the third point of the outline is used. Formally, it means that

$$(rel(\underline{g}, \underline{v}) \Rightarrow (\underline{v}^* \neq \underline{0} \Rightarrow rel(\underline{g}^*, \underline{v}^*)). \tag{3}$$

If (3) has been proved, it can be applied in (2*):

$$P^*_{succ}(\mu, \underline{g}^*) \geq (q-1)^{-\mu} \sum_{\underline{g} \in (H \setminus \{1\})^\mu} \sum_{\underline{v}: rel(\underline{g}, \underline{v})} P_{S_\mu}(\underline{v} \mid \underline{g}) \, P_{S_\mu}(\underline{v}^* \neq \underline{0} \mid \underline{g}, \underline{v}). \tag{3*}$$

Finally, as the fourth point of the outline, it will be proved that whenever $\underline{g}$ is a tuple of generators and $rel(\underline{g}, \underline{v})$ holds, then

$$P_{S_\mu}(\underline{v}^* \neq \underline{0} \mid \underline{g}, \underline{v}) = 1 - q^{-1}. \tag{4}$$

Substituting (4) into (3*) yields

$$P^*_{succ}(\mu, \underline{g}^*) \geq (q-1)^{-\mu} (1 - q^{-1}) \sum_{\underline{g} \in (H \setminus \{1\})^\mu} \sum_{\underline{v}: rel(\underline{g}, \underline{v})} P_{S_\mu}(\underline{v} \mid \underline{g}). \tag{4*}$$

It seems fairly clear that for any μ-tuple of generators, $\underline{g}$,

$$\sum_{\underline{v}: rel(\underline{g}, \underline{v})} P_{S_\mu}(\underline{v} \mid \underline{g}) = P_{succ}(\mu, \underline{g}), \tag{5}$$

because the choice of $\underline{v}$ within $\tilde{A}^*_\mu$, once $\underline{g}$ is given, is carried out by $\tilde{A}$, and thus the sum on the left side is the probability that $\tilde{A}$ successfully computes a $\underline{g}$-relation $\underline{v}$, but (5) will be proved formally below. Then one obtains from (4*)

$$\begin{aligned} P^*_{succ}(\mu, \underline{g}^*) &\geq (q-1)^{-\mu} (1 - q^{-1}) \sum_{\underline{g} \in (H \setminus \{1\})^\mu} P_{succ}(\mu, \underline{g}) \\ &\geq (1 - q^{-1}) \sum_{\underline{g} \in (H \setminus \{1\})^\mu} |(H \setminus \{1\})^\mu|^{-1} P_{succ}(\mu, \underline{g}) \\ &= (1 - q^{-1}) \, P_{succ,av}(\mu). \end{aligned}$$

Finally, the overall success probability of $\tilde{A}^*$ is at least as large as that of each iteration, because $\tilde{A}^*$ cannot stop unsuccessful in any previous iteration, according to (1). Moreover, the additional outputs of $\tilde{A}^*_\mu$ do not make any difference in the success probabilities. Hence for $2 \leq \mu \leq Qmu(k)$,

$$P^*_{succ}(\underline{g}^*) \geq (1 - q^{-1}) \, P_{succ,av}(\mu).$$

This is (0), which finishes the proof.

Now Formulas (1) to (5) have to be proved. Those that do not involve probabilities, (1) and (3), are proved first.

Proof of (1). Let $(\underline{g}, \underline{v}, \underline{v}^*) \in [S_\mu]$ with $\underline{g} \notin (H \setminus \{1\})^\mu$ be given. This means $g_i = 1$ for some i. As g_i is defined as $\underline{g}^{*\underline{r}_i}$, and $\underline{r}_i \neq \underline{0}$ by construction, the output $\underline{v}^* = \underline{r}_i$ of $\tilde{A}^*_\mu$ is indeed a $\underline{g}^*$-relation.

Proof of (3). Let $(\underline{g}, \underline{v}, \underline{v}^*) \in [S_\mu]$ be given, where $\underline{g}$ is a tuple of generators and $rel(\underline{g}, \underline{v})$ and $\underline{v}^* \neq \underline{0}$ hold. It has to be shown that $\underline{g}^{*\underline{v}^*} = 1$. The preconditions imply that $\underline{v}^* = red(\underline{v}, \underline{R})$ for some matrix $\underline{R} \in \mathbb{Z}_q^{\mu \times 2}$, i.e., for $j := 1, 2$,

$$v_j^* = \sum_{i=1}^{\mu} v_i\, r_{i,j}.$$

Thus, using $\underline{g} = ext(\underline{g}^*, \underline{R})$ in the fourth equality and $rel(\underline{g}, \underline{v})$ in the last one,

$$\underline{g}^{*\underline{v}^*} = \prod_{j=1}^{2} g_j^{*v_j^*} = \prod_{j=1}^{2} \prod_{i=1}^{\mu} g_j^{*v_i r_{i,j}} = \prod_{i=1}^{\mu} \prod_{j=1}^{2} (g_j^{*r_{i,j}})^{v_i} = \prod_{i=1}^{\mu} g_i^{v_i} = \underline{g}^{\underline{v}} = 1.$$

Proof of (2) and (4). The proofs of (2) and (4) both involve counting matrices $\underline{R}$ that lead to the events under consideration. The following sets are defined (for all $\underline{g} \in H^{\mu}$ and $\underline{v} \in \mathbb{Z}_q{}^{\mu}$):

$$\begin{aligned}
\mathcal{R} &:= \{\underline{R} \in \mathbb{Z}_q{}^{\mu \times 2} \mid (r_{i,1}, r_{i,2}) \neq (0, 0) \text{ for all } i\},\\
\mathcal{R}_{poss}(\underline{g}^*, \underline{g}) &:= \{\underline{R} \in \mathcal{R} \mid ext(\underline{g}^*, \underline{R}) = \underline{g}\},\\
\mathcal{R}_{unlucky}(\underline{g}^*, \underline{g}, \underline{v}) &:= \{\underline{R} \in \mathcal{R} \mid ext(\underline{g}^*, \underline{R}) = \underline{g} \wedge \underline{v}^* := red(\underline{v}, \underline{R}) = \underline{0}\}, \text{ and}\\
\mathcal{R}_{lucky}(\underline{g}^*, \underline{g}, \underline{v}) &:= \mathcal{R}_{poss}(\underline{g}^*, \underline{g}) \setminus \mathcal{R}_{unlucky}(\underline{g}^*, \underline{g}, \underline{v}).
\end{aligned}$$

Intuitively, $\mathcal{R}$ is the set of matrices from which $\underline{R}$ is chosen in Step 1 of $\tilde{A}_{\mu}^*$, and $\mathcal{R}_{poss}(\underline{g}^*, \underline{g})$ is the subset of the matrices that are possible if one knows that $\underline{g}^*$ has been transformed into $\underline{g}$. Among the possible matrices, $\mathcal{R}_{unlucky}(\underline{g}^*, \underline{g}, \underline{v})$ contains those that will result in $\underline{v}^* = \underline{0}$ if $\tilde{A}$ outputs $\underline{v}$ when it is called in Step 3 of $\tilde{A}_{\mu}^*$, and $\mathcal{R}_{lucky}(\underline{g}^*, \underline{g}, \underline{v})$ contains the others.

Below, it will be shown that if both $\underline{g}^*$ and $\underline{g}$ are tuples of generators and if $rel(\underline{g}, \underline{v})$ holds, then

$$|\mathcal{R}_{poss}(\underline{g}^*, \underline{g})| = q^{\mu} \tag{6}$$

and

$$|\mathcal{R}_{unlucky}(\underline{g}^*, \underline{g}, \underline{v})| = q^{\mu-1}. \tag{7}$$

First, however, (2) and (4) are derived from (6) and (7). As to (2), note that $P_{S_{\mu}}(\underline{g}')$ is completely determined by the first two steps of $\tilde{A}_{\mu}^*$, i.e.,

$$P_{S_{\mu}}(\underline{g}') = P(\underline{g} = \underline{g}' \setminus \underline{R} \in_R \mathcal{R};\ \underline{g} := ext(\underline{g}^*, \underline{R})) = \frac{|\mathcal{R}_{poss}(\underline{g}^*, \underline{g}')|}{|\mathcal{R}|} = \frac{q^{\mu}}{(q^2-1)^{\mu}}.$$

As this is independent of $\underline{g}'$ and there are $(q-1)^{\mu}$ tuples of generators altogether, (2) follows immediately.

To prove (4), one has to compute (for any μ-tuple of generators, $\underline{g}'$, and if $rel(\underline{g}', \underline{v}')$ holds)

$$P_{S_{\mu}}(\underline{v}^* \neq \underline{0} \mid \underline{g}', \underline{v}') = \frac{P_{S_{\mu}}(\underline{g}', \underline{v}', \underline{v}^* \neq \underline{0})}{P_{S_{\mu}}(\underline{g}', \underline{v}')}.$$

The probabilities $P_{S_{\mu}}$ are defined as follows:

$$\begin{aligned}
P_{S_{\mu}}(\underline{g}', \underline{v}') &= P(\underline{g} = \underline{g}', \underline{v} = \underline{v}' \setminus \underline{R} \in_R \mathcal{R};\ \underline{g} := ext(\underline{g}^*, \underline{R});\\
&\qquad \underline{v} \leftarrow \tilde{A}(\text{`1'}^k, \text{`1'}^{\mu}, q, desc, \underline{g});\ \underline{v}^* := red(\underline{v}, \underline{R}))\\
&= \sum_{\underline{R}:\underline{g}'=ext(\underline{g}^*,\underline{R})} |\mathcal{R}|^{-1}\ P_{\tilde{A}(\text{`1'}^k, \text{`1'}^{\mu}, q, desc, \underline{g}')}(\underline{v}'),
\end{aligned}$$

and, similarly,

$$P_{S_\mu}(\underline{g}', \underline{v}', \underline{v}^* \neq \underline{0}) = \sum_{\substack{\underline{R}:\underline{g}'=ext(\underline{g}^*,\underline{R}) \\ red(\underline{v}',\underline{R})\neq \underline{0}}} |\mathcal{R}|^{-1} \, P_{\tilde{A}('1'^k,'1'^\mu,q,desc,\underline{g}')}(\underline{v}').$$

Thus the conditional probability is

$$P_{S_\mu}(\underline{v}^* \neq \underline{0} \mid \underline{g}', \underline{v}') = \frac{|\mathcal{R}_{lucky}(\underline{g}^*, \underline{g}', \underline{v}')|}{|\mathcal{R}_{poss}(\underline{g}^*, \underline{g}')|} = \frac{q^\mu - q^{\mu-1}}{q^\mu} = 1 - q^{-1}.$$

(Note that (6) and (7) could be applied because $\underline{g}^*$ and $\underline{g}'$ consist of generators and $\underline{v}' \neq \underline{0}$.) This proves (4).

Proof of (6) and (7). First, note that the restrictions "$\underline{R} \in \mathcal{R}$" in the definitions of $\mathcal{R}_{poss}(\underline{g}^*, \underline{g})$ and $\mathcal{R}_{unlucky}(\underline{g}^*, \underline{g}, \underline{v})$ can be replaced by "$\underline{R} \in \mathbb{Z}_q^{\mu \times 2}$": As $\underline{g}$ is a tuple of generators, the condition $ext(\underline{g}^*, \underline{R}) = \underline{g}$ implies $\underline{r}_i \neq \underline{0}$ for each i.

The remaining equations defining these sets can be written as linear equations for the entries of the matrix $\underline{R}$: Let $e := log_{g_1^*}(g_2^*)$ and $\gamma_i := log_{g_1^*}(g_i)$ for $i := 1, \ldots, \mu$. (Note that nobody needs to compute these logarithms, they just exist.) Then

$$ext(\underline{g}^*, \underline{R}) = \underline{g} \Leftrightarrow \forall i\colon g_1^{*r_{i,1}} g_1^{*e\, r_{i,2}} = g_1^{*\gamma_i} \Leftrightarrow \forall i\colon r_{i,1} + e\, r_{i,2} = \gamma_i \text{ (in } \mathbb{Z}_q).$$

Written as a matrix, and with two extra rows for $red(\underline{v}, \underline{R}) = \underline{0}$, this system of equations is

$$\left(\begin{array}{ccc|ccc} 1 & & 0 & e & & 0 \\ & \ddots & & & \ddots & \\ 0 & & 1 & 0 & & e \\ \hline v_1 & \cdots & v_\mu & 0 & \cdots & 0 \\ 0 & \cdots & 0 & v_1 & \cdots & v_\mu \end{array}\right) \begin{pmatrix} r_{1,1} \\ | \\ r_{\mu,1} \\ r_{1,2} \\ | \\ r_{\mu,2} \end{pmatrix} = \begin{pmatrix} \gamma_1 \\ | \\ \gamma_\mu \\ 0 \\ 0 \end{pmatrix}.$$

Obviously, the first μ rows are linearly independent. This proves (6). As $\underline{v} \neq \underline{0}$, the last row is not a linear combination of the first μ rows. This would already suffice if (7) had been formulated as an inequality, but one can also see that Row $\mu + 1$ is a linear combination of the others: By subtracting appropriate multiples of the first μ rows, one transforms it into

$$(0 \;\ldots\; 0 \mid -e\, v_1 \;\ldots\; -e\, v_\mu \,\|\, -\sum_{i=1}^{\mu} \gamma_i v_i),$$

and the right side of this is 0, because $\underline{v}$ is a $\underline{g}$-relation. Hence this row is now a multiple of the last row. Thus (7) has been proved, too.

Proof of (5). Let $\underline{g}$ be a μ-tuple of generators. One has to compute

$$\sum_{\underline{v}:rel(\underline{g},\underline{v})} P_{S_\mu}(\underline{v} \mid \underline{g}) = \Big(\sum_{\underline{v}:rel(\underline{g},\underline{v})} P_{S_\mu}(\underline{g}, \underline{v}) \Big) \,/\, P_{S_\mu}(\underline{g}).$$

As in the proof of (2) and (4), the denominator is

$$P_{S_\mu}(\underline{g}) = |\mathcal{R}_{poss}(\underline{g}^*, \underline{g})| \; |\mathcal{R}|^{-1},$$

and the numerator is

$$\sum_{\underline{v}:rel(\underline{g},\underline{v})} P_{S_\mu}(\underline{g}, \underline{v}) = \sum_{\underline{v}:rel(\underline{g},\underline{v})} \sum_{\underline{R}:\underline{g}=ext(\underline{g}^*,\underline{R})} |\mathcal{R}|^{-1} P_{\tilde{A}(\text{'}1\text{'}^k,\text{'}1\text{'}^\mu,q,desc,\underline{g})}(\underline{v})$$

$$= \sum_{\underline{v}:rel(\underline{g},\underline{v})} P_{\tilde{A}(\text{'}1\text{'}^k,\text{'}1\text{'}^\mu,q,desc,\underline{g})}(\underline{v}) \Big(\sum_{\underline{R}:\underline{g}=ext(\underline{g}^*,\underline{R})} |\mathcal{R}|^{-1} \Big)$$

$$= P(rel(\underline{g},\underline{v}) \setminus \underline{v} \leftarrow \tilde{A}(\text{'}1\text{'}^k,\text{'}1\text{'}^\mu,q,desc,\underline{g}))(|\mathcal{R}_{poss}(\underline{g}^*,\underline{g})|\ |\mathcal{R}|^{-1})$$

$$= P_{succ}(\mu, \underline{g})\ |\mathcal{R}_{poss}(\underline{g}^*, \underline{g})|\ |\mathcal{R}|^{-1}.$$

Hence, as claimed in (5), the quotient is

$$\sum_{\underline{v}:rel(\underline{g},\underline{v})} P_{S_\mu}(\underline{v} \mid \underline{g}) = P_{succ}(\mu, \underline{g}).$$

This finishes the proof of Lemma 8.42 (and thus also of Theorem 8.41). □

Remark 8.43. Theorem 8.41 really does not hold for arbitrary group orders q, instead of primes ones. As an example, consider a family of cyclic groups $H_{2q,desc}$ of order $2q$, such as $\mathbb{Z}_p^*$ for $p = 2q + 1$. Then each $H_{2q,desc}$ has exactly one element w of order 2, and each generator g fulfils $g^q = w$. Already for two generators g_1 and g_2, this yields $g_1{}^q g_2{}^0 = w = g_1{}^0 g_2{}^q$. Hence one can easily find the collision $((q, 0), (0, q))$.

More generally, if the group order is fq for a small factor f, then $g := g_1{}^q$ and $g^* := g_2{}^q$ are generators of the small subgroup of order f. Hence one can easily find the discrete logarithm $e := log_g(g^*)$ and obtain $g_1{}^{q\,e} g_2{}^0 = g_1{}^0 g_2{}^q$. ♦

Pair Exponentiation as Bundling Homomorphisms

After all the mathematical and computational preparations, it is quite clear that pair exponentiation in a family of groups of prime order where the discrete logarithm is hard yields a collision-intractable family of bundling homomorphisms. (It was first used in this way in [HePe93].) It only remains to be decided how the security parameters are related, because the family of groups has only one, k, whereas the family of bundling homomorphisms has two, say k^* and τ^* for distinction. The following facts are known:

- The purpose of τ^* is to guarantee that the bundling degree is at least 2^{τ^*}.
- The bundling degree of pair exponentiation is the group order q (Corollary 8.4).
- The family of groups guarantees $q > 2^k$.

Hence, if k^* and τ^* are given, it seems reasonable to use $k := \max(k^*, \tau^*)$ when selecting a group. This leads to the following construction.

Construction 8.44. Let a family of groups of prime order be given (Definition 8.19a). The corresponding **family of pair exponentiations as bundling homomorphisms** is defined by the following components, which are written with an asterisk to distinguish them from the components of the underlying family of groups:

- Key generation gen^*: On input $('1'^{k^*}, '1'^{\tau^*})$, set $k := \max(k^*, \tau^*)$ and call the group-generation algorithm $gen('1'^k)$. It produces a pair $(q, desc)$. Now choose a pair $\underline{g}$ of generators of $H_{q,desc}$ randomly. Output
$$K^* := (q, desc, \underline{g}).$$
- Sets of keys: For all $k^*, \tau^* \in \mathbb{N}$, a key $K^* := (q, desc, \underline{g})$ for the bundling homomorphisms is considered both good and acceptable if $(q, desc)$ is an acceptable group description and $\underline{g}$ really consists of two generators. Thus
$$\begin{aligned}(q, desc, \underline{g}) \in Good^*_{k^*,\tau^*} &:= All^*_{k^*,\tau^*} \\ &:\Leftrightarrow (q, desc) \in All_{\max(k^*,\tau^*)} \wedge \underline{g} \in (H_{q,desc} \setminus \{1\})^2.\end{aligned}$$
- For each $K^* = (q, desc, \underline{g}) \in All^*$, the homomorphism $h^*_{K^*}$ is pair exponentiation with respect to $\underline{g}$, and $G^*_{K^*}$ and $H^*_{K^*}$ are its domain and codomain, i.e.,
$$\begin{aligned} G^*_{(q,desc,\underline{g})} &:= \mathbb{Z}_q \times \mathbb{Z}_q \quad \text{(additive)}, \\ H^*_{(q,desc,\underline{g})} &:= H_{q,desc}, \end{aligned}$$
and
$$h^*_{(q,desc,\underline{g})}(\underline{x}) := exp_{\underline{g}}(\underline{x}) = \underline{g}^{\underline{x}}.$$
- A polynomial-time algorithm h^* that, on input $(q, desc, \underline{g}) \in All^*$ and $\underline{x}$, outputs $\underline{g}^{\underline{x}}$, is constructed from the assumed algorithms that compute the group operations as described in Section 8.3.
- Additionally, the following polynomial-time algorithms have been required (where the first one is probabilistic): With a first input $(q, desc, \underline{g}) \in All^* = Good^*$, they
  - choose random elements in $\mathbb{Z}_q \times \mathbb{Z}_q$ with uniform distribution,
  - test membership in $\mathbb{Z}_q \times \mathbb{Z}_q$ and $H_{q,desc}$, and
  - compute the group operations in $\mathbb{Z}_q \times \mathbb{Z}_q$ and $H_{q,desc}$.

  All this is clear for $\mathbb{Z}_q \times \mathbb{Z}_q$, and for $H_{q,desc}$, such algorithms are given in the family of groups. (Note that one can also choose random elements in $H_{q,desc}$ efficiently.) ♦

Theorem 8.45 (Pair exponentiation as bundling homomorphisms). If the discrete logarithm in the given family of groups of prime order is hard (Definition 8.19b), Construction 8.44 is a collision-intractable family of bundling homomorphisms. ♦

Proof. The properties from Definitions 8.29a to d and 8.30a have to be shown.

A. Good and acceptable keys (8.29a). The set inclusions follow immediately from the construction and Definition 8.19aα. The length of the first two components of acceptable keys, q and $desc$, is bounded by a polynomial in k, and thus also in k^* and τ^*, by Definition 8.19aα, and for the other two components, this holds by Remark 8.20.

B. The length restriction (8.29b) is clear for $\mathbb{Z}_q \times \mathbb{Z}_q$, and for $H_{q,desc}$, it is Remark 8.20.

C. Bundling property (8.29c). Let $k^*, \tau^* \in \mathbb{N}$ and $K^* = (q, desc, \underline{g}) \in Good^*_{k^*,\tau^*}$ be given and $z \in h^*_{(q,desc,\underline{g})}(\mathbb{Z}_q \times \mathbb{Z}_q)$. It has to be shown that z has at least 2^{τ^*} preimages. As q is prime and the order of $H_{q,desc}$ is q by Definition 8.19aβ, Corollary 8.4 states that z has q preimages, and, also with Definition 8.19aβ, $q \geq 2^k \geq 2^{\tau^*}$.

D. Collision-intractability (8.29d). Assume that there were a probabilistic polynomial-time algorithm $\tilde{A}^*$ that computed collisions better than permitted in Definition 8.29d, i.e., there is a polynomial *Qtau* and a constant $c > 0$ such that $\forall k_0^* \ \exists k^* \geq k_0^* \ \exists \tau^* \leq Qtau(k^*)$:

$$\begin{aligned} k^{*-c} \ &\leq \ \mathrm{P}((\underline{x}, \underline{x}') \text{ is an } exp_{\underline{g}}\text{-collision} \setminus (q, desc, \underline{g}) \leftarrow gen^*(\text{`}1\text{'}^{k^*}, \text{`}1\text{'}^{\tau^*}); \\ &\qquad\qquad (\underline{x}, \underline{x}') \leftarrow \tilde{A}^*(\text{`}1\text{'}^{k^*}, \text{`}1\text{'}^{\tau^*}, (q, desc, \underline{g}))) \\ &= \ \mathrm{P}((\underline{x}, \underline{x}') \text{ is an } exp_{\underline{g}}\text{-collision} \setminus k := \max(k^*, \tau^*); \\ &\qquad\qquad (q, desc) \leftarrow gen(\text{`}1\text{'}^k); \ \underline{g} \in_R (H_{q,desc} \setminus \{1\})^2; \\ &\qquad\qquad (\underline{x}, \underline{x}') \leftarrow \tilde{A}^*(\text{`}1\text{'}^{k^*}, \text{`}1\text{'}^{\tau^*}, (q, desc, \underline{g}))) \\ &=: \ P_{\tilde{A}^*, k^*, \tau^*}. \end{aligned}$$

This will be led to a contradiction with Theorem 8.41, the collision-intractability of tuple exponentiation, for the case $Qmu = 2$: An algorithm $\tilde{A}$ is constructed such that, for the same constant c: $\forall k_0 \ \exists k \geq k_0$:

$$\begin{aligned} k^{-c} \ &\leq \ \mathrm{P}((\underline{x}, \underline{x}') \text{ is an } exp_{\underline{g}}\text{-collision} \setminus (q, desc) \leftarrow gen(\text{`}1\text{'}^k); \\ &\qquad\qquad \underline{g} \in_R (H_{q,desc} \setminus \{1\})^2; \ (\underline{x}, \underline{x}') \leftarrow \tilde{A}(\text{`}1\text{'}^k, \text{`}1\text{'}^2, q, desc, \underline{g})) \\ &=: \ P_{\tilde{A},k}. \end{aligned}$$

To overcome the difference between k^* and k, the algorithm $\tilde{A}$ is defined as follows: On input ('1'^{k}, '1'^{2}, q, $desc$, $\underline{g}$), all pairs (k^*, τ^*) with $k = \max(k^*, \tau^*)$ are tried one by one, i.e., $\tilde{A}^*$ is run on input ('1'$^{k^*}$, '1'$^{\tau^*}$, $(q, desc, \underline{g})$). As soon as a result $(\underline{x}, \underline{x}')$ is an $exp_{\underline{g}}$-collision, $\tilde{A}$ outputs it and stops.

Obviously, there are less than $2k$ pairs to be tried; hence $\tilde{A}$ runs in polynomial time. Moreover, its success probability is at least the maximum of the success probabilities of the individual iterations, because no unsuccessful stop in a previous iteration is possible.

Hence, if k_0 is given, let $k_0^* := k_0$. There exist numbers $k^* \geq k_0^*$ and $\tau^* \leq Qtau(k^*)$ with $P_{\tilde{A}^*,k^*,\tau^*} \geq k^{*-c}$. Let $k := \max(k^*, \tau^*)$. Thus $k \geq k_0$ and $P_{\tilde{A},k} \geq P_{\tilde{A}^*,k^*,\tau^*} \geq k^{*-c} \geq k^{-c}$.

E. Groups and homomorphisms (8.30a). For each $K^* = (q, desc, \underline{g}) \in All^*$, the sets $\mathbb{Z}_q \times \mathbb{Z}_q$ and $H_{q,desc}$ are Abelian groups and $h^*_{(q,desc,\underline{g})}$ is a homomorphism between them according to Lemma 8.2a. □

Pair Exponentiation as Hiding Homomorphisms

Now pair exponentiation is turned into a collision-intractable family of hiding homomorphisms. This is the use of pair exponentiation from [BoCP88] and later [Bos92, ChHP92, Pede92]. The construction can be generalized to longer tuples if commitments on longer strings are needed.

Construction 8.46. Let a family of groups of prime order be given. The corresponding **family of pair exponentiations as hiding homomorphisms** is defined by the following components, which are written with an asterisk to distinguish them from the components of the underlying family of groups:

- Key generation gen^*: On input '1'^{k}, let $(q, desc) \leftarrow gen(\text{'1'}^k)$, and choose a pair $\underline{g}$ of generators of $H_{q,desc}$ randomly. Output
$$K^* := (q, desc, \underline{g}).$$
- Sets of keys: For all $k \in \mathbb{N}$,
$$\begin{aligned} K^* := (q, desc, \underline{g}) \in Good^*_k &:= All^*_k \\ &:\Leftrightarrow (q, desc) \in All_k \wedge \underline{g} \in (H_{q,desc} \setminus \{1\})^2. \end{aligned}$$
- For each $K^* = (q, desc, \underline{g}) \in All^*$, the homomorphism $h^*_{K^*}$ is pair exponentiation and $\pi^*_{K^*}$ is the projection to the first component. Thus
$$\begin{aligned} S^*_{(q,desc,\underline{g})} &:= \mathbb{Z}_q, \\ G^*_{(q,desc,\underline{g})} &:= \mathbb{Z}_q \times \mathbb{Z}_q, \\ H^*_{(q,desc,\underline{g})} &:= H_{q,desc}, \end{aligned}$$
and
$$\begin{aligned} h^*_{(q,desc,\underline{g})}(\underline{x}) &:= exp_{\underline{g}}(\underline{x}) = \underline{g}^{\underline{x}}, \\ \pi^*_{(q,desc,\underline{g})}((x_1, x_2)) &:= x_1. \end{aligned}$$
- Polynomial-time algorithms h^* and π^* can be constructed in the canonical way.
- A probabilistic polynomial-time algorithm $choose^*$ that selects a random extended value for a given secret x_1 merely chooses x_2 in $\mathbb{Z}_q$ with uniform distribution and outputs (x_1, x_2).
- Polynomial-time algorithms that compute "$\in_R$" (probabilistically), "$\in$", and the group operations can easily be constructed for $\mathbb{Z}_q$ and $\mathbb{Z}_q \times \mathbb{Z}_q$, and for $H_{q,desc}$, they are given in the family of groups. ♦

Theorem 8.47 (Pair exponentiation as hiding homomorphisms). If the discrete logarithm in the given family of groups of prime order is hard, Construction 8.46 is a collision-intractable family of hiding homomorphisms. ♦

Proof. It has to be shown that Definitions 8.31a, b, d, 8.33a, and the simpler version of the hiding property that replaces Definition 8.31c for homomorphisms according to Lemma 8.34, are fulfilled.

A. Good and acceptable keys (8.31a). Clear with Definition 8.19aα and Remark 8.20.

B. The length restriction (8.31b) is clear for $\mathbb{Z}_q \times \mathbb{Z}_q$, and for $H_{q,desc}$, it is Remark 8.20.

C. Collision-intractability (8.31d). One can even prove real collision-intractability (which is obviously stricter than that with respect to any reflexive relation), i.e., for every probabilistic polynomial-time algorithm $\tilde{A}^*$: $\forall c > 0\ \exists k_0\ \forall k \geq k_0$:
$$\begin{aligned} \mathrm{P}((\underline{x}, \underline{x}') \text{ is an } exp_{\underline{g}}\text{-collision} \setminus (q, desc, \underline{g}) \leftarrow gen^*(\text{'1'}^k); \\ (\underline{x}, \underline{x}') \leftarrow \tilde{A}^*(\text{'1'}^k, (q, desc, \underline{g}))) \\ < k^{-c}. \end{aligned}$$

If one substitutes *gen** by its definition, this is exactly Theorem 8.41, the collision-intractability of tuple exponentiation, for the case $Qmu = 2$ (except that $\tilde{A}$ has an additional input '1'^{2}, which it can forget at once).

D. Groups and homomorphisms (8.33a). For each $K^* = (q, desc, \underline{g}) \in All^*$, the sets $\mathbb{Z}_q$, $\mathbb{Z}_q \times \mathbb{Z}_q$ and $H_{q,desc}$ are Abelian groups, $h^*_{(q,desc,\underline{g})}$ is a homomorphism between them according to Definition 8.19aβ and Lemma 8.2a, and any projection $\pi^*_{(q,desc,\underline{g})}$ is a homomorphism, too.

E. Hiding property (8.34). Let $K^* = (q, desc, \underline{g}) \in Good^*$. It has to be shown that the product homomorphism $\psi^*_{K^*} := (h^*_{K^*}, \pi^*_{K^*})$: $G^*_{K^*} \to h^*_{K^*}(G^*_{K^*}) \times S^*_{K^*}$ is surjective, i.e., for each $z \in h^*_{K^*}(G^*_{K^*}) \subseteq H_{q,desc}$ and each $x_1 \in \mathbb{Z}_q$, there exists $\underline{x} \in \mathbb{Z}_q \times \mathbb{Z}_q$ with $exp_{\underline{g}}(\underline{x}) = z$ and $\underline{x} = (x_1, x_2)$ for some x_2. This is exactly Lemma 8.3. □

Tuple Exponentiation as Fixed-Size Hash Functions

Now tuple exponentiation is turned into collision-intractable families of fixed-size hash functions. This was first done in [ChHP92]; the construction was extended for the use in incremental signature schemes in [BeGG94]. In particular, one can use pair exponentiation, but larger tuples turn out to be more efficient.

Fixed-size hash functions have been defined as functions on strings: If k^* is the security parameter of the family of hash functions, then

$$hash^*_{K^*}\colon \{0, 1\}^{k^*} \to \{0, 1\}^{len^*(k^*)}$$

with $len^*(k^*) < k^*$ (if k^* is at least some value k^*_{len}). In contrast, the given tuple exponentiations are of the form

$$exp_{\underline{g}}(\underline{x})\colon \mathbb{Z}_q^{\ \mu} \to H_{q,desc}.$$

The codomains are considered first. As the elements of a group $H_{q,desc}$ may be strings of different length, one may have to pad them. Suppose that they are of the length $length(k)$ afterwards, where k is the security parameter of the family of groups.

One cannot simply use *length* as *len**, because $length(k) \geq k$ (recall $q > 2^k$). Thus, given k^*, one must first compute a smaller k with $length(k) < k^*$. For efficiency in the subsequent construction of normal hash functions, it is even required that $length(k) < k^* - 1$. Hence a function *make_small* is needed with $length(make\_small(k^*)) < k^* - 1$ for all $k^* \geq k^*_{len}$, but nevertheless, for computational security, $make\_small(k^*)$ should only be smaller than k^* by a polynomial factor.

The following definition describes the resulting requirements on the encoding of $H_{q,desc}$.

Definition 8.48. A **fixed-length encoding** for a given family of groups (of prime order) has the following components:

- A monotonically (but not necessarily strictly) increasing function *length*: $\mathbb{N} \to \mathbb{N}$ (which denotes the length of the values after the encoding).
- A family of injective functions $(code_{k,q,desc})_{k \in \mathbb{N}, (q,desc) \in All_k}$, where

$$code_{k,q,desc}: H_{q,desc} \rightarrow \{0, 1\}^{length(k)}.$$

- A function *make_small*: $\mathbb{N} \rightarrow \mathbb{N}$ and a value $k^*_{len} \in \mathbb{N}$ (which denotes from where on *make_small* makes values small enough).
- Polynomial-time algorithms that compute *length* and *make_small* in unary and *code*. The latter means that, on input ('1'^{k}, q, $desc$, g^*), the output is $code_{k,q,desc}(g^*)$.

These components must have the following additional properties:

a) For all $k^* \in \mathbb{N}$ with $k^* \geq k^*_{len}$,
$$length(make\_small(k^*)) < k^* - 1.$$
b) Constants $C, c > 0$ exist such that for all $k^* \in \mathbb{N}$,
$$C\, make\_small(k^*)^c \geq k^*. \qquad \blacklozenge$$

Remark 8.49. For every family of groups of prime order, a fixed-length encoding exists: According to Remark 8.20, the length of the group elements is polynomially bounded in k, say by $C' k^{c'}$ with $C', c' > 0$. If C' and c' are known explicitly, the rest of this remark is constructive. Moreover, to show a fairly useful construction, assume that two more functions may be given:

- A monotonically increasing function *len* that is a closer bound on the length of the group elements and a polynomial-time algorithm that computes *len* in unary, such that constants $D, d \in \mathbb{R}$ with $D, d > 0$ exist where $\forall k\ \forall (q, desc) \in All_k$ $\forall g^* \in H_{q,desc}$:
$$D k^d \leq len(k) \leq C' k^{c'} \wedge |g^*| \leq len(k).$$
- One may want the hash function to reduce the message length by more than the 1 or 2 bits required above. Hence let a monotonically increasing function len_0 be given, which is to be approximated by len^* from below. A polynomial-time algorithm that computes len_0 in unary and a value $k^*_{len_0} \in \mathbb{N}$ are also needed such that for all $k^* \geq k^*_{len_0}$,
$$len_0(k^*) < k^* - 1;$$
and constants $C'', c'' > 0$ have to exist such that for all k^*,
$$C''\, len_0(k^*)^{c''} \geq k^*.$$

For instance, one can use $len_0(k^*) := (k^* \text{ div } E) + 1$ for any $E \in \mathbb{N}\backslash\{1\}$ and $k^*_{len_0} := 5$.

Now a fixed-length encoding is given by the following components:

- $length(k) := len(k) + |len(k)|_2$. Obviously, *length* is monotonically increasing.
- $code_{k,q,desc}$ pads a group element to exactly the length $len(k)$ and prefixes the original length as a binary number with fixed length $|len(k)|_2$ (i.e., with leading zeros). Obviously, these functions are injective.
- *make_small* is defined by
$$make\_small(k^*) := \max\{k \in \mathbb{N} \mid length(k) \leq len_0(k^*)\}$$
if $length(1) \leq len_0(k^*)$, and as 1 otherwise, and
$$k^*_{len} := \max\{k^*_{len_0}, \min\{k^* \in \mathbb{N} \mid length(1) \leq len_0(k^*)\}\}.$$

- Polynomial-time algorithms that compute *length* in unary and *code* can be constructed in a natural way. Moreover, as *length* is monotonically increasing, *make_small* in unary can, e.g., be computed by trying $k := 1, 2, \ldots$. One needs at most $(D^{-1}\, len_0(k^*))^{d^{-1}}$ trials, i.e., the algorithm is polynomial-time.

The two additional properties required in Definition 8.48 remain to be shown.

a) A value $k := make\_small(k^*)$ is defined such that $length(k) \le len_0(k^*) \le k^* - 1$ if $length(1) \le len_0(k^*)$ and $k^* \ge k^*_{len_0}$. For $k^* \ge k^*_{len}$ the latter condition is fulfilled by definition, and the former holds because len_0 is monotonically increasing and $length(1) \le len_0(k^*_{len})$.

b) The definition of *make_small* implies

$$C''\,(length(make\_small(k^*) + 1))^{c''} \ge C''\, len_0(k^*)^{c''} \ge k^*$$

for all k^*. Moreover, an upper bound on $length(k)$ is $2C'k^{c'}$. Hence

$$C''(2C'(make\_small(k^*) + 1)^{c'})^{c''} \ge k^*.$$

Let $c := c'c''$ and let C^* be a constant such that $(k' + 1)^c \le C^* k'^{\,c}$ for all $k' \in \mathbb{N}$. Furthermore, let $C := C''(2C')^{c''}C^*$. Then $C\, make\_small(k^*)^c \ge k^*$ for all k^*, as required. ♦

Now the domains of the desired fixed-size hash functions are considered. The inputs are of length k^* and must be represented as elements of $\mathbb{Z}_q{}^{\mu}$ for some μ, where q has to be generated from $k := make\_small(k^*)$, i.e., only μ remains to be adapted. The family of groups guarantees

$$q > 2^k.$$

Strings of k bits can be interpreted as numbers modulo q in a canonical way. Hence the input must be partitioned into $\mu := \lceil k^*/k \rceil = \lceil k^* / make\_small(k^*) \rceil$ blocks of length k. Now it is useful that the collision-intractability of tuple exponentiation has been proved for tuples of variable length μ.

This leads to the following construction.

Construction 8.50. Let a family of groups of prime order and a fixed-length encoding for it be given (Definitions 8.19a and 8.48). The corresponding **family of tuple exponentiations as fixed-size hash functions** has the following components, which are written with an asterisk to distinguish them from the components of the underlying family of groups:

- Key generation *gen**: On input '1'$^{k^*}$, compute '1'^{k} with $k := make\_small(k^*)$, and $\mu := \lceil k^*/k \rceil$. Generate a group as $(q, desc) \leftarrow gen(\text{'}1\text{'}^k)$, and choose a μ-tuple $\underline{g}$ of generators of $H_{q,desc}$ randomly. Output
$$K^* := (\text{'}1\text{'}^{k^*}, q, desc, \underline{g}).$$
- Acceptable keys: For all $k^* \in \mathbb{N}$,
$$K^* = (\text{'}1\text{'}^{k''}, q, desc, \underline{g}) \in All^*_{k^*}$$
$$:\Leftrightarrow k'' = k^* \wedge (q, desc) \in All_k \wedge \underline{g} \in (H_{q,desc}\setminus\{1\})^{\mu}$$
for $k := make\_small(k^*)$ and $\mu := \lceil k^*/k \rceil$.

- The function len^* is defined by $len^*(k^*) := length(make\_small(k^*))$, as explained above, and the polynomial-time algorithm that computes it in unary is the composition of those for *length* and *make_small*. The value that denotes from where on the hash functions are length-reducing is k_{len}^*.
- For each $k^* \in \mathbb{N}$ and $K^* = (\text{'1'}^{k^*}, q, desc, g) \in All^*_{k^*}$, the function
$$hash^*_{K^*}: \{0, 1\}^{k^*} \rightarrow \{0, 1\}^{len^*(k^*)}$$
is defined as follows: Let $k := make\_small(k^*)$ and $\mu := \lceil k^*/k \rceil$. The input m is split into μ blocks of length k, where the last one is padded with zeros.[141] These blocks are interpreted as numbers in binary, say $m_1, \ldots, m_\mu$, and let $\underline{m} := (m_1, \ldots, m_\mu)$. Then
$$hash^*_{K^*}(m) := code_{k,q,desc}(\underline{g}^{\underline{m}}).$$
- The polynomial-time algorithm $hash^*$ can be constructed in a canonical way along the description of the functions $hash^*_{K^*}$. ♦

Theorem 8.51 (Tuple exponentiation as fixed-size hash functions). If the discrete logarithm in the given family of groups is hard, Construction 8.50 is a collision-intractable family of fixed-size hash functions. ♦

Proof. The properties required in Definition 8.36a to c remain to be shown.

a) Acceptable keys. The fact that all correctly generated keys are acceptable follows immediately from the construction and Definition 8.19aα. The length of acceptable keys is polynomial in k and μ according to Definition 8.19aα and Remark 8.20, and thus polynomial in k^*, because k and μ are computed from k^* in unary in polynomial time.

b) Length-reducing. $len^*(k^*) = length(make\_small(k^*)) < k^*$ for all $k^* \geq k_{len}^*$ follows immediately from Definition 8.48a.

c) Collision-intractability. The conversion of strings of length k^* (such as m) into μ-tuples of numbers of binary length k (such as $\underline{m}$), is denoted by underlining, as in the construction. Assume the contrary of the theorem. Then a probabilistic polynomial-time algorithm $\tilde{A}^*$ and a constant $c^* > 0$ exist such that $\forall k_0^* \, \exists k^* \geq k_0^*$:

$$\begin{aligned} k^{*-c^*} \;\leq\;& P(hash^*_{K^*}(m) = hash^*_{K^*}(m') \wedge m \neq m' \wedge m, m' \in \{0, 1\}^{k^*} \setminus \\ & \quad K^* \leftarrow gen^*(\text{'1'}^{k^*});\ (m, m') \leftarrow \tilde{A}^*(\text{'1'}^{k^*}, K^*)) \\ =\;& P(code_{k,q,desc}(\underline{g}^{\underline{m}}) = code_{k,q,desc}(\underline{g}^{\underline{m}'}) \wedge m \neq m' \wedge m, m' \in \{0, 1\}^{k^*} \setminus \\ & \quad k := make\_small(k^*);\ \mu := \lceil k^*/k \rceil;\ (q, desc) \leftarrow gen(\text{'1'}^{k}); \\ & \quad \underline{g} \in_R (H_{q,desc} \setminus \{1\})^{\mu};\ (m, m') \leftarrow \tilde{A}^*(\text{'1'}^{k^*}, \text{'1'}^{k^*}, q, desc, \underline{g})). \end{aligned}$$

Let $\mathcal{K}^*$ be the set of values k^* with this property, and define an algorithm $\tilde{A}'$ as $\tilde{A}^*$ followed by the conversion of m and m' into μ-tuples of numbers, and without the redundant parameter '1'^{k^*}. Both $code_{k,q,desc}$ and this conversion are injective. Hence for all $k^* \in \mathcal{K}^*$:

141 One need not indicate how long the original message is, because its length k^* is fixed.

$$k^{*-c^*} \le \mathrm{P}(\underline{g}^{\underline{m}} = \underline{g}^{\underline{m}'} \wedge \underline{m} \ne \underline{m}' \wedge \underline{m}, \underline{m}' \in \mathbb{Z}_q{}^{\mu} \setminus k := make\_small(k^*); (q, desc) \leftarrow gen(`1\text{'}^k); \mu := \lceil k^*/k \rceil; \underline{g} \in_R (H_{q,desc} \setminus \{1\})^{\mu}; (\underline{m}, \underline{m}') \leftarrow \tilde{A}'(`1\text{'}^{k^*}, q, desc, \underline{g}))$$
$$=: P_{succ,\tilde{A}'}(k^*).$$

This is to be led to a contradiction with Theorem 8.41, i.e., there should be a probabilistic polynomial-time algorithm $\tilde{A}$, a polynomial *Qmu*, and a constant $c > 0$ such that $\forall k_0\ \exists k \ge k_0\ \exists \mu \le Qmu(k)$:

$$k^{-c} \le \mathrm{P}((\underline{x}, \underline{x}') \text{ is an } exp_{\underline{g}}\text{-collision} \setminus (q, desc) \leftarrow gen(`1\text{'}^k); \underline{g} \in_R (H_{q,desc} \setminus \{1\})^{\mu}; (\underline{x}, \underline{x}') \leftarrow \tilde{A}(`1\text{'}^k, `1\text{'}^{\mu}, q, desc, \underline{g}))$$
$$=: P_{succ,\tilde{A}}(k, \mu).$$

The algorithm $\tilde{A}$ is defined as follows: On input $(`1\text{'}^k, `1\text{'}^{\mu}, q, desc, \underline{g})$, it tries the values k^* with $\lceil k^*/k \rceil = \mu$ and $make\_small(k^*) = k$ one by one (if there aren't any, it stops): For each such k^*, it calls $\tilde{A}'(`1\text{'}^{k^*}, q, desc, \underline{g})$. If $\tilde{A}'$ outputs a collision, $\tilde{A}$ outputs that collision, too, and stops.

$\tilde{A}$ works in polynomial time, because there are only k possible values k^* with $\lceil k^*/k \rceil = \mu$. Secondly, the values k^* have been selected so that $\tilde{A}'$ is run on tuples of the same sizes k and μ as in $P_{succ,\tilde{A}'}(k^*)$. Thirdly, the success probability of $\tilde{A}$ is at least as large s that of any of its iterations, because $\tilde{A}$ cannot stop unsuccessfully in another iteration, i.e., $P_{succ,\tilde{A}}(k, \mu) \ge P_{succ,\tilde{A}'}(k^*)$ for all values k^* that are tried.

Let C' and c' be the constants with $C'\, make\_small(k^*)^{c'} \ge k^*$ for all k^*. It is shown that $\tilde{A}$ yields the desired contradiction for the constant $c := c^*(c' + 1)$ and the polynomial $Qmu := C'\, k^{c'-1} + 1$.

Let k_0 be given, and without loss of generality $k_0 \ge C'$. Then there is $k^* \ge k_0^* := C'\, k_0^{c'}$ with $P_{succ,\tilde{A}'}(k^*) \ge k^{*-c^*}$. Let $k := make\_small(k^*)$ and $\mu := \lceil k^*/k \rceil$. Then

$$k \ge (C'^{-1}k^*)^{c'^{-1}} \ge (C'^{-1}k_0^*)^{c'^{-1}} = k_0$$

and $\quad P_{succ,\tilde{A}}(k, \mu) \ge P_{succ,\tilde{A}'}(k^*) \ge k^{*-c^*} \ge (C'\, k^{c'})^{-c^*} \ge (k^{c'+1})^{-c^*} = k^{-c}.$

Finally, $\quad \mu \le k^*/k + 1 \le C'\, k^{c'}/k + 1 = Qmu(k).$ □

Hash Functions from Tuple Exponentiation

The construction in the previous subsection only yielded fixed-size hash functions. A construction of (normal) hash functions, i.e., for inputs of arbitrary length, from fixed-size hash functions was presented and proved in [Damg90a] (following similar ad hoc constructions by various authors). The definitions of both these notions in [Damg90a] are not identical to those used here, but they are also uniform and can easily be shown to be equivalent with two exceptions: First, in the place of the sets All_k, the sets of correctly generated keys are used. One can easily see that these sets do not change the proof. Secondly, the fixed-size hash functions are required to be length-reducing for all k there. Hence the construction for $k < k_{len}$ has to be changed here. This only concerns a finite number of k's and therefore does not affect the only complicated property, collision-intractability. Hence only the result is presented in the notation used here, and Figure 8.9 illustrates it.

Construction 8.52. (Part of the proof of Theorem 3.1 in [Damg90a].) Let a collision-intractable family of fixed-size hash functions be given with $len(k) < k - 1$ for all $k \geq k_{len}$. The corresponding **family of hash functions** is defined by the following components, which are written with an asterisk to distinguish them from the components of the underlying family of fixed-size hash functions:

- On input $'1'^{k^*}$, the key-generation algorithm gen^* computes $'1'^k$, where $k := \max(k^*, k_{len})$, and generates a key as $K \leftarrow gen('1'^k)$. Accordingly, the sets of all acceptable keys and the length function are $All^*_{k^*} := All_k$ and $len^*(k^*) := len(k)$.
- For each $K \in All^*_{k^*} = All_k$, the function

$$hash^*_K: \{0, 1\}^+ \rightarrow \{0, 1\}^{len(k)} = \{0, 1\}^{len^*(k^*)}$$

is defined as follows: The input m is split into blocks of length $k - len(k) - 1$ and the last block is padded with zeros. Let d be the number of zeros used. Call the blocks $m_1, \ldots, m_n$, and add a block m_{n+1} that contains the binary representation of d with leading zeros. (d fits into one block because $|d|_2 \leq d$.) Now m is hashed iteratively: In each step, the next block and the result of the previous step are hashed together. One additional bit is included so that first blocks can be distinguished from the others. If || denotes concatenation, the intermediate results are defined as

$$r_1 := hash_K('0'^{len(k)+1} \,||\, m_1)$$

and, for $i := 2, \ldots, n+1$,

$$r_i := hash_K(r_{i-1} \,||\, '1' \,||\, m_i).$$

The final result is $hash^*_K(m) := r_{n+1}$.

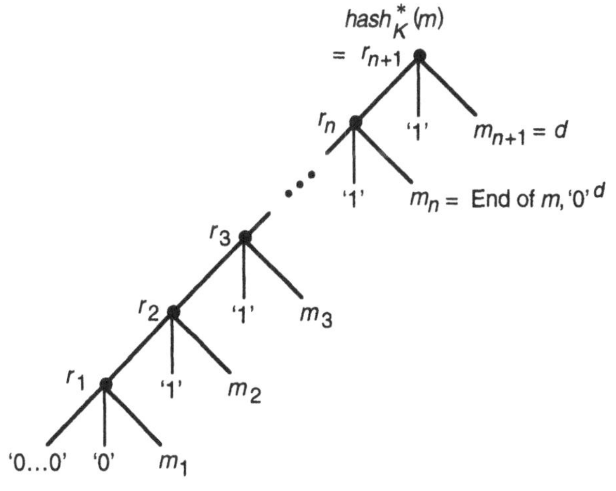

Figure 8.9. Construction of a hash function from a fixed-size hash function.
Each node value is computed by one application of the fixed-size hash function to the concatenation of its three children.

- The polynomial-time algorithm *hash** that computes the whole family of functions can be derived in a canonical way from the description of $hash*_K$. ♦

Theorem 8.53. (Adapted from [Damg90a, Theorem 3.1]). Construction 8.52 is a collision-intractable family of hash functions. ♦ □

Remark 8.54. This family of hash functions can be augmented by short collision proofs according to Remark 8.37: The reduction used in the proof of the theorem yields a (rather obvious) algorithm to construct a collision of the underlying family of fixed-size hash functions from any collision of the new family (for all acceptable keys, although it is only needed for correctly generated keys in the proof of collision-intractability). ♦

Concrete Parameter Choice for Hash Functions

As the construction of hash functions was in several steps, it may be useful to summarize the result for the concrete case of subgroups of prime fields, as in Definition 8.21 and Construction 8.22, and to study how the parameters should be chosen. In particular, the algorithm *gen* is considered variable, i.e., the relation between the lengths of q and p, and the function *make_small*.

For simplicity, only algorithms *gen* are considered that, on input '1'^{k}, always generate a prime p of the precise length *len_p*(k). In this case, the elements of $H_{q,p}$ are numbers of length *len_p*(k), if a representation with leading zeros is used, and no additional fixed-length encoding is needed, i.e., *length*(k) := *len_p*(k) and $code_{k,q,desc}$ is the identity.

In a concrete case, everything amounts to a choice of values k, l, and μ, such that the fixed-size hash functions are of the form

$$hash_{K^*}: \{0, 1\}^{\mu k} \to \{0, 1\}^l,$$
$$hash_{K^*}(m) = \underline{g}^{\underline{m}},$$

where $K^* = (\text{'1'}^{\mu k}, q, p, \underline{g})$ with $q > 2^k$, $|p|_2 = l$, and $\underline{g}$ is a μ-tuple of generators of $H_{q,p}$, and the tuple $\underline{m}$ is obtained from the message m by dividing m into μ blocks of length k and interpreting them as numbers. (In the general construction, k^* may also be slightly smaller than μk.)

In practice, one will choose l first, because it must be adapted to the current state of the art of computing discrete logarithms; e.g., l might be 512. (In contrast, the primary security parameter in Definition 8.36 and thus in Construction 8.50 is $k^* \approx \mu k$.)

If these fixed-size hash functions are used in the construction of normal hash functions, each application of $hash_{K^*}$ deals with approximately $\mu k - l$ bits of the message. One must minimize the time needed per message bit. Let

- $mm(l)$ be the time needed for one modular multiplication of l-bit numbers, and
- $\eta(\mu, k)$ the average number of multiplications needed for μ-tuple exponentiation with k-bit exponents. This depends on the exponentiation algorithm. However, assume that
  - $\eta(\mu, k)$ is at most linear in k, or, more precisely, $\eta(\mu, k)/k \geq \eta(\mu, l)/l$ for $k \leq l$. (This is true for both the naive version of individual exponentiations

and the μ-tuple exponentiation algorithm shown in Section 8.3, because they need precomputations.)

- $\eta(\mu, k)$ is at most linear in μ, or, more precisely, $\eta(\mu, k)/\mu \geq \eta(\mu', l)/\mu'$ for $\mu \leq \mu'$. (Otherwise one should change the algorithm by splitting long tuples into smaller ones.)

The time needed per message bit is approximately (for fixed l and any μ, $k < l$):

$$time\_per\_bit(\mu, k) := \frac{mm(l)\ \eta(\mu, k)}{\mu k - l} \geq \frac{mm(l)\ \eta(\mu, l)\ k/l}{\mu k - l} = \frac{mm(l)\ \eta(\mu, l)}{\mu l - l^2/k}$$

$$> \frac{mm(l)\ \eta(\mu, l)}{\mu l - l} = time\_per\_bit(\mu, l).$$

Hence q should be of about the same length l as p. Then

$$time\_per\_bit(\mu, l) = \frac{mm(l)}{l}\ \frac{\eta(\mu, l)}{\mu}\ \frac{\mu}{\mu - 1}$$

is even strictly monotonically decreasing with μ. Hence μ should be rather large. Practical limits are given by the overhead resulting from padding short messages.

Table

The following table summarizes the most important parameters of the constructions of collision-intractable families of bundling homomorphisms, hiding homomorphisms, and fixed-size hash functions based on the discrete-logarithm assumption. Note that the main use of fixed-size hash functions is in the construction of real hash functions.

	Bundling	Hiding	Fixed-size hash
Parameters	k^*, τ^*	k	k^*
Keys	$K = (q, desc, g)$ with $\mu = 2$ and $k := max(k^*, \tau^*)$	$K = (q, desc, g)$ with $\mu = 2$	$K = (\text{'}1\text{'}^{k^*}, q, desc, g)$ with $k := make\_small(k^*)$ and $\mu := \lceil k^*/k \rceil$
Functions	$h_K(\underline{x}) := \underline{g}^{\underline{x}}$	$h_K(\underline{x}) := \underline{g}^{\underline{x}}$, $\pi_K((x_1, x_2)) := x_1$	$hash_K(m) :=$ $code_{k,q,desc}(\underline{g}^{\underline{m}})$

Table 8.2. Overview of the constructions in the discrete-logarithm case

8.5.4 Constructions from Claw-Intractable Pairs of Permutations

This section contains the constructions of some types of function families defined in Section 8.5.2 from a claw-intractable family of permutation pairs. An overview is given by the left half of the constructions in Figure 8.7. For some constructions, the underlying family may be weak, for others, it must be strong.

The basic idea is from [GoMR88]; it was first applied to hash functions in [Damg88] and to bundling and hiding functions in [Pfit89, PfWa90].

The construction principle is always the iteration of the given permutations or functions, as shown in Figures 8.2 and 8.3, i.e., the functions B and B_σ constructed in Definition 8.5. The idea why such constructions are collision-intractable is shown in Figure 8.10: If one has a collision of the iterated function B, one knows two paths of applications of f_0 and f_1 that end at the same value z. Hence, except for the case where one path is a part of the other, those paths must meet at some point, coming from different directions. At this point, one has a claw between f_0 and f_1, if f_0 and f_1 are permutations.

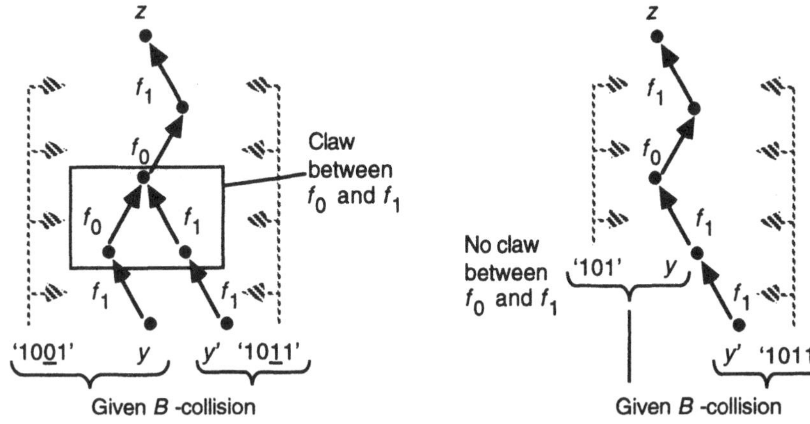

Figure 8.10. How collisions can be used to find claws.
On the left, one sees how a claw is found where the two paths ending at z meet; on the right, one sees the exception where one of the two bit strings is a prefix of the other.

The common part of the two paths corresponds to the common prefix of the two bit strings that are the first parameters of the iterated function B. (Recall that these bit strings are evaluated back to front.) Hence a collision leads to a claw if and only if neither of the two strings is a prefix of the other. For instance, this is clear if only bit strings of a fixed length σ are considered at the same time, as in the functions B_σ.

Lemma 8.55. (Finding claws in collisions). Whenever a claw-intractable family of permutation pairs is given (strong or weak, see Definitions 8.26 and 8.27), the corresponding algorithm *claw_from_collision* is defined as follows.[142] (Remember that with the conventions from Definition 8.5, the iterated functions are called B_K.) It works on inputs of the form (K, x, x') with $K \in All$, where $x = (b, y)$ and $x' = (b', y')$ with $b, b' \in \{0, 1\}^+$ and $y, y' \in D_K$.

---

142 More formally, one would have to define *claw_from_collision* as an operator mapping a family of permutation pairs to an algorithm, but, similar to the notations "B" etc. from Definition 8.5, the additional notation would not be justified.

claw_from_collision: On input (K, x, x'), determine the common prefix b^* of b and b'. If $b^* = b$ or $b^* = b'$, stop with an error message: one of the strings was a prefix of the other. Otherwise, without loss of generality, let $b =: b^* \| 0 \| b_0$ and $b' =: b^* \| 1 \| b_1$ (where b_0 or b_1 may be the empty string). Compute $z_0 := B_K(b_0, y)$ and $z_1 := B_K(b_1, y')$, i.e., evaluate the parts of the two paths before they meet. Output (z_0, z_1).

a) This algorithm works in polynomial time.

b) It outputs a claw whenever
   - (x, x') is a B_K-collision,
   - neither of the first components of x and x' is a prefix of the other, and
   - $f_{0,K}$ and $f_{1,K}$ are permutations (i.e., if $K \in Good$ if the given family is strong, and only if K has been generated correctly if the given family is weak).

c) One can extend the algorithm to find either a claw or an $f_{0,K}$- or $f_{1,K}$-collision even for all acceptable keys, i.e., if only the first two preconditions of Part b) hold: After the operations described above, test if (z_0, z_1) is a claw. If not, i.e., $f_{0,K}(z_0) \neq f_{1,K}(z_1)$, continue to follow the paths, which are now both defined by b^*: If $b^* = b_1 b_2 \ldots b_l$, define values $z_j^{(l+1)} := f_{j,K}(z_j)$ and $z_j^{(i)} := f_{b_i,K}(z_j^{(i+1)})$ for $i := l, \ldots, 1$ and $j := 0, 1$. After each step, compare $z_0^{(i)}$ and $z_1^{(i)}$. Let i be the first (i.e., maximal) value where they are equal. Output $(z_0^{(i+1)}, z_1^{(i+1)})$. ♦

Proof. a) The major part of the computation is the applications of B_K. Polynomial-time algorithms for the individual permutations (or functions) are given, and the number of times they are applied is bounded by the length of the strings.

b) Let $z := B_K(x) = B_K(x')$. As neither of the first components, b and b', is a prefix of the other, *claw_from_collision* really outputs a pair (z_0, z_1). With the definition of B_K and the partitions of the strings b and b', one has (see Figure 8.10)

$$z = B_K(b^*(f_{0,K}(z_0))) = B_K(b^*(f_{1,K}(z_1))).$$

As $f_{0,K}$ and $f_{1,K}$ are permutations, $B_K(b^*, \bullet)$ is injective according to Lemma 8.6a. This yields $f_{0,K}(z_0) = f_{1,K}(z_1)$, as required.

c) Now the case where *claw_from_collision* does not produce a claw remains to be considered. Then the very first pair, $(z_0^{(l+1)}, z_1^{(l+1)})$, is unequal by definition. The last pair, $(z_0^{(1)}, z_1^{(1)})$, is (z, z). Hence there must be a first pair that is equal, and the previous pair is an $f_{b_i,K}$-collision. □

In the following subsections, the complete function families are presented.

Bundling Functions

Construction 8.56. Let a weak claw-intractable family of permutation pairs be given (see Definition 8.27). The corresponding family of **iterated permutations as bundling functions** is defined by the following components, which are written with an asterisk to distinguish them from the components of the family of permutation pairs:

- Key generation gen^*: On input ('1'^{k}, '1'$^{\tau^*}$), call gen('1'^{k}) to generate a key K (i.e., the description of a permutation pair). Output[143]
$$K^* := (K, \text{'1'}^{\tau^*}).$$
- Sets of keys: A key K^* of the form described above is considered good or acceptable if K is good or acceptable, respectively, and τ^* is correct. Thus for all $k, \tau^* \in \mathbb{N}$,
$$Good^*_{k,\tau^*} := \{(K, \text{'1'}^{\tau^*}) \mid K \in Good_k\}$$
and
$$All^*_{k,\tau^*} := \{(K, \text{'1'}^{\tau^*}) \mid K \in All_k\}.$$
- For each $K^* = (K, \text{'1'}^{\tau^*}) \in All^*$, the function $h^*_{K^*}$ is the function $B_{\tau^*,K}$ that results if Definition 8.5 is applied to $f_{0,K}$ and $f_{1,K}$, and $G^*_{K^*}$ and $H^*_{K^*}$ are its domain and codomain, i.e.,
$$G^*_{(K,\text{'1'}^{\tau^*})} := \{0, 1\}^{\tau^*} \times D_K,$$
$$H^*_{(K,\text{'1'}^{\tau^*})} := D_K,$$
and
$$h^*_{(K,\text{'1'}^{\tau^*})}(b, y) := B_{\tau^*,K}(b, y) = f_{b_1,K}(f_{b_2,K}(\ldots f_{b_{\tau^*},K}(y)\ldots)),$$
where $b_1, b_2, \ldots, b_{\tau^*}$ are the individual bits of b.
- A polynomial-time algorithm h^* that, on input $(K, \text{'1'}^{\tau^*}) \in All^*$ and $(b, y) \in \{0, 1\}^{\tau^*} \times D_K$, outputs $B_{\tau^*,K}(b, y)$, can be constructed in a canonical way from the assumed algorithms that compute the underlying permutations or functions.
- Additionally, polynomial-time algorithms (where the first one is probabilistic) have been required that, with a first input $(K, \text{'1'}^{\tau^*}) \in All^*$,
  - choose random elements in $\{0, 1\}^{\tau^*} \times D_K$, where the distribution must be uniform if $K \in Good^*$, and
  - test membership in $\{0, 1\}^{\tau^*} \times D_K$ and D_K.

  Such algorithms can be constructed in a canonical way from those given in the family of permutation pairs. (Note that one can also choose random elements in the codomains efficiently.) ♦

Theorem 8.57 (Iterated permutations as bundling functions). If a strong claw-intractable family of permutation pairs is given, Construction 8.56 defines a collision-intractable family of bundling functions. If the underlying family is weak, all properties except for the bundling property are still guaranteed.[144] ♦

Proof. The properties required in Definition 8.29a to d remain to be proved.

a) Good and acceptable keys. Both the set inclusions and the restriction on the length of all acceptable keys are an immediate consequence of the corresponding parts of Definition 8.26a.

b) The length restrictions follow immediately from those for D_K (Definition 8.26b).

---

143 The parameter '1'$^{\tau^*}$ is needed because the algorithms performing random choices and membership tests need τ^*, and they have only the key, and not the security parameters, among their inputs.

144 This statement will be used in the factoring case when n is not a generalized Blum integer: In that case, the bundling property can be proved in a different way.

c) Bundling property. If the underlying family is strong and $K^* \in Good^*$, then $K \in Good$ and hence $f_{0,K}$ and $f_{1,K}$ are permutations by Definition 8.26c. Thus the bundling property follows from Lemma 8.6b.

d) Collision-intractability can be shown according to Figure 8.10: Assume the contrary. Hence a probabilistic polynomial-time algorithm $\tilde{A}^*$, a polynomial $Qtau$, and a constant $c > 0$ exist such that for an infinite set $\mathcal{K}$ of values k, there is a $\tau^* \leq Qtau(k)$ with

$$\begin{aligned} k^{-c} \;\leq\;& \mathrm{P}(B_{\tau^*,K}(x) = B_{\tau^*,K}(x') \wedge x \neq x' \wedge x, x' \in \{0,1\}^{\tau^*} \times D_K \setminus \\ & \quad K \leftarrow gen(\text{'1'}^k);\ K^* := (K, \text{'1'}^{\tau^*}); \\ & \quad (x, x') \leftarrow \tilde{A}^*(\text{'1'}^k, \text{'1'}^{\tau^*}, (K, \text{'1'}^{\tau^*}))) \\ =:\;& P_{succ,\tilde{A}^*}(k, \tau^*). \end{aligned}$$

(Note that gen^*, $h^*_{K^*}$, and $G^*_{K^*}$ have already been substituted by their definitions.)

It is shown that the following algorithm $\tilde{A}$ contradicts Definition 8.26d for the same constant c: On input $(\text{'1'}^k, K)$, try all values τ^* with $\tau^* \leq Qtau(k)$ as follows:

1. Call $\tilde{A}^*(\text{'1'}^k, \text{'1'}^{\tau^*}, (K, \text{'1'}^{\tau^*}))$.
2. If the output is a pair (x, x'), where $x = (b, y)$ and $x' = (b', y')$ with $b, b' \in \{0, 1\}^{\tau^*}$ and $y, y' \in D_K$, call $claw\_from\_collision(K, x, x')$.
3. Test if the output of $claw\_from\_collision$ is a claw (z_0, z_1). If yes, $\tilde{A}$ outputs this claw and stops.

First, it is clear that $\tilde{A}$ works in polynomial time.

Secondly, whenever K is a correctly generated key, $K \in [gen(\text{'1'}^k)]$, and $\tilde{A}^*$ within $\tilde{A}$ succeeds in finding a collision (x, x'), where $x = (b, y)$ and $x' = (b', y')$, then $\tilde{A}$ succeeds in finding a claw: $x, x' \in \{0, 1\}^{\tau^*} \times D_K$ implies that b and b' are of equal length. Hence, if one of them were a prefix of the other, they would be equal. However, $B_{\tau^*,K}(b, y) = B_{\tau^*,K}(b', y')$ would then imply $y = y'$, too, because $B_{\tau^*,K}(b, \bullet)$ is injective. This contradicts $x \neq x'$. Thus neither of b and b' is a prefix of the other, and *claw_from_collision* succeeds by Lemma 8.55. (Note that injectivity and Lemma 8.55 can be used even if the given family is weak, because only correctly generated keys are considered here.)

Thirdly, the success probability of $\tilde{A}$ on a certain input is at least as large as that of any of its trials, because $\tilde{A}$ cannot stop unsuccessfully in any of the previous trials. Hence for all $k \in \mathcal{K}$, there is a $\tau^* \leq Qtau(k)$ such that

$$\begin{aligned} & \mathrm{P}(f_{0,K}(z_0) = f_{1,K}(z_1) \wedge z_0, z_1 \in D_K \setminus K \leftarrow gen(\text{'1'}^k);\ (z_0, z_1) \leftarrow \tilde{A}(\text{'1'}^k, K)) \\ & \quad \geq\; \mathrm{P}(f_{0,K}(z_0) = f_{1,K}(z_1) \wedge z_0, z_1 \in D_K \setminus \\ & \qquad\qquad K \leftarrow gen(\text{'1'}^k);\ (x, x') \leftarrow \tilde{A}^*(\text{'1'}^k, \text{'1'}^{\tau^*}, (K, \text{'1'}^{\tau^*})); \\ & \qquad\qquad (z_0, z_1) \leftarrow claw\_from\_collision(K, x, x')) \\ & \quad \geq\; P_{succ,\tilde{A}^*}(k, \tau^*) \\ & \quad \geq\; k^{-c}. \end{aligned}$$

□

Hiding Functions

In contrast to the discrete-logarithm case, the sets of secrets for the hiding functions to be constructed are not automatically given. Instead, Lemma 8.6a implies that any restriction $B_{\tau,K}$ to strings of a fixed length has a hiding property. Thus one obtains many families of hiding functions, depending on the choice of τ. However, one cannot make the strings arbitrarily long as a function of k so as not to give attackers arbitrarily much time to break the claw-intractability of the underlying permutation pairs. Hence the usual restriction is made that τ can be computed from k in unary in polynomial time.

Construction 8.58. Let

- a strong claw-intractable family of permutation pairs (see Definition 8.26), and
- a function *tau*: $\mathbb{N} \to \mathbb{N}$ and a polynomial-time algorithm that computes *tau* in unary

be given. The corresponding **family of iterated permutations as hiding functions** is defined by the following components, which are written with an asterisk to distinguish them from the components of the family of permutation pairs:

- Key generation *gen**: On input '1'^{k}, call *gen*('1'^{k}) to generate a key K (i.e., the description of a permutation pair), and compute '1'$^{\tau*}$:= '1'$^{tau(k)}$. Output
$$K^* := (K, \text{'1'}^{\tau*}).$$
- Sets of keys: A key K^* of the form described above is considered good or acceptable if K is good or acceptable, respectively, and the second component is correct. Thus for all $k \in \mathbb{N}$,
$$Good^*_k := \{(K, \text{'1'}^{tau(k)}) \mid K \in Good_k\}$$
and
$$All^*_k := \{(K, \text{'1'}^{tau(k)}) \mid K \in All_k\}.$$
- For each $K^* = (K, \text{'1'}^{\tau*}) \in All^*$, the function $h^*_{K^*}$ is the function $B_{\tau*,K}$ resulting if Definition 8.5 is applied to $f_{0,K}$ and $f_{1,K}$, and $\pi^*_{K^*}$ is the projection to the first component, i.e., the secret is the string. Thus
$$G^*_{(K,\text{'1'}^{\tau*})} := \{0, 1\}^{\tau*} \times D_K,$$
$$H^*_{(K,\text{'1'}^{\tau*})} := D_K,$$
$$S^*_{(K,\text{'1'}^{\tau*})} := \{0, 1\}^{\tau*},$$
and
$$h^*_{(K,\text{'1'}^{\tau*})}(b, y) := B_{\tau*,K}(b, y),$$
$$\pi^*_{(K,\text{'1'}^{\tau*})}(b, y) := b.$$
- Polynomial-time algorithms h^* and π^* can be constructed in a canonical way.
- A probabilistic polynomial-time algorithm *choose** that, with a first input $K^* = (K, \text{'1'}^{\tau*}) \in All^*$, selects a random extended value for a given secret b merely chooses an element y of D_K randomly and outputs (b, y). If $K^* \in Good^*$, then $K \in Good$, and hence the distribution is uniform by Definition 8.26.
- Polynomial-time algorithms that compute "$\in_R$" (probabilistically) and "$\in$" in $S^*_{K^*}$ are clear, and those for "$\in$" in $G^*_{K^*}$ and $H^*_{K^*}$ can easily be constructed from that for the sets D_K from the family of permutation pairs.

Theorem 8.59 (Iterated permutations as hiding functions). If a strong claw-intractable family of permutation pairs (and a function *tau* with an algorithm as specified) is given, Construction 8.58 is a collision-intractable family of hiding functions. ♦

Proof. The properties required in Definition 8.31a to d remain to be proved.

a) Good and acceptable keys: The set inclusions follow immediately from the constructions. The length of good keys is polynomial in k according to Definition 8.26a and because τ^* is computed from k in unary in polynomial time.

b) The length restrictions follow immediately from those for D_K (Definition 8.26b).

c) Hiding property: For each $K^* = (K, \text{'1'}^{\tau^*}) \in Good^*$:

- For all $b \in \{0, 1\}^{\tau^*}$, the set $\pi^*_{K^*}{}^{-1}(b)$ is $\{b\} \times D_K$, and thus its size is independent of b.
- For each public value $z \in D_K$ and each secret $b \in \{0, 1\}^{\tau^*}$, the set $h^*_{K^*}{}^{-1}(z) \cap \pi^*_{K^*}{}^{-1}(b)$ consists of those pairs (b, y) with $B_{\tau^*,K}(b, y) = z$. According to Lemma 8.6a, the size of any such set is 1.

d) Not only collision-intractability with respect to equal π-images, but real collision-intractability can be shown: By substituting the definitions of gen^*, $h^*_{K^*}$, $\pi^*_{K^*}$, and $G^*_{K^*}$ into Definition 8.31, one sees that it suffices to show that for every probabilistic polynomial-time algorithm $\tilde{A}^*$: $\forall c > 0\ \exists k_0\ \forall k \geq k_0$:

$$P(B_{tau(k),K}(x) = B_{tau(k),K}(x') \wedge x \neq x' \wedge x, x' \in \{0, 1\}^{tau(k)} \times D_K \setminus K \leftarrow gen(\text{'1'}^k);\ K^* := (K, \text{'1'}^{tau(k)});\ (x, x') \leftarrow \tilde{A}^*(\text{'1'}^k, K^*)) < k^{-c}.$$

There exists a polynomial *Qtau* that is an upper bound on *tau*. Hence this formula is a special case of what has been shown in Part d) of the proof of Theorem 8.57. □

Hash Functions

In the construction of hash functions from a claw-intractable family of permutation pairs, the messages more or less correspond to the string parameter of the function B, but two additional aspects have to be considered:

- Arbitrarily long messages must be hashed. However, for collision-intractability, none of the possible strings should be a prefix of another one (see Figure 8.10). Hence a prefix-free code must be applied to the messages before the function B. (One could apply the same idea to hiding functions, if one wanted to hide secrets of different length.)
- The outputs of a function B_K are elements of D_K, but the outputs of a hash function should be strings from a set $\{0, 1\}^{len(k)}$. Thus a fixed-length encoding for the elements of D_K is needed, similar to Definition 8.48. However, the situation is much easier here, because it is not required that $len(k) < k$, and one can therefore take any natural encoding, without transformations between k and k^*.

This leads to the following definition.

Definition 8.60 (Components for hash functions from permutation pairs).

a) A **prefix-free encoding of arbitrarily long strings** consists of

- a function
$$prefix\_free: \{0, 1\}^* \rightarrow \{0, 1\}^+,$$
where $prefix\_free(m)$ is not a prefix of $prefix\_free(m')$ for any strings $m \neq m'$ (and, in particular, $prefix\_free(m) \neq prefix\_free(m')$), and
- a polynomial-time algorithm that computes *prefix_free*.

b) A **standard prefix-free encoding**, $prefix\_free^*$, is computed by the following algorithm: On input $m \in \{0, 1\}^+$, determine the length $\lambda := |m|$. If $|\lambda|_2 \leq 31$ (which is the only realistic case in practice), represent λ as a binary number of 32 bits and prefix it to m, which is padded at the left with zeros so that its length is also a multiple of 32.[145] Thus
$$prefix\_free^*(m) := \lambda \,||\, m,$$
where both λ and m are padded on the left with zeros.

If λ has more than 31 bits, the length field must be extended: λ is partitioned into blocks of 31 bits, say $\lambda_1, \ldots, \lambda_n$ (with the most significant bits on the left, as usual, and with leading zeros). They are represented in 32-bit words, where the leftmost bit is used to indicate whether another word of the length field follows, i.e.,
$$prefix\_free^*(m) := \text{'1'}\lambda_1 \,||\, \ldots \,||\, \text{'1'}\lambda_{n-1} \,||\, \text{'0'}\lambda_n \,||\, m.$$

c) A **fixed-length encoding** for a claw-intractable family of permutation pairs (strong or weak) has the following components:

- A function $length$: $\mathbb{N} \rightarrow \mathbb{N}$.
- A family of injective functions $(code_{k,K})_{k \in \mathbb{N}, K \in All_k}$, where
$$code_{k,K}: D_K \rightarrow \{0, 1\}^{length(k)}.$$
- Polynomial-time algorithms that compute *length* in unary and *code*. The latter means that $code_{k,K}(x)$ is computed from ('1'^{k}, K, x). ♦

The length restriction (Definition 8.26b) implies that a fixed-length encoding exists for each claw-intractable family of permutation pairs. However, to base a construction on it, one must effectively know one. ♦

Construction 8.61. Let a weak claw-intractable family of permutation pairs, a fixed-length encoding for it, and a prefix-free encoding on arbitrarily long strings be given. The corresponding **family of iterated permutations as hash functions** is defined by the following components, which are written with an asterisk to distinguish them from the components of the family of permutation pairs:

- Key generation gen^*: On input '1'^{k}, call gen('1'^{k}) to generate a key K, choose an element y^* of D_K randomly (using the algorithm given in the claw-intractable family of permutation pairs), and output

[145] The number 32 is used because the length of the fields should be compatible with the word length on standard computers, to keep the code simple.

$$K^* := (\text{`}1\text{'}^k, K, y^*).$$

- Acceptable keys: For all $k \in \mathbb{N}$, a key K^* of the form described above is considered acceptable if k is correct, K is acceptable, and y^* is in the correct domain. Thus

$$All^*_k := \{(\text{`}1\text{'}^k, K, y^*) \mid K \in All_k \wedge y^* \in D_K\}.$$

- The function len^* is identical to *length* from the given fixed-length encoding, and so is the algorithm to compute it in unary.
- For each $k \in \mathbb{N}$ and $K^* = (\text{`}1\text{'}^k, K, y^*) \in All^*_k$, the function

$$hash^*_{K^*}: \{0, 1\}^+ \to \{0, 1\}^{len^*(k)}$$

  is defined as follows: First, the message is encoded with the prefix-free encoding. Then it is used as the string parameter in B_K, and the other parameter is the element y^* given in the key. Finally, the result is brought to the fixed length by an application of *code*. Thus

$$hash^*_{(\text{`}1\text{'}^k,\, K,\, y^*)}(m) := code_{k,K}(B_K(prefix\_free(m), y^*)).$$

- The polynomial-time algorithm $hash^*$ can be constructed in a canonical way from the algorithms given for $prefix\_free, f_0, f_1$, and *code*. ♦

Theorem 8.62 (Iterated permutations as hash functions). If a weak claw-intractable family of permutation pairs is given, Construction 8.61 defines a collision-intractable family of hash functions. ♦

Proof. The properties required in Definition 8.35a and b remain to be proved.

a) Acceptable keys: The set inclusion follows immediately from the definitions. The length of acceptable keys is polynomial in k because of Definition 8.26a and b (referred to in Definition 8.27).

b) Collision-intractability: Assume, to the contrary, that there were a probabilistic polynomial-time algorithm $\tilde{A}^*$ and a constant $c > 0$ such that $\forall k_0\, \exists k \geq k_0$

$$\begin{aligned} k^{-c} \;\leq\; & \mathrm{P}(hash^*_{K^*}(m) = hash^*_{K^*}(m') \wedge m \neq m' \wedge m, m' \in \{0, 1\}^+ \setminus \\ & \qquad K \leftarrow gen(\text{`}1\text{'}^k);\, y^* \in_R D_K;\, K^* := (\text{`}1\text{'}^k, K, y^*); \\ & \qquad (m, m') \leftarrow \tilde{A}^*(\text{`}1\text{'}^k, K^*)) \\ =:\; & P_{succ,\tilde{A}^*}(k). \end{aligned}$$

(Note that gen^* has already been substituted by its definition.) It is shown that the following algorithm $\tilde{A}$ contradicts Definition 8.26d:

1. On input $(\text{`}1\text{'}^k, K)$, select $y^*$ from $D_K$ randomly, let $K^* := (\text{`}1\text{'}^k, K, y^*)$, and call $\tilde{A}^*(\text{`}1\text{'}^k, K^*)$.
2. If the output is a pair of strings, (m, m'), let $b := prefix\_free(m)$ and $b' := prefix\_free(m')$, and call $claw\_from\_collision(K, (b, y^*), (b', y^*))$.
3. If *claw_from_collision* does not stop with an error message, its result (z_0, z_1) is used as the output of $\tilde{A}$, too.

It is clear that $\tilde{A}$ works in polynomial time.

Furthermore, whenever K is a correctly generated key, i.e., $K \in [gen(\text{`}1\text{'}^k)]$, and $\tilde{A}^*$ within $\tilde{A}$ succeeds in finding a $hash^*_{K^*}$-collision (m, m'), then $\tilde{A}$ succeeds in finding a claw: $hash^*_{K^*}(m) = hash^*_{K^*}(m')$ means $code_{k,K}(B_K(b, y^*)) = code_{k,K}(B_K(b', y^*))$. As $code_{k,K}$ is injective, this implies $B_K(b, y^*) = B_K(b', y^*)$. As $m \neq m'$, neither of b and b' is a prefix of the other. Hence *claw_from_collision* succeeds according to Lemma 8.55. Thus

$$
\begin{aligned}
&P(f_{0,K}(z_0) = f_{1,K}(z_1) \wedge z_0, z_1 \in D_K \setminus K \leftarrow gen(\text{'1'}^k);\ (z_0, z_1) \leftarrow \tilde{A}(\text{'1'}^k, K)) \\
&= \ P(f_{0,K}(z_0) = f_{1,K}(z_1) \wedge z_0, z_1 \in D_K \setminus \\
&\qquad\qquad K \leftarrow gen(\text{'1'}^k);\ y^* \in_R D_K;\ K^* := (\text{'1'}^k, K, y^*); \\
&\qquad\qquad (m, m') \leftarrow \tilde{A}^*(\text{'1'}^k, K^*); \\
&\qquad\qquad b := prefix\_free(m);\ b' := prefix\_free(m'); \\
&\qquad\qquad (z_0, z_1) \leftarrow claw\_from\_collision(K, (b, y^*), (b', y^*))) \\
&\geq \ P_{succ,\tilde{A}^*}(k) \\
&\geq \ k^{-c}.
\end{aligned}
$$

□

Remark 8.63. This family of hash functions can be augmented by short collision proofs according to Remark 8.37: Given a collision of the new family, one can use the extended version of *claw_from_collision* from Lemma 8.55c to compute either a claw of the underlying family of permutation pairs, or a collision of one of its functions. As the latter is impossible for correctly generated keys, where the functions are permutations, it is clearly infeasible to find collision proofs. ♦

8.5.5 Constructions in the Factoring Case

This section contains the constructions of function families, as defined in Section 8.5.2, on the factoring assumption. An overview is given in the right half of the constructions in Figure 8.7, and some details are summarized in Table 8.3.

Basically, the constructions are special cases of those described in the previous section, based on the permutation pairs from Definition 8.10. (The origin of the constructions is the same as in the previous section, too: The basic idea is from [GoMR88]; it was first applied to hash functions in [Damg88] and to bundling and hiding functions in [Pfit89, PfWa90].)

Hence this section starts with the construction of claw-intractable families of permutation pairs from these functions. In addition to the results that are then a consequence of Section 8.5.4, most function families in this section are families of homomorphisms, and one can use the results of Section 8.2.3 to show a bundling property even if only a weak claw-intractable family of permutation pairs is given.

Squaring and Doubling as Claw-Intractable Permutation Pairs

The constructions in Section 8.2.3 had different properties depending on whether n was a generalized Blum integer or any element of $4\mathbb{N} + 1$. Thus two different families of good keys, *Good* and *Good_weak* are provided; they lead to a strong and a weak claw-intractable family of permutation pairs, respectively.

Construction 8.64. The **strong** and **weak GMR family of permutation pairs** are defined as follows:

- Key generation: The algorithm *gen* is an algorithm gen_{Will} for the uniform generation of Williams integers with two factors p, q of binary length k as in the factoring assumption. (However, see Section 8.4.1, "Generation of Uniformly Distributed Williams Integers" for discussions of realistic algorithms.)
- Sets of keys: In both families, an integer n is an acceptable key if it is not too long and an element of $4\mathbb{N} + 1$. In the weak family, all these keys are also considered good, whereas in the strong family, only generalized Blum integers are good. Thus for all k,

$$All_k := Good\_weak_k := \{n \in 4\mathbb{N} + 1 \mid |n|_2 \leq 2k\},$$

and $$Good_k := \{n \in GeneralBlum \mid |n|_2 \leq 2k\}.$$

- For each key $K = n \in All$, the domain D_K is $RQR_n^>$, and the function pair is that from Definition 8.10, i.e., $f_{0,n}(x) = x^2$ and $f_{1,n}(x) = 4 \circ x^2$.
- Polynomial-time algorithms f_0 and f_1 can be constructed in the canonical way from the algorithms for $\mathbb{Z}_n$ mentioned in Section 8.3.
- Additionally, polynomial-time algorithms have been required (where the first one is probabilistic) that, with a first input $n \in All = 4\mathbb{N} + 1$,
  - choose random elements in $RQR_n^>$, where the distribution must be uniform if $n \in Good$ or $Good\_weak$, respectively, and
  - test membership in $RQR_n^>$.

  The algorithm for random choice in the weak family repeatedly generates a random element y of $\mathbb{Z}_n{}^*$ and computes its Jacobi symbol modulo n, until $y \in \mathbb{Z}_n{}^*(+1)$; then it outputs the class $\{\pm y\}$. In the strong family, the following faster algorithm can be used, because $RQR_n^>$ is then equal to $RQR_n^<$ for $n \in Good$: Generate $y' \in_R \mathbb{Z}_n{}^*$, let $y := y'^2$, and use the class $\{\pm y\}$.

  The membership test, on input (n, y), simply verifies that $1 \leq y < n/2$ and $(\frac{y}{n}) = 1$. ♦

Lemma 8.65. (Adapted from [GoMR88].) On the factoring assumption (Definition 8.18), Construction 8.64 defines a strong and a weak claw-intractable family of permutation pairs. ♦

Proof.

a) Good and acceptable keys: All correctly generated keys are obviously good and $Good_k \subseteq All_k$, and the length of all acceptable keys is bounded by the polynomial $2k$.

b) Length restrictions: The length of the elements of D_n for $n \in All$ is restricted by $|n|_2$.

c) Permutations: In the strong family, the functions $f_{0,n}$ and $f_{1,n}$ are permutations for all keys $n \in Good$ by Lemma 8.11a. In the weak family, they are at least permutations for all correctly generated keys, because those keys are a subset of the good keys of the strong family.

d) Claw-intractability. Assume, to the contrary, that there were a probabilistic polynomial-time algorithm $\tilde{A}$ and a constant $c > 0$ such that $\forall k_0\ \exists k \geq k_0$:

$$P(x^2 = 4 \circ x'^2 \wedge x, x' \in RQR_n^{\geq} \setminus n \leftarrow gen_{Will}(\text{'1'}^k);\ (x, x') \leftarrow \tilde{A}(\text{'1'}^k, n))\ \geq\ k^{-c}.$$

An equality $x^2 = 4 \circ x'^2$ in $RQR_n^{\geq}$ implies $x^2 = 4x'^2$ for the representatives in $\mathbb{Z}_n^*$, because the only alternative would be $x^2 = -4x'^2$, but both x^2 and $4x'^2$ are obviously elements of the group QR_n and -1 is not (see Section 8.1.3).

Now one can conclude that $(x + 2x')(x - 2x') \equiv 0 \bmod n$, i.e., n divides this product. However, one can easily see that n does not divide any of the factors, i.e., $x \neq \pm 2x'$ in $\mathbb{Z}_n$: As n is a Williams integer (here is the only place where this fact is used), 2 has the Jacobi symbol -1, whereas x, x', and -1 have the Jacobi symbol $+1$, and the Jacobi symbol is multiplicative.

Thus one of the two factors of n, say p, divides $x + 2x'$ and the other divides $x - 2x'$. Hence the greatest common divisor of n and $x + 2x'$ is p.

Thus it has been shown that the following algorithm $\tilde{F}$ factors Williams integers with the same probability as $\tilde{A}$ finds claws: On input n, compute k as $\lceil |n|_2/2 \rceil$ and call $\tilde{A}(\text{'1'}^k, n)$. Whenever the output is a pair (x, x'), output $p := \gcd(n, x + 2x')$. □

Iterated Squaring and Doubling as Bundling Homomorphisms

The construction of a collision-intractable family of bundling homomorphisms from iterated squaring and doubling is basically Construction 8.56, based on the claw-intractable families of permutation pairs from Construction 8.64. The new points are:

- Of course, one needs algorithms that compute the group operations.
- The bundling property is shown even for the weak GMR family of permutation pairs.
- The functions $B_{\tau,n}$ with a string parameter are replaced by the functions $B^*_{\tau,n}$ with an integer parameter, because those are homomorphisms. For the relation between them, note that the function *num* from Lemma 8.12, which converts strings to numbers, is invertible on the strings of any fixed length τ, i.e., one can define num_τ^{-1}: $\{0, \ldots, 2^\tau - 1\} \rightarrow \{0, 1\}^\tau$.

This yields the following construction. (Note that one can derive a second family by restricting *Good* to good keys from the strong GMR family of permutation pairs, i.e., to generalized Blum integers, according to Remark 8.38a.)

Construction 8.66. The **family of iterated squaring and doubling as bundling homomorphisms** has the following components:

- Key generation *gen*: On input $(\text{'1'}^k, \text{'1'}^\tau)$, call $gen_{Will}(\text{'1'}^k)$ to generate a Williams integer n and let
$$K := (n, \text{'1'}^\tau).$$
- Sets of keys: A key K of the form described above is considered both good and acceptable if n is weakly good and τ is correct. Thus, for all $k, \tau \in \mathbf{N}$,
$$Good_{k,\tau} := All_{k,\tau} := \{(n, \text{'1'}^\tau) \mid n \in 4\mathbb{N} + 1 \wedge |n|_2 \leq 2k\}.$$

- For each $K = (n, \text{'1'}^\tau) \in All$, the groups are (see Definition 8.14)

$$G_K := G_{\tau,n} = \{0, \ldots, 2^\tau - 1\} \times RQR_n^>,$$
$$H_K := RQR_n^>,$$

  and the homomorphism can be written as

$$h_K(a, y) := B^*_{\tau,n}(a, y) = 4^a \circ y^{2^\tau} = B_{\tau,n}(num_\tau^{-1}(a), y).$$

- The polynomial-time algorithms that compute h and perform random choices (probabilistically) and membership tests can be constructed canonically as in Construction 8.56 from those in Construction 8.64. (Note that the conversions num and num_τ^{-1} can be computed very efficiently.)
- Polynomial-time algorithms that compute the group operations in the family of groups H_K are clear. Now the groups G_K are considered:
  - Multiplication is $(a, y) * (a', y') = ((a + a') \bmod 2^\tau, y \circ y' \circ 4^{(a+a') \operatorname{div} 2^\tau})$.
    - The computation of $(a + a') \bmod 2^\tau$ and $(a + a') \operatorname{div} 2^\tau$ with additions and shifts takes time $O(\tau)$.
    - As a and a' are smaller than 2^τ, the exponent of 4 can only be 0 or 1. Hence no computation is needed there.
    - A modular multiplication by 4 is two iterations of a shift and possibly a subtraction, i.e., $O(|n|_2)$.
    - Thus the main operation is the computation of $y \circ y'$, which is basically a modular multiplication, and therefore $O(|n|_2^2)$.

    As the algorithm has $K = (n, \text{'1'}^\tau)$ as an input, all this is polynomial in the input length.
  - The neutral element is always (0, 1).
  - The main operation in the computation of a group inverse is the computation of a modular inverse; altogether, it is $O(\tau) + O(|n|_2^3)$. ♦

Theorem 8.67 (Iterated squaring and doubling as bundling homomorphisms). On the factoring assumption, Construction 8.66 defines a collision-intractable family of bundling homomorphisms. ♦

Proof. According to Theorem 8.16, G_K and H_K are groups and h_K a homomorphism (actually, into $RQR_n^< \subseteq H_K$) for all $K \in All$. The set inclusions with good and acceptable keys are obvious, the length of all acceptable keys is polynomial in k and τ, and the length of group elements is polynomial in K. The bundling property is Lemma 8.17. Collision-intractability follows from Theorem 8.57 and Lemma 8.65, because each collision of $B^*_{\tau,n}$ can easily be transformed into one of $B_{\tau,n}$ because the family of inverses num_τ^{-1} is efficiently computable. □

Iterated Squaring and Doubling as Hiding Homomorphisms

The construction of collision-intractable families of hiding homomorphisms from iterated squaring and doubling is basically Construction 8.58, based on the strong claw-intractable family of permutation pairs from Construction 8.64. Similar to the case with bundling homomorphisms, the functions $B_{\tau,n}$ are replaced by $B^*_{\tau,n}$.

Construction 8.68. Let a function *tau*: $\mathbb{N} \to \mathbb{N}$ and a polynomial-time algorithm that computes *tau* in unary be given. The corresponding **family of iterated squaring and doubling as hiding homomorphisms** has the following components:

- Key generation *gen*: On input '1'^{k}, call gen_{Will}('1'^{k}) to generate a Williams integer n, and compute '1'$^\tau$:= '1'$^{tau(k)}$. Output
$$K := (n, \text{'1'}^\tau).$$
- Sets of keys: A key K of the form described above is considered good and acceptable if n is good or acceptable, respectively, and τ is correct. Thus, for all $k \in \mathbb{N}$,
$$Good_k := \{(n, \text{'1'}^{tau(k)}) \mid n \in GeneralBlum \wedge |n|_2 \le 2k\}$$
and
$$All_k := \{(n, \text{'1'}^{tau(k)}) \mid n \in 4\mathbb{N} + 1 \wedge |n|_2 \le 2k\}.$$
- For each $K = (n, \text{'1'}^\tau) \in All$, the groups are
$$G_K := G_{\tau,n} = \{0, \ldots, 2^\tau-1\} \times RQR^>_n,$$
$$H_K := RQR^>_n,$$
$$S_K := \{0, \ldots, 2^\tau-1\} = (\mathbb{Z}_{2^\tau}, +),$$
and the homomorphisms are
$$h_K(a, y) := B^*_{\tau,n}(a, y) = 4^a \circ y^{2^\tau} = B_{\tau,n}(num_\tau^{-1}(a), y),$$
$$\pi_K(a, y) := a.$$
- The algorithms h, π, *choose*, the random choice in S_K, and the membership tests can be taken from Construction 8.58 (given those in Construction 8.64), and those for the group operations from Construction 8.66. ♦

Theorem 8.69 (Iterated squaring and doubling as hiding homomorphisms). On the factoring assumption, Construction 8.68 defines a collision-intractable family of hiding homomorphisms. ♦

Proof. The construction is a collision-intractable family of hiding functions according to Theorem 8.59 and Lemma 8.65. (The replacement of $B_{\tau,n}$ by $B^*_{\tau,n}$ can be handled as in the proof of Theorem 8.67.) The functions h_K are homomorphisms between groups G_K and H_K according to Theorem 8.16, and S_K is obviously an Abelian group, too. It remains to be shown that π_K is a homomorphism. This is not completely trivial, although π_K is simply a projection, because G_K as a group is not the direct product of $\mathbb{Z}_{2^\tau}$ and RQR_n, but one can immediately see it from the definition of the operation:
$$\pi_K((a, y) * (a', y')) = (a + a') \bmod 2^\tau = \pi_K((a, y)) + \pi_K((a', y')). \qquad \square$$

Iterated Squaring and Doubling as Hash Functions

Before Construction 8.61 can be applied to the weak claw-intractable family of permutation pairs from Construction 8.64, a fixed-length encoding must be fixed. The sets to be encoded are $RQR_n^{>}$ with $|n|_2 \le 2k$. One can simply represent all their elements as binary numbers of length $2k$ with leading zeros. Furthermore, the standard prefix-free encoding, *prefix_free**, is used for the messages. This yields the following construction.

Construction 8.70. (Adapted from [Damg88].) The family of **iterated squaring and doubling as hash functions** has the following components:

- Key generation *gen*: On input '1'^{k}, call gen_{Will}('1'^{k}) to generate a Williams integer n, and choose an element y^* of $RQR_n^{>}$ randomly. Output
$$K := (\text{'1'}^k, n, y^*).$$
- Acceptable keys: For all $k \in \mathbb{N}$,
$$All_k := \{(\text{'1'}^k, n, y^*) \mid n \in 4\mathbb{N}+1 \wedge |n|_2 \le 2k \wedge y^* \in RQR_n^{>}\}.$$
- For all $k \in \mathbb{N}$, $len(k) := 2k$.
- For each $K := (\text{'1'}^k, n, y^*) \in All_k$, the actual hash function is
$$hash_K\colon \{0, 1\}^+ \to \{0, 1\}^{2k}$$
with
$$hash_K(m) := B_n(prefix\_free^*(m), y^*),$$
where the result, from $RQR_n^{<}$ in its standard representation, is interpreted as a string with leading zeros.
- A polynomial-time algorithm for *hash* is given in Construction 8.61. ♦

Theorem 8.71 (Iterated squaring and doubling as hash functions). (Adapted from [Damg88].) On the factoring assumption, Construction 8.70 is a collision-intractable family of hash functions. Moreover, it can be equipped with short collision proofs according to Remark 8.37. ♦

Proof. This is a special case of Theorem 8.62 and Remark 8.63. □

Remark 8.72. One can write $hash_K(m) = 4^{num(prefix\_free^*(m))} \circ y^{*2^{\lambda^*}}$, where λ^* is the length of the encoded message, $prefix\_free^*(m)$. If the party that has generated the key applies the hash function, this can be used to improve efficiency greatly: The Chinese remainder theorem can be used to evaluate $hash_K(m)$ modulo the factors p and q of n separately, and the exponents, which may be quite long, can first be reduced modulo $p-1$ and $q-1$. ♦

Table

The following table summarizes the most important parameters of the constructions of collision-intractable families of bundling homomorphisms, hiding homomorphisms, and hash functions based on the factoring assumption.

	Bundling	Hiding	Hash
Parameters	k, τ	k	k
Keys	$K = (n, \text{'1'}^{\tau})$	$K = (n, \text{'1'}^{tau(k)})$	$K = (\text{'1'}^{k}, n, y^*)$
Requirements on n in good keys	$n \in 4\mathbf{N} + 1$, $\lvert n\rvert_2 \le 2k$	$n \in GeneralBlum$, $\lvert n\rvert_2 \le 2k$	$n \in 4\mathbf{N} + 1$, $\lvert n\rvert_2 \le 2k$, $y^* \in RQR_n^>$
Functions	$h_K(a, y) := 4^a \cdot y^{2^\tau}$	$h_K(a, y) := 4^a \cdot y^{2^{tau(k)}}$, $\pi_K(a, y) := a$	$hash_K(m) :=$ $B_n(prefix\_free^*(m), y^*))$

Table 8.3. Overview of the constructions in the factoring case.
With the hash functions, the "requirement on n in good keys" refers to acceptable keys, because they have no stricter notion of good keys.

9 Constructions for One Message Block

In this chapter, constructions of standard fail-stop signature schemes for signing one message block are presented. Generalizations to schemes where a large number of messages of arbitrary length can be signed follow in Chapter 10.

The chapter concentrates on efficient schemes where a whole message block is signed at once. Constructions with bit-by-bit signing are not presented; they were all mentioned in Section 6.1.2, "Cryptologic Assumptions and Efficiency".

Section 9.1 contains definitions of standard fail-stop signature schemes with prekey for signing message blocks. Section 9.2 presents a construction framework for such schemes from bundling homomorphisms. The reason why it is not simply called a construction is that one gap in the security proofs remains to be filled depending on the actual family of bundling homomorphisms. Sections 9.3 and 9.4 contain concrete implementations of this construction framework based on the abstract discrete-logarithm assumption and the factoring assumption, respectively. A brief overview of the efficiency is given in Section 9.5.

Historically, the first of these efficient schemes was presented in [HePe93], and the construction framework, from [HePP93], is a generalization of that scheme.

9.1 Definition of Schemes for Signing Message Blocks

In this section, a formal definition of schemes for signing message blocks, instead of real messages from a fixed message space, is given. Furthermore, some notation for schemes where only one message or message block can be signed is introduced.

All the following constructions yield schemes with prekey, and the message blocks that can be signed only depend on the prekey *prek*, i.e., one can use message-block spaces M_{prek}. Hence only this case is defined. First, the definitions of the components, Definitions 7.1 and 7.31, are adapted, and then the simplified security criteria from Theorem 7.34. As in Section 7.3, it is tacitly assumed that all schemes are with only one risk bearer; see Section 7.5 for extensions.

Definition 9.1. A standard fail-stop signature scheme with prekey for **signing message blocks** is defined like a standard fail-stop signature scheme with prekey, except that there is no fixed message space *M*. Instead, there is a family of message-block spaces

$$MFam := (M_{prek})_{prek \in All}.$$

Any main key pair based on a prekey *prek* is used for messages from M_{prek}. More precisely, the domains of the second parameter, *m*, of the algorithms *sign*, *test*, and *prove* can be restricted as follows, depending on the first parameter:

- *test*: Recall from the end of Definition 7.31 that *test* only needs to be defined for first parameters $pk \in PK\_All$. They are of the form $(prek, mk)$. For any $prek \in All$, let
$$PK(prek) := \{pk = (prek, mk) \mid pk \in PK\_All\}.$$
For all $pk \in PK(prek)$, the domain of the parameter m must comprise M_{prek}.
- *sign* and *prove*: Recall from the end of Definition 7.31 that only original temporary keys $sk\_temp \in SK\_Temp_{orig}(prek)$ for some $prek \in All$ have to be considered. For such an sk_temp, the domain of the parameter m in $test(pk, m, s)$ must comprise M_{prek}, and the same holds for any sk_temp_{new} derived from it by signing messages from M_{prek}. Denote the set of all temporary secret keys that can occur together with *prek* in this way by
$$SK\_Temp(prek).$$

Such a scheme is called secure if it fulfils the criteria from Theorem 7.34 with the modification that the messages are restricted to M_{prek} in the definition of

- the effectiveness of authentication, and
- the possible histories and the set of successful forgeries (Definition 7.12, used in the security for the signer). In particular, one has to write $Hist(prek, sk, N)$ now, because *prek* is not necessarily a component of *sk* (whereas for all public keys that can actually occur, it is). ♦

Remark 9.2. One could adapt the original security definitions (Definition 7.15) in a similar way to message-block spaces M_{pk} and prove an analogue of Theorem 7.34, i.e., that the simplified security criteria imply the original ones. ♦

Definition 9.3. Any standard fail-stop signature scheme (with prekey or not, and with a real message space or for signing message blocks) with the set $Message\_bounds = \{1\}$ is called a **one-time** signature scheme (with the same attributes). A one-time signature scheme for signing message blocks is also called a scheme for **signing one message block**.

With one-time signature schemes, slightly simplified notation can be used:

- As the message bound N is always 1, it can be omitted from the parameters, i.e., $par := (\text{'}1\text{'}^k, \text{'}1\text{'}^\sigma)$.
- The message bound N can be omitted in the definition of the histories, i.e., one can write $Hist(sk)$ or $Hist(prek, sk)$, respectively. All message sequences in possible histories consist of zero or one message. In the latter case, the sequences can be replaced by the messages themselves, i.e., a history can be written as $hist = (m, s)$ and the functional version of signing one message as $s := sign^{(f)}(sk, m)$. ♦

9.2 General Construction Framework

In this section, a framework for constructing standard fail-stop signature schemes with prekey for signing one message block from a collision-intractable family of bundling homomorphisms is described. Two parameters (the exact family of message-block spaces and a function *tau*) are left open; they depend on the actual choice of the family of bundling homomorphisms. Some lemmas are proved that reduce the security of the scheme to one property of the family of bundling homomorphisms and the parameters that were left open. Thus for each particular implementation of the construction framework, one has to specify these two parameters and to prove this property, see Sections 9.3 and 9.4.

Construction 9.4 (General construction framework). Let the following parameters be given:

- A collision-intractable family *BundFam* of bundling homomorphisms. The same notation is used for its components as in Definitions 8.29 and 8.30. Furthermore, let *CorrFam* be the family of correct key distributions from *BundFam*, i.e., $Corr_{k,\tau} := gen(\text{'1'}^k, \text{'1'}^\tau)$ for all $k, \tau \in \mathbb{N}$.
- An algorithm *all_test* that decides membership in *AllFam*, i.e., on input ('1'^k, '1'^τ, K), it decides if $K \in All_{k,\tau}$ in time polynomial in the first two inputs alone.
- A zero-knowledge proof scheme (gen°, *ZKP*) with generation algorithm, goodness predicate, and external verifiability for the keys of the bundling homomorphisms, i.e., for the pair (*CorrFam*, *GoodFam*).[146]
- A function *tau* that maps two positive integers k and σ to an integer $\tau \geq \sigma$, and a polynomial-time algorithm *tau** that computes *tau* in unary. (This function will be used to determine the bundling degree, 2^τ, of the bundling homomorphism to be used from the security parameters of the signature scheme.)
- A family *MFam* of message-block spaces consisting of integers, parametrized by all acceptable keys of the bundling homomorphisms and two security parameters, i.e., $MFam := (M_{k,\sigma,K})_{k,\sigma \in \mathbb{N}, K \in All}$, with $M_{k,\sigma,K} \subseteq \mathbb{Z}$ for all k, σ, and K.

The corresponding standard fail-stop signature scheme with prekey for signing one message block is defined by the following components. (Recall that the special components for schemes with prekey from Definition 7.31, the message-block spaces, and the remaining components from Definition 7.1 are needed.) They are written with an asterisk if their names would otherwise collide with those from an underlying scheme.

- Key generation:
  - Prekey generation: A prekey is primarily a key of the family of bundling homomorphisms, i.e., it specifies one such homomorphism. The security parameter k for this homomorphism is the same k as that for the signature scheme, whereas τ is chosen as $tau(k, \sigma)$. The zero-knowledge proof scheme is adapted accordingly. Additionally, the security parameters are in the prekey. This means:
    - Correct prekey distributions: For all $k, \sigma \in \mathbb{N}$:

$$prek \leftarrow Corr^*_{k,\sigma} :\Leftrightarrow K \leftarrow Corr_{k,tau(k,\sigma)};\ prek := (\text{'1'}^k, \text{'1'}^\sigma, K).$$

146 As usual, an implementation of this construction is particularly simple if the zero-knowledge proof scheme is only a local verification algorithm.

- Good prekeys: $Good^*_{k,\sigma} := \{(`1'^k, `1'^\sigma)\} \times Good_{k,tau(k,\sigma)}$ for all $k, \sigma \in \mathbb{N}$.
- All acceptable prekeys: $All^*_{k,\sigma} := \{(`1'^k, `1'^\sigma)\} \times All_{k,tau(k,\sigma)}$ for all $k, \sigma \in \mathbb{N}$.
- Zero-knowledge proof scheme and *all_test**: The prekey-generation algorithm gen_B is defined by

  $$(prek, aux) \leftarrow gen_B(`1'^k, `1'^\sigma)$$
  $$:\Leftrightarrow (K, aux) \leftarrow gen^\circ(`1'^k, `1'^{tau(k,\sigma)});\ prek := (`1'^k, `1'^\sigma, K).$$

  (Note that $`1'^{tau(k,\sigma)}$ can be computed with $tau^*$.) The prover's algorithm, $P^*$, on input $(`1'^k, `1'^\sigma, prek, aux)$ with *prek* as above, calls $P(`1'^k, `1'^{tau(k,\sigma)}, K, aux)$. The verifying algorithms *all_test**, $V^*$, and $Obs^*$, on input $(`1'^k, `1'^\sigma, prek)$ with *prek* as above, call *all_test*, $V$, and *Obs*, respectively, on input $(`1'^k, `1'^{tau(k,\sigma)}, K)$.

- Main key generation gen_A: On input $(par^*, prek)$ with $par^* = (`1'^k, `1'^\sigma)$ and $prek = (`1'^k, `1'^\sigma, K) \in All^*_{k,\sigma}$, the essential part of the secret key is a pair of random values from G_K, and the main public key consists of their images under the bundling homomorphism. Thus for $i := 1, 2$:

  $$sk_i \in_R G_K,$$
  $$mk_i := h_K(sk_i),$$

  and[147]

  $$sk\_temp := (K, 0, sk_1, sk_2),$$
  $$mk := (mk_1, mk_2).$$

  Signing will be deterministic, hence

  $$sk = sk\_temp.$$

- Main public key test *mk_test*: It is tested that both components of *mk* are elements of the correct group. That is, on input $(par^*, prek, (mk_1, mk_2))$, where $par^* = (`1'^k, `1'^\sigma)$ and $prek = (`1'^k, `1'^\sigma, K) \in All^*$, it is tested that $mk_1, mk_2 \in H_K$.

- Message-block spaces: For each $prek = (`1'^k, `1'^\sigma, K) \in All^*$, the message-block space M_{prek} is simply $M_{k,\sigma,K}$ from the underlying family *MFam*.
- Signing: The domain of the first parameter, *sk*, of the algorithm *sign* is

  $$SK\_Temp := \{(K, i, sk_1, sk_2) \mid K \in All \wedge i \in \{0, 1\} \wedge sk_1, sk_2 \in G_K\}.$$

  Moreover, *sign* can be defined for all $m \in \mathbb{Z}$, which includes all message-block spaces. If $sk\_temp = (K, 0, sk_1, sk_2) \in SK\_Temp$, then $sign(sk\_temp, m) := (s, sk\_temp_{new})$ with

  $$s := sk_1 + m\, sk_2$$

  and $sk\_temp_{new} := (K, 1, sk_1, sk_2)$. If $sk\_temp = (K, 1, sk_1, sk_2) \in SK\_Temp$, then $sign(sk\_temp, m) :=$ *'key_used_up'*.

---

147 K must be a component of *sk_temp* because signing was defined with *sk_temp* and m as the only inputs. One might even let *sk_temp* contain *mk*, too; then *mk* need not be recomputed in *prove*. The component "0" is a counter.

- Test: A value s is an acceptable signature on a message block m if s is in the correct group[148] and fulfils the homomorphic image of the signing equation. Thus, if $pk = (prek, (mk_1, mk_2))$, where $prek = (\text{'1'}^k, \text{'1'}^\sigma, K) \in All^*$, which implies $K \in All$, and $mk_1, mk_2 \in H_K$, and if $m \in \mathbb{Z} \supseteq M_{prek}$, then
$$test(pk, m, s) = \text{TRUE} \;:\Leftrightarrow\; s \in G_K \wedge h_K(s) = mk_1 \cdot mk_2{}^m \text{ (in } H_K).$$
- Proving forgeries: On input $sk\_temp = (K, i, sk_1, sk_2) \in SK\_Temp$, a message block $m \in \mathbb{Z}$ (which includes all the message-block spaces) and a value s' that is supposed to be a forged signature on m, the algorithm *prove* first tests whether s' is an acceptable signature on m, i.e., whether $test(pk, m, s') = \text{TRUE}$. (Here, K and mk can be recomputed from sk, and the rest of pk is not needed.) If yes, the correct signature s on the same message block is computed, i.e., $s := sk_1 + m\, sk_2$. If $s \neq s'$, the output is
$$proof := (s, s').$$
Otherwise the output is *not_a_forgery*.
- Verifying proofs of forgery: Valid proofs of forgery are h_K-collisions. More precisely, on input a pair $(prek, proof)$, where $prek = (\text{'1'}^k, \text{'1'}^\sigma, K) \in All^*$, which implies $K \in All$, and where *proof* is a pair (s, s'),
$$verify\_simple(prek, (s, s')) = \text{TRUE}$$
$$:\Leftrightarrow\; s, s' \in G_K \wedge s \neq s' \wedge h_K(s) = h_K(s'). \qquad \blacklozenge$$

The following lemmas prove the properties that all implementations of the general construction framework have. It turns out that the only desired property that cannot be proved once and for all is a certain aspect of the security for the signer.

Lemma 9.5.

a) All implementations of Construction 9.4 (i.e., for all parameters *BundFam*, *all_test*, (*gen°*, *ZKP*), *tau*, and *MFam* of the prescribed types) are components of a standard fail-stop signature scheme with prekey for signing one message block (i.e., they fulfil Definition 9.1).

b) Moreover, they are polynomial-time in the interface inputs alone.

c) They fulfil effectiveness of authentication according to Criterion 1 of Theorem 7.34 (with the modification from Definition 9.1). ♦

Proof sketch.

A. First, the properties that are implicitly required in the definition of the components in Definitions 7.1 and 7.31 are verified, including the property to be polynomial-time in the interface inputs alone.

- The domain of the first parameter, *pk*, of *test* comprises all the values that can actually occur; this can immediately be seen if one adapts the end of Definition 7.31 to one-time schemes.
- All the algorithms are polynomial-time in the correct parameters. This is clear if one recalls that the definition of bundling homomorphisms contains algorithms

[148] This test is needed because the behaviour of the algorithm h outside its intended domain has not been defined.

for random choice in G_K, membership tests in G_K and H_K (polynomial-time in K alone), and the group operations in both G_K and H_K, and that multiplication of elements of an additive group with elements of $\mathbb{Z}$, which is defined by repeated addition, can be evaluated with the fast algorithms for exponentiation. As to *test* and *verify_simple* being polynomial-time in the interface inputs alone, note that the length of elements $s' \in G_K$ is polynomial in K because of Definition 8.29b.

- It is fairly clear that the adapted zero-knowledge proof scheme is indeed a zero-knowledge proof scheme for the adapted distributions. In particular, the condition $\tau := tau(k, \sigma) \geq \sigma$ guarantees that the error probability in the soundness, which is smaller than $2^{-\tau-1}$, is also smaller than $2^{-\sigma-1}$, and the computational security parameter, on which the zero-knowledge property mainly relies, is unchanged.

B. Now the properties required explicitly in Definition 7.31 are verified. (Property c has already been shown in Part A.)

a) Good and acceptable prekeys. The fact that $[Corr^*_{k,\sigma}] \subseteq Good^*_{k,\sigma} \subseteq All^*_{k,\sigma}$ for all $k, \sigma \in \mathbb{N}$ follows immediately from the corresponding property of the family of bundling homomorphisms (Definition 8.29a), and so does the fact that the length of all acceptable prekeys is polynomial in k and σ, if one recalls that *tau* is polynomial-time computable in unary.

b) It is clear that all correctly generated main public keys are acceptable to *mk_test*; and the length of acceptable main public keys is polynomial in *par** and *prek* by Definition 8.29b.

C. Effectiveness of authentication. Let parameters $par^* = (\text{'1'}^k, \text{'1'}^\sigma)$, a prekey $prek = (\text{'1'}^k, \text{'1'}^\sigma, K) \in All^*_{k,\sigma}$, a key pair $(sk, mk) \in [gen_A^{(f)}(par^*, prek)]$, a message block $m \in M_{prek}$, and its correct signature $s := sign^{(f)}(sk, m)$ be given. By construction, $sk = (K, 0, sk_1, sk_2)$ with $sk_1, sk_2 \in G_K$ and $mk = (mk_1, mk_2)$ with $mk_i = h_K(sk_i)$ for $i = 1, 2$, and $s = sk_1 + m\ sk_2$. As G_K is a group, $s \in G_K$, and the homomorphism property yields $h_K(s) = h_K(sk_1) \cdot h_K(sk_2)^m = mk_1 \cdot mk_2{}^m$, i.e., $test(pk, m, s) =$ TRUE.

D. Finally, the remaining properties required explicitly in Definition 7.1 are verified. (Property d has already been shown in Part A.)

a) The condition on *SK_Temp* is obviously fulfilled: With the end of Definition 7.31, one can immediately see that all original temporary secret key are of the form required in *SK_Temp* with $i = 0$, and the construction of *sign* implies that the temporary secret keys that can be reached later only differ by having $i = 1$ instead.

b) Let $sk = (K, 0, sk_1, sk_2) \in SK\_Temp$. It has to be shown that any output $proof \neq not\_a\_forgery$ of *prove* is a valid proof of forgery for any public key *pk* that can arise from the same execution of key generation. By construction, $proof = (s, s')$ with $s \neq s'$. Hence the second condition of *verify_simple* is true. Moreover, as effectiveness of authentication has already been shown,

$test(pk, m, s)$ = TRUE, and $test(pk, m, s')$ = TRUE has been verified in *prove*. This implies $s, s' \in G_K$ and

$$h_K(s) = mk_1 \cdot mk_2{}^m = h_K(s'),$$

i.e., the other two conditions of *verify_simple*.

c) The condition about reaching the message bound, 1, is obviously fulfilled. □

Lemma 9.6. All implementations of Construction 9.4 have the following properties:

a) Security for the risk bearer according to Criterion 2 of Theorem 7.34.

b) A step towards the security for the signer: Any successful forgery that is not the correct signature is a provable forgery. (Thus this construction has all the properties from the basic construction idea in Section 6.3.1, see Figures 6.6 to 6.8.)

More precisely: For all parameters $par^* = (\text{‘}1\text{’}^k, \text{‘}1\text{’}^\sigma)$, all prekeys $prek \in All^*_{k,\sigma}$, all pairs $(sk, mk) \in [gen_A{}^{(f)}(par^*, prek)]$ and $pk := (prek, mk)$, and all possible histories $hist \in Hist(prek, sk)$: If $f = (m', s') \in Forg(\text{TRUE}, pk, hist)$, then

$$s' \neq sign^{(f)}(sk, m') \Rightarrow provable(sk, pk, hist, f). \qquad \blacklozenge$$

Proof.

a) Assume the contrary. Then there are a probabilistic polynomial-time algorithm $\tilde{A}^*$, a polynomial $Qsig$ and a constant $c > 0$ such that $\forall k_0\ \exists k \geq k_0\ \exists \sigma \leq Qsig(k)$:

$$\begin{aligned} k^{-c} \leq\ & \mathrm{P}(s, s' \in G_K \wedge s \neq s' \wedge h_K(s) = h_K(s') \setminus \\ & \qquad K \leftarrow gen(\text{‘}1\text{’}^k, \text{‘}1\text{’}^{tau(k,\sigma)});\ prek := (\text{‘}1\text{’}^k, \text{‘}1\text{’}^\sigma, K); \\ & \qquad (s, s') \leftarrow \tilde{A}^*(\text{‘}1\text{’}^k, \text{‘}1\text{’}^\sigma, prek)) \\ =:\ & P_{succ,\tilde{A}^*}(k, \sigma). \end{aligned}$$

(Note that *verify_simple* and $Corr^*_{k,\sigma}$ have already been substituted by their definitions.) To lead this to a contradiction with the collision-intractability from Definition 8.29d, a probabilistic polynomial-time algorithm $\tilde{A}$ will be constructed such that for some polynomial $Qtau$ and the same constant $c > 0$ as above: $\forall k_0\ \exists k \geq k_0\ \exists \tau \leq Qtau(k)$

$$\begin{aligned} k^{-c} \leq\ & \mathrm{P}(h_K(s) = h_K(s') \wedge s \neq s' \wedge s, s' \in G_K \setminus \\ & \qquad K \leftarrow gen(\text{‘}1\text{’}^k, \text{‘}1\text{’}^\tau);\ (s, s') \leftarrow \tilde{A}(\text{‘}1\text{’}^k, \text{‘}1\text{’}^\tau, K)) \\ =:\ & P_{succ,\tilde{A}}(k, \tau). \end{aligned}$$

The algorithm $\tilde{A}$ is defined as follows: On input $(\text{‘}1\text{’}^k, \text{‘}1\text{’}^\tau, K)$, it searches for all values σ with $\tau = tau(k, \sigma)$; at most $\sigma := 1, \ldots, \tau$ have to be tried because $tau(k, \sigma) \geq \sigma$. It stops if no such σ exists. Otherwise, for each such σ, it calls $\tilde{A}^*(\text{‘}1\text{’}^k, \text{‘}1\text{’}^\sigma, (\text{‘}1\text{’}^k, \text{‘}1\text{’}^\sigma, K))$. If an output (s, s') is an h_K-collision, $\tilde{A}$ outputs this collision and stops.

It is clear that $\tilde{A}$ is polynomial-time. Secondly, the values σ have been selected so that $\tilde{A}$ is run on prekeys corresponding to its parameters k and σ. Thirdly, the success probability of $\tilde{A}$ is at least as large as that of any of its trials, because no unsuccessful stop in a previous trial is possible, i.e., $P_{succ,\tilde{A}}(k, \tau) \geq P_{succ,\tilde{A}^*}(k, \sigma)$ for all values σ that are tried.

Let *Qtau* be a polynomial with $Qtau(k) \geq tau(k, \sigma)$ for all k and all $\sigma \leq Qsig(k)$. Such a polynomial exists because *tau* is polynomial-time computable in unary, i.e., a polynomial Q with $tau(k, \sigma) \leq Q(k, \sigma)$ exists, and Q can be chosen so that it is monotonically increasing with σ for any fixed k. Then let $Qtau(k) := Q(k, Qsig(k))$.

Now let k_0 be given. There exist $k \geq k_0$ and $\sigma \leq Qsig(k)$ such that $k^{-c} \leq P_{succ,\tilde{A}^*}(k, \sigma)$. Let $\tau := tau(k, \sigma)$. Then $\tau \leq Qtau(k)$, and σ is tried when $\tilde{A}$ runs on input ('1'^{k}, '1'$^\tau$, K). Hence $P_{succ,\tilde{A}}(k, \tau) \geq P_{succ,\tilde{A}^*}(k, \sigma) \geq k^{-c}$.

b) This is a trivial consequence of the fact that both s and s' pass the test and the constructions of *prove* and *verify_simple*. □

Thus all the security properties except for the security for the signer have now been proved. For the latter, one has to compute the probability with which a computationally unrestricted attacker can guess exactly the correct signature, because this was just shown to be the only way of making an unprovable forgery.

This probability is certainly related to the bundling degree. If the attacker forges immediately after key generation, the only information he has about *sk* is the public key, i.e., the prekey and the images of sk_1 and sk_2 under the bundling homomorphism. Hence $2^{2\tau}$ secret keys are possible at that time, and they are all equally probable because they are chosen with uniform distribution in the construction. However, the attacker may gain more information about the secret key when the signer signs a message block m (which may even be chosen by the attacker). One can see that this restricts the choice to 2^τ possible secret keys. If all these secret keys led to different correct signatures on another message block m', the proof would be finished: The attacker could only guess the correct signature with probability $2^{-\tau}$. However, this is not always the case. Then the attacker can choose that value s' as his forged signature on m' that is correct for the largest number of possible secret keys, and thus with the highest likelihood.

This likelihood is computed in the following lemma.

Lemma 9.7 (Likelihood of guessing the correct signature). Let parameters par^* = ('1'^{k}, '1'$^\sigma$) and $\tau := tau(k, \sigma)$, a prekey $prek$ = ('1'^{k}, '1'$^\sigma$, K) $\in Good^*_{k,\sigma}$, a public key $pk = (prek, mk)$, a history $hist = (\underline{m}, \underline{s})$, and a successful forgery $f = (m', s')$ be given.

a) If *hist* is non-empty, i.e., $hist = (m, s)$, where s is an acceptable signature on m, let

$$m_\Delta := m' - m \neq 0.$$

Then the a-posteriori probability that s' is the correct signature on m', given all the information an attacker has, is at most

$$2^{-\tau}\, |T_{K,m_\Delta}|,$$

where $$T_{K,m_\Delta} := \{d \in G_K \mid h_K(d) = 1 \wedge m_\Delta\, d = 0\}.^{149}$$

149 Recall that, according to the conventions after Definition 8.30, the domain G_K of a bundling homomorphism is written additively and the codomain H_K multiplicatively. Hence "0" and "1" are the neutral elements in these two groups.

The probability space is defined as in Theorem 7.34 with the simplifications from Definition 9.3 (i.e., only $par^* = (\text{`}1\text{'}^k, \text{`}1\text{'}^\sigma)$ needs to be considered). Hence the formal claim is

$$P_{par^*,prek}(sign^{(f)}(sk, m') = s' \mid mk, sign^{(f)}(sk, m) = s) \leq 2^{-\tau} |T_{K,m_\Delta}|.$$

b) If the history is still empty, the attacker cannot do better: For any $m \neq m'$ and $m_\Delta := m' - m$, the following holds, too:

$$P_{par^*,prek}(sign^{(f)}(sk, m') = s' \mid mk) \leq 2^{-\tau} |T_{K,m_\Delta}|. \quad \blacklozenge$$

Remark 9.8. Equivalent expressions for T_{K,m_Δ} (where "T" stands for "torsion") are

$$\begin{aligned} T_{K,m_\Delta} &= \{d \in G_K \mid h_K(d) = 1 \wedge \text{ord}(d) \mid m_\Delta\} \\ &= \{d \in \ker(h_K) \mid \text{ord}(d) \mid m_\Delta\}. \end{aligned} \quad \blacklozenge$$

Proof of Lemma 9.7. Let the parameters k, σ, and τ and a prekey $prek \in Good^*_{k,\sigma}$ with $prek = (\text{`}1\text{'}^k, \text{`}1\text{'}^\sigma, K)$ be fixed in the proof. Hence $K \in Good_{k,\tau}$, and h_K is a homomorphism of bundling degree 2^τ.

a) Recall that the probabilities $P_{par^*,prek}(E)$ are defined by the generation of sk and mk from $prek$, i.e., in the given case by uniformly random choice of sk_1 and sk_2 in G_K. Hence the probability of an event E that can be expressed as a predicate $pred$ about sk_1 and sk_2 is

$$P_{par^*,prek}(E) = |\{(sk_1, sk_2) \mid pred(sk_1, sk_2)\}| \;/\; |G_K|^2,$$

i.e., the number of pairs (sk_1, sk_2) fulfilling the predicate divided by the number of all such pairs.

Let SK be the set of possible keys, given the public key and the history, i.e.,[150]

$$\begin{aligned} SK := \{(sk_1, sk_2) \in G_K \times G_K \mid \\ h_K(sk_1) = mk_1 \wedge h_K(sk_2) = mk_2 \wedge sk_1 + m\, sk_2 = s\}. \end{aligned} \quad (1)$$

The desired probability can be expressed as

$$\begin{aligned} &P_{par^*,prek}(sign^{(f)}(sk, m') = s' \mid mk, sign^{(f)}(sk, m) = s) \\ &= \frac{|\{(sk_1, sk_2) \in SK \mid sk_1 + m' sk_2 = s'\}|}{|SK|}. \end{aligned} \quad (2)$$

First, the size of SK is determined. The claim is that

$$SK = \{(s - m\, sk_2, sk_2) \mid h_K(sk_2) = mk_2\}. \quad (3)$$

The inclusion "$\subseteq$" is clear: sk_1 has been substituted by the last equation from (1). For the other inclusion, "$\supseteq$", the second and third equation are clear, and it remains to be shown that $h_K(s - m\, sk_2) = mk_1$. The fact that s is an acceptable signature on m means $h_K(s) = mk_1\, mk_2{}^m$. Thus the homomorphism property yields

$$h_K(s - m\, sk_2) = h_K(s)\, h_K(sk_2)^{-m} = h_K(s)\, mk_2{}^{-m} = mk_1.$$

---

150 For this proof, SK is simply defined by the following equation. But it is in fact the set of possible keys in the sense of Definition 7.16 (except that the components $prek$ and 0 have been omitted) when the zero-knowledge proof in key generation has been replaced by a trusted oracle, as in all the criteria from Theorem 7.34.

This proves (3). The size of SK is therefore the number of preimages of mk_2, i.e.,

$$|SK| \geq 2^{\tau}. \tag{4}$$

Secondly, one needs to know for how many possible secret keys the forged signature s' is correct, i.e., how many pairs $(sk_1, sk_2) \in SK$ satisfy the equation

$$sk_1 + m' \, sk_2 = s'. \tag{5}$$

According to (3), sk_1 is always $s - m \, sk_2$; hence (5) is equivalent to

$$(m' - m) \, sk_2 = s' - s. \tag{6}$$

This equation may be unsolvable, but if any solution sk_2' exists (with $h_K(sk_2') = mk_2$, because only pairs $(sk_1, sk_2) \in SK$ are considered), any other sk_2 is a solution if and only if $(m' - m) \, sk_2 = (m' - m) \, sk_2'$. Hence, in this case, the numerator of (2) is

$$\begin{aligned} &|\{(s - m \, sk_2, sk_2) \mid h_K(sk_2) = h_K(sk_2') \wedge (m' - m)(sk_2 - sk_2') = 0\}| \\ &= \quad |\{sk_2 \mid h_K(sk_2 - sk_2') = 1 \wedge m_\Delta (sk_2 - sk_2') = 0\}| \\ &= \quad |\{d \mid h_K(d) = 1 \wedge m_\Delta \, d) = 0\}| \\ &= \quad |T_{K,m_\Delta}|. \end{aligned} \tag{7}$$

Substituting (7) and (4) into (2) yields that the desired probability is at most $2^{-\tau} |T_{K,m_\Delta}|$, as claimed.

b) Instead of proving this directly, one can show that for any predicate *pred* and any random variables X, Y defined on the secret key, if $P_{par,prek}(pred(sk) \mid X = x, Y = y) \leq \varepsilon$ for some ε has already been shown for all y that can occur together with x, then $P_{par,prek}(pred(sk) \mid X = x) \leq \varepsilon$ holds, too:

$$\begin{aligned} &P_{par,prek}(pred(sk) \mid X = x) \\ &\quad = \sum_y P_{par,prek}(Y = y \mid X = x) \, P_{par,prek}(pred(sk) \mid Y = y, X = x) \\ &\quad \leq \sum_y P_{par,prek}(Y = y \mid X = x) \cdot \varepsilon \\ &\quad \leq \varepsilon. \end{aligned}$$

In the given case, the predicate is $sign^{(f)}(sk, m') = s'$, the random variable X is the main public key, and Y is the signature s on one fixed m. □

Now it is summarized what has to be done to make an implementation of the general construction framework secure for the signer. It has just been shown that the a-posteriori probability of a forgery being unprovable is bounded by $2^{-\tau} |T_{K,m_\Delta}|$. It has to be bounded by $2^{-\sigma-1}$, according to Criterion 3 from Theorem 7.34 in the version of Definitions 9.1 and 9.3. Hence an upper bound on $|T_{K,m_\Delta}|$ is needed, and then τ has to be chosen sufficiently larger than σ. The exact condition is summarized in the following theorem.

Theorem 9.9. Construction 9.4 yields a secure standard fail-stop signature scheme with prekey for signing one message block if the following condition holds for the parameters *BundFam*, *MFam*, and *tau* (i.e., the family of bundling homomorphisms, the message-block spaces, and the function that determines the bundling degree): Let $t_{k,\sigma,K}$ denote the maximum size of T_{K,m_Δ}, i.e., for all $k, \sigma \in \mathbb{N}$ and $K \in Good$,

$$t_{k,\sigma,K} := \max(\{|T_{K,m_\Delta}| \mid m_\Delta \in (M_{k,\sigma,K} - M_{k,\sigma,K}) \setminus \{0\}\}),$$

where, as usual, $M_{k,\sigma,K} - M_{k,\sigma,K} := \{m' - m \mid m', m \in M_{k,\sigma,K}\}$. The condition is that for all parameters $k, \sigma \in \mathbb{N}$ and all keys $K \in Good_{k,tau(k,\sigma)}$ of the family of bundling homomorphisms,

$$tau(k, \sigma) \geq \sigma + 1 + \log_2(t_{k,\sigma,K}). \qquad \blacklozenge$$

Proof. It has to be shown that Definition 9.1, with the abbreviations from Definition 9.3, is fulfilled. Lemmas 9.5 and 9.6 cover all the requirements except for the security for the signer, i.e., Criterion 3 of Theorem 7.34. If values $pk = (prek, mk)$ with $prek = (\text{'}1\text{'}^k, \text{'}1\text{'}^\sigma, K)$ and $hist = (\underline{m}, \underline{s})$ are given, where $hist$ is a possible history, Lemma 9.7 can be applied. Together with Lemma 9.6, it immediately yields

$$P_{par^*,prek}(provable(sk, pk, hist, f) \mid mk, sign^{(f)}(sk, \underline{m}) = \underline{s}) \geq 1 - 2^{-\tau} |T_{K,m_\Delta}|$$

for all successful forgeries f and some $m_\Delta := m' - m$ with $m, m' \in M_{k,\sigma,K}$ and $m' \neq m$. Thus $(mk, hist) \in GoodInf(\text{'}1\text{'}^k, \text{'}1\text{'}^\sigma, prek)$ if one can show that $2^{-\tau} |T_{K,m_\Delta}| \leq 2^{-\sigma-1}$ for $\tau := tau(k, \sigma)$ and for all these values m_Δ. This holds if $2^{-\tau} t_{k,\sigma,K} \leq 2^{-\sigma-1}$, or, equivalently, $\tau \geq (\sigma + 1) + \log_2(t_{k,\sigma,K})$. □

9.3 Implementation Based on the Discrete-Logarithm Assumption

In this section, an efficient standard fail-stop signature scheme with prekey for signing one message block is shown where the security for the risk bearer can be proved on the abstract discrete-logarithm assumption. Recall that this scheme (for subgroups of prime fields) is due to [HePe93].

Of course, in the present context, the scheme is constructed by using the family of pair exponentiations as bundling homomorphisms from Section 8.5.3 in the general construction framework from Section 9.2.

In the following, the remaining parameters are defined and the security is proved. Then the resulting scheme is summarized, and finally, the complexity of the scheme is evaluated briefly.

Definition 9.10 (Discrete-logarithm scheme). Let a family of groups of prime order be given (see Definition 8.19a). The corresponding standard fail-stop signature scheme with prekey for signing one message block, called a discrete-logarithm scheme, is defined as the result of Construction 9.4 with the following parameters:

- *BundFam*, the collision-intractable family of bundling homomorphisms, is given by Construction 8.44, i.e., pair exponentiation in the given family of groups. Its components are written with a prime if their names would otherwise collide with those from the given family of groups, in particular, *gen'* and *AllFam'*.

- The algorithm *all_test*, on input ('1'^{k}, '1'$^\tau$, K), where $K = (q, desc, g)$, decides if $K \in All'_{k,\tau}$ as follows. First it uses *group_verification*('1'$^{\max(k,\tau)}$, q, $desc$) to decide if $(q, desc) \in All_{\max(k,\tau)}$. If yes, it tests if $g \in (H_{q,desc} \setminus \{1\})^2$.
- As *GoodFam* = *AllFam* in the given family *BundFam*, the good keys are locally verifiable, too, i.e., the zero-knowledge proof scheme (*gen°*, *ZKP*) is derived with Lemma 7.28 from *gen'* and the local verification algorithm V := *all_test*. (Of course, this algorithm only needs to be carried out once in A and *res*.)
- The function that determines the bundling degree is simply defined by

$$tau(k, \sigma) := \sigma + 1,$$

and *tau** is the canonical algorithm to compute *tau* in unary.
- The family *MFam* of message-block spaces is defined as follows: For all $k, \sigma \in \mathbb{N}$ and $K = (q, desc, g) \in All'$,

$$M_{k,\sigma,K} := \{0, 1, \ldots, q-1\}. \qquad \blacklozenge$$

Theorem 9.11. If the discrete logarithm in the given family of groups is hard, the corresponding discrete-logarithm scheme from Definition 9.10 is secure. ♦

Proof. According to Theorem 9.9, one only has to verify that for all parameters k, $\sigma \in \mathbb{N}$ and all keys $K = (q, desc, g) \in Good'_{k,tau(k,\sigma)}$ of the family of bundling homomorphisms,

$$tau(k, \sigma) \;\geq\; \sigma + 1 + \log_2(t_{k,\sigma,K}).$$

By definition of *tau*, it is sufficient to prove $\log_2(t_{k,\sigma,K}) = 0$, i.e.,

$$t_{k,\sigma,K} \;=\; 1. \qquad (*)$$

By definition, $t_{k,\sigma,K}$ is the maximum of the sizes of the sets

$$T_{K,m_\Delta} \;=\; \{d \in \ker(h_K) \mid \operatorname{ord}(d) \mid m_\Delta\}$$

with $m_\Delta \in (M_{k,\sigma,K} - M_{k,\sigma,K}) \setminus \{0\} = \pm\{1, \ldots, q-1\}$. The group G_K in Construction 8.44 is the additive group $\mathbb{Z}_q \times \mathbb{Z}_q$. Hence

$$T_{K,m_\Delta} \;\subseteq\; \{d \in \mathbb{Z}_q \times \mathbb{Z}_q \mid \operatorname{ord}(d) \mid m_\Delta\}.$$

As the group order is q^2, the order of every element d is a factor of q^2 (actually only 1 or q). The only factor of q^2 that divides a number $m_\Delta \in \pm\{1, \ldots, q-1\}$ is 1, and the only element d of order 1 is the neutral element (0, 0). This proves $|T_{K,m_\Delta}| = 1$ for all m_Δ, and thus (*). □

As the construction is spread out in a modular way over several definitions, it seems useful to summarize the result. For even more concreteness, this is done for subgroups of prime fields, i.e., on a concrete discrete-logarithm assumption (Definition 8.21b).

Lemma 9.12 (Summary of the discrete-logarithm scheme for subgroups of prime fields). If a family of subgroups of prime fields according to Construction 8.22 is given, the corresponding discrete-logarithm scheme from Definition 9.10 has the following components that are actually used.[151]

- Key generation:
  - Prekey generation:
    - Prekey-generation algorithm gen_B: On input $par^* = (\text{'1'}^k, \text{'1'}^\sigma)$, call the group-generation algorithm $gen(\text{'1'}^{\max(k,\sigma+1)})$. It produces a pair (q, p) of primes. Now choose a pair (g, g^*) of generators of the group $H_{q,p}$ randomly (where $H_{q,p}$ is the unique subgroup of order q of $\mathbb{Z}_p^*$). Hence the complete prekey is
    $$prek := K := (q, p, g, g^*).$$
    It is guaranteed that $q > 2^{\max(k,\sigma+1)}$ and $q \mid (p - 1)$ and $|p|_2 \leq len\_p(\max(k, \sigma+1))$.
    - Local verification algorithm *all_test* (for acceptable and good prekeys): On input $(\text{'1'}^k, \text{'1'}^\sigma, prek)$ with $prek = (q, p, g, g^*)$: First, *group_verification* is called on input $(\text{'1'}^{\max(k,\sigma+1)}, q, p)$. It computes $l := len\_p(\max(k, \sigma+1))$ and verifies that $|q|_2 \leq |p|_2 \leq l$, and, if yes, that $q > 2^{\max(k,\sigma+1)}$ and $q \mid (p - 1)$, and that q and p are prime. Secondly, it is verified that g and g^* are generators of $H_{q,p}$ by testing that they are in $\mathbb{Z}_p^*$ (in the correct representation) and that $g^q = g^{*q} = 1$, but neither g nor g^* is 1.
  - Main key generation gen_A: On input $(\text{'1'}^k, \text{'1'}^\sigma, prek)$ with $prek = (q, p, g, g^*)$, a pair of random values sk_1, sk_2 is chosen from $\mathbb{Z}_q \times \mathbb{Z}_q$, i.e.,
  $$sk := sk\_temp := (prek, 0, (x_1, y_1), (x_2, y_2)),$$
  where x_1, y_1, x_2, and y_2 are random numbers modulo q. The corresponding main public key is the pair (mk_1, mk_2) of images under the bundling homomorphism, pair exponentiation, i.e.,
  $$mk := (mk_1, mk_2)$$
  with $$mk_1 := g^{x_1} g^{*y_1} \wedge mk_2 := g^{x_2} g^{*y_2}.$$
  - Main public key test *mk_test* (on input $(\text{'1'}^k, \text{'1'}^\sigma, prek, mk)$ with $prek = (q, p, g, g^*)$ and $mk = (mk_1, mk_2)$): Instead of testing that mk_1 and mk_2 are elements of $H_{q,p}$, it is usually sufficient to test that they are in $\mathbb{Z}_p^*$: The length restrictions are still fulfilled, and the only other property that could be violated by enlarging the set of acceptable main public keys is that *test* works in polynomial time for all public keys that can possibly occur, and any usual multiplication algorithm works on the entire $\mathbb{Z}_p$.

---

151 The following components from Construction 9.4 are *not* used: The families of correct prekey distributions and sets of good and all acceptable prekeys (only the generation and verification algorithms are used); the zero-knowledge proof scheme, except for the generation algorithm, because it only repeats *all_test*; and the security parameters as components of the prekey.

- Message-block spaces: For a prekey $prek = (q, p, g, g^*)$, the message-block space is $M_{prek} := \{0, 1, \ldots, q-1\}$.
- Signing: If the secret key is $sk = (prek, 0, sk_1, sk_2)$ with $prek = (q, p, g, g^*)$, the correct signature on a message block $m \in \{0, 1, \ldots, q-1\}$ is $sk_1 + m\ sk_2$ in $\mathbb{Z}_q \times \mathbb{Z}_q$, i.e.,
$$sign^{(f)}(sk, m) := (x_1, y_1) + m\,(x_2, y_2) = (x_1 + m\,x_2, y_1 + m\,y_2).$$
- Test: If the public key is $pk = (prek, (mk_1, mk_2))$ with $prek = K = (q, p, g, g^*)$, a value s is an acceptable signature on a message block m if and only if
  - s is in the correct group, i.e., s is a pair (x, y) of numbers modulo q, and
  - $h_K(s) = mk_1\ mk_2{}^m$, i.e.
$$g^x\, g^{*y} = mk_1\, mk_2{}^m.$$
- Proving forgeries: Given a secret key as above and a supposed forgery (m, s'), it is first tested if s' is an acceptable signature on m. If yes, the correct signature s on the same message block is computed. If $s' \neq s$, the result is
$$proof := (s, s'),$$
and otherwise, *not_a_forgery*.
- Verifying proofs of forgery: Valid proofs of forgery are h_K-collisions. Thus if the prekey is $prek = K = (q, p, g, g^*)$, a value $proof = (s, s')$, where $s = (x, y)$ and $s' = (x', y')$, is considered valid iff
$$x, y, x', y' \in \mathbb{Z}_q \wedge (x, y) \neq (x', y') \wedge g^x\, g^{*y} = g^{x'}\, g^{*y'}.$$ ♦

Proof. Everything can be verified by straightforward substitution of Definition 9.10, Constructions 9.4, 8.44, and 8.22, and Definition 8.21. □

Remark 9.13. Instead of the proof of forgery according to the general construction framework, $e := log_g(g^*)$ could be defined to be the valid proof of forgery, because it is shorter and easier to verify (and shows more intuitively that someone has broken the discrete-logarithm assumption in its concrete instantiation). This does not alter the security, because there are polynomial-time algorithms that transform either type of proof of forgery into the other (cf. Lemma 8.40). ♦

This section ends with a short evaluation of the efficiency of the scheme from Lemma 9.12. Only the length of values that are sent or stored and the time complexity of the algorithms is presented. The consequences for the overall communication and time complexity of the transactions and the space complexity of the entities is then easy to see with the simple structure of standard fail-stop signature schemes.

To obtain readable results, some simplifications are made:

- It is assumed that $\max(k, \sigma+1)$ is always k. This is reasonable, because error probabilities of 2^{-100} seem negligible enough for any real-world purpose, i.e., 100 is a reasonable upper bound on σ, whereas k will be larger.
- It is assumed that the group-generation algorithm *gen* generates q of length $|q|_2 \approx k$, and this is simplified by assuming $|q|_2 = k$.

  In contrast, $|p|_2$ may be larger. In practice, two usual choices for similar situations are $k = 160$ and $|p|_2 = 512$ or $k = |p|_2 = 512$; see Section 8.4.2.

Lemma 9.14 (Complexity of the discrete-logarithm scheme for subgroups of prime fields). In the following, the complexity of the scheme from Lemma 9.12 is summarized on the assumption that $max(k, \sigma+1) = k$, and, slightly simplified, $|q|_2 = k$ and $|p|_2 = l := len\_p(k)$.

a) Lengths (in bits):
   - Prekey: $k + 3l$.
   - Secret key, both the temporary and the complete one: $4k$ (in addition to the prekey).
   - Main public key: $2l$.
   - Signature (on a k-bit message block): $2k$.
   - Proof of forgery: $4k$, or, if Remark 9.13 is used, k.

b) Time complexity:
   - Key generation.
     - Prekey generation is of the same order of complexity as key generation in ordinary digital signature schemes: It is dominated by the primality tests needed for the generation of two primes, q and p. This means approximately one exponentiation per number tested for primality with the Rabin-Miller test. Hence the number of exponentiations is determined by the density of primes of the chosen size (see Section 8.1.5); however, many numbers can be excluded by trial division as usual.
     - Prekey verification: A fixed small number of exponentiations, such as 12 (with 5 iterations of the basic Rabin-Miller primality test for q and p each).
     - Main key generation: Generation of 4 random numbers and two pair exponentiations, which require less than $4k$ modular multiplications of numbers of length l.
     - Main key test: Negligible.
   - Signing requires two multiplications modulo q. This is extremely efficient, even in comparison with ordinary digital signature schemes.
   - Testing a signature can be sped up by computing $g^x g^{*y} (mk_2^{-1})^m$ and verifying that it equals mk_1. The inversion of mk_2 can be precomputed. Then, even with a simple 3-tuple exponentiation algorithm (see Section 8.3), less than $2k$ modular multiplications of numbers of length l are needed.

     To avoid a modular inversion altogether, one can even replace mk_2 in the public key by mk_2^{-1}, because the signer's entity can compute it as $g^{-x_2} g^{*-y_2}$ with $-x_2, -y_2 \in \mathbb{Z}_q$ just as fast as mk_2.

     Thus testing is not as efficient as signing, but still of the same order as signing or testing in ordinary digital signature schemes, such as RSA (see Section 2.4).
   - Computing proofs of forgery: One test and one signing operation.

- Verifying proofs of forgery: Either one pair exponentiation to compute $g^{x-x'} g^{*y-y'}$ (less than $2k$ modular multiplications of numbers of length l) or, with Remark 9.13, one exponentiation. ♦□

Remark 9.15 (Small message spaces). The message-block spaces $M_{prek} = \{0, \ldots, q-1\}$ are very simple. In particular, random choice of a message block and membership tests can be carried out efficiently, if they are needed in an application.

Moreover, one can already construct one-time fail-stop signature schemes for real finite message spaces M: One only needs a number $k_0 \in \mathbb{N}$ and a polynomial-time computable injection ι of M into the set $\{0, \ldots, 2^{k_0} - 1\}$. The scheme is changed so that any $k < k_0$ is replaced by k_0. This does not alter the security. Then one can map M into M_{prek} with ι for all acceptable prekeys. ♦

Remark 9.16 (Many risk bearers). Extensions to many risk bearers are comparatively simple in the discrete-logarithm case, because prekey generation can be decomposed into the uniformly random choice of a string r of a certain length, where r need not be secret, and a deterministic algorithm that computes *prek* from r. This can be exploited as in Section 7.5.2, "Special Versions", Item 2.

The details of this decomposition depend on the underlying group-generation algorithm *gen* (see Section 8.4.2, "Generation Algorithms"). For instance, the first part of r can be used as a starting value for the search for a prime q in steps of 2. If the primality test is probabilistic, one can use more trusted random bits there. Alternatively, one can trust the fact that even with a probabilistic primality test, all honest participants obtain identical results with an exponentially small error probability. (To preclude that attackers can claim that this happened nevertheless, one might let a centre publish its result and a witness for each number it found composite. Other participants may challenge this result if it is incorrect or if they have a witness proving compositeness of the number q the centre found prime.)

The second prime, p, can be generated similarly. It may even be determined deterministically, e.g., as the smallest prime of the form $dq + 1$ with $d \geq 1000$.

The generators g and g^* are chosen by raising random numbers modulo p to the d-th power. For the random numbers, one either chooses a larger number and reduces it modulo p, which yields a small bias in the distribution, or one needs enough random bits to repeat the choice of numbers of the correct length until two of them are smaller than p with an exponentially small error probability. ♦

9.4 Implementations Based on the Factoring Assumption

In this section, efficient standard fail-stop signature schemes with prekey for signing one message block are shown where the security for the risk bearer can be proved on the factoring assumption. The schemes apply the family of iterated squaring and doubling as bundling homomorphisms in the general construction framework from Section 9.2.

There are two classes of such schemes. The main difference is that one has a small set of really good prekeys and the other a larger set of prekeys that are not quite so good. With the really good prekeys, the remaining parameters are quite small, but a real zero-knowledge proof is needed to verify that a prekey is good. In the other class, the remaining parameters are larger, but good prekeys can be verified locally. The class with real zero-knowledge proofs was already presented in [HePP93, PePf95].

Apart from that, this section is structured like Section 9.3.

Definition 9.17 (Factoring schemes). Let a function *rho*: $\mathbb{N} \times \mathbb{N} \to \mathbb{N}$ and an algorithm to compute *rho* in unary in polynomial time be given. (This function will determine the size of the message blocks as a function of the security parameters.) Two corresponding standard fail-stop signature schemes with prekey for signing one message block, called **factoring scheme with zero-knowledge proof** and **factoring scheme with local verifiability**, are defined as the result of Construction 9.4 with the following parameters. The two schemes are distinguished by indices "*z*" and "*l*" where necessary.

- *BundFam*, the collision-intractable family of bundling homomorphisms, is given by Construction 8.66, i.e., iterated squaring and doubling.

  However, in the scheme with zero-knowledge proof, *GoodFam* is replaced by $GoodFam_z$ where $Good_{z,k,\tau} := \{(n, \text{'1'}^{\tau}) \mid n \in GeneralBlum \wedge |n|_2 \le 2k\}$; this is possible by Remark 8.38a.
- The algorithm *all_test*, on input ('1'^{k}, '1'$^\tau$, K), where $K = (n, \text{'1'}^{\tau'})$, verifies that $\tau' = \tau$ and $n \in 4\mathbb{N} + 1$ and $|n|_2 \le 2k$.
- The generation algorithm, $gen°$, of the zero-knowledge proof scheme is the same as in *BundFam*, except that in the scheme with zero-knowledge proof, the factors p and q of n are the auxiliary output (this was assumed to be possible in Section 8.4.1). The component *ZKP* is different in the two schemes:
  1. In the scheme with zero-knowledge proof: Local verification that τ is correct and $|n|_2 \le 2k$, and the zero-knowledge proof scheme from [GrPe88] with the modifications sketched in Section 8.1.3, "Recognizing Generalized Blum Integers", are combined.
  2. In the scheme with local verifiability: As *GoodFam* = *AllFam* in the given family *BundFam*, the good keys are locally verifiable, too, i.e., the zero-knowledge proof scheme is derived from *all_test* with Lemma 7.28. (Of course, this algorithm only needs to be carried out once in *A* and *res*.)
- Functions tau_z and tau_l that determine the bundling degree in the schemes with local verifiability and with zero-knowledge proof, respectively, are defined as follows:

$$tau_z(k, \sigma) := \sigma + 1 + rho(k, \sigma),$$
$$tau_l(k, \sigma) := \sigma + 1 + rho(k, \sigma) + 2k.$$

  Polynomial-time algorithms that compute tau_z and tau_l in unary are clear.
- In both schemes, the family *MFam* of message-block spaces is defined by

$$M_{k,\sigma,K} := \{0, 1, \ldots, 2^{rho(k,\sigma)} - 1\}$$

  for all $k, \sigma \in \mathbb{N}$ and $K \in All$. ♦

Theorem 9.18. On the factoring assumption, the two schemes from Definition 9.17 are secure for any function *rho*. ♦

Proof. According to Theorem 9.9, only the one condition made there has to be verified. Let parameters $k, \sigma \in \mathbb{N}$ be fixed, ™$\rho := rho(k, \sigma)$, and

$$\tau_z := tau_z(k, \sigma) \text{ and } \tau_l := tau_l(k, \sigma).$$

The condition is that

$$\begin{aligned} & tau_z(k, \sigma) \geq \sigma + 1 + \log_2(t_{k,\sigma,K}) && \text{for all } K \in Good_{z,k,\tau_z} \\ \text{and} \quad & tau_l(k, \sigma) \geq \sigma + 1 + \log_2(t_{k,\sigma,K}) && \text{for all } K \in Good_{k,\tau_l}. \end{aligned}$$

By definition of tau_z and tau_l, it is sufficient to prove that $\log_2(t_{k,\sigma,K})$ is at most ρ or $\rho + 2k$, respectively, i.e.,

$$\begin{aligned} & t_{k,\sigma,K} \leq 2^{\rho} && \text{for all } K \in Good_{z,k,\tau_z} \\ \text{and} \quad & t_{k,\sigma,K} \leq 2^{\rho+2k} && \text{for all } K \in Good_{k,\tau_l}. \end{aligned} \qquad (*)$$

By definition, $t_{k,\sigma,K}$ is the maximum of the sizes of the sets

$$T_{K,m_\Delta} = \{d \in \ker(h_K) \mid \text{ord}(d) \mid m_\Delta\}$$

with $m_\Delta \in (M_{k,\sigma,K} - M_{k,\sigma,K}) \setminus \{0\} = \pm\{1, \ldots, 2^{\rho} - 1\}$. A key of the family of bundling homomorphisms is of the form $K = (n, \text{'1'}^{\tau})$, and the corresponding group G_K is $G_{\tau,n} = \{0, \ldots, 2^{\tau} - 1\} \times RQR_n^{>}$ with the operation $*$ from Definition 8.14. If $d = (a, y) \in G_{\tau,n}$, then

$$\Big(\text{ord}(d) \mid m_\Delta \;\Rightarrow\; (a, y)^{m_\Delta} = (0, 1) \quad (\text{in } G_{\tau,n}) \\ \Rightarrow\; m_\Delta\, a \bmod 2^{\tau} = 0 \quad (\text{in } \mathbb{Z}) \Big).$$

The second implication was obtained by comparing the first components of the pairs. Hence

$$T_{K,m_\Delta} \subseteq \{(a, y) \in G_{\tau,n} \mid h_K(a, y) = 1 \wedge m_\Delta\, a \equiv 0 \bmod 2^{\tau}\}.$$

Now the two schemes are considered separately.

1. Scheme with zero-knowledge proof: $K \in Good_{z,k,\tau_z}$ means $K = (n, \text{'1'}^{\tau_z})$, where $n \in GeneralBlum$. As $h_K = B^*_{\tau_z,n}$, Lemma 8.11b says that for each a, there is exactly one y with $h_K(a, y) = 1$. (Similar to Section 8.5.5, the lemma can be applied to $B^*_{\tau_z,n}$, instead of $B_{\tau_z,n}$ because of the bijection $num_{\tau_z}^{-1}$ from parameters a to strings b.) Thus

$$\begin{aligned} |T_{K,m_\Delta}| &\leq |\{a \in \mathbb{Z}_{2^{\tau_z}} \mid m_\Delta\, a \equiv 0 \bmod 2^{\tau_z}\}| \\ &= \gcd(2^{\tau_z}, m_\Delta) \\ &\leq |m_\Delta| \\ &< 2^{\rho}. \end{aligned}$$

2. Scheme with local verifiability: For $K \in Good_{k,\tau_l}$, only a much weaker bound is shown:

$$\begin{aligned} |T_{K,m_\Delta}| &\leq |\{a \in \mathbb{Z}_{2^{\tau_l}} \mid m_\Delta\, a \equiv 0 \bmod 2^{\tau_l}\}| \cdot |RQR_n^{>}| \\ &< \gcd(2^{\tau_l}, m_\Delta) \cdot n \\ &\leq |m_\Delta| \cdot 2^{2k} \\ &< 2^{\rho+2k}. \end{aligned}$$

Hence (∗), and thus the theorem, has been proved in both cases. □

Similar to Lemma 9.12, the resulting constructions are now summarized (except for the details of the zero-knowledge proof scheme).

Lemma 9.19 (Summary of the factoring schemes). The factoring schemes from Definition 9.17 with the function *rho* have the following components that are actually used:

- Key generation:
  - Prekey generation:
    - Prekey-generation algorithm gen_B: On input $par^* = (\text{'1'}^k, \text{'1'}^\sigma)$, it calls $gen_{Will}(\text{'1'}^k)$ to generate a Williams integer n. It sets $\rho := rho(k, \sigma)$ and
    $$\tau := \sigma + 1 + \rho \quad \text{and} \quad \tau := \sigma + 1 + \rho + 2k$$
    in the schemes with zero-knowledge proof and with local verifiability, respectively, and
    $$K := (n, \text{'1'}^\tau) \quad \text{and} \quad prek := (\text{'1'}^k, \text{'1'}^\sigma, K).$$
    In the scheme with zero-knowledge proof, the factors p and q of n are retained.
    - Zero-knowledge proof scheme: In both schemes, it is verified that the security parameters in *prek* are correct and that $|n|_2 \le 2k$.
    Furthermore, the zero-knowledge proof scheme from [GrPe88] with the modifications sketched in Section 8.1.3 is used to prove that n is a generalized Blum integer, or it is locally verified that $n \in 4\mathbb{N} + 1$, respectively.
  - Main key generation gen_A: On input $(\text{'1'}^k, \text{'1'}^\sigma, prek)$ with *prek* as above, a pair of random values sk_1, sk_2 is chosen from $G_{\tau,n} = \{0, \ldots, 2^\tau - 1\} \times RQR_n^>$, i.e.,
  $$sk := (prek, 0, (a, y), (a', y')).$$
  The random choice of y (and similarly y') in $RQR_n^>$ works as follows: In the scheme with zero-knowledge proof, $\tilde{y}$ is chosen randomly in $\mathbb{Z}_n$, and $y := \tilde{y}^2$ or $y := -\tilde{y}^2$, whichever is smaller than $n/2$, is used. In the scheme with local verifiability, a number y is chosen repeatedly, until it has the Jacobi symbol +1, and then negated if it is greater than $n/2$.
  The corresponding main public key is the pair (mk_1, mk_2) of images under the bundling homomorphism, i.e.,
  $$mk_1 := 4^a \circ y^{2^\tau} \wedge mk_2 := 4^{a'} \circ y'^{\,2^\tau}.$$
  The computations can be carried out in $\mathbb{Z}_n^*$, except for one possible final negation to make the result smaller than $n/2$.
  - Main public key test *mk_test*: Instead of testing that mk_1 and mk_2 are elements of $RQR_n^>$, one can simply test that they are in $\mathbb{Z}_n$, similar to Lemma 9.12.
- Message-block spaces: For a prekey $prek = (\text{'1'}^k, \text{'1'}^\sigma, K)$, the message-block space is $M_{prek} := \{0, 1, \ldots, 2^\rho - 1\}$, where $\rho := rho(k, \sigma)$.

- Signing: If the secret key is $sk = (prek, 0, sk_1, sk_2)$ with $prek = (\text{'1'}^k, \text{'1'}^\sigma, K)$ and $K = (n, \text{'1'}^\tau)$, the correct signature on a message block $m \in \{0, 1, \ldots, 2^\rho - 1\}$ is $sk_1 * sk_2{}^m$ in $G_{\tau,n}$, i.e.,

$$sign^{(f)}(sk, m) := (a, y) * (a', y')^m,$$

which is computed by applying a usual exponentiation algorithm to $(G_{\tau,n}, *)$.

- Test: If the public key is $pk = (prek, (mk_1, mk_2))$ with $prek = (\text{'1'}^k, \text{'1'}^\sigma, K)$ and $K = (n, \text{'1'}^\tau)$, a value s is an acceptable signature on a message block m if and only if
  - s is in the correct group, i.e., s is pair $(\ddot{a}, \ddot{u})$ of numbers with $0 \le \ddot{a} < 2^\tau$ and $0 < \ddot{u} < n/2$, and the Jacobi symbol of $\ddot{u}$ is $+1$, and
  - $h_K(s) = mk_1 \circ mk_2{}^m$, i.e.

$$4^{\ddot{a}} \circ \ddot{u}^{2^\tau} = mk_1 \circ mk_2{}^m$$

  in $RQR_n^{>}$, i.e., in $\mathbb{Z}_n^*$ with final mappings to numbers smaller than $n/2$.

- Proving forgeries: Given a secret key as above and a supposed forgery (m, s'), it is first tested if s' is an acceptable signature on m. If yes, the correct signature s on the same message block is computed. If $s' \ne s$, the result is

$$proof := (s, s'),$$

and otherwise, *not_a_forgery*.

- Verifying proofs of forgery: Valid proofs of forgery are h_K-collisions. Thus if *proof* is a pair (s, s'), where $s = (\ddot{a}, \ddot{u})$ and $s' = (\ddot{a}', \ddot{u}')$, it is considered valid iff[152]

$$\ddot{a}, \ddot{a}' \in \mathbb{Z}_{2^\tau} \wedge \ddot{u}, \ddot{u}' \in RQR_n^{>} \wedge (\ddot{a}, \ddot{u}) \ne (\ddot{a}', \ddot{u}') \wedge 4^{\ddot{a}} \circ \ddot{u}^{2^\tau} = 4^{\ddot{a}'} \circ \ddot{u}'^{2^\tau}. \quad \blacklozenge$$

Proof. Everything can be verified by straightforward substitution of Constructions 9.4, 8.66, and 8.64. □

Remark 9.20. In the scheme with local verifiability, the random choice of sk_1 and sk_2 is rather inefficient because of the computation of Jacobi symbols. One could avoid this if the bundling homomorphism were based on $RQR_n^{<}$, instead of $RQR_n^{>}$. However, no polynomial-time membership test in $RQR_n^{<}$ is known, and hence Definition 8.29 is not fulfilled. Nevertheless, it is now shown that the random choice in the main key generation of the signature scheme can be restricted to $RQR_n^{<}$, while maintaining the weaker membership tests for $RQR_n^{>}$ in *test* and in *verify_simple*.

Obviously, the only property of the scheme that could be affected by this restriction of the secret key space is the security for the signer. (Effectiveness of authentication holds for each key individually.) Furthermore, Lemma 9.6b is unchanged; hence only the likelihood of guessing the correct signature has to be reconsidered. The functions h_K on the restricted domains are the functions $B_{\tau,n}^{*<}$, which are still of bundling degree 2^τ by Lemma 8.17b. Hence Lemma 9.7 can be proved for them, too. Thus an upper bound on the sizes of the sets $T_{K,m_\Delta}^{<} = \{d \in G_{\tau,n}^{<} \mid h_K(d) = 1 \wedge$

[152] Recall that the computation of the Jacobi symbol is necessary to exclude trivial claws such as $(2x)^2 = 4(x)^2$. The computation of a Jacobi symbol in *test* is necessary to guarantee that if the signature is a successful forgery, it will pass this verification.

$m_\Delta\, d = 0\}$ remains to be computed. These sizes are obviously at most as large as in the original scheme. ♦

Remark 9.21. Instead of the proof of forgery according to the general construction framework, any factor p of n could be defined to be a valid proof of forgery. Obviously, this still guarantees the security for the risk bearer on the factoring assumption. In the scheme with zero-knowledge proof, this obviously does not weaken the security for the signer, because the reductions in the proofs of Theorem 8.57 and Lemma 8.65 yield a polynomial-time algorithm that computes such a factor from a proof of forgery in the previous sense for all good keys. In the scheme with local verifiability, where the functions are not necessarily permutations, the extended version of *claw_from_collision* from Lemma 8.55 must be used to find either a claw or an $f_{0,K}$- or $f_{1,K}$-collision. The collision can be used to factor just as a claw in the proof of Lemma 8.65. (That n does not divide any of the factors arising is clear, because the two preimages x, x' in a collision are different, and they are defined as classes modulo $\{\pm 1\}$. ♦

Finally, the complexity is summarized. For this, recall that a multiplication in $G_{\tau,n}$ is mainly one multiplication modulo n (see Construction 8.66).

Lemma 9.22 (Complexity of the factoring schemes). In the following, the complexity of the schemes from Definition 9.17 and Lemma 9.19 is summarized. To avoid confusion when comparing the results with those of the discrete-logarithm scheme, where the size of k is usually different, the length $l := |n|_2$ ($=2k$) is used as a parameter.

The schemes with zero-knowledge proof and with local verifiability can be treated together if one uses the abbreviation

$$\tau := \sigma + 1 + \rho \quad \text{and} \quad \tau := \sigma + 1 + \rho + l,$$

respectively.

a) Lengths (in bits):
   - Prekey: $3/2\ l + \sigma + \tau$; and actually, only the number n of length l has to be sent, because the security parameters are assumed to be known.
   - Secret key, both the temporary and the complete one: $2(\tau + l)$ (in addition to the prekey).
   - Main public key: $2l$.
   - Signature (on a ρ-bit message block): $\tau + l$.
   - Proof of forgery: $2(\tau + l)$, or, if Remark 9.21 is used, l.

b) Time complexity:
   - Key generation:
     - Prekey generation is of the same order of complexity as key generation in ordinary digital signature schemes: As in the discrete-logarithm case, it is dominated by the primality tests needed for the generation of two primes.
     - Prekey verification:

    - In the scheme with zero-knowledge proof: Quite inefficient; the exact complexity depends on the coin-flipping protocol used.
    - In the scheme with local verifiability: Negligible.
  - Main key generation:
    - In the scheme with zero-knowledge proof: Generation of four random numbers and $2\tau + 2$ squarings modulo a number of length l.
    - In the scheme with local verifiability: Generation of random numbers (six on average, because half of all numbers have the Jacobi symbol +1), the computation of Jacobi symbols (four on average) and 2τ squarings modulo numbers of length l.
  - Main key test: Negligible.
- Signing requires one exponentiation in $G_{\tau,n}$ with a number of length ρ, which corresponds to one exponentiation in $\mathbb{Z}_n$ with the same exponent. (Thus, in contrast to the discrete-logarithm scheme, signing is not significantly more efficient than testing.)
- Testing a signature $s = (\ddot{a}, \ddot{u})$ on a message block m starts with the computation of a Jacobi symbol.

  The main test can be sped up by computing $4^{\ddot{a}} \circ \ddot{u}^{2^\tau} \circ (mk_2^{-1})^m$ and verifying that it equals mk_1. (The inversion of mk_2 can be precomputed, or one can use mk_2^{-1} in the main public key; then $mk_2 \in \mathbb{Z}_n^*$ must be tested in *mk_test*.) There are simple measures to improve upon a straightforward 3-tuple exponentiation algorithm (see Section 8.3): The exponent m is only of length ρ, whereas the first two exponents are of length $\tau \geq \sigma + 1 + \rho$. Hence the first part of the evaluation of exponents from left to right is just the computation of a value $4^{\ddot{a}*} \circ \ddot{u}^{2^{\tau-\rho}}$, which needs exactly $\tau - \rho$ squarings. In the second part, one can continue to multiply with factors 4 by doubling instead of multiplication, and thus the only factors that need to be multiplied into the intermediate results are powers of mk_2^{-1}. Hence for the second part, the number of multiplications can be reduced as in normal exponentiation, which yields ρ squarings and about 0.2ρ multiplications. Hence the total number of multiplications and squarings is about $\tau + 0.2\rho$.

  If the recipient is the risk bearer, his entity can use the Chinese remainder theorem to speed up testing, because it knows the factors of the prekey.
- Computing proofs of forgery: One test and one signing operation.
- Verifying proofs of forgery: Either one computes $4^{\ddot{a}-\ddot{a}'} \circ (\ddot{u} \circ \ddot{u}'^{-1})^{2^\tau}$ with one inversion and τ squarings, or, with Remark 9.21, one only tests if p is a non-trivial divisor of n. ♦□

Remark 9.23 (Small message spaces). As with the discrete-logarithm scheme, the message-block spaces are very simple, so that random choice of a message block and membership tests can be carried out efficiently, if they are needed in an application.

Moreover, it is trivial to construct one-time fail-stop signature schemes for real finite message spaces M: One can use $M := \{0, \ldots, 2^\rho - 1\}$ for any $\rho \in \mathbb{N}$ and define $rho(k, \sigma) := \rho$ for all k, σ. ♦

9.5 Complexity Overview

The most important complexity parameters for the discrete-logarithm scheme and the factoring schemes are summarized in Table 9.1. To enable a comparison of the schemes, the complexity parameters are presented as functions of input parameters that yield similar message-block spaces and security. This means:

- For similar message spaces, k in the discrete-logarithm scheme is set equal to ρ in the factoring schemes. Note, however, that ρ is arbitrary, whereas k is restricted by something like $160 \le k \le |p|_2$.
- For similar security, the same σ is used in both schemes, and, with the current state of factoring and computing discrete logarithms, $l = |p|_2$ in the discrete-logarithm scheme is set equal to $l = |n|_2$ in the factoring schemes.

To avoid ambiguity, only the parameters ρ, σ, and l (and no k) are used in Table 9.1.

Random number generation, which occurs in prekey and main key generation, has been omitted, because real random numbers are needed, and the speed depends very much on the type of the implementation (physical or involving the user). Furthermore, Remark 9.20 has been used.

	Discrete-logarithm scheme	Factoring scheme with zero-knowledge proof	Factoring scheme with local verifiability
Prekey generation	Similar to ordinary digital signature schemes	Rather inefficient prekey verification	Similar to ordinary digital signature schemes
Main key generation	$\approx 4\rho$ multiplications	$\approx 2(\sigma + \rho)$ multiplications	$\approx 2(\sigma + \rho + l)$ multiplications
sign	2 multiplications	$\approx 1.2\rho$ multiplications	$\approx 1.2\rho$ multiplications
test	$< 2\rho$ multiplications	$< 2l + \sigma + 1.2\rho$ multiplications	$< 3l + \sigma + 1.2\rho$ multiplications
Length of *prek*	$\approx \rho + 3l$	$\approx l$	$\approx l$
Length of *mk*	$\approx 2l$	$\approx 2l$	$\approx 2l$
Length of *sk*	$\approx 4\rho$	$\approx 2(\sigma + \rho + l)$	$\approx 2(\sigma + \rho + 2l)$
Length of a signature	$\approx 2\rho$	$\approx \sigma + \rho + l$	$\approx \sigma + \rho + 2l$

Table 9.1. Important complexity parameters of the efficient schemes for signing one message block.
Lengths are in bits; multiplications are modulo a number of length l, except for the two multiplications in *sign* in the discrete-logarithm scheme, where the modulus is only of length ρ. The parameters ρ, l, and σ are discussed in the text above.

Prekey generation and main key generation have been considered separately, because in the subsequent constructions with tree authentication, main key generation from the underlying one-time signature scheme will be used very often, but prekey generation only once.

As a result, one can say that the discrete-logarithm scheme is generally more efficient and clearly the scheme of choice if one regards the two underlying computational assumptions as equally trustworthy. Nevertheless, the factoring schemes are comparable in most parameters and thus an alternative if one trusts the factoring assumption more. Interactive prekey verification will often be difficult in practice, hence the scheme with local verifiability may be preferable although it is inferior in the remaining parameters.

10 Signing Many Long Messages

In Chapter 9, constructions of standard fail-stop signature schemes with prekey for signing one message block or one message from a small message space were presented. These constructions are now extended so that an arbitrary number of messages of arbitrary length can be signed.

An informal overview was given in Section 6.3.1, Subsections "Signing Long Messages (Message Hashing)", "Signing Many Messages (Tree Authentication)", and "Simplifications with Fixed Recipient". The scheme for signing many messages without trees from [Pfit94] is not yet presented in the following.

10.1 Message Hashing

As sketched in Section 6.3.1, message hashing is used to reduce messages of arbitrary length to a fixed length, so that a signature scheme for signing message blocks can be applied.

Overview

If one combines message hashing with fail-stop signature schemes, the following conditions have to be fulfilled:

- Collision-intractable families of hash functions have to be used.
- A collision of the hash function counts as a valid proof of forgery.
- A signer's entity must store each message m it has signed, so that it can indeed show a collision if a computationally unrestricted attacker finds another message m' with the same hash value and uses the signature on m for m'. (Note that there was no need to store the message in the constructions in Chapter 9.)
- The key for the family of hash functions, i.e., the description of the particular function used, must be chosen by the risk bearer's entity (because collision-intractability is only guaranteed against parties who did not generate this key). Hence in schemes with prekey, this key is a part of the prekey.
- The parameters must be chosen so that each hash value is an element of the message-block space of the underlying signature scheme. In general, this makes parameter transformations similar to Construction 8.50 necessary.

In the following, first a general theorem about combinations of hash functions and standard fail-stop signature schemes with prekey is presented formally. If a concrete fail-stop signature scheme based on a factoring or discrete-logarithm assumption is used, it is natural to combine it with a family of hash functions based on the same assumption. These special cases are considered afterwards.

General Construction

The construction in this section is formalized so that it yields one-time standard fail-stop signature schemes with prekey that fulfil the simplified security criteria for such schemes from Theorem 7.34, because the constructions in Sections 10.2 to

10.4 are based on such schemes. Hence it is assumed that the underlying scheme for signing message blocks is with prekey, too. This comprises all the constructions in Chapter 9. A similar construction for schemes with arbitrary key generation would not be difficult. Remember that schemes with prekey were tacitly assumed to be with only one risk bearer; see Section 7.5 for generalizations. However, a restriction to one-time schemes is not made.

In addition to a family of hash functions in the sense of Definition 8.35, one needs a method to verify that keys are acceptable before they are used. As no difference between good and all acceptable keys had to be made with hash functions, local verifiability is assumed.

The following construction, although lengthy, is canonical, but it is the only formal test whether the definition of schemes for signing message blocks is suitable in relation to the definition of schemes for fixed message spaces.

Construction 10.1. Let the following parameters be given:

- *SigScheme*, a standard fail-stop signature scheme with prekey for signing message blocks from a family *MFam*, and with a set *Message_bounds*.
- *HashFam*, a collision-intractable family of hash functions. Its components are distinguished from those of *SigScheme* by superscripts °.
- A local verification algorithm for *AllFam*°, i.e., an algorithm *all_test*° that, on input ('1'$^{k^\circ}$, K°) decides if $K^\circ \in All^\circ{}_{k^\circ}$ in time polynomial in the first input alone.
- Components for embedding hash values into message-block spaces:
  - A function *make_small*: $\mathbb{N} \to \mathbb{N}$ (which derives a suitable security parameter for the hash functions from the given parameter k).
  - A value $k_\iota^\circ \in \mathbb{N}$ (which denotes from where on the embedding works).
  - A family of embeddings of the codomains of the hash functions into message-block spaces of the signature scheme, i.e., a family of injective functions
  $$\iota_{k,prek}: \{0, 1\}^{len^\circ(make\_small(k))} \to M_{prek}$$
  for all $k \geq k_\iota^\circ$ and all $prek \in All_{k,\sigma}$ for some $\sigma \in \mathbb{N}$.
  - Polynomial-time algorithms that compute *make_small* in unary and ι.

  These components must have the following additional property: Constants $D, d > 0$ exist such that $D\, make\_small(k)^d \geq k$ for all $k \in \mathbb{N}$.

The corresponding standard **fail-stop signature scheme with message hashing** for the general message space $M = \{0, 1\}^+$ and the same set *Message_bounds*, and also with prekey, is defined by the following components, which are distinguished from those of the underlying schemes by asterisks.

- Key generation:
  - Prekey generation: Prekeys primarily consist of one prekey of *SigScheme* and one key of *HashFam*. More precisely:
    - Correct prekey distribution: Let parameters $k^*, \sigma \in \mathbb{N}$ be given, and let
    $$k := \max(k^*, k_\iota^\circ).$$

Correct prekeys are triples

$$prek^* := (\text{'1'}^k, prek, K^\circ),$$

where *prek* is distributed according to $Corr_{k,\sigma}$, and K° according to $gen^\circ(\text{'1'}^{k^\circ})$ with $k^\circ := make\_small(k)$. (In particular, K° and *prek* are independent.)

- Sets of prekeys: Prekeys of the form described above are acceptable if the two keys from underlying schemes in them are acceptable and k is correct. They are good if, in addition, the prekey from the underlying scheme is good. Thus, for all $k^*, \sigma \in \mathbb{N}$ and with $k := \max(k^*, k_\iota^\circ)$,

$$All^*_{k^*,\sigma} := \{\text{'1'}^k\} \times All_{k,\sigma} \times All^\circ_{make\_small(k)}$$

and

$$Good^*_{k^*,\sigma} := \{\text{'1'}^k\} \times Good_{k,\sigma} \times All^\circ_{make\_small(k)}.$$

- Zero-knowledge proof scheme and *all_test**: The prekey-generation algorithm $gen_B{}^*$ is defined as

$$\begin{aligned}
&(prek^*, aux) \leftarrow gen_B{}^*(\text{'1'}^{k^*}, \text{'1'}^\sigma)\\
&\quad :\Leftrightarrow k := \max(k^*, k_\iota^\circ);\ k^\circ := make_small(k);\\
&\qquad (prek, aux) \leftarrow gen_B(\text{'1'}^k, \text{'1'}^\sigma);\ K^\circ \leftarrow gen^\circ(\text{'1'}^{k^\circ});\\
&\qquad prek^* := (\text{'1'}^k, prek, K^\circ),
\end{aligned}$$

where k and k° are computed in unary.

Similarly, *all_test**, on input $(\text{'1'}^{k^*}, \text{'1'}^\sigma, prek^*)$ with $prek^* = (\text{'1'}^{k'}, prek, K^\circ)$ computes $k := \max(k^*, k_\iota^\circ)$ and $k^\circ := make\_small(k)$ in unary. Then it tests if $k' = k$ and calls $all\_test(\text{'1'}^k, \text{'1'}^\sigma, prek)$ and $all\_test^\circ(\text{'1'}^{k^\circ}, K^\circ)$. The output is TRUE if all these tests yield TRUE.

In the zero-knowledge proof scheme, V^* and Obs^* start with *all_test** (but in practice, *all_test** is carried out only once). Then a zero-knowledge proof from *SigScheme* is carried out for the component *prek* of $prek^*$ with the parameters $k := \max(k^*, k_\iota^\circ)$ and σ; the details are canonical.

- Main key generation $gen_A{}^*$: On input parameters $par^* = (\text{'1'}^{k^*}, \text{'1'}^\sigma, \text{'1'}^N)$ with $N \in Message\_bounds$ and a prekey $prek^* = (\text{'1'}^k, prek, K^\circ) \in All^*_{k^*,\sigma}$, call $gen_A(\text{'1'}^k, \text{'1'}^\sigma, \text{'1'}^N, prek)$ to generate a key pair (*sk_temp*, *mk*). Let

$$sk\_temp^* := (sk\_temp, prek^*, \varepsilon)$$

and

$$mk^* := mk.$$

- Main public key test *mk_test**: On input $(par^*, prek^*, mk)$ with par^* as above and $prek^* = (\text{'1'}^k, prek, K^\circ) \in All^*_{k^*,\sigma}$, call $mk\_test((\text{'1'}^k, \text{'1'}^\sigma, \text{'1'}^N), prek, mk)$.

- Signing: The domain *SK_Temp** of the first parameter of *sign** consists of values

$$sk\_temp^* = (sk\_temp, prek^*, \underline{m}^*)$$

where $prek^* = (\text{'1'}^k, prek, K^\circ) \in All^*$ and $sk\_temp \in SK\_Temp(prek)$, and $\underline{m}^*$ is a sequence of messages from $\{0, 1\}^+$.

On input (sk_temp^*, m^*), the message is hashed and mapped into the message-block space as

$$m := \iota_{k,prek}(hash^\circ_{K^\circ}(m^*)).$$

This is possible for the following reasons:

- $\iota_{k,prek}$ exists because $k \ge k_\iota^\circ$ and $prek \in All_{k,\sigma}$ for some σ,
- $hash^\circ_{K^\circ}(m^*) \in \{0, 1\}^{len^\circ(make\_small(k))}$ because $K^\circ \in All^\circ_{make\_small(k)}$, and
- all parameters for ι are available.

Now, $m \in M_{prek}$. It can therefore be signed with *sk_temp* by Definition 9.1. Let

$$(sk\_temp_{new}, s) \leftarrow sign(sk\_temp, m).$$

If the result is *'key_used_up'* instead, that is the output. Otherwise, the correct signature in the new scheme is simply

$$s^* := s,$$

and the new temporary secret key is

$$sk\_temp^*_{new} := (sk\_temp_{new}, prek^*, \underline{m}^*_{new}),$$

where $\underline{m}^*_{new}$ is obtained by appending m^* to $\underline{m}^*$.

- Test: The input to *test** is a triple (pk^*, m^*, s) with $pk^* = (prek^*, mk) \in PK\_All^*$. Hence $prek^*$ is of the form $(\text{'1'}^k, prek, K^\circ)$, and one easily sees that $pk := (prek, mk) \in PK(prek)$, i.e., *pk* can be used to test message blocks from M_{prek}. The message is hashed and mapped into the message-block space as $m := \iota_{k,prek}(hash^\circ_{K^\circ}(m^*)) \in M_{prek}$ (which is possible for the same reasons as in *sign**), and the result is

$$acc := test(pk, m, s).$$

- Proving forgeries: The input to *prove** is a triple (sk_temp^*, m^*, s') with $sk\_temp^* = (sk\_temp, (\text{'1'}^k, prek, K^\circ), \underline{m}^*) \in SK\_Temp^*$. First, $m := \iota_{k,prek}(hash^\circ_{K^\circ}(m^*)) \in M_{prek}$ is computed (which is possible for the same reasons as in *sign**). Then one tries to compute a proof of forgery in the underlying scheme as $proof \leftarrow prove(sk\_temp, m, s')$. If this works, the result is

$$proof^* := (\text{'normal\_proof'}, proof).$$

Otherwise, one searches through $\underline{m}^*$, i.e., the previously signed messages, to see if a message m^*_i collides with m^* under $hash^\circ_{K^\circ}$. If yes, the output is

$$proof^* := (\text{'collision'}, (m^*_i, m^*)),$$

and otherwise *not_a_forgery*.

- Verifying proofs of forgery: The input to *verify_simple** is a pair $(prek^*, proof^*)$ with $prek^* = (\text{'1'}^k, prek, K^\circ) \in All^*$. Depending on the first component of $proof^*$, it is verified that the second component is either a $hash^\circ_{K^\circ}$-collision or a valid proof of forgery in the underlying scheme, i.e., it passes $verify\_simple(prek, proof)$.

The functional version of the secret key in the new scheme is $sk^* = (sk, prek^*, \varepsilon)$, because hashing is deterministic. ♦

Theorem 10.2 (Message hashing). Construction 10.1 defines components of a standard fail-stop signature scheme with prekey for the message space $\{0, 1\}^+$. If the underlying scheme *SigScheme* for signing message blocks is secure (according to Definition 9.1), the new scheme fulfils the criteria from Definition 7.34 and is therefore secure. (However, it is not polynomial-time in the interface inputs alone; see Remark 10.3.) ♦

Proof sketch.

A. Most of the properties that are implicitly required in the definitions of the components in Definitions 7.1 and 7.31 have already been verified within Construction 10.1, in particular, that all algorithms are defined on sufficiently large domains. Moreover, one can easily see from the construction that all the algorithms are polynomial-time in the correct parameters, and the adapted zero-knowledge proof scheme, where only the parameter k has been changed on a finite number of values, is a zero-knowledge proof scheme again.

B. The three properties required in Definition 7.1 follow immediately from the construction and the corresponding properties of the underlying scheme.

C. The properties required in Definition 7.31:

a) The set inclusions for prekeys follow immediately from the corresponding properties of *SigScheme* and *HashFam*. The length of all acceptable prekeys is polynomial in k and σ, because those of the underlying schemes are and *make_small* is polynomial-time computable in unary.

b) Similarly, the set inclusion and length restriction on main public keys follow immediately from those in *SigScheme*.

D. Hence the criteria from Theorem 7.34 remain to be proved.

a) Effectiveness of authentication follows immediately from that in the underlying scheme: The hash function and the embedding used in both *sign** and *test** are deterministic and the temporary secret keys *sk_temp* from the underlying scheme are updated correctly, and the correct signature s on $m = \iota_{k,prek}(hash^\circ_{K^\circ}(m^*))$ in the underlying signature scheme is acceptable in the underlying signature scheme. Moreover, as effectiveness of authentication holds for all values k, the change between k and k^* does not matter.

b) Security for the risk bearer. Assume the contrary, i.e., there is a probabilistic polynomial-time algorithm $\tilde{A}^*$, a constant $c^* > 0$, and a polynomial $Qsig$ such that for an infinite set $\mathcal{K}^*$ of values k^* there exists $\sigma \le Qsig(k^*)$ with

$$\begin{aligned}P(&verify\_simple^*(prek^*, proof^*) = \text{TRUE} \setminus \\ &\qquad k := \max(k^*, k_\iota^\circ);\ k^\circ := make\_small(k); \\ &\qquad prek \leftarrow Corr_{k,\sigma};\ K^\circ \leftarrow gen^\circ(\text{`}1\text{'}^{k^\circ});\ prek^* := (\text{`}1\text{'}^k, prek, K^\circ); \\ &\qquad proof^* \leftarrow \tilde{A}^*(\text{`}1\text{'}^{k^*}, \text{`}1\text{'}^\sigma, prek^*)) \\ \ge\ & k^{*-c^*}.\end{aligned}$$

(Note that $Corr^*_{k,\sigma}$ has already been substituted by its definition.)

As k only differs from k^* on a finite set, the same formula holds with $k = k^*$. Let $c := c^*+1$. Whenever $verify\_simple^*(pk^*, proof^*) = \text{TRUE}$ holds, $proof^*$ contains a component $proof$ with $verify\_simple(prek, proof) = \text{TRUE}$ or a $hash^\circ_{K^\circ}$-collision (m^*_i, m^*). Thus there is

1. either an infinite set $\mathcal{K}$ of values k where $\sigma \le Qsig(k)$ exists such that the probability of *verify_simple(prek, proof)* = TRUE is at least $k^{-c^*}/2 \ge k^{-c}$,
2. or the same for collisions.

These probabilities are still in the space defined by the new scheme. One can now derive attacker algorithms on the underlying schemes that have at least the same probability of success.

For *SigScheme*, an algorithm $\tilde{A}$ is defined that uses $\tilde{A}^*$ and simulates the actions of the risk bearer's entity with respect to the family of hash functions on its own. Thus, on input ('1'^{k}, '1'$^\sigma$, *prek*), it computes $k^\circ := make\_small(k)$; $K^\circ \leftarrow gen^\circ(\text{'1'}^{k^\circ})$; $prek^* := (\text{'1'}^k, prek, K^\circ)$; $proof^* \leftarrow \tilde{A}^*(\text{'1'}^k, \text{'1'}^\sigma, prek^*)$. If *proof** contains a component *proof*, $\tilde{A}$ outputs that. In Case 1, this immediately yields a contradiction to the security for the risk bearer in *SigScheme*.

For *HashFam*, one proceeds similarly, but a parameter transformation is necessary: First an algorithm $\tilde{A}^\circ$ is defined that simulates the actions of the risk bearer's entity with respect to the underlying signature scheme, i.e., on input ('1'^{k}, '1'$^\sigma$, K°), it computes $prek \leftarrow Corr_{k,\sigma}$; $prek^* := (\text{'1'}^k, prek, K^\circ)$; $proof^* \leftarrow \tilde{A}^*(\text{'1'}^k, \text{'1'}^\sigma, prek^*)$. If *proof** contains a $hash^\circ_{K^\circ}$-collision, $\tilde{A}^\circ$ outputs that. In Case 2, this yields: For all $k \in \mathcal{K}$, there exists $\sigma \le Qsig(k)$ with

$$\begin{aligned} k^{-c} \;\le\; & \mathrm{P}(hash^\circ_{K^\circ}(m^*_i) = hash^\circ_{K^\circ}(m^*) \wedge m^*_i \ne m^* \setminus k^\circ := make\_small(k); \\ & \qquad K^\circ \leftarrow gen(\text{'1'}^{k^\circ});\ (m^*_i, m^*) \leftarrow \tilde{A}^\circ(\text{'1'}^k, \text{'1'}^\sigma, K^\circ)) \\ =:\; & P_{succ,\tilde{A}^\circ}(k, \sigma). \end{aligned}$$

Secondly, an algorithm $\tilde{A}^\circ_{D,d}$ for the values D, d that were required to exist for *make_small* is defined as follows: On input ('1'$^{k^\circ}$, K°), it tries all the pairs (k, σ) with $1 \le k \le D\,k^{\circ d}$ and $make\_small(k) = k^\circ$ and $\sigma \le Qsig(k)$. For each one, it runs $\tilde{A}^\circ(\text{'1'}^k, \text{'1'}^\sigma, K^\circ)$. If an output is a $hash^\circ_{K^\circ}$-collision (m^*_i, m^*), then $\tilde{A}^\circ_{D,d}$ outputs this collision and stops.

Obviously, $\tilde{A}^\circ_{D,d}$ works in polynomial time, and its success probability $P_{succ,\tilde{A}^\circ_{D,d}}(k^\circ)$ for any k° is at least $P_{succ,\tilde{A}^\circ}(k, \sigma)$ for each pair (k, σ) that is tried on input k°, because no unsuccessful stop in a previous trial is possible.

Now, if $k^\circ_0 \ge D$ is given, there exists $k \ge k_0 := D\,k^\circ_0{}^d$ with $k \in \mathcal{K}$, i.e., there exists $\sigma \le Qsig(k)$ with $P_{succ,\tilde{A}^\circ}(k, \sigma) \ge k^{-c}$. Let $k^\circ := make\_small(k)$. Then $k^\circ \ge k^\circ_0$ and (k, σ) is tried on input k°, and therefore $P_{succ,\tilde{A}^\circ_{D,d}}(k^\circ) \ge k^{-c} \ge (D\,k^{\circ d})^{-c} \ge k^{\circ\,-(d+1)c}$.

c) Security for the signer. Let parameters $par^* = (\text{'1'}^{k^*}, \text{'1'}^\sigma, \text{'1'}^N)$, a prekey $prek^* = (\text{'1'}^k, prek, K^\circ) \in Good^*_{k^*,\sigma}$, and values *mk* and $hist^* = (\underline{m}^*, \underline{s})$ be given, where a value sk^*_0 exists with $(sk^*_0, mk) \in [gen_A{}^{*(f)}(par^*, prek^*)]$ and $hist^* \in Hist^*(sk^*_0, N)$. It has to be shown that $(mk, hist^*) \in GoodInf^*(par^*, prek^*)$.

For this, let a successful forgery $f^* = (m^*, s')$ in the new scheme be given. It has to be shown that (recall that the probability is over sk^*):

$$\begin{aligned} & \mathrm{P}_{par^*,prek^*}(provable^*(sk^*, pk^*, hist^*, f^*) \mid mk, sign^{*(f)}(sk^*, \underline{m}^*) = \underline{s}) \\ & \quad \ge\; 1 - 2^{-\sigma-1}. \end{aligned}$$

If m^* is a $hash^\circ_{K^\circ}$-collision with any of the messages in $\underline{m}^*$, the forgery is provable with probability 1. (Note that the value *sk_temp* actually used in *prove** on these parameters contains the complete message sequence $\underline{m}^*$ from *hist**.)

Otherwise, $m := \iota_{k,prek}(hash^\circ{}_{K^\circ}(m^*))$ has not been signed in the underlying scheme yet (because of the injectivity of $\iota_{k,prek}$); hence it does not occur in the history of the underlying scheme, which is defined as $hist := (\underline{m}, \underline{s})$, where $\underline{m}$ is the sequence of message blocks $m_i := \iota_{k,prek}(hash^\circ{}_{K^\circ}(m^*_i))$. Moreover, $test^*(pk^*, m^*, s') = $ TRUE implies $test(pk, m, s') = $ TRUE for $pk := (prek, mk)$. Hence $f := (m, s')$ is a successful forgery in the underlying scheme, i.e., an element of $Forg$(TRUE, pk, $hist$).

Whenever f is provable in the underlying scheme, then so is f^* in the new scheme, i.e., if $proof := prove^{(f)}(sk, m, s', hist)$ is a valid proof of forgery with respect to pk, then $proof^* := prove^{*(f)}(sk^*, m^*, s', hist^*)$ equals ('*normal_proof*', *proof*) and is valid with respect to pk^*. Hence it suffices to prove

$$P_{par^*,prek^*}(provable(sk, pk, hist, f) \mid mk, sign^{*(f)}(sk^*, \underline{m}^*) = \underline{s}) \geq 1 - 2^{-\sigma-1}.$$

The security of the underlying scheme implies that the same formula holds in the probability space defined by the underlying scheme, i.e.,

$$P_{par,prek}(provable(sk, pk, hist, f) \mid mk, sign^{(f)}(sk, \underline{m}) = \underline{s}) \geq 1 - 2^{-\sigma-1},$$

where par is derived from par^* by replacing k^* with $k := \max(k^*, k_\iota^\circ)$. The only difference between the probability spaces is that the values sk^* in the former contain fixed components K° and ε. The conditions, if translated into formulas about sk, are identical, too. This finishes the proof. □

Remark 10.3 (Availability of service). As announced in a footnote to Definition 7.1, the component *verify_simple** of Construction 10.1 is not polynomial-time in the interface inputs alone (nor *verify** in pk^*, whereas *test** and *prove** are), even if all the components of the underlying signature scheme for signing message blocks have this property (as in the constructions in Chapter 9): There is no upper bound on the length of valid proofs of forgery of the form $proof^* = $ ('*collision*', (m^*_i, m^*)). However, if the family of hash functions can be equipped with short collision proofs according to Remark 8.37, this can be repaired: In the algorithm *prove**, any collision is transformed into a short collision proof, and in *verify_simple**, only a short collision proof has to be verified with *verify_collision*, which is polynomial-time in K° alone.

All the constructions of families of hash functions in Section 8.5 had this property (Remarks 8.54 and 8.63 and Theorem 8.71). ♦

Remark 10.4 (Conditions of embedding). The condition about the embedding of hash values into the message spaces is no serious restriction: It can eventually be applied even if the underlying signature scheme allows only one bit to be signed, e.g., if one has an embedding of {0, 1} into all the message-block spaces. First, one can achieve that more bits can be signed by mere replication, i.e., main key generation from the underlying scheme is carried out $Q(k)$ times, where Q is polynomial-time computable in unary, and each key pair is used to sign one bit. One can easily see that this construction (with a logarithmic increase in σ) is secure. Then one uses $Q := len^\circ$, the function that determines the length of the hash values. ♦

Remark 10.5 (Complexity of *prove).** The time complexity of *prove** in Construction 10.1 is at least linear in N, in contrast to *sign** and *test**, because of the search for a previously signed message that collides with the message in the forgery. In the following, this construction is primarily applied to one-time signature schemes (which are then used in tree authentication); hence the factor is 1 and it was not worth while making a better formal construction. Generally, one could get rid of this factor by storing the previously signed messages more efficiently, e.g., by storing their hash values in a hash table. In concrete schemes, one can usually do even better, because the failure to prove the forgery in the underlying signature scheme shows with which message it collides. (Compare Remark 10.25, or consider how message hashing would work when added to a scheme that already offers tree authentication; see Sections 10.2 to 10.4.) ♦

Remark 10.6 (Two variants of '*broken*'). If a collision of the hash function occurs as a proof of forgery, it is sufficient to choose a new hash function, whereas one can retain the prekey *prek* from the underlying scheme and the values *sk* and *mk*. As the keys of the hash functions were assumed to be locally verifiable, only the risk bearer(s) have to publish a new key of a hash function after such a proof of forgery, whereas the signers need not send any new information. This may be helpful if one decides to use fast, but not provably collision-intractable hash functions.

At the interface, this means that the output '*broken*' has a parameter *which_assumption* that indicates which assumption was broken, as mentioned in Section 5.2.4, "Dispute". The range might be {'*hash*', '*sig_scheme*'}. ♦

Hashing in the Discrete-Logarithm Case

As the main issue in the combination of fail-stop signature schemes and families of hash functions is concrete block lengths, it is useful to restrict oneself to concrete discrete-logarithm assumptions, here those from Definition 8.21. Thus the standard fail-stop signature scheme for signing one message block summarized in Lemma 9.12 and the hash functions from Construction 8.52, based on the fixed-length hash functions from Construction 8.50, are combined. The exact group-generation algorithms (which may be different for the hash functions and the underlying signature scheme) and the components for the embedding remain to be chosen. As before, all values used with hash functions will be distinguished by $^\circ$.

As in the subsection "Concrete Parameter Choice for Hash Functions" at the end of Section 8.5.3, the value $l^\circ = len\_p^\circ(k^\circ)$ that determines the length of the prime p° used for the hash functions must be regarded as given by the state of the art of computing discrete logarithms, and k°, which determines the size of the corresponding prime q°, should be almost equal to l°. The length of the hash values is l°. The security parameter k° corresponds to $make\_small(k)$ with $k = \max(k^*, k_l^\circ)$ in Construction 10.1. The message-block space of the underlying signature scheme is $M_{prek} = \{0, 1, \ldots, q\}$, where $q \geq 2^k$ is guaranteed. There are two possibilities:

1. One fits the hash values into the message-block space directly. This works if $k \geq l^\circ$. One will then use a generation scheme where $l := len\_p(k) \approx k$, i.e., l will be a little larger than l° (e.g., $l^\circ = 512$, $k = 512$, $l = 528$).

2. One divides the hash values into several smaller blocks, which are signed individually. (Hence several one-time keys must be prepared to sign one message.) Then one can use $k < l^\circ$, and one will use a key generation where $l = len\_p(k) \approx l^\circ$ (e.g., $l^\circ = 512$, $k = 176 > \frac{512}{3}$, $l = 512$).

As the complexity of hashing is always the same, one can use Lemma 9.14 to compare these possibilities. If one neglects overheads from message blocking, the differences between the different values of l and l°, and from exponentiation algorithms being slightly less than linear in the size of the exponents, the following differences remain: Main public keys grow linearly with the number of blocks used (i.e., with l° / k), whereas the complexity of signing decreases more or less linearly with them.

Remark 10.7. One can try to use the same prekey for the hash function and the underlying signature scheme. If the hash value is signed in one block, this does not work, but it works in the closely related schemes with $p = 2q + 1$ and the factor group $H'_{q,p} = \mathbb{Z}_p^*/\{\pm 1\}$, as mentioned in Section 8.4.2, "Other Concrete Discrete-Logarithm Assumptions". If the hash value is signed in several blocks, it works, but a problem is that hash functions were most efficient when q was almost as large as p, whereas the idea about blocking in the signature scheme was to use q much shorter than p. Of course, a new security proof would be needed in any case, but it is not more complicated than that of Construction 10.1. (A related proof of a construction based on strong claw-intractable families of permutation pairs was given in [Pfit89, PfWa90].) ♦

As a conclusion, it will usually be optimal to sign each hash value as one message block and to use primes q°, p°, q, and p of approximately equal size, because signing is so much more efficient than testing that its exact complexity does not seem to matter in most applications, whereas longer main public keys are a disadvantage in the following constructions with tree authentication.

With fast, but not provably collision-intractable hash functions, small q's, e.g., of length 160, can be used in the signature scheme.

Hashing in the Factoring Case

If one combines the standard fail-stop signature schemes for signing one message block from Definition 9.17 with message hashing, there are no particular problems, because the function *rho* can be used to adapt the message-block spaces.

If the family of hash functions from Construction 8.70 is used, the hash values are of length $2k^\circ$, if k° is the security parameter used for the hash function. Hence one can use the same $k := k^\circ$ for the signature scheme and $rho(k, \sigma) := 2k$.

Remark 10.8. The same number n can be used in the prekey of the underlying signature scheme and for the hash function. (Of course, this needs a proof, but it is not more complicated than the one with separate keys.) ♦

With fast, but not provably collision-intractable hash functions, *rho* can be smaller, e.g., the constant 160.

10.2 Bottom-up Tree Authentication

The construction of bottom-up tree authentication is sketched in Figure 10.1, and it was briefly described in Section 2.4. It is based on a collision-intractable family of hash functions and any one-time standard fail-stop signature scheme with prekey. Signatures and keys in the underlying one-time fail-stop signature scheme and the scheme now to be constructed are distinguished by calling them "one-time" and "new", respectively, and one-time main "public" keys are written in quotes, because they are no longer public.

A complete formal description and a proof of a special case of bottom-up tree authentication (an optimized construction from strong claw-intractable families of permutation pairs) can be found in [Pfit89, PfWa90]. Hence only a sketch is presented here, whereas top-down tree authentication is treated in more detail.

For simplicity, only complete binary trees are considered. One could use trees of any other shape, but the shape must be fixed during main key generation (in contrast to the following top-down tree authentication), and it must be clear from the public key.

Construction sketch 10.9. Let the following parameters be given:

- *SigScheme*, a one-time standard fail-stop signature scheme with prekey for a message space M (see Definition 7.31).
- *HashFam*, a collision-intractable family of hash functions. Its components are distinguished by superscripts °.

The corresponding standard **fail-stop signature scheme with bottom-up tree authentication** (also with prekey) for the same message space has the following components, which are written with an asterisk (see Figure 10.1): The set *Message_bounds* is the set of powers of 2.

- Key generation:
  - Prekey generation: A prekey $prek^*$ in the new scheme consists of a prekey $prek$ from the underlying scheme and a key K° of the hash function, both generated from the original security parameters. Sets of good and acceptable prekeys and the corresponding verification algorithm and zero-knowledge proof scheme are combinations of those from the underlying schemes (similar to Construction 10.1, but without parameter transformations).
  - Main key generation: On input the parameters and a new prekey $prek^*$, N one-time key pairs (sk_temp_j, mk_j) based on $prek$ are generated. The values mk_j are used as the leaves of a binary tree. The value of each inner node is the hash value of its two children (regarded as one message). The new temporary secret key sk_temp^* consists of the whole tree and a counter for the messages already signed, initialized with zero. But only the final hash value, i.e., the root of the tree, is published as the main public key mk^* of the new scheme.

    The main public key test verifies that mk^* is a possible hash value, i.e., that its length is $len^\circ(k)$.

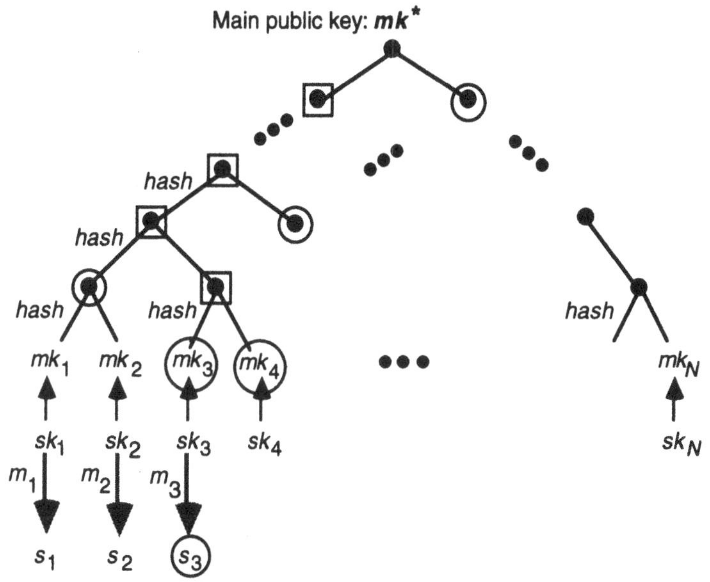

Figure 10.1. Fail-stop signature scheme with bottom-up tree authentication.
Thin black arrows denote the relation between a one-time secret key and the corresponding one-time main "public" key, broad grey arrows denote one-time signatures, and the tree is constructed by repeatedly hashing pairs of values. Values *sk_temp* are abbreviated as *sk*.

For instance, the complete correct signature s^* on m_3 consists of the encircled nodes. To test it, the recipient's entity reconstructs the nodes in squares.

- Signing: For any $j \le N$, the complete correct new signature s^* on the j-th message, m_j, contains
  - the number j,
  - the correct one-time signature s_j on m_j using sk_temp_j,
  - the corresponding value mk_j, and
  - the branch from mk_j to the root mk^*, so that the authenticity of mk_j is guaranteed; more precisely, this means that the other children of all the nodes on this branch belong to the signature (see Figure 10.1).

  (Hence the length of the new signature is logarithmic in N.) The value sk_temp_j is updated in this process. If $j > N$, the output is *'key_used_up'*.
- Test: To test a new signature s^* of the form described above, one first tests the one-time signature s_j with respect to the claimed value mk_j. Then one reconstructs the values on the path to the root and tests if this path ends at the correct main public key mk^*. (That is, one starts by hashing mk_j and its claimed neighbour, and iteratively hashes each intermediate result with its claimed neighbour until one obtains a value mk' that should be the root value; this is compared with mk^*.)

- Proving forgeries: A proof of forgery *proof** in the new scheme should be either a collision of the hash function or a valid proof of forgery in the one-time scheme. It can be found by comparing the branch in the forged signature with the correct signature on the same message at the same leaf j, starting at the common root mk^*. If no collision of the hash function is found, both signatures contain the same value mk_j, i.e., the one-time signature s_j' in the forged signature is a forgery in the one-time scheme, and one can try to prove it in that scheme.
- Verifying proofs of forgery: It is verified that the proof is either a collision of the hash function or a valid proof of forgery in the one-time scheme.

To make the components polynomial-time in the interface inputs alone, each value mk_j that is received in a signature is first tested with *mk_test*, and it is verified that each value that should be an inner node of the tree, and thus a hash value, is of length $len^{\circ}(k)$. Similarly, a collision in a valid proof of forgery must either consist of acceptable one-time main "public" keys or values of length $len^{\circ}(k)$. ♦

Theorem 10.10 (Bottom-up tree authentication). Construction 10.9 defines the components of a standard fail-stop signature scheme with prekey for signing an arbitrary number of messages. If the underlying signature scheme fulfils the simplified security criteria from Theorem 7.34, the new scheme fulfils them, too, and is therefore secure.

Moreover, the new scheme is polynomial-time in the interface inputs alone if the underlying signature scheme is. ♦

Proof sketch. The implicit and explicit requirements from Definitions 7.1 and 7.31 and the property to be polynomial-time in the interface inputs alone are easy to see. Among the criteria from Theorem 7.34, effectiveness of authentication is also easily derived from the construction.

The security for the risk bearer follows from the fact that valid proofs of forgery of the underlying one-time signature scheme and collisions of the hash functions are assumed to be infeasible to construct. (Formally, the two infeasibility conditions are combined as in the proof of Theorem 10.2, but without parameter transformations.) Note that the fact that many one-time key pairs are based on the same prekey *prek* makes no formal difference at all in Criterion 2 of Theorem 7.34.

As to the security for the signer, one first shows that, as claimed in the sketch of the construction, any successful forgery either yields a collision of the hash function or contains a successful forgery (m_j, s_j') of the one-time signature scheme. Moreover, it is clear that the new forgery is provable whenever the one-time forgery is. Hence it remains to be shown that the probability that an attacker can make a successful and unprovable one-time forgery is not significantly greater within the new scheme than if the one-time scheme is used alone. This is fairly clear, because any forgery in the new scheme is at one particular leaf j, and the other leaves and the inner nodes of the tree do not give the attacker more information about sk_temp_j than mk_j and *prek*. □

Remark 10.11 (Security for the signer forwards). Currently, security for the signer backwards has been assumed in the one-time scheme and proved in the new scheme. If one wanted to obtain a similar theorem for security forwards, one would have to increase the parameter σ in Construction 10.9 by adding $\log_2(N)$, because the attacker has more chances to come into a situation where he can make an unprovable successful forgery. The same holds for the following constructions. ♦

Remark 10.12 (Optimization). Bottom-up tree authentication can be optimized in several ways.

- Special hash functions that only map a message-block space $M_{K^\circ}{}^2$ into M_{K°, instead of being applicable to arbitrary messages, can be used. They were called 2-fold folding functions in [PfWa90], and at least on the factoring assumption, they can be more efficient than the general construction.
- The same hash function can be used for message hashing within the underlying one-time signature scheme and in the tree.
- If the hash function and the one-time signature scheme are based on the same assumption, the same prekey can be used for them.
- One can apply measures that are not specific to fail-stop signature schemes, e.g., ternary trees or the key-reconstruction mechanism of [Vaud92] (although the latter only helps a little in the case of fail-stop signature schemes, because the one-time keys cannot be generated pseudo-randomly). ♦

10.3 Top-Down Tree Authentication

This section and Section 10.4 are closely related.

1. In this section, a natural fail-stop version of top-down tree authentication is presented. It can be based on any one-time standard fail-stop signature scheme with prekey where arbitrarily long messages can be signed (and thus, in particular, on the schemes from Chapter 9 combined with message hashing). In this construction, the public key is short and only a small amount of private storage is needed immediately after the keys have been chosen. However, a long temporary secret key accumulates until the end.
2. In Section 10.4, additional measures are added so that the amount of private storage is small all the time. Those measures are constructed specifically for the general construction framework from Section 9.2 and thus for the efficient schemes based on factoring and discrete logarithms.

The basic idea of top-down tree authentication (here immediately presented for fail-stop signature schemes with prekey) is that the signer's entity starts with one key pair (sk, mk) of an underlying one-time signature scheme; the main public key of this pair is the main public key of the new scheme, too. The entity then generates two new one-time key pairs (sk_0, mk_0) and (sk_1, mk_1) and uses the original secret key to sign one message containing the two new "public" keys; the message can be interpreted as "the following are my next two 'public' keys … ". Now the entity has two authenticated one-time key pairs it can still use. Next, it generates four new one-time key pairs and signs two of the new "public" keys with sk_0 and the other two with sk_1, which yields four authenticated one-time key pairs. In the following step, eight new keys can be authenticated, and so on in a tree-like fashion. Finally, when there are enough one-time keys, they can be used to sign real messages. The important point is that when such a signature is tested, only the original main public key mk, and not all the other one-time main "public" keys must have been published, and only those on the branch from the root to the leaf used are sent with the signature, similar to the hash values in bottom-up tree authentication.

What makes top-down tree authentication more flexible than bottom-up tree authentication is that the entity need not generate all the one-time key pairs in advance, in contrast to the basic idea described above. Instead, it can start with not much more than the leftmost branch of the tree. Details can be seen in Construction 10.13 and Figure 10.2.

As in Section 10.2, only complete binary trees are considered formally, although one could use trees of any other shape. This time, one need not even fix the shape during key generation; in particular, one can allow $N = \infty$ (see Remark 10.17). Moreover, the construction is first presented in a simple form (Construction 10.13), and then in a version with reduced storage (Lemma 10.15).

As in Section 10.2, the words "one-time" and "new" are used to distinguish signatures and keys in the underlying scheme from those in the scheme to be constructed.

Construction 10.13. Let a one-time standard fail-stop signature scheme with prekey for the message space $M = \{0, 1\}^+$ be given (see Definition 7.31). The corresponding standard **fail-stop signature scheme with top-down tree authentication** (also with prekey) is constructed as follows (see Figure 10.2): The set *Message_bounds* is the set of powers of 2.

- Key generation:
  - Prekey generation and verification are identical to that of the one-time scheme. Hence a prekey in the new scheme is just one prekey *prek* of the one-time scheme.
  - Main key generation is almost identical to that of the one-time scheme: A one-time key pair (*sk_temp*, *mk*) based on *prek* is chosen, *mk* is the main public key, and the main public key test is identical. The temporary secret key in the new scheme is *sk_temp** := (*sk_temp*, *par*, *prek*, *j*), where *par* are the parameters, as usual, and j is a string initialized with d zeros, where $N = 2^d$. It serves as a counter of the number of messages already signed. (The message number i in the previous sense is $j + 1$, if j is interpreted as a binary number.)

    Note, however, that signing will be probabilistic, and hence the functional version sk^* of the secret key is longer.
- Signing (*sign**): Signing takes place in a complete binary tree with N leaves. Only the root exists at the beginning; the other nodes are created on demand. Each node is denoted by a bit string l, where the root is Node ε and the children of Node l are Nodes $l0$ and $l1$ (for each l of length $< d$, where $N = 2^d$).

At the end, i.e., when the message bound has been reached, each Node l will be labeled with a one-time key pair (sk_temp_l, mk_l); all these pairs are based on *prek*. Initially, only the root is labeled with (sk_temp, mk).

A one-time secret key at an inner node is used to sign the pair of one-time main "public" keys of its two children; a one-time secret key at a leaf is used to sign a real message. Thus at the end, each node will also be labeled with a one-time signature s_l, where $(s_l, sk\_temp_{new,l})$ is computed as $sign(sk\_temp_l, (mk_{l0}, mk_{l1}))$ if $|l| < d$ and as $sign(sk\_temp_l, m_l)$ for a real message m_l otherwise; sk_temp_l is replaced with $sk\_temp_{new,l}$ in this process. Moreover, the leaves are labeled with the real messages. Figure 10.2 shows such a tree at an early stage.

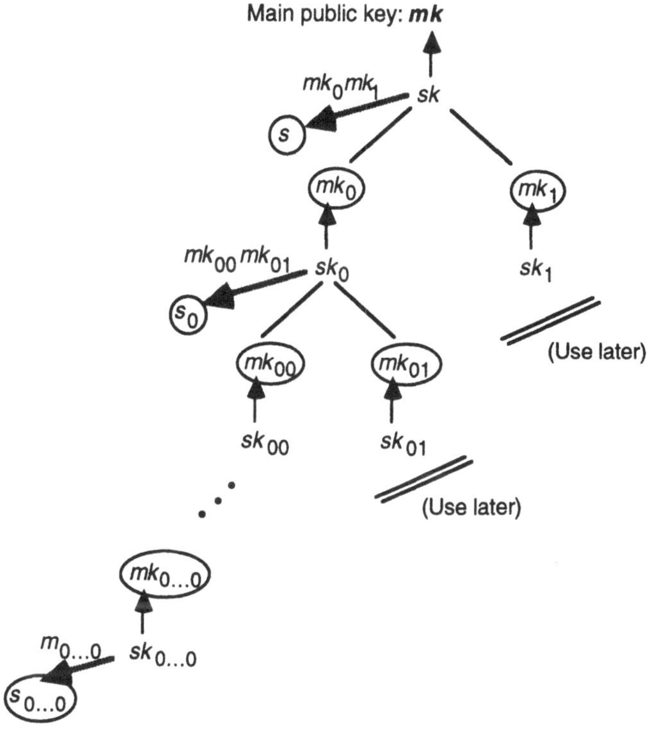

Figure 10.2. Fail-stop signature scheme with top-down tree authentication.
Thin black arrows denote the relation between a one-time secret key and the corresponding one-time main "public" key, broad grey arrows denote one-time signatures, and normal lines only indicate a tree, but are not related to a computation. The values *sk_temp* are abbreviated as *sk*.

The figure shows the temporary secret key after the first real message, $m_{0...0}$, has been signed. The complete new signature on $m_{0...0}$ consists of the encircled nodes.

At any time, the temporary secret key is of the form

$$sk\_temp^* := (tree, par, prek, j),$$

where *tree* denotes the current labeling of the tree and j the leaf where the next real message is to be signed.

A complete signature in the new scheme is one branch of this tree. More precisely, the correct signature on m_j is

$$s^* := (j, s_j, \underline{mk}, \underline{s}),$$

where j is the current string from *sk_temp**, s_j the correct one-time signature on m_j with sk_temp_j, $\underline{mk}$ the sequence of one-time main "public" keys on the path from mk_j to the root *mk* and at the immediate other children of that path, and $\underline{s}$ the sequence of one-time signatures on the path. (See Figure 10.2 for the signature on $m_{0...0}$; formalizations are canonical.) When all the leaves have been used, the output is *'key_used_up'* instead.

Thus, to sign the first real message, the one-time key pairs on the leftmost branch and their immediate other children have to be generated. After that, the tree is gradually constructed from left to right: When m_j has been signed (i.e., the $(j+1)$-st real message), the branch to Node j and all the nodes to the left of it are completely labeled, and the right siblings of the nodes on this branch (if there are any) are labeled with a one-time key pair, but not yet with a one-time signature.

Note that if there is time, the one-time key pairs that are needed next and the one-time signatures at inner nodes can be precomputed.

- Test (*test**): Given a signature s^* of the form described above, all the one-time main "public" keys in it are tested with *mk_test* and then the one-time signatures with *test*, where the top one-time signature is tested with respect to the correct main public key *mk*. (The form of the path is known from j.)
- Proving forgeries (*prove**): A proof of forgery in the new scheme is simply a valid proof of forgery in the one-time scheme. On input *sk_temp**, a message m_j', and a supposed forged signature $s^{*\prime} = (j, s_j', \underline{mk}', \underline{s}')$, such a proof is found as follows: For simplicity, it is first tested if $s^{*\prime}$ is a correct signature on m_j', and if m_j' has not really been signed at Node j. If not, the output is *not_a_forgery*.[153]

  Now the one-time main "public" keys in the forged signature are compared with those on the same branch in *sk_temp**, starting at the common root *mk*. The goal is to find a node l where the forged signature "links in" to the correct tree. This means that the same mk_l is used in $\underline{mk}'$ and in *sk_temp**, but the message m_l' signed at this node in the forged signature has not been signed at this node in the correct tree. (Depending on the position of Node l, m_l' is the real message m_j' or the pair of the next two one-time main "public" keys; in the correct tree, either no message yet or a different message has been signed at Node l.)

  Finally, the algorithm tries to compute a proof of forgery in the one-time scheme as $proof \leftarrow prove(sk\_temp_l, m_l', s_l')$ and outputs the result.

153 One can save time by not testing parts that are identical to the corresponding parts in *sk_temp** or that are not used in the rest of the algorithm. Furthermore, this preliminary test does not imply that $(m_j', s^{*\prime})$ is a successful forgery, because m_j' might have been signed at another leaf of the tree before, but it guarantees that a valid proof of forgery will be found.

- Verifying proofs of forgery (*verify_simple**) works just as in the one-time scheme. ♦

Theorem 10.14 (Top-down tree authentication). Construction 10.13 defines the components of a standard fail-stop signature scheme with prekey for signing an arbitrary number of messages. If the underlying one-time signature scheme fulfils the simplified security criteria from Theorem 7.34, then the new scheme fulfils them, too, and is therefore secure.

Moreover, the new scheme is polynomial-time in the interface inputs alone if the underlying one-time signature scheme is. ♦

Proof sketch. The implicit and explicit requirements from Definitions 7.1 and 7.31 and the property to be polynomial-time in the interface inputs alone are easy to see. Among the criteria from Theorem 7.34, effectiveness of authentication is easily derived from that in the one-time scheme, and the security for the risk bearer is completely identical to that in the underlying one-time scheme. (Recall that the fact that the signer's entity bases many one-time key pairs on the same prekey makes no formal difference at all in Criterion 2 of Theorem 7.34.)

The security for the signer is shown as follows: First, the algorithm *prove** finds a successfully forged one-time signature in every successfully forged new signature. Secondly, it can prove the new forgery whenever it can prove the one-time forgery. Thirdly, the probabilities are related in a way that the probability of a new forgery being unprovable is not higher than that of a one-time forgery (stand-alone) being unforgeable. Now this proof is carried out in more detail.

Let parameters *par*, a prekey $prek \in Good_{k,\sigma}$, and *mk* and $hist^* = (\underline{m}^*, \underline{s}^*)$ be given, where sk^*_0 exists with $(sk^*_0, mk) \in [gen_A{}^{*(f)}(par, prek)]$ and $hist^* \in Hist^*(sk^*_0, N)$. It has to be shown that $(mk, hist^*) \in GoodInf^*(par, prek)$.

For this, let a successful forgery $f^* \in Forg^*(\text{TRUE}, pk, hist^*)$ in the new scheme be given, where $pk = (prek, mk)$. It has to be shown that (recall that the probability is over sk^*):

$$P^*_{par,prek}(provable^*(sk^*, pk, hist^*, f^*) \mid mk, sign^{*(f)}(sk^*, \underline{m}^*) = \underline{s}^*) \geq 1 - 2^{-\sigma-1}.$$

Let $f^* = (m_j', (j, s_j', \underline{mk}', \underline{s}'))$. Moreover, as the security definition is in functional notation, whereas Construction 10.13 is algorithmic, let the current value *sk_temp** be redefined in terms of the history, i.e., as the result of applying *sign** to the messages from $\underline{m}^*$, given the original temporary secret key and the random string from sk^*.

First, the successfully forged one-time signature is identified formally. The precondition that f^* is a successful forgery implies that it passes *test**. In particular, the path $\underline{mk}'$ starts at the correct root *mk*, which is also the root in *sk_temp**. However, a successful forgery cannot be contained in *sk_temp** entirely, because it would then be a signature that the signer really made. Hence, if one starts at the root and follows the path to the leaf indicated by *j*, the first difference yields a node *l* where the forged signature links into the correct tree as defined above, i.e., the same mk_l is used in $\underline{mk}'$ and in *sk_temp**, but the message m_l' signed at this node in the forged signature has not been signed at this node in *sk_temp**. Let $f_l := (m_l', s_l')$ and $pk_l := (prek, mk_l)$, and let $hist_l := (\underline{m}_l, \underline{s}_l)$ be the history at Node *l*, i.e., (m_l, s_l) if a message m_l has already been signed at Node l in *sk_temp** and the empty sequences otherwise. Clearly, $f_l \in Forg(\text{TRUE}, pk_l, hist_l)$.

One can easily see from the construction of *prove** and *verify_simple** that $provable(sk_l, pk_l, hist_l, f_l)$ implies $provable^*(sk^*, pk, hist^*, f^*)$, where sk_l is defined as the original sk_temp_l and the random string needed for signing at Node l.[154] Hence it suffices to show that

$$P^*_{par,prek}(provable(sk_l, pk_l, hist_l, f_l) \mid mk, sign^{*(f)}(sk^*, \underline{m}^*) = \underline{s}^*) \geq 1 - 2^{-\sigma-1}.$$

The security of the one-time scheme implies a similar-looking formula in the probability space defined by a stand-alone application of the one-time scheme:

$$P_{par,prek}(provable(sk_l, pk_l, hist_l, f_l) \mid mk_l, sign^{(f)}(sk_l, \underline{m}_l) = \underline{s}_l) \geq 1 - 2^{-\sigma-1}.$$

Hence it suffices to show that the two probabilities are equal. This is clear[155], because the new probabilities $P^*_{par,prek}$ are defined by the independent random generation of many one-time key pairs and can therefore be partitioned, and the additional information that is given in the condition in the first probability, but not in the second one, does not concern the one-time key pair (sk_l, mk_l). (The only point where one might expect a problem is the one-time signature immediately above Node l, because there, mk_l is a part of the message. But even that does not restrict the possible values sk_l.) □

In Construction 10.13, all the information that is generated is also stored in *sk_temp** for simplicity, i.e., the one-time key pairs, the one-time signatures at the nodes, and the real messages. The next lemma shows how much of this information can be deleted.

Lemma 10.15 (Storage reduction). One can make the following changes to Construction 10.13 without reducing the security:

- In signing:
  - The real messages at the leaves are not stored in *sk_temp**.[156]
  - In the long run, only the one-time temporary secret key sk_temp_l is stored at a Node l, but neither the one-time main "public" key mk_l nor the one-time signature s_l. More precisely, mk_l and s_l can be deleted when they are no longer needed in the path of any future signature. Hence, when the counter j is updated to $j + 1$, and if j^* denotes the common prefix of j and $j + 1$ (as strings), the values at the nodes below Node j^*0 and s_{j^*0} are deleted (but mk_{j^*0} not yet).
- In the algorithm *prove**: As the one-time algorithm *prove* only has sk_temp_l, m_l', and s_l' as inputs, it is fairly clear that the values that have been deleted do not really matter. However, they were used for finding the node l with the success-

154 This change from the algorithmic construction to the functional security statement is a little abbreviated: It may not be clear a priori which part of the random string in *sk* is needed for signing at Node l.

155 If it is not, compare the proof of Theorem 10.20.

156 However, the real message may be contained in the updated one-time temporary secret key $sk\_temp_{new\,j}$.

ful one-time forgery. Now, instead, one only tests the values mk_l' with *mk_test* and then immediately starts at the root and calls $prove(sk\_temp_\varepsilon, m'_\varepsilon, s'_\varepsilon)$ to prove that s'_ε is a one-time forgery. If the output is *not_a_forgery*, one continues with the next node on the path (to Node j), and so on until either a value $proof \neq$ *not_a_forgery* occurs; then *prove** outputs it and stops; or the leaf is reached unsuccessfully, then the output is *not_a_forgery*. ♦

Proof. It is clear that the algorithm *sign** would not have needed the deleted information, and that the new algorithm *prove** does not need it either and works in time polynomial in the correct parameters. (Recall that it was not only defined on successful forgeries.) The only security property that could be affected is the security for the signer. However, the new algorithm *prove** cannot stop unsuccessfully before reaching Node l where the forged signature links into the correct tree, and if it arrives there, it behaves just like the old algorithm and therefore finds a valid proof of forgery with the same probability. □

Remark 10.16 (Other efficiency improvements).

a) Trees of other shapes, e.g., ternary trees, can be used.

b) One can use subtrees constructed with bottom-up tree authentication in the place of individual one-time key pairs in top-down tree authentication (i.e., one signs the main "public" key at the root of a new bottom-up tree with an already existing one-time secret key) to combine the flexibility of the top-down construction with the shorter signatures of the bottom-up construction. This is particularly useful if one trusts a fast hash function in the bottom-up construction.

If a concrete one-time signature scheme is given, there may be further efficiency improvements.

c) If the one-time signature scheme is a combination of the general construction framework (Construction 9.4) and message hashing (Construction 10.1), one can omit some redundant values: If the parameters of the new scheme are $par = (\text{‘}1\text{’}^{k*}, \text{‘}1\text{’}^{\sigma}, \text{‘}1\text{’}^{N})$, and $k := \max(k^*, k_l^\circ)$ as before, the prekey can be shortened to

$$prek^* = (\text{‘}1\text{’}^{k}, \text{‘}1\text{’}^{\sigma}, K, K^\circ),$$

where K denotes a bundling homomorphism and K° a hash function. The one-time secret keys at the nodes can be shortened to

$$sk\_temp_l = (sk_{l,1}, sk_{l,2}),$$

if one stores the real messages signed at the leaves separately in *sk_temp**. The other values would be K and a local counter i_l from Construction 9.4, and *prek** and $\underline{m}^*$ from Construction 10.1. The first three can be derived from the components *prek** and j of *sk_temp**, and $\underline{m}^*$, which is either ε or the message m_l signed at this node, is stored separately if m_l is a real message and can be reconstructed from the secret keys at the children of Node l otherwise.

d) One can use a more efficient scheme for signing message blocks of certain sizes at the inner nodes, because only two one-time main "public" keys are signed there, not messages of arbitrary length. ♦

Remark 10.17 (Flexible tree shape). Instead of fixing the shape of the tree in the scheme and a message bound N during key generation, one can leave them open. The shape must then be indicated in the signatures. For instance, the signer's entity can decide dynamically whether a node becomes a leaf or an inner node. To indicate this, one additional bit is prefixed to the value m_l signed at any node l. If one uses the message bound ∞, the components are no longer polynomial-time in the interface inputs alone, because one may have to test arbitrarily long signatures. ♦

10.4 Top-Down Tree Authentication with Small Amount of Private Storage

In the constructions in the previous two sections, the length of the secret key is linear in the message bound, i.e., the number of messages to be signed. It is shown in Chapter 11 that this cannot be avoided if one defines "secret key" in the functional way of Definition 7.3a, i.e., including all the secret random bits that the signer's entity ever uses.

However, it is now shown that a secret key of this size never needs to exist completely at the same time: In the following construction, the signer's entity only needs a small amount of private storage, whereas the rest of its information can be stored in authentic, but not necessarily secret storage. As mentioned in Section 5.4.1, "Some Special Properties", this can be an advantage in practice.

It is still an open question if the overall storage complexity of the signer's entity has to grow linearly with the message bound. Note, however, that in typical applications, ordinary digital signature schemes also require that such a large amount of information can be stored in an authentic way, because the signatures are stored by the entities of their recipients so that they are available in disputes.

A large amount of private storage is needed in Construction 10.13 because all the values sk_temp_l must be stored secretly so that one-time forgeries at any node of the tree can be proved. The basic idea that will be used to reduce private storage in this construction is to store those sk_temp_l's that are no longer used for signing in encrypted form (in an authentic way, but not secretly) and to store only the encryption key secretly. The idea is shown in Figure 10.3.

At first sight, this may seem impossible: The secrecy scheme used for this purpose must be information-theoretically secure to keep the sk_temp_l's secret from a computationally unrestricted attacker against the security for the signer; but with a one-time pad, which is the most efficient perfect information-theoretically secure secrecy scheme, the key would be just as long as the encrypted message (see [Shan49] or Section 2.2), and thus the amount of private storage would not be reduced. However, a special form of encryption will be used where each individual sk_temp_l remains information-theoretically secret, although information about the ensemble of sk_temp_l's becomes known.

It is now shown how this can be done when top-down tree-authentication is combined with the special one-time signature schemes derived from the general construction framework, Construction 9.4. One also has to take into account that an attacker has a-priori information about an encrypted sk_temp_l, because he may know the corresponding one-time main "public" key and signature. For instance, if the one-time signature is $s_l = sk_{l,1} + m_l\, sk_{l,2}$, the signer's entity should use the message and the signature as a part of the encryption of sk_l, because they can certainly not give an attacker new information about sk_temp_l. Then only $sk_{l,2}$ remains to be encrypted, because $sk_{l,1}$ can be reconstructed from it.

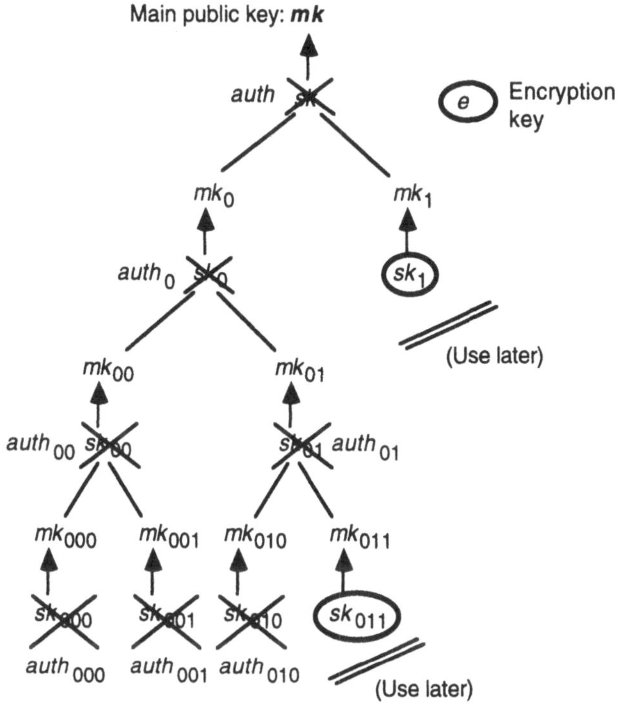

Figure 10.3. Top-down tree authentication with small amount of private storage.
Values *sk_temp* are abbreviated as *sk*. The figure shows the situation after three real messages have been signed. Only the encircled values have to be in private storage. Values crossed out have been deleted. The remaining values are in authentic storage, where $auth_l$ is the information stored in authentic storage instead of sk_l, i.e., (m_l, s_l, c_l) in Construction 10.19.

As before, thin black arrows denote the relation between a one-time secret key and the corresponding one-time main "public" key and normal lines only indicate a tree, but are not related to a computation.

Before the construction can be presented, or at least before it can be proved, one needs an additional definition for the distinction between private and authentic storage. For brevity, it is only made for schemes with one risk bearer and with prekey.

Definition 10.18 (Distinction of private and authentic storage). A secure standard fail-stop signature scheme with prekey and with a distinction between private and authentic storage is a special case of Definition 7.31 (and thus 7.1) and Theorem 7.34 with the following additional properties:

a) All values $sk\_temp \in SK\_Temp$ consist of two parts,

$$sk\_temp = (sk\_temp\_priv, sk\_temp\_auth).$$

The intuitive meaning is that *sk_temp_priv* is stored in private storage, whereas *sk_temp_auth* is in authentic, but not necessarily secret storage.

b) An extension of the functional version of signing is defined so that it reflects all the values that were ever in authentic storage (in extension of Definition 7.3b): $sign\_ext^{(f)}(sk, \underline{m})$ for $\underline{m} = (m_1, \ldots, m_i)$ is defined like $sign^{(f)}(sk, \underline{m})$, except that it also outputs the sequence

$$\underline{auth} := (sk\_temp\_auth_0, \ldots, sk\_temp\_auth_i),$$

where $sk\_temp\_auth_0$ is the second component of the original temporary secret key, and each $sk\_temp\_auth_j$ is the second component of the temporary secret key after signing m_j. Hence one can write

$$(\underline{s}, \underline{auth}) := sign\_ext^{(f)}(sk, \underline{m}).$$

c) The set of possible extended histories is defined as follows (in extension of Definition 7.12a, because the view of the attacker is now extended by the values in authentic storage):

$$Hist\_ext(sk, N) :=$$
$$\{(\underline{m}, \underline{s}, \underline{auth}) \mid \exists j \in \mathbb{N}: j \le N \wedge \underline{m} \in M^j \wedge (\underline{s}, \underline{auth}) = sign\_ext^{(f)}(sk, \underline{m})\}.$$

d) In the security for the signer (Criterion 3 of Theorem 7.34), the definition of the set of good information known to the attacker is modified by using extended histories: If $pk = (prek, mk)$ and $hist\_ext = (\underline{m}, \underline{s}, \underline{auth})$, and its restriction to a usual history is $hist := (\underline{m}, \underline{s})$, then

$$(mk, hist\_ext) \in GoodInf\_ext(par, prek) :\Leftrightarrow \forall f \in Forg(\text{TRUE}, pk, hist):$$
$$P_{par,prek}(provable(sk, pk, hist, f) \mid mk, sign\_ext^{(f)}(sk, \underline{m}) = (\underline{s}, \underline{auth}))$$
$$\ge 1 - 2^{-\sigma-1}.$$

e) The **extended security for the signer** is: For all parameters *par* as before, all prekeys $prek \in Good_{k,\sigma}$, all key pairs $(sk, mk) \in [gen_A^{(f)}(par, prek)]$, and all possible extended histories $hist\_ext \in Hist\_ext(sk, N)$,

$$(mk, hist\_ext) \in GoodInf\_ext(par, prek).$$ ♦

Note that these definitions imply that anything stored in authentic storage in a formal construction can be moved into private storage without weakening the security, i.e., formal constructions should make minimal use of private storage. This may be interesting if private storage is the memory of a hand-held device and authentic storage is on a back-up device or on diskettes; then, of course, information that is still needed for signing does not have to be moved out of the hand-held device.

Now the construction sketched above is shown in more detail and with a concrete encryption scheme. Recall that it was illustrated in Figure 10.3.

Construction 10.19. Let a one-time fail-stop signature scheme be given that is a combination of the general construction framework (Construction 9.4) and message hashing (Construction 10.1).

The corresponding standard **fail-stop signature scheme with top-down tree authentication and a small amount of private storage** (with prekey and with a distinction between private and authentic storage) is constructed by using the given one-time scheme in top-down tree authentication (Construction 10.13) with the following modifications:

- In the key-generation protocol, the signer's entity chooses an additional value $e \in G_K$ randomly as an encryption key. (Recall from Remark 10.16c that the prekey is of the form $prek = (\text{`}1\text{'}^k, \text{`}1\text{'}^\sigma, K, K^\circ)$, where K is a key of a family of bundling homomorphisms.) It keeps e secret all the time. Thus $sk\_temp\_priv :=$ (e, sk_temp) and $sk\_temp\_auth := (par, prek, j)$.
- In signing: One-time key pairs, one-time signatures, and complete signatures are generated as in Construction 10.13. The rules for storing them are as follows:
  - If a one-time key pair (sk_temp_l, mk_l) has been generated, but not yet used for signing, sk_temp_l is stored secretly, i.e., as a component of sk_temp_priv, whereas mk_l is a component of sk_temp_auth.
  - According to Remark 10.16c, one-time secret keys can be of the shortened form $sk\_temp_l = (sk_{l,1}, sk_{l,2})$.
  - If the one-time secret key $sk\_temp_l = (sk_{l,1}, sk_{l,2})$ has been used up by signing a message m_l (which may be a real message or a pair of one-time main "public" keys), it is processed as follows:
    - The second half, $sk_{l,2}$, is encrypted as $c_l := sk_{l,2} + e$ (in G_K).
    - The value $auth_l := (m_l, s_l, c_l)$ consisting of the message, the one-time signature, and the ciphertext is stored in sk_temp_auth.
    - Then sk_temp_l is removed from private storage.
- In the algorithm *prove**: When the node l has been found where the forgery links into the correct tree and the one-time secret key sk_temp_l is needed for proving the one-time forgery, the algorithm reconstructs it as follows: It retrieves $auth_l = (m_l, s_l, c_l)$, decrypts $sk_{l,2} = c_l - e$, and recomputes $sk_{l,1} =$ $s_l - \tilde{m}_l\, sk_{l,2}$, where $\tilde{m}_l := \iota_{k,prek'}(hash^\circ{}_{K^\circ}(m_l))$ with $prek' := (\text{`}1\text{'}^k, \text{`}1\text{'}^\sigma, K)$. ♦

Theorem 10.20 (Top-down tree authentication with small amount of private storage).

a) Construction 10.19 defines the components of a standard fail-stop signature scheme with prekey for signing an arbitrary number of messages. If the underlying fail-stop signature scheme for signing one message block is secure according to Theorem 9.9, Construction 10.19 is secure, too (in the sense of Definition 10.18).

b) At any time, private storage is only needed for the encryption key e and at most d one-time secret keys sk_temp_l, where d is the depth of the tree, i.e., $N = 2^d$. ♦

Proof. a) The only really interesting part of the proof is that the additional information stored non-secretly does not weaken the security for the signer — the requirements from Definitions 7.1 and 7.31 are easy to see, and effectiveness of authentication and the security for the risk bearer are unchanged in comparison with Theorem 10.14. (Recall from Theorem 10.2 that the security of the underlying scheme according to Definition 9.1 implies that in combination with message hashing, it fulfils the criteria of Theorem 7.34, and hence Theorem 10.14 can be applied.)

Similar to the proof of Theorem 10.14, let parameters *par*, a prekey $prek = (\text{'1'}^k, \text{'1'}^\sigma, K, K^\circ) \in Good_{k,\sigma}$, and values *mk* and $hist\_ext^* = (\underline{m}^*, \underline{s}^*, \underline{auth}^*)$ be given, where a value sk^*_0 exists with $(sk^*_0, mk) \in [gen_A{}^{*(f)}(par, prek)]$ and $hist\_ext^* \in Hist\_ext^*(sk^*_0, N)$. It has to be shown that $(mk, hist\_ext^*) \in GoodInf\_ext^*(par, prek)$.

For this, let a successful forgery $f^* = (m_j', (j, s_j', \underline{mk}', \underline{s}')) \in Forg^*(\text{TRUE}, pk, hist^*)$ be given, where $pk = (prek, mk)$ and $hist^* = (\underline{m}^*, \underline{s}^*)$, and let $prek' := (\text{'1'}^k, \text{'1'}^\sigma, K)$.

As before, one shows that in the given forgery f^*, the algorithm *prove** finds a successful one-time forgery $f_l = (m_l', s_l') \in Forg(\text{TRUE}, pk_l, hist_l)$, and one can see from the construction of *prove** and *verify** that $provable(sk_l, pk_l, hist_l, f_l)$ implies $provable^*(sk^*, pk, hist^*, f^*)$ — the only addition to Theorem 10.14 is here that one has to show that sk_temp_l is reconstructed correctly in *prove**. Hence it remains to be shown that

$$P^*_{par,prek}(provable(sk_l, pk_l, hist_l, f_l) \mid mk, sign\_ext^{*(f)}(sk^*, \underline{m}^*) = (\underline{s}^*, \underline{auth}^*)) \\ \geq 1 - 2^{-\sigma-1}$$

(where the probability is over sk^*).

If the signer's entity has already signed a message m_l at this node, and if (m_l, m_l') is a $hash^\circ{}_{K^\circ}$-collision, this collision is a valid proof of forgery with probability 1. (Recall that K° is a part of the prekey and therefore fixed in the probability.) Thus only the remaining case is considered further. Let $\tilde{m}_l' := \iota_{k,prek'}(hash^\circ{}_{K^\circ}(m_l'))$. As $\iota_{k,prek'}$ is injective, $(\tilde{m}_l', s_l')$ is a successful forgery in the one-time scheme without message hashing.

Lemma 9.6b guarantees that this one-time forgery is provable unless s_l' is the correct one-time signature on $\tilde{m}_l'$ at Node *l*. Intuitively, it remains to be shown that the additional information in $\underline{auth}^*$ does not make it easier for an attacker to guess this correct signature. Formally, it suffices to show that

$$P^*_{par,prek}(sign^{(f)}(sk_l, \tilde{m}_l') = s_l' \mid mk, sign\_ext^{*(f)}(sk^*, \underline{m}^*) = (\underline{s}^*, \underline{auth}^*)) \\ \leq 2^{-\sigma-1}. \qquad (*)$$

In contrast to the proof of Theorem 10.14, the probability cannot simply be partitioned into those for the individual one-time keys, because there is the encryption with the same key *e*. Hence the possible secret keys are counted as in the proof of Lemma 9.7. Only the worst case is considered where the attacker has maximal information about the secret key, i.e., where $\underline{m}^*$ is of maximal length *N* and hence a one-time signature s_l on a message m_l has already been issued at every node of the tree. In any other case, the attacker cannot do better (by the general formula in the proof of Lemma 9.7b).

Denote the corresponding hash values by $\tilde{m}_l := \iota_{k,prek'}(hash^\circ{}_{K^\circ}(m_l))$ and the possible secret keys sk^* by $(e, \underline{sk})$, where $\underline{sk}$ is the family of the values sk_λ at all nodes λ.[157]

As e and the values $sk_{\lambda,1}$ and $sk_{\lambda,2}$ at all nodes λ are chosen independently and uniformly from G_K, the probability of an event E expressed as a predicate *pred* about $sk^* = (e, \underline{sk})$ is

$$P^*_{par,prek}(E) = |\{(e, \underline{sk}) \mid pred(e, \underline{sk})\}| \;/\; |G_K|^{(4N-1)}.$$

The $4N-1$ values are two at each of the $2N-1$ nodes of the tree and e.

The conditions about a certain sk_λ given by the values mk_λ, m_λ, and s_λ contained in $\underline{auth}^*$ are the same as in Formulas (1) and (3) of Lemma 9.7. Hence the set of the possible secret keys that fulfil the condition of the probability in (∗) is

$$SK^* = \{(e, \underline{sk}) \mid \forall \lambda: (sk_{\lambda,1} = s_\lambda - \tilde{m}_\lambda\, sk_{\lambda,2} \wedge h_K(sk_{\lambda,2}) = mk_{\lambda,2} \wedge c_\lambda = sk_{\lambda,2} + e)\}.$$

It is now shown that any value $sk'_{l,2} \in G_K$ with $h_K(sk'_{l,2}) = mk_{l,2}$ (intuitively: that the attacker guesses) occurs in exactly one tuple in SK^*, say $tup(sk'_{l,2})$. Uniqueness is easy to see: The encryption key can only be $e' := c_l - sk'_{l,2}$, and the one-time secret key at any other node λ must then be

$$sk'_{\lambda,2} := c_\lambda - e' = sk'_{l,2} + c_\lambda - c_l$$

(and $sk'_{\lambda,1}$ is uniquely determined by $sk'_{\lambda,2}$ anyway). Conversely, it must be shown that this tuple is in SK^*, i.e., $h_K(sk'_{\lambda,2}) = mk_{\lambda,2}$ for all λ. On the one hand,

$$h_K(sk'_{\lambda,2}) = h_K(sk'_{l,2}) \cdot h_K(c_\lambda) \,/\, h_K(c_l) = mk_{l,2} \cdot h_K(c_\lambda) \,/\, h_K(c_l). \qquad (**)$$

On the other hand, the real encryption key e and the real values $sk_{\lambda,2}$ and $sk_{l,2}$ (i.e., from the secret key sk^*_0 whose existence was required above) fulfil

$$h_K(c_\lambda) = h_K(sk_{\lambda,2}) \cdot h_K(e) = mk_{\lambda,2} \cdot h_K(e)$$

and

$$h_K(c_l) = h_K(sk_{l,2}) \cdot h_K(e) = mk_{l,2} \cdot h_K(e).$$

Substituted into (∗∗), this yields $h_K(sk'_{\lambda,2}) = mk_{\lambda,2}$. Hence indeed, any $sk'_{l,2} \in G_K$ with $h_K(sk'_{l,2}) = mk_{l,2}$ occurs in exactly one tuple $tup(sk'_{l,2})$ in SK^*. The size of SK^* is therefore the number of preimages of $mk_{l,2}$, i.e.,

$$|SK^*| \geq 2^\tau,$$

where $\tau := tau(k, \sigma)$ is the intermediate parameter that determines the bundling degree of h_K.

Secondly, one needs to know for how many possible secret keys the forged one-time signature s'_l is correct, i.e., how many of them satisfy the equation $sign^{(f)}(sk_l, \tilde{m}'_l) = s'_l$ from (∗). This is just a one-time signature at Node l and equivalent to Equation (5) in the proof of Lemma 9.7. Hence the number of

157 As in Section 10.3, this partitioning of the random string is a little simplified.

solutions $sk'_{l,2}$ is $|T_{K,m_\Delta}|$, where $m_\Delta := \tilde{m}'_l - \tilde{m}_l$, and each of them determines exactly one solution $tup(sk'_{l,2})$ in SK^*.

Hence the probability in (*) is at most $2^{-\tau} |T_{K,m_\Delta}|$ and thus at most $2^{-\sigma-1}$, because the underlying scheme is secure according to Theorem 9.9.

b) It has to be shown that at any time, at most one one-time key pair per level of the tree has already been generated, but not yet used for signing. (These are marked "use later" in Figures 10.2 and 10.3.) If the last real message signed was m_j, all the one-time keys on the branch to Node j and to the left of it have been used for signing, and the only further one-time key pairs that have already been generated are those immediate children of the nodes on this path that are to the right of the path.

Hence, if this construction is applied to a binary complete tree, as assumed above, the amount of private storage needed is only logarithmic in the message bound, N. □

Remark 10.21. One can even achieve that the amount of private storage is constant (as a function of N) by using a list-shaped tree instead of the complete binary tree. For instance, the left child of each node can be a real message and only the right child a new one-time main "public" key (see Figure 10.4). Then only two secret sk_temp_l's are needed at any time: For instance, when m_2 is signed in Figure 10.4, sk and sk_1 have already been moved out to authentic storage, sk_3 has just been generated, and sk_2 is needed for signing. However, later signatures are very long. Thus the list-shaped version should only be used if there is a fixed recipient, see Section 10.6. ♦

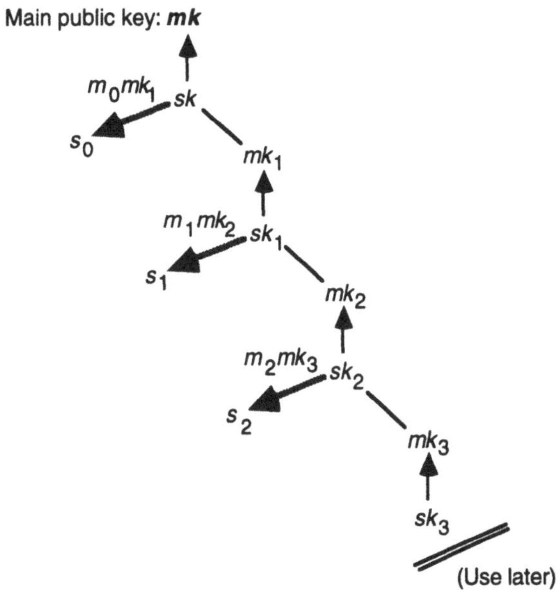

Figure 10.4. List-shaped tree authentication.
The same graphical conventions as in Figure 10.2 are used.

Recall that trees of other shapes can also be used, e.g., ternary trees or trees where one decides dynamically whether a node l is used to sign a real message or more one-time main "public" keys, see Remarks 10.16 and 10.17.

10.5 Discrete-Logarithm Scheme with Shorter Secret Key

In this section, a standard fail-stop signature scheme with prekey is shown where N messages can be signed with a secret key of total length $(2N+2)k$ (not counting the prekey). The smallest upper bound in the previous sections was $4Nk$, achieved by using the one-time scheme based on the concrete discrete-logarithm assumption N times (see Lemma 9.14).[158] The scheme, which was first published in [HePe93] as personal communication by me, is a variant of an earlier scheme by the authors of [HePe93], which is mentioned in Remark 10.24 below.

It is a variant of the discrete-logarithm scheme where half of each one-time secret key is reused for the next signature. For simplicity, it is immediately presented with subgroups of prime fields, i.e., in a form similar to Lemma 9.12. Moreover, the length of the public key is not minimized for the moment, and the scheme is presented for message blocks; see Remark 10.25.

Construction 10.22. Let a generation scheme for subgroups of prime fields be given (Definition 8.21). A corresponding standard fail-stop signature scheme with prekey for signing an arbitrary number of message blocks (with *Message_bounds* = $\mathbb{N}$), called the **discrete-logarithm scheme with minimized secret key**, is given by the following components:

- Key generation:
  - Prekey-generation algorithm: On input $par^* = (\text{'1'}^k, \text{'1'}^\sigma, \text{'1'}^N)$, a prekey
  $$prek := K := (q, p, g, g^*)$$
  is chosen as in Lemma 9.12. In particular, p and q are primes, and g and g^* are generators of the group $H_{q,p}$, the unique subgroup of order q of $\mathbb{Z}_p{}^*$.
  - Local verification algorithm: Identical to Lemma 9.12.
  - Main key generation: The secret key is of the form
  $$\begin{aligned} sk = sk\_temp &:= (prek, 0, sk_1, \ldots, sk_{N+1}) \\ &:= (prek, 0, (x_1, y_1), (x_2, y_2), \ldots, (x_{N+1}, y_{N+1})), \end{aligned}$$
  where all the values x_i and y_i are randomly and independently chosen numbers modulo q. The corresponding main public key consists of the images under the bundling homomorphism,
  $$mk := (mk_1, \ldots, mk_{N+1}) := (g^{x_1} g^{*y_1}, \ldots, g^{x_{N+1}} g^{*y_{N+1}}).$$

---

158 This is a slightly simplified comparison, because k is not directly comparable between schemes relying on different cryptologic assumption. However, the two schemes just mentioned do rely on the same assumption, and it was shown in Section 9.5 that with choices of security parameters that seem reasonable at present, the secret keys in the constructions based on the factoring assumption are longer.

- Main public key test: Each value mk_i is tested as in Lemma 9.12.
- The message-block space for $prek = (q, p, g, g^*)$ is $M_{prek} := \{1, \ldots, q-1\}$. (Note that 0 has now been excluded.)
- Signing: The correct signature on the j-th message block, $m \in \{1, \ldots, q-1\}$, (i.e., $sign^{(f)}(sk, j, \underline{m})$ for any message sequence $\underline{m}$ with $m_j = m$) is the triple
$$s \ := \ (j, x_j + m\, x_{j+1}, y_j + m\, y_{j+1}).$$
It will also be written $sign^{(f)}(sk, j, m_j)$, because it does not depend on the rest of the sequence. In the algorithmic version, the second component of *sk_temp* is incremented, and if it is already N when *sign* is called, the output is '*key_used_up*'.
- Test: If the public key is $pk = (prek, mk)$ with *prek* and *mk* of the form described above, a value s is an acceptable signature on the message block m if and only if
  - s is a triple (j, x, y) where $j \in \{1, \ldots, N\}$ and x and y are numbers modulo q, and
  - $h_K(x, y) = mk_j\, mk_{j+1}{}^m$, i.e.,
$$g^x\, g^{*y} \ = \ mk_j\, mk_{j+1}{}^m.$$
- Proving forgeries: Given a supposed forgery (m, s'), it is first tested if s' is an acceptable signature on m. If yes, and if $s' = (j, x', y')$, the correct signature s on the same message block in the same position j is computed, i.e., $s = (j, x, y) = (j, x_j + m\, x_{j+1}, y_j + m\, y_{j+1})$. If $s' \neq s$, the result is
$$proof \ := \ ((x, y), (x', y')).$$
Otherwise the output is *not_a_forgery*.
- Verifying proofs of forgery: As in Lemma 9.12, valid proofs of forgery are h_K-collisions. ♦

Theorem 10.23 (Discrete-logarithm scheme with minimized secret key). If the discrete logarithm is hard for the given generation scheme for subgroups of prime fields, Construction 10.22 is a standard fail-stop signature scheme with prekey for signing message blocks. It fulfils the simplified security criteria from Theorem 7.34 and is therefore secure. Moreover, it is polynomial-time in the interface inputs alone. ♦

Proof. The implicit and explicit requirements from Definitions 7.1 and 7.31 are obviously fulfilled, and effectiveness of authentication and the security for the risk bearer are shown as in Lemma 9.12. Furthermore, it is clear that every successful forgery f that is not the correct signature in the same position j in the sequence is provable. It remains to be shown that the reuse of halves of the one-time secret keys does not increase the likelihood with which such a forgery is the correct signature. Thus, with all the quantifiers as in Criterion 3 of Theorem 7.34 in the version of Definition 9.1, it has to be shown that for $f = (m', s')$ with $s' = (j, x', y')$:
$$P_{par,prek}(sign^{(f)}(sk, j, m') = s' \mid mk, sign^{(f)}(sk, \underline{m}) = \underline{s}) \ \leq \ 2^{-\sigma-1} \qquad (*)$$
(where the probability is over sk).

It suffices to show this for the worst case, where the signer has already signed N messages, i.e., the length of $\underline{m}$ is N, and the history therefore contains maximum information about sk (see the proof of Lemma 9.7b).

Similar to the proof of Lemma 9.7a, first the size of the set SK of the possible secret keys that fulfil the condition in (∗) is determined, i.e.,

$$\begin{aligned} SK := \{&(prek, 0, (x_1, y_1), (x_2, y_2), \ldots, (x_{N+1}, y_{N+1})) \\ &\mid (g^{x_1} g^{*y_1}, \ldots, g^{x_{N+1}} g^{*y_{N+1}}) = (mk_1, \ldots, mk_{N+1}) \\ &\wedge (l, x_l + m_l x_{l+1}, y_l + m_l y_{l+1}) = s_l \text{ for } l := 1, \ldots, N\}. \end{aligned}$$

All these equations can be written as linear equations over the field $\mathbb{Z}_q$. Let $e := log_g(g^*)$ and $\gamma_l := log_g(mk_l)$ for $l := 1, \ldots, N+1$ and $s_l =: (v_l, w_l)$ for $l := 1, \ldots, N$. (Note that nobody needs to compute these logarithms, they just exist.) Then the equations are

$$\begin{pmatrix} 1 & 0 & m_1 & & & & & & \\ & 1 & 0 & m_1 & & & & 0 & \\ & & 1 & 0 & m_2 & & & & \\ & & & 1 & 0 & m_2 & & & \\ & & & & \ddots & & & & \\ & 0 & & & & 1 & 0 & m_N & \\ & & & & & & 1 & 0 & m_N \\ \hdashline 1 & e & & & & & & & \\ & & 1 & e & & & 0 & & \\ & 0 & & & \ddots & & & & \\ & & & & & & & 1 & e \end{pmatrix} \begin{pmatrix} x_1 \\ y_1 \\ x_2 \\ \vdots \\ x_{N+1} \\ y_{N+1} \end{pmatrix} = \begin{pmatrix} v_1 \\ w_1 \\ v_2 \\ w_2 \\ \vdots \\ v_N \\ w_N \\ \hdashline \gamma_1 \\ \vdots \\ \gamma_{N+1} \end{pmatrix}.$$

It is now shown that the rank of the matrix L in this equation is $2N + 1$. For this, the following submatrix of L is considered (from Rows $2j - 1$, $2j$, $2N + j$, and $2N + j + 1$ for some $j \le N$):

$$\begin{matrix} 1 & 0 & m_j & 0 \\ 0 & 1 & 0 & m_j \\ 1 & e & 0 & 0 \\ 0 & 0 & 1 & e. \end{matrix}$$

One can easily see that the rank of this submatrix is 3 and that the third row is a linear combination of the others and can therefore be removed. By performing this step for $j := 1, \ldots, N$ in this order, all the rows $(0 \ldots 0\ 1\ e\ 0 \ldots 0)$ are deleted, except for the last one. The rank of the resulting matrix is clearly $2N + 1$.

Furthermore, the equations are solvable because the correct secret key is a solution. Hence the number of solutions is $|SK| = q$.

It is now shown that the equation $sign^{(f)}(sk, j, m') = s'$ from (∗) holds for at most one out of these possible secret keys (i.e., the forged signature is correct for at most one of these keys). The additional signature introduces two new equations corresponding to new matrix rows

$$\begin{matrix} 0\ldots0 & 1 & 0 & m' & 0 & 0\ldots0 \\ 0\ldots0 & 0 & 1 & 0 & m' & 0\ldots0 \end{matrix}$$

with the first 1 in Column $2j$–1. It has to be shown that the rank of the new matrix is $2N + 2$. First, the submatrix defined by the forged signature and the j-th signature the signer really made is transformed into

$$\begin{matrix} 1 & 0 & m_j & 0 \\ 0 & 1 & 0 & m_j \\ 0 & 0 & 1 & 0 \\ 0 & 0 & 0 & 1\,. \end{matrix}$$

(It was used that $m' \neq m_j$ by definition of a successful forgery.) Now the next two rows of the original matrix are transformed into

$$\begin{matrix} 0\ldots0 & 0 & 0 & 0 & 0 & m_{j+1} & 0 & 0\ldots0 \\ 0\ldots0 & 0 & 0 & 0 & 0 & 0 & m_{j+1} & 0\ldots0\,. \end{matrix}$$

As 0 was excluded from the message-block space, one can divide by m_{j+1} and repeat this step for the messages $m_{j+2}, \ldots, m_N$. The rank of the resulting matrix is clearly $2N + 2$.

As all the components of the secret key (except for *prek*, which is fixed in the probability) are chosen independently and uniformly, this implies that the probability in (∗) is at most $1/q < 2^{-\sigma-1}$, as desired. □

Remark 10.24 (An alternative). [HePe93] contains a related scheme where the keys are of the same size as in Construction 10.22, but the signatures need not contain the message number. Hence the signature length is only $2k$, instead of $2k + |N|_2$. However, the complexity of signing grows linearly in N in that scheme, i.e., it is unsuitable for most practical applications. Moreover, $|N|_2 \approx \log_2(N)$ is much smaller than k. (This is not only natural in most applications, but necessary for the security of this scheme: As N operations are considered feasible in *sign*, it is also feasible to compute discrete logarithms modulo numbers of length $\log_2(N)$, and thus k must be larger.) ♦

Remark 10.25 (Combinations). Construction 10.22 can be combined with several other constructions:

- It can be combined with message hashing so that messages of arbitrary length can be signed. (Recall that Construction 10.1 was not only for one-time signature schemes.)
- If message hashing is used, the algorithm *prove* does not need to search among all the previously signed message for a collision with the message m', because a successful forgery (m, s') with $s' = (j, x', y')$ is provable in the underlying scheme unless it collides with m_j.

- One can use bottom-up tree authentication so that the public key is short. (This does not follow from Theorem 10.10, but it is easy to see.)
- One can use subtrees of this form in top-down tree authentication in the place of individual one-time key pairs. ♦

10.6 The Case of a Fixed Recipient

In the case with a fixed recipient, efficiency can be improved significantly, because the recipient's entity can store information from previously received signatures.

Optimized Standard Constructions

With all forms of tree authentication, the algorithms *sign* and *test* can be optimized as follows: The signer's entity only sends that part of the branch that is different from the previous signature, and the recipient's entity only tests that part. Thus, two new nodes must be sent and tested on average — independent of the depth of the tree and thus the message bound (because the tree has $2N-1$ nodes altogether). The maximum occurs in the middle of the tree. One can also try to level the differences out, similar to [Vaud92].

List-Shaped Trees

One can also use top-down tree authentication with a list-shaped tree where a message and a new one-time main "public" key are signed at the same node. (See Figure 10.4 and Remark 10.21, but the construction can be based on any one-time standard fail-stop signature scheme with prekey for the message space $\{0, 1\}^+$.) In this case, only one new node of the tree must be produced, sent, and tested during each authentication. Thus signing and testing are reduced to the following procedures:

- Signing: Let the current one-time secret key be sk_i. A new one-time key pair (sk_{i+1}, mk_{i+1}) is generated; this can be done off-line before the new message is known. The correct signature s^* on a message m_i is (mk_{i+1}, s_i), where s_i is a one-time signature with sk_i on the pair (m_i, mk_{i+1}).
- Testing: On input a message m_i and a supposed signature $s^* = (mk_{i+1}, s_i)$, the new one-time main "public" key is tested with *mk_test* and then the new one-time signature with $test(mk_i, (m_i, mk_{i+1}), s_i)$, where the current one-time main "public" key mk_i is taken from local memory. If the result is TRUE, the overall result is TRUE, too, and mk_i is replaced by mk_{i+1} as the current one-time main "public" key.

If a court's entity has to decide in a dispute, it must test the signature with respect to the original public key *mk*. There are two possibilities:

- The recipient's entity has to send the whole list.
- One uses an interactive protocol with the signer's entity, i.e., 3-party disputes at the recipient's discretion (Section 5.2.8, "Important Combinations") to make the

complexity of a dispute logarithmic in N: With logarithmic search, one first finds an index $l \leq i$ where the signer and the recipient agree on mk_l, but not on the pair (m_l, mk_{l+1}) signed with respect to it. Then it suffices to solve the dispute regarding this one-time signature.

Note that this scheme is not a standard fail-stop signature scheme.

11 Lower Bounds

Lower bounds should to provide answers to the following two types of questions:

1. How close to the optimum are the existing constructions?
2. Is there necessarily a certain price in efficiency to pay for more security, and in particular, for information-theoretic security instead of computational security?

In the present context, the first question is mainly interesting for fail-stop signature schemes.

The second question is studied for the difference between signature schemes with ordinary, fail-stop, and information-theoretic security. Moreover, one can ask how much an increase in security within a given security type affects the attainable efficiency (see Figure 11.1). With a requirement that is fulfilled information-theoretically with an error probability, such an increase is expressed by the security parameter σ that determines the bound on the error probability. Handling computational security is more complicated; this is discussed in the introduction to Section 11.3.

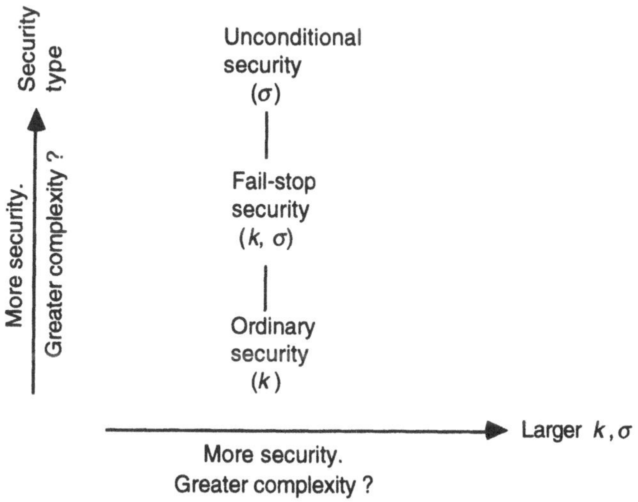

Figure 11.1. Some questions about lower bounds

Actually, not arbitrary signature schemes with fail-stop security according to Chapter 5 are considered at present, but only standard fail-stop signature schemes as defined in Chapter 7, and security for the signer backwards and error-free effectiveness of authentication, at least in the case where all parties carry out key generation correctly, are assumed.[159]

---

[159] I expect the lower bounds to hold more generally, but the following proofs would have to be changed, because the message sequence can no longer be fixed.

The lower bounds proven below concern the length of keys and signatures. This yields lower bounds on the communication complexity of initialization and authentication and on the space complexity of the entities.[160] Similar lower bounds have been investigated for other cryptologic schemes with information-theoretic security properties, e.g., encryption schemes [Shan49] and authentication codes, starting with [GiMS74] (see [SaTo94] for more references). Combinations of information-theoretic and computational security as in the following do not seem to have been considered before. Large parts of this chapter have been presented in [HePP93, PePf95].

Section 11.1 sketches the information-theoretic background. Section 11.2 introduces random variables used throughout large parts of this chapter. Section 11.3 investigates the length of secret keys and Section 11.4 that of signatures and public keys of standard fail-stop signature schemes. Information-theoretically secure signature schemes are studied in Section 11.5. Section 11.6 answers some of the questions posed above, i.e., it compares the lower bounds to the known upper bounds and compares lower bounds of different classes of schemes.

11.1 Information-Theoretic Background

The following lower bounds are primarily proved on entropies of random variables, such as the random variable of the secret key generated with a probabilistic key-generation protocol. This automatically yields lower bounds on the length of the values of these random variables (such as individual secret keys), because a random variable with the entropy l cannot be coded with less than l bits on average.

For the formal theorems and proofs, it is useful if the reader is familiar with elementary information theory (see [Shan48] and [Gall68, Sections 2.2 and 2.3]). The most important notions are briefly repeated in the notation of [Gall68]. It is assumed that a common probability space is given where all the random variables are defined. Capital letters denote random variables and small letters the corresponding values, and terms like $\mathrm{P}(x)$ are abbreviations for probabilities like $\mathrm{P}(X = x)$. The joint random variable of X and Y is written as X, Y. The entropy of a random variable X is

$$\mathrm{H}(X) := -\sum_{x} \mathrm{P}(x) \log_2(\mathrm{P}(x)).$$

(All the random variables occurring in entropies in the following are finite, i.e., their range only contains a finite number of values x.) $\mathrm{H}(X \mid Y)$ denotes the conditional entropy of X when Y is known and $\mathrm{I}(X ; Y)$ the mutual information between X and Y. They are defined as follows:

$$\mathrm{H}(X \mid Y) := -\sum_{x,y} \mathrm{P}(x, y) \log_2(\mathrm{P}(x \mid y)),$$

[160] This does not mean that bounds on time complexity would not be interesting. However, on the one hand, no approach at proving non-trivial ones seems to be known, and on the other hand, efficiency differences between existing signature schemes with different degrees of security primarily concern communication and storage complexity.

and $$\mathrm{I}(X ; Y) := \mathrm{H}(X) - \mathrm{H}(X \mid Y).$$

Furthermore, the conditional mutual information between X and Y when Z is known is defined as

$$\mathrm{I}(X ; Y \mid Z) := \mathrm{H}(X \mid Z) - \mathrm{H}(X \mid Y, Z).$$

(Actually, only the first two of these formulas are definitions in [Gall68]; the last two are Formulas (2.2.17) and (2.2.26).) The following rules will often be used (for any random variables X, Y, and Z in the common probability space):

$$\mathrm{H}(X) \geq 0, \quad (1)$$
$$\mathrm{H}(X, Y) = \mathrm{H}(X) + \mathrm{H}(Y \mid X), \quad (2)$$
$$\mathrm{I}(X ; Y) = \mathrm{I}(Y ; X), \quad (3)$$
$$\mathrm{I}(X ; Y) \geq 0, \quad (4)$$

and their counterparts with an additional condition:

$$\mathrm{H}(X \mid Y) \geq 0, \quad (1')$$
$$\mathrm{H}(X, Y \mid Z) = \mathrm{H}(X \mid Z) + \mathrm{H}(Y \mid X, Z), \quad (2')$$
$$\mathrm{I}(X ; Y \mid Z) = \mathrm{I}(Y ; X \mid Z), \quad (3')$$
$$\mathrm{I}(X ; Y \mid Z) \geq 0. \quad (4')$$

Moreover, if Y is a function f of X, the conditional entropy of Y given X is zero:

$$\mathrm{H}(f(X) \mid X) = 0. \quad (5)$$

Remark 11.1. Rules (1), (1'), and (5) follow immediately from the definitions, (2), (4), and (4') are (2.2.21), (2.3.5), and (2.3.11) in [Gall68], and (3) follows immediately from (2.2.22). (2') and (3') can be shown as follows:[161]

$$\begin{aligned}
\mathrm{H}(X, Y \mid Z) &= \mathrm{H}(X, Y, Z) - \mathrm{H}(Z) && \text{(Rule (2))}\\
&= \mathrm{H}(X, Z) + \mathrm{H}(Y \mid X, Z) - \mathrm{H}(Z) && \text{(Rule (2))}\\
&= \mathrm{H}(Z) + \mathrm{H}(X \mid Z) + \mathrm{H}(Y \mid X, Z) - \mathrm{H}(Z) && \text{(Rule (2))}\\
&= \mathrm{H}(X \mid Z) + \mathrm{H}(Y \mid X, Z)
\end{aligned}$$

and
$$\begin{aligned}
\mathrm{I}(X ; Y \mid Z) &= \mathrm{H}(X \mid Z) - \mathrm{H}(X \mid Y, Z)\\
&= \mathrm{H}(X \mid Z) - (\mathrm{H}(X, Y \mid Z) - \mathrm{H}(Y \mid Z)) && \text{(Rule (2'))}\\
&= \mathrm{H}(Y \mid Z) - (\mathrm{H}(X, Y \mid Z) - \mathrm{H}(X \mid Z))\\
&= \mathrm{H}(Y \mid Z) - \mathrm{H}(Y \mid X, Z) && \text{(Rule (2'))}\\
&= \mathrm{I}(Y ; X \mid Z).
\end{aligned}$$
♦

Additionally, Jensen's inequality for the special case of the logarithm function is often needed (see, e.g., [Fell71]): If $p_i \geq 0$ and $x_i > 0$ for all i, and the sum of the p_i's is 1, then

$$\log_2\Big(\sum_i p_i x_i\Big) \geq \sum_i p_i \log_2(x_i).$$

161 A more systematic way is to see that any entropy or mutual information with an additional condition Z is the weighted sum over the same terms with a condition z (over all values z), and those are terms of the simpler structure in the probability space induced by conditioning over z. Hence the simpler formulas can be applied.

11.2 Random Variables in Fail-Stop Signature Schemes

The next two sections consider lower bounds on standard fail-stop signature schemes. This section introduces the random variables used for this purpose.

For the lower bounds, only the case where all parties execute the key-generation protocol honestly is needed. Note that one is interested in lower bounds on the length of *correct* keys and signatures; hence this restriction does not exclude the interesting cases. (But it is not trivial that all lower bounds can be proved with this restriction; anyway, cases where authentication or disputes are carried out dishonestly will be needed.)

Moreover, in each situation, fixed parameters $par = (\text{'1'}^k, \text{'1'}^\sigma, \text{'1'}^N)$ and a fixed finite message sequence $\underline{m} = (m_1, \ldots, m_i)$ with $i \leq N$ can be used.

Under these conditions, the functional version of the definitions in Section 7.1 already has the necessary structure with a common probability space where all the random variables can be defined: All values are deterministic functions of the results of key generation, and thus ultimately random variables in the probability space defined by the random strings used in key generation (because the protocol itself and the parameters have been fixed).[162] Some of these random variables are now given names.

Definition 11.2. Let the components of a standard fail-stop signature scheme (according to Definitions 7.1 or 7.2 and 7.3), a tuple of parameters, $par = (\text{'1'}^k, \text{'1'}^\sigma, \text{'1'}^N)$ with $k, \sigma \in \mathbb{N}$ and $N \in$ *Message_bounds*, and a message sequence $\underline{m} = (m_1, \ldots, m_i) \in M^i$ with $i \in \mathbb{N}$ and $i \leq N+1$ be given.

Then key generation, $Gen^{(f)}(par)$, defines a probability space. The following random variables are defined in it:

- PK and SK are the random variables of the public and the secret key, respectively, i.e., they are defined by the components pk and sk of the outcome of $Gen^{(f)}(par)$.
- For all $j \leq i$ with $j \neq N+1$, let S_j denote the random variable of the correct signature s_j on m_j in this context, i.e.,
$$S_j := sign^{(f)}(SK, j, \underline{m}).$$
If $i = N+1$, there is one message more than the message bound, hence m_{N+1} cannot be signed correctly in the strict sense. Therefore its "correct" signature is defined as if m_N had not been signed. Thus let
$$\underline{m}_{\setminus N} := (m_1, \ldots, m_{N-1}, m_{N+1})$$
and
$$S_{N+1} := sign^{(f)}(SK, N, \underline{m}_{\setminus N}).$$

---

[162] Recall, however, that a lower bound on the length of the secret key in the functional version does not mean that this key must exist all the time in the algorithmic version. In practice, it is only a lower bound on the overall number of secret random bits needed, but they may be generated and deleted dynamically, as in Section 10.4. In contrast, lower bounds on public keys and signatures apply to the algorithmic version, too.

- For all $j \le i$, let $Hist_j$ denote the random variable of the history up to the j-th signature, i.e.,
$$Hist_j := ((m_1, \ldots, m_j), (S_1, \ldots, S_j)).$$
Note that the first component is constant, and that the values of $Hist_j$ for $j \ne N{+}1$ are possible histories in the sense of Definition 7.12.
- $SK_{\underline{m}}$ is the part of SK that is actually used: If the value of SK is $sk = (sk\_temp, r_A)$, the corresponding value $sk_{\underline{m}}$ of $SK_{\underline{m}}$ consists of sk_temp and that part of r_A that is used when $\underline{m}$ is signed in the case $i \le N$, and when $(m_1, \ldots, m_N)$ or $\underline{m}_{\backslash N}$ is signed in the case $i = N + 1$. In particular, one can write
$$S_j = sign^{(f)}(SK_{\underline{m}}, j, \underline{m})$$
for all $j \le i$ with $j \ne N{+}1$ and, if $i = N{+}1$,
$$S_{N+1} = sign^{(f)}(SK_{\underline{m}}, N, \underline{m}_{\backslash N}).$$

The probabilities in this space were called $P_{B,par}(E)$ in Definition 7.17, but they will be abbreviated as $P(E)$ when the probability space is clear from the context. ♦

The random variables defined above, except for SK, are always finite, because the running time of the corresponding algorithms is deterministically polynomial. Moreover, any lower bound on the length of the values of $SK_{\underline{m}}$ is also valid for SK.

Remark 11.3. As each correct signature is a deterministic function of the part of the secret key (in the functional version) that is actually used and the message sequence, Rule (5) implies for $j := 1, \ldots, i$,
$$H(S_j \mid SK_{\underline{m}}) = 0.$$
♦

11.3 Lower Bound on the Secret Random Bits Needed

The greatest difference between existing fail-stop signature schemes and ordinary digital signature schemes is the overall number of secret random bits a signer's entity needs, i.e., the length of the secret key in the sense of the functional version of the definition. In all existing constructions, it grows linearly with the message bound, i.e., the number of messages that can be signed. It is now proved that this cannot be avoided.

To keep the notation simple, only finite message bounds N are considered. For the case $N = \infty$, one can show in the same way that the part of the secret key needed to sign $N' \in \mathbb{N}$ messages grows linearly with N'. (Hence the complete secret key is infinite, but as it does not have to exist completely at any given time, it is more interesting to know how many new random bits are needed per message signed.)

Overview

From the informal description in Section 6.3.1, "Basic Construction Idea" it seems easy to see that the signer's entity needs a lot of secretly chosen random bits:

1. Even a computationally unrestricted attacker must not be able to guess the correct signature on a given message with significant probability of success.
2. Hence the entropy of the correct signature is large.
3. As this holds for each additional signature, even when some signatures are already known, the entropies of the signatures can be added, and therefore the overall entropy of the secrets in the signer's entity is large.

Statement 1 was required explicitly in the basic construction idea, but now it must be derived from the definitions. Informally, this is done as follows:

1.1 In general, applying *prove* to a correct signature should not yield a valid proof of forgery; otherwise the signer could prove her own signatures to be forgeries. (The probability is over the choice of the keys; it will be seen that the messages can be fixed.)

1.2 Thus, on average, even a computationally unrestricted attacker must not be able to guess those correct signatures, because the signer's entity cannot disavow them by applying *prove*.

If Statement 1.1 were simply required without error probability in the definition of fail-stop signature schemes, a formal proof of the intended lower bound would be easy and would yield

$$H(SK \mid PK) \geq (N+1)\sigma.$$

However, there are useful secure fail-stop signature schemes where the attacker sometimes *does* know correct signatures on new messages, and the signer's entity can prove them to be forgeries. For instance, in schemes with message hashing, a computationally unrestricted attacker knows the correct signatures on all the messages with the same hash value as a message that has really been signed. Hence, only an average version of Statement 1.1 can be derived from Definition 7.11, i.e., the security for risk bearers (or, more generally, the correctness of *'broken'*).

Remark 11.4. The desired lower bound cannot possibly be proved from the security for the signer alone. To see this, consider the following counterexample: Suppose that an ordinary digital signature scheme is used, but the signer is simply allowed to tell the court that a signature was forged. Then the security for the signer is guaranteed information-theoretically and nevertheless, the signer's entity does not need many random bits. (Of course, the risk bearer has no security at all.) ♦

That the security for risk bearers is needed is a problem, because Definition 7.11, like all computational cryptologic definitions, is asymptotic, i.e., security is only guaranteed for k sufficiently large. Thus, in a certain sense, one can only derive lower bounds for $k \geq k_0$, for an unknown k_0. This seems unsatisfactory: Nobody would have doubted that one needs arbitrarily long keys if one makes k sufficiently large, because in the definitions, k primarily determines the size of the problem instances and only secondarily the security.

However, the real purpose of lower bounds is to say "whenever one has certain requirements on the security, one has to pay the following price in terms of efficiency". In this section, this is more precisely: "If the error probability in the security for the signer is at most $2^{-\sigma}$, and the risk bearers want some security, too, then at least the following number of random bits is needed (as a function of σ and the security for risk bearers)".

To quantify the security for risk bearers, it suffices for the present purpose to consider the case from Statement 1.1 above, i.e., the probability that the signer can compute a valid proof of forgery simply by applying the algorithm *prove* to her own correct signatures. In practice, one will require this probability to be at most, say, 2^{-40}, or, more generally, $2^{-\sigma^*}$ for some σ^*. The following lower bounds are proved as functions of this parameter σ^* (in addition to σ).

Details

To formalize the proof sketched above, first the quantification of the security for risk bearers is defined formally.

Definition 11.5. Let the components of a standard fail-stop signature scheme (Definitions 7.1 or 7.2 and 7.3) and a parameter $N \in \mathbb{N} \cap Message\_bounds$ be given. For every message sequence $\underline{m} = (m_1, \ldots, m_{N+1}) \in M^{N+1}$, a polynomial-time algorithm $\tilde{A}_{\underline{m}}$ is defined that a cheating signer could use to compute proofs of forgery from her own correct signatures after taking part in key generation correctly. (This algorithm is very efficient and stupid and should be rather useless!)

On input the results of key generation, i.e., $(par, acc, ids_{Risk,out}, pk, sk\_temp_0)$ with $par = (\text{'1'}^k, \text{'1'}^\sigma, \text{'1'}^N)$:

1. For $i := 1, \ldots, N$, it signs the i-th message as $(s_i, sk\_temp_i) \leftarrow sign(sk\_temp_{i-1}, m_i)$. Then it signs the last message, m_{N+1}, as if m_N had not been signed (as in Definition 11.2), i.e., as $(s_{N+1}, sk\_temp_{N+1}) \leftarrow sign(sk\_temp_{N-1}, m_{N+1})$. It stores the intermediate results.
2. It tries to prove that one of these signatures is a forgery with respect to the previous temporary secret key, i.e., $proof_i \leftarrow prove(sk\_temp_{i-1}, m_i, s_i)$ for $i := 1, \ldots, N+1$. If $proof_i \neq not\_a\_forgery$, $\tilde{A}_{\underline{m}}$ outputs it and stops.[163]

For any $\sigma, \sigma^*, k \in \mathbb{N}$, the parameter k is said to be large enough to provide the **security level σ^* for risk bearers against $\tilde{A}_{\underline{m}}$** for the given σ if the success probability of $\tilde{A}_{\underline{m}}$ is at most $2^{-\sigma^*}$.

This probability is defined as in Definition 7.11 with $\tilde{A}_{\underline{m}}$ in the role of $\tilde{A}_2$. Hence, with $par = (\text{'1'}^k, \text{'1'}^\sigma, \text{'1'}^N)$ and with simplifications due to the fact that $\tilde{A}_1$ is the correct A, the condition for one risk bearer is

$$\begin{aligned} &P(acc = \text{TRUE} \wedge verify(pk, proof) = \text{TRUE} \setminus \\ &\quad (acc, ids_{Risk,out}, pk, sk\_temp_0) \leftarrow Gen(par); \\ &\quad proof \leftarrow \tilde{A}_{\underline{m}}(par, acc, ids_{Risk,out}, pk, sk\_temp_0)) \\ &< 2^{-\sigma^*}. \end{aligned}$$

The case with more risk bearers is defined in the same way. ♦

Remark 11.6. Under the preconditions of Definition 11.5, security for risk bearers (Definition 7.11) immediately implies that for all $\sigma, \sigma^* \in \mathbb{N}$, a value

[163] One can interleave Steps 1 and 2 so that one never has to store more than two temporary secret keys.

$k_0 \in \mathbb{N}$ exists such that all $k \geq k_0$ provide the security level σ^* for risk bearers against $\tilde{A}_{\underline{m}}$ for the given σ. (The polynomials *Qsig* and *Qn* can be the constants σ and N, respectively.) Hence Definition 11.5 does not make any new assumptions. ♦

What Definition 11.5 does is bypass the problem that the size of this k_0 is unknown, because it is clear that any k used in practice must be large enough to provide this security level, and hence one can derive lower bounds from the concrete formula for this security level, whereas the asymptotic formula in Definition 7.11 is useless for such a purpose.

Note that it would be impossible to require k to be large enough to provide the same security level against all polynomial-time algorithms instead of only $\tilde{A}_{\underline{m}}$, because once k is fixed, there is a finite problem, and all finite problems can be perfectly solved by some asymptotically polynomial-time algorithm. However, the given $\tilde{A}_{\underline{m}}$ is not only asymptotically polynomial-time, but definitely feasible at the given k, because it is of the same complexity as *sign* and *prove*, which must be carried out by the correct entities for the same k. Requirements of this type are well-known in practice, e.g., when one requires k to be large enough to make the success probability of all known factoring algorithms small.

As a first step towards lower bounds, it is stated what a certain security level for risk bearers means in the terminology with random variables.

Lemma 11.7. Let the components of a standard fail-stop signature scheme, parameters $\sigma \in \mathbb{N}$ and $N \in \mathbb{N} \cap Message\_bounds$, and a message sequence $\underline{m} \in M^{N+1}$ be given. Furthermore, let the signature scheme provide correctness of initialization and let the parameter k be large enough to provide the security level σ^* for risk bearers against $\tilde{A}_{\underline{m}}$ for the given σ. Then for all $i \leq N+1$, with the notation from Definition 11.2,

$$P(provable(SK, PK, Hist_{i-1}, (m_i, S_i))) < 2^{-\sigma^*}. \qquad \blacklozenge$$

Proof. Let $i \leq N+1$ be fixed. The success probability of $\tilde{A}_{\underline{m}}$ is at least as large as the probability that its intermediate result $proof_i$ is a valid proof of forgery, because no unsuccessful stop for a smaller value i is possible. The functional version of the corresponding part of $\tilde{A}_{\underline{m}}$ is the following deterministic function $\tilde{A}^{(f)}{}_{\underline{m},i}$: On input $(par, acc, ids_{Risk,out}, pk, sk)$ with $par = (\text{'1'}^k, \text{'1'}^\sigma, \text{'1'}^N)$:

1. For $j := 1, \ldots, i-1$, let $s_j := sign^{(f)}(sk, j, \underline{m})$. Then $hist_{i-1} := ((m_1, \ldots, m_{i-1}), (s_1, \ldots, s_{i-1}))$ and $s_i := sign^{(f)}(sk, i, \underline{m})$ or $s_{N+1} := sign^{(f)}(sk, N, \underline{m}_{\setminus N})$ if $i \leq N$ or $i = N+1$, respectively.
2. Output $proof_i := prove^{(f)}(sk, pk, hist_{i-1}, (m_i, s_i))$.

Hence one has

$$\begin{aligned} P(&acc = \text{TRUE} \wedge verify(pk, proof) = \text{TRUE} \setminus \\ &\quad (acc, ids_{Risk,out}, pk, sk) \leftarrow Gen^{(f)}(par); \\ &\quad proof := \tilde{A}^{(f)}{}_{\underline{m},i}(par, acc, ids_{Risk,out}, pk, sk)) \\ &< 2^{-\sigma^*}. \end{aligned} \qquad (*)$$

This is not completely trivial, because a different part of the random string from sk is used when applying *prove* in this formula and in the corresponding one for the original $\tilde{A}_{\underline{m}}$. However, in both cases, the random string used is independent of that used to produce $hist_{i-1}$ and s_i, and thus the probabilities are equal.

Correctness of initialization (Definition 7.9) implies that the condition "acc = TRUE" can be omitted in (*).

Finally, as $\tilde{A}^{(f)}_{\underline{m},i}$ is deterministic, the probability is in the probability space considered in Definition 11.2. Hence one can write (*) with random variables and immediately obtains the desired result. □

Now the theorem about the lower bound on the length of the secret key is formulated:

Theorem 11.8 (Lower bound on the secret random bits needed). Let a secure standard fail-stop signature scheme be given that fulfils security for the signer backwards, including Definition 7.17f, and error-free effectiveness of authentication if the risk bearers' entities act correctly. Moreover, let parameters $\sigma, \sigma^* \in \mathbb{N}$ and $N \in \mathbb{N} \cap Message\_bounds$ (and R in the case with several risk bearers) and any sequence $\underline{m}$ of N+1 pairwise distinct messages be fixed. Let $\sigma' := \min(\sigma, \sigma^*)$. For any k large enough to provide the security level σ^* for risk bearers against the algorithm $\tilde{A}_{\underline{m}}$ for the given σ,

$$\mathrm{H}(SK_{\underline{m}} \mid PK) \geq (N+1)(\sigma' - 1). \quad \blacklozenge$$

Remark 11.9.

a) Security against $\tilde{A}_{\underline{m}}$ is only required for one message sequence $\underline{m}$ in Theorem 11.8. The contrary is that *all* these algorithms work. Thus the precondition is very weak.

b) If the message space is very small, Theorem 11.8 does not make a statement for $N \geq |M|$. However, one can then prove a similar statement with $\mathrm{H}(SK_{\underline{m}} \mid PK) \geq |M|(\sigma' - 1)$. ♦

The proof of Theorem 11.8 uses two lemmas. The first one formalizes Statement 1 from the overview, i.e., that correct signatures cannot be guessed with significant probability of success.

Lemma 11.10. With the preconditions and notation of Theorem 11.8: For each $i \leq N$+1 and each pair (pk, $hist_{i-1}$) of possible values of PK and $Hist_{i-1}$, let $s^*(pk, hist_{i-1})$ denote the optimal guess an attacker who has seen pk and $hist_{i-1}$ can make at the correct signature on the next message, m_i. (For $i = N$+1, "correct" is understood as in Definition 11.2.) Thus $s^*(pk, hist_{i-1})$ is defined so that

$$\mathrm{P}(S_i = s^*(pk, hist_{i-1}) \mid pk, hist_{i-1}) \geq \mathrm{P}(S_i = s \mid pk, hist_{i-1})$$

for all values s (representing other potential signatures).

Then this guess is still not very good on average:

$$\mathrm{P}(S_i = s^*(PK, Hist_{i-1})) \leq 2^{-\sigma'+1}. \quad \blacklozenge$$

Proof. Let i be fixed.

a) It is first shown that the best guess at the correct signature is at least a successful forgery, i.e., for all possible pairs (pk, $hist_{i-1}$),

$$(m_i, s^*(pk, hist_{i-1})) \in Forg(\text{TRUE}, pk, hist_{i-1}).$$

The fact that the message is new, i.e., $m_i \notin M(hist_{i-1})$, follows from the precondition that the sequence $\underline{m}$ consists of pairwise distinct messages. The signature is acceptable, i.e., $test(pk, m_i, s^*(pk, hist_{i-1})) = \text{TRUE}$, because it is correct with non-zero probability and error-free effectiveness of authentication after correct key generation was assumed. More precisely, the definition of s^* implies that $P(S_i = s^*(pk, hist_{i-1}) \mid pk, hist_{i-1}) \neq 0$, because S_i must assume some value with non-zero probability. Hence a secret key sk_0 exists where (sk_0, pk) is a possible outcome of $Gen^{(f)}(par)$ and $sign^{(f)}(sk_0, i, \underline{m}) = s^*(pk, hist_{i-1})$ or, for $i = N+1$, $sign^{(f)}(sk_0, N, \underline{m}_N) = s^*(pk, hist_N)$. Now error-free effectiveness of authentication after the execution of $Gen^{(f)}(par)$ yields $test(pk, m_i, s^*(pk, hist_{i-1})) = \text{TRUE}$.

b) The probability of the guess being correct is first partitioned according to whether it is a provable forgery or not:

$$\begin{aligned}
&P(S_i = s^*(PK, Hist_{i-1}))\\
&= P(S_i = s^*(PK, Hist_{i-1}) \wedge provable(SK, PK, Hist_{i-1}, (m_i, S_i)))\\
&\quad + P(S_i = s^*(PK, Hist_{i-1}) \wedge \neg provable(SK, PK, Hist_{i-1}, (m_i, s^*(PK, Hist_{i-1}))))\\
&\le P(provable(SK, PK, Hist_{i-1}, (m_i, S_i)))\\
&\quad + P(\neg provable(SK, PK, Hist_{i-1}, (m_i, s^*(PK, Hist_{i-1}))))\\
&\le 2^{-\sigma^*} + P(\neg provable(SK, PK, Hist_{i-1}, (m_i, s^*(PK, Hist_{i-1})))). \qquad (1)
\end{aligned}$$

For the first summand, Lemma 11.7 was used. The second summand means that the best guess of an attacker is not provable to be a forgery. As it was shown to be a successful forgery in Part a), the security for the signer can be applied. Definition 7.17f yields for all pairs $(pk, hist_{i-1})$ of possible values of PK and $Hist_{i-1}$, and with simplifications due to the fact that $\tilde{B}$ is the correct B,

$$P_{B,par}(provable(sk, pk, hist_{i-1}, (m_i, s^*(pk, hist_{i-1}))) \mid pk, hist_{i-1}) \ge 1 - 2^{-\sigma-1},$$

or, expressed with the random variables,

$$\begin{aligned}
&P(provable(SK, pk, hist_{i-1}, (m_i, s^*(pk, hist_{i-1}))) \mid PK = pk, Hist_{i-1} = hist_{i-1})\\
&\quad \ge 1 - 2^{-\sigma-1}.
\end{aligned}$$

Hence

$$\begin{aligned}
&P(\neg provable(SK, PK, Hist_{i-1}, (m_i, s^*(PK, Hist_{i-1}))))\\
&= \sum_{pk, hist_{i-1}} P(pk, hist_{i-1})\, P(\neg provable(SK, pk, hist_{i-1}, (m_i, s^*(pk, hist_{i-1})))\\
&\qquad\qquad \mid PK = pk, Hist_{i-1} = hist_{i-1})\\
&\le \sum_{pk, hist_{i-1}} P(pk, hist_{i-1})\, 2^{-\sigma-1}\\
&= 2^{-\sigma-1}. \qquad (2)
\end{aligned}$$

Substituting (2) into (1) yields the desired result. □

This result is used in the next lemma to prove a lower bound corresponding to Statement 2 from the overview.

Lemma 11.11. With the preconditions and notation of Theorem 11.8, for the given message sequence $\underline{m}$, and for each $i \le N+1$:

$$H(S_i \mid PK, Hist_{i-1}) \ge \sigma' - 1. \qquad \blacklozenge$$

Proof. With the definition of conditional entropy and Jensen's inequality,

$$\begin{aligned} H(S_i \mid PK, Hist_{i-1}) &= -\sum_{s_i, pk, hist_{i-1}} P(s_i, pk, hist_{i-1}) \log_2(P(s_i \mid pk, hist_{i-1})) \\ &\ge -\log_2\Big(\sum_{s_i, pk, hist_{i-1}} P(s_i, pk, hist_{i-1})\, P(s_i \mid pk, hist_{i-1})\Big). \end{aligned}$$

It suffices to show that the argument of the logarithm is at most $2^{-\sigma'+1}$.[164] In fact, with the definition of the best guess s^* and Lemma 11.10,

$$\begin{aligned} &\sum_{s_i, pk, hist_{i-1}} P(s_i, pk, hist_{i-1})\, P(s_i \mid pk, hist_{i-1}) \\ &\le \sum_{s_i, pk, hist_{i-1}} P(s_i, pk, hist_{i-1})\, P(S_i = s^*(pk, hist_{i-1}) \mid pk, hist_{i-1}) \\ &= \sum_{pk, hist_{i-1}} \Big(P(S_i = s^*(pk, hist_{i-1}) \mid pk, hist_{i-1}) \sum_{s_i} P(s_i, pk, hist_{i-1})\Big) \\ &= \sum_{pk, hist_{i-1}} \big(P(S_i = s^*(pk, hist_{i-1}) \mid pk, hist_{i-1})\, P(pk, hist_{i-1})\big) \\ &= P(S_i = s^*(PK, Hist_{i-1})) \\ &\le 2^{-\sigma'+1}. \end{aligned}$$

□

Proof of Theorem 11.8. First, it is shown by induction over i that the entropy of all correct signatures together is large, i.e., for all $i \le N+1$:

$$H(Hist_i \mid PK) \ge i\,(\sigma' - 1). \qquad (*)$$

For $i = 1$, (*) is just Lemma 11.11; and if (*) has already been proved for $i-1$, it can be proved for i with a rule from Section 11.1:

$$\begin{aligned} H(Hist_i \mid PK) &= H(Hist_{i-1}, S_i \mid PK) \\ &= H(Hist_{i-1} \mid PK) + H(S_i \mid PK, Hist_{i-1}) && \text{(Rule (2'))} \\ &\ge (i-1)(s' - 1) + (s' - 1) \\ &= i\,(s' - 1). \end{aligned}$$

It is now used that $Hist_{N+1}$ is a deterministic function of $SK_{\underline{m}}$. By Rule (5), this implies $H(Hist_{N+1} \mid PK, SK_{\underline{m}}) = 0$, and therefore

$$\begin{aligned} H(SK_{\underline{m}} \mid PK) &= H(SK_{\underline{m}}, Hist_{N+1} \mid PK) - H(Hist_{N+1} \mid PK, SK_{\underline{m}}) && \text{(Rule (2'))} \\ &= H(SK_{\underline{m}}, Hist_{N+1} \mid PK) \\ &= H(Hist_{N+1} \mid PK) + H(SK_{\underline{m}} \mid Hist_{N+1}, PK) && \text{(Rule (2'))} \\ &\ge H(Hist_{N+1} \mid PK) && \text{(Rule (1'))} \\ &\ge (N+1)(\sigma' - 1). \end{aligned}$$

□

164 One can *not* prove that the individual values $\log_2(P(s_i \mid pk, hist_{i-1}))$ are at least σ, which would greatly simplify the proof: This is the fact mentioned in the overview that an attacker sometimes *does* know the correct signature.

11.4 Length of Signatures and Public Keys

Signatures and public keys in existing fail-stop signature schemes are not much longer than in ordinary digital signature schemes. Hence the lower bounds are very small, too.

Overview

The basic idea why fail-stop signatures might have to be longer than ordinary digital signatures at all is the following (see Figure 6.6). Let a message *m* be given.

1. It must have at least 2^{σ} acceptable signatures; otherwise the correct signature could be guessed with a too high probability by a computationally unrestricted attacker.
2. For unforgeability, it must be infeasible for a computationally restricted attacker to find acceptable signatures at all. Thus the density of the set of acceptable signatures within the signature space should be small, e.g., at most $2^{-\sigma^*}$ for some σ^*.

Hence one can expect the size of the signature space to be at least $2^{\sigma+\sigma^*}$. Formally, only $2^{\sigma+\sigma^*-1}$ is proved, but on the other hand, it is proved more generally that the entropy of the correct signature on each message is at least $\sigma + \sigma^* - 1$.

The asymptotic character of the definition of unforgeability, which is used in Statement 2, is treated in the same way as in Section 11.3, i.e., a very efficient algorithm is fixed that an attacker might use to try to compute acceptable signatures: The attacker generates a completely unrelated key pair and hopes that a signature made with the new secret key is also acceptable with respect to the real public key. Of course, this algorithm should be very stupid from the point of view of an attacker, but security against it is sufficient to derive lower bounds.

Details

First, the security against the stupid forging algorithm mentioned above is defined precisely.

Definition 11.12. Let the components of a standard fail-stop signature scheme and a parameter $N \in$ *Message_bounds* be given. For every message sequence $\underline{m} = (m_1, \ldots, m_i) \in M^i$ with $i \in \mathbb{N}$ and $i \le N$, a (very efficient and stupid) polynomial-time non-interactive forging algorithm $\tilde{F}_{\underline{m}}$ is defined.

On input the public outcomes of key generation, i.e., $(par, acc, ids_{Risk,out}, pk)$ with $par = (\text{'1'}^k, \text{'1'}^{\sigma}, \text{'1'}^N)$:

1. $\tilde{F}_{\underline{m}}$ generates a new key pair (sk_temp^*, pk^*) by carrying out all the algorithms of *Gen* correctly.
2. It signs the messages from $\underline{m}$ correctly, starting with its own sk_temp^*, and outputs the last message and signature, (m_i, s_i), as a proposed forgery for the given key *pk*.

For any σ, σ^*, $k \in \mathbb{N}$, the parameter k is said to be large enough to provide the **security level σ^* against forgery by $\tilde{F}_{\underline{m}}$** for the given σ if the probability that the output s_i of $\tilde{F}_{\underline{m}}$ is an acceptable signature on m_i is at most $2^{-\sigma^*}$.

The probability space is as in the definition of unforgeability (Definition 7.22). Hence, with $par := (\text{'}1\text{'}^k, \text{'}1\text{'}^\sigma, \text{'}1\text{'}^N)$ and simplifications due to the fact that $\tilde{B}$ is the correct B and that no history is produced because $\tilde{F}_{\underline{m}}$ is non-interactive, the condition for one risk bearer is

$$\begin{aligned} P_{\tilde{F}_{\underline{m}}}(par) \; := \; & \mathrm{P}(test(pk, m_i, s_i) = \mathrm{TRUE} \setminus \\ & \quad (acc, ids_{Risk,out}, pk, sk) \leftarrow Gen^{(f)}(par); \\ & \quad (m_i, s_i) \leftarrow \tilde{F}_{\underline{m}}(par, acc, ids_{Risk,out}, pk)) \\ \le \; & 2^{-\sigma^*}. \end{aligned}$$

The case with more risk bearers is defined in the same way. ♦

Remark 11.13. Similar to Remark 11.6, unforgeability in k alone, which holds on the assumptions of Theorem 11.15 (by Theorem 7.24b), implies that for all σ, $\sigma^* \in \mathbb{N}$, a value k_0 exists such that all $k \ge k_0$ provide the security level σ^* against forgery by $\tilde{F}_{\underline{m}}$ for the given σ. (Even if one only assumes security for the signer forwards and thus Theorem 7.24a, this still holds for $\sigma^* < \sigma$.) ♦

As in Section 11.3, the first step towards lower bounds is to state what a certain security level against forgery means in the functional terminology of Definition 11.2.

Lemma 11.14. Under the conditions of Definition 11.12, the success probability of the simple forging algorithm is

$$P_{\tilde{F}_{\underline{m}}}(par) = \sum_{pk, s_i : test(pk, m_i, s_i) = \mathrm{TRUE}} \mathrm{P}(PK = pk)\ \mathrm{P}(S_i = s_i). \qquad ♦$$

Proof. By the definition of $\tilde{F}_{\underline{m}}$,

$$\begin{aligned} P_{\tilde{F}_{\underline{m}}}(par) \; = \; & \mathrm{P}(test(pk, m_i, s_i) = \mathrm{TRUE} \setminus \\ & \quad (acc, ids_{Risk,out}, pk, sk) \leftarrow Gen^{(f)}(par); \\ & \quad (acc^*, ids_{Risk,out}{}^*, pk^*, sk^*) \leftarrow Gen^{(f)}(par); \\ & \quad s_i := sign^{(f)}(sk^*, i, \underline{m})). \end{aligned}$$

This probability is not in the common probability space from Definition 11.2, because $\tilde{F}_{\underline{m}}$ is probabilistic. However, $\tilde{F}_{\underline{m}}$ defines a second, independent copy of that space, and the overall probability can therefore be partitioned into products of two probabilities in that space. For this, the condition is expressed in a form that can be partitioned, too:

$$\begin{aligned} & P_{\tilde{F}_{\underline{m}}}(par) \\ & = \sum_{pk', s_i' : test(pk', m_i, s_i') = \mathrm{TRUE}} \mathrm{P}(pk = pk' \wedge s_i = s_i' \setminus \\ & \qquad\qquad (acc, ids_{Risk,out}, pk, sk) \leftarrow Gen^{(f)}(par); \\ & \qquad\qquad (acc^*, ids_{Risk,out}{}^*, pk^*, sk^*) \leftarrow Gen^{(f)}(par); \\ & \qquad\qquad s_i := sign^{(f)}(sk^*, i, \underline{m})) \end{aligned}$$

$$= \sum_{pk', s_i': test(pk', m_i, s_i') = \text{TRUE}} P(pk = pk' \setminus (acc, ids_{Risk,out}, pk, sk) \leftarrow Gen^{(f)}(par)) \; P(s_i = s_i' \setminus (acc^*, ids_{Risk,out}^*, pk^*, sk^*) \leftarrow Gen^{(f)}(par); s_i := sign^{(f)}(sk^*, i, \underline{m}))$$

$$= \sum_{pk', s_i': test(pk', m_i, s_i') = \text{TRUE}} P(PK = pk')\, P(S_i = s_i').$$

Finally, one can substitute pk' by pk and s_i' by s_i. □

Theorem 11.15 (Lower bounds on the length of signatures and public keys). Let a standard fail-stop signature scheme, parameters $\sigma, \sigma^*, k \in \mathbb{N}$ and $N \in \mathbb{N} \cap Message\_bounds$ (and R in the case with several risk bearers), and a sequence $\underline{m}^*$ of N+1 pairwise distinct messages be given. Moreover, let all the preconditions of Theorem 11.8 be fulfilled, and let k be large enough to provide the security level σ^* against forgery by $\tilde{F}_{\underline{m}}$ for the given σ, where $\underline{m}$ is a prefix of $i \le N$ messages of $\underline{m}^*$.

a) If $\sigma' := \min(\sigma, \sigma^*)$ as before, the entropy of the random variable S_i is

$$H(S_i) \ge \sigma' + \sigma^* - 1.$$

b) The entropy of the public key is

$$H(PK) \ge \sigma^*.$$ ♦

The following lemma formalizes Statement 2 from the overview. The fact that the number of acceptable signatures, given the public key, is much smaller than the complete signature space is generalized as follows: The public key contains a lot of information about the correct signature.

Lemma 11.16. With the preconditions and notation of Theorem 11.15, the mutual information between the public key and a correct signature is

$$I(S_i\,; PK) \ge \sigma^*.$$ ♦

Proof. One can easily see from the definitions or [Gall68] (2.2.7) that for all random variables X and Y,

$$I(X\,; Y) = -\sum_{x,y: P(x,y) \ne 0} P(x, y) \log_2(P(x) / P(x \mid y)).$$

Hence with Jensen's inequality,

$$I(S_i\,; PK) \ge -\log_2\Big(\sum_{s_i, pk: P(s_i, pk) \ne 0} P(s_i, pk)\, P(s_i) / P(s_i \mid pk)\Big)$$

$$= -\log_2\Big(\sum_{s_i, pk: P(s_i, pk) \ne 0} P(s_i)\, P(pk)\Big).$$

It suffices to show that the argument of the logarithm is at most $2^{-\sigma^*}$. First, error-free effectiveness of authentication after correct execution of *Gen* implies

$$(P(s_i, pk) \ne 0 \Rightarrow test(pk, m_i, s_i) = \text{TRUE}),$$

because the precondition means that a result of key generation exists where *pk* is the public key and s_i the correct signature. Together with Lemma 11.14, this yields

$$\sum_{s_i, pk: \mathrm{P}(s_i, pk) \neq 0} \mathrm{P}(s_i)\,\mathrm{P}(pk) \leq \sum_{s_i, pk: test(pk, m_i, s_i) = \mathrm{TRUE}} \mathrm{P}(s_i)\,\mathrm{P}(pk).$$
$$= \mathrm{P}_{\tilde{F}_{\underline{m}}}(par)$$
$$\leq 2^{-\sigma^*},$$

which remained to be shown. □

Proof of Theorem 11.15. a) By the definition of mutual information, Lemma 11.16 means

$$\mathrm{H}(S_i) - \mathrm{H}(S_i \mid PK) \geq \sigma^*.$$

As all the preconditions of Theorem 11.8 were assumed, one can apply Lemma 11.11; it yields

$$\mathrm{H}(S_i \mid PK, Hist_{i-1}) \geq \sigma' - 1.$$

With the definition of conditional mutual information and Rule (4'), this yields

$$\mathrm{H}(S_i \mid PK) = \mathrm{I}(S_i\,; Hist_{i-1} \mid PK) + \mathrm{H}(S_i \mid PK, Hist_{i-1}) \geq \sigma' - 1,$$

and therefore

$$\mathrm{H}(S_i) \geq \mathrm{H}(S_i \mid PK) + \sigma^* \geq \sigma' + \sigma^* - 1.$$

b) With Lemma 11.16 and Rules (3) and (1') from Section 11.1,

$$\sigma^* \leq \mathrm{I}(S_i\,; PK) = \mathrm{I}(PK\,; S_i) = \mathrm{H}(PK) - \mathrm{H}(PK \mid S_i) \leq \mathrm{H}(PK).$$ □

Schemes with Prekey

For fail-stop signature schemes with prekey (see Section 7.3), one obtains slightly stronger results.

Remark 11.17. If a scheme with prekey is given and all the preconditions of Theorem 11.15 hold, one can use a forging algorithm $\tilde{F}^*_{\underline{m}}$ that only carries out main key generation again to generate a new pair (*sk**, *mk**) based on the same prekey *prek*. In this case, a proof analogous to those of Lemma 11.16 and Theorem 11.15, with an additional average over *prek* everywhere, yields

$$\mathrm{H}(S_i \mid Prek) \geq \sigma' + \sigma^* - 1$$

and

$$\mathrm{H}(PK \mid Prek) \geq \sigma^*.$$ ♦

If, as usual in such schemes, *pk* is a function of *prek* and the original temporary secret key *sk_temp*, one can derive one more lower bound on the secret key.

Remark 11.18. If a scheme with prekey is given and all the preconditions of Theorem 11.15 hold, and if the public key is a function of the original temporary secret key and the prekey, then

$$\mathrm{H}(SK_{\underline{m}^*} \mid Prek) \geq (N + 2)(\sigma' - 1).$$

To show this, first the usual rules are applied:

$$\begin{aligned} H(SK_{\underline{m}^*} \mid Prek) &= H(SK_{\underline{m}^*}, PK \mid Prek) - H(PK \mid SK_{\underline{m}^*}, Prek) && \text{(Rule (2'))} \\ &= H(PK \mid Prek) + H(SK_{\underline{m}^*} \mid PK, Prek) - 0. && \text{(Rules (2'), (5))} \end{aligned}$$

The prekey is part of the public key, hence $H(SK_{\underline{m}^*} \mid PK, Prek) = H(SK_{\underline{m}^*} \mid PK)$ and

$$\begin{aligned} H(SK_{\underline{m}^*} \mid Prek) &= H(PK \mid Prek) + H(SK_{\underline{m}^*} \mid PK) \\ &\geq \sigma^* + (N+1)(\sigma' - 1) \\ &\geq (N+2)(\sigma' - 1). \end{aligned}$$ ♦

11.5 Lower Bounds on Information-Theoretically Secure Signature Schemes

In this section, information-theoretically secure signature schemes are considered — at least a standard class of them in a conventional definition. The main goal of this section in the given context is to find out the price to pay for better security than that offered by fail-stop signature schemes. It turns out that this price is very high.

Existing constructions of information-theoretically secure signature schemes were sketched in Section 6.3.4. They were very complex in several respects. Among these, the signature length is now considered primarily. It is proved that the (average) length of a signature grows linearly in the number of participants who can test it, either as a recipient or as a court. In other words, it is shown that signatures are at least as long as if they consisted of an independent part for each of the different test keys of these parties, i.e., the signatures cannot be shortened by a suitable combination. As a consequence, lower bounds on the length of the keys are obtained.

Definitions

First, a conventional definition of those properties of information-theoretically secure signature schemes that are needed in the proofs is given. Actually, a rather small set of such properties is sufficient to prove the lower bounds. However, some restrictions are made, too.

The main restriction, in conventional terms, is that a probabilistic function *sign* and a deterministic non-interactive function *test* exist, where each signature is supposed to pass the test of several other participants, called **testers**. In the classification of Chapter 5, this can be justified for several classes of schemes, e.g.:

1. Schemes with non-interactive authentication and no dependence on the recipient. Then, as usual, *test* is used by the recipient's entity in authentication, and the recipients are the testers.
2. Schemes with 2-party disputes where the recipient's entity only sends a signature to the court's entity. This may also be fulfilled if authentication depends on the recipient, as in Section 10.6. Then the courts are the testers.

Another restriction is that some properties are required without error probability. As ordinary digital signature schemes fulfil these restrictions, it was natural to assume them for information-theoretically secure signature schemes in [HePP93, PePf95]. Anyway, I expect the lower bounds to hold more generally.

The subset of security properties needed to prove the lower bounds only considers the case where all the entities, even those of the attackers, carry out key generation correctly, and neither active attacks on recipients nor provisions for finite transferability are used. Moreover, in the first class of schemes considered above, only unforgeability, and no requirement on disputes, is considered, and in the second class, with the same conventional definition, only the requirement of the signer on disputes, and not that of the recipient. (This suggests that one can prove more stringent bounds by using more requirements.)

Finally, it is not used that the correct algorithms should work in polynomial time. Hence the definition is immediately made in a functional form corresponding to Definition 7.3. In particular, the secret key *sk* is assumed to include all the random bits the signer's entity will ever use.

Definition 11.19 (Rudimentary standard information-theoretically secure signature schemes). The components of a rudimentary standard information-theoretically secure signature scheme (in functional notation) for a non-empty message space $M \subseteq \{0, 1\}^+$ and a non-empty set $Message\_bounds \subseteq \mathbb{N} \cup \{\infty\}$ are a triple $(Gen^{(f)}, sign^{(f)}, test)$ where

- $Gen^{(f)}$, the key-generation protocol, is a multi-party protocol defined by a pair of probabilistic interactive functions, $(A^{(f)}, B^{(f)})$ (where $A^{(f)}$ is supposed to be executed by the signer's entity and $B^{(f)}$ by each entity of a tester), and arbitrary types of channels. (For concreteness, one can assume that in any execution, there is a private point-to-point channel between each pair of entities and a reliable broadcast channel for each one.)

  $A^{(f)}$ expects an initial input $par := (\text{'1'}^\sigma, \text{'1'}^N, \text{'1'}^R)$, where $\sigma \in \mathbb{N}$ is a security parameter, N the message bound, and R the number of testers, and $B^{(f)}$ expects an input (par, x), where $x \in \{1, ..., R\}$ denotes the internal identity of that particular tester's entity.

  $A^{(f)}$ outputs a triple (acc, ids_{out}, sk), where sk is called a secret key, and $B^{(f)}$ outputs a triple (acc, ids_{out}, t), where t is called a test key. Thus $Gen^{(f)}$ defines probabilistic assignments of the form

  $$(\underline{acc}, \underline{ids}_{out}, sk, t_1, ..., t_R) \leftarrow Gen^{(f)}(par),$$

  where each t_x denotes the output parameter t of the entity with the identity x, and $\underline{acc} := (acc, acc_1, ..., acc_R)$ and $\underline{ids}_{out} := (ids_{out}, ids_{out,1}, ..., ids_{out,R})$ are defined similarly. Note that different entities running $B^{(f)}$ will usually obtain different test keys, because they take different internal random choices. Usually, only the keys are of interest; then the notation

  $$(sk, t_1, ..., t_R) \leftarrow Gen^{*(f)}(par)$$

  is used. Probabilities in the space defined by this assignment are denoted by

  $$P_{par}$$

- $sign^{(f)}$ is a deterministic function that, on input a secret key sk and a message sequence $\underline{m} = (m_1, ..., m_i) \in M^i$ with $i \in \mathbb{N}$ and $i \leq N$, outputs a sequence

$\underline{s} = (s_1, \ldots, s_i)$ of signatures. The definition must respect prefixes, i.e., $sign^{(f)}(sk, (m_1, \ldots, m_j)) = (s_1, \ldots, s_j)$ for $j \le i$. The projection to the j-th signature is denoted by an additional parameter j, i.e.,

$$s_j := sign^{(f)}(sk, j, \underline{m}).$$

- *test* is a deterministic function that, on input a triple (t_x, m, s), where t_x is a test key and $m \in M$ a message, outputs a value $acc \in \{\text{TRUE}, \text{FALSE}\}$. If the output is TRUE, s is called an acceptable signature on m for this test key.

These components must have the following properties:

a) Rudimentary error-free effectiveness and correctness of initialization: If key generation is carried out correctly, it is accepted.

   More precisely: For all parameters *par* as above and all tuples $(\underline{acc}, \underline{ids}_{out}, sk, t_1, \ldots, t_R) \in [Gen^{(f)}(par)]$, all the components of $\underline{acc}$ are TRUE, and all those of $\underline{ids}_{out}$ are $\{1, \ldots, R\}$.

b) Rudimentary error-free effectiveness of authentication: If key generation has been carried out correctly, all correct signatures are acceptable for everybody.

   More precisely: For all parameters *par* as above, all tuples $(sk, t_1, \ldots, t_R) \in [Gen^{*(f)}(par)]$, all message sequences $\underline{m} = (m_1, \ldots, m_i) \in M^i$ with $i \in \mathbb{N}$ and $i \le N$, and all $x \in \{1, \ldots, R\}$:

$$s_i = sign^{(f)}(sk, i, \underline{m}) \Rightarrow test(t_x, m_i, s_i) = \text{TRUE}.$$

c) Rudimentary unforgeability or security for the signer (in the first or second class of schemes mentioned above): If key generation is carried out correctly, no subset of testers can forge signatures so that another tester accepts them with significant likelihood.

   More precisely (similar to the definition of security for the signer backwards, Definition 7.17):

   - The set of possible histories, given a secret key *sk* and a message bound *N*, is

     $Hist(sk, N) := \{(\underline{m}, \underline{s}) \mid \exists j \in \mathbb{N}: j \le N \wedge \underline{m} \in M^j \wedge \underline{s} = sign^{(f)}(sk, \underline{m})\}.$

     The set *M(hist)* of previously signed messages in a given history is the same as in Definition 7.12b.

   - For all parameters *par* as above, all sets of attacking testers, $X \subset \{1, \ldots, R\}$, and all honest testers $y \in \{1, \ldots, R\} \setminus X$, the set *GoodInf(par, X, y)* of good information known to the attacker is defined as follows: For any tuple $t_X := (t_x)_{x \in X}$ of test keys of the attackers and any history $hist = (\underline{m}, \underline{s})$,

$$\begin{aligned}&(t_X, hist) \in GoodInf(par, X, y)\\ &\quad :\Leftrightarrow \forall f = (m, s) \text{ with } m \in M \setminus M(hist):\\ &\qquad P_{par}(test(t_y, m, s) = \text{TRUE} \mid t_X, sign^{(f)}(sk, \underline{m}) = \underline{s}) \le 2^{-\sigma}.\end{aligned}$$

     Thus the information known to the attacker is called good if no matter how the attacker selects a forgery f, the likelihood that it is accepted by the honest tester y is very small.

   - With the same notation, the set *GoodKeys(par, X, y)* of good keys is defined as follows:

$(sk, t_1, \ldots, t_R) \in GoodKeys(par, X, y)$
$:\Leftrightarrow \forall hist \in Hist(sk, N)\colon (t_X, hist) \in GoodInf(par, X, y).$

- Rudimentary unforgeability or security for the signer means that for all parameters *par* as above, all sets of attackers $X \subset \{1, \ldots, R\}$ and all honest testers $y \in \{1, \ldots, R\} \setminus X$, all the outcomes of key generation are good keys, i.e., $[Gen^{*(f)}(par)] \subseteq GoodKeys(par, X, y)$. ♦

Recall that this is a very weak notion of security, but it will only be used to prove lower bounds.

Very similar to Section 11.2, some random variables are defined in the probability space induced by the correct execution of $Gen^{(f)}$ on given parameters *par*.

Definition 11.20 (Random variables). Let the components of a rudimentary standard information-theoretically secure signature scheme, a tuple of parameters, $par = (\text{'1'}^\sigma, \text{'1'}^N, \text{'1'}^R)$ with $\sigma, R \in \mathbb{N}$ and $N \in Message\_bounds$, and a message sequence $\underline{m} = (m_1, \ldots, m_i) \in M^i$ with $i \in \mathbb{N}$ and $i \le N+1$ be given.

Then key generation, $Gen^{(f)}(par)$, defines a probability space. The following random variables are defined in it:

- *SK* is the random variable of the secret key, i.e., it is defined by the output parameter *sk* of $Gen^{(f)}(par)$. Similarly, for each $x \in \{1, \ldots, R\}$, T_x is the random variable of the test key t_x, and for each $X \subseteq \{1, \ldots, R\}$, T_X is random variable of the tuple t_X.
- For all $j \le i$ with $j \ne N+1$, let S_j denote the random variable of the correct signature s_j on m_j in this context, i.e.,
$$S_j := sign^{(f)}(SK, j, \underline{m}).$$
If $i = N+1$, let $\underline{m}_{\setminus N} := (m_1, \ldots, m_{N-1}, m_{N+1})$ as before, and
$$S_{N+1} := sign^{(f)}(SK, N, \underline{m}_{\setminus N}).$$
- For all $j \le i$, let $Hist_j$ denote the random variable of the history up to the j-th signature, i.e.,
$$Hist_j := ((m_1, \ldots, m_j), (S_1, \ldots, S_j)).$$
- $SK_{\underline{m}}$ is the part of *SK* that is actually used for signing $\underline{m}$. In the given functional notation, the value of $SK_{\underline{m}}$ can be defined as the shortest prefix of *sk* that uniquely determines the correct signatures on all the messages from $\underline{m}$. Hence one can write
$$S_j = sign^{(f)}(SK_{\underline{m}}, j, \underline{m})$$
for $j \le i$ with $j \ne N+1$ and, if $i = N+1$,
$$S_{N+1} = sign^{(f)}(SK_{\underline{m}}, N, \underline{m}_{\setminus N}).$$

The probabilities in this space were called P_{par} in Definition 11.19, but they will be abbreviated as P when the space is clear from the context. ♦

Lower Bounds

The basic idea why information-theoretically secure signatures must be long is the following: If some attackers want to forge a signature on a message *m*, they can determine the set of signatures acceptable under all their test keys, see Figure 11.2. Still, within this set, the density of signatures acceptable to another tester must not exceed $2^{-\sigma}$. Inductively, this implies that the size of the original signature space must be at least $2^{R\sigma}$. In Theorem 11.21, this result is more generally proved for entropies.

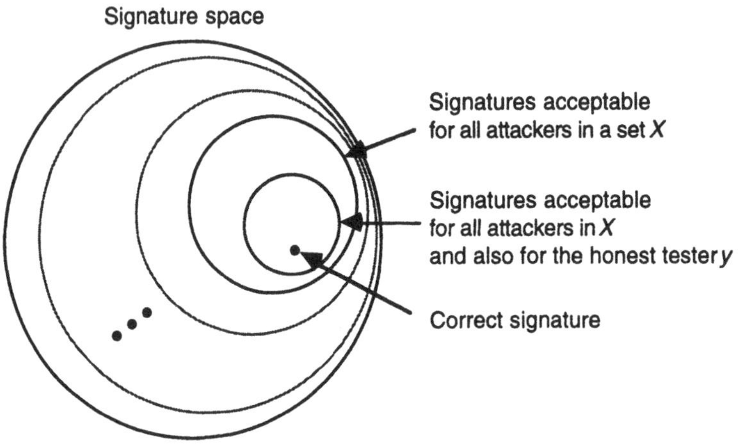

Figure 11.2. Acceptable and correct signatures in a rudimentary information-theoretically secure signature scheme.
The size of the smallest circle is at most $2^{-\sigma}$ times that of the second one. Similarly, one can consider successively larger circles corresponding to smaller sets of attackers.

For simplicity, only finite message bounds N are considered from now on, similar to Section 11.3.

Theorem 11.21. Let a rudimentary standard information-theoretically secure signature scheme, parameters par = ('1'$^{\sigma}$, '1'^{N}, '1'^{R}) with $\sigma, R \in \mathbb{N}$ and $N \in \mathbb{N} \cap$ *Message_bounds*, a sequence $\underline{m}$ of N+1 pairwise distinct messages, and $i \leq N+1$ be given. Then the conditional entropy of the i-th correct signature, given the previous ones, is large:

$$\mathrm{H}(S_i \mid Hist_{i-1}) \geq R\,\sigma. \qquad \blacklozenge$$

The basic idea for the proof is formalized similar to Lemma 11.16: Even if some test keys are known, any other test key still gives a lot of information about the correct signature.

Lemma 11.22. With the preconditions and notation of Theorem 11.21: For any set $X \subseteq \{1, \ldots, R\}$ (representing attacking testers) and any $y \in \{1, \ldots, R\} \backslash X$:

$$\mathrm{I}(S_i\,;\,T_y \mid T_X, Hist_{i-1}) \geq \sigma. \qquad \blacklozenge$$

Proof. For readability, the joint random variable $T_X, Hist_{i-1}$ is abbreviated as Z, and a pair $(t_X, hist_{i-1})$ as z. The definitions or [Gall68], (2.2.23) imply that the conditional mutual information can be written as

$$\mathrm{I}(S_i\,;T_y \mid Z) \;=\; \sum_z \mathrm{P}(z)\,\mathrm{I}(S_i\,;T_y \mid z)$$

with $$\mathrm{I}(S_i\,;T_y \mid z) \;=\; -\sum_{s_i,t_y:\mathrm{P}(s_i,t_y|z)\neq 0} \mathrm{P}(s_i, t_y \mid z)\,\log_2(\mathrm{P}(s_i \mid z)\,/\,\mathrm{P}(s_i \mid t_y, z)).$$

It suffices to show

$$\mathrm{I}(S_i\,;T_y \mid z) \;\geq\; \sigma \tag{1}$$

for any possible value z of Z. With Jensen's inequality,

$$\begin{aligned}\mathrm{I}(S_i\,;T_y \mid z) \;&\geq\; -\log_2\Big(\sum_{s_i,t_y:\mathrm{P}(s_i,t_y|z)\neq 0} \mathrm{P}(s_i, t_y \mid z)\,\mathrm{P}(s_i \mid z)\,/\,\mathrm{P}(s_i \mid t_y, z)\Big)\\ &=\; -\log_2\Big(\sum_{s_i,t_y:\mathrm{P}(s_i,t_y|z)\neq 0} \mathrm{P}(s_i \mid z)\,\mathrm{P}(t_y \mid z)\Big).\end{aligned} \tag{2}$$

Rudimentary error-free effectiveness of authentication (Definition 11.19b) implies

$$(\mathrm{P}(s_i, t_y \mid z) \neq 0 \;\Rightarrow\; \mathit{test}(t_y, m_i, s_i) = \mathrm{TRUE}),$$

because the precondition means that a result of key generation exists where t_y is the y-th test key and s_i the correct signature on m_i. Hence for any value s_i that is possible given z,

$$\begin{aligned}\sum_{t_y:\mathrm{P}(s_i,t_y|z)\neq 0} \mathrm{P}(t_y \mid z) \;&\leq\; \sum_{t_y:\mathit{test}(t_y,m_i,s_i)=\mathrm{TRUE}} \mathrm{P}(t_y \mid z)\\ &=\; \mathrm{P}(\mathit{test}(T_y, m_i, s_i) = \mathrm{TRUE} \mid z).\end{aligned} \tag{3}$$

Now rudimentary unforgeability or security for the signer can be applied. It states that $z \in \mathit{GoodInf}(\mathit{par})$, and thus, in the notation with random variables,

$$\mathrm{P}_{\mathit{par}}(\mathit{test}(T_y, m_i, s_i) = \mathrm{TRUE} \mid z) \;\leq\; 2^{-\sigma}. \tag{4}$$

(The precondition $m_i \in M \setminus M(\mathit{hist}_{i-1})$ is clear, because $\underline{m}$ consists of pairwise distinct messages.) Substituting (4) into (3) and taking the average over s_i yields

$$\sum_{s_i,t_y:\mathrm{P}(s_i,t_y|z)\neq 0} \mathrm{P}(s_i \mid z)\,\mathrm{P}(t_y \mid z) \;\leq\; \sum_{s_i} \mathrm{P}(s_i \mid z)\,2^{-\sigma} \;=\; 2^{-\sigma}. \tag{5}$$

Finally, (5) and (2) yield (1), which remained to be shown. □

Proof of Theorem 11.21. The following generalization of the theorem is proved by induction over the size of X: For all $X \subseteq \{1, \ldots, R\}$:

$$\mathrm{H}(S_i \mid T_X, \mathit{Hist}_{i-1}) \;\geq\; (R - |X|)\,\sigma. \tag{*}$$

For $|X| = |R|$, this is Rule (1'). If (*) has been proved for all sets X of size $\rho + 1 \leq R$, it can be proved for all sets X of size ρ as follows: Let $y \in \{1, \ldots, R\}\setminus X$, and note that the joint random variable T_X, T_y is $T_{X\cup\{y\}}$. Hence with the definition of conditional mutual information and Lemma 11.22,

$$\begin{aligned}\mathrm{H}(S_i \mid T_X, \mathit{Hist}_{i-1}) \;&\geq\; \mathrm{I}(S_i\,;T_y \mid T_X, \mathit{Hist}_{i-1}) + \mathrm{H}(S_i \mid T_{X\cup\{y\}}, \mathit{Hist}_{i-1})\\ &\geq\; \sigma + (R - (|X| + 1))\,\sigma\\ &\geq\; (R - |X|)\,\sigma.\end{aligned}$$

This finishes the proof of (∗). For $X = \varnothing$, the joint random variable T_X contains no random variable at all, and hence (∗) is the theorem. □

Theorem 11.23. With the preconditions and notation of Theorem 11.21:

a) The secret key grows linearly in both the number of messages to be signed and the number of testers:

$$\mathrm{H}(SK_{\underline{m}}) \geq (N+1)R\,\sigma.$$

b) Test keys also grow linearly in the number of messages to be signed: For all sets $X \subseteq \{1, \ldots, R\}$ and all $y \in \{1, \ldots, R\} \setminus X$:

$$\mathrm{H}(T_y \mid T_X) \geq (N+1)\,\sigma.$$ ♦

Proof. Part a) is derived from Theorem 11.21 with induction over i exactly as Theorem 11.8 was derived from Lemma 11.11.

Part b) is proved in a similar way from Lemma 11.22 with an analogue of Rule (2) for mutual information ([Gall68] (2.2.29)):

$$\mathrm{I}(X\,;Y,Z) = \mathrm{I}(X\,;Y) + \mathrm{I}(X\,;Z \mid Y). \tag{1}$$

This formula can be used with an additional condition W. Validity of that version can be seen by applying (1) three times:

$$\begin{aligned}\mathrm{I}(X\,;Y,Z \mid W) &= \mathrm{I}(X\,;Y,Z,W) - \mathrm{I}(X\,;W)\\ &= (\mathrm{I}(X\,;Y,W) - \mathrm{I}(X\,;W)) + (\mathrm{I}(X\,;Y,Z,W) - \mathrm{I}(X\,;Y,W))\\ &= \mathrm{I}(X\,;Y \mid W) + \mathrm{I}(X\,;Z \mid Y,W). \qquad (2)\end{aligned}$$

The following generalization of the theorem is proved by induction: For all $i \in \{1, \ldots, N+1\}$:

$$\mathrm{I}(T_y\,;Hist_i \mid T_X) \geq i\,\sigma. \tag{3}$$

For $i = 1$, (3) is just Lemma 11.22 (with Rule (3')); and if (3) has been proved for $i-1$, it holds for i because

$$\begin{aligned}\mathrm{I}(T_y\,;Hist_i \mid T_X) &= \mathrm{I}(T_y\,;Hist_{i-1}, S_i \mid T_X)\\ &= \mathrm{I}(T_y\,;Hist_{i-1} \mid T_X) + \mathrm{I}(T_y\,;S_i \mid Hist_{i-1}, T_X) && \text{(with (2))}\\ &\geq (i-1)\,\sigma + \sigma && \text{(with (3) and Lemma 11.22)}\\ &= i\,\sigma.\end{aligned}$$

This finishes the proof of (3). For $i = N+1$, and with the definition of conditional mutual information, one obtains

$$\begin{aligned}\mathrm{H}(T_y \mid T_X) &= \mathrm{I}(T_y\,;Hist_{N+1} \mid T_X) + \mathrm{H}(T_y \mid Hist_{N+1}, T_X)\\ &\geq \mathrm{I}(T_y\,;Hist_{N+1} \mid T_X) && \text{(Rule (1'))}\\ &\geq (N+1)\,\sigma.\end{aligned}$$ □

11.6 Comparison

This section answers the two questions raised at the beginning of this chapter by evaluating how well the existing constructions of standard fail-stop signature schemes meet the lower bounds and by comparing the lower bounds with similar bounds on ordinary digital signature schemes and standard information-theoretically secure signature schemes.

A Table

Table 11.1 shows the lower bounds proved in this chapter in comparison with the upper bounds achieved in the constructions from Chapter 10. Hence the length of the secret key (in the functional sense, i.e., primarily denoting the secret random bits used), the length of the public key, the length of a signature, and moreover the amount of private storage needed are shown. Note that the maximum length of the temporary secret key is longer than the secret key in some constructions, but always by less than a factor of 2.

The abbreviated names of the constructions mean bottom-up tree authentication (10.9), top-down tree authentication (10.13), top-down tree authentication with a small amount of private storage (10.19), the discrete-logarithm scheme with minimized secret key (10.22) without combination with tree authentication, and the construction with a list-shaped tree for a fixed recipient from Section 10.6. The first column of lower bounds is for standard fail-stop signature schemes (Sections 11.3 and 11.4), the second one for standard information-theoretically secure signature schemes (Section 11.5); here the length of a test key has been entered in the row with the public keys.

Length of	Bottom-up	Top-down	Top-down +	Improved discr. log.	Fixed recipient	Lower bound	Info.-th. secure
sk	$4Nk$	$8Nk$	$8Nk$	$(2N+2)k$	$4Nk$	$(N+1)(\sigma'-1)$	$(N+1)R\sigma$
private storage	$4Nk$	$8Nk$	$4k\log_2 N$	$(2N+2)k$	$10k$	—	—
mk	$2\sigma^*$	$2\sigma^*$	$2\sigma^*$	$(N+1)l$	$2\sigma^*$	σ^*	$(N+1)\sigma$
signature	$2k + 4l + 2\sigma^* \log_2 N$	$(2k + 4l) \cdot \log_2 N$	$(2k + 4l) \cdot \log_2 N$	$2k + \log_2 N$	$2k + 2l$	$\sigma' + \sigma^* - 1$	$R\sigma$

Table 11.1. Comparison of constructions and lower bounds of standard fail-stop signature schemes with one risk bearer.
Some small constants are omitted. Details of the terminology are explained in the surrounding text.

The parameters have their usual meaning from the previous sections. In particular, N is the message bound, R in the information-theoretically secure signature schemes is the number of testers (i.e., recipients or courts or both, depending on the class of schemes), and k, l, σ, σ^*, and $\sigma' := \min(\sigma, \sigma^*)$ are security parameters with $k \le l$ and where σ^* determines the concrete security for risk bearers. As all the constructions of fail-stop signature schemes are with prekey, and the same prekey can be used for several signers, only the main public key is shown.

For the upper bounds on standard fail-stop signature schemes, the constructions are based on the discrete-logarithm scheme (Lemmas 9.12 and 9.14). Bottom-up tree authentication is evaluated for the case where the risk bearers trust a fast hash function with output length $2\sigma^*$ (i.e., they trust that collisions cannot be found significantly faster than with the so-called birthday attack, where random hash values are computed and stored until one of them occurs twice). For fairness, it is assumed that the main public key in the top-down constructions is also hashed with this function.

Recall from Remark 10.24 that a scheme exists where the key length and the private storage are the same as in Construction 10.22 and the signature length is only $2k$, but that it has disadvantages in other respects and $\log_2(N)$ must be dominated by k in these schemes anyway.

Comparison of Upper and Lower Bounds

The differences between k and l in the upper bounds and σ and σ^* in the lower bounds are as follows. Usually, σ and σ^* would be chosen of equal size, say between 20 to 100, whereas l must be at least 500 to give sufficient computational security. It is assumed that k can be moderately small, say 160; but it should be at least $2\sigma^*$ to provide practical security against general discrete-logarithm algorithms such as Shanks's baby-step-giant-step method (see, e.g., the overview [LeLe90]). If one believes that variants of the discrete-logarithm problem exist that cannot be solved in subexponential time, e.g., on elliptic curves, one can assume that l is very close to $k = 2\sigma^*$. Then the lower bounds are met by the upper bounds except for factors of not much more than 4.

The two most important questions not answered by the bounds and constructions in the table are:

- Is it possible to make the length of both public keys and signatures simultaneously independent of N in the general case without a fixed recipient? This was achieved in [Pfit94], based on [BeMa94], but on a very strong cryptologic assumption and with some computational disadvantages.
- What is the minimum overall storage? So far, it is always linear in N, but no lower bound is known.

Comparison of Classes of Schemes

If standard fail-stop signature schemes are compared with ordinary digital signature schemes, the most obvious difference in complexity is that the number of secret random bits needed in a standard fail-stop signature scheme is linear in the number of messages to be signed, which is not the case with ordinary digital signature schemes. (But recall that this does not imply a similar lower bound on the amount of private storage needed.) Public keys are of the same length both in practice and in theory (the same lower bound σ^* holds for ordinary digital signature schemes by the same proof), if one does not count the prekey. For signatures, the minima differ by a factor of about 2. However, the fail-stop signature schemes that one would use in practice do not achieve this minimum.

Information-theoretically secure schemes, in contrast, even with the rudimentary security requirements made above, have much higher lower bounds, at least in applications where a large number of participants may have to test any given signature.

Some Conclusions on Fail-Stop Signature Schemes

Altogether, the existing schemes and the lower bounds suggest that fail-stop signature schemes provide the most viable way of protecting the signers in digital signature schemes information-theoretically. Note, however, that one should prove lower bounds on information-theoretically secure signature schemes with a more general structure than that assumed in Section 11.5 before ruling them out completely. Furthermore, the upper bounds on fail-stop signature schemes were with one risk bearer and are only valid for more risk bearers if these risk bearers have a (cryptologic or noncryptologic) method to choose mutually trusted random bits for the prekey.

Recall that for the practical use of fail-stop signatures, a combination of bottom-up and top-down tree authentication is recommended to combine the shorter signatures of the former (at least if a fast hash function is used) with the greater flexibility and faster key generation of the latter. Two additional decisions have to be made in an implementation for real life: First, one needs a source for the real random bits. A hardware random-number generator would be useful, but currently, user participation is needed. Random bits might be collected as a background process; if this is not good enough, one could advertize typing random characters as a part of the warning function. Secondly, recall that if message hashing is used, the messages have to be stored to provide for proofs of forgery if the hash function is broken. One can leave this to the user, or let the implementation of the signature scheme store copies, or try to get help from other programs, e.g., the operating system or the e-mail program, in warning users if they attempt to delete such messages.

References

ABA95 American Bar Association: Digital Signature Guidelines; Information Security Committee, Science and Technology Section, American Bar Association, Draft, Oct. 5, 1995.

ABEP90 Mireille Antonie, Jean-François Brakeland, Marc Eloy, Yves Poullet: Legal requirements facing new signature technologies; Eurocrypt '89, LNCS 434, Springer-Verlag, Berlin 1990, 273-287.

AbTu91 Martín Abadi, Mark R. Tuttle: A Semantics for a Logic of Authentication; 10th Symposium on Principles of Distributed Computing (PoDC), 1991, ACM, New York 1991, 201-216.

AdHu87 Leonard M. Adleman, Mind-Deh A. Huang: Recognizing Primes In Random Polynomial Time; 19th Symposium on Theory of Computing (STOC) 1987, ACM, New York 1987, 462-469.

AdPR83 Leonard M. Adleman, Carl Pomerance, R. S. Rumely: On distinguishing prime numbers from composite numbers; Annals of Mathematic 117 (1983) 173-206.

AGLL95 Derek Atkins, Michael Graff, Arjen K. Lenstra, Paul C. Leyland: The Magic Words are Squeamish Ossifrage; Asiacrypt '94, LNCS 917, Springer-Verlag, Berlin 1995, 263-277.

Akl82 Selim G. Akl: Digital Signature with Blindfolded Arbitrators who cannot form Alliances; 1982 IEEE Symposium on Security and Privacy, IEEE Computer Society Press, 129-135.

Ande94 Ross J. Anderson: Why Cryptosystems Fail; Communications of the ACM 37/11 (1994) 32-40.

AnLe81 Tom Anderson, Pete A. Lee: Fault Tolerance — Principles and Practice; Prentice Hall, Englewood Cliffs, New Jersey, 1981.

Aßma89 Ralf Aßmann: Assembler-Implementierung von modularer Langzahlarithmetik; Studienarbeit, Institut für Rechnerentwurf und Fehlertoleranz, Universität Karlsruhe 1989.

Bach88 Eric Bach: How to generate factored random numbers; SIAM Journal on Computing 17/2 (1988) 179-193.

BaDG88 José Luis Balcázar, Josep Díaz, Joaquim Gabarró: Structural Complexity I; EATCS Monographs on Theoretical Computer Science 11, Springer-Verlag, Berlin 1988.

Bale93 D. Balenson: Privacy Enhancement for Internet Electronic Mail, Part III: Algorithms, Modes, and Identifiers; Internet RFC 1423, TIS, Feb. 1993.

BCDP91 Joan Boyar, David Chaum, Ivan Damgård, Torben Pedersen: Convertible Undeniable Signatures; Crypto '90, LNCS 537, Springer-Verlag, Berlin 1991, 189-205.

BDPW90 Mike V. D. Burmester, Yvo Desmedt, Fred Piper, Michael Walker: A general zero-knowledge scheme; Eurocrypt '89, LNCS 434, Springer-Verlag, Berlin 1990, 122-133.

Beav90 Donald Beaver: Security, Fault Tolerance, and Communication Complexity in Distributed Systems; Ph. D. Thesis, Division of Applied Sciences, Harvard University, Cambridge, Massachusetts, May 1990.

Beav91 Donald Beaver: Secure Multiparty Protocols and Zero Knowledge Proof Systems Tolerating a Faulty Minority; Journal of Cryptology 4/2 (1991) 75-122.

Beav95 Donald Beaver: Factoring: The DNA Solution; Asiacrypt '94, LNCS 917, Springer-Verlag, Berlin 1995, 419-423.

BeGG94 Mihir Bellare, Oded Goldreich, Shafi Goldwasser: Incremental cryptography: the case of hashing and signing; Crypto '94, LNCS 839, Springer-Verlag, Berlin 1994, 216-233.

BeGG95 Mihir Bellare, Oded Goldreich, Shafi Goldwasser: Incremental Cryptography and Application to Virus Protection; 27th Symposium on Theory of Computing (STOC) 1995, ACM, New York 1995, 45-56.

BeGo90 Mihir Bellare, Shafi Goldwasser: New Paradigms for Digital Signatures and Message Authentication Based on Non-interactive Zero-knowledge Proofs; Crypto '89, LNCS 435, Springer-Verlag, Heidelberg 1990, 194-211.

BeGo93 Mihir Bellare, Oded Goldreich: On Defining Proofs of Knowledge; Crypto '92, LNCS 740, Springer-Verlag, Berlin 1993, 390-420.

BeGW88 Michael Ben-Or, Shafi Goldwasser, Avi Wigderson: Completeness theorems for non-cryptographic fault-tolerant distributed computation; 20th Symposium on Theory of Computing (STOC) 1988, ACM, New York 1988, 1-10.

BeMa94 Josh Benaloh, Michael de Mare: One-Way Accumulators: A Decentralized Alternative to Digital Signatures; Eurocrypt '93, LNCS 765, Springer-Verlag, Berlin 1994, 274-285.

BeMi88 Mihir Bellare, Silvio Micali: How to sign given any trapdoor function; 20th Symposium on Theory of Computing (STOC) 1988, ACM, New York 1988, 32-42.

BeMi92 Mihir Bellare, Silvio Micali: How to Sign Given Any Trapdoor Permutation; Journal of the ACM 39/1 (1992) 214-233.

Bena87 Josh Cohen Benaloh: Verifiable Secret-Ballot Elections; Ph. D. Thesis, Yale University, Sept. 1987.

BéQu95 Philippe Béguin, Jean-Jasques Quisquater: Fast Server-Aided RSA Signatures Secure Against Active Attacks; Crypto '95, LNCS 963, Springer-Verlag, Berlin 1995, 57-69.

BeRo93 Mihir Bellare, Phillip Rogaway: Random Oracles are Practical: A Paradigm for Designing Efficient Protocols; 1st Conference on Computer and Communications Security, 1993, ACM, New York 1993, 62-73.

BeRo94 Mihir Bellare, Phillip Rogaway: Entity Authentication and Key Distribution; Crypto '93, LNCS 773, Springer-Verlag, Berlin 1994, 232-249.

BeVa93 Ethan Bernstein, Umesh Vazirani: Quantum Complexity Theory; 25th Symposium on Theory of Computing (STOC) 1993, ACM, New York 1993, 11-20.

BeYu93 Mihir Bellare, Moti Yung: Certifying Cryptographic Tools: The Case of Trapdoor Permutations; Crypto '92, LNCS 740, Springer-Verlag, Berlin 1993, 442-460.

BGB86 BGB • Bürgerliches Gesetzbuch; (29. ed) dtv-Band 5001 (Beck-Texte), Deutscher Taschenbuch Verlag, München 1986.

BGMW93 Ernest Brickell, Daniel M. Gordon, Kevin S. McCurley, David B. Wilson: Fast exponentiation with precomputation; Eurocrypt '92, LNCS 658, Springer-Verlag, Berlin 1993, 200-207.

BiBT94 Ingrid Biehl, Johannes Buchmann, Christoph Thiel: Cryptographic protocols based on discrete logarithms in real-quadratic orders; Crypto '94, LNCS 839, Springer-Verlag, Berlin 1994, 56-60.

BiSh93 Eli Biham, Adi Shamir: Differential Cryptanalysis of the Data Encryption Standard; Springer-Verlag, New York 1993.

Bisk93 Joachim Biskup: Sicherheit von IT-Systemen als "sogar wenn – sonst nichts – Eigenschaft"; Verläßliche Informationssysteme (VIS '93), DuD Fachbeiträge 16, Vieweg, Wiesbaden 1993, 239-254.

BJKS94 Jürgen Bierbrauer, Thomas Johansson, Gregory Kabatianskii, Ben Smeets: On Families of Hash Functions via Geometric Codes and Concatenation; Crypto '93, LNCS 773, Springer-Verlag, Berlin 1994, 331-342.

Blak79 G. R. Blakley: Safeguarding cryptographic keys; AFIPS Conference Proceedings Vol. 48, National Computer Conference (NCC) 1979, 313-317.

Bleu90 Gerrit Bleumer: Vertrauenswürdige Schlüssel für ein Signatursystem, dessen Brechen beweisbar ist; Studienarbeit, Institut für Rechnerentwurf und Fehlertoleranz, Universität Karlsruhe 1990.

BlFM88 Manuel Blum, Paul Feldman, Silvio Micali: Non-interactive zero-knowledge and its applications; 20th Symposium on Theory of Computing (STOC) 1988, ACM, New York 1988, 103-112.

BlMa94 Daniel Bleichenbacher, Ueli M. Maurer: Directed acyclic graphs, one-way functions and digital signatures; Crypto '94, LNCS 839, Springer-Verlag, Berlin 1994, 75-82.

BlMi84 Manuel Blum, Silvio Micali: How to Generate Cryptographically Strong Sequences of Pseudo-Random Bits; SIAM Journal on Computing 13/4 (1984) 850-864.

BlPW91 Gerrit Bleumer, Birgit Pfitzmann, Michael Waidner: A remark on a signature scheme where forgery can be proved; Eurocrypt '90, LNCS 473, Springer-Verlag, Berlin 1991, 441-445.

Blum82 Manuel Blum: Coin Flipping by Telephone — A Protocol for Solving Impossible Problems; compcon spring 1982, 133-137.

BoCh93 Jurjen Bos, David Chaum: Provably Unforgeable Signatures; Crypto '92, LNCS 740, Springer-Verlag, Berlin 1993, 1-14.

BoCo90 Jurjen Bos, Matthijs Coster: Addition chain heuristics; Crypto '89, LNCS 435, Springer-Verlag, Heidelberg 1990, 400-407.

BoCP88 Jurjen Bos, David Chaum, George Purdy: A Voting Scheme; unpublished manuscript, presented at the rump session of Crypto '88.

BoFL91 Joan Boyar, Katalin Friedl, Carsten Lund: Practical Zero-Knowledge Proofs: Giving Hints and Using Deficiencies; Journal of Cryptology 4/3 (1991) 185-206.

BoKK90 Joan F. Boyar, Stuart A. Kurtz, Mark W. Krentel: A Discrete Logarithm Implementation of Perfect Zero-Knowledge Blobs; Journal of Cryptology 2/2 (1990) 63-76.

BoLi95 Dan Boneh, Richard J. Lipton: Quantum Cryptanalysis of Hidden Linear Functions; Crypto '95, LNCS 963, Springer-Verlag, Berlin 1995, 424-437.

Bos92 Jurjen Bos: Practical Privacy; Proefschrift (Ph. D. Thesis), Technische Universiteit Eindhoven 1992.

Boyd86 Colin Boyd: Digital Multisignatures; IMA Conference on Coding and Cryptography, Cirencester 1986, proceedings published 1989.

Bran93 Stefan Brands: An Efficient Off-line Electronic Cash System Based On The Representation Problem; Centrum voor Wiskunde en Informatica (CWI), Report CS-R9323, Amsterdam 1993.

Bran94 Stefan Brands: Untraceable Off-line Cash in Wallet with Observers; Crypto '93, LNCS 773, Springer-Verlag, Berlin 1994, 302-318.

Bran95 Stefan Brands: Restrictive Blinding of Secret-Key Certificates; Eurocrypt '95, LNCS 921, Springer-Verlag, Berlin 1995, 231-247.

Bras88 Gilles Brassard: Modern Cryptology — A Tutorial; LNCS 325, Springer-Verlag, Berlin 1988.

Bras90 Gilles Brassard: How to improve signature schemes; Eurocrypt '89, LNCS 434, Springer-Verlag, Berlin 1990, 16-22.

BrCC88 Gilles Brassard, David Chaum, Claude Crépeau: Minimum Disclosure Proofs of Knowledge; Journal of Computer and System Sciences 37 (1988) 156-189.

BrCh94 Stefan Brands, David Chaum: Distance-Bounding Protocols; Eurocrypt '93, LNCS 765, Springer-Verlag, Berlin 1994, 344-359.

BrCr90 Gilles Brassard, Claude Crépeau: Sorting out zero-knowledge; Eurocrypt '89, LNCS 434, Springer-Verlag, Berlin 1990, 181-191.

BrDL93 Jørgen Brandt, Ivan Damgård, Peter Landrock: Speeding up Prime Number Generation; Asiacrypt '91, LNCS 739, Springer-Verlag, Berlin 1993, 440-449.

BrOd92 Ernest F. Brickell, Andrew M. Odlyzko: Cryptanalysis: A Survey of Recent Results; in: Gustavus J. Simmons (ed.): Contemporary Cryptology - The Science of Information Integrity; IEEE Press, Hoes Lane 1992, 501-540.

Brow94 Julian Brown: A Quantum Revolution For Computing; New Scientist 24/1944 (Sept. 1994) 21-24.

BrSt88 Ernest F. Brickell, Doug R. Stinson: Authentication Codes with Multiple Arbiters; Eurocrypt '88, LNCS 330, Springer-Verlag, Berlin 1988, 51-55.

BuAN90 Michael Burrows, Martin Abadi, Roger Needham: A Logic of Authentication; ACM Transactions on Computer Systems 8/1 (1990) 18-36.

BüPf89 Holger Bürk, Andreas Pfitzmann: Digital Payment Systems Enabling Security and Unobservability; Computers & Security 8/5 (1989) 399-416.

BüPf90 Holger Bürk, Andreas Pfitzmann: Value Exchange Systems Enabling Security and Unobservability; Computers & Security 9/8 (1990) 715-721.

CaPS95 Jan L. Camenisch, Jean-Marc Piveteau, Markus A. Stadler: Blind Signatures Based on the Discrete Logarithm Problem; Eurocrypt '94, LNCS 950, Springer-Verlag, Berlin 1995, 428-432.

CBDP91 David Chaum, Joan Boyar, Ivan Damgård, Torben Pedersen: Undeniable Signatures: Applications and Theory; manuscript, Matematisk Institut, Århus, July 1, 1991.

ChAn90 David Chaum, Hans van Antwerpen: Undeniable signatures; Crypto '89, LNCS 435, Springer-Verlag, Heidelberg 1990, 212-216.

Chau85 David Chaum: Security without Identification: Transaction Systems to make Big Brother Obsolete; Communications of the ACM 28/10 (1985) 1030-1044.

Chau88 David Chaum: The Dining Cryptographers Problem: Unconditional Sender and Recipient Untraceability; Journal of Cryptology 1/1 (1988) 65-75.

Chau89 David Chaum: Privacy Protected Payments – Unconditional Payer and/or Payee Untraceability; SMART CARD 2000: The Future of IC Cards, IFIP WG 11.6 International Conference 1987, North-Holland, Amsterdam 1989, 69-93.

Chau90 David Chaum: Showing credentials without identification: Transferring signatures between unconditionally unlinkable pseudonyms; Auscrypt '90, LNCS 453, Springer-Verlag, Berlin 1990, 246-264.

Chau91 David Chaum: Zero-knowledge undeniable signatures; Eurocrypt '90, LNCS 473, Springer-Verlag, Berlin 1991, 458-464.

Chau91a David Chaum: Some Weaknesses of "Weaknesses of Undeniable Signatures"; Eurocrypt '91, LNCS 547, Springer-Verlag, Berlin 1991, 554-556.

Chau92 David Chaum: Achieving Electronic Privacy; Scientific American (Aug. 1992) 96-101.

Chau95 David Chaum: Designated Confirmer Signatures; Eurocrypt '94, LNCS 950, Springer-Verlag, Berlin 1995, 86-91.

ChCD88 David Chaum, Claude Crépeau, Ivan Damgård: Multiparty unconditional secure protocols; 20th Symposium on Theory of Computing (STOC) 1988, ACM, New York 1988, 11-19.

ChDG88 David Chaum, Ivan B. Damgård, Jeroen van de Graaf: Multiparty Computations ensuring privacy of each party's input and correctness of the result; Crypto '87, LNCS 293, Springer-Verlag, Berlin 1988, 87-119.

ChEG88 David Chaum, Jan-Hendrik Evertse, Jeroen van de Graaf: An improved protocol for demonstrating possession of discrete logarithms and some generalizations; Eurocrypt '87, LNCS 304, Springer-Verlag, Berlin 1988, 127-141.

Chen94 Lidong Chen: Oblivious Signatures; 3rd European Symposium on Research in Computer Security (ESORICS 94), LNCS 875, Springer-Verlag, Berlin 1994, 161-172.

ChEv87 David Chaum, Jan-Hendrik Evertse: A secure and privacy-protecting protocol for transmitting personal information between organizations; Crypto '86, LNCS 263, Springer-Verlag, Berlin 1987, 118-167.

ChFN90 David Chaum, Amos Fiat, Moni Naor: Untraceable Electronic Cash; Crypto '88, LNCS 403, Springer-Verlag, Berlin 1990, 319-327.

ChHe91 David Chaum, Eugène van Heijst: Group signatures; Eurocrypt '91, LNCS 547, Springer-Verlag, Berlin 1991, 257-265.

ChHP92 David Chaum, Eugène van Heijst, Birgit Pfitzmann: Cryptographically Strong Undeniable Signatures, Unconditionally Secure for the Signer; Crypto '91, LNCS 576, Springer-Verlag, Berlin 1992, 470-484.

ChPe93 David Chaum, Torben Pryds Pedersen: Wallet Databases with Observers; Crypto '92, LNCS 740, Springer-Verlag, Berlin 1993, 89-105.

ChPe95 Lidong Chen, Torben P. Pedersen: New Group Signature Schemes; Eurocrypt '94, LNCS 950, Springer-Verlag, Berlin 1995, 171-181.

ChRo91 David Chaum, Sandra Roijakkers: Unconditionally Secure Digital Signatures; Crypto '90, LNCS 537, Springer-Verlag, Berlin 1991, 206-214.

Clev86 Richard Cleve: Limits on the Security of Coin Flips When Half the Processors are Faulty; 18th Symposium on Theory of Computing (STOC) 1986, ACM, New York 1986, 364-369.

CoLe87 Henri Cohen, Arjen K. Lenstra: Implementation of a New Primality Test; Mathematics of Computation 48/177 (1987) 103-121.

CoSV94 Don Coppersmith, Jacques Stern, Serge Vaudenay: Attacks on the Birational Permutation Signature Schemes; Crypto '93, LNCS 773, Springer-Verlag, Berlin 1994, 435-443.

CrDa95 Ronald Cramer, Ivan Damgård: Secure Signature Schemes based on Interactive Protocols; Crypto '95, LNCS 963, Springer-Verlag, Berlin 1995, 297-310.

CrDS94 Ronald Cramer, Ivan Damgård, Berry Schoenmakers: Proofs of partial knowledge and simplified design of witness hiding protocols; Crypto '94, LNCS 839, Springer-Verlag, Berlin 1994, 174-187.

CrGT95 Claude Crépeau, Jeroen van de Graaf, Alain Tapp: Committed Oblivious Transfer and Private Multi-Party Computation; Crypto '95, LNCS 963, Springer-Verlag, Berlin 1995, 110-123.

DaLP93 Ivan Damgård, Peter Landrock, Carl Pomerance: Average Case Error Estimates for the Strong Probable Prime Test; Mathematics of Computation 61/203 (1993) 177-194.

Damg88 Ivan Bjerre Damgård: Collision free hash functions and public key signature schemes; Eurocrypt '87, LNCS 304, Springer-Verlag, Berlin 1988, 203-216.

Damg88a Ivan Bjerre Damgård: The Application of Claw Free Functions in Cryptography – Unconditional Protection in Cryptographic Protocols; Aarhus University, Computer Science Department, DAIMI PB – 269 (ISSN 0105-8517), May 1988.

Damg90 Ivan Bjerre Damgård: Payment Systems and Credential Mechanisms with Provable Security Against Abuse by Individuals; Crypto '88, LNCS 403, Springer-Verlag, Berlin 1990, 328-335.

Damg90a Ivan B. Damgård: A design principle for hash functions; Crypto '89, LNCS 435, Springer-Verlag, Heidelberg 1990, 416-427.

DaPP94 Ivan B. Damgård, Torben P. Pedersen, Birgit Pfitzmann: On the Existence of Statistically Hiding Bit Commitment Schemes and Fail-Stop Signatures; Crypto '93, LNCS 773, Springer-Verlag, Berlin 1994, 250-265.

DaPr80 Donald W. Davies, Wyn L. Price: The Application of Digital Signatures Based on Public Key Cryptosystems; 5th International Conference on Computer Communication (ICCC) 1980, "Computer Communications: Increasing Benefits for Society"; Atlanta, Oct. 27-30, 1980, 525-530.

DaPr85 Donald W. Davies, Wyn L. Price: Digital Signatures — An Update; Seventh International Conference on Computer Communication (ICCC) 1984, "The New World of the Information Society"; Elsevier (North-Holland), 1985, 843-847.

DaPr89 Donald W. Davies, Wyn L. Price: Security for Computer Networks, An Introduction to Data Security in Teleprocessing and Electronic Funds Transfer; (2nd ed.) John Wiley & Sons, New York 1989.

Davi82 George Davida: Chosen Signature Cryptanalysis of the RSA (MIT) Public Key Cryptosystem; TR-CS-82-2, University of Wisconsin, Milwaukee, Oct. 1982. (Quoted in [Merr83].)

DeFr92 Yvo Desmedt, Yair Frankel: Shared generation of authenticators and signatures; Crypto '91, LNCS 576, Springer-Verlag, Berlin 1992, 457-469.

DeMe82 Richard A. DeMillo, Michael Merritt: Chosen Signature Cryptanalysis of Public Key Cryptosystems; Technical Memorandum, School of Information and Computer Science, Georgia Institute of Technology, Atlanta, Georgia, Oct. 25, 1982.

Denn84 Dorothy E. Denning: Digital Signatures with RSA and Other Public-Key Cryptosystems; Communications of the ACM 27/4 (1984) 388-392.

DES77 Specification for the Data Encryption Standard; Federal Information Processing Standards Publication 46 (FIPS PUB 46), Jan. 15, 1977.

Desm88 Yvo Desmedt: Society and group oriented cryptography: a new concept; Crypto '87, LNCS 293, Springer-Verlag, Berlin 1988, 120-127.

Desm88a Yvo Desmedt: Subliminal-Free Authentication and Signature; Eurocrypt '88, LNCS 330, Springer-Verlag, Berlin 1988, 23-31.

DeYu91 Yvo Desmedt, Moti Yung: Weaknesses of Undeniable Signature Schemes; Eurocrypt '91, LNCS 547, Springer-Verlag, Berlin 1991, 205-220.

Dier91 Rüdiger Dierstein: The Concept of Secure Information Processing Systems and Their Basic Functions; Computer Security and Information Integrity (IFIP/Sec '90), North-Holland, Amsterdam 1991, 133-149.

DiHe76 Whitfield Diffie, Martin E. Hellman: New Directions in Cryptography; IEEE Transactions on Information Theory 22/6 (1976) 644-654.

DoDN91 Danny Dolev, Cynthia Dwork, Moni Naor: Non-Malleable Cryptography; 23rd Symposium on Theory of Computing (STOC) 1991, ACM, New York 1991, 542-552.

DoDw91 Danny Dolev, Cynthia Dwork: On-The-Fly Generation of Names and Communication Primitives; part of a manuscript, IBM Research Division, Almaden Research Center, San Jose, received from Cynthia Dwork by e-mail, Dec. 13, 1991.

DoLe95 Bruce Dodson, Arjen K. Lenstra: NFS with Four Large Primes: An Explosive Experiment; Crypto '95, LNCS 963, Springer-Verlag, Berlin 1995, 372-385.

DoSt83 Danny Dolev, H. Raymond Strong: Authenticated Algorithms for Byzantine Agreement; SIAM Journal on Computing 12/4 (1983) 656-666.

DoYa81 Danny Dolev, Andrew C. Yao: On the Security of Public Key Protocols; 22nd Symposium on Foundations of Computer Science (FOCS) 1981, IEEE Computer Society, 1981, 350-357.

DSS91 Announcing a Digital Signature Standard; Federal Information Processing Standards Publication (FIPS PUB XX), Draft, Aug. 19, 1991.

DSS92 CACM: The Digital Signature Standard Proposed by NIST; Communications of the ACM 35/7 (1992) 36-40.

DwNa94 Cynthia Dwork, Moni Naor: An efficient existentially unforgeable signature scheme and its applications; Crypto '94, LNCS 839, Springer-Verlag, Berlin 1994, 234-246.

ElGa85 Taher ElGamal: A Public Key Cryptosystem and a Signature Scheme Based on Discrete Logarithms; IEEE Transactions on Information Theory 31/4 (1985) 469-472.

Euro93 Eurocrypt '92 Panel Report: Trapdoor Primes and Moduli; Eurocrypt '92, LNCS 658, Springer-Verlag, Berlin 1993, 194-199.

EvGM90 Shimon Even, Oded Goldreich, Silvio Micali: On-line/off-line digital signatures; Crypto '89, LNCS 435, Springer-Verlag, Heidelberg 1990, 263-275.

EvHe92 Jan-Hendrik Evertse, Eugène van Heyst: Which new RSA signatures can be computed from some given RSA signatures?; Journal of Cryptology 5/1 (1992) 41-52.

EvKW74 Arthur Evans, William Kantrowitz, Edwin Weiss: A User Authentication Scheme Not Requiring Secrecy in the Computer; Communications of the ACM 17/8 (1974) 437-442.

EvSY84 Shimon Even, Alan L. Selman, Yacov Yacobi: The Complexity of Promise Problems with Applications to Public-Key Cryptography; Information and Control 61 (1984) 159-173.

EvYa80 Shimon Even, Yacov Yacobi: Cryptocomplexity and NP-Completeness; 7th International Colloquium on Automata, Languages and Programming (ICALP), LNCS 85, Springer-Verlag, Heidelberg 1980, 195-207.

FeFS88 Uriel Feige, Amos Fiat, Adi Shamir: Zero-Knowledge Proofs of Identity; Journal of Cryptology 1/2 (1988) 77-94.

Fell71 William Feller: An Introduction to Probability Theory and Its Applications — Volume II; (2nd ed.) John Wiley & Sons, New York 1971.

Fiat90 Amos Fiat: Batch RSA; Crypto '89, LNCS 435, Springer-Verlag, Heidelberg 1990, 175-185.

FINN89 David Feldman, Russell Impagliazzo, Moni Naor, Noam Nisan, Steven Rudich, Adi Shamir: On Dice and Coins: Models of Computation for Random Generation; 16th International Colloquium on Automata, Languages and Programming (ICALP), LNCS 372, Springer-Verlag, Heidelberg 1989, 319-340.

FiSh87 Amos Fiat, Adi Shamir: How to Prove Yourself: Practical Solutions to Identification and Signature Problems; Crypto '86, LNCS 263, Springer-Verlag, Berlin 1987, 186-194.

Fitz89 Karen Fitzgerald: The quest for intruder-proof computer systems; Encryption, smart cards, and fingerprint readers are among the tools employed by organizations requiring data security; IEEE spectrum 26/8 (1989) 22-26.

FoPf91 Dirk Fox, Birgit Pfitzmann: Effiziente Software-Implementierung des GMR-Signatursystems; Verläßliche Informationssysteme (VIS '91), Informatik-Fachberichte 271, Springer-Verlag, Heidelberg 1991, 329-345.

Fox91 Dirk Fox: Effiziente Softwareimplementierung asymmetrischer Kryptosysteme und der zugrundeliegenden modularen Langzahlarithmetik; Diplomarbeit, Institut für Rechnerentwurf und Fehlertoleranz, Universität Karlsruhe, April 1991.

Fox91a Dirk Fox: Buchbesprechung zu: „Jürgen W. Goebel, Jürgen Scheller: Elektronische Unterschriftsverfahren in der Telekommunikation, Rechtliche Rahmenbedingungen und Einzelfragen"; Datenschutz und Datensicherung DuD 15/9 (1991) 491-494.

FrGY92 Matthew Franklin, Zvi Galil, Moti Yung: An Overview of Secure Distributed Computing; Columbia University, Dep. of Computer Science, TR CUCS-008-92, March 24, 1992.

FrYu93 Matthew Franklin, Moti Yung: Secure and Efficient Off-Line Digital Money; 20th International Colloquium on Automata, Languages and Programming (ICALP), LNCS 700, Springer-Verlag, Heidelberg 1993, 265-276.

FrYu95 Yair Frankel, Moti Yung: Cryptanalysis of the Immunized LL Public Key Systems; Crypto '95, LNCS 963, Springer-Verlag, Berlin 1995, 287-296.

FuOO91 Atsushi Fujioka, Tatsuaki Okamoto, Kazuo Ohta: Interactive Bi-Proof Systems and Undeniable Signature Schemes; Eurocrypt '91, LNCS 547, Springer-Verlag, Berlin 1991, 243-256.

GaHY86 Zvi Galil, Stuart Haber, Moti Yung: Symmetric Public-Key Encryption; Crypto '85, LNCS 218, Springer-Verlag, Berlin 1986, 128-137.

GaHY89 Zvi Galil, Stuart Haber, Moti Yung: Symmetric Public-Key Cryptosystems; Bellcore TM ARH-013160, 13th July 1989.

GaJo80 Michael R. Garey, David S. Johnson: Computers and Intractability — A Guide to the Theory of NP-Completeness; 2nd Printing, W. H. Freeman, New York 1980.

Gall68 Robert G. Gallager: Information Theory and Reliable Communication; John Wiley & Sons, New York 1968.

Garf95 Simson Garfinkel: PGP Pretty Good Privacy; O'Reilly & Associates, Sebastopol 1995.

GiMS74 E. N. Gilbert, F. J. Mac Williams, N. J. A. Sloane: Codes which detect deception; The Bell System Technical Journal 53/3 (1974) 405-424.

Gira88 Marc Girault: Hash-functions using modulo-N operations; Eurocrypt '87, LNCS 304, Springer-Verlag, Berlin 1988, 217-226.

Gira91 Marc Girault: Self-certified public keys; Eurocrypt '91, LNCS 547, Springer-Verlag, Berlin 1991, 490-497.

GoKi86 Shafi Goldwasser, Joe Kilian: Almost All Primes Can be Quickly Certified; 18th Symposium on Theory of Computing (STOC) 1986, ACM, New York 1986, 316-329.

Gold87 Oded Goldreich: Two Remarks Concerning the Goldwasser-Micali-Rivest Signature Scheme; Crypto '86, LNCS 263, Springer-Verlag, Berlin 1987, 104-110.

Gold91 Oded Goldreich: A Uniform-Complexity Treatment of Encryption and Zero-Knowledge; Technical Report no. 685, Computer Science Department, Technion, Haifa, Israel, July 1991.

Gold93 Oded Goldreich: A Uniform-Complexity Treatment of Encryption and Zero-Knowledge; Journal of Cryptology 6/1 (1993) 21-53.

Gold95 Oded Goldreich: Foundations of Cryptography (Fragments of a Book); Department of Computer Science and Applied Mathematics, Weizmann Institute of Science, Rehovot, Israel, 1995 and ftp.wisdom.weizmann.acil//pub/oded/bookfrag.

GoLe91 Shafi Goldwasser, Leonid Levin: Fair Computation of General Functions in Presence of Immoral Majority; Crypto '90, LNCS 537, Springer-Verlag, Berlin 1991, 77-93.

GoMc93 Daniel M. Gordon, Kevin S. McCurley: Massively Parallel Computation of Discrete Logarithms; Crypto '92, LNCS 740, Springer-Verlag, Berlin 1993, 312-323.

GoMi84 Shafi Goldwasser, Silvio Micali: Probabilistic Encryption; Journal of Computer and System Sciences 28 (1984) 270-299.

GoMR84 Shafi Goldwasser, Silvio Micali, Ronald L. Rivest: A "Paradoxical" Solution to the Signature Problem; 25th Symposium on Foundations of Computer Science (FOCS) 1984, IEEE Computer Society, 1984, 441-448.

GoMR85 Shafi Goldwasser, Silvio Micali, Charles Rackoff: The Knowledge Complexity of Interactive Proof-Systems; 17th Symposium on Theory of Computing (STOC) 1985, ACM, New York 1985, 291-304.

GoMR88 Shafi Goldwasser, Silvio Micali, Ronald L. Rivest: A Digital Signature Scheme Secure Against Adaptive Chosen-Message Attacks; SIAM Journal on Computing 17/2 (1988) 281-308.

GoMR89 Shafi Goldwasser, Silvio Micali, Charles Rackoff: The Knowledge Complexity of Interactive Proof Systems; SIAM Journal on Computing 18/1 (1989) 186-207.

GoMT82 Shafi Goldwasser, Silvio Micali, Po Tong: Why and How to Establish a Private Code on a Public Network; 23rd Symposium on Foundations of Computer Science (FOCS) 1982, IEEE Computer Society, 1982, 134-144.

GoMW87 Oded Goldreich, Silvio Micali, Avi Wigderson: How to play any mental game – or – a completeness theorem for protocols with honest majority; 19th Symposium on Theory of Computing (STOC) 1987, ACM, New York 1987, 218-229.

GoMW91 Oded Goldreich, Silvio Micali, Avi Wigderson: Proofs that Yield Nothing But Their Validity or All Languages in NP Have Zero-Knowledge Proof Systems; Journal of the ACM 38/1 (1991) 691-729.

GoMY83 Shafi Goldwasser, Silvio Micali, Andrew Yao: On signatures and authentication; Crypto '82, Plenum Press, New York 1983, 211-215.

GoMY83a Shafi Goldwasser, Silvio Micali, Andy Yao: Strong Signature Schemes; 15th Symposium on Theory of Computing (STOC) 1983, ACM, New York 1983, 431-439.

GoOr94 Oded Goldreich, Yair Oren: Definitions and Properties of Zero-Knowledge Proof Systems; Journal of Cryptology 7/1 (1994) 1-32.

Gord85 John Gordon: Strong Primes are Easy to Find; Eurocrypt '84, LNCS 209, Springer-Verlag, Berlin 1985, 216-223.

Gord93 Daniel M. Gordon: Designing and Detecting Trapdoors for Discrete Log Cryptosystems; Crypto '92, LNCS 740, Springer-Verlag, Berlin 1993, 66-75.

Gord93a Daniel M. Gordon: Discrete logarithms in GF(p) using the number field sieve; SIAM Journal on Discrete Mathematics 6/1 (1993) 124-138.

GoSc91 Jürgen W. Goebel, Jürgen Scheller: Elektronische Unterschriftsverfahren in der Telekommunikation; DuD-Fachbeiträge 12, Vieweg, Braunschweig 1991.

Gray92 James W. Gray III: Toward a Mathematical Foundation for Information Flow Security; Journal of Computer Security 1/3,4 (1992) 255-294.

GrPe88 Jeroen van de Graaf, René Peralta: A simple and secure way to show the validity of your public key; Crypto '87, LNCS 293, Springer-Verlag, Berlin 1988, 128-134.

GrSe88 Joachim Grollmann, Alan L. Selman: Complexity measures for public-key cryptosystems; SIAM Journal on Computing 17/2 (1988) 309-335.

GrYa89 Ronald L. Graham, Andrew C. Yao: On the Improbability of Reaching Byzantine Agreements; 21st Symposium on Theory of Computing (STOC) 1989, ACM, New York 1989, 467-478.

Guin91 Daniel Guinier: The Multiplication of Very Large Integers Using the Discrete Fast Fourier Transform; ACM SIGSAC Review 9/3 (1991) 26-36.

GuQu91 Louis Claude Guillou, Jean-Jacques Quisquater: Precautions taken against various potential attacks in ISO/IEC DIS 9796; Eurocrypt '90, LNCS 473, Springer-Verlag, Berlin 1991, 465-473.

Hass64 Helmut Hasse: Vorlesungen über Zahlentheorie; (2. ed.) Grundlehren der Mathematischen Wissenschaften vol. 59, Springer-Verlag, Berlin 1964.

HaWr79 G. H. Hardy, E. M. Wright: An Introduction to the Theory of Numbers; (5th ed.) Oxford at the Clarendon Press, Oxford 1978.

Heij92 Eugène van Heijst: Special Signature Schemes; Proefschrift (Ph. D. Thesis), Technische Universiteit Eindhoven, 6.7.1992.

HePe93 Eugène van Heyst, Torben P. Pedersen: How to Make Efficient Fail-stop Signatures; Eurocrypt '92, LNCS 658, Springer-Verlag, Berlin 1993, 366-377.

HePP93 Eugène van Heijst, Torben Pryds Pedersen, Birgit Pfitzmann: New Constructions of Fail-Stop Signatures and Lower Bounds; Crypto '92, LNCS 740, Springer-Verlag, Berlin 1993, 15-30.

HoMP95 Patrick Horster, Markus Michels, Holger Petersen: Meta-Message Recovery and Meta-Blind Signature Schemes Based on the Discrete Logarithm Problem and Their Applications; Asiacrypt '94, LNCS 917, Springer-Verlag, Berlin 1995, 224-237.

ImLL89 Russell Impagliazzo, Leonid A. Levin, Michael Luby: Pseudo-random Generation from One-way Functions; 21st Symposium on Theory of Computing (STOC) 1989, ACM, New York 1989, 12-24.

ImRu89 Russell Impagliazzo, Steven Rudich: Limits on the Provable Consequences of One-way Permutations; 21st Symposium on Theory of Computing (STOC) 1989, ACM, New York 1989, 44-61.

IrRo90 Kenneth Ireland, Michael Rosen: A Classical Introduction to Modern Number Theory; (2nd ed.) GTM 84, Springer-Verlag, New York 1990.

ISO95 ISO/IEC JTC 1/SC 21 N9214: Open Systems Interconnection, Data Management and Open Distributed Processing; Proposed Draft Amendment ISO/IEC 9594-2/4, 9594-6-2, 9594-7/1, 9594-8/1, 12.05.1995.

ISO91 ISO/IEC 9594-8: Information technology — Open Systems Interconnection — Specification — The Directory — Part 8: Authentication framework; ISO International Standard, First edition 15.12.1990, with Technical Corrigendum 1, 15.12.1991.

JoCh86 Wiebren de Jonge, David Chaum: Attacks on Some RSA Signatures; Crypto '85, LNCS 218, Springer-Verlag, Berlin 1986, 18-27.

JoSm95 Thomas Johansson, Ben Smeets: On A^2-codes including arbiter's attacks; Eurocrypt '94, LNCS 950, Springer-Verlag, Berlin 1995, 456-460.

Kahn67 David Kahn: The Codebreakers, The Story of Secret Writing; Macmillan Publishing Co., New York, 1967.

Kali91 Burton S. Kaliski Jr.: An Overview of the PKCS Standards; RSA Data Security, Inc., 10 Twin Dolphin Drive, Redwood City, CA 94065, USA, June 3, 1991.

Kent93 Stephen T. Kent: Internet Privacy Enhanced Mail; Communications of the ACM 36/8 (1993) 48-60.

Kili91 Joe Kilian: Achieving Zero-Knowledge Robustly; Crypto '90, LNCS 537, Springer-Verlag, Berlin 1991, 313-325.

Knut81 Donald E. Knuth: The Art of Computer Programming, Vol. 2: Seminumerical Algorithms; (2nd ed.) Addison-Wesley, Reading 1981.

Kobl87 Neal Koblitz: A Course in Number Theory and Cryptography; GTM 114, Springer-Verlag, Berlin 1987.

Kobl87a Neal Koblitz: Elliptic Curve Cryptosystems; Mathematics of Computation 48/177 (1987) 203-209.

Kobl89 Neal Koblitz: Hyperelliptic Cryptosystems; Journal of Cryptology 1/3 (1989) 139-150.

Kobl91 Neal Koblitz: Elliptic Curve Implementation of Zero-Knowledge Blobs; Journal of Cryptology 4/3 (1991) 207-213.

Kran86 Evangelos Kranakis: Primality and Cryptography; Wiley-Teubner Series in Computer Science, B. G. Teubner, Stuttgart 1986.

Krum86 Heiko Krumm: Spezifikation und Verifikation von Kommunikationsprotokollen; Skript zur Vorlesung im WS 85/86, Institut für Informatik III, Universität Karlsruhe, 1986.

LABW92 Butler Lampson, Martin Abadi, Michael Burrows, Edward Wobber: Authentication in Distributed Systems: Theory and Practice; ACM Transactions on Computer Systems 10/4 (1992) 265-310.

Lamp79 Leslie Lamport: Constructing Digital Signatures from a One-Way Function; SRI Intl. CSL-98, Oct. 1979.

Lang95 Susan K. Langford: Threshold DSS Signatures without a Trusted Party; Crypto '95, LNCS 963, Springer-Verlag, Berlin 1995, 397-409.

LaOd91 Brian A. LaMacchia, Andrew M. Odlyzko: Computation of Discrete Logarithms in Prime Fields; Designs, Codes and Cryptography 1/1 (1991) 47-62.

Lare83 Karl Larenz: Allgemeiner Teil des deutschen Bürgerlichen Rechts; (6. ed.), Verlag C. H. Beck, München, 1983.

LeLe90 A. K. Lenstra, H. W. Lenstra, Jr: Algorithms in Number Theory; in: J. van Leeuwen (ed.): Handbook of Theoretical Computer Science; Elsevier, 1990, 673-715.

LeLe93 A. K. Lenstra, H. W. Lenstra: The Development of the number field sieve; Lecture Notes in Mathematics 1554, Springer-Verlag, Berlin 1993.

LeMo95 Reynald Lercier, François Morain: Counting the number of points on elliptic curves over finite fields: strategies and performances; Eurocrypt '95, LNCS 921, Springer-Verlag, Berlin 1995, 79-94.

LiLe95 Chae Hoon Lim, Pil Joong Lee: Security and Performance of Server-Aided RSA Computation Protocols; Crypto '95, LNCS 963, Springer-Verlag, Berlin 1995, 70-83.

Lini83 Peter F. Linington: Fundamentals of the Layer Service Definitions and Protocol Specifications; Proceedings of the IEEE 71/12 (1983) 1341-1345.

Lips81 John D. Lipson: Elements of algebra and algebraic computing; Addison-Wesley, Reading, Mass. 1981.

MaIm91 Tsutomu Matsumoto, Hideki Imai: Human Identification Through Insecure Channel; Eurocrypt '91, LNCS 547, Springer-Verlag, Berlin 1991, 409-421.

MaKI90 Tsutomu Matsumoto, Koki Kato, Hideki Imai: Speeding up Secret Computations with Insecure Auxiliary Devices; Crypto '88, LNCS 403, Springer-Verlag, Berlin 1990, 497-506.

MaPn91 Zohar Manna, Amir Pnueli: The Temporal Logic of Reactive and Concurrent Systems: Specification; Springer-Verlag, New York 1991.

Maur92 Ueli M. Maurer: Some Number-theoretic Conjectures and Their Relation to the Generation of Cryptographic Primes; 2nd IMA Symposium on Cryptography and Coding, 1989; Oxford University Press, 1992, 173-191.

Maur95 Ueli M. Maurer: Fast Generation of Prime Numbers and Secure Public-Key Cryptographic Parameters; Journal of Cryptology 8/3 (1995) 123-155.

McCu90 Kevin S. McCurley: The Discrete Logarithm Problem; in: Carl Pomerance (ed.): Cryptology and Computational Number Theory; Proceedings of Symposia in Applied Mathematics, Volume 42, American Mathematical Society, Providence 1990, 49-74.

Mead95 Catherine A. Meadows: Formal Verification of Cryptographic Protocols: A Survey; Asiacrypt '94, LNCS 917, Springer-Verlag, Berlin 1995, 133-150.

MeMa82 Carl H. Meyer, Stephen M. Matyas: Cryptography — A New Dimension in Computer Data Security; (3rd printing) John Wiley & Sons, 1982.

MeOV93 Alfred J. Menezes, Tatsuaki Okamoto, Scott Vanstone: Reducing Elliptic Curve Logarithms to Logarithms in a Finite Field; IEEE Transactions on Information Theory 39/5 (1993) 1639-1646.

Merk80 Ralph C. Merkle: Protocols for Public Key Cryptosystems; 1980 IEEE Symposium on Security and Privacy, IEEE Computer Society Press, 122-134.

Merk82 Ralph C. Merkle: Protocols for Public Key Cryptosystems; AAAS Selected Symposium 69, Secure Communications and Asymmetric Cryptosystems; Westview Press, Boulder, Colorado 1982, 73-104.

Merk88 Ralph C. Merkle: A digital signature based on a conventional encryption function; Crypto '87, LNCS 293, Springer-Verlag, Berlin 1988, 369-378.

Merk90 Ralph C. Merkle: A certified digital signature (That antique paper from 1979); Crypto '89, LNCS 435, Springer-Verlag, Heidelberg 1990, 218-238.

Merr83 Michael John Merritt: Cryptographic Protocols; Ph. D. Dissertation, School of Information and Computer Science, Georgia Institute of Technology, Feb. 1983.

MeVa93 Alfred J. Menezes, Scott A. Vanstone: Elliptic Curve Cryptosystems and Their Implementation; Journal of Cryptology 6/4 (1993) 209-224.

Meye91 Carl H. Meyer: Merkle DEA Digital Signature Scheme; BeCEEP 4th International Symposium on Cryptographic Security for Data Processing and Data Communication, Berlin, Nov. 11-15, 1991, Handouts.

Miha94 Preda Mihailescu: Fast Generation of Provable Primes Using Search in Arithmetic Progressions; Crypto '94, LNCS 839, Springer-Verlag, Berlin 1994, 282-293.

Mill76 Gary L. Miller: Riemann's Hypothesis and Tests for Primality; Journal of Computer and System Sciences 13 (1983) 300-317.

Mill86 Victor S. Miller: Use of Elliptic Curves in Cryptography; Crypto '85, LNCS 218, Springer-Verlag, Berlin 1986, 417-426.

MiOI91 Shoji Miyaguchi, Kazuo Ohta, Masahiko Iwata: Confirmation that Some Hash Functions are not Collision Free; Eurocrypt '90, LNCS 473, Springer-Verlag, Berlin 1991, 326-343.

MiRo91 Silvio Micali, Phillip Rogaway: Secure Computation (Chapters 1-3); Laboratory for Computer Science, MIT, Cambridge, Mass., distributed at Crypto '91.

MiRS88 Silvio Micali, Charles Rackoff, Bob Sloan: The Notion of Security for Probabilistic Cryptosystems; SIAM Journal on Computing 17/2 (1988) 412-426.

Mont85 Peter L. Montgomery: Modular Multiplication without trial division; Mathematics of Computation 44 (1985) 519-512.

Naor91 Moni Naor: Bit Commitment Using Pseudorandomness; Journal of Cryptology 4/2 (1991) 151-158.

NaYu89 Moni Naor, Moti Yung: Universal One-way Hash Functions and their Cryptographic Applications; 21st Symposium on Theory of Computing (STOC) 1989, ACM, New York 1989, 33-43.

NaYu90 Moni Naor, Moti Yung: Public-key Cryptosystems Provably Secure against Chosen Ciphertext Attacks; 22nd Symposium on Theory of Computing (STOC) 1990, ACM, New York 1990, 427-437.

NOVY93 Moni Naor, Rafail Ostrovsky, Ramarathnam Venkatesan, Moti Yung: Perfect Zero-Knowledge Arguments for NP Can Be Based on General Complexity Assumptions; Crypto '92, LNCS 740, Springer-Verlag, Berlin 1993, 196-214.

NRVR95 David Naccache, David M'Raihi, Dan Raphaeli, Serge Vaudenay: Can D.S.A. be Improved? Complexity Trade-Offs with the Digital Signature Standard; Eurocrypt '94, LNCS 950, Springer-Verlag, Berlin 1995, 77-85.

NyRu95 Kaisa Nyberg, Rainer R. Rueppel: Message Recovery for Signature Schemes Based on the Discrete Logarithm Problem; Eurocrypt '94, LNCS 950, Springer-Verlag, Berlin 1995, 182-193.

OhOk93 Kazuo Ohta, Tatsuaki Okamoto: A Digital Multisignature Scheme Based on the Fiat-Shamir Scheme; Asiacrypt '91, LNCS 739, Springer-Verlag, Berlin 1993, 139-148.

Okam88 Tatsuaki Okamoto: A Digital Multisignature Scheme Using Bijective Public-Key Cryptosystems; ACM Transactions on Computer Systems 6/4 (1988) 432-441.

Okam94 Tatsuaki Okamoto: Designated confirmer signatures and public-key encryption are equivalent; Crypto '94, LNCS 839, Springer-Verlag, Berlin 1994, 61-74.

OkOh91 Tatsuaki Okamoto, Kazuo Ohta: How to Utilize the Randomness of Zero-Knowledge Proofs; Crypto '90, LNCS 537, Springer-Verlag, Berlin 1991, 456-475.

OkSS93 Tatsuaki Okamoto, Kouichi Sakurai, Hiroki Shizuya: How intractable is the discrete logarithm for a general finite group; Eurocrypt '92, LNCS 658, Springer-Verlag, Berlin 1993, 420-428.

Oren87 Yair Oren: On the cunning power of cheating verifiers: some observations about zero-knowledge proofs; 28th Symposium on Foundations of Computer Science (FOCS) 1987, IEEE Computer Society, 1987, 462-471.

Pede91 Torben Pryds Pedersen: Distributed Provers with Applications to Undeniable Signatures; Eurocrypt '91, LNCS 547, Springer-Verlag, Berlin 1991, 221-242.

Pede92 Torben Pryds Pedersen: Non-Interactive and Information-Theoretic Secure Verifiable Secret Sharing; Crypto '91, LNCS 576, Springer-Verlag, Berlin 1992, 129-140.

PePf95 Torben Pryds Pedersen, Birgit Pfitzmann: Fail-Stop Signatures; accepted for SIAM Journal on Computing, submitted 25.2.1993, revised 21.3.1995.

PeSL80 Marshall Pease, Robert Shostak, Leslie Lamport: Reaching Agreement in the Presence of Faults; Journal of the ACM 27/2 (1980) 228-234.

Pfit88 Birgit Pfitzmann: Vergleich der algebraischen und kryptographischen Modellierung von Kryptoprotokollen; Studienarbeit, Institut für Rechnerentwurf und Fehlertoleranz, Universität Karlsruhe 1988.

Pfit89 Birgit Pfitzmann: Für den Unterzeichner unbedingt sichere digitale Signaturen und ihre Anwendung; Diplomarbeit, Institut für Rechnerentwurf und Fehlertoleranz, Universität Karlsruhe 1989.

Pfit91 Birgit Pfitzmann: Neu und sicher: Digitale Fail-stop-Signaturen; KES – Zeitschrift für Kommunikations- und EDV-Sicherheit 7/5 (1991) 321-326.

Pfit91a Birgit Pfitzmann: Fail-stop Signatures; Principles and Applications; Compsec '91, 8th world conference on computer security, audit and control, Elsevier, Oxford 1991, 125-134.

Pfit93 Birgit Pfitzmann: Sorting Out Signature Schemes; 1st Conference on Computer and Communications Security 1993, ACM, New York 1993, 74-85.

Pfit94 Birgit Pfitzmann: Fail-Stop Signatures Without Trees; Hildesheimer Informatik-Berichte 16/94, ISSN 0941-3014, Institut für Informatik, Universität Hildesheim, June 1994.

PfWa90 Birgit Pfitzmann, Michael Waidner: Formal Aspects of Fail-stop Signatures; Interner Bericht 22/90, Fakultät für Informatik, Universität Karlsruhe, Dec. 1990.

PfWa91 Birgit Pfitzmann, Michael Waidner: Fail-stop-Signaturen und ihre Anwendung; Verläßliche Informationssysteme (VIS'91), Informatik-Fachberichte 271, Springer-Verlag, Heidelberg 1991, 289-301.

PfWa91a Birgit Pfitzmann, Michael Waidner: Fail-stop Signatures and their Application; Securicom 91, 9th Worldwide Congress on Computer and Communications Security and Protection, Paris, March 19-22, 1991, 145-160.

PfWa92 Birgit Pfitzmann, Michael Waidner: Unconditional Byzantine Agreement for any Number of Faulty Processors; 9th Symposium on Theoretical Aspects of Computer Science (STACS 92), LNCS 577, Springer-Verlag, Heidelberg 1992, 339-350.

PfWa92a Birgit Pfitzmann, Michael Waidner: How to Break and Repair a "Provably Secure" Untraceable Payment System; Crypto '91, LNCS 576, Springer-Verlag, Berlin 1992, 338-350.

PfWa92b Birgit Pfitzmann, Michael Waidner: Unconditionally Untraceable and Fault-tolerant Broadcast and Secret Ballot Election; Hildesheimer Informatik-Berichte 3/92, ISSN 0941-3014, Institut für Informatik, Universität Hildesheim, April 1992.

PfWa94 Birgit Pfitzmann, Michael Waidner: A General Framework for Formal Notions of "Secure" System; Hildesheimer Informatik-Berichte 11/94, ISSN 0941-3014, Institut für Informatik, Universität Hildesheim, April 1994.

PfWP90 Birgit Pfitzmann, Michael Waidner, Andreas Pfitzmann: Rechtssicherheit trotz Anonymität in offenen digitalen Systemen; Datenschutz und Datensicherung DuD 14/5-6 (1990) 243-253, 305-315.

Pive93 Jean-Marc Piveteau: New signature scheme with message recovery; Electronics Letters 29/25 (1993) 2185.

PoHe78 Stephen C. Pohlig, Martin E. Hellman: An Improved Algorithm for Computing Logarithms over GF(p) and its Cryptographic Significance; IEEE Transactions on Information Theory 10/1 (1978) 106-110.

Poin95 David Pointcheval: A New Identification Scheme Based on the Perceptrons Problem; Eurocrypt '95, LNCS 921, Springer-Verlag, Berlin 1995, 319-328.

Poll74 John M. Pollard: Theorems on factorization and primality testing; Proceedings of the Cambridge Philosophical Society 76 (1974) 521-528.

Pord93 Ulrich Pordesch: Risiken elektronischer Signaturverfahren; Datenschutz und Datensicherung DuD 17/10 (1993) 561-569.

PoRS93 Ulrich Pordesch, Alexander Roßnagel, Michael J. Schneider: Erprobung sicherheits- und datenschutzrelevanter Informationstechniken mit Simulationsstudien; Datenschutz und Datensicherung DuD 17/9 (1993) 491-497.

PPSW95 Andreas Pfitzmann, Birgit Pfitzmann, Matthias Schunter, Michael Waidner: Vertrauenswürdiger Entwurf portabler Benutzerendgeräte und Sicherheitsmodule; Verläßliche IT-Systeme (VIS '95); DuD Fachbeiträge, Vieweg, Wiesbaden 1995, 329-350.

PPSW96 Andreas Pfitzmann, Birgit Pfitzmann, Matthias Schunter, Michael Waidner: Mobile User Devices and Security Modules: Design for Trustworthiness; IBM Research Report RZ 2784 (#89262) 02/05/96, IBM Research Division, Zürich, Feb. 1996.

Purd74 George B. Purdy: A High Security Log-in Procedure; Communications of the ACM 17/8 (1974) 442-445.

QuCo82 Jean-Jacques Quisquater, C. Couvreur: Fast Decipherment Algorithm for RSA Public-Key Cryptosystem; Electronics Letters 18/21 (1982) 905-907.

RaBe89 Tal Rabin, Michael Ben-Or: Verifiable Secret Sharing and Multiparty Protocols with Honest Majority; 21st Symposium on Theory of Computing (STOC) 1989, ACM, New York 1989, 73-85.

Rabi78 Michael O. Rabin: Digitalized Signatures; in: R. A. DeMillo, D. P. Dobkin, A. K. Jones, R. J. Lipton (ed.): Foundations of Secure Computation; Academic Press, N.Y. 1978, 155-166.

Rabi79 Michael O. Rabin: Digitalized Signatures and Public-Key Functions as Intractable as Factorization; Laboratory for Computer Science, MIT, MIT/LCS/TR-212, Jan. 1979.

Rabi80 Michael O. Rabin: Probabilistic algorithm for primality testing; J. Number Theory 12/ (1980) 128-138.

RaSi92 Charles Rackoff, Daniel R. Simon: Non-Interactive Zero-Knowledge Proof of Knowledge and Chosen Ciphertext Attack; Crypto '91, LNCS 576, Springer-Verlag, Berlin 1992, 433-444.

ReSc95 E. Rescorla, A. Schiffmann: The Secure HyperText Transport Protocol, Version 1.1; Internet-Draft, Enterprise Integration Technologies, July 1995, http://www.eit.com/projects/s-http/draft-ietf-wts-shttp-00.txt.

RiSA78 Ronald L. Rivest, Adi Shamir, Leonard Adleman: A Method for Obtaining Digital Signatures and Public-Key Cryptosystems; Communications of the ACM 21/2 (1978) 120-126, reprinted: 26/1 (1983) 96-99.

Romp90 John Rompel: One-Way Functions are Necessary and Sufficient for Secure Signatures; 22nd Symposium on Theory of Computing (STOC) 1990, ACM, New York 1990, 387-394.

Rooi94 Peter de Rooij: On Schnorr's Preprocessing for Digital Signature Schemes; Eurocrypt '93, LNCS 765, Springer-Verlag, Berlin 1994, 435-439.

RoSc62 J. B. Rosser, L. Schoenfield: Approximate Formulas for Some Functions of Prime Numbers; Illinois J. Math. 6 (1962) 64-94.

SaDi93 Jörg Sauerbrey, A. Dietel: Resource requirements for the application of addition chains in modulo exponentiation; Eurocrypt '92, LNCS 658, Springer-Verlag, Berlin 1993, 174-182.

SaTo94 Reihaneh Safavi-Naini, L. Tombak: Optimal Authentication Systems; Eurocrypt '93, LNCS 765, Springer-Verlag, Berlin 1994, 12-27.

Schn91 Claus P. Schnorr: Efficient Signature Generation by Smart Cards; Journal of Cryptology 4/3 (1991) 161-174.

Schn92 Claus P. Schnorr: Comparison of the DSA of NIST and the Signature Schemes of ElGamal and Schnorr; 2. GMD-SmartCard Workshop, Feb. 4-5, 1992, GMD, Rheinstr. 75, D-6100 Darmstadt (now 64295).

Schn96 Bruce Schneier: Applied Cryptography: Protocols, Algorithms, and Source Code in C; John Wiley & Sons, New York 1996.

Schö85 Uwe Schöning: Complexity and Structure; LNCS 211, Springer-Verlag, Berlin 1985.

ScHö95 Claus P. Schnorr, H. H. Hörner: Attacking the Chor-Rivest cryptosystem by improved lattice reduction; Eurocrypt '95, LNCS 921, Springer-Verlag, Berlin 1995, 1-12.

Schu94 Matthias Schunter: Spezifikation von Geheimhaltungseigenschaften für reaktive kryptologische Systeme; Diplomarbeit, Institut für Informatik, Universität Hildesheim, Jan. 1994.

Schu95 Matthias Schunter: Vertrauen als integraler Bestandteil kryptografischer Spezifikationen; Trust Center, Grundlagen, Rechtliche Aspekte, Standardisierung, Realisierung, DuD Fachbeiträge, Vieweg, Wiesbaden 1995, 173-179.

ScSc83 Richard D. Schlichting, Fred B. Schneider: Fail-Stop Processors: An Approach to Designing Fault-Tolerant Computing Systems; ACM Transactions on Computer Systems 1/3 (1983) 222-238.

ScSt71 Arnold Schönhage, Volker Strassen: Schnelle Multiplikation großer Zahlen; Computing 7/ (1971) 281-292.

Sham79 Adi Shamir: How to Share a Secret; Communications of the ACM 22/11 (1979) 612-613.

Sham85 Adi Shamir: Identity-Based Cryptosystems and Signature Schemes; Crypto '84, LNCS 196, Springer-Verlag, Berlin 1985, 47-53.

Shan48 Claude E. Shannon: A Mathematical Theory of Communication; The Bell System Technical Journal 27 (1948) 379-423, 623-656.

Shan49 Claude E. Shannon: Communication Theory of Secrecy Systems; The Bell System Technical Journal 28/4 (1949) 656-715.

Shor94 Peter W. Shor: Algorithms for Quantum Computation: Discrete Logarithms and Factoring; 35th Symposium on Foundations of Computer Science (FOCS) 1994, IEEE Computer Society, 1994, 124-134.

SHS92 Secure Hash Standard (SHS); NIST Federal Register, 31.1.1992, essential parts by e-mail from Dennis Branstad.

Simm84 Gustavus J. Simmons: The Prisoners' Problem and the Subliminal Channel; Crypto '83, Plenum Press, New York 1984, 51-67.

Simm88 Gustavus J. Simmons: Message authentication with arbitration of transmitter/receiver disputes; Eurocrypt '87, LNCS 304, Springer-Verlag, Berlin 1988, 151-165.

Ster90 Jacques Stern: An alternative to the Fiat-Shamir protocol; Eurocrypt '89, LNCS 434, Springer-Verlag, Berlin 1990, 173-180.

SyMe93 Paul Syverson, Catherine Meadows: A Logical Language for Specifying Cryptographic Protocol Requirements; 1993 IEEE Symposium on Research in Security and Privacy, IEEE Computer Society Press, Los Alamitos 1993, 165-177.

Tane88 Andrew S. Tanenbaum: Computer Networks; (2nd ed.) Prentice-Hall, Englewood Cliffs 1988.

ToWo87 Martin Tompa, Heather Woll: Random self-reducibility and zero knowledge proofs of possession of information; 28th Symposium on Foundations of Computer Science (FOCS) 1987, IEEE Computer Society, 1987, 472-482.

Vaud92 Serge Vaudenay: One-time identification with low memory; Eurocode 92, CISM Courses and Lectures 339, Springer-Verlag, Wien 1992, 217-228.

Vern26 G. S. Vernam: Cipher Printing Telegraph Systems for Secret Wire and Radio Telegraphic Communications; Journal American Institute of Electrical Engineers XLV (1926) 109-115.

Waid91 Michael Waidner: Byzantinische Verteilung ohne kryptographische Annahmen trotz beliebig vieler Fehler; Universität Karlsruhe, Fakultät für Informatik, Dissertation, Oct. 24, 1991.

WaPf89 Michael Waidner, Birgit Pfitzmann: Unconditional Sender and Recipient Untraceability in spite of Active Attacks – Some Remarks; Fakultät für Informatik, Universität Karlsruhe, Interner Bericht 5/89, March 1989.

WaPf90 Michael Waidner, Birgit Pfitzmann: The Dining Cryptographers in the Disco: Unconditional Sender and Recipient Untraceability with Computationally Secure Serviceability; Eurocrypt '89, LNCS 434, Springer-Verlag, Berlin 1990, 690.

WeCa81 Mark N. Wegman, J. Lawrence Carter: New Hash Functions and Their Use in Authentication and Set Equality; Journal of Computer and System Sciences 22 (1981) 265-279.

Wilh93 Jan-Peter Wilhelms: Fail-stop-Signaturen — Eine Implementierung; program and manual, Institut für Informatik, Universität Hildesheim 1993.

Wilh94 Jan-Peter Wilhelms: Effizienzuntersuchungen neuerer Fail-stop-Signaturschemata; Diplomarbeit, Institut für Informatik, Universität Hildesheim, June 1994.

Will80 Hugh C. Williams: A Modification of the RSA Public-Key Encryption Procedure; IEEE Transactions on Information Theory 26/6 (1980) 726-729.

Will82 Hugh C. Williams: A p+1 method of factoring; Mathematics of Computation 39 (1982) 225-234.

Yao82 Andrew C. Yao: Protocols for Secure Computations; 23rd Symposium on Foundations of Computer Science (FOCS) 1982, IEEE Computer Society, 1982, 160-164.

Yao82a Andrew C. Yao: Theory and Applications of Trapdoor Functions; 23rd Symposium on Foundations of Computer Science (FOCS) 1982, IEEE Computer Society, 1982, 80-91.

YeLa95 Sung-Ming Yen, Chi-Sung Laih: Improved Digital Signature Suitable for Batch Verification; IEEE Transactions on Computers 44/7 (1995) 957-959.

Yuva79 Gideon Yuval: How to Swindle Rabin; Cryptologia 3/3 (1979) 187-189.

Zimm93 Philip Zimmermann: PGP – Pretty Good Privacy, Public Key Encryption for the Masses, User's Guide, Volume I: Essential Topics, Volume II: Special Topics; Version 2.6.2, Oct. 11, 1994, see <http://www.mantis.co.uk/pgp/pgp.html> for sources.

ZPO86 ZPO • Zivilprozeßordnung; (17. ed) dtv-Band 5005 (Beck-Texte), Deutscher Taschenbuch Verlag, München 1986.

Symbols

Greek letters are treated as a form of latin letters sounding similar; other symbols and numbers are at the beginning of the alphabet.

Index

Springer-Verlag and the Environment

We at Springer-Verlag firmly believe that an international science publisher has a special obligation to the environment, and our corporate policies consistently reflect this conviction.

We also expect our business partners – paper mills, printers, packaging manufacturers, etc. – to commit themselves to using environmentally friendly materials and production processes.

The paper in this book is made from low- or no-chlorine pulp and is acid free, in conformance with international standards for paper permanency.

Lecture Notes in Computer Science

For information about Vols. 1–1071

please contact your bookseller or Springer-Verlag

Vol. 1072: R. Kasturi, K. Tombre (Eds.), Graphics Recognition. Proceedings, 1995. X, 308 pages. 1996.

Vol. 1073: J. Cuny, H. Ehrig, G. Engels, G. Rozenberg (Eds.), Graph Grammars and Their Application to Computer Science. Proceedings, 1994. X, 565 pages. 1996.

Vol. 1074: G. Dowek, J. Heering, K. Meinke, B. Möller (Eds.), Higher-Order Algebra, Logic, and Term Rewriting. Proceedings, 1995. VII, 287 pages. 1996.

Vol. 1075: D. Hirschberg, G. Myers (Eds.), Combinatorial Pattern Matching. Proceedings, 1996. VIII, 392 pages. 1996.

Vol. 1076: N. Shadbolt, K. O'Hara, G. Schreiber (Eds.), Advances in Knowledge Acquisition. Proceedings, 1996. XII, 371 pages. 1996. (Subseries LNAI).

Vol. 1077: P. Brusilovsky, P. Kommers, N. Streitz (Eds.), Mulimedia, Hypermedia, and Virtual Reality. Proceedings, 1994. IX, 311 pages. 1996.

Vol. 1078: D.A. Lamb (Ed.), Studies of Software Design. Proceedings, 1993. VI, 188 pages. 1996.

Vol. 1079: Z.W. Raś, M. Michalewicz (Eds.), Foundations of Intelligent Systems. Proceedings, 1996. XI, 664 pages. 1996. (Subseries LNAI).

Vol. 1080: P. Constantopoulos, J. Mylopoulos, Y. Vassiliou (Eds.), Advanced Information Systems Engineering. Proceedings, 1996. XI, 582 pages. 1996.

Vol. 1081: G. McCalla (Ed.), Advances in Artificial Intelligence. Proceedings, 1996. XII, 459 pages. 1996. (Subseries LNAI).

Vol. 1082: N.R. Adam, B.K. Bhargava, M. Halem, Y. Yesha (Eds.), Digital Libraries. Proceedings, 1995. Approx. 310 pages. 1996.

Vol. 1083: K. Sparck Jones, J.R. Galliers, Evaluating Natural Language Processing Systems. XV, 228 pages. 1996. (Subseries LNAI).

Vol. 1084: W.H. Cunningham, S.T. McCormick, M. Queyranne (Eds.), Integer Programming and Combinatorial Optimization. Proceedings, 1996. X, 505 pages. 1996.

Vol. 1085: D.M. Gabbay, H.J. Ohlbach (Eds.), Practical Reasoning. Proceedings, 1996. XV, 721 pages. 1996. (Subseries LNAI).

Vol. 1086: C. Frasson, G. Gauthier, A. Lesgold (Eds.), Intelligent Tutoring Systems. Proceedings, 1996. XVII, 688 pages. 1996.

Vol. 1087: C. Zhang, D. Lukose (Eds.), Distributed Artificial Intelliegence. Proceedings, 1995. VIII, 232 pages. 1996. (Subseries LNAI).

Vol. 1088: A. Strohmeier (Ed.), Reliable Software Technologies – Ada-Europe '96. Proceedings, 1996. XI, 513 pages. 1996.

Vol. 1089: G. Ramalingam, Bounded Incremental Computation. XI, 190 pages. 1996.

Vol. 1090: J.-Y. Cai, C.K. Wong (Eds.), Computing and Combinatorics. Proceedings, 1996. X, 421 pages. 1996.

Vol. 1091: J. Billington, W. Reisig (Eds.), Application and Theory of Petri Nets 1996. Proceedings, 1996. VIII, 549 pages. 1996.

Vol. 1092: H. Kleine Büning (Ed.), Computer Science Logic. Proceedings, 1995. VIII, 487 pages. 1996.

Vol. 1093: L. Dorst, M. van Lambalgen, F. Voorbraak (Eds.), Reasoning with Uncertainty in Robotics. Proceedings, 1995. VIII, 387 pages. 1996. (Subseries LNAI).

Vol. 1094: R. Morrison, J. Kennedy (Eds.), Advances in Databases. Proceedings, 1996. XI, 234 pages. 1996.

Vol. 1095: W. McCune, R. Padmanabhan, Automated Deduction in Equational Logic and Cubic Curves. X, 231 pages. 1996. (Subseries LNAI).

Vol. 1096: T. Schäl, Workflow Management Systems for Process Organisations. XII, 200 pages. 1996.

Vol. 1097: R. Karlsson, A. Lingas (Eds.), Algorithm Theory – SWAT '96. Proceedings, 1996. IX, 453 pages. 1996.

Vol. 1098: P. Cointe (Ed.), ECOOP '96 – Object-Oriented Programming. Proceedings, 1996. XI, 502 pages. 1996.

Vol. 1099: F. Meyer auf der Heide, B. Monien (Eds.), Automata, Languages and Programming. Proceedings, 1996. XII, 681 pages. 1996.

Vol. 1100: B. Pfitzmann, Digital Signature Schemes. XVI, 396 pages. 1996.

Vol. 1101: M. Wirsing, M. Nivat (Eds.), Algebraic Methodology and Software Technology. Proceedings, 1996. XII, 641 pages. 1996.

Vol. 1102: R. Alur, T.A. Henzinger (Eds.), Computer Aided Verification. Proceedings, 1996. XII, 472 pages. 1996.

Vol. 1103: H. Ganzinger (Ed.), Rewriting Techniques and Applications. Proceedings, 1996. XI, 437 pages. 1996.

Vol. 1104: M.A. McRobbie, J.K. Slaney (Eds.), Automated Deduction – CADE-13. Proceedings, 1996. XV, 764 pages. 1996. (Subseries LNAI).

Vol. 1105: T.I. Ören, G.J. Klir (Eds.), Computer Aided Systems Theory – CAST '94. Proceedings, 1994. IX, 439 pages. 1996.

Vol. 1106: M. Jampel, E. Freuder, M. Maher (Eds.), Over-Constrained Systems. X, 309 pages. 1996.

Vol. 1107: J.-P. Briot, J.-M. Geib, A. Yonezawa (Eds.), Object-Based Parallel and Distributed Computation. Proceedings, 1995. X, 349 pages. 1996.

Vol. 1108: A. Díaz de Ilarraza Sánchez, I. Fernández de Castro (Eds.), Computer Aided Learning and Instruction in Science and Engineering. Proceedings, 1996. XIV, 480 pages. 1996.

Vol. 1109: N. Koblitz (Ed.), Advances in Cryptology – Crypto '96. Proceedings, 1996. XII, 417 pages. 1996.

Vol. 1110: O. Danvy, R. Glück, P. Thiemann (Eds.), Partial Evaluation. Proceedings, 1996. XII, 514 pages. 1996.

Vol. 1111: J.J. Alferes, L. Moniz Pereira, Reasoning with Logic Programming. XXI, 326 pages. 1996. (Subseries LNAI).

Vol. 1112: C. von der Malsburg, W. von Seelen, J.C. Vorbrüggen, B. Sendhoff (Eds.), Artificial Neural Networks – ICANN 96. Proceedings, 1996. XXV, 922 pages. 1996.

Vol. 1113: W. Penczek, A. Szałas (Eds.), Mathematical Foundations of Computer Science 1996. Proceedings, 1996. X, 592 pages. 1996.

Vol. 1114: N. Foo, R. Goebel (Eds.), PRICAI'96: Topics in Artificial Intelligence. Proceedings, 1996. XXI, 658 pages. 1996. (Subseries LNAI).

Vol. 1115: P.W. Eklund, G. Ellis, G. Mann (Eds.), Conceptual Structures: Knowledge Representation as Interlingua. Proceedings, 1996. XIII, 321 pages. 1996. (Subseries LNAI).

Vol. 1116: J. Hall (Ed.), Management of Telecommunication Systems and Services. XXI, 229 pages. 1996.

Vol. 1117: A. Ferreira, J. Rolim, Y. Saad, T. Yang (Eds.), Parallel Algorithms for Irregularly Structured Problems. Proceedings, 1996. IX, 358 pages. 1996.

Vol. 1118: E.C. Freuder (Ed.), Principles and Practice of Constraint Programming — CP 96. Proceedings, 1996. XIX, 574 pages. 1996.

Vol. 1119: U. Montanari, V. Sassone (Eds.), CONCUR '96: Concurrency Theory. Proceedings, 1996. XII, 751 pages. 1996.

Vol. 1120: M. Deza. R. Euler, I. Manoussakis (Eds.), Combinatorics and Computer Science. Proceedings, 1995. IX, 415 pages. 1996.

Vol. 1121: P. Perner, P. Wang, A. Rosenfeld (Eds.), Advances in Structural and Syntactical Pattern Recognition. Proceedings, 1996. X, 393 pages. 1996.

Vol. 1122: H. Cohen (Ed.), Algorithmic Number Theory. Proceedings, 1996. IX, 405 pages. 1996.

Vol. 1123: L. Bougé, P. Fraigniaud, A. Mignotte, Y. Robert (Eds.), Euro-Par'96. Parallel Processing. Proceedings, 1996, Vol. I. XXXIII, 842 pages. 1996.

Vol. 1124: L. Bougé, P. Fraigniaud, A. Mignotte, Y. Robert (Eds.), Euro-Par'96. Parallel Processing. Proceedings, 1996, Vol. II. XXXIII, 926 pages. 1996.

Vol. 1125: J. von Wright, J. Grundy, J. Harrison (Eds.), Theorem Proving in Higher Order Logics. Proceedings, 1996. VIII, 447 pages. 1996.

Vol. 1126: J.J. Alferes, L. Moniz Pereira, E. Orlowska (Eds.), Logics in Artificial Intelligence. Proceedings, 1996. IX, 417 pages. 1996. (Subseries LNAI).

Vol. 1127: L. Böszörményi (Ed.), Parallel Computation. Proceedings, 1996. XI, 235 pages. 1996.

Vol. 1128: J. Calmet, C. Limongelli (Eds.), Design and Implementation of Symbolic Computation Systems. Proceedings, 1996. IX, 356 pages. 1996.

Vol. 1129: J. Launchbury, E. Meijer, T. Sheard (Eds.), Advanced Functional Programming. Proceedings, 1996. VII, 238 pages. 1996.

Vol. 1130: M. Haveraaen, O. Owe, O.-J. Dahl (Eds.), Recent Trends in Data Type Specification. Proceedings, 1995. VIII, 551 pages. 1996.

Vol. 1131: K.H. Höhne, R. Kikinis (Eds.), Visualization in Biomedical Computing. Proceedings, 1996. XII, 610 pages. 1996.

Vol. 1132: G.-R. Perrin, A. Darte (Eds.), The Data Parallel Programming Model. XV, 284 pages. 1996.

Vol. 1133: J.-Y. Chouinard, P. Fortier, T.A. Gulliver (Eds.), Information Theory and Applications. Proceedings, 1995. XII, 309 pages. 1996.

Vol. 1134: R. Wagner, H. Thoma (Eds.), Database and Expert Systems Applications. Proceedings, 1996. XV, 921 pages. 1996.

Vol. 1135: B. Jonsson, J. Parrow (Eds.), Formal Techniques in Real-Time and Fault-Tolerant Systems. Proceedings, 1996. X, 479 pages. 1996.

Vol. 1136: J. Diaz, M. Serna (Eds.), Algorithms - ESA '96. Proceedings, 1996. XII, 566 pages. 1996.

Vol. 1137: G. Görz, S. Hölldobler (Eds.), KI-96: Advances in Artificial Intelligence. Proceedings, 1996. XI, 387 pages. 1996. (Subseries LNAI).

Vol. 1138: J. Calmet, J.A. Campbell, J. Pfalzgraf (Eds.), Artificial Intelligence and Symbolic Mathematical Computation. Proceedings, 1996. VIII, 381 pages. 1996.

Vol. 1139: M. Hanus, M. Rogriguez-Artalejo (Eds.), Algebraic and Logic Programming. Proceedings, 1996. VIII, 345 pages. 1996.

Vol. 1140: H. R. Kuchen, S. Doaitse Swierstra (Eds.), Programming Languages: Implementations, Logics, and Programs. Proceedings, 1996. XI, 479 pages. 1996.

Vol. 1141: W. Ebeling, I. Rechenberg, H.-P. Schwefel, H.-M. Voigt (Eds.), Parallel Problem Solving from Nature — PPSN IV. Proceedings, 1996. XVII, 1.050 pages. 1996.

Vol. 1142: R.W. Hartenstein, M. Glesner (Eds.), Field-Programmable Logic. Proceedings, 1996. X, 432 pages. 1996.

Vol. 1143: T.C. Fogarty (Ed.), Evolutionary Computing. Proceedings, 1996. VIII, 305 pages. 1996.

Vol. 1144: J. Ponce, A. Zisserman, M. Hebert (Eds.), Object Representation in Computer Vision. Proceedings, 1996. VIII, 403 pages. 1996.

Vol. 1145: R. Cousot, D.A. Schmidt (Eds.), Static Analysis. Proceedings, 1996. IX, 389 pages. 1996.